Footprint London

Charlie Godfrey-Faussett
2nd edition

"London is on the whole the most possible form of life."

Henry James, *Notebooks*

London Highlights

1 Hampstead
Highbrow London looking down from the hills to the north of the city

2 Notting Hill and Portobello
The media darlings' location, location, location of choice and a decent market

3 V&A
Absorbing and awe-inspiring collection of decorative arts down the ages, the mother of South Ken's museums

4 Buckingham Palace and St James's Park
The Royal stamping ground and luscious greenery

5 National Gallery and National Portrait Gallery
The best things about Trafalgar Square, superbly generous and enlightening picture collections

6 Theatreland
West End shows from the sublime to the ridiculous centred round Shaftesbury Avenue

7 Covent Garden
A tourist honeypot – a fine old covered market turned boutique shopper's paradise

8 British Museum
The daddy, 'illuminating world cultures' like nowhere else on earth

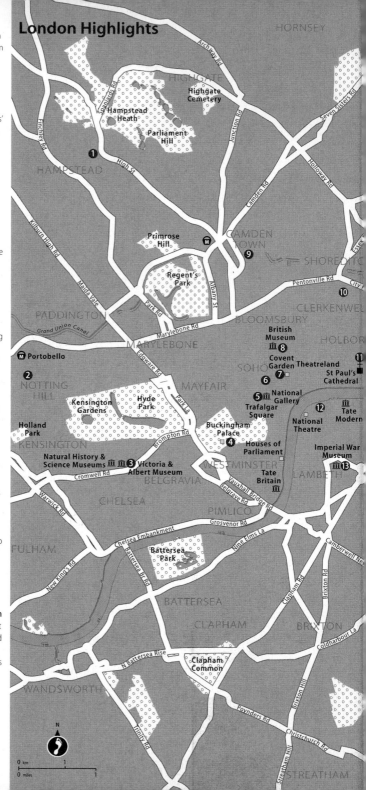

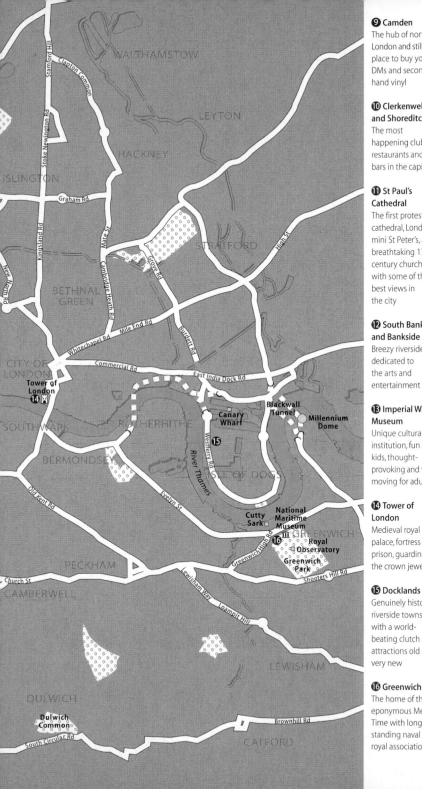

9 Camden
The hub of north London and still the place to buy your DMs and second-hand vinyl

10 Clerkenwell and Shoreditch
The most happening clubs, restaurants and bars in the capital

11 St Paul's Cathedral
The first protestant cathedral, London's mini St Peter's, a breathtaking 17th-century church with some of the best views in the city

12 South Bank and Bankside
Breezy riverside dedicated to the arts and entertainment

13 Imperial War Museum
Unique cultural institution, fun for kids, thought-provoking and very moving for adults

14 Tower of London
Medieval royal palace, fortress and prison, guarding the crown jewels

15 Docklands
Genuinely historic riverside towns with a world-beating clutch of attractions old and very new

16 Greenwich
The home of the eponymous Mean Time with long-standing naval and royal associations

Contents

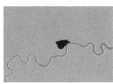

East London

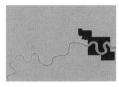

North London

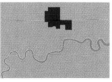

West London

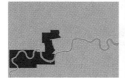

South London

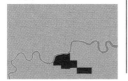

Keep abreast of London's changing landscape in a flight on the London Eye.

Winging it
Wind, water and pigeons in the air round Trafalgar Square.

A foot in the door

Much to its own surprise, London is still one of the world's great cities. Endlessly diverting and diverse, it provides no room for complacency but plenty for hope and admiration. And it largely has visitors to thank for the fact. The Romans were the first, sticking around long enough to establish a vital western trading post for their empire. Then the Normans made it the capital of the country they had conquered. Later, as London built its own empire, successive generations of British, European and global immigrants created a unique, expansive city on the banks of the little river Thames. Neither ancient nor modern, although old and new, London still does tradition, with Beefeaters in the Tower, Buckingham Palace, Piccadilly and trooping the colour. There may have been an attempt to banish pigeons from Trafalgar Square; and St Paul's is being given a good bath; but Nelson still tops his column, the cathedral looms over the water, Westminster shimmers at dusk, the buses (although not routemasters) are still red and many of the cabs still black. But this London has been joined by another in a different spirit, with equally distinctive sights. They've been called New London: the London Eye, Tate Modern, the Millennium Bridge and even the ill-fated Millennium Dome. And just about every venerable museum and art gallery has enjoyed a designer makeover. Erudite and grand, while something of London stands still, it's continually moving on. A kind of quantum city. Boasting the busiest airport in the world, it's a backward-looking, optimistic mongrel town, where dreams can turn sour or golden overnight. With magnificent trees, a tidal river and changeable weather, plus a thriving culture and driven soul, London is one of the most engaging and invigorating places on the planet.

Contemporary London

This century is London's twenty-first. And like all grown-up cities, it comes of age with a fair share of problems. Top of the list of grumbles for Londoners and visitors are the exorbitant cost of everything, overcrowded and unreliable tube trains, slow buses and bad air. The good news is that finally there seems to be a determination to do something about it. All the major museums and galleries are free, the city centre congestion charge has had a very desirable effect and cycling has become almost pleasurable. Far from stuffy, London daily performs an astonishing balancing act between preserving its particular civilized atmosphere and generating exciting new ideas. As well as an extraordinary cultural life – more music, performance and treasure-house museums than any other European city – it now boasts a

Temple of the contemporary
Powerhouse of modern art: the Turbine Hall at Tate Modern.

restaurant, bar and hotel scene to match. Old-fashioned boozers rub shoulders with sleek designer bars. Not a week passes without something opening up or somewhere going under. London also solidly resists feverish hype. No picture too rosy will ever fit. In many parts it remains a very hard and uncomfortable place to be. And yet, among its population of some seven million – speaking about 300 different languages and a quarter from ethnic minorities – the rich still keep house in close proximity to the poor. And though race relations are still difficult, the city is far from being segregated or impersonal. In its own distinctive style, it continues to seduce, enthral and inspire. It may be a masculine place, with Old Father Thames winding through its heart, but as Shakespeare wrote of the similarly irresistible Cleopatra: "Age cannot wither her, nor custom stale her infinite variety."

Caution, wet surface
The troubled Diana memorial water feature in Hyde Park, which is now again open.

1 Sam Wanamaker's brainchild, Shakespeare's Globe Theatre, on Bankside Pier. ▶▶ See page 244.

2 The stainless steel lion and unicorn of Queen Elizabeth gate into Hyde Park, a tribute to the Queen Mother. ▶▶ See page 158.

3 One of the temporary summer pavilions at the Serpentine Gallery. Each year sees a new piece of architecture. ▶▶ See page 158.

4 Spectacular blooms at the Columbia Flower market in the East End every Sunday morning. ▶▶ See page 271.

5 Signs in English and Bengali in Brick Lane, which has long been a focus for immigrants starting with the Huguenots in the 17th century. ▶▶ See page 260.

6 Pride in the Park, the capital's full-on gay and lesbian festival, where some let it all hang out whether they mean to or not. ▶▶ See page 28.

7 The Great Court, the highlight of Norman Foster's British Museum makeover, and the largest covered square in Europe. ▶▶ See page 193.

8 Royal Opera House's new refurbishment includes the Floral Hall, a successful conclusion to the debate about spending public money on elitist pursuits. ▶▶ See page 95.

9 Rise, like cream, to the surface in Norman Foster's Jubilee line extension station at Canary Wharf. ▶▶ See page 273.

10 Fuller's brewery (based in Chiswick) cashes in on the butcher's chic of Smithfield meat market in Clerkenwell. ▶▶ See page 214.

11 Mad dogs and Englishmen: snow-surfing on Primrose Hill. ▶▶ See page 301.

12 Piccadilly Circus: fast traffic and fast food in the frenetic heart of Tourist London. ▶▶ See page 117.

Gastropolis

Among the city's innumerable highlights, the transformation of the restaurant scene ranks as one of London's most phenomenally successful quick-change acts. Areas where you would once have been pushed to find anything much better than a curry or chips have metamorphosed into gastronomic hotspots. Grand hotels now boast the most fashionable chefs and happening dining rooms. A prolific variety of different cuisines are offered in almost any conceivable setting to suit every wallet. The quality of the fresh ingredients on menus and the skill with which they're handled has made London a choice destination for global gourmets, as well as a generally satisfying experience for more casual foodies. Arguably it all began in Soho, where you can still find some of the best cooking in the capital. Mayfair and St James's, next door, are besieged by discerning diners looking for an exquisite meal. In Clerkenwell several restaurants make the most of their proximity to Smithfield meat market. And in the west, Kensington, Chelsea and Notting Hill all cater expertly to the celebrity crowd. Some trends are worth noting. Brazilian food has arrived in style, joining a wide array of Thai food joints, Japanese noodle bars and more formal Asian restaurants that sprang up in the 1990s.

The business of art

Showbusiness has long been the best business in London. No other European city stages anything like such vibrant theatre and music. And these traditionally strong performers have been joined by a brisk stand-up comedy circuit and booming art scene. The lion's share of the city's live

Sundial, Tower Bridge and new City Hall in the background.

Summertime at Kew Gardens.

entertainment value is divided between the commercial West End, with its inimitable 'theatreland', and the South Bank, home to an eclectic collection of state-subsidized arts venues. Beyond these two poles are a host of other star destinations: indie music rocks, jazz swings and dance beats break in Camden, Soho and Shoreditch; challenging drama hits the boards in Islington; orchestras tune up in Marylebone; weird films flicker on the Mall. The fine arts too have rarely been more popular: Tate Modern is their contemporary flagship, while the East End is still a creative powerhouse.

Ebb and flow

The soul of the city and the force of nature in the history, culture and geography of the place is the tidal river Thames. No trip to the capital is complete without a jaunt along, across, upon or beside the river. Pick almost any point for a satisfying perspective on London: from Hampton Court and the Royal Botanic Gardens at Kew to Greenwich and the sea, bridged, embanked and even barred, the Thames still marks time. It flows softly past the medieval Tower of London; the designer warehouses on Butler's Wharf; the skyscrapers of Docklands; the pubs and pumphouses in Wapping and the arts and entertainment on Bankside and the South Bank. It drifts beside the fine arts and decorative antiques at Somerset House; below the London Eye, Big Ben and the Houses of Parliament by Westminster Bridge; Tate Britain on Millbank; the gardens of Battersea Park, Chelsea and Fulham and the riverside bars of Hammersmith and Putney. The rising tide reaches as far as Teddington Lock, well beyond the mansions of Richmond, the rugby at Twickenham and Kingston bridge. London still leans towards the river, the city's most remarkable, perennial, ever-changing sight.

Is it a plane...
... or a Gherkin? The Swiss Re insurance building at No. 1 St Mary Axe, Lothbury.

Essentials

Footprint features

Planning your trip

Where to go

London is a city often seen in a hurry. If time is very limited, then the one unmissable sight remains **Tate Modern**. Whatever your reaction to the contents or industrial style of this huge gallery of contemporary art, its position on the river puts it at the heart of the beast. In order to see as much of London as possible in a day, it's best to avoid wasting time on public transport. Stick with the riverside walks instead. Thanks to the new footbridges, an easy three-mile (one hour) stroll takes in several of the major London sights. From **Trafalgar Square**, walk down Northumberland Avenue to the **Embankment** and cross over the Golden Jubilee footbridge to the **South Bank**. From the southern bridge there are great views of the London Eye, Big Ben and Houses of Parliament. Unless you want a closer look at the attractions of **County Hall**, turn left to walk along the river past the **Royal Festival Hall** to Waterloo Bridge. Here you can decide whether to walk on to **Tate Modern** and **Shakespeare's Globe** before heading over the Millennium Footbridge to **St Paul's**, or to cross Waterloo Bridge (which gives some of the finest views of the City) and carry straight on through **Covent Garden** to find the **British Museum** in Bloomsbury. After a look around St Paul's, the restaurants and clubs of **Clerkenwell** and **Smithfield** or **Shoreditch** are close at hand for an evening's entertainment. The British Museum is a short walk from the restaurants and bars of **Soho** and the **West End**.

Less energetic and just as rewarding perhaps would be to spend the morning at Tate Modern, the afternoon at St Paul's, and the evening in a bar or restaurant somewhere near Smithfield. With an extra day, the half-hour skyride on offer at the London Eye is definitely worth the ticket price, although even with its sophisticated boarding system, precious time can still sometimes be lost in the queue.

Alternatively, the **Great Court at the British Museum** defies old-fashioned fustiness and casts the Museum's frankly mind-boggling collection of antiquities in a new light. A visit here can also easily be combined with a taste of the peculiar small-scale charm and beauty of **Sir John Soane's Museum** in Lincoln's Inn Fields.

On a similar scale to the British Museum, the **Victoria and Albert Museum** in South Kensington is an extraordinary neo-gothic shrine to art and design packed with innumerable marvellous things. Less aesthetic and more historical insights can be found either at the **Imperial War Museum** or the **Tower of London**. At the gateway to south London, the Imperial War Museum is the most disturbing, its compelling exhibition on the Holocaust putting the military hardware and World War memorabilia on display into perspective. The Tower of London, downriver near the splendid Tower Bridge, is a proper medieval castle, a very well-preserved relic riddled with stories of the pursuit and abuse of royal power.

With more time, essential destinations further afield are the venerable old **Tate Britain** on the river near Victoria, dedicated to the latest in British contemporary, modern and historical art including Turner's dramatic oil paintings; the superhip bars, restaurants and shops of **Notting Hill** in the west; the loud and grungey music and market mecca of **Camden** or the views of the city from genteel **Primrose Hill** or **Hampstead** in the north; and the nightlife of **Shoreditch** to the east. Day trips south to the revamped Dulwich Picture Gallery or a river trip to Kew and Hampton Court also rank with the best that London has to offer.

London at a glance → *See map of central London, page 20.*

1 Trafalgar Square The centre of London. The pigeons banished and north side pedestrianized but here is the monumental hotch-potch heart of the beast, with Nelson on his column and the National Gallery to boot. ▸▸ *See page 56.*

2 The Strand, Embankment and Aldwych The main road between Westminster and the City, east out of the Square, where the admin office blocks of Empire sprang up after the 18th century, the first at Somerset House, overlooking the 19th century's great sanitary achievement: the Victoria Embankment. ▸▸ *See page 64.*

3 Leicester Square and Chinatown The diminutive showbiz epicentre of the West End boasts a statue of Shakespeare unfazed by the movie premieres all around, the theatrical first nights on Shaftesbury Avenue, the bookselling bonanza on Charing Cross Road and Chinese cuisine next door. ▸▸ *See page 73.*

4 Soho The West End's late-night party zone sleezily converts the film, music and TV frenzy here by day into some of the best restaurants, gay bars, cinemas and drinking clubs in the capital. ▸▸ *See page 81.*

5 Covent Garden Just north of the Strand is a tourist honeypot: a sympathetic conversion of central London's beautiful old covered market into a boutique shopping mall with no traffic and a hint of culture. ▸▸ *See page 92.*

6 Mayfair and Regent Street West of Soho beyond the glorified sweep of big-name retailers on Regent Street, Mayfair remains the most moneyed, swanky and occasionally discreet home of haute couture, cuisine and hospitality. ▸▸ *See page 102.*

7 Piccadilly and St James's The land that time forgot. Beyond the neon hoardings of Piccadilly Circus, Piccadilly heads west with panache, freighted with Fortnum and Mason's, the Royal Academy and the Ritz, dividing Mayfair from the gentleman's clubland of St James's and Buckingham Palace. ▸▸ *See page 114.*

8 Oxford Street London's not very prepossessing High Street, just north of Soho, lined with department stores and all the big names in retail. ▸▸ *See page 128.*

9 Westminster and Whitehall Just south of Trafalgar Square on the river stands the seat of central government in the UK: the sub-Venetian grandeur of Whitehall, the golden Victorian pinnacles of the Houses of Parliament and Big Ben, beside the crowning Gothic glory of Westminster Abbey. ▸▸ *See page 136.*

10 Victoria, Belgravia and Pimlico A bustling transport hub, Victoria disturbs the creamy stuccoed dignity of Belgravia and Pimlico. Highlights include Westminster Cathedral and the Brit art and Turners on the river at Tate Britain. ▸▸ *See page 147.*

11 Knightsbridge, South Kensington and Hyde Park West of Belgravia and almost as affluent, Knightsbridge and South Ken boast luxury shopping a go-go and three wonderful old museums – of Science, of Natural History, and of the decorative arts at the V&A – all on the edge of the city's most famous park. ▸▸ *See page 155.*

12 Chelsea South Kensington's naughty neighbour has grown out of its swinging, punk rock days to become a chi chi shopping strip along the King's Road backed up by a clutch of venerable visitor attractions. ▸▸ *See page 169.*

Essentials Planning your trip

Central London at a glance

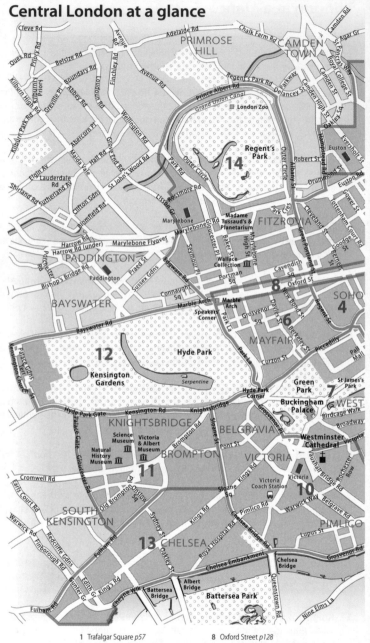

N

0 metres 500
0 yards 500

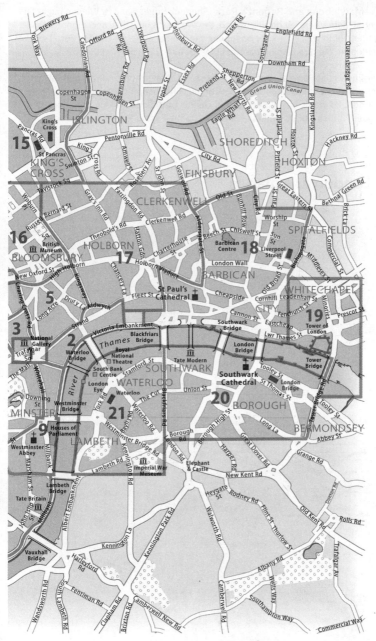

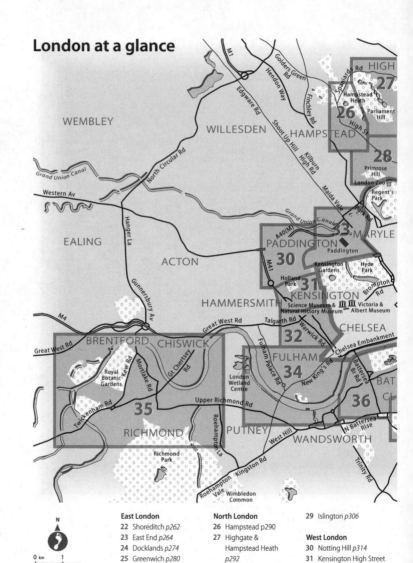

14 Marylebone and Regent's Park Sherlock Holmes and Dr Watson might still feel at home here, snooping round the Wallace Collection and glorious flower gardens of Regent's Park, or observing the animal antics in London Zoo. Less so perhaps in the new fashion parade of Marylebone High St. ▸▸ *See page 177.*

15 Euston, St Pancras and King's Cross All change at the railway termini for the north, with the channel tunnel rail link under construction due to open at St Pancras in 2006. London's seedy backyard is cleaning up its act, taking a leaf out of the modern British Library's billions of books on the Euston Rd. ▸▸ *See page 186.*

London at a glance

16 Bloomsbury and Fitzrovia The academic heart of London: home to the British Museum and on the other side of the Tottenham Court Rd, the offices and playgrounds of London's advertising and media gurus. ▸▸ *See page 192.*

17 Holborn and Clerkenwell The most famous way through Holborn's courts of law was Fleet St. Once the busiest news mill in the world, it's all quiet now, though a buzz can still be heard in Clerkenwell, just across the Farringdon Rd. ▸▸ *See page 206.*

18 & 19 The City and the Tower of London Where it all began. St Paul's cathedral, lots of other beautiful churches, the Bank of England, Guildhall and Museum of London, all surrounded by massive offices mashing up other people's money. ▸▸ *See page 218.*

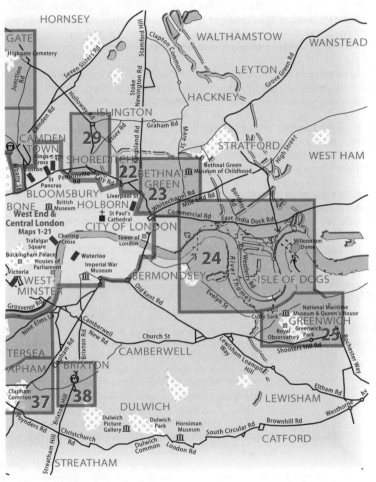

20 Southwark, Bankside, Borough and Bermondsey For a long time the City's disreputable neighbour on the south side of the river and now accessible across the Millennium Bridge from St Paul's, or along the riverside walk from the South Bank, and laden with an extraordinary array of attractions: Borough Market the best of them. ▸▸ *See page 236.*

21 South Bank and Waterloo Across the river from Trafalgar Square and Covent Garden, the concrete culture bunkers of the largest arts centre in Europe have been joined by the dizzying delights of the London Eye and the Saatchi Gallery in County Hall. Close by, the Imperial War Museum is a place to pause for thought and rememberance. ▸▸ *See page 249.*

22-24 East End and Docklands Some of the most happening nightlife in London in Shoreditch, Hoxton, Brick Lane and Spittalfields have given the old East End a much-needed shot in the arm. On the river, Docklands has become a gleaming extension of the teeming money-driven life of the City. ▸▸ *See page 260.*

25 Greenwich Across the river from Docklands, London's stately 18th-century port retains the atmosphere of a small town, harbouring the salty delights of the National Maritime Museum and timely interest of the Royal Observatory. ▸▸ *See page 278.*

26-29 North London Beyond Regent's Park, Camden draws in the punters with its markets, music and mayhem while Primrose Hill and Hampstead are historic villages with precious breathing space and great views. To the east, Islington buzzes with bars, fringe theatres and antiques. ▸▸ *See page 287.*

30-35 West London Beyond Marble Arch and Hyde Park, Bayswater boasts a huge number of hotels. Next door Notting Hill was once a hip multicultural haven, now going the same way as Chelsea, if anything even hotter for the shopper. ▸▸ *See page 311.*

36-38 South London Some way beyond the South Bank, Brixton town is the cannabis capital of the UK, Clapham its more gentrified neighbour. ▸▸ *See page 355.*

When to go

Climate

The English obsession with the weather can largely be put down to its unpredictable nature. London's climate is generally milder than in the rest of the country and although temperatures rarely drop to freezing or below, they can fluctuate considerably from one day to the next, with temperatures averaging around 6°C (43°F) in winter and 18°C (64°F) in summer, although in July and August it is not unusual for them to soar to 30°C (86°F). Despite its reputation, the average annual rainfall is fairly low – around 60 cm – although you should come prepared for wet weather at any time of year.

❧ Recorded weather information:
T0891-500401.
Weather forecast websites:
www.met-office.gov.uk,
www.bbc.co.uk/weather.

Tour operators

There are hundreds of tours of London offered by companies organizing sightseeing by coach, mini-coach, bus, boat, taxi, private driver-guides or on foot. These tours can last for anything from 2-3 hours to a full day. Sightseeing tour coaches should carry the LTB 'Approved Sightseeing Tour' sticker and it is advisable to make sure that your guide is a trained Blue Badge Guide. Other than the companies listed below, the **25** London Tourist Board, **Visit London** ① *2 More London Riverside, SE1 2RR, T0870-1566366, www.visitlondon.com*, will have more information.

Sightseeing tours → *See also guided walks page 44.*

Big Bus Company, 48 Buckingham Palace Rd, SW1, T020-7233 9533, www.bigbus.co.uk. Daily sightseeing tours from hop-on, hop-off, open-top double-decker buses. Tickets include a river cruise and a choice of walking tours. The commentary is live, or digitally recorded in 12 languages. £18 adults, £8 children.

Black Taxi tours of London, T020-7935 9363, www.blacktaxitours.co.uk. Sightseeing tours in licensed taxi cabs. Commentary from trained London 'cabbies'. Two-hour day and night tours. Hotel pick-up and return. Costs £80 (£85 at night) for up to five people.

Evan Evans Tours, T020-7950 1777, www.evanevans.co.uk. Half- and full-day coach tours of London with stop-offs at key sights. Prices start at £16 for adults (£10 for children between 3 and 16). Sightseeing trips to major tourist destinations outside London also available, as are tours in Japanese and Spanish.

London Duck Tours, T020-7928 3132, T020-8249 6055, www.londonducktours.co.uk. Starting at County Hall, these 'road and river' tours of London last 80 mins, The DUKW 'splashes down' (in a yellow amphibious WWII vehicle) into the Thames at Lacks Dock, Vauxhall for the river part of the tour lasting about 30 minutes, after setting off from the London Eye. Tours cost £18.50 for adults and £14 for children; family tickets are also available. Booking advisable during holiday season.

Driver-guides operating general and special-interest tours for individuals and small groups in and around London are another option. The **Driver-Guides Association** (DGA), T020-8874 2745, www.driver-guides.org.uk, can provide details of professional blue-badge driver-guides throughout the country.

Essentials Planning your trip

Finding out more

The best way of finding out more information for your trip to London is to contact the British Tourist Authority (BTA) in your country (see below) or the head office of the London Tourist Board (LTB), **Britain and London Visitor Centre** (BLVC) ① *1 Lower Regent St, SW1, tube: Piccadilly Circus, Mon 0930-0630, Tue-Fri 0900-0630, Sat-Sun 1000-1600; Jun-Sep Sat-Sun 1000-1700*. The BLVC can provide a wealth of free literature and information such as maps, city guides, events calendars and accommodation brochures. Travellers with special needs should also contact their nearest BTA office.

Useful websites

www.londontown.com Information on accommodation, transport and sights, events and attractions. Also has a very useful page with tips and ideas for travellers on a tight budget.

www.bbc.co.uk/london For up to date news and a guide to what's going on.

www.thefridayproject.co.uk/lbl Eclectic online insider's guide to London, published weekly.

genuki.org.uk Great place to start genealogical research, with a huge number of links.

www.guardian.co.uk This newspaper's website has excellent London listings.

www.sky.co.uk/news Another excellent news site.

www.tfl.gov.uk/tfl Transport for London's website, with all the information you need to get around London.

www.thisislondon.com Up-to-date news, business information and weather.

www.timeout.com The ultimate listings guide to what's on in London.

www.visitlondon.com Official London tourist board website (see above).

Discount passes

The **London Pass** covers entry to over 60 varied attractions from the Tower of London and the London Dungeon to river boat rides and ten-pin bowling. Prices start at £17.50 for a one-day adult pass and £12 for children. It can be purchased online at www.londonpass.com or at London Transport and Tourist Information Centres and at Exchange International bureaux de change.

The **GoSeeCard**, www.london-gosee.com, a one-, three- or seven-day discount pass gives visitors access to around 17 London museums and galleries. The card costs £10, £16 or £26 per adult; a family card (two adults and up to four children) is also available at £32 for three days or £50 for seven days. But before buying it, make sure you will get you money's worth: you'd need to see at least two museums per day (check prices in individual entries) – bear in mind that some of the big museums and galleries don't charge, and that in other cases (for example the Natural History and Science Museums) entry is free for children and senior citizens.

British tourist authorities overseas

The BTA is an excellent source of information for visitors to England. More information can be obtained from their website (www.bta.org.uk), or from the offices listed below:

Australia Level 16, The Gateway, 1 Macquarie Pl, Circular Quay, Sydney NSW 2000, T02-9377 4400, F02-93774499.

Belgium and Luxembourg 306 Av Louise, 1050 Brussels, T2-6463510, F2-6463986.

Canada 111 Avenue Rd, Suite 450, Toronto, Ontario MR5 3J8, T416-9256326, F416-9612175.

Denmark Montergade 3, 1116 Copenhagen K, T33-339188, F33-140136.

France Maison de la Grande-Bretagne, 19 Rue des Mathurins, 75009 Paris, T1-4451 5620, F1-44515621.

Germany, Austria and Switzerland Taunustrasse 52-60, 60329 Frankfurt, T69-2380711.

Ireland 18/19 College Green, Dublin 2, T1-6708000, F1-6708244.

Italy Corso Vittorio Emanuele II No 337, 00186 Rome, T6-68806821, F6-6879095.

Netherlands Stadhouderskade 2 (5e), 1054 ES Amsterdam, T20-6855051, F20-6186868.

New Zealand 17th Floor, Fay Richwhite Building, 151 Queen St, Auckland 1, T09-3031446, F09-3776965.

South Africa Lancaster Gate, Hyde Park Lane, Hyde Park 2196, Johannesburg, T011-3250342.

USA 7th Flr, 551 Fifth Av, New York, NY 10176-0799, T212-986-2200. 10880 Wiltshire Blvd, Suite 570, Los Angeles, CA 90024, T310-4702782.

Language

Courses

Thousands of people come to London each year to study English, but finding the right course can be confusing and time-consuming. First of all make sure you choose an organization that is accredited by the **British Council**. There are about 100 accredited schools, colleges and universities in London offering a wide range of courses at all levels and for all ages. They can all arrange accommodation and many organize social activities for students as well. Type of course, cost, class size and location of college may influence your decision. Executive courses, for example, are normally more expensive, in small groups, or one-to-one, and they usually offer more expensive accommodation arrangements. There are general programmes, examination courses, or those specializing in business or other kinds of English. Courses can be

means you live in the house of a trained EFL teacher. Summer courses are often held
in the cities universities and colleges.

English in Britain, www.englishinbritain.co.uk, lists the accredited schools and
colleges in London and the rest of the UK. From the website you'll be able to search the
database, contact the schools and colleges, visit their websites, and book a course.

Disabled travellers

Most visitors should not experience too many problems on arrival as all London
airports are modern and equipped to help passengers with special needs. Express
service transport from the airports to the city centre (ie via Heathrow or Gatwick
Express) is also easily accessible for wheelchair users. Eurostar trains and Waterloo
International (the Eurostar terminal) are also accessible, although each train takes a
maximum of only two wheelchairs). If you are disabled you should contact the travel
officer of your national support organization before travelling. They can provide
literature or put you in touch with travel agents specializing in tours for the disabled.

Accommodation in London can be problematic. Many of the large, modern and
more expensive hotels do have disabled facilities, but most of the smaller hotels are
not designed to cater for people with disabilities or can only accommodate people with
limited mobility. Of the seven YHA youth hostels, only the **Rotherhithe** hostel (see page
276) has access for wheelchairs. **Holiday Care Service** ① *To845-1249971 (from UK only)*
T44-(0)20-8760 0072, *www.holidaycare.org.uk*, is an organization that provides
information on holidays and accommodation suitable for disabled visitors.

Public transport is still quite bad too: access to most **underground** stations is via
numerous steps or escalators and extreme crowding at peak times make things
difficult for anyone with mobility problems. However, some newer tube stations and
the DLR stations are wheelchair accessible, and an increasing number of low-floor
accessible **buses** are being introduced. **Transport for London** ① *To20-7222 1234*,
www.tfl.gov.uk, publishes various booklets with information on access to buses and
the tube as well as Braille maps and recorded guides (all free). They also give
information and advice to disabled travellers.

Most, if not all, London **taxis** are now wheelchair accessible (look out for the
illuminated chair symbol when the 'for hire' symbol is on). If ordering a taxi in advance
from one of the hire services, you must state it is needed for a disabled person. People
with impaired mobility are welcome on **Thames river services** and step-free access is
now available from most major piers. Newer craft have dedicated wheelchair spaces.

On the national rail network, wheelchair users, and blind or partially sighted
people are automatically given 30-50% discount on train fares; those with other
disabilities are eligible for the **Disabled Person's Railcard**, which gives a third off tickets
for the disabled person and one other. There are no reductions on national buses.

The **www.londontown.com** website has an informative *Guide to Disabled London*
with information on accommodation, attractions, nightlife, shopping, travelling and
sightseeing in the capital. There are ideas for everything from easy-access walks along
the Thames, suitable for wheelchair users, to listening-and-touching tours of St Paul's
Cathedral aimed specifically at blind and partially sighted visitors.

Information and organizations

Access in London. A guide published by
www.accessproject-phsp.org. Includes
information on the practicalities of getting
around and access to the main places of
interest, entertainment and

accommodation in London. Also
has an extensive list of useful c
ontact organizations.
Artsline, T020-7388 2227,
www.dircon.co.uk/artsline. Has detailed

information and publications on arts, attractions and entertainment for disabled people in London.
Can Be Done, 11 Woodcock Hill, Harrow, HA3 0XP, T020-8907 2400, www.canbedone.co.uk. Arrange holidays for disabled visitors in accommodation which suits each individual's requirements.

The Royal Association for Disability and Rehabilitation (RADAR), www.radar.org.uk. Publish *Holidays in Britain and Ireland*, an annual guide on travelling in the UK.
The Royal National Institute for the Blind, T020-7388 1266. Publishes a *Hotel Guide Book* for blind and partially sighted people. They also have maps for the blind of London and other cities.

Gay and lesbian travellers

London has the most thriving gay scene in the UK. Its centre has long been in Soho, now more exuberant and well-established than ever, where Old Compton St and Rupert St boast a host of gay bars, cafés and restaurants. Almost every part of the city though is home to equally congenial spots for gay visitors. In particular Earl's Court in the west, Islington and Stoke Newington in the north and Vauxhall and Brixton in the south, have all developed reputations for the quality of their gay and lesbian nightlife. Flyers for club nights at various venues around town can be found at most of the West End bars listed below. Otherwise check *Time Out*, the *Pink Paper* or the *Gay Times* for details of what's on where when you visit. In late July (usually the last Saturday), Pride in the Park is the capital's full-on gay and lesbian festival, now a ticketed event that fills Hyde Park with a colourful and confident crowd celebrating the culmination of the Pride Parade from the Embankment. See **www.prideparade.org** or **www.prideinthepark.com** for more details.
▸▸ *See individual area listings sections for gay and lesbian-friendly, pubs, bars and clubs etc.*

Contacts

Gay's the Word, 66 Marchmont St, T020-7278 7654. One of London's premier gay and lesbian bookshops.
Liberty Cars, 330 Old St, T020-7734 1313 or T020-7739 9080. Gay-friendly car service.

London Lesbian and Gay Switchboard, T020-7837 7324, www.queery.org.uk. Popular help and information line.
Soho Centre for Health Care, 20 Soho Sq. Tue 1730-2100. Walk-in hepatitis vaccinations.

Travelling with children

Although London, with its busy roads, crowded pavements and bad weather, may not appear immediately child-friendly, the city remains one of the most exciting places in the world for children and teenagers. Babies can happily be wheeled around its lovely parks, gardens and open squares and every major museum and art gallery caters for infants as well as the very young. And there's no shortage of child-orientated attractions. Somewhere near the top of any long list of these (and free to enter) are the **Natural History Museum** and **Science Museum** (see page 162 and 160), both wonderfully entertaining and educational in presenting their world-class collections. Others include the **Horniman Museum** (page 362), the **London Transport Museum** (page 95) and (more expensively) **London Zoo** (page 182). And then there are places like the **London Dungeon** (page 244) and **Madame Tussaud's** (page 183), irresistible to kids if not so much to paying adults. **HMS Belfast** (page 244), the **Tower of London** (page 232) and **Tower Bridge** (page 234) are very enjoyable old-fashioned treats and still definitive London experiences for seven to 11s. Perhaps best of all is the **river**: from the London Eye via Tate Modern to Greenwich, no one under 16 can fail to be impressed.

Working in London

Citizens of **European Union** (EU) countries can live and work in Britain freely without a visa, but **non-EU residents** need a permit to work legally. This can be difficult to obtain without the backing of an established company or employer in the UK. **Note:** Visas should be obtained from a British mission overseas before entering the UK.

Visitors from **Commonwealth countries** who are aged between 17 and 27 can apply for a working-holidaymaker's visa which permits them to do casual (ie non-career orientated) work for up to two years in the UK. Adverts for typical working-holidaymaker jobs (pub or restaurant work, clerking, book-keeping, etc) can always be found in the pages of *TNT*, *SX*, or other magazines distributed free outside train and tube stations in London.

‡ *For more details, contact your nearest British Embassy, Consulate or High Commission, or the Foreign and Commonwealth Office in London, www.fco.gov.uk.*

An option for citizens of some **non-Commonwealth** countries is to come to the UK on an 'au pair' placement in order to learn English by living with an English-speaking family for a maximum of two years. In return for helping in the home (up to a maximum of five hours per day), the au pair is given a 'reasonable allowance' and two days off each week. This can be a very good way to learn English and to live rent free in London, but check out the precise conditions of your placement (as far as possible) before you take it up.

If you want to **study** in the UK you must first prove you can support and accommodate yourself without working in the UK and without recourse to public funds. Your studies should take up at least 15 hours a week for a minimum of six months. Once you are studying, you are allowed to do 20 hours of casual work per week in the term time and you can work full time during the holidays if you want. The type of job you do will depend largely on how much English you speak; students with very little or no English often do office cleaning or similar work.

In **North America**, **full-time students** can obtain temporary work or study permits through the Council of International Education Exchange (CIEE), 205 E 42nd Street, New York, NY 10017, T212-8222600, www.ciee.org. Also, **Commonwealth** citizens with a parent or grandparent born in the UK can apply for a **Certificate of Entitlement to the Right of Abode**, allowing them to work in Britain.

Before you travel

Visas and immigration

Visa regulations are subject to change, so it is essential to check with your local British embassy, consulate or high commission before leaving home. Citizens of all European countries – except Albania, Bosnia, Bulgaria, Macedonia, Romania, and all former Soviet republics (other than the Baltic states) – require only a passport to enter Britain and can generally stay for up to three months. Citizens of Australia, Canada, New Zealand, South Africa or the USA can stay for up to six months, providing they have a return ticket and sufficient funds to cover their stay. Citizens of most other countries require a visa from the commission or consular office in the country of application.

The **Foreign Office's website** (www.fco.gov.uk), provides details of British immigration and visa requirements. The **Immigration Advisory Service** (IAS) ① *County House, 190 Great Dover St, London SE1 4YB, T020-73576917, www.vois.org.uk/ias*, offers free and confidential advice to anyone applying for entry clearance into the UK.

For **visa extensions** contact the **Home Office** ① *Immigration and Nationality Department, Lunar House, Wellesley Rd, Croydon, London CR9, T020-8686 0688*, before your existing visa expires. Citizens of **Australia, Canada, New Zealand, South Africa** or the **USA** wishing to stay longer than six months will need an Entry Clearance Certificate from the British Embassy or High Commission in their country.

British embassies abroad

Australia High Commission: Commonwealth Av, Yarralumla, Canberra, ACT 2600, T02-6270 6666, www.uk.emb.gov.au.

Canada High Commission: 80 Elgin St, Ottawa, K1P 5K7, T613-2371530, www.britain-in-canada.org.

France 9 Av Hoche, 8e, Paris, T01-4266 3810, www.amb-grandebretagne.fr

Germany Wilhelmstrasse 70-71, 10117 Berlin, T030-20457-0, www.britischebotschaft.de.

Ireland 29 Merrion Rd, Ballsbridge, Dublin 4, T01-2053700, www.britishembassy.ie.

Netherlands Koningslaan 44, 1075AE Amsterdam, T20-6764343, www.britain.nl.

New Zealand High Commission: 44 Hill St, Wellington, T04-4726049, www.britain.org.nz.

South Africa 91 Parliament St, Cape Town 8001, T21-4617220, www.britain.org.za.

USA 3100 Massachusetts Av NW, Washington DC 20008, T1-202-588 7800, www.britain-info.org, regional consulates in 12 other cities.

Customs

Visitors from EU countries do not have to make a declaration to customs on entry into the UK. There is no longer any duty-free shopping. Visitors from non-EU countries are allowed to import 200 cigarettes, or 250g of tobacco, two litres of wine, and two litres of fortified wine or one litre of spirits.

There are various import restrictions, most of which should not affect the average tourist, and tight **quarantine restrictions** which apply to animals brought from overseas (except for Ireland). For more information on British import regulations, contact **HM Customs and Excise** ① *Dorset House, Stamford St, London SE1 9PJ, T020-7928 3344, www.hmce.gov.uk.*

Many goods in Britain are subject to a **Value Added Tax** (VAT) of 17.5%, with the major exception of books and food. Visitors from non-EU countries can save money through the Retail Export Scheme, which allows a refund of VAT on goods to be taken out of the country. Note that not all shops are participants in the scheme and that VAT cannot be reclaimed on hotel bills or other services.

What to take

You'll be able to find everything you could possibly need for your trip in London, so you can pack light and buy stuff as you go along. Given the climate, however, you should bring a lightweight waterproof jacket and a warm sweater whatever the time of year. Also bring light clothes in the summer.

A padlock can be handy for locking your bag if you are staying in one of London's Youth Hostel Association hostels, *www.yha.org.uk*. All necessary linen is included in the cost of the room so it is not necessary to take a sleeping bag or sheet. Other useful items include an alarm clock and an adaptor plug for electrical appliances.

Insurance

Insurance is crucial if things go seriously wrong. A good insurance policy should cover you in case of theft, loss of possessions or money (often including cash), the cost of any medical and dental treatment, cancellation of flights, delays in travel arrangements, accidents, missed departures, lost baggage, lost passport, and personal liability and legal expenses. There's nearly always small print: some policies exclude 'dangerous activities' such as scuba diving, skiing, horse riding or even trekking. Older travellers should note that some companies won't cover people over 65 years old, or may charge high premiums. Not all policies cover ambulance, helicopter rescue or emergency flights home. Find out if your policy pays medical expenses direct to the hospital or doctor, or if you have to pay and then claim the money back later. If the latter applies, make sure you keep all records. Whatever your policy, if you have something stolen, make sure you get a copy of the police report, as you will need this to substantiate your claim.

Before shopping around for prices, check whether your credit card and home insurance companies already offer overseas travel within your policy. If not, a good place to start is **STA Travel** at www.sta-travel.com. Travellers from North America can try **Travel Guard**, T1-800-8261300, www.noelgroup.com; **Access America**, T1-800- 2848300; **Travel Insurance Services** T1-800-9371387; and **Travel Assistance International**, T1-800-8212828. Travellers from Australia could also try www.travelinsurance.com.au.

Money

Currency
The British currency is the pound sterling (£), divided into 100 pence (p). Coins come in denominations of 1p, 2p, 5p, 10p, 20p, 50p, £1 and £2.

Exchange
Traveller's cheques The safest way to carry money is in travellers' cheques. These are available for a small commission from all major banks. **American Express** (Amex), **Visa** and **Thomas Cook** cheques are widely accepted and are the most commonly issued by banks. You'll normally have to pay commission again when you cash each cheque. This will usually be 1%, or a flat rate. No commission is payable on Amex cheques cashed at Amex offices. Make sure you keep a record of the cheque numbers and the cheques you've cashed separate from the cheques themselves, so that you can get a full refund of all uncashed cheques should you lose them. It's best to bring sterling cheques to avoid changing currencies twice. Also note that in Britain travellers' cheques are rarely accepted outside banks, so you'll need to cash them in advance and keep a good supply of ready cash.

Credit cards and ATMs Most hotels, shops and restaurants in London accept the major credit cards Access/MasterCard, Visa and Amex), though some places may charge for using them. Some smaller establishments such as B&Bs may only accept cash. You can withdraw cash from selected banks and ATMs (or cashpoints as they are called in Britain) with your cash card. Your bank or credit card company will give you a list of locations where you can use your card. Visa card and Access/MasterCard holders can use all major High Street banks (**Barclays, HSBC, Lloyds TSB, NatWest, Royal Bank of Scotland** and **Bank of Scotland**).

Banks and bureaux de change Branches of the main High Street banks – **Barclays, HSBC, Lloyds TSB, NatWest, Royal Bank of Scotland** and **Bank of Scotland** – are easily found throughout London. Bank opening hours are Monday-Friday 0930-1600 or 1700. Some larger branches may open later on Thursdays and on Saturday mornings. Banks tend to offer very similar exchange rates and are usually the best places to change money and cheques. Outside banking hours you'll have to use a **bureau de change**, which can be easily found in central London and also at airports and train stations. Post offices also change money, at competitive rates of exchange and without commission.

⠸ London for free

Enjoying London need not cost an arm and a leg. As in life, many of the best things in town are free. Top of the list are the city's parks and most of its major museums and art galleries. Exploring the rolling green acres of **Hyde Park**, strolling the flower gardens of **Regent's Park** or lazing around in **St James's Park** should only set you back the price of an ice cream. Less well-known pieces of green worth seeking out include **Postman's Park** with its memorial wall of self-sacrificing heroes and **Victoria Embankment Gardens** with their free lunchtime concerts and diverting monuments. The **British Museum**, **Victoria and Albert**, **Natural History and Science Museums** ask only for voluntary donations. As at **Tate Modern**, **Tate Britian** and the **National Gallery**, they only charge for special exhibitions. Commercial art galleries are also always worth a look for nothing, as are many of the fine art auctions at **Sotheby's** and **Christie's**. The vast majority of London's churches, including the Byzantine splendour of **Westminster Cathedral** and most of Wren's masterpieces in the City, still make no plea to your purse on the door: St Paul's Cathedral and Westminster Abbey are the big exceptions. If you're prepared to queue, the **Houses of Parliament** are also free to enter, as are the central criminal courts at the **Old Bailey** and civil courts at the **Royal Courts of Justice**. The libraries of London are another safe bet: the **Guildhall Library** holds a particularly impressive collection on the City; the **British Library** stages free exhibitions in its huge building on the Euston Rd; and many of the borough libraries provide free access to the internet. State and military papers can be searched (with some form of ID) at the **Public Record Office** in Kew (T020-8392 5200) or family records dug up in Finsbury. And countless events around town are free of charge: lunchtime classical music concerts in the music schools and churches; the **Changing of the Guard**; **gun salutes** in Hyde Park; street festivals; **BBC TV** shows in Shepherd's Bush and **ITV shows** on the South Bank; or even **glassblowing in Bermondsey**. Imagination and perseverance are just as likely to guarantee a good time as a heavy wallet.

Note: some private bureaux charge high commissions for changing cheques; those at international airports, however, often charge less than banks and will change pound sterling cheques for free. Another option is **Exchange International** which has over 20 branches throughout central London and offers good exchange facilities; Thomas Cook and other major travel agents also operate bureaux de change with reasonable rates. Avoid changing money or cheques in hotels, as the rates are usually very poor.

Money transfers If you need money urgently, the quickest way to have it sent to you is to have it **wired** to the nearest agent via **Western Union** www.westernunion.com, or **Moneygram** www.moneygram.com. Charges are on a sliding scale, ie it will cost proportionately less to wire out more money. Money can also be wired by **Thomas Cook** www.thomascook.com or **American Express** www.americanexpress.com, though this may take a day or two, or transferred via a bank draft, but this can take up to a week.

London is expensive. Accommodation will probably cost at least £20 a night (for a bed in a dorm), or £50 a night for a room of your own. A minimum of £20 a day will be required to feed, transport and entertain yourself, but expect to spend double that. By staying in YHA youth hostels – some include a substantial breakfast in the price – and by getting around on foot or using London Transport Travelcards (see page), costs can be kept to a minimum of around £30 per person per day. Those staying in slightly more upmarket B&Bs or guest houses, eating out every evening at pubs or modest restaurants and visiting tourist attractions, such as castles or museums, can expect to pay around £60 per person per day. Single travellers will have to pay more than half the cost of a double room in most places and should budget on spending around 60% of what a couple would spend. In order to enjoy London to the full then you'll need at least £70 per day, without being extravagant. That said, many of the best things in the city are free: most of the major museums, art galleries, the riverside and parks for example.

Youth and student discounts

There are various official youth and student ID cards available. The most useful is the **International Student ID Card** (ISIC), which soon pays for itself through a series of discounts, including most forms of local transport, cheap or free admission to museums, theatres and other attractions, and cheap meals in some of the city's restaurants. US and Canadian citizens are also entitled to emergency medical coverage with the card, and there's a 24-hour hotline to call in the event of medical, legal or financial emergencies.

If you're aged under 26 but not a student, you can apply for a **Federation of International Youth Travel Organizations** (FIYTO) card, or a **Euro 26 Card**, which give you much the same discounts. If you're 25 or younger you can qualify for a **Go-25 Card**, which gives you the same benefits as an ISIC card. These discount cards are issued by discount travel agencies and hostelling organizations.

Getting there

Air → *For airport information, see page 36.*

The majority of visitors to Britain fly to one of London's five airports. The largest of these, Heathrow, is the busiest airport in the world with direct flights to most major cities on all continents. More and more people are turning to budget airlines, which offer a variety of routes throughout Europe. Note, however, that the main hubs in London (Stansted and Luton) are not that near to the city itself and will require some extra overland travel.

Buying a ticket

There are a mind-boggling number of outlets for buying your plane ticket and finding the best deal can be a confusing business. **Fares** will depend on the season. Ticket prices are highest from around early June to mid-September, which is the tourist high season. Fares drop in the months either side of the peak season – mid-September to early November and mid-April to early June. They are cheapest in the low season, from November to April, although prices tend to rise sharply over Christmas and the New Year. It's also worth noting that flying at the weekend is normally more expensive.

One of the best ways of finding a good deal is to use the internet. There are a number of sites where you can check out prices and even book tickets. You can search in the travel sections of your web browser or try the sites of the discount travel

Discount flight agents in North America

Air Brokers International, 323 Geary St, Suite 411, San Francisco, CA94102, T1-800-8833273, www.airbrokers.com. Consolidator and specialist in RTW and Circle Pacific tickets.

Discount Airfares Worldwide On-Line, www.etn.nl/discount.htm. A hub of consolidator and discount agent links.

STA Travel, 5900 Wiltshire Blvd, Suite 2110, Los Angeles, CA 90036, T1-800-7770112, www.sta-travel.com. Discount student/youth travel discount company with branches in New York, San Francisco, Boston, Miami, Chicago, Seattle and Washington DC.

Travel CUTS, 187 College St, Toronto, ON M5T 1P7, T1-800-6672887, www.travelcuts.com. Specialist in student discount fares, IDs and other travel services. Branches in other Canadian cities.

companies and agents and the budget airlines listed in this section. Also worth trying are: **www.expedia.com**, **www.lastminute.com**, **www.e-bookers.com**, **www.cheapflights.co.uk**, **www.deckchair.com**, **www.flynowww.com**, **www.dialaflight.co.uk**, **www.opodo.com** and **www.travelocity.com**.

Airport tax All tickets are subject to taxes (£10-20 depending on route), insurance charge (around £6) and passenger service charge, which varies according to airport. This adds up quickly – for economy-fare flights within the UK and from EU countries expect additions of £20-30. For inter-continental flights, this will rise to around £60-70.

Flights from North America
There are non-stop flights to London Heathrow and Gatwick airports from many US and Canadian cities, including Atlanta*, Boston, Calgary, Chicago, Cincinnati*, Dallas*, Denver, Detroit, Halifax, Honolulu, Houston, Las Vegas*, Los Angeles, Miami, Minneapolis*, Montreal, New York, Orlando*, Philadelphia, Phoenix, Portland, San Diego, San Francisco, Santa Cruz*, Seattle, Tampa*, Toronto, Vancouver and Washington DC, and many more connections to other cities.
* Flights from these cities are to London Gatwick airport.

For low-season Apex fares expect to pay US$200-450 from New York and other East Coast cities, and US$300-600 from the West Coast. Prices rise to around US$500-800 from New York and US$400-900 from the West Coast in the summer months. Low-season Apex fares from Toronto and Montreal cost around CAN$600-700, and from Vancouver around CAN$800-900, rising to $750-950 and $950-1150 during the summer.

Flights from Australia and New Zealand
The cheapest scheduled flights to London Heathrow from Australia or New Zealand are via Asia with **Gulf Air, Royal Brunei** or **Thai Airways**. They charge A$1300-1500 in low season and up to A$1800 in high season, and involve a transfer en route. Flights via Africa start at around A$2000 and are yet more expensive via North America. Flights to and from Perth via Africa or Asia are a few hundred dollars cheaper. The cheapest scheduled flights from New Zealand are with **Korean Air, Thai Airways** or **JAL**, all of whom fly via their home cities for around NZ$2000-2300. The most direct route is via North America with **United Airlines**, via Chicago or Los Angeles. Fares range from around NZ$2800 in low season to NZ$3200 in high season.

Flights from Europe and Ireland
In addition to regular flights operated by the major national carriers, the surge in **budget airline** routes means that you can fly from practically anywhere in Europe, to London's Stansted, Gatwick or Luton airports. The budget airlines specialize in routes

from provincial and smaller cities. The flight consolidator **www.opodo.com** can often
offer good rates, but it's worth noting that flight consolidators do not include budget
airline fares – you'll have to search those out separately. Fares for a return ticket can
range from €15 to €300 on a scheduled flight. Budget airlines offer no frills: no meals,
no reserved seating and baggage restrictions. However, you can sometimes travel for
as little as €5. Check terms and airport location before booking: **www.basiqair.com**,
www.bmibaby.com, **www.easyjet.com**, **www.flybe.com**, **www.ryanair.com**,
www.virgin-express.com.

Rail

Eurostar, T0990-186186, www.eurostar.com, operates high-speed trains to London
Waterloo from Paris (three hours) and Brussels (two hours 40 minutes) via Lille (two
hours). Standard-class tickets to Paris and Brussels range from £70 for a weekend day
return to £300 for a fully flexible mid-week return. There are substantial discounts for
children (4-11 years) and for passengers who are under 26 years on the day of travel. It is
worth keeping an eye open for special offers, especially in the low season. All other rail
connections will involve some kind of ferry crossing (see below). For full details on rail
services available, contact your national railway or **Rail Europe**, www.raileurope.com, for
information on routes, timetables, fares and discount passes.

Road

If you're driving from continental Europe you can take the **Eurotunnel Shuttle Service**,
T0800-969992, www.eurotunnel.com, a freight train which runs 24 hours a day, 365
days a year, and takes you and your car from Calais to Folkestone (about 2 hours'
drive from London) in 35-45 minutes. Fares are per carload, regardless of the number
of passengers, and range from £135 one way to £270 return depending on the time of
year or how far in advance you book. For bookings, call T08705-353535. Foot
passengers cannot cross on the Shuttle.

Coach National Express's **Eurolines** ① T0990-143219, www.eurolines.com,
operates services between London's Victoria Coach Station and many European
destinations. Channel crossings are made by both the ferry and Eurotunnel and
tickets are cheaper if booked at least seven days in advance. This is a good option for
travellers on a tight budget, as fares are less than half those of Eurostar.

Getting to London from within the UK

Rail
There are four main companies operating frequent rail services between London and
other towns and cities in England, Scotland and Wales: **GNER** ① T0345-225225,
leaves from King's Cross and run up the east coast to the East Midlands, Yorkshire,
Northeast England and Scotland; **Virgin** ① T08457-222333, trains operate a
cross-country and a west coast service from Euston to the Midlands, the northwest
and Scotland. **Scotrail** ① T08457-550033, www.scotrail.co.uk, operates the
Caledonian Sleeper service if you wish to travel overnight to Scotland. Trains to Wales
and the west of England are run by **First Great Western** ① T0845-7000125,
www.great-western-trains.co.uk, from Paddington Station in London. **National Rail
Enquiries**① T0845-7484950, www.railtrack.co.uk, are very helpful for information on
rail services and fares.

Bus National Express ℹ *To8705-808080*, *www.gobycoach.com*, operates from Victoria Coach Station and has a nationwide network with over 1000 destinations. Tickets can be bought at bus stations or from a huge number of agents throughout the country.

Touching down

Airport information

London Heathrow Airport

London Heathrow Airport (LHR), Hounslow, Middlesex, TW6 1JH, To870-0000123, is the world's busiest international airport and it has four terminals, so when leaving London, it's important to check which terminal to go to before setting out for the airport. Transport for London and British Rail have travel information points in Terminals 1, 2 and 4. Bus and coach sales/information desks are located in all four terminals. There are hotel reservations desks in the arrivals area of each terminal (a booking fee is charged). For general enquiries, passengers with special needs should contact the Call Centre, To870-0000123. If further help or advice concerning travel arrangements is required call Heathrow Travelcare To20-8745 7495.

By train and tube The airport is on the **London Underground** Piccadilly Line, which runs trains every 5-9 minutes to the centre of London and beyond, with an approximate journey time of 50 minutes. There are two stations: one serving Terminals 1, 2, and 3; the other for Terminal 4. The first train from central London arrives at Terminal 4 at 0629 (0749 on Sun) and the last arrives at 0107 (0008 on Sun). Allow a further five minutes to reach the station for Terminals 1, 2 and 3. Details of timetables and fares are available on To20-7222 1234 (24 hours). **Heathrow Express**, To845-6001515, www.heathrowexpress.co.uk, non-stop train to and from Paddington Station in central London. The journey takes 15 minutes to Terminals 1, 2 and 3, and 20 minutes to Terminal 4. Trains depart every 15 minutes between 0510 and 2340, 365 days a year. There is plenty of luggage space and wheelchairs and pushchairs are catered for. Some airlines have check-in facilities at Paddington. Tickets cost £12 (single), £22 (return). A £2 premium is charged for tickets purchased on board the train. Discounted fares are available and tickets purchased via the website are also cheaper. Children travel free when accompanied by an adult.

By bus An **Airlink**, To990-747777, 'Hotel Hoppa' shuttle service serves most major hotels near the airport. **Airbus A2**, To20-8400 6655, runs every 30 minutes throughout the day to and from a number of stops in central London. During the night, the **N97** bus connects Heathrow with central London. **National Express**, To8705-808080, runs coaches from Victoria Coach Station every 30 minutes. Airlinks also operates frequent coach services between Heathrow, Gatwick, Luton, Stansted and other airports.

By car/taxi Heathrow is 16 miles west of London at Junctions 3 and 4 on the M4 motorway. A taxi from Heathrow Airport to central London takes approximately one hour and should cost around £40. There are taxi desks in the Arrivals area of all four terminals (Terminal 1, To20-8745 7487; Terminal 2, To20-8745 5408; Terminal 3, To20-8745 4655; Terminal 4, To20-8745 7302).

London Gatwick Airport

London Gatwick Airport (LGW), Gatwick, West Sussex, RH6 0JH, To870-0002468. London's second airport 28 miles south of the capital has two terminals, North and

Touching down

Business hours Banks, post offices and other city businesses: 0900-1700 Mon-Fri. **Shops**: usually more flexible 0900-2000 Mon-Sat in some cases and increasingly on Sun from 1100-1700. **Pubs**: 1100-2300 (1200-2230 on Sun). **Restaurants**: often stop serving lunch at 1400 and dinner at 2200.

Electricity The current in Britain is 240V AC. Plugs have three square pins and adapters are widely available.

Emergencies For **police**, **fire brigade** and **ambulance** dial 999.

Laundry Coin-operated launderettes are easy to find in residential areas of London. The average cost for a wash and tumble dry is about £4. A service wash where someone will do your washing for you, costs around £6.

Time Greenwich Mean Time (GMT) is used from late October to late March, after which time the clocks go forward an hour to British Summer Time (BST). GMT is five hours ahead of US Eastern Standard Time and 10 hours behind Australian Eastern Standard Time.

Toilets Public toilets are found at all train and bus stations. They may charge 20p but are generally clean with disabled and baby-changing facilities. Those in department stores, pubs or restaurants are usually better – and easier to find – than public toilets in the street.

Weights and measures Imperial and metric both used. Distances on roads are measured in miles and yards, drinks are poured in pints and gills, but generally nowadays, the metric system is used elsewhere.

Essentials Touching down

South, with all the facilities including car hire, currency exchange, 24-hour banking, Flight Shops (T08000-747787), Hotel Reservations Desks (T01293-504549) and a Travel Shop in the South Terminal (T01293-506783). There are many help points for passengers with special needs and free wheelchair assistance or help with baggage to reach check-in.

By train All trains arrive at the South Terminal where there is a fast link to the North Terminal. A number of airlines offer check-in facilities at London's Victoria Station. The fastest service is the non-stop 30-minute **Gatwick Express**, T0990-301530, which runs to and from London Victoria every 15 minutes during the day, and hourly throughout the night. Standard tickets cost £10.50 single and £20 return; first-class and cheap-day returns are available. **Thameslink** rail services run from King's Cross, Farringdon, Blackfriars and London Bridge stations.

By bus Airbus A5 operates hourly to/from Victoria Coach Station. For further information call the Airport Travel Line, T0990-747777.

By car Gatwick is at Crawley, off Junction 9 on the M23 motorway, about an hour's drive from central London. A taxi to central London for up to 4 people costs around £75.

London Luton Airport

London Luton Airport (LTN), Luton, Bedfordshire, LU2 9LU, T01582-405100. Luton airport, about 30 miles north of central London, deals particularly with flights operated by budget airlines. All the usual facilities are available plus fax, internet, a children's play area and an airport chapel. There is also a Skyline Travel Shop, T01582-726454.

By train Regular **Thameslink** trains leave from London Bridge, Blackfriars, Farringdon and King's Cross stations to Luton Airport Parkway station; a free shuttle bus service operates between the station and the airport terminal. The Thameslink station at King's Cross is about 100 yards east of the main station, along the Pentonville Road.

By bus Green Line coaches run to and from Victoria Coach Station, Hyde Park Corner, Marble Arch, George Street and Baker Street in central London.

By car The airport is southeast of Luton, 2 miles off the M1 at Junction 10. The 30-mile journey into London will take around 50 minutes, and costs around £55 by taxi. Two companies operate from outside the terminal.

Stansted Airport

Stansted Airport (STN), CM24 1RW, T08700-000303, 35 miles northeast of London (near Cambridge), is another budget airline hub. Terminal facilities include car hire, ATMs, 24-hour currency exchange, shops, restaurants and bars. There's a *Book and Go* Travel Shop, T08700-102015, a hotel reservations desk, T01279-661220, and AAS Assistance, T01279-663213, for passengers with special needs and also left luggage.

By train Stansted Express, T0845-8500150, runs trains every 15 minutes from London's Liverpool Street Station to the main terminal building. The journey takes 45 minutes and costs £13 single and £23 open return.

By bus Airbus A6 runs every hour from Victoria Coach Station, Hyde Park Corner, Marble Arch and Baker Street. **Airbus A7** also runs hourly from Victoria Coach Station, Embankment and Aldgate. The journey takes around 1 hour 30 minutes. **Jetlink**, T08705-747777, operates a frequent service between London's four main airports.

By car The airport is north of London by Junction 8 of the M11. The 35-mile journey to/from central London takes around an hour to 1 hour 30 minutes depending on traffic.

Local customs and laws

In general, customs and laws are the same as you would encounter in any other western country. Informal clothing is acceptable, except at special events that specify a dress code. If you are planning to work in London, business clothes may be appropriate. Visitors may find the British to be reserved, and, as in most countries, politeness is appreciated.

Tipping

Tipping is at the customer's discretion. In a restaurant you should leave a tip of 10-15% if you are satisfied with the service. If the bill already includes a service charge, you needn't add a further tip. Tipping is not normal in pubs or bars. Taxi drivers expect a tip, usually of around 10%. As in most other countries, porters, bellboys and waiters in more upmarket hotels rely on tips to supplement their meagre wages.

Prohibitions

If you use mace or pepper spray for self defence at home, you should note that both are illegal in the UK, and if you are caught carrying or using them, you may be arrested. Marijuana is illegal, as are all the usual drugs. However, under a recently introduced law, police may turn a blind eye to possession of small amounts of cannabis.

Safety

Generally speaking, London is a safe place to visit, though, like in any big city, sensible precautions need to be taken to guard against pickpockets. Even at night you should feel relatively safe as there are usually plenty of people milling about, especially around Soho, Leicester Square and Piccadilly. Places to be especially vigilant against pickpockets are in tube stations and while travelling on the tube. Assault in Central London is comparatively rare, though women travellers are advised never to get into an empty tube carriage on their own. You should also avoid deserted and unlit streets at night.

The greatest annoyance in Central London is likely to be the unwanted attention of drunks, particularly at the weekend. You'll probably find this amusing, or at worst, slightly irritating. It often consists of someone sitting next to you on the night bus or last tube, off their face and trying to chat you up before falling asleep on your shoulder and dribbling, or perhaps puking up on your shoes. Rather more worrying is if you're stuck in a tube carriage on your own with a nutcase screaming obscenities in your general direction. Best thing to do in this situation is to simply get off at the next populated station platform. Other popular places for freaks, or those intent on harm, are any of the city's parks or open spaces, and these should be avoided after dark.

Trafalgar Square late at night can be a bit chaotic, as this is where most revellers congregate to try and remember which night bus they should be taking, but in reality the most dangerous people around here are those selling distinctly dodgy-looking hot dogs.

Getting around

Public transport is generally fairly efficient, although it can be expensive. Fortunately, there's a whole raft of discount passes and tickets which can cut the price considerably. There are five **Travel Information Centres** in London underground stations (Heathrow 1,2,3, King's Cross, Liverpool Street, Oxford Circus and St James's Park), three at National Rail stations (Euston, Paddington and Victoria), several at bus stations, including Hammersmith, and also in the arrival halls of Terminals 1, 2 and 3 at Heathrow Airport. They all provide free travel advice, maps and timetables. They also sell travelcards and bus passes as well as guide books, sightseeing tours and entry tickets to many London attractions. For 24-hour information call T020-7222 1234, www.tfl.gov.uk. You can get specific advice here on the best way of getting from A to B anywhere within London on any type of transport.

Rail

Tube

The London underground, or tube, is the fastest way of getting around town and most Londoners use it. The 12 lines are colour coded, the map (see page) is easy to follow and the system is relatively straightforward to use. However, it is worth avoiding during rush hour (0800-0930 and 1700-1830) if at all possible. Crime is not a serious problem on the tube in Central London although, as with anywhere else, beware of pickpockets and don't choose an empty carriage, especially at night. Services run from 0530 until just after midnight, with fewer trains run on Sundays and public holidays.

The underground is divided into six **fare zones**, with Zone 1 covering central London. Travel between two stations within Zone 1 costs £2.00 (child £0.60); a journey crossing into Zone 2 will cost £2.30 (child £0.80). Anyone planning to make more than two journeys in one day will save money by buying a Day Travelcard (£6 peak, £4.70 off-peak), a 3-day Travelcard (£15), or Family Travelcard £2.70 per adult and £0.80 per child for one day's travel (you need to be two adults and have at least one child with you). A carnet of 10 zone 1 tickets costs £15 and is valid for at least a year.

The **Docklands Light Railway (DLR)**, operating as part of the tube system, runs from Bank and Tower Gateway to the Cutty Sark for Maritime Greenwich and beyond. It is a scenic route, passing through the revived Docklands area and Canary Wharf and can be used by travelcard holders. Guided tours on weekend services make a good (and cheap) tour option.

Road

Bicycle ⟩⟩ *See cycle map, p458*

Cycle lanes are still not the norm in London and, compared with some European or Scandinavian cities, London is not an easy ride for cyclists. Make sure you always wear a helmet and never leave your bike unlocked. A 1000-mile cycle network is planned for the city and several organizations and direct action groups are continually pressing for improvements to convince the Greater London Authority of the importance of making London more bicycle friendly.

The best known is the **London Cycling Campaign** ① *T020-7928 7220, www.lcc.org.uk, Mon-Fri, 1400-1700 only*. Their magazine *London Cyclist*, publishes a diary of rides and related events for all London. They also publish the *Brand New Central London Map*, a cycling map with traffic-free routes, safe cycle crossings and bike shops. Other publications include the *Ordnance Survey Cycle Tours Around London*, which has 24 one-day routes within a 60-mile radius of the capital; and the *London Cycle Guide* by Nick Crowther, which details 25 routes in and around the city.

> ⚑ *www.cycling.uk.com is a cycling information station with over 200 links to other useful sites.*

The **London Bicycle Tour Company** ① *1a Gabriel's Wharf, 56 Upper Ground, SE1, T020-7928 6838, www.londonbicycle.com*, rent bikes with full insurance (helmets provided), and operate guided cycle tours along four different routes: *The Royal West Tour* (9 miles, 3 ½ hours on Sunday afternoons); *The East Tour* (9 miles, 3 ½ hours on Tuesday and Thursday afternoons); and *Night Ride* (historical trips round pubs). Tours all leave from the company's base and cost around £15. You are advised to book in advance.

Every summer thousands of people take part in long-distance cycle rides (often in aid of charity) from London to cities as far afield as Brighton, Paris and Brussels.

Bus ⟩⟩ *See bus map, p460*

The big, red 'routemaster' double-decker buses, introduced in 1959, were a London institution, part of the fabric of the city. Now, sadly, these have been phased out in favour of more modern, if less iconic, buses, but no matter where you are in London there will always be a bus route nearby. Bus stops are either compulsory or request stops. Buses always stop at **compulsory stops** (red symbol on a white background) unless they are full; at **request stops** (white symbol on a red background) they will only stop if you put out your hand. To get off at a request stop, ring the bell once and in good time to let the driver know.

> ⚑ *The No 11 bus route is one of the best sightseeing trips in town.*

Daytime buses, like the London underground, run until about 0030. After that, an extensive system of **night buses** takes over. Most areas of Greater London are within reach of at least one night bus service. All night bus route numbers start with the letter 'N'. Most of the central London night buses pass through Trafalgar Square (see box). The standard single Zone 1 day and night bus fare is £1.20. A day bus pass costs £3 (£1 child)

Buses are a great way of getting to know the city, especially from the top deck, but it may take substantially longer to reach your destination by bus than by tube. Most buses require a ticket to be bought before boarding, either at one of the machines at stops, or by using a travelcard.

Car

If you are only planning to spend a short time in London, don't bother hiring a car, it's not worth it. Traffic-clogged central London is still a nightmare to drive in, despite the newly introduced congestion charges of £5 per day (congestion charging area marked out with a white 'C' on a red background on the road and on signs) Monday-Friday 0700

▸ Night buses

Night buses run hourly along more than 50 routes from about 2300 until dawn; most pass through Trafalgar Square, a good place to head for if you are unsure of which bus you need. The Central London Bus Guide, which includes a night bus map, is provided free at Travel Information Centres (see page 39). Alternatively, call London Transport Information T020-7222 1234 (lines are very busy).

The following is a selection of 10 popular routes:
N5 Trafalgar Sq – Hampstead – Hendon – Edgware
N9 Aldwych – Trafalgar Sq – Hammersmith – Putney – Richmond – Kingston
N11 Liverpool St – Trafalgar Sq – Fulham – Hammersmith – Wembley

N12 Notting Hill Gate – Trafalgar Sq – Elephant – Camberwell – Peckham – Dulwich
N14 Tottenham Court Rd – Piccadilly Circus – Fulham – Putney – Roehampton
N31 Camden Town – Kilburn – Kensington – Earl's Court – Chelsea – Clapham Junction
N52 Victoria – Trafalgar Sq – Notting Hill – Ladbroke Grove – Willesden
N97 Trafalgar Square – Earl's Court – Hammersmith – Hounslow – Heathrow Airport
N159 Marble Arch – Trafalgar Sq – Brixton – Streatham – Croydon – New Addington
N207 Holborn – Shepherd's Bush – Ealing – Southall – Uxbridge

Essentials Getting around

and 1830. Indeed, Londoners themselves tend to use public transport during the day, saving their cars for night and weekends. Apart from the heavy traffic and complicated web of one-way streets, parking is hard to find and very expensive. The charge can be paid on the day at any one of 300 Paypoint-equipped shops, petrol stations or car parks until 2200. Failure to pay before 2400 incurs another £5 penalty fee, after which time the driver owes Transport for London £80. Call T0845-9001234 for more details, or look up www.cclondon.com. Beware of parking illegally too, as you are very likely to get a ticket or else be clamped or towed away and impounded (in which case you should call T020-7747 4747). This can set you back anywhere between £80 and £240.

Rules and regulations To drive in the UK you must have a current driving licence. Although foreign nationals may use their own licence for one year, international driving permits, available from your country of origin, may be required for some rentals, especially if your own licence is not in English. Visitors importing their own vehicle should also have their vehicle registration or ownership document. Make sure you're adequately insured. In all of the UK you **drive on the left**. **Speed limits** are 30 miles per hour (mph) in built-up areas, 70 mph on motorways and dual carriageways and 60 mph on most other roads.

▸ *www.dvla.gov.uk has details of every aspect of driving in the UK. The AA and RAC websites are excellent for route planning information.*

Motoring organizations It's advisable to join one of the main UK motoring organizations during your visit for their **24-hour breakdown assistance**. The two main ones in Britain are the **Automobile Association** (*AA*) ① *T0800-444999, www.theaa.co.uk*, and the **Royal Automobile Club** (*RAC*) ① *T0800-550550, www.rac.co.uk*. One year's membership starts from £40 for the AA and £38 for the RAC. They also provide many other services, including a reciprocal agreement for free assistance with many overseas motoring organizations. Check to see if your organization is included. Both companies can extend their cover to include Europe.

Their **emergency numbers** are: *AA* To800-887766; *RAC* To800-828282. You can call these numbers even if you're not a member, but you'll have to a pay a large fee.

Car hire

Car hire is expensive in London and you may be better off making arrangements in your home country for a fly/drive deal through one of the main multi-national companies. The minimum you can expect to pay is around £150 per week for a small car. Always check and compare conditions, such as mileage limitations, excess payable in the case of an accident, etc. Small, local hire companies often offer better deals than the larger multinationals. Most companies prefer payment with a credit card – some insist on it – otherwise you'll have to leave a large deposit (£100 or more). You need to have had a full driver's licence for at least one year and to be aged between 21 (25 for some companies) and 70. **Motorcycle hire** is very expensive, ranging from around £200 up to £350 per week.

Car hire companies

Britain
Avis, T0870 6060100.
Budget, T0800-181181.
Europcar, T0345-222525.
Hertz, T0990-996699.
Holiday Autos, T0870-4000011.
National Car Rental, T020-7278 2273.
Thrifty, T0990-168238.

North America
Alamo, T800-5229696, www.goalamo.com.
Avis, T800-3311084, www.avis.com.
Budget, T800-5270700,
www.budgetrentacar.com.
Dollar, T800-4216868, www.dollar.com.
Hertz, T800-6543001, www.hertz.com.

Holiday Autos, T800-4227737,
www.holiday/colauto.com.
National, T800-CAR-RENT,
www.nationalcar.com.
Thrifty, T800-3672277, www.thrifty.com.

Australia
Avis, T1800-225533.
Budget, T1300-362848.
Hertz, T1800-550067.

New Zealand
Avis, T 09-5262847.
Budget, T09-3752222.
Hertz, T09-3676350.

Taxi → *If in doubt, it's best to stick to black cabs – at least they know their way around the city.*
London's black cabs are almost as much of an institution as the old routemaster buses. Licensed cabs can be hailed in the street when the yellow 'For Hire' sign is displayed; they all have meters which start ticking as soon as you get in, and fares increase by the minute thereafter. Surcharges are added late at night and for luggage or extra passengers. Most 'cabbies' will expect a tip of between 10 and 15%. Any comments or complaints should be made to the **Public Carriage Office** T020-7230 1631, whilst lost property should be reported to T020-7833 0996 (make a note of your taxi's licence number and the driver's badge number). For 24-hour **Radio Taxis** call T020-7272 0272.

As well as black cabs there are also regular taxis, which are known as **minicabs**. It is advisable to book these directly from the cab office, as there are many unlicensed cab drivers operating in Central London. Minicabs can be more economical, especially during busy times, as they charge a flat fee for the journey instead of using a meter, but you will need to know the going rate for a particular journey in order to avoid being ripped off.

River

Boat ▸▸ *See river map, p456*

Daily services operate from most central London piers. Riverboats travel to and from Greenwich and the Thames Barrier in the east, and as far as Hampton Court in the west. There are over 20 piers along this stretch of the Thames and apart from Hampton Court Palace and the sights at Greenwich, the river gives access to Kew Gardens, Richmond Park and many of the central London attractions. Tickets for most trips can be bought at the pier or, in some cases, on the boat.

The direct, 50-minute Westminster to Greenwich route is operated by **Westminster Passenger Services** *To20-7930 4097, www.wpsa.co.uk*. A single adult ticket costs £6.80 (return £7.70). There are concessions for children and senior citizens and family tickets are also available. They also run the 3½-hour Westminster-Kew-Richmond-Hampton Court route, between 1 April and 30 October . Adult single £13.50 (child £6.75) return £19.50 (child £9.75). All of these fares are discounted by a third if you have a travelcard. The 50-minute 'Multilingual Circular Cruises', with a taped commentary in seven languages, operate from Waterloo and Embankment piers and are run by **Catamaran Cruisers** *To20-7987 1185, www.catamarancruisers.co.uk*. Tickets cost £7.00 (adults), £5.00 (children), £19.50 (family) with concessions for students and senior citizens. Sailings depart hourly from Embankment at 10.45. Other one-hour long **Circular Cruises** *To20-7936 2033*, leave from Westminster Pier and cost £6.80 for adults and £3.40 for children (discounted by a third with a travelcard). Shorter 25-30-minute trips between Westminster Pier and Tower Pier are operated by **City Cruises** *To20-7237 5134*. Adults £5.60 single, £6.80 return (children half price).

Other riverboat options are the **lunch and dinner cruises** operated by: **Woods River Cruises** *To20-7481 2711, www.woodsrivercruises.co.uk*; **Bateaux London** *To20-7925 2215, www.bateauxlondon.com*; and **City Cruises** *To20-7237 5134, www.citycruises.com*.

Several companies offer trips on traditional narrow boats along **Regent's Canal** between Camden Lock and Little Venice taking in Regent's Park and London Zoo: **London Waterbus Company** *To20-7482 2660* (50 mins, £5.50 adult); **Jenny Wren** *To20-7485 4433* (90 mins, £7 adult, £3.50 child) (also operates a restaurant boat, *My Fair Lady* for private charters); and **Jason's Canal Boat Trip** *To20-7286 3428* (45 mins £6/7 single/return adults, £4.50/5.50 child). For further information, go to www.canalmuseum.org.uk/boat-trip.htm.

On foot

London is a wonderfully walkable city. And there are an increasing number of places in the thick of things where you can escape the traffic entirely. There are the gorgeous Royal parks obviously, and the hilltop expanse of Hampstead Heath, as well as a decent clutch of central locations that are positively pedestrian-friendly. Shoppers in Covent Garden and Carnaby Street avoid running the gauntlet of maniac drivers and thundering buses. The riverside walk along the South Bank and Bankside is mercifully free of fumes. Leicester Square provides a fairly safe haven to watch the world go by. And the north side of Trafalgar Square now joins up with the National Gallery so that art lovers can mooch up to a Botticelli from Landseer's lions without risking life and limb. Walking is an excellent way to get to know London whether it be on your own with a map or book or as part of a group on an organized tour. More and more companies are running these tours, either pre-booked or regular, turn-up-and-go walks that leave from the same place at a fixed time every week. There are walks in the morning, afternoon or evening, seasonal walks, and dozens of special-interest walks, from Dickens and Jack the Ripper, to Bohemians and Bluestockings, to Bishops, Brothels and the Bard. There are also ghost walks, haunted pubs, mystery pubs, Clubland, and the Beatles, or perhaps Beautiful Belgravia, Hidden Hampstead and Little Venice... Most of these walks last between 1½ and 2 hours and cost about £5 for adults with discounts for students (accompanied children usually go free).

Guided walks One of the best-known companies, **The Original London Walks** *T020-7624 3978, www.walks.com*, have over 200 walks to choose from. Some other companies are: **Mystery Walks** *T07957-388280, www.tourguides.org.uk (Jack the Ripper Tour*, Sun, Wed and Fri at 1900) *Haunted London Ghost Tour* (Tue at 1900), £5 adults £4 students; and **Stepping Out** *T020-8881 2933*.

Guided historical tours of the Houses of Parliament (see page 142) were introduced for the first time in 2000. For information, T020-7219 4272 (Commons) and T020-7219 3107 (Lords).

Other enjoyable walks are around London's many parks, gardens and cemeteries. One of these is the circular **Diana Princess of Wales Memorial Walk**, a 7-mile route through St James's Park, Green Park, Hyde Park and Kensington Gardens, taking in the newly opened, typically controversial **Diana Memorial Fountain**, a slippery, circular water feature in Hyde Park, south of the Serpentine, between the Lido and the main road. Royal Parks information: T020-7298 2000. Also try www.london.walks.com.

Sleeping

Accommodation in central London has always been expensive and most rooms for hire are small by international standards. That said, at most prices standards have improved dramatically in recent years. Fierce competition has meant that hostels have cleaned up their act and even the smartest hotels have been forced to do deals, especially during the quieter months (January to March, October and November). A wave of designer hotels opened in the city in the late 1980s and 90s and most of the famous and luxurious older names felt they needed to spruce themselves up as a result. They're usually cheaper at weekends.

London's grandest hotels are almost all in **Mayfair** (page 108), **Knightsbridge** (page 165) and **Belgravia** (page 152), with a sprinkling east towards the City. The most central areas with the largest selection of less expensive rooms – either in Hotels or B&Bs – are on the fringes of these districts, in **Victoria** (page 152), **Earl's Court** (page 324), **Bayswater** (page 331) and **Bloomsbury** (page 202). Many are cheaper at weekends and most mid-range hotels include breakfast in the price, although it's worth checking.

A room in these districts is likely to cost between £50 and £70 per person per night – at the very least. Try the seven YHA London hostels, www.yha.org.uk, well spread out around the city for anything cheaper. All are open 24 hours and charge between £19 and £24 a night for dormitory accommodation. Some even have rooms with en suite facilities. Other hostels can be found in Bloomsbury and Bankside. Also check out the halls of residence of various London University colleges (see pages 165 and 347), where student rooms are let during vacations. Book well ahead, especially for the youth hostels and other budget options, but also keep an eye out for last-minute offers.

For self catering and short lets try **Holiday Serviced Apartments**, PO Box 226, Northwood, Middlesex, HA6 2ZJ, T020-7373 4477, www.holidayapartments.co.uk. From £450 a week self-catering serviced apartments in central London.

⁞ Sleeping price codes

AL	over £280	C	£50-£80
L	£180-£280	D	£30-£50
A	£100-£180	E	£15-£30
B	£80-£100	F	under £15

Prices refer to the cost per night for a standard double room with en suite bathroom (or a single bed in a dorm) in high season.

Camping is also a possibility. Try: **Lea Valley Campsite**, Sewardstone Rd, Chingford E4 7RA, T020-8529 5689, Apr-Oct only, £6.15 per person per night, £2.50 for electricity; or **Crystal Palace Caravan Club**, Crystal Palace Parade, London, SE19 1UF, T020 8778 7155, £5 per pitch plus £4 per adult low season, £10 per pitch plus £5 per adult in high season.

Eating ⇥ *See also restaurant guide, p427*

London's restaurant scene continues to mature at a heady rate. Broadly speaking, a couple of decades ago Londoners and visitors alike were faced with a choice between forking out astronomic amounts for haute cuisine in luxury surroundings or settling for a curry or chips. Nowadays, the range of excellent food on offer in almost every setting and price bracket can be equally baffling. A good meal has become an essential part of a top night on the town. That said, the city does remain a notoriously expensive place in which to eat out compared to the British regions, much of Europe and North America. Compensation of a kind can be found in the sheer variety of different cuisines available – from Africa to Yemen via Poland and New Zealand; in the quality of the fresh ingredients appearing on menus across the capital; and in the extraordinary array of different places they can be enjoyed – from snack bars, burger joints and pubs via cafés and brasseries to silver-service fine dining restaurants. Some trends are worth noting. The late '90s witnessed a boom in Japanese noodle bars and more formal restaurants, now well-established. They joined a healthy spate of Thai food joints, many of them very good value. Turkish, Spanish and Lebanese cooking have also enjoyed a renaissance. And then there's the continuing Anglo-Italian love affair, demonstrated in first-rate performances almost every night from kitchens all over the city. Traditional British fare can still be found too, now elevated to heights way beyond boiled cabbage and bully beef. So where do you start looking for this exciting cultural turnaround? Arguably it all began in Soho, where you can still find some of the best cooking in the capital. Elsewhere in the West End, Mayfair and St James's are the gourmets' favourite destination. Clerkenwell is another, with several superb restaurants capitalising on their proximity to Smithfield meat market. In the end though, with a little care, it's true to say that even the fussiest eaters are unlikely to be disappointed in almost every part of London. The city is now confidently one of the world's great gastronomic centres.

Like any major tourist centre, London has its fair share of overpriced mediocrity, but this is easily avoided. For example, if you're shopping in the West End, a slight detour into the streets of Soho, choc-full of excellent bars, cafés and restaurants, offers refuge from the culinary wasteland of Oxford Street. Similarly, Chinatown's myriad restaurants are an appealing alternative to the bland chains of Piccadilly and Leicester Square. Just across Charing Cross Road, Covent Garden may look like

Eating price codes

♕♕♕ **Expensive** (£40 and above)
♕♕ **Mid-range** (£20-40)
♕ **Cheap** (£20 and under)

Prices are based on a two-course evening meal for one, without service charge or drink. Places which are considerably cheaper than £20 are described as such in the listing.

a tourist trap, but has some tasty secrets up its sleeve, and if money's no object, then Mayfair's finest can deliver the goods with impeccable manners and no shortage of style. Red-blooded carnivores, meanwhile, should head for trendy Clerkenwell, where several chic eateries are taking advantage of neighbouring Smithfield meat market.

Beyond the West End and Central London there are many more treats in store. Wealthy areas such as Clapham in South London, Islington and Hampstead in the north and Notting Hill in the west boast many excellent eating establishments. Take note, however, that in some of the more painfully hip joints, style may rule over substance. Not so much 'you are what you eat' as 'you are where you're seen to eat'.

Alternatively, you can always set off in search of one of Britain's favourite dishes – curry. Two districts in the city are *sans pareil* when it comes to Asian cuisine. Brick Lane, in the East End, is jam-packed with seriously good curry houses, where a full meal may stretch your waistline but not your budget, while way out west in Southall authentic Indian food comes so cheap they're practically giving it away.

Entertainment

No visit to the capital is complete without checking out its extraordinary cultural life. What other European city offers anything like such vibrant live music or theatre? And these traditionally strong performers have been joined by a brisk stand-up comedy circuit and popularized art scene. Even the sorry decline in the number of independent rep cinemas seems to have slowed. In central London, the lion's share is divided between the **West End**, with its grand 'theatreland', Covent Garden and blockbusting cinemas in Leicester Square; and the **South Bank**, home to the state-subsidized Royal National Theatre, National Film Theatre and the eclectic fare provided by the South Bank Centre itself. Beyond these two poles spin a host of other star attractions: indie music rocks, jazz swings and dance beats break in **Camden**, **Soho** and **Shoreditch**; challenging theatricals hit the boards in Islington and Hampstead; orchestras tune up in **Marylebone**; comedians leave audiences ga-ga in pubs and weird films flicker on **The Mall**. Prepare to be entertained, very entertained.

▶▶ *For specific Cinema, Music, Theatre and other listings see the relevant area's listings section and for more information and background on the arts scene in London, see also the Background chapter pages 419-424.*

Where to buy tickets

For a picture of what's on where and when, the best listings are to be found in *Time Out* magazine, London's entertainment bible, and the traditional music fan's weekly, the *New Musical Express* (NME). London's daily newspaper, the *Evening*

Standard, also publishes the very handy 'Hot Tickets' as a supplement on Thursdays.
www.bigmouth.co.uk is the UK's most comprehensive gig guide; and you can buy tickets online. Tickets range hugely in cost and are almost always available directly from the individual venues. Alternatively try: **Stargreen Box Office**, 20-21a Argyll St, Oxford Circus, W1, T020-7734 8932, www.stargreen.com; **Ticketweb**, T020-7771 2000, www.ticketweb.co.uk; and the ubiquitous **TicketMaster**, T020-7344 4444, www.ticketmaster.co.uk. Stargreen also prints an expansive free sheet listing upcoming gigs. If worst comes to worst there are always ticket touts, though prices are hugely inflated and there's no guarantee that the ticket you buy will be genuine.

Festivals and events

London is not naturally a festival city. It's simply too large to get into the spirit – royal funerals seemingly the obvious exception. Many of the best events capitalize on the river, though, and throughout the year innumerable individual festivals and festivities enliven other parts of the city. Some are important dates in the social calendar: the Chelsea Flower Show, Wimbledon, the Proms, the Boat Race and Notting Hill Carnival, all in their different ways are enjoyed by ardent fans and are also annual occasions unique to the city. Others, like the Lord Mayor's Show, Trooping the Colour and Beating the Retreat are colourful anachronisms that indulge an enthusiasm for pomp and circumstance. And still more display local communities celebrating their own identity. Whatever the time of year, in this city there's always likely to be some kind of celebration of something going on near you.
▸▸ *See also relevent area listings sections.*

Calendar of events

January
Chinese New Year A procession down Gerrard St with dances and masks reflecting whichever Chinese year is being ushered in.
London Art Fair, T020-7359 3535, www.londonart fair.co.uk. (5 days mid-Jan.) Jamboree of barely affordable contemporary art in the Business Design Centre, Islington.
London International Festival of Mime, T020-7637 5661, www.mimefest.co.uk. (2 weeks mid-Jan). The largest of its kind in the world. Shows at the Barbican Centre, ICA and South Bank Centre.

March
Oxford and Cambridge Boat Race. www.theboatrace.org. (Usually last weekend in Mar.) Since 1829, England's two most ancient universities have thrashed it out on the river. A big social event. See also page 51.

April
Flora London Marathon, T020-7620 4117; www.london-marathon.co.uk. (Mid-Apr.) 26-mile mass jog from Greenwich to Westminster by more than 30,000 participants, some professional, others in fancy dress, including one guy recently in full diving gear. Entry forms are distributed in *Marathon News* (a free magazine available in specialist sports stores). Overseas visitors wanting to receive copies of the entry form should send a self-addressed envelope (stating the number you require), with two international reply coupons to: Overseas Entry Co-ordinator, 91 Walkden Rd, Walkden, Manchester, M28 7BQ, England. All entry forms should be submitted for ballot six months prior to the race.
London Harness Horse Parade, T020-8871 7530. (Easter Mon). An event that dates from 1885, an impressive procession of dray and cart horses round Battersea Park.

May
Chelsea Flower Show, T0870-906378 (public), T0870-9063780 (RHS members), www.rhs.org.uk. (5 days at end of May.) Possibly the world's most prestigious celebration of the art of gardening, in the

grounds of the Royal Hospital. Admission £10-£27 depending on the time of day.

May Fayre and Puppet Festival, Alternative Arts, T020-7375 0441. (2nd Sun of the month.) A celebration of the first Punch and Judy show, in the churchyard of St Paul's Church, Covent Garden.

Beating the Retreat, T020-7414 2479. (3 evenings late in the month). Annual tattoo on Horse Guards' Parade celebrating the return of the troops back to barracks. Colourful and very British, it's followed by a military band concert.

June

Royal Academy Summer Exhibition, T020-7300 8000, www.royalacademy.org.uk. Staggering exhibition of mainly amateur and semi-professional artistic talent.

Spitalfields Festival, T020-7377 0287, www.spitalfieldsfestival.org.uk. (2 weeks in mid-June and 2 weeks before Christmas.) Baroque, gospel and classical music recitals in Christ Church Spitalfields and other venues.

Trooping the Colour (on 2nd or 3rd Sat). Book well ahead for this ceremonial celebration of the Queen's official birthday, or enjoy the procession for free on the Mall. For grandstand seats, write in with an SAE for up to 2 tickets per person for the day itself, or an unrestricted number for the two rehearsals on the Saturdays before (minus Her Majesty) to Brigade Major, HQ Household Division, Horseguards, Whitehall, London, SW1A 2AX, T020-7414 2479.

Wimbledon Lawn Tennis Championships, T020-8946 2244, www.wimbledon.org. (2 weeks end Jun and beginning Jul.) The world's favourite and still an important fixture in the British social diary.

City of London Festival, T020-7377 0540, www.colf.org. (2 or 3 weeks, end of Jun and start of Jul.) Classical music, jazz, visual arts and literature invade a variety of livery company HQs and City churches (including St Paul's).

July

Hampton Court Palace Flower Show, T020-7834 4333, www.rhs.org.uk. The Royal Horticultural Society's annual flowerfest (larger and less posh than Chelsea) in a tremendous setting.

Greenwich and Docklands Festival, T020-8305 1818; www.festival.org. (2 or 3 weeks from beginning of month.) Vibrant and very successful arts festival featuring traditional markets, music, dance, theatre and fireworks.

Clerkenwell Festival, T020-7251 6311, www.clerkenwell.org. (19th or nearest Sun.) Based around the Italian festival of Our Lady of Mount Carmel in the RC church of St Peter's, Clerkenwell Rd, followed by a street festival, with a big Friday music night.

BBC Henry Wood Promenade Concerts, www.bbc.co.uk/proms. (Late Jul to mid-Sep.) 'The Proms', a series of classical concerts at the Royal Albert Hall and on the last night more like a rugby match.

Shoreditch Festival, 182 Hoxton St, T020-7613 2727. (Sun mid-Jul.) Organized by Shoreditch Ourway, a local festival in fashionable Hoxton continuing to celebrate the area's indigenous spirit.

Kenwood Open Air Concerts, T020-8348 1286. (Weekends through Jul and Aug.) Open-air lakeside concerts with fireworks in the grounds of the grand Adam house overlooking London.

August

Notting Hill Carnival, www.nottinghill carnival.org.uk. (Last Sun and Mon.) What began in 1966 as a small celebration of local Afro-Caribbean culture has exploded over the years into a full-blooded spectacular with DJ-driven sound systems, floats, steel bands, food stalls and very large crowds.

September

Thames Festival, T020-7401 2255. (Sun mid-Sep.) Hugely popular culmination of the summer-long Coin Street Festival on Sun, usually featuring an illuminated procession and river-related events.

London Open House, www.londonopen house.org. (2 days in mid-Sep.) A celebration of the city's architecture and rare opportunity to see inside more than 400 buildings, most not normally open to the public. Book in advance for the more interesting places.

October

Costermongers' Pearly Harvest Festival Service, T020-7766 1100. (1st Sun, 1430.) Cockney fruit 'n' veg sellers assemble in their Pearly King and Queen outfits (covered in buttons) at St Martin-in-the-Fields, Trafalgar Sq.

★ Five of the best markets

Those who love rooting around for a bargain won't be disappointed by London's markets. Everyone has their own favourite, but here are five of the best:

Brick Lane, E1 (page 266). Sundays 0700-1300. Mainly second-hand, including clothes, bric-a-brac, books, records and some furniture.
Camden Market, Camden High Street, NW1 (page 299). Saturday and Sunday 0900-1700. Everything under the sun, but especially techno-clubby gear and retro clothing.

Greenwich, SE5 (page 286). Sundays 0900-1700. Retro clothes, bric-a-brac, antiques, more for the retro purists than Camden.
Portobello Road, Notting Hill, W11 (page 321). Fridays and Saturdays 0800-1800. Antiques at the beginning, then retro clothes, records, junk and books. Prices drop as you head into Golborne Road.
Spitalfields Market, Commercial Street, E1 (page 265). Open Sunday 1100-1500. Clothes, books, paintings, organic food, jewellery, antiques, bric-a-brac.

November
Lord Mayor's Show, T020-7606 3030, www.corpoflondon.gov.uk. (2nd Sat.) Huge and very jolly procession (featuring the likes of pewterers, basketweavers, big bands and lots of charity floats) led by the Mayor in his State coach, from the Guildhall up Fleet St and back along the river, with fireworks on the Thames between Blackfriars and Waterloo bridges.

Shopping

A very broad summary of the shopping areas in London goes like this: **Oxford St** and **Regent St** for *Selfridges*, *Hamleys*, other department stores and big brands; **Tottenham Court Rd** for computers and electronics; **Charing Cross Rd** and **Bloomsbury** for books new and secondhand; **Soho** and **Carnaby Street** for urban streetwear and style accessories; **Covent Garden** for clothes, both new and second-hand, specialist foods and gifts; **Bond St** and **Mayfair** for high fashion and expensive jewellery; **St James's** for bespoke boots, hats and wine; **Clerkenwell** for crafts and independent designers; **Knightsbridge** for more high fashion, *Harrods* and *Harvey Nichols*; and **Chelsea** or **Notting Hill** for one-off and independent fashion, music, gift and book retailers. And then there are the markets, some of them the most evocative places to get into the spirit of the city: **Brick Lane** on a Sunday for just about everything; **Portobello** on Saturdays, **Bermondsey** on Friday mornings, or **Alfie's** during the week, all for antiques and bric-a-brac; and **Camden** at the weekend for furniture, gifts, clothes, accessories and general mayhem. ▸▸ *For more details see individual area listings sections.*

Opening hours Most shops open at 0930 or 1000 and close at 1730 or 1800. Many shops in busy areas also open on Sundays. On Thursdays the shops on Oxford Street stay open until 2000. During the Christmas season, and the summer and winter sales, opening hours are usually extended. **Bliss Chemist** ① *5-6 Marble Arch W1*, T020-7723 6116, is a late-night pharmacy open until midnight throughout the year.

Essentials Shopping

Sport and activities

Launched under the banner 'leaping for London', the city's bid to host the Olympics in 2012 has pushed this already sports-mad city to fever pitch. Of course football has long been the main focus of attention, although interested visitors may find it next to impossible to obtain tickets for a big match. The same is almost as true for the other big spectator sports: attending the tennis at Wimbledon, cricket at Lord's and the Oval, or rugby at Twickenham requires serious planning. Much easier events to see ad hoc include horse racing, greyhound racing, and the boat races on the river. And there are masses of ways to get active and involved as well. Swimming, water sports, ice-skating, horse riding, golf, boating, running or dry-slope skiing: you name it, London does it.

Boating

Rowing boats for a paddle around can be hired in the summer in **Hyde Park**, **Regent's Park** and **Battersea Park**.

Cricket

The definitive summer sport is played from Apr-Sep. London's two main grounds are **The Oval**, Kennington, T020-7582 7764, and **Lord's**, T020-7432 1066. Test Match tickets usually need to be bought well in advance, but you should be able to get seats for county matches on the day.

Dry-slope skiing

Alexandra Palace Ski Centre, T020-8888 2284; **Crystal Palace Ski School**, T020-8778 0131; **Hillingdon Ski Centre**, Uxbridge, T01895-58506; **Profiles Ski Centre**, Orpington, T01689-78239; **Woolwich Ski Slope Army Barracks**, T020-8317 1726.

Football

Tickets to see Premier League London clubs like Arsenal, Chelsea, Tottenham Hotspur or West Ham can be pretty hard to come by. Try calling the **Premier League**, T020-7298 1600 or the **Football League**, T01772-325800. Tickets for Premiership matches start at about £20.

Golf

There's a driving range at the **Regent's Park Golf and Tennis School**, Outer Circle, T020-7724 0643, www.rpgts.co.uk. Non- members can only play before 1600 and not at weekends. £5 for a bucket of balls. Booking advisable. A full list of golf courses can be found at www.londongolf.info.

Greyhound racing

Most easily accessible from central London are the tracks at: **Walthamstow**, Chingford Rd, T020-8531 4255; and **Wimbledon**, Plough Lane, T020-8946 8000. First race at 1930.

Horse racing

You'll need to travel a bit further to put your money on the horses. The nearest racetracks to the capital are a shortish train ride away at **Ascot**, T01344-622211; **Epsom**, T01372-726311; **Sandown Park**, T01372-463072; and **Windsor**, T01753-498400. Admission prices for the general public start at about £6. Flat racing: early Mar-early Nov. Steeplechasing: Oct-Apr.

Horse riding

In **Hyde Park**, T020-7723 2813, £30 per hour (with an escort). You can also ride in **Richmond Park** and on **Hampstead Heath**.

Ice-skating

Somerset House (see page 68). Open-air ice-skating can be enjoyed in the 18th-century courtyard in Dec and Jan daily 1000-2200. Tickets cost £9.50/£11.00 for adults and £6 for children including skate hire per hour, but book first to avoid the queues on T0870-1660423 or www.ticketmaster.co.uk.
Broadgate Ice Rink, near Liverpool St tube station, T020-7505 4068. Another open-air option (open from Oct until Apr). Entry costs £6 for adults (plus £2 skate hire) and £4 for children (plus £1 for skates).
There are also year-round indoor ice rinks at: **Leisurebox**, T020-7229 0172 (Queensway); **Streatham**, T020-8769 7771 (Streatham Station, South London).

Outdoor swimming

Available (and really only sensible) in the summer only at: **Serpentine Lido**, Hyde Park, T020-7298 2100; **Hampstead Heath Ponds**, T020-7485 4491; **Evian Lido**, Brockwell Park, Brixton, T020-7274 3088; and **Pools on the Park**, Richmond, T020-8940 0561.

Oxford and Cambridge Boat Race

You can witness this traditional contest for supremacy between England's two most famous universities from either bank of the Thames along the whole length of the course, but the best viewpoints are **Putney Bridge**, **Putney Embankment** and **Bishop's Park** at the start of the race, **Hammersmith** and **Barnes** in the middle, and **Duke's Meadows** and **Chiswick Bridge** at the finish. The race is usually held in the last weekend in March.

Rugby

Twickenham Rugby Football Ground, T020-8744 3111 (ticket information line), hosts the main national and international matches. The season last from early Sep-Apr (although a few matches may run into May).

Tennis

If you want Centre Court or Court 1 seats for Wimbledon you'll need to contact the **All England Lawn Tennis Club**, Church Rd, Wimbledon, **T** 020-8946 2244, at least six months in advance. Otherwise you can get there early and queue on the day (some people camp out overnight) to watch play on the outside courts. Determined fans can usually buy cut-price returned tickets later in the afternoon for some Centre Court action. Tennis can be played at the **Regent's Park Tennis Centre**, York Bridge, T020-7486 4216 or the **Regent's Park Golf and Tennis School**, Outer Circle, T020-7724 0643, www.rpgts.co.uk. Non-members can only play before 1600 and not at weekends. £5 for a bucket of balls. Three Tennis Courts, £15 an hour. Booking advised.

Watersports

Docklands Sailing and Watersports Centre, Crossharbour and London Arena DLR station, T020-7537 2626, www.dswc.org. Sailing, canoeing, rowing and Chinese dragon-boat racing (no power sports). Membership £15 a day. Pre-booking essential at weekends.

Health → *Medical emergency: dial 999 or 112 (both free) for an ambulance.*

No vaccinations are required for entry into Britain. Citizens of **EU** countries and Iceland, Liechtenstein, Norway or Switzerland are entitled to free medical treatment at National Health Service hospitals and health centres on production of an E111 form. As a result of recent changes to European law a new E111 form was introduced in 2004. Be aware that old ones are no longer valid and ensure you have an up to date form for your visit. More information is available from Post Offices and the Department of Health, www.dh.gov.uk/travellers. During 2005, the UK will adopt the European Health Insurance Card (EHIC) which will eventually fully replace the E111 form. Australia and New Zealand also have reciprocal health-care arrangements with Britain. Citizens of other countries will have to pay for all medical services, except accident and emergency care given at Accident and Emergency (A&E) Units at most (but not all) National Health hospitals. Health insurance is therefore strongly advised for citizens of non-EU countries.

Pharmacists (or chemists) can dispense only a limited range of drugs without a doctor's prescription. Most pharmacies are open during normal shop hours, though some are open late; **Bliss Chemist** ① *5 Marble Arch, W1*, open till midnight every day.

Doctors' surgeries are usually open from around 0830-0900 till 1730-1800, though times vary. Outside surgery hours you can go to the casualty department of the local hospital for any complaint requiring urgent attention. For the address of the nearest hospital or doctor's surgery, T0800-665544.

Charing Cross Hospital, Fulham Palace Rd, W6 8RF, T020-8846 1234.

Chelsea Royal Hospital, Royal Hospital Rd, SW3, T020-7730 0161.

Guy's Hospital, St Thomas St, SE1 9RT, T020-7955 5000.

St Thomas's Hospital, Lambeth Palace Rd, SE1 7EH, T020-7928 9292.

Keeping in touch

Communications

Internet

There are cafés all over London where you can access the internet. **easyEverything**, probably the biggest and cheapest option (access from £1), has five locations in central London: 9-16 Tottenham Court Road (Oxford Street end); 7 Strand (Trafalgar Square end); 358 Oxford Street (opposite Bond Street tube station); 9-13 Wilton Road, Victoria (opposite main line station); 160-166 Kensington High Street. For other options, www.allinlondon.co.uk/directory, has a directory of about 70 internet cafés in different areas of the capital. Local libraries also often provide cheap or free internet access.

Post

Most post offices are open Monday-Friday 0900-1730 and Saturday 0900-1230. Smaller sub-post offices operate out of newsagents. Details of your local branch and the services offered can be obtained from the Customer Helpline T0845-7223344.

Stamps can be bought at post offices and from vending machines outside as well as from many newsagents and supermarkets. Airmail letters of less than 20g cost 40p to Europe. To the USA and Australia it costs 47p for 10g and 68g for 20g. For more information: T0845-740740, www.royalmail.com.

Telephone

Most public **payphones** are operated by British Telecom (*BT*) and are widespread throughout London. *BT* payphones take either coins (20p, 50p, £1 and occasionally £2) or **phonecards**, which are available at newsagents, post offices and supermarkets displaying the *BT* logo. These cards come in denominations of £3, £5, £10 and £20. Some payphones also accept credit cards (Delta, Visa and Diners Club). Calls are cheapest between 1800 and 0800 Monday-Friday and all day Saturday and Sunday. The **phone code** for the whole of London is **020**. You don't need to use the area code if calling from within London. Any number prefixed by **0800** or **0500** is free to the caller; **0345** and **0845** numbers are charged at local rates and **0990** numbers at the national rate. Premium rates, charged on numbers prefixed by **090**, vary from number to number and can be very high (up to £2 per minute from a public payphone); the operator (T100) will tell you how much your call will cost.

Operator: T100. International operator: T155. Directory enquiries: T192. Overseas directory enquiries: T153.

To **call London** from overseas, dial 011 from USA and Canada, 0011 from Australia and 00 from New Zealand, followed by 44, then 20 (ie the area code, minus the first zero), then the number. ·

To **call overseas from London** dial 00 followed by the country code and the number (minus the fist zero). Country codes include: **Australia** 61; **France** 33; **Ireland** 353; **New Zealand** 64; **South Africa** 27; **USA** and **Canada** 1.

Media

Newspapers

London is media central for the UK and you just can't escape it. There is a huge variety of national newspapers and competition between them is fierce. The national dailies are divided into two distinct camps; the **tabloids**, which are more downmarket; and the **broadsheets**, which are generally of a higher standard. Foreign visitors may find the broadsheets easier to understand as they tend to use less slang than the tabloids.

The broadsheets include *The Times* and *The Daily Telegraph*, which are politically conservative, and *The Guardian* and *The Independent*, which have more of a liberal/left-wing leaning. There's also the distinctively coloured and very serious *Financial Times*, which focuses on business and finance. The Saturday editions of these papers carry their own listings guides with useful reviews of movies, clubs, restaurants, theatre, etc. The broadsheets' Sunday versions are huge and would take most of your holiday to read thoroughly. They include the *Independent on Sunday*, *Sunday Times*, *Sunday Telegraph* and the *Observer* (a stablemate of *The Guardian*).

The list of tabloids (known also as redtops) comprises *The Sun* and *The Mirror* which are the most popular and provide celebrity gossip and extensive sports coverage, the *Daily Mail* and *Daily Express* which are right-wing and aimed directly at 'Middle England'. Then there's the *Daily Star* and *The Sport* and the less said about them the better. The tabloids have their own Sunday versions, which, are, if anything, even more salacious: these include the notorious *News of the World*; the *Sunday Mirror*, *Sunday People* and *Sunday Sport*.

London's daily is the *Evening Standard* with local news and views and a useful *ES Magazine* on Fridays which contains some good features.

Free publications, usually distributed at tube stations, include the daily *Metro*, which has listings for that evening including free things to do, or the magazines *TNT* and *Southern Cross* which also have listings and ads for good travel deals.

Foreign newspapers and **magazines**, including *USA Today* and *International Herald Tribune*, are available in larger newsagents. *Time* and *Newsweek* are also widely available.

Magazines

There are thousands of mags available and the choice is bewildering. The women's market is particularly saturated, and men's titles are growing, too. The best for a guide to what's on in London is *Time Out*, which also has some interesting features. Those looking for political comment of a left-wing nature should read the *New Statesman*, while *The Spectator* provides a right-wing viewpoint on the world. For a satirical, and very funny, look at British politics, check out the weekly *Private Eye*.

For music fans the *NME* gives reviews of gigs and new releases. The dashing gentleman about town should pick up his copy of *The Chap*, which provides the last word on sartorial elegance.

Television

There are five main television channels in the UK; the publicly funded BBC 1 and 2, and the independent commercial stations, Channel 4, Channel 5 and ITV. The rather limited offerings of the main five channels is greatly expanded by the various digital cable TV companies, such as *Sky Digital*, which currently has 170 channels, and *ONdigital*. These include movie channels such as *FilmFour*, *Sky Movies* and the *Movie Channel*, as well as sports-only channels like *Sky Sports*.

Essentials Keeping in touch

54 Radio

The BBC network also broadcasts several radio channels, most of which are based in London. These include: *Radio 1* (98.8 FM) aimed at a young audience; *Radio 2* (89.1 FM) targeting a more mature audience; *Radio 3* (91.3 FM) which plays mostly classical music; *Radio 4* (93.5 FM) which is talk-based and features arts, drama and current affairs; and *Radio 5 Live* (693, 909 MW) which is a mix of sport and news. *BBC London Live* (94.9 FM) is a talk-based station, a poor replacement for the much-missed *GLR* which was far and away the most intelligent radio station in the capital, if not the world. There is also a large number of local **commercial radio stations**, including *Capital FM* (95.8 FM) which is London's biggest station playing mainstream chart stuff. There's also *Smooth FM* (102.2 FM), formerly *Jazz FM* which, in an attempt to rebrand itself, is aiming at a more mainstream market than the old 'Jazz' label allowed for, and *XFM* (104.9 FM) for dedicated indie-kids.

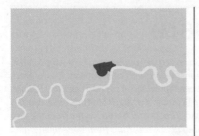

West End

Trafalgar Square

Trafalgar Square is the centre of London, avoided by Londoners whenever possible, unless to make their voices heard at demonstrations and celebrations. It's the lynch pin of the West End's tourist triangle between Piccadilly Circus and Leicester Square. On its north side, Pall Mall slides west into St James's while St Martin's Place wiggles northwards to become Charing Cross Road. The Strand hurtles in the from the east and the City, but it's the breadth of Whitehall approaching from Westminster and Parliament to the south that explains the prominence of the square in London's geography. This is where the administrative offices of government meet the people, and the monarch comes too, with The Mall marching straight up from Buckingham Palace into the southwest corner through Admiralty Arch.

Nelson's Column, Landseer's lions and the two large fountains give the square some dignity, inspiring a sense of occasion. Meanwhile pigeon-feeding has been outlawed and the pedestrianization of the north side of the square has transformed access to the National Gallery, one of the most comprehensive collections of fine art in the world. Along with the National Portrait Gallery behind it, these two treasure houses are the best reasons for a visit here, unless you just want to sit around in the centre of things. During the day the square must be one of the most polyglot places in town, teeming with visitors from every corner of the globe. ➤➤ For Eating and other listings see pages 63-63.

History

This area has always been an important crossroads and has become the place from which all distances to London are measured. Seven hundred years ago, the Abbot of Westminster's fields and gardens lay to the southwest, while Whitehall was no more than a track heading south to the abbey itself. In Henry II's reign, the church of St Martin-in-the-Fields in the northeast corner would have lived up to its name. The king's mews occupied the area, housing falconers, clerks (Geoffrey Chaucer among them), and later, under the Stuarts, court officials.

The original site of the Charing Cross, the last of a series of crosses placed by Edward I to commemorate the 12 resting places of his beloved Eleanor's funeral procession (a 19th-century imitation of it now stands on the forecourt of Charing Cross Station), is marked by a statue of Charles I, looking majestically down Whitehall towards his place of execution, Banqueting House. Propaganda is nothing new – Charles I was 5' 4", but the sculptor, Le Sueur, was obliged by contract to ensure that 'the figure of his majesty King Charles proportionate six foot'.

The area first won the title Trafalgar Square in 1835 in celebration of Horatio Nelson's defence of British naval supremacy at the Battle of Trafalgar in 1805 – its redesign was the product of John Nash's Charing Cross Improvement Scheme of the 1830s. Sir Edwin Landseer's lions only finally settled at the column's base in 1867. They had caused the sculptor endless difficulties after the ageing lion posing for him died, forcing Landseer to use the decomposing corpse as a model. The naval theme continues with statues of Admirals Cunningham, Jellicoe and Beatty, and Admiralty Arch – once the offices of the First Sea Lord – framing the entrance to The Mall.

The square also has a history of political activism: the Chartists demanded constitutional reforms here in 1848; artist and writer William Morris and George Bernard Shaw joined a march against the Reform Bill in 1887, an event known as Bloody Sunday; George Orwell slept here in the course of his research for *Down and Out in Paris and London* and this is where the Poll Tax demonstration of 1990 turned

★ Don't miss in the West End...

1. **National Galleries** Marvel at the European art or British faces down the ages at the National Gallery or National Portrait Gallery in Trafalgar Square, page 59.
2. **Somerset House** Falling in 'Love Actually' at the Somerset House ice rink in winter or with the fine art and antiques in the Courtauld and Gilbert Collections or Hermitage Rooms there, page 68.
3. **Leicester Square** Get in line for a half-price theatre ticket at the tickets booth or dodge the crowd barriers for the latest movie premiere, page 73.
4. **Soho** Hit Soho for a coffee by day or drinks by night and watch the world go by without its wife, page 81.
5. **Shopping** Get your designer streetwear, shoes, gifts and accessories in 'Carnaby' off Regent St, page 85, and Seven Dials near Covent Garden, page 96; or go window-shopping along Old and New Bond streets, South Molton Street and down the Burlington Arcade in Mayfair, page 103.
7. **Royal London** Pop into Fortnum's for tea and royal groceries, page 118, before strolling through St James's or Green Park to visit Buckingham Palace or the Queen's Gallery, page 122.

nasty. More recently, millions converged on the Square to protest against the government's decision to go to war in Iraq.

Sights ⊖ *Charing Cross, Leicester Sq.* ⊖ *See p460.*

Around the square

The square has a formidable focal point in **Nelson's Column**. Nelson is just about the only military commander ever to have been truly taken to heart by the British people. Even so, it took 40 years after he was mortally wounded while defeating Napoleon's navy at Trafalgar for his Column finally to be erected. In a fit of patriotic fervour in 1843, two days after the anniversary of the battle, 14 people ate a dizzy supper of rump steak on the top. Then the statue of the one-armed hero, three times life size and sporting his eye-patch and three-cornered hat, was hoisted into position on his granite Corinthian column, facing southwest so that he could review the fleet in Portsmouth. Around the base the bronze relief sculptures were cast from captured French cannons, celebrating his victories at Copenhagen, the Nile, and Cape St Vincent, as well as Trafalgar.

1 Trafalgar Square

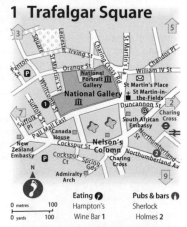

0 metres 100	
0 yards 100	

Eating 🍴	Pubs & bars 🍺
Hampton's	Sherlock
Wine Bar **1**	Holmes **2**

West End walkabout

A common mistake many visitors to London make is to slavishly take the tube everywhere, when it would be far quicker to walk. This is especially true around the West End. It only takes 10 minutes to walk from Piccadilly Circus to Covent Garden, by which time the tube traveller would still be queuing for a ticket. Similarly, Tottenham Court Road tube station is only a 10-minute walk from Leicester Square, and Oxford Circus is a mere 10 minutes on foot from Piccadilly Circus. However, on a Saturday afternoon you may want to take a tube from Oxford Circus to Tottenham Court Road to avoid the hordes of shoppers.

Several other monuments in the square are more easily missed. Set into the **north wall** on a bronze plate, between the statues of Admirals Jellicoe and Cunningham, are the definitive Imperial Standards of Length: the inch, the foot and the yard, solemnly marked out between stubby brass pegs. The inscription claims that the thing is accurate 'at 62 degrees Fahrenheit'. In the **northeastern corner**, the equestrian statue of George IV in a toga was originally intended for the top of Marble Arch but no one has ever bothered to put it there. The long-empty pedestal in the **northwest corner**, now known as the Fourth Plinth, has become a unique temporary public space for national and international contemporary art. Sculptures planned at time of writing include Marc Quinn's 'Alison Lapper Pregnant', a monumental marble statue of a disabled expectant mother and friend of the artist; and in 2006, Thomas Schütte's 'Hotel for the Birds', a perspex cityscape where pigeons may or may not be able to feel at home.

The oldest and finest of the buildings surrounding the square is undoubtedly the **Church of St Martin-in-the-Fields** ① *T020-7766 1100. Mon-Fri 0745-1800, Sat 0845-1800, Sun 0745-1930*. Like St Mary-le-Strand nearby, but on a larger scale, it's an impressive fusion of classical and baroque by James Gibbs, dating from 1722-1726. The interior is less remarkable, although beautifully proportioned, and includes a font from the original medieval church. Regular concerts are also given here (see page 63) and there's an excellent café in the crypt (see page 63) and a brass rubbing centre. Notables such as Joshua Reynolds, Hogarth, and Charles II's mistress Nell Gwyn are buried in the churchyard.

Over Duncannon Street to the south, opposite the entrance to the church's crypt, is **South Africa House** ① *T020-7451 7299, for details of tours*, the home of the South African High Commission. Built in 1933, the exterior features various African animals carved in stone. The refurbished interior can be visited by pre-arranged groups, phone for details.

Continuing clockwise round the square, beyond Northumberland Avenue and Whitehall, is **Admiralty Arch**. Designed by Aston Webb in 1910, the triple-arched building provided a grand gateway to The Mall and Webb's new east front for Buckingham Palace as well as offices for the First Sea Lord, the commander of the Royal Navy. He has now moved out and the Arch has become government offices. Traffic goes through the arches on either side, the central arch being reserved for royal processions.

Canada House ① *5 Trafalgar Sq, T020-7258 6600, www.dfait-maci.gc.ca/london,* *Mon-Fri 1000-1800, library Mon-Fri 1000-1300,* is where the consular and cultural arms of the Canadian High Commission are based. Formerly the Royal College of Physicians and Union Club, it hosts art exhibitions in two galleries, with Canadian artists, Canadian music, library, Canadian newspapers, and email for use by Canadians or anyone doing Canadian research. Free movies are also shown here at 1300 on Thursday (for more information T020-7258 6421).

★ National Gallery

① *T020-7747 2885, www.nationalgallery.org.uk. Daily 1000-1800, Wed 1000-2100. Free. Free guided tours from Sainsbury Wing Level 0 daily at 1130 and 1430, also 1800 and 1830 on Wed, 1230 and 1530 Sat, audio guide also available.*

Stretching along the north side of the square, and easily its finest asset, is the National Gallery, housing more than 2000 Western European paintings dating from the 13th century to 1900. The collection began with the purchase by the government in 1824 of 38 paintings from the financier John Julius Angerstein. Originally housed in Pall Mall, the present building was purpose built and completed by 1838. Artificial lighting, to extend the winter opening hours, was only introduced as recently as 1935. The Sainsbury Wing, specially designed to house the earliest paintings, was finished in 1991. More recently, the Getty entrance to the East Wing from Trafalgar Square was opened, complete with café, cloakrooms and information desks. The refurbishment of the main Portico Entrance includes more room for the Micro Gallery, a computerized pictorial database of the entire collection allowing visitors to locate their favourite pictures, plan and print out a personalized tour, or browse through genres, periods, themes or artists. The gallery as a whole is now much more accessible to its five million or so visitors each year than it's ever been before. Although it may not possess as many masterpieces as the Louvre, the Prado or the Hermitage, it glories in a comprehensive selection of outstanding work from all the great schools of European painting down the ages.

The **main entrance**, up the steps beneath the grand portico and 'pepperpot' dome, overlooks Trafalgar Square, well above the traffic, and there's a great view past Nelson's Column down Whitehall towards the Palace of Westminster, enough to make you feel as though you really have found the middle of London. Once inside, the bustle of bag-checking and orientation tends to distract visitors from the curious floor mosaics by **Boris Anrep** on the stairway leading up to the central hall. Only completed in 1952 after nearly a quarter of a century's labour, they depict a weird cavalcade of early and mid-20th century celebrities personifying the Muses and 'Modern Virtues' such as Lucidity and Defiance. They're also the only examples of modern art permanently on show in the gallery. If you want to put them in the correct chronological order in which the rest of the Gallery's collection is arranged you'll need to save them for your exit, by starting a visit instead at the side entrance at street level in the Sainsbury Wing.

The Sainsbury Wing: paintings from 1250-1500 » See also p415
① *On the ground floor of the Sainsbury Wing is the Gallery's main shop while the basement is reserved for special exhibitions. The stairs up to the main galleries take you past the restaurant on the first floor.*

The 16 rooms of the Sainsbury Wing, on the left at the top of the stairs, are broadly arranged in chronological order. In the first room, 51, the most significant exceptions are two masterpieces of the early Renaissance by **Leonardo da Vinci**. In a special alcove of its own, behind his *Virgin of the Rocks*, is the gallery's most fragile and precious possession, a charcoal and chalk cartoon on paper of *The Virgin and Child with St Anne and St John the Baptist*. Carefully restored after being attacked by a maniac with a shotgun in the 1980s, the dim lighting establishes a suitably devotional mood. Most of the pictures in this wing have religious and devout themes, with a strong Italian and Dutch emphasis. Painted at a time when all western nations were under spiritual sway of the Pope, they would look best in flickering candlelight.

One of the most significant early works, **Giotto**'s *The Pentecost*, executed in 1306, was the last in a series of seven panels for an Italian church altarpiece. The two figures in the foreground were almost certainly painted by the artist himself, as opposed to his assistants, and demonstrate the early moves he made towards three- dimensionality and psychological accuracy. One of the first oil paintings in the collection, in room 56, **Jan van Eyck**'s meticulous *Arnolfini Marriage* uses the play of light to astonishing effect, right down to the tiny reflection of the painter himself at his easel in the convex mirror behind the complacent newly weds. The same artist's *Man in a Turban* could well be a self-portrait, inscribed with the motto 'As I can', an abbreviation of the Flemish proverb 'As I can, not as I would wish'.

Piero della Francesca's *Baptism of Christ* is unmissable, hung in a key position at the far end of room 66, and showing the most important moment in the life of John the Baptist, with the Holy Spirit hovering overhead, a dove that could almost be a cloud. **Crivelli**'s *Annunciation, with St Emidius*, nearby, is an extraordinary study in deep architectural perspective. **Botticelli**'s *Mystic Nativity* is the only surviving painting with his signature, a strange composition based on the book of Revelations that the artist probably used for his private devotions. His *Venus and Mars* is one of the few secular paintings in the wing.

Another brilliant and moving piece of composition is **Raphael**'s *The Ansidei Madonna*, with St John looking up at the source of the light, his pose reflected by the Christ-child's posture in the lap of the Virgin as they gaze upon a book, leading the viewer on to St Nicholas on the right, also rapt in study. The same artist's *Saint Catherine of Alexandria* (in room 8 of the West Wing) shows the influence of Leonardo in the saint's twisting pose. The peculiar *Wilton Diptych* (room 53) was probably commissioned by Richard II as an affirmation of his divine right to rule, showing the king in the company of angels and his saintly predecessors. Cleaning in 1992 revealed a castle on a green island in a silver sea painted onto the tiny orb above the banner of St George, the patron saint of England.

The West Wing: paintings from 1510-1600

Leaving the Sainsbury Wing, the High Renaissance begins in the West Wing, in the main body of the gallery, starting with the Wohl Room and three outstanding **Titian**s, *Bacchus and Ariadne*, *Noli Me Tangere* and the possible self-portrait *Portrait of a Man*. This last work makes interesting comparison with **Raphael**'s beautiful portrait of the soldier pontiff *Pope Julius II*. In the same wing, *The Entombment* and *The Manchester Madonna* are both exceptionally rare things, paintings by **Michelangelo**, both unfinished (room 2). Look out too for **Tintoretto**'s dynamic *Saint George and the Dragon* and **Holbein**'s *Christina of Denmark*. Henry VIII commissioned Holbein to paint his prospective bride full face so he could inspect all her blemishes. (Even though there were none, the marriage came to naught.) Ten years earlier, the same artist's *Lady with a Squirrel and a Starling* is more fun, the squirrel's tail modestly covering his demure subject's cleavage. The Venetian master **Correggio**'s *Madonna of the Basket* is one of the most perfectly

66 99 Although it may not possess as many masterpieces as the Louvre, the Prado or the Hermitage, it glories in a comprehensive selection of outstanding work from all the great schools of European painting down the ages...

preserved paintings in the gallery, while the sombre hue of **El Greco's** *Christ Driving the Traders from the Temple* has been taken to reflect the seriousness of the Counter Reformation. Mythological subjects also became increasingly popular at this time, such as **Bronzino's** impressive *Allegory with Venus and Cupid*. Other paintings here mark the birth of landscape painting.

The North Wing: paintings from 1600-1700

The North Wing, comprising the back rooms of the gallery, houses 17th-century paintings, with a stronger emphasis on landscapes and especially rich in the Spanish and Dutch schools, including **Velázquez's** extraordinary play on the nature of 'looking', *The Rokeby Venus* (room 30). The first room (15) includes two remarkable paintings by **Claude Lorrain**, *Seaport with the Embarkation of the Queen of Sheba* and *Landscape with the Marriage of Isaac and Rebekah*. Thanks to a clause in **Turner's** will, that 19th-century British landscape painter's *Sun Rising through Vapour* and *Dido Building Carthage* hang alongside those of his hero. This wing is also home to the collection's wonderful array of **Rubens**, **Poussin** and also **Rembrandt** paintings, including the delightfully light touch of the latter's *Woman Bathing in a Stream*, the thoroughness of *Self Portrait Aged 34* (room 23) and the atmospheric and dramatic *Belshazzar's Feast*. Look out too for **Frans Hals'** spontaneous rendition of a *Young Man Holding a Skull* and **Caravaggio's** compelling *Supper at Emmaus*.

The East Wing: paintings from 1700-1900

Unsurprisingly, the most crowded part of the gallery is often the East Wing, where the collection of works by **Van Gogh**, **Gauguin**, **Cézanne**, **Degas**, **Monet** and **Renoir** draw in admirers of the Impressionists and Post-Impressionists. Eighteenth-century British landscape and portraiture are also well represented, with some beautiful family portraits by **Gainsborough** (room 35) and **Stubbs**, and several works, including *The Haywain*, by **John Constable**, England's greatest landscape painter (room 34). **Goya's** lively portrait of the Duke of Wellington is also worth seeking out, as is **William Hogarth's** irresistible and satirical *Marriage Settlement*. No visit to the gallery is complete without a look at **Turner's** shimmering *Rain, Steam and Speed*.

Despite the popularity of the gallery, it's just large enough to mean that there are always some rooms away from the bustle of visitors jostling to find their favourites. Equally, there's far too much to see in one visit. Plans are afoot to provide more areas for quiet contemplation in an attempt to prevent the gallery from becoming too crowded for its own good. The late opening on Wednesdays is often a good time to avoid the crush.

★ Five of the best late-night bars

- **Salvador and Amanda**, Great Newport St, Leicester Square, page 78.
- **Circus**, Upper James St, Soho, page 86.
- **Sak**, Greek St, Soho, page 89.
- **Café Bohème**, Old Compton St, Soho, page 88.
- **Atlantic Bar and Grill**, Glasshouse St, Soho, page 88.

★ National Portrait Gallery

① *To20-7306 0055, information ext 216, recorded information To20-7312 2463, www.npg.org.uk. Mon-Wed, Sat, Sun 1000-1800, Thu and Fri 1000-2100. Free. Lectures Tue 1500 and Thu 1310, Sat and Sun 1300 or 1500, free; Thu 1900, admission charge; Fri music nights 1830, free. IT Gallery does print outs: black and white free, colour postcard £5.50, colour A4 £17.50.*

Tucked away behind the National Gallery, up Charing Cross Road, the National Portrait Gallery is a shrine to British history pictured in the portraits of those who have shaped it. Attracting fewer visitors than the National Gallery, and much smaller, it can be almost as rewarding. Directly beyond the old main entrance, visitors arrive in a soaring lobby, ready to be whisked up an escalator to the earliest pictures in the collection, now hung in purpose-built rooms on the second floor.

It might come as a disappointment that there are no medieval works here, the earliest being an impressive portrait of Henry VII, but the **Tudor Galleries** more than make up for their absence. Modelled on an Elizabethan Long Room, they include the only portrait of Shakespeare known to have been taken from life, **Holbein**'s Henry VIII, several striking images of Elizabeth I and many of her famous courtiers. Further on, the Stuarts and 17th century galleries are even more colourful and extraordinary: a leggy full-length celebration of James I's toyboy, George Villiers, Duke of Buckingham; **Van Dyck**'s weird allegorical portrait redeeming the nymphomaniac Venetia, Lady Digby; a sensitive picture of the philosopher Thomas Hobbes, most famous for his assertion that life is 'nasty, brutish and short'; and a vivid likeness of a jaded Charles II.

On the same floor, the vibrancy of those early years gives way to the formal elegance and poise of the 18th century, with works by **Joshua Reynolds**, **Thomas Gainsborough** and **Hogarth**. Don't miss the birth of Romanticism in the Regency galleries beyond.

On the first floor, the galleries given over to the Victorians are powerfully evocative of the age of Empire, full of Roman-style busts and severe expressions, including a haunting picture of Charles Darwin. A surprisingly modern-looking Henry James ushers in the 20th century, a wavy see-through gallery design marking a significant change in mood. In the small room before it, in a massive and strange picture of First World War statesmen, Winston Churchill takes centre stage lit by a prophetic shaft of sunlight.

The **Balcony Gallery** in the Ondaatje Wing displays images and sculptures of movers and shakers in Britain since the 60s. On the way back to the ground floor, which is given over to special temporary exhibitions, the entire collection can be searched in the comfort of the IT Gallery and favourite pictures printed out. The gallery also runs a series of lectures, opens late on Thu and Fri, and has a smart restaurant and bar with great views over the old roofs of the National Gallery towards Big Ben.

❶ Eating

Trafalgar Square *p56, map p57*
Trafalgar Square is not really the place to look for good restaurants. Better to try St James's or Covent Garden nearby, although there are a few interesting exceptions
🍴 **Portrait Rooftop Restaurant**, on the top floor of the National Portrait Gallery, T020-7312 2490. Does a fine modern British menu, served up briskly and efficiently in swish non-smoking surroundings, but people really come here for the views. Open 1000-1715 Mon-Wed and at the weekends, and 1000-2200 with last orders at 2015 on Thu and Fri. The same hours apply to the bar, where you can also enjoy some fairly expensive snacks and are allowed to smoke.

There are a surprising number of good-value options close to the Square.
🍴 **Café in the Crypt**, under St Martin-in-the-Fields, Trafalgar Sq, T020-7839 4342. Closes at 1930 daily but is an atmospheric location to enjoy some reasonably priced salads, hot soups and meals served canteen-style to the strains of classical music.
🍴 **Hampton's Wine Bar**, 15 Whitcomb St, WC2, T020-7839 2823. A middle-of-the-road wine bar and restaurant doing the likes of Eggs Benedict for under a tenner, tucked away in a new development beside the National Gallery and popular with local office workers, closed weekends.
🍴 **Portrait Café**, in the basement of the Portrait Gallery. Serves excellent coffee, cakes and sandwiches during the day.
Brasserie in the Sainsbury Wing, National Gallery. A pleasant spot for lunch. There's also a good café in the Getty Entrance.

❶ Pubs and bars

Trafalgar Square *p56, map p57*
Again, this is not the best place to look for a drink, although the *Portrait Gallery's Rooftop Bar*, makes an interesting venue.

The Sherlock Holmes, 10 Northumberland Av, WC2, T020-7930 2644. A cosy, very busy pub with a central bar surrounded by Holmes memorabilia.

❷ Entertainment

Trafalgar Square *p56, map p57*
Music
St Martin-in-the-Fields, T020-7839 8362. Free lunchtime concerts on Mon, Tue and Fri at 1305, also Candlelit Baroque concerts on Thu, Fri and Sat at 1930, choral evensong on Sun at 1700. £6-15.

❸ Festivals and events

Trafalgar Square *p56, map p57*
St Martin-in-the-Fields hosts the Pearly Kings and Queens at the **Costermongers' Harvest Festival Service** in early **Oct**, a good-natured Cockney fancy-dress knees-up. Most other festivals in Trafalgar Square are best avoided, including the one at New Year. The Sea Cadets parade on **Trafalgar Day**, Sat nearest to **21 Oct**, celebrates Nelson's victory. The lights on the **Christmas Tree**, an annual gift from Norway in gratitude for British help during the Second World War, are switched on some time in Nov.

❹ Shopping

Trafalgar Square *p56, map p57*
Europa Food and Wine, a useful late-night supermarket on the corner of Whitehall and Trafalgar Square.
National Gallery, T020-7747 2870. Has 3 shops, the main one in the Sainsbury Wing, with an extensive array of books on art and art history, postcards and gift ideas like Van Gogh sunflower umbrellas or oven gloves.
National Portrait Gallery Shop, T020-7306 0055 (ext 223). Smaller, packed with postcards and posters of famous Brits down the ages.

● *For an explanation of sleeping and eating price codes used in this guide, see inside the*
● *front cover. Other relevant information is found in Essentials, see pages 44-46.*

The Strand, Embankment and Aldwych

Once one of the most important streets in town, linking Westminster with the City, the Strand was upstaged in the late 19th century by the building of the Victoria Embankment. Even so, this north bank of the river still provides an impressive southern border for Covent Garden. The Strand itself has some interesting old-established specialist shops like Stanley Gibbons and Twinings Tea, while the Embankment provides great views of the South Bank and Waterloo Bridge. Grand government buildings around the Aldwych are sterling examples of the architectural legacy of the Empire and its administration. The Courtauld Gallery is one of the most exceptional small collections of fine art in the city. It can be found in Somerset House, one of London's – if not Europe's – finest 18th-century buildings, opened up fully to the public for the first time in 2000 and now one of the riverside's more exotic attractions. It combines the art hoard of the Courtauld Gallery and the glitz of the Gilbert Collection with a high-tech waterjet display and a glimpse in the Hermitage Rooms of treasures from the great St Petersburg museum. Other discoveries waiting to be made here include the Queen's Chapel of the Savoy, the York Water Gate, the Royal Society of Arts and a 'Roman' bath. ▸▸ *For Sleeping, Eating and other listings see pages 70-73.*

History

The Strand was the link between the City and the village of Charing, and thence on to Whitehall. Streams flowed gently into the Thames across its path as the Strand tracked its way through fields from the edge of the City at Temple Bar to what is now Trafalgar Square. In the 10th century a Danish community settled here, probably those who had married Englishwomen before Alfred the Great drove the Danes out. St Clement Danes now occupies the site of their church.

Medieval mansions sprang up in the 13th century, the grandest of which was the Savoy Palace along the south side. The **Savoy Chapel** is on the site of the original chapel (incidentally, the first church in London to be lit by electricity), while the grand **Savoy Hotel** (the largest in Europe when it opened in 1886) now covers the site of the original palace, which was finally destroyed by the Peasants' Revolt in 1381. Mansions for bishops and nobles and the inns of court swept down to the Thames, and although they were torn down by the 17th-century entrepreneur Dr Nicholas Barbon, today's street names indicate those who once resided here (Durham, Exeter, Devereux, Sussex). The current Somerset House is an 18th-century replacement of the palace built by the Lord Protector Somerset in 1547-1550, and the York Water Gate remains an elegant monument to the grand residences that lined the street.

During the course of the 16th and 17th centuries, when Whitehall and Parliament emerged as the focus of political power, so the Strand's traffic grew. Barbon's transformation of the street to more wood-framed, modest housing saw the Strand develop into a haven for taverns, alehouses, coffeehouses and chophouses (*Twinings Tea*, at No 216, settled here in 1706). Meanwhile, pickpockets and prostitutes exploited the narrow alleyways. During the course of the 19th century theatres emerged (the *Adelphi*, *Vaudeville* and *Savoy* remain), hotels set up residence, and restaurants (*Simpson's*), music halls, and smoking rooms made it popular with lawyers (the Royal Courts of Justice were erected in the 1870s), and also among literary figures. Pepys, Coleridge, George Eliot, Shaw, Galsworthy and Hardy all lived on or around the street.

Meanwhile, in the late 19th century, London continued expanding into the Thames. According to Tacitus, the growth of the river's banks began with the Romans, and it underwent further development at various points thereafter. The Embankment was the creation of London's drainage king, Sir Joseph Bazalgette, who in the late 1860s began to build the Albert, Victoria and Chelsea embankments. The delays over the construction of the District line held up proceedings until Bazalgette lost patience and went ahead regardless. The gardens were integrated into the plans, and Cleopatra's Needle, a gift from the Turkish viceroy of Egypt, arrived in 1878. This granite obelisk from c1475 BC was intended to stand before Parliament, but the ground was subsiding, so it now watches over the river. Below it is buried a time-capsule, containing, among the obvious newspapers, coins and bible, photos of the best-looking women of the day – no doubt Cleopatra herself would have featured in her own time.

The 20th century saw the more notable additions of Bush House, synonymous with the voice of the BBC World Service, and the commonwealth High Commissions such as Australia and Zimbabwe (the male nude statues on the front of Zimbabwe House were 'modified' in response to popular outrage). Disraeli described the Strand as 'perhaps the greatest street in Europe' – it would be an ambitious claim now, but its renown is certainly well deserved.

2 Strand, Embankment & Aldwych

See London at a glance, p19-24, for related maps.

Sleeping
One Aldwych **1** *B2*
Royal Adelphi **2** *C1*
Savoy **3** *B2*
Strand Continental **4** *A3*
Strand Palace **5** *B2*

Eating
Admiralty **1** *B2*
Bank **2** *A2*
Cabman's Shelter **3** *C2*

India Club **4** *A3*
Simpson's-in-the-Strand **6** *B2*
Smollensky's **7** *B2*
Thai Pot Express **8** *A3*

Pubs & bars
Club Bar at Waldorf
  Hilton **14** *A2*
Coal Hole **9** *B2*
Gordon's **11** *C2*
Ship & Shovel **12** *C1*

Tattershall Castle **13** *C2*
Wellington **15** *B2*

Entertainment
Adelphi Theatre **1** *B2*
Aldwych Theatre **2** *A2*
Heaven **3** *C1*
Playhouse Theatre **4** *C1*
Savoy **5** *B2*
Strand Theatre **6** *A2*
Vaudeville Theatre **7** *B2*

Sights
Charing Cross, Embankment and Temple (closed Sun). *See p460*

Emerge from Charing Cross train or tube station and you'll find yourself on the Strand. Apart from its width, first impressions reveal little of this vital thoroughfare's glory days in the 18th and 19th centuries, when it was every fashionable Londoner's favourite riverside prom. To catch a glimpse of those times, turn right down Villiers Street, and then right again through **The Arches**, an atmospheric sunken shopping arcade beneath the station.

Craven Passage, at the end, which oddly enough cuts the Ship and Shovel pub in half, brings you into **Craven Street**, sloping down towards **Northumberland Avenue** and the river. Here is one of the most complete rows of Georgian houses in the centre of the city. Number 36 was Benjamin Franklin's home in the 1750s; it's now a Grade I listed building and is in the process of being transformed into a 'living' museum by the Friends of Benjamin Franklin House. The **Benjamin Franklin Museum** should be fully open some time in 2006, in time to celebrate the 300th anniversary of his birth, but it can be visited before then by arrangement ① *T020-7930 9121.*

Left at the end of Craven Street, past the Playhouse Theatre, you're directly beneath postmodernist Terry Farrell's **Embankment Place**, one of his love-'em-or-loathe-'em '90s developments, spectacularly lit at night. Passing beneath it brings you out in front of Embankment tube station at the foot of Villiers Street. From here you can walk through the station, past the flower and fruit'n'veg stalls, onto the Embankment itself (see below) and then over the river via the **Hungerford Millennium Foot Bridges**. Opened in 2002, these wide walkways are slung either side of the old Hungerford railway bridge, built in 1864 to bring trains into the new Charing Cross station. There are spectacular views to the west of the Houses of Parliament and London Eye, and to the east of Waterloo Bridge, the South Bank and St Paul's beyond.

Victoria Embankment and around

Constructed in the late 1860s, the Victoria Embankment between Westminster and Blackfriars bridges was an amazing feat of engineering led by Sir Joseph Bazalgette, commemorated here with a bronze bust. Its 8 ft-thick granite walls still protect both the Circle and District tube line and the largest sewer the world had yet found necessary from the brunt of the current on this outside bend of the river. The road above soon became the most popular route between the City and Westminster. Today it is lined with noble plane trees and monuments although its sunny south-facing views are disturbed by the continual roar of traffic.

Cleopatra's Needle

Cleopatra's Needle is easily the oldest thing around here, and just about the oldest monument in London exposed to the weather. The pink granite obelisk is one of a pair that once stood in Heliopolis, long before the Egyptian queen with the famous nose, although the inscriptions on the stone apparently refer to her. It was given to George IV by the viceroy of Egypt in 1820 but only made it to the banks of the Thames over 50 years later after an extremely hazardous voyage in which several sailors' lives were lost. Its companion is in New York's Central Park. The First World War bomb-scarred bronze sphinxes are late 19th-century, replaced the wrong way round after cleaning in the 1920s.

● *In 1917, Cleopatra's Needle earned the odd distinction of being the first London monument*
● *to be hit in an air attack.*

ⓘ *Basic tearoom and café with plastic tables and chairs outside, throughout the year 0730-1930 daily. The gardens are also a pleasant place to take a picnic.*

Escape the fumes in Victoria Embankment Gardens, where the free lunchtime and evening entertainment manages to make itself heard above the din of the road. In high season, afternoon and evening events in the old bandstand range from dance, mime and poetry to world music and brass bands, organized by **Alternative Arts** ⓘ *T020-7375 0441*. They can be enjoyed from the comfort of ranks of stripy blue deckchairs. You'll be surrounded by lunching office workers and statues of famous folk, notably the great Scottish bard, Robert Burns.

On the north side of the gardens, near Villiers Street, the **York Water Gate** is all that remains of York House, the 17th-century home of James I's favourite, George Villiers, Duke of Buckingham. He has left most of the many parts of his name on the surrounding streets. Before his time, York House was also the birthplace and later the home of the great natural philosopher Sir Francis Bacon. The grand old stone gate was probably designed by Inigo Jones. Its position demonstrates how much wider the river was before the construction of the Victoria Embankment. Today the foot of the gate is lapped not by the Thames but by the waters of an ornamental pond.

Buckingham Street, overlooking the water gate, has also been home, at different times, to Samuel Pepys, Peter the Great, David Hume, Rousseau and the novelist Henry Fielding. At the top of the street, the **Proud Galleries** ⓘ *5 Buckingham St, T020-7839 4942,* is a lively young media-driven exhibition space, often putting on controversial shows, usually of photography and contemporary art.

Royal Society of Arts

ⓘ *T020-7451 6874, and for groups by appointment T020-7451 6825 (or for details of the regular series of public lectures and lunchtime events staged by the RSA). Tours of the 18th-century interior take place at lunchtime on the 1st Fri of every month.*

Turning right takes you into John Adam Street and brings you to the front door of the **Royal Society of Arts**, at No 8. One of the few remaining original buildings from the Adam brothers' ambitious Adelphi development, it was purpose built by Robert Adam for the 'Royal Society for the Encouragement of Arts, Manufactures and Commerce' in 1774. A product of mid-18th-century 'coffee house' culture, the Society's eminent members still meet up regularly to share ideas, discuss the latest issues in the arts, design and technology, and promote new projects. There's an interesting view of the back of the building from the Strand.

Queen's Chapel of the Savoy

ⓘ *T020-7836 7221. Tue-Fri 1130-1530 (closed Aug/Sep), services on Sun and Wed.*
Round the corner, back on the Strand, pass the Savoy Hotel and then duck right beneath it down Savoy Buildings, through the white-tiled bowels of the hotel, past the staff entrance into Savoy Hill. Here stands the incongruous little stone tower of the Queen's Chapel of the Savoy, an often unremarked little piece of Royal London and *the* place for fashionable weddings in the 19th century. Built on the site of John of Gaunt's Savoy Palace, which was burnt down during the Peasants' Revolt of 1381, it was restored by Queen Victoria and became the chapel of the Royal

❋ *The BBC broadcast its first daily radio programmes in 1922 from the building over the road, moving to Broadcasting House 10 years later.*

Victorian Order in 1937. Heraldic copper plaques mark the pews of the different knights in the splendid late-Gothic interior, its flat ceiling decorated with the Royal Arms above the monarch's seat at the west end.

★ Somerset House

① T020-7845 4600, www.somerset-house.org.uk. Courtauld Institute and Gallery T020-7848 2526, www.courtauld.ac.uk. Gilbert Collection T020-7240 4080, www.gilbert-collection.org.uk. Hermitage Rooms T020-7845 4630. Daily 1000-1800 (last admission 1715). Standard admission to each of the collections £5, concessions £4, full-time students, under 18's, unwaged free. Any two collections: £8, concessions £7. All three collections: £12, concessions £11. For ice-skating details see page 50.

Further east along the Strand, on the right, stands Somerset House, one of the most important 18th-century buildings in Europe. It was designed by Sir William Chambers in 1776 for George III's Naval office, with the wings on the Strand purpose-built for the fledgling Royal Academy of Arts (founded in 1768 and relocated to Piccadilly in 1837), the Royal Society, and the Society of Antiquaries. Appropriately enough, since 1990, this northern wing has been occupied by the **Courtauld Institute and Gallery**. In 2000 the southern buildings were opened up to display the **Gilbert Collection** and **Hermitage Rooms**, providing access for the first time to the river frontage. The terrace, which can also be reached from Waterloo Bridge, is a sunny spot to take some tea, slightly marred by the traffic noise from the Embankment below. The entrance to Somerset House from the Embankment takes you through the original water gate on the river.

Courtauld Institute and Gallery

Founded by the textile magnate Samuel Courtauld in memory of his wife Elizabeth, who died on Christmas day 1931, the Courtauld Institute, now attached to the University of London, has become the foremost academy of fine art history in the country. The Courtauld Gallery, on the right-hand side as you enter Somerset House from the Strand, gains its special character from its role as a teaching aid to the Institute as well as from the beautifully proportioned rooms that it now occupies. Ascending the wonderful winding stairway, apparently designed to inspire the terror that the time considered necessary to the appreciation of the Sublime, the rooms on three floors afford a delightful potted introduction to Western painting.

‡ The gallery is free on Mon 1000-1400 except Bank Holidays. If you're looking for a particular painting, it's worth phoning ahead to check that it's not out on loan.

Five major collections are displayed, particular strengths being European medieval art, including the **Master of Flemalle**'s tripytch of The Entombment, a masterpiece of early Dutch painting, the Italian and Northern Renaissance schools, the Baroque and 18th-century British portraiture. Among the many remarkable works on show, look out for **Botticelli**'s altarpiece for the Augustinian convent of Sant' Elisabetta in Florence; Martin Luther's friend **Lucas Cranach**'s Adam and Eve; **Brueghel**'s dramatic Landscape with the Flight into Egypt; and **Rubens**' strange, star-studded Landscape by Moonlight.

For many the highlight of a visit remains Courtauld's own collection of Impressionists and Post-Impressionists: a copy of **Manet**'s Déjeuner sur l'herbe and, even more extraordinary, his Bar at the Folies-Bergère, vie for attention with famous works by **Degas, Pissarro, Monet, Renoir, Seurat, Gauguin, Van Gogh** and **Cezanne**. Since 2002 the gallery has been enhanced by permanent loans from a series of private collections, notably some very fine work by the Fauve group, including **Derain, Vlaminck** and **Matisse**, and a representative variety of paintings by **Kandinsky** and the German expressionists. Also popular is Roger Fry's collection of work by the Bloomsbury Group including his own and artists like **Vanessa Bell** and **Duncan Grant** as well as some Chinese and non-Western art. Regular temporary exhibtions are mounted.

The great central courtyard of Somerset House has been re-christened the **Edmond J** **Safra Fountain Court** ① *the fountains operate from 1000-2300, with short displays on the hour and half hour, and main displays at 1300, 1800, and 2200; open-air ice-skating can be enjoyed here in winter, see page 50*, and blessed with a diverting but controversial computer-operated water feature. Fifty fountains arranged in 10 rows of five spurt straight up out of the ground with varying force, reaching a height of about 15 ft. In daylight the effect is more comical than impressive, but the display is best seen after dark when the lights in place beneath the waterjets transform them into sparkling columns of luminesence. The reservoir for the fountains is located in the two storeys beneath the courtyard, a reminder that Somerset House was built facing the river, its front three times higher than its back. The fountains have been criticized for upsetting the intended effect of the quad's classical proportions, but they make an appropriately wacky introduction to the wonders of the Gilbert Collection now on display in the riverside wings of the building.

The Gilbert Collection

This is London's latest museum of decorative art. Arthur Gilbert was born in London in 1913 and moved to California in 1949. With the profits from his successful adventures in real estate he began an extraordinary and costly collection of gold and silverware, precious snuff boxes and peculiar Roman micromosaics, among other things. Described as the single most generous gift ever made to the nation, his collection went on display in purpose-built galleries in the southern wing of Somerset House in 2000.

The effect of so many expensive objects gathered together and lovingly lit in the designer galleries is fairly overwhelming. They include one of the earliest gold vessels in the world, from Bronze Age Anatolia, a Maharajah's silver howdah from Rajasthan, and a pair of silver-gilt royal gates given to a monastery in a Kiev by Catherine the Great. An audio guide, which often proves more interesting than the objects themselves, tells the history of some of the items. The most bizarre exhibit must be the recreation of Gilbert's study, complete with a waxwork replica of the collector himself.

The Hermitage Rooms

The most recent addition to the exotic collections at Somerset House are The Hermitage Rooms, designed to exhibit changing selections of artefacts from the great St Petersburg museum. The five rooms have been decorated in the Imperial style of the Winter Palace, with replica chandeliers, gilded chairs and marquetry floors. The first room shows a live feed to St Petersburg, looking across Palace Square, and a six-minute video taking you on a tour of the Hermitage itself. There's also a shop selling souvenirs inspired by the Hermitage.

The Strand

Back on the Strand, the church marooned on its traffic island in front of King's College London is **St Mary-le-Strand** ① *Mon-Fri 1100-1530*. A striking blend of Italian Baroque and Renaissance, it was the first public building designed by the Scotsman James Gibbs, from 1714-17. Free lunchtime recitals are usually given here on Wednesdays at 1300. The pulpit was carved by Grinling Gibbons and oddly enough, this is where Bonnie Prince Charlie secretly converted to Anglicism after his disastrous defeat at Culloden.

Bush House, now the home of the **BBC World Service**, was designed by Americans in 1920 and sensitively embraces the church. The shop (see Shopping page 72) sells World Service merchandise, BBC videos, books, CDs and cassettes,

★ Five of the best cheap eats

- **India Club**, Strand, page 71.
- **Pizzico**, Haymarket, Leicester Square, page 77.
- **Hamburger Union**, Dean St, Soho, page 87.
- **Poetry Society**, Betterton St, Covent Garden, page 98.
- **ICA Café**, The Mall, St James's, page 125.

and technical books on radio production. Next door is the mighty façade of **India House**, dating from 1930. **Australia House** is on the other side of Melbourne Place. Built during the First World War, Australian stone, wood and marble were used in its construction. The entrance is decorated with statues of Exploration and Shearing and Reaping; up above are the Horses of the Sun.

The other church at the end of the Strand is **St Clement Danes** ① *T020-7242 8282, Mon-Fri 0830-1630, Sat 0900-1530, Sun 0900-1230.* Named after the Danish settlement at Aldwych in Saxon times, this is probably not the St Clement's whose bells say 'Oranges and Lemons' although tradition would have it so. This was also Dr Johnson's church. It was badly bombed in the Blitz, and became the RAF church; the USAF donated the organ.

Just down the hill from here is London's only **'Roman' Bath** ① *5 Strand Lane, off Surrey St, T020-7641 5264, May-Sep, every Wed 1300-1700 by appointment only, with 24 hrs notice during office hours, free.* Whether or not you've booked an appointment, you can peer through grubby windows at ground level at its sunken brickwork, fed by the Holy Well nearby. It has been known about since at least the late 18th century and Dickens mentions it in *David Copperfield*. No one has yet proven that it is Roman, although it almost certainly does date back at least to Shakespeare's day.

● Sleeping

The Strand, Embankment and Aldwych *p64, map p65*

AL One Aldwych, 1 Aldwych, WC2, T020-7300 1000, www.onealdwych.co.uk. Award-winning modern designer hotel close to Covent Garden, with 105 rooms, complete with an extensive art collection, huge swimming pool and plenty of subtle and not-so-subtle style notes. £315 for a standard double. Still one of the most fashionable London hotels, with impeccable service.

AL The Savoy, Strand, WC2, T020-7836 4343, www.savoy-group.co.uk. 207 rooms, single £329, double £393-£417, suite £535-£1610. Opened by Richard D'Oyly Carte in 1889, retains reputation for the understated and traditional British comfort of its 263 rooms. The great Escoffier was the first chef, inventing the Peach Melba for Australian Dame Nellie Melba after she had been singing in Manon Lescaut at Covent Garden. Cesar Ritz was its first manager. Superb views over the river from the 4th floor and above.

Art deco luxury on the top floor and funky new cuisine in the old-fashioned Savoy Grill. Service can occasionally be shambolic.

A Strand Palace, Strand, WC2, T0870-4008702, www.strandpalacehotel.co.uk. First opened in 1909, freshly refurbished but rather impersonal rooms (all 784 of them on 9 floors), popular with corporate travellers but also in a great position near Covent Garden for tourists. Standard rate about £125 including breakfast.

C Royal Adelphi, 21 Villiers St, WC2, T020-7930 8764, www.royaladephi.co.uk. Very central, basic small hotel with 47 rooms, on busy little Villiers St off the Strand next to Charing Cross station, not much changed since the 60s. Clean enough and friendly though with a 24-hr bar. £68 standard double.

D Strand Continental, 142 Strand, WC2, T020-7836 4880. Basic but very convenient Indian hotel with hot and cold water in 24 bedrooms. Above the *India Club* restaurant. Good value at £40 for a double.

❶ Eating

The Strand, Embankment and Aldwych *p64, map p65*

₩₩₩ The Admiralty, T020-7845 4646. The modern British food here has won some praise, making booking essential later in the week. A smart place to take your time with the river beckoning beyond the terrace outside (where there's a separate and less expensive brasserie operation, open in the summer only).

₩₩₩ Bank, 1 Kingsway, on the corner of Aldwych, WC2, T020-7379 9797. More of a buzz can be found here. Brave the designer shards of plate glass suspended from the ceiling of this bank-branch-conversion to enjoy some top-quality fish and modern European dishes. The set pre-theatre and lunch menus are particularly good value at £13.50 for 2 courses. Booking is essential. It's also open on Sun, for brunch, lunch and dinner.

₩₩₩ Savoy Grill, in *The Savoy Hotel*, Strand, WC2, T020-7836 4343. Good old-fashioned English food, closed in Aug and insists on jacket and tie, no denims or trainers.

₩₩₩ Simpson's-in-the-Strand,100 Strand, WC2, T020-7836 9112. Provides good old-fashioned English food, including famous full English breakfasts during the week, in a formal, upper-crust environment any day for lunch and dinner.

₩ Smollensky's, 105 Strand, WC2, T020-7497 2101. Has become an institution. It's a reasonably good-value family restaurant, American in style and generosity, often packed with hungry kids at the weekends. Jazz bands play here on Sun evenings, as well as a pianist throughout the week and DJ's from Thu to Sat.

₮ India Club, 143 Strand, WC2, T020-7836 0650. A world apart from the area's many cafés and fast-food joints, this is easily the most characterful place to eat cheaply around here. Pay up to £10 for old-style curries at formica tables on linoleum floors with yellow walls. A very Indian institution, since 1950. It also has the unusual advantage (in central London) of being unlicensed:

take your own booze and they won't even charge you 'corkage'. Open Mon-Sat 1200-1430, 1800-2250.

₮ Thai Pot Express, 148 Strand, WC2, T020-7497 0904. A smart, woody place for slightly more expensive Thai food.

Cafés and sandwich bars

Cabman's Shelter, Embankment Pl. Another interesting option doing low-price takeaway teas and very basic rolls.

Savoy, Strand, WC2, T020-7836 4343. Top-notch teas can be taken daily between 1500-1730. They cost about £20.

❶ Pubs and bars

The Strand, Embankment and Aldwych *p64, map p65*
Pubs

Apart from a few notable exceptions listed here, pubs in this area tend to be big, busy and commercial. Otherwise this is an area that excels in sophisticated and expensive hotel bars.

Coal Hole, 91 Strand, WC2, T020-7836 7503. Has real ales, tables outside and lots of decorative plasterwork.

The Ship and Shovel, Craven Passage. The best traditional pub in the area. It survived the renovation of Charing Cross in the 1990s and opened another version of itself across the passage a year ago. **No 1 Craven** is a new old-fashioned little place with a snug. Does good beers and food.

The Wellington, 351 Strand, WC2, T020-7557 9881. Another good bet, on a prominent corner site at the end of Waterloo Bridge. Its standard pub grub is very reasonably priced.

Bars

American Bar, at the *Savoy*, Strand, WC2, T020-7836 4343. Has a dress code, no smoking area and claims to be the 1st place a Martini was put together in Britain (shaken, not shtirred, of courshe).

Axis Bar, at *One Aldwych Hotel*, 1 Aldwych. Smarter than *Lobby Bar*, above the restaurant and done up in art deco style.

● *For an explanation of sleeping and eating price codes used in this guide, see inside the*
● *front cover. Other relevant information is found in Essentials, see pages 44-46.*

The Club Bar, at *Waldorf Hilton*, Aldwych, WC2, T020-7836 2400. Unusually for a hotel this pulls a very good if expensive pint and the atmosphere is not as formal as you might expect.

Gordon's, 47 Villiers St, WC2, T020-7930 1408. A subterranean wine bar at the bottom of Villiers St. Exceptional wines can be enjoyed in the candlelit gloom of its convivial vaults. It also serves up fairly expensive salad bar-style food.

Lobby Bar, at *One Aldwych Hotel*, 1 Aldwych, WC2, T020-7300 1000. Less stuffy, somewhere to enjoy sculpture and design as well as good-value cocktails.

The Tattershall Castle, T020-7839 6548. A pub-ship that does bar food with a barbecue on deck through Jul and Aug. There are good views of the Eye from its position upstream of Hungerford Bridge.

⦿ Entertainment

The Strand, Embankment and Aldwych *p64, map p65*
Dance
Waldorf Hilton, T020-7836 2400. Tea dances on Sat from 1430-1700 on Sun 1600-1830. Need to book, £25 per person including tea, with scones and cakes. Different big bands.

Music
Rock, folk and jazz Smollensky's, jazz. **Waldorf**, in Palm Court. Jazz brunch on Sun 1200-1430, £40 per person, need to book.

Nightclubs
Heaven, under the arches, off Villiers St, WC2, T020-7930 2020, www.heaven-london.com. Once the foremost gay nightclub in the city, Heaven has been joined by many others but is still going strong. Mon 1030-0300 is *Popcorn*, a disco mix, indie music and house. Wed 1030-0300 is *Fruit Machine*, hard house, disco, soul. Sat (£5) 1000-0500, commercial house, funky house. 3 different rooms, 1 members' bar (7 bars). 1st Thu every month *Bedrock* (£7-8), which is a straight night. All are cheaper before 1130 with a flyer, no booking, just queue. *Bedrock* and Sat are the busiest nights.

Theatre
Adelphi Theatre, Strand, WC2, T020-7344 0055. Opened in 1806, it is the oldest theatre still standing on the Strand, and has been rebuilt 3 times since , most recently in 1900.

Aldwych Theatre, Aldwych, WC2, T020-7416 6003. Built as a pair with Strand Theatre to the south in 1905, the 2 theatres stand either side of the Waldorf. Before the Second World War it staged Ben Travers' farces and became the London home of the Royal Shakespeare Company in 1960 before the company moved to the Barbican in 1982. Box office open Mon-Sat 1000-2000.

Playhouse Theatre, Northumberland Av, WC2, T020-7839 4292.

Savoy Theatre, Strand, WC2, T020-7836 8888. Older than the hotel, the theatre was built in 1881 by Richard d'Oyly Carte for Gilbert and Sullivan's operas. It was the first public place in London to be electrically lit. The art deco interior was fully restored after a fire in 1990.

Strand Theatre, Aldwych, WC2, T020-7930 8800. Opened in 1905 as one of a pair with the Aldwych Theatre. Donald Wolfit performed Shakespeare here at lunchtimes during the Blitz.

Vaudeville Theatre, Strand, WC2, T020-7836 9987. Opened in 1870, this attractive little theatre was given a make-over in the 20s. Since then it has staged a successful variety of musicals and comedies.

⦿ Shopping

The Strand, Embankment and Aldwych *p64, map p65*
This isn't an area that you'd choose to mount a shopping expedition but there are several interesting specialist shops worth a look if you happen to be passing. When the theatres on the Strand closed down, the philatelists and numismatists that had colonized the street stayed on. Nowadays only 2 stamp emporia are left.

A H Baldwin & Sons, 11 Adelphi Terr, WC2, T020-7930 6879. Open by appointment during the week, is the UK's 2nd largest numismatist. They're the 4th generation of a family firm dealing in coins and medals.

BBC World Service Shop, Bush House Arcade, Strand, WC2, T020-7557 2576. Has videos and cassettes, books, souvenirs and umbrellas.

Davenport's Magic Shop, 7 Charing Cross Underground Arcade, Strand, WC2, T020-7836 0408. in the tube station. A family business that has been catering to the needs of magicians amateur and professional since 1898. Closed on Sun.

The London Camera Exchange, 98 Strand, WC2, T020-7379 0200. A reliable independent dealing in new and second-hand cameras.

Penfriend, Bush House Arcade, Strand, WC2, T020-7836 9809. Under the wing of the World Service, scribblers of the world can unite here, has a wide selection of antique and new pens.

The Stamp Centre, 79 Strand, WC2, T020-7836 2579. Has less cachet than Stanley Gibbons and hence lower prices.

Stanley Gibbons International, 399 Strand, WC2, T020-7836 8444. Founded in 1856 and is the Harrods of world stamp collecting.

R Twining & Co, 216 Strand, WC2, T020-7353 3511. Another old family business, but on a much grander scale, they've been importing and exporting fine tea and coffee on this site since 1706 and won't let you forget it. There's even a museum.

Woodhams at One, 1 Aldwych, WC2, T020-7300 0777. For a special thank you present perhaps, they do the flowers for the designer hotel, also spectacular bouquet deliveries in a smart box complete with their own water for £30-£50.

Leicester Square and around

Leicester Square always gets bad press, written off as a charmless tourist-trap. The criticisms are still justified – not too many of the businesses round here expect to see the same face twice – but since the little square's pedestrianization and refurbishment, it has provided a much-needed focal point for the entertainment scene in the West End. Just about everyone looking for fun in central London ends up passing through here eventually: Soho, Covent Garden, Piccadilly and Mayfair are all within easy walking distance. During the day Leicester Fields, the gardens in the middle, are usually packed with people sitting about deciding what to do next.

In the evenings the after-work crowds can make crossing the square almost impossible. The two main draws are the cinemas, not only the blockbusting first-run multiscreens surrounding the square, but also places like the cult rep Prince Charles, or the fashionable Curzon Soho, and the nightclubs, like Sound, Equinox and the Hippodrome. And then there's the Comedy Store, the place that set many comedians on the road to stardom in the 1970s. Just north of the square lies Chinatown, only a couple of streets of shops and restaurants but still an area with one of the most distinctive cultural identities in the capital. It squeezes into a little niche between the square itself, Shaftesbury Avenue, the high street of 'Theatreland', and Charing Cross Road, the bookseller's favourite address. ▸▸ *For Sleeping, Eating and other listings see pages 76-80.*

History

Leicester Square derives its name from the grand Leicester House that dominated the area in the mid-17th century. The fields sloping south were slowly surrounded by grand houses, creating a square, while in the latter part of the century the area behind the Earl of Leicester's house was developed by Nicholas Barbon, the entrepreneur who tore down the mansions that lined the Strand. It remained primarily residential until the mid-18th century, when the construction of New Coventry Street led to the emergence of coffee houses, taverns, hotels and hotel restaurants. Nevertheless it remained a distinguished address – John Dryden, Edmund Burke and Sir Joshua

Reynolds lived here, while Hogarth executed many of his more notable works in a gallery he built off his house at No 30.

As the area became less residential, the Survey of London observed "Leicester Square was essentially masculine – its popularity with the demi-monde meant that there was no place for unescorted ladies". In later Victorian times oyster rooms and theatres, such as the Alhambra and Empire, emerged, and Turkish baths became the vogue. The Hippodrome became a venue of almost Roman proportions – water shows were put on here, as well as music hall and circus acts. The central garden's fortunes also fluctuated. Originally available to commoners to graze their livestock, its heyday was in the mid-19th century when the Great Globe was constructed by James Wylde, a geographer, to capitalize on the mass of visitors drawn by the Great Exhibition of 1851. Standing 60 ft high and 40 ft in diameter, visitors ascended a four-stage gallery constructed on the inside, viewing the world's surface reproduced on a scale of one inch to one mile. It was sold for scrap 10 years later. Despite a cleaning up of the garden itself in 1992, the square's current status as a popular tourist attraction continues to mystify Londoners.

The area north of the square, now called **Chinatown** (although a pale imitation of its namesake in New York), has only relatively recently become the focal point for the city's Chinese community. Before that, Gerrard Street and the smaller streets around housed nightclubs, strip-joints and other such clubs – the author Graham Greene commenting that "half the blackmail or swindling cases lived in Gerrard Street". Although opium dens run by the likes of Brilliant Chang existed in the '20s, it is only since the '50s that Chinese businesses began moving in from their earlier community near the docks in Limehouse.

Sights ⊖ *Leicester Sq and Piccadilly Circus.* ⦿ *See p460.*

Leicester Square

Leicester Square itself is surprisingly small, and since being cleaned up is in fact quite attractive. Sloping downhill from the Empire cinema, it's ringed by big cinemas catching the eye with the titles of the current Hollywood blockbusters. **Leicester Fields** is the leafy garden in the middle, complete with a statue of Shakespeare, a copy of the one in Westminster Abbey. He's surrounded on the edge of the garden by busts of famous locals like Hogarth, Newton, and Joshua Reynolds as well as a modern statue of Charlie Chaplin with the mawkish inscription 'the comic genius who gave pleasure to so many'. Indeed the big film premieres at the Odeon cinema on the eastside of the Square still regularly draw huge crowds of stargazers.

On the south side, the **London Information Centre** ① *T020-7292 2333, daily 0800-2300*, shares a modern chalet-style building with **tkts**, the only official half-price theatre ticket outlet (see Theatre, page 79). The Information Centre dispenses free advice, maps and posters and can additionally book hotels and tours for free.

Dedicated sightseers and art-lovers won't want to miss the church of **Notre Dame de France** ① *5 Leicester Pl, T020-7437 9363, daily 0930-2000*, on the north side of the Square. Originally a panoramic playhouse, which explains its unusual round design, it became the Eglise Française Catholique de Londres in 1865. Bombed out in 1940 it was almost entirely rebuilt in 1955 when Jean Cocteau was commissioned to decorate the Chapelle du Saint Sacrement. His mural is an energetic depiction of the Annunciation, Mary at the foot of the Cross, and the Assumption. An Aubusson tapestry hangs over the altar and Boris Anrep did the mosaics.

Chinatown

Leicester Place and Leicester Street both head north into Chinatown. It may be tiny in comparison to other cities', but then this is not really the home of London's Chinese community, more like its market place. **Lisle Street** is lined with restaurants and supermarkets, while pedestrianized **Gerrard Street** has been 'themed' with Chinoiserie street furniture and gates to complement another stretch of busy restaurants. Both streets meet in **Newport Place**, where a little bandstand-cum-pagoda has become a bustling meeting point.

3 Leicester Square & around

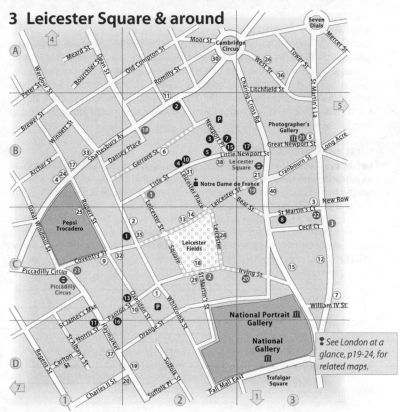

West End Leicester Square & around

> ✽ See London at a glance, p19-24, for related maps.

0 metres 100
0 yards 100

Sleeping 🛏
Manzi's & Restaurant **1** *B2*
Radisson Edwardian
  Hampshire **2** *C2*
St Martin's Lane **3** *C3*

Eating 🍴
1997 **1** *C2*
Aroma II **2** *B2*
Canton **3** *B2*
Fung Shing **5** *B2*
Imperial City **4** *B2*
Jen Café **7** *B2*
J Sheekey **8** *C3*
Mr Kong **10** *B2*
Pizzico **11** *D1*
Stockpot **13** *C2*
Tokyo Diner **15** *B2*
West End
  Kitchen **16** *D1*
Zipangu **17** *B3*

Pubs & bars 🍺
Cork & Bottle **19** *B3*
De Hems **18** *B2*
Oxygen **20** *C3*
Salisbury **22** *C3*
Salvador &
  Amanda **21** *B3*
Tiger Tiger **23** *C1*

Entertainment 🎭
Albery **3** *B3*
Apollo **4** *B1*
Arts Theatre **5** *B3*
Bar Room Bar **6** *B2*
Coliseum **7** *C3*
Comedy Store **9** *C1*
Comedy Theatre **10** *C2*
Curzon Soho **11** *B2*
Duke of York's **12** *C3*
Empire **13** *C2*
Equinox **14** *C2*
Garrick **15** *C3*
Gielgud **17** *B1*
Haymarket
  Theatre Royal **19** *D2*
Her Majesty's **20** *D2*
Hippodrome **21** *B3*
Lyric Shaftesbury **24** *B1*

New Ambassadors
  26 *A3*
Odeon Wardour St **2** *C2*
Odeon Leicester
  Square & Odeon
  Mezzanine **28** *C2*
Odeon Panton St **1** *C2*
Odeon West End **29** *C2*
Other Cinema **25** *C1*
Palace Theatre **30** *A2*
Prince Charles **31** *B2*
Prince of Wales **32** *C1*
Queen's Theatre **33** *B1*
Sound **35** *C2*
St Martin's **36** *A3*
TKTs **18** *C2*
UGC Haymarket **37** *D1*
Vue West End **38** *B2*
Wyndham's **40** *B3*

★ Five of the best late night food stops

- **1997**, Wardour St, Leicester Square, page 77
- **Café Bohème**, Old Compton Street, Soho, page 88.
- **Café Lazeez**, Dean St, Soho, page 88
- **The Wolesley**, Piccadilly, page 125
- **Tesco Metro**, Oxford St, page 132.

Shaftesbury Avenue → For theatre listings, see page 79.

Shaftesbury Avenue runs along the northern boundary of Chinatown and Covent Garden, from Piccadilly Circus to High Holborn. Since the late 19th century, this street has most famously been the heart of West End 'theatreland', as the street signs now indicate. Six theatres were opened up along its west side in the decades either side of 1900, including the *Lyric*, the *Apollo*, the *Globe* (now the *Gielgud*), the *Queen's* and the grand *Palace Theatre* on Cambridge Circus. Before then, the most important theatres were on the Haymarket.

Charing Cross Road

Cambridge Circus is where Shaftesbury Avenue crosses the Charing Cross Road as it heads north to Tottenham Court Road and south to Trafalgar Square. Charing Cross Road has long been to books what Shaftesbury Avenue is to theatres. South of Cambridge Circus, almost every shop on the east side is stacked full of books new and second-hand, while small pedestrian alleyways like Cecil Street and St Martin's Court run through into St Martin's Lane lined with some of the city's foremost specialist booksellers. The **Photographer's Gallery** ① *5-8 Great Newport St, WC2, T020-7831 1772*, mounts regular exhibitions of promising new work and has a good café.

⬤ Sleeping

Leicester Square *p73, map p75*
L The Radisson Edwardian Hampshire, Leicester Sq, WC2, T020-7859 9399, www.radissonedwardian.com. Once the Dental Hospital but now a plush 5-star hotel with great views from the Penthouse Suite. No single rooms. A straightforward, well-run smart hotel bang in the middle of town.
L St Martin's Lane, 45 St Martin's Lane, WC2, T0800-634 5500, www.morganshotelgroup.com. Formerly Ian Schrager's media favourite, designed by minimalist Philippe Starck, with a restaurant doing classic French and modern European on the side, the awesome *Light Bar* and the *Seabar* for seafood. Rooms have a contemporary designer edge.
B Manzi's, 1-2 Leicester St, WC2, T020-7734 0224, www.manzis.co.uk. 70 years old, with 17 smallish, clean rooms, above the famous fish restaurant right in the

thick of Chinatown near Leicester Square, Manzi's is popular with business travellers as well as tourists. £88 for a double including breakfast.

⑦ Eating

Leicester Square *p73, map p75*
The obvious destination around here is Chinatown, although the choice can be bewildering. The best bet is to join a crowded restaurant, especially if the crowd is Chinese, and don't insist on too much English explanation from either menu or staff. A traditional feature of Hong Kong/Cantonese cuisine, dim sum, are tasty little dumplings and snacks, often excellent value but not usually served after about 1700. If you're not a fan of Chinese cooking, either splash out on some celebrity dining or head for Soho or Covent Garden (see p86 and p97).

Asia de Cuba, St Martin's Lane Hotel, 45 St Martin's Lane, WC2, T020-7300 5588. More loud and lively and just about as star-studded as *J Sheekey*, with an imaginative menu fashionably fusing Asian and Latin American cuisine. Book well ahead at the weekend.

J Sheekey, 28-32 St Martin's Ct, WC2, T020-7240 2565. A name that has long been associated with fish, and was given a sympathetic overhaul by the people responsible for *The Ivy* and *Le Caprice*. Now it remains the most stylish place around for top-quality seafood, fairly traditional and exclusive. Book well ahead for the weekend.

Fung Shing, 15 Lisle St, WC2, T020-7437 1539, www.ipi.co.uk/funshing. Has long had a good reputation for its seafood and Cantonese cooking. It was one of the first restaurants in London to serve up Chinese haute cuisine and standards reportedly remain high.

Manzi's, 1-2 Leicester St, WC2, T020-7734 0224. Has been around for over 70 years, drawing in a generally sedate crowd of regulars, often an elder statesman or two, who come for its old-fashioned Italian service and traditional ways with fish.

At the lower end of this price range, but also taking their cookery seriously, the following 2 Chinatown restaurants are particularly exceptional:

Aroma II, 118-120 Shaftesbury Av, W1, T020-7437 0377, on a busy corner opposite the Curzon Soho cinema. A large, modern restaurant with a wide choice of Cantonese and, more unusually, Beijing dishes.

Imperial China, White Bear Yard, 25a Lisle St, WC2, T020-7734 3388. Another large restaurant, with the added attraction of being hidden away in the tranquility of its own courtyard off Lisle St. Recently completely redecorated, it does very good dim sum until 1700 as well as good value Cantonese dishes.

Many Chinatown restaurants can serve a meal for under £10, although the quality varies widely.

1997, 19 Wardour St, W1, T020-7734 2868. A busy place named after the year of Hong Kong's handover. It's open almost 24 hrs for consistently good-value Cantonese cooking.

Canton Restaurant, 11 Newport Pl, WC2, T020-7437 6220. This is a reliable old-timer at the upper end of this price range.

Jen Café Tea Specialist, 4-8 Newport Pl, T020-7287 9708. Equally true to its roots, a basic place for a cuppa chrysanthemum tea.

Mr Kong, 21 Lisle St, WC2, T020-7437 7923. Serves up some excellent Mandarin dishes and stays open until 0230.

Pizzico, 66 Haymarket, SW1, T020-7839 3641. Altogether more upbeat and contemporary, this is a new venture by the Spaghetti House chain, where the pizzas are excellent value for the area. Open all day until 2330 Fri and Sat, 2300 other nights, Sun 2230.

Stockpot, 40 Panton St, SW1, T020-7839 5142. For something other than Oriental food this branch of a chain (see also p133, 166 and 175) has been doing inexpensive, unfancy British food for years, as has its former partner over the road, the

West End Kitchen, 5 Panton St, SW1, T020-7839 4241.

Tokyo Diner, 2 Newport Pl, WC2, T020-7287 8777. Of the Japanese restaurants in Chinatown, the Tokyo Diner remains many people's favourite, as much for its cheerful service as its sushi and noodles.

Zipangu, 8 Little Newport St, WC2, T020-7437 5042. Another popular Japanese.

Cafés

Leicester Square has no shortage of cafés but some of them can charge an extortionate and tourist-bleeding £3.50 for a coffee. One of the several ice cream parlours might be a better bet.

● *For an explanation of sleeping and eating price codes used in this guide, see inside the*
● *front cover. Other relevant information is found in Essentials, see pages 44-46.*

☏ Pubs and bars

Leicester Square *p73, map p75*
Cork and Bottle, Cranbourn St, just off Charing Cross Rd, almost opposite the Warner Village cinema. A long-established subterranean wine bar which is a good place to enjoy some oysters washed down with a good bottle of Chablis, very popular with office workers on Fri nights.
De Hems, Macclesfield St, T020-7437 2494. A very lively place, unusual for being the only authentically Dutch pub in London.
The Light Bar, St Martin's Lane Hotel, T020- 7300 5599. Stride confidently or book into this place if you are looking for an awesome designer drinking experience surrounded by models and media darlings.
Oxygen, 17 Irving St, WC2, T020-7930 0907. Open late, the ground floor is large and dark, the first floor brighter, and you can buy its namesake here if you're having trouble breathing in the crush.
The Salisbury, 90 St Martin's Lane, WC2, T020-7836 5863. Easily the grandest old boozer in the area, its gleaming Victorian interior fully renovated and as popular as ever (sometimes too popular), especially with tourists and theatregoers.
Salvador and Amanda, 8 Great Newport St, WC2, T020-7240 1551. Subterranean designer tapas bar with a good range of cocktails. Open til 0200 during the week and 0300 Fri and Sat.
Tiger Tiger, 29 Haymarket, SW1, T020-7930 1885. A good party venue, this is a huge place with 4 bars decorated in a weird variety of styles that's quite fun.

☺ Entertainment

Leicester Square *p73, map p75*
Cinema
Leicester Square and the surrounding area boasts the densest population of cinemas and theatres in London. All these cinemas show a wide variety of new releases.
Empire, 5-6 Leicester Sq, bookings T0870-1020030 plus 50p booking fee, on the north side of the square. 3-screen picture palace, where most world and national premieres take place.
Odeon Leicester Square, 22-24 Leicester Sq, WC2, T0871-2244007, on the east side, formerly the Alhambra Music Hall. Now the largest cinema in the West End, huge screen.
Odeon Panton St, 11-18 Panton St, WC2, T0871-2244007, just off the square itself. A small 2-screen cinema.
Odeon Wardour St, 10 Wardour St, WC2, T0871-2244007. A small 3-screen cinema that often shows more offbeat releases.
Odeon West End, 40 Leicester Sq, T0871- 2244007, on the south side of the square. Much more pleasant, Screen 2 is larger than Screen 1.
UGC Haymarket, 63-65 Haymarket, T0871-2002000. Shows mainstream new releases on its 2 screens.
Vue West End, 3 Cranbourne St, T0870-2406020, programme information T020-7437 4347; enquiries T020-7437 3484; advance booking T020-7437 4343. A refurbished 9-screen multiplex.

Independent cinemas and others
Curzon Soho, 93-107 Shaftesbury Av, W1, T020-7734 2255, recorded information line T020-7439 4805. Does fashionable first-runs, private screenings, and has a good coffee shop and bar.
OTHER Cinema, 11 Rupert St, W1, T020-7437 0757, booking T0207-734 1506. A very comfortable 2-screen arthouse cinema.
Prince Charles, Leicester Pl, WC2, today's films T020-7734 9127, this week's films T0901-2727007. Altogether different, a popular inexpensive cult repertory cinema club with regular theme nights and late night screenings.

Comedy
Comedy Store, 1a Oxendon St, SW1, T0870- 0602340. The trailblazing comedy venue that's now almost too popular for its own good but still has many of the best line-ups. Tue-Sun 1830 for 2000; Fri, Sat midnight, doors open 2300. Each show 2¼ hrs. £12-15, few tickets on the

door. Food and bar. Best arrive early at this now legendary and often sold-out comedy dive.

Music
Classical and opera London Coliseum, St Martin's Lane, T020-7632 8300, www.eno.org. The home of English National Opera, and all operas are sung in English. Recently magnificently restored to its original glory, it is one of the largest theatres in London and also stages ballet and full-scale touring productions. £3-22 with standbys for students.
Rock, folk and jazz Bar Room Bar, 32 Gerrard St, W1 T020-7494 1482. Usually has live jazz on Tue and funky bands on Sat nights.
Sound, 10 Wardour St, W1, T020-7287 1010. Live music happens in some of the clubs, like this one, on Fri nights. With Talent Scout £5, 1930-2200 (see below).

Nightclubs
Two massive dance clubs have long been synonymous with Leicester Square, and both are usually avoided by most Londoners. These mega party venues are popular with tourists and Brits who've come into town for the night. They go on until about 0300:
Equinox, Leicester Sq, WC2, T020-7437 1446. Wed-Sat, £8-£12, Fri night with Kiss FM.
Hippodrome, Leicester Sq, T020-7437 4311. Thu-Sat, £12-£20.
Sound, 10 Wardour St, W1, T020-7287 1010. Another in a similar mould with marginally more credibility, open Mon-Wed until 2400, Thu-Sat, 2200-0400.

Theatre
tkts, occupies the same building as the London Information Centre on the south side of Leicester Square. Run by the Society of London Theatre (SOLT), T020-7557 6700. The official half-price ticket booth that offers discounted tickets on a first-come-first- served basis so there's usually a queue. Open Mon-Sat 1000-1900, Sun 1200-1500.

Comedy Theatre, Panton St, WC2, T0870-0606637. A little late 19th-century

theatre most famous recently for staging the *Little Shop of Horrors*.
Haymarket Theatre Royal, Haymarket, SW1, T0870-9013356. There's been a theatre on this site since 1720, famous for staging Oscar Wilde's *Ideal Husband* and in 1914 the first London production of Ibsen's *Ghosts*.
Her Majesty's, Haymarket, SW1, T0870-1602878. Originally built by Sir John Vanbrugh in 1704, managed by William Congreve, and later staged many of the first performances of Handel's work. Burnt down in 1789, then rebuilt as an opera house, witnessing London premieres of *Fidelio*, *Carmen*, and Wagner's *Ring* cycle. Rebuilt again in 1897 under the management of Herbert Beerbohm Tree, founder of RADA. Lloyd Webber's *Phantom of the Opera* has been running here since 1986.
Prince of Wales Theatre, Coventry St, W1, T0870-8500393. Since 1884 this large theatre has been dedicated to musicals and vaudeville.

The following are all on **Shaftesbury Avenue**, between Piccadilly Circus and Cambridge Circus.
Albery Theatre, St Martin's Lane, T0870-0606621. Opened in 1903 as the *New Theatre*, where Gielgud made his name before the war, Eliot's *Cocktail Party*, Dylan Thomas' *Under Milk Wood*, and in the 60s Lionel Bart's *Oliver!* premièred here.
Apollo, T0870-7494 5070, nearest to Piccadilly Circus. Majors on musicals.
Arts Theatre, 6-7 Great Newport St, WC2, T020-7836 3334. Opened in 1927 as theatre club, most famous for staging Samuel Beckett's *Waiting for Godot* for the first time on 3 Aug 1955, and it still often stages interesting new writing.
Duke of York's, St Martin's Lane, T0870-0606623. First theatre in St Martin's Lane, originally called the *Trafalgar Square Theatre*, often shows decent dramas.
Garrick Theatre, Charing Cross Rd, WC2, T0870-8901104. Also built in 1889, once famous for a long run of *No Sex Please We're British*.
Gielgud Theatre, T020-7494 5065. Built in 1906, now usually shows plays casting stars as the name suggests (was called The Globe).
Lyric Shaftesbury, T0870-8901107. Built

in 1888, famous in the 1950s for staging plays by TS Eliot and later Alan Bennett, now tends towards West End dramas and star vehicles.

New Ambassadors, West St, T0870-0606627. Strong on drama, especially since the departure of the Royal Court which used it as a temporary space while its home in Sloane Square was being refurbished.

Palace Theatre, T020-7434 0909. Built as an opera house in 1888, staged the *Sound of Music* in the 1960s, *Jesus Christ Superstar* in the 70s, and is now comprehensively renovated.

Queen's Theatre, T020-7494 5040. Built as twin to The Globe, now stages a wide mix of classics, musicals and new plays, currently home to long-runner *Les Miserables*.

St Martin's, West St, WC2, T0870-1628787. *The Mousetrap*, 5th decade of Agatha Christie's whodunnit, staged here since 1974, sharing its title with the play that catches the conscience of the king in *Hamlet*.

Wyndham's Theatre, Charing Cross Rd, T020-7369 1736. Built in 1899, famous for its radical dramas, a tradition that it struggles gamely to maintain.

❀ Festivals and events

Leicester Square *p73, map p75*
Chinese New Year, in **Jan or Feb**, is celebrated in Chinatown with a procession down Gerrard St with masks reflecting whichever Chinese year is being ushered in. The **Chinese mid-Autumn Festival**, in **mid-Sep**, sees the area lively up itself with stage performances and dancing. During **Dec** the gardens are taken over by a **Christmas fair ground**, with all the traditional rides like dodgems and roundabouts but sadly no ferris wheel.

✪ Shopping

Leicester Square *p73, map p75*
Books
Books, books, books! Charing Cross Rd is still one of the best places in London to rummage around for any and every out-of-print, remaindered or second-hand

book as well as new titles. Most special and antiquarian items of interest can be found just off the road on Cecil Court, St Martin's Court and Caxton Walk.

Any Amount of Books, 56 Charing Cross Rd, T020-7836 3697. A rambling treasure trove of battered second-hand.

Henry Pordes Books, 58-60 Charing Cross Rd, T020-7836 9031. Another good general second-hand boook shop, specializing in art, literature and cinema.

Motor Books, 33 St Martin's Court, WC2, T020-7836 5376. Stock a range that will satisfy the most frustrated or devoted mechanic, everything about anything that moves with a motor.

Shipley's, south of Cambridge Circus, on Charing Cross Rd itself, there are 3 branches of this place: T020-7240 4157, for photography and film, and T020-7240 1559, for design, and further down the street, their original shop **Shipley Art Booksellers**, 70 Charing Cross Rd, T020-7836 4872, an independent that has been around for over 100 years, specializing in new, rare and out of print books on the fine arts.

G Smith and Sons, 74 Charing Cross Rd, WC2, T020-7836 7422. Bookshops apart, smokers should not miss this traditional tobacconist extraordinaire.

Sportspages, Caxton Walk, 94-96 Charing Cross Rd, WC2, T020-7240 9604, just beyond Cambridge Circus. Every sport imaginable.

Watkins Books, 19 Cecil Court, WC2, T020-7836 2182. Specialists in mysticism, the occult and New Age titles.

❶ Directory

Leicester Square *p73, map p75*
Libraries **Westminster Central Reference Library**, St Martin's St, on the site of Newton's house, Mon-Fri 1000-2000, Sat 1000-1700. Business library, T020-7641 4634; **General reference library**, T020-7641 4636 1000-2000; Arts and design library, T020-7641 4638 (only open 1300-2000.) **Tourist offices** **London Information Centre**, in the middle of Leicester Sq, T020-729 22333. Visitor inform-ation and hotel booking, sightseeing and entertainment tickets. Daily special offers such as half price hotels . Open daily 0800-2300.

Soho

Soho has always been the West End at its least respectable and most lively, and remains the only part of central London that comes close to keeping the same hours as New York. More clearly defined than many, the area is bordered to the north by Oxford Street, to the east by the Charing Cross Road, to the west by Regent Street, and to the south by Shaftesbury Avenue. And it has more character (and characters) per square yard than all those big names put together. That's partly because people still actually live here and are proud of the place. Unlike New Yorkers, though, they need their sleep. The influx of late-night partygoers, chain bars and mega-restaurants has received almost as much opposition as the sex industry that once pervaded the area. Even so, here the West End's late-night party zone sleazily converts the daytime film, music and TV frenzy into some of the best restaurants, pubs, gay bars, cafés, music and drinking clubs in the capital. Soho Square in the east and Golden Square in the west provide the only breathing spaces in a maze of old streets. In the east, Old Compton Street and Rupert Street have become the heart of the capital's gay scene. In the west, Carnaby St and Kingly St have been reborn as epicentres of street fashion, recapturing something of the spirit that made them famous in the 1960s. ⤖ *For Sleeping, Eating and other listings see pages 85-91.*

History

The name Soho derives from a medieval hunting or coursing cry, 'So-ho'. The farmland belonged to the Abbot and convent of Abingdon, before being handed over to Henry VIII in the course of the dissolution of the monasteries, and was briefly a royal park for Whitehall Palace. By the end of the 17th century, however, parts of the land were sold off to various nobles and the 1670s and 1680s saw rapid development, and with it the influx of refugees from abroad. Greeks fled here from persecution under the Ottomans – hence Greek Street, and French Huguenots sought refuge from Louis XIV's intolerance.

The French connection was to last through to the Second World War, with the French House restaurant on Dean Street (see page 87) serving as the unofficial HQ of the Free French Forces. Although the wealthier residents headed west to Mayfair towards the end of the 18th century, the area grew famous for its craftsmen and artisans – the Soho Tapestries flourished, the Soho Bazaar on the site of King Square (now Soho Square) housed stalls and counters for jewellery, millinery, gloves and lace for much of the 19th century, and Josiah Wedgwood's London warehouse lay on Greek Street.

Predictably, the cosmopolitan flavour of the area attracted writers and artists to both live and drink in its taverns and coffee-houses. Canaletto had a studio in Beak Street; William Blake was born on Marshall Street and returned to the area later in life; Shelley was sent down from Oxford and came to Poland Street; William Hazlitt's house (which has now been transformed into a cosy and exclusive hotel) remains on Frith Street; and a seven year-old Mozart touted his talents on Dean Street. Karl Marx lived at No 28 Dean Street in dingy attic rooms (three of his children died here), while Verlaine and Rimbaud lodged briefly on Old Compton Street following the fall of the Paris Commune.

By the mid-18th century Soho had become severely overcrowded – there were 327 inhabitants per acre in 1851, so the cholera epidemic of 1854 spread rampantly. The burial ground of St Anne's Church was set 6 ft above the ground to accommodate some 10,000 bodies and six hospitals were built in the area. Soho also became a centre of entertainment. Restaurants such as the Café Royale opened, and were frequented by the likes of Beardsley, GB Shaw, DH Lawrence and Katherine Mansfield, while Kettner's bedrooms were visited by Wilde with his young acolytes, and Edward VII and Lillie Langtry.

4 Soho

See London at a glance, p19-24, for related maps.

0 metres 100
0 yards 100

Sleeping
Courthouse **3** B2
Hazlitt's **1** B5
Sanderson **2** A3
Soho **4** C4
YHA Oxford St **5** B3

Eating
Alastair Little **1** C5
Andrew Edmonds **3** C3
Bar Italia **26** C5
Beatroot **4** C4
Blue Room **28** B5
Busaba Eathai **5** C4
Café Emm **6** C5
Café España **7** C5
Café Lazeez **8** B5
Centrale **9** C6
Chiang Mai **10** B5
Circus **11** D3
Country Life **13** E3
Ed's Easy Diner **15** C5
French House
 Dining Room **16** C5
Garden Café **17** C2
Gay Hussar **19** B5
Hamburger Union **22** B5
Jimmy's **21** C5
Kettners **23** C6
Kulu Kulu **24** D3
L'Arena **25** B5
La Trouvaille **2** C2
Maison Bertaux **29** C6
Mildred's Wholefood
 Café **31** B5
Misato **32** D5
Mar I Terra **18** E3
Masala Zone **20** C3
Nani's **69** A2
Patisserie Valerie **33** C5
Pizzeria Malletti **34** B3
Pollo **35** C6
Ramen Seto **37** C1
Randall & Aubin **38** C4
Red Fort **39** C5
Richard Corrigan At
 Lindsay House **27** C5
RYO **40** D3
Satsuma **41** C5
Spiga **44** C5
Star Café **45** B4
Sugar Club **46** D2
Tartuffo **14** B5
Toucan **48** B5

Pubs & bars
Alphabet **51** C3
Atlantic Bar & Grill **52** E3
Café Boheme **53** C6
Coach & Horses **54** C6
Dog & Duck **55** B5

Germans, Italians, Polish and Russian Jews, Greeks and Swiss were included among the residents, but Soho also began to gravitate towards a centre for the media. John Logie Baird gave the first demonstration of television in his rooms above what is now *Bar Italia*, publishers such as Bloomsbury, and film companies like Twentieth Century Fox set up in Soho Square – the *Groucho Club* on Dean Street continues this tradition. The sex industry took hold in the 1960s, but the Soho Society managed to restrict its spread. Soho is now known as a 'gay' area, with several gay bars dotting Rupert Street and Old Compton Street; one, the *Admiral Duncan*, was bombed in 1999 by a lone bigot.

Sights

◉ *Leicester Sq, Oxford Circus, Piccadilly Circus, Tottenham Court Rd.* ◉ *See p460.*

Shopfronts, restaurant windows, doorways, alleys and, most important of all, other people are the sights of Soho, all packed so close together that somewhere, somehow, here you can reasonably expect to find your heart's desire.

Soho Square

Soho Square is one of the few breathing spaces, formerly the site of Monmouth House, the home of Charles II's bastard son James Scott, who rebelled unsuccessfully against James II, crying 'soho!' as he went into battle. Now a weather-beaten statue of his father by Caius Gabriel Cibber stands in front of a mock Tudor toolshed, and the gardens are the favourite summer lunchtime snackspot of office workers and resting cycle couriers.

On either side of the square stand the French protestant church and St Patrick's Catholic church. The **House of St Barnabas** ① *T020-7437 1894, by appointment, call to check details*, on the corner of the square where it meets Greek Street, is a beautiful Georgian building with a very old mulberry tree in the garden. It's been a hostel for single homeless women since 1851. Tours of the fine interior, including the charming Victorian chapel, in 13th-century French Gothic style, usually take place on the first day of every month.

Edge **57** *A5*
Freedom **59** *C4*
French House **58** *C5*
Lab **61** *B6*
Phoenix **56** *B6*
Player **60** *B4*
Rupert St **63** *D4*
Sak **64** *B5*
Shaston Arms **62** *C2*
Three Greyhounds **65** *C6*
Two Floors **66** *D2*
Yard **67** *D4*

Entertainment ♪
100 Club **11** *A3*
Astoria **12** *A6*
Borderline **14** *B6*

Candy Bar **1** *B4*
Colony Room **13** *C5*
London Palladium **3** *B1*
Madame Jo Jo's **4** *C4*
Mean Fiddler **12** *A6*
Pop **5** *A5*
Prince Edward
  Theatre **6** *C6*
Ronnie Scott's **7** *C5*
Salsa! **8** *B6*
Soho Theatre
  & Writer's Centre **9** *B5*
St Moritz **10** *C4*
Trap **2** *C4*

⁑ Sex and clubs and rock 'n' roll

Soho has long been associated with sex and vice. Central London's notorious one-square-mile district was home to some 300 prostitutes in the 1950s and when they moved elsewhere in the 60s, Soho turned to other methods, such as 'clipping' (getting the customer to pay before sending them to a fictitious address, and then disappearing). Around this time, the number of strip and drinking clubs increased dramatically. The most famous, Raymond Revue Bar, is still doing business, though most have now closed.

From the late 60s Soho became the centre of the porn industry. While pornographic magazines were shipped over from the continent in Danish Bacon lorries, the Obscene Publications Squad (OPS) was being bribed to turn a blind eye. But in 1972 a new commissioner of the Metropolitan Police was appointed to clean up Soho and the OPS was suspended. In the early 80s new legislation requiring all sex shops to be licensed came into effect.

Soho was also one of the centres of British bohemia as well as the culinary capital of Britain. Its drinking clubs are still famous: The Colony Room, on Dean Street, has always been a favourite haunt of hard-drinking British artists, from Francis Bacon to Damien Hirst, and the Groucho, once the epitome of Thatcherite excess, still serves the inflated egos of medialand.

Soho also has mighty impressive music credentials. Ronnie Scott's was the first outlet in the capital for modern jazz, while the Marquee (now closed) played host to the Yardbirds and the Rolling Stones. Its dance clubs, such as The Wag and Beat Route were at the cutting edge of late 70s/early 80s music and its most famous late-night coffee bar, Bar Italia on Frith Street, still gives homeward-bound clubbers the coolest of caffeine kicks.

Soho's most recent cultural incarnation, as the capital's big gay heart only confirms its status as London's Left Bank or Greenwich Village.

Greek Street, Frith Street and Dean Street

Running south down to Shaftesbury Avenue from Soho Square, roughly parallel to the Charing Cross Road, are **Greek Street** and **Frith Street**. The **Frith Street Gallery** ① 59-60 Frith St, T020-7494 1550, picks up on their tone by putting on shows of cutting-edge contemporary art. The length of **Dean Street** lies one block further west. Even though each is crowded with highly individual shops, restaurants and bars, these three streets and the alleyways between them are so

⁑ *These streets form the core of 'high' Soho, with Dean St perhaps the most happening of the three.*

similar in atmosphere and appearance that they can easily baffle the inexperienced Soho partygoer.

Old Compton Street

Just before reaching Shaftesbury Avenue they all cross **Old Compton Street**, the area's unofficial high street. The street has also become the main artery of the gay scene, while its junction with Greek Street and Moor Street must be one of the most characteristic and crowded spots in the area.

● *The Hospital for Diseases of Women in Soho Square was the first of its kind in the world, although it had to change its name to simply the Hospital for Women since many people thought it only dealt with venereal disease.*

★ **Five of the best West End cafés**

- **Bar Italia**, Frith St, Soho, page 88.
- **Maison Malnowski**, Neal St, Covent Garden, page 98.
- **Coffee Republic**, South Molton St, Mayfair, page 111.
- **Mokaris**, Jermyn St, St James's, page 125.
- **Carluccio's**, St Christopher's Place, Oxford St, page 131.

Wardour Street

Meard Street, a fine row of Georgian houses, links Dean Street with **Wardour Street**, the main north-south axis dividing this part of the area from 'low' Soho to the west. Wardour Street is still synonymous with the film industry, even though few British film companies can afford much office space here, most of it being taken up by advertising production companies.

On the corner of Wardour Street and Old Compton Street, only the tower of the Church of St Anne survived the Blitz, but it now houses the **Soho Society** ① *T020-7439 4303*. Among the many projects and campaigns in support of the area currently being undertaken by the Society is the quest for the Museum of Soho's new home.

Berwick Street

Brewer Street continues the march of Old Compton Street westwards, heading into the newly branded 'West Soho'. Just along here on the right, a little passage called Walker's Court leads through into Berwick Street, home to the West End's one and only pukka **fruit 'n' veg market**. Since 1995 the stalls piled high with bargain comestibles have only been allowed on one side of the street, making for more space on the road but threatening the future of the market. Even so, a jostle down this street of a busy weekday lunchtime remains one of Soho's unmissable treats. The market does not take place on Sundays.

★ Carnaby Street and around

This west side of Soho is generally more seedy and money-grabbing than boho high Soho. Nearer Regent Street, around **Carnaby Street**, it also becomes even more fashion-conscious, especially along Newburgh Street. Carnaby Street itself, a bye-word for anything groovy in the 1960s, has begun to reclaim some of the cachet that it let slip in the 1980s after becoming a tourist trap trading on its heyday. Other streets nearby well worth exploring for their bars, clubs, shops and restaurants are **Kingly Street** and **Beak Street**. Just south of these, **Golden Square** is like a piece of Mayfair that has slipped the wrong side of Regent Street. Although nothing remains of its early 18th-century origins, it is distinguished by the faceless offices of media multinationals. The rose bushes were given in gratitude by the city of Sofia.

● Sleeping

Soho *p81, map p82*

L Courthouse, 19-21 Great Marlborough St, WC2, T020-7297 5555, www.thecourthouse-hotel.com. As the name suggests, this is a conversion of an old magistrates court with lots of pale green slate and water features in the lobby, contemporary styling in the bedrooms (116 of them) and a restaurant called Silk in the old wood-panelled courtroom itself. Three original cells have been preserved in the bar, maybe for the kind of drinkers who want to start where they'll have to try hard to avoid ending up.

L Hazlitt's, 6 Frith St, W1, T020-7434 1771, www.hazlittshotel.com. 23 individual period rooms of great character, in memory of the London essayist, this classic hotel is many people's London favourite. With a discreet entrance and very busy at weekends, there's no restaurant or bar as yet but plenty round about in the liveliest streets in Soho.

L Sanderson, 50 Berners St, W1, T020-7300 9500, www.morganshotelgroup.com. 150 rooms. The latest and most fashionable in London in the ultra-modern Philippe Starck-designed chain that includes the *St Martin's Lane Hotel*. Ultra-chic *Spoon Plus* restaurant, *Purple Bar* for residents only, and *Long Bar* open to the public until 0100 nightly. Romantic and luxurious, more traditional than St Martin's, in many rooms the bathrooms are separated from bedrooms with white silk curtains.

L Soho, 4 Richmond Mews, W1, T020-7559 3000, www.sohohotel.com. The latest in the Firmdale Hotel group that includes the Covent Garden and Charlotte St hotels, designed by owner Kit Kemp, 85 individual and contemporary British rooms, more comfortable than minimal. Top chef Robin Reed runs the restaurant and the Refuel Bar has already become somewhere to be seen for the media set's movers and shakers.

E YHA Oxford St, 14 Noel Street, Soho, W1, T0870 770 5984 (within UK), +44 20 7734 1618 (outside UK), oxfordst@yha.org.uk. £22.60 a night, under-18s £18.20. Open every day including Christmas and New Year, reception 0700-2300. Small (75 beds, so booking ahead essential), with self-catering accommodation only, this 2-star hostel could hardly be closer to all the late night action.

⦿ Eating

Soho *p81, map p82*
Just about every type of cooking under the sun is available somewhere in Soho: the problem is deciding exactly where and how to enjoy what. In fact, the sheer number of good mid-range and cheap restaurants in Soho has been largely responsible for the area's popularity for some time. Many of the places listed here will need to be booked.

Circus Restaurant and Bar, 1 Upper James St, W1, T020-7534 4000. Try this if *The Sugar Club* is full, more expensive, and stuffed with smart suits and fashionistas, the downstairs bar is lavish and late.

Richard Corrigan at Lindsay House, 21 Romilly St, W1, T020-7439 0450. Makes similar waves with his modern British menu. The great man himself is still very much in charge while the 18th-century atmosphere of his Soho townhouse creates an appreciative mood.

Andrew Edmonds, 46 Lexington St, W1, T020-7437 5708. Other gourmet dining options in the area, such as this place, can offer more quiet pleasures. Excellent modern European cooking at reasonable prices is served up in a cosy, candlelit atmosphere here. Booking ahead strongly recommended.

Gay Hussar, 2 Greek St, W1, T020-7437 0973. The discerning, predominantly grey-haired customers at one of Soho's best-loved institutions have long been tucking into gigantic servings of Hungarian food in the clubby, old-fashioned intimacy of this place.

Alastair Little, 49 Frith St, W1, T020-7734 5183. For a slightly more zippy dining experience this trailblazer of Anglo-Italian cooking no longer runs the kitchen here but it continues to come up with the freshest of well-prepared goods, majoring in fish.

The Red Fort, 77 Dean St, W1, T020- 7437 2115. Indian cuisine is not particularly well represented in Soho. One of the best can be found here. Smart and formal, specializing in delicacies from Uttar Pradesh.

The Sugar Club, 21 Warwick St, W1, T020-7437 7776. Still one of the most fun and fashionable smart eateries in Soho, a dressed-up crowd flock here for New Zealand-Asian fusion food in a see-and-be-seen setting. Downstairs is quieter, away from the buzzy bar.

La Trouvaille, 12a Newburgh St, W1 T020-7287 8488, on the other side of Soho. Mon-Sat 1200-1500, 1800-2300. A 'find' that does a terrific set lunch at £20 for 3 courses, a wacky but supremely competent small restaurant bursting with Gallic flair.

♥♥ **Chiang Mai**, 48 Frith St, W1, T020-7437 7444. Offers a peaceful, intimate venue for some decidedly elegant Thai food.

♥♥ **L'Arena**, 6 Greek St, W1, T020-7734 2334. For more traditional Italian favourites, try this well-starched place.

♥♥ **French House Dining Room**, 49 Dean St, W1, T020-7437 2477. A modern British menu in laid-back, old-school style above the estimable Soho institution. Booking is almost essential and it can get smoky.

♥♥ **Mar I Terra**, 17 Air St, W1 T020-7734 1992. A dinky new branch of the Waterloo Spanish restaurant, its toothsome menu served up in a bright little place close to Piccadilly Circus.

♥♥ **Randall and Aubin**, 16 Brewer St, W1, T020-7287 4447. Slightly more expensive, but another long-timer in the area, this is popular for fish, a bustling bistro-style seafood stop with its bar-stool counters and open kitchen. Good for oysters and champagne in the afternoon.

♥♥ **Spiga**, 84-86 Wardour St, W1, T020-7734 3444. Offers excellent contemporary recipes in appropriately spare and stylish settings.

♥♥ **Tartuffo**, 63-64 Frith St, W1, T020-7734 4545. Very cheerful Italian place doing the classics better than others round here.

♥ **Café Emm**, 17 Frith St, T020-7437 0723. Another good, cheap choice and effortlessly informal, where the portions are as huge as its popularity.

♥ **Centrale**, 16 Moor St, W1, T020-7437 5513. Small and not-as-hectic old-school Italian fast-food joint, serving up great bowlfuls of comfort food at very low prices. A tremendous business-like service and very popular with students. Last orders at 2130.

♥ **Ed's Easy Diner**, Old Compton St, T020-7434 4439, also at 38 Shaftesbury Av. A good place to take the kids. An American-style diner that does classic junk food better than most, serving great big greasy cheeseburgers, fries and luscious milkshakes.

♥ **Hamburger Union**, 25 Dean St, W1 T020-7437 6004. Even better than *Ed's Easy Diner* for burgers, much appreciated by young and old, where all the meat is organic, freshly grilled and served up on long, clean communal tables with great views of the passing streetlife.

♥ **Jimmy's**, 23 Frith St, W1, T020-7437 9521. The Greek equivalent of *Centrale* and *Pollo*. A brilliantly busy vibe, and also very popular with students.

♥ **Kettners**, 29 Romilly St, W1, T020-7734 6112. The longest-standing home of the pizza around here, where no booking is required and the savoury flatbreads are still exceptional value given the faded grandeur of the decor.

♥ **Masala Zone**, 9 Marshall St, W1 T020-7287 9966. A busy and bustling Indian restaurant specializing in street food from Mumbai and recipes from southwest India, serving food all day and often understandably packed out.

♥ **Pizzeria Malletti**, 26 Noel St, T020-7439 4096. For a takeaway lunchtime pizza, the authenticity of this place is hard to beat.

♥ **Pollo**, 20 Old Compton St, W1, T020-7734 5917. Old-school Italian fast-food joint, serving up great bowlfuls of comfort food at very low prices, this is the best known and biggest place, has a bustling atmosphere, last orders at 2330.

♥ **Toucan**, 19 Carlisle St, W1, T020-7437 4123. The dive bar beneath here serves up filling platefuls of good-quality Irish nosh.

Healthy eating

♥ **Busaba Eathai**, 106-110 Wardour St, W1, T020-7255 8686. Altogether more hip than most, but also busier and slightly more expensive, a 'Thai casual dining room' with communal tables and large windows looking out onto Wardour St, open 1200-2330.

♥ **Country Life**, 3-4 Warwick St, W1, T020-7434 2922. Very good-value vegan place. No alcohol or smoking. Closes at 2130.

♥ **Mildred's Wholefood Café**, 58 Greek St, W1, T020-7494 1634. Vegetarians are well catered for and many make for this place which is licensed, clean and non-smoking.

★ Five of the best West End DJ Bars

- **Lab**, Old Compton St, Soho, page 89.
- **Player**, Broadwick St, Soho, page 89.
- **Pop**, Soho St, Soho, page 90.
- **Trap**, Wardour St, Soho, page 90.
- **AKA**, West Central St, Covent Garden, page 98.

West End Soho Listings

¶ **Satsuma**, 56 Wardour St, W1, T020-7437 8338. A well-established Japanese place doing fine ramen soups and bento boxes.

For healthy-eating 21st-century style though, four Japanese noodle and sushi bars win the day:

¶ **Kulu Kulu**, 76 Brewer St, W1, T020-7734 7316. Sushi on a travellator.

¶ **Misato**, 11 Wardour St, W1, T020-7734 0808. Sushi on a travellator, very quick, high-quality lunches.

¶ **RYO**, 84 Brewer St, W1, T020-7287 1318. An efficient noodle bar.

¶ **Ramen Seto**, 19 Kingly St, W1, T020-7434 0309. A good noodle bar.

Cafés and sandwich bars

In Soho, the epicentre of London's café culture, almost every other door opens on tempting cakes, coffees, pastries, sandwiches and full meals. The following five of the best have all been around a long time:

Bar Italia, 22 Frith St, football and coffee crazy, open 24 hrs daily (except Mon) and still as hip as ever;

Maison Bertaux, 28 Greek St, W1, T020-7437 4520, French patisserie heaven, as is

Patisserie Valerie, 44 Old Compton St.

Café España, 63 Old Compton St, W1, T020-7494 1271;

Star Café, 22 Great Chapel St, W1, T020-7437 8778. Check tablecloths presided over indomitably by the same family since 1936.

Other newer and very acceptable café options include:

Beatroot, 82 Berwick St, W1, T020-7437 8591, an excellent funky fresh-food café located bang on Berwick St market, open until 2100;

The Blue Room, 3 Bateman St, W1, T020-7437 4827; worth seeking out for its fresh way with ingredients, laid back atmosphere and friendly staff;

Café Lazeez, in Soho Theatre, 21 Dean St, W1, T020-7434 9393, new place open until 0100, a functional-looking bar, restaurant and café with huge windows that just about manages to be all things to all people;

The Garden Café, 4 Newburgh St, W1, T020- 7494 0044, on the other side of Soho, a sweet place that comes into its own when the sun shines, with its quirky and colourful little back garden.

❶ Pubs and bars

Soho *p81, map p82*

At weekends the crowds of revellers make streets like Old Compton and Greek almost impassable. After 1800 throughout the week, finding a pub or bar with room to sit down can be a challenge, not just in the new wave of designer and chain bars, but also in those pubs that have been around for years.

Alphabet, 61-63 Beak St, W1, T020-7439 2190. Has become the favourite place to be seen if you're in advertizing. Arrive early to ensure a seat.

Atlantic Bar and Grill, 20 Glasshouse St, W1, T020-7734 4888. Still going strong after becoming the most fashionable dive of the 90s. Book a table at the restaurant if you want guaranteed entry, although the louche comfort of *Dick's Bar* is the main attraction.

Café Bohème, 13-17 Old Compton St, W1, T020-7734 0623. Open 0800-0300, Fri and Sat, admission £4 after 2200, (last orders for bar snacks 0230 daily). One of the bars that led the way for late-night Soho, a relaxed, continental-style brasserie on a busy corner with a top-notch restaurant attached. Expect to queue if arriving late.

The Coach and Horses, 29 Greek St, W1, T020-7437 5920. Has long established itself as the archetypal Soho boozer, thanks to its famously rude landlord and alcoholic regulars like the late Jeffrey Bernard. It's still a refreshingly unpretentious place for a plain pint and a very good value old-style ham sandwich.

Dog and Duck, 18 Bateman St, W1, T020-7494 0697. This remains the film industry's favourite old-fashioned boozer, a busy little corner pub on 2 floors pumping very good beer.

French House, 49 Dean St, W1, T020-7437 2799, formerly the *Yorkminster*. The other favourite haunt of the Soho set, cosy, where the wine is very good and beer served in halves only, with an unpretentious restaurant upstairs.

Three Greyhounds, 25 Greek St, W1, T020-7287 0754. Usually less crowded, unless pre- or post-theatre, with its strange mock-Swiss interior and serving reasonably good home-made food.

Lab, 12 Old Compton St, T020-7437 7820. 70s design and contemporary music policy, popular with students.

The Phoenix, 1 Phoenix St, WC2, T020-7836 1077. Back on the other side of Soho, another late bar beckons downstairs with plenty of character and an equally uncertain door policy. Arrive before 2000 to be sure of gaining access to this bric-a-brac filled cellar just off the Charing Cross Rd that also does a wide range of hearty bar meals.

Player, 8 Broadwick St, W1, T020-7494 9125. Has DJs at the weekend in an otherwise chilled out and subtly sophisticated basement bar that's members only after 2300, so find your spot before then.

Sak, 49 Greek St, T020-7439 4159. A marginally more grown-up designer style bar (murals and astro turf) open until 0300 most nights.

Shaston Arms, Marshall St, W1. Probably the best old-fashioned pub in the area: it pumps superb Badger beer and seems itself to have wandered into town from deepest Dorset.

The Toucan, 19 Carlisle St, W1, T020-7437 4123. An Irish pub boasting the best Guiness in Soho with plenty of scruffy charm and not too themed either.

Two Floors, 3 Kingly St, in West Soho, W1, T020-7439 1007. Pretty much kicked off the boom in style bars in this part of town and remains popular.

Gay bars

Most of the bars in Soho welcome gay or straight customers but some are more out and proud than others. See also clubs below.

Admiral Duncan, 54 Old Compton St, T020-7437 5300. Mon-Sat 1200-2300, Sun 1200-2230. Traditional and long-standing old boozer that's gone from strength to strength after being horrifically bombed by a lone bigot in the late 1990s.

BarCode, 3-4 Archer St, T020-7734 3342. Mon-Sat 1600-0100, Sun 1600-2230. £3 after 2300 on Fri, Sat. Round the corner from Rupert St, cruisey place popular with boyz and a club downstairs at the weekends.

The Box, 32 Monmouth St, T020-7240 5828. Mon-Sat 1100-2330, Sun 1200-2330. Over 10 years old, and one of the original West End gay bars popular with a happy mix of regulars and tourists.

Candy Bar, 4 Carlisle St, T020-7494 4041, www.thecandybar.co.uk. One of the original Soho late-night lesbian bars, laid back but increasingly lively as the night progresses.

The Edge, 11 Soho Sq, W1, T020-7439 1313. A vast 5-floor gay pleasuredome that does food during the day.

First Out, 52 St Giles High St, T020-7240 8042. Mon-Sat 1000- 2300, Sun 1100-2330. Another venerable old- timer: slightly staid café by day and more happening joint in the evenings, attracting a good spread of customers.

Freedom, 60 Wardour St, W1, T020-7734 0071. Has a predominantly gay clientele but has long made a point of welcoming people of any sexual persuasion, open until 0300 Mon-Sat, with the clubby basement hotting up after 2200 on Fri and Sat.

Rupert Street, 50 Rupert St, W1, T020-7292 7141. Remains one the more fashionable of the gay bars.

The Yard, 57 Rupert St, W1, T020-7437 2652. The most homely and comfortable place.

☻ Entertainment

Soho *p81, map p82*
Music
Rock, folk and jazz **Astoria**, 157 Charing Cross Rd, T020-7434 9592, next door to *The Mean Fiddler* and twice the size. Hosts more mainstream indie and rock bands.
Borderline, Orange Yard, off Mannette St, T020-7534 6971. A club of the more intimate variety, and the bands are generally new and unheard of. It is, however, a very nice venue, and has its place in London music folklore as the stage where REM played in 1991 under the more than faintly ridiculous moniker of Bingo Handjob.
The Colony Room Club, 47 Dean St. Tiny, intimate and strange, hosts *Showtime* on the 1st Sun of every month, with surprise special guests (often an impossibly glamorous chanteuse or 2), hosted by Phil Dirtbox. 2030, £3 on the door.
Gazza's Rockin Blues, 159 Wardour St, W1 T020-7437 0525, in the basement of *St Moritz*. Another regular treat is this Thu night session. It's been going for at least the last 25 years.
The Mean Fiddler (formerly *LA2*), 165 Charing Cross Rd, T020-7434 9592, T020-7344 0044 for bookings. The grunge brigade head here for their doses of live indie and rock, admission £8-20.
Ronnie Scott's, 47 Frith St, W1, T020-7439 0747. Legendary jazz club, open 2030, admission Mon-Thu £15, Fri and Sat £20, still smokin' like a train and often needs to be booked at least a fortnight in advance.

Nightclubs
Candy Bar (see Gay bars above). Lesbian bar that is more like a club, till 0200.
Madame Jo Jo's, 8-10 Brewer St, W1, T020-7734 3040. One of the most happening small clubs, hosts a variety of polysexual extravaganzas: Fri is Deep Funk (£6 before 2300, £8 after) also northern soul; new jazz, broken beats and soulful house at Groove Sanctuary, Sat (same prices as Fri), and Club Noir on Wed, (£5) has bands, electro rock and pop.
Pop,14 Soho St, W1, T020-7734 4004. An expensive retro designer bar that is more like a club, till 0500 on Sat £10 after 2100, till 0400 on Fri, £10 after 2100, and till 0330 Mon to Thu, £5 after 2100.

Salsa!, 96 Charing Cross Rd, WC2, T020-7379 3277, beneath *Waterstone's* bookshop. One of London's best Latin nights. Mon Salsa, Tue Brazilian, Fri Introduction to Latin dance with free lesson at 1830, Thu Cuban Salsa, Sat and Sun Salsa club nights. From 2100 £4 during the week, weekends £2 at 1900, £4 at 2000, £8 at 2100. Until 0200. No trainers.
Shadow Lounge, 5 Brewer St, T020-7287 7988, www.shadow-lounge.co.uk. Mon-Wed 2200-0300, Thu-Sat 2100-0300. Funky and handbag house throughline at one of Soho's most fashionable gay nightspots, although much more mellow early in the evenings. The sunken dance floor gets very busy by 2230 at weekends. Ring beforehand to be put on the paying guest list to guarantee entry.
Trap, 201 Wardour St, W1, T020-7434 3820, email trap@traplondon.com to get in (guest list only). A designer style bar with a cutting-edge R&B music policy.

Theatre
London Palladium, Argyll St, W1, T0870-890 1108. A vast entertainment house since 1910 that now specializes in musical spectaculars.
Prince Edward Theatre, Old Compton St, W1, T020-7447 5400. A large 1930s theatre, now usually staging blockbusting musicals.
Soho Theatre and Writers' Centre, 21 Dean St, W1, T020-7478 0100. Excellent brand new base for new playwriting in the West End.

☻ Festivals and events

Soho *p81, map p82*
The **Soho Jazz Festival** takes place in the last week of **Jul** each year, bringing a host of top names into the area for some smokin' sounds in a variety of venues.

○ Shopping

Soho *p81, map p82*
Bookshops
On Charing Cross Rd, north of Cambridge Circus, you will find several large shops for new books.

Foyles, 113-119 Charing Cross Rd, WC2, T020-7437 5660. There's the inimitable, rambling and extraordinary range of new titles on 4 floors here, open until 2000 Mon-Sat and also open on Sun until 1800. Almost every fairly recently published book could well be here somewhere, but it may take sometime to find at this huge indomitable independent. They also stage an interesting variety of literary events and talks.

Nearby are branches of **Borders**, **Books Etc**, **Blackwells** and **Waterstones**.

European Bookshop, 5 Warwick St, W1, T020-7734 5259. Has a wide range of European language books.

Grant and Cutler, 55-57 Great Marlborough St, W1, T020-7734 2012. One of the most famous foreign-language bookshops in the city.

A Moroni and Son, 68 Old Compton St, W1, T020-7437 2847. A large international newsagent, open until about 2130 most nights except Mon and Sun.

Clothing and jewellery

Head to West Soho for latest street fashions.
Carhartt, Newburgh St. Own-label womenswear.
Plum, 79 Berwick St, W1, T020-7734 0812. Skateboard stuff, labels like Komodo, and trendy jeans.
Slinky's, 10 Walker Ct, W1, T020-7434 1716. One of several fetishwear outlets, full of rubber and bondage stuff.

Carnaby St, Kingly St and Newburgh St are the place to look for the hippest designer labels in the area:
Great Frog, 10 Ganton St, T020-7439 9357. Make silver jewellery beloved by celebs as well as lesser mortals.
Merc, 10 Carnaby St, T020-7734 1469. Was one of the originals on the street, completely reinvented and still up-to-the-minute.
Puma, in the freshly redeveloped Kingly Court. This is Puma's only outlet in London alongside other fashionable brand retailers. In East Soho, fashion shops are thinner on the ground but include the following:
American Retro, 35 Old Compton St, W1,

T020-7734 3477.
Kokon To Zai, 57 Greek St, W1, T020-7434 1316. Supercool, for dance music and gear.

Food and drink

Algerian Coffee Stores, 52 Old Compton St, W1, T020-7437 2480. For good coffee, teas, and things needed for their careful preparation.
The Vintage House, 42 Old Compton St, W1, T020-7437 2592. Fine wines and spirits.

Miscellaneous

Anything Left-Handed, 57 Brewer St, W1, T020-7437 3910. A quirky one-off selling exactly what its name suggests.
The Eye Company, Optometrist and Contact Lens Practitioner, 159 Wardour St, W1, T020- 7434 0988. A good place to pick up some fashionable (and expensive) sunglasses by various big names, and they also do eye tests.
Scribbler, 104 Wardour St, W1, T020-7439 2199. Has a wacky range of cards and wrapping paper.
Sendean, 9-12 St Anne's Ct, T020-7439 8418. Reliable camera repairers.
Vintage Magazine Store, 39-43 Brewer St, W1, T020-7439 8525. Vintage magazines (yep, you guessed it) and also has a few old movie posters and postcards.

⚑ Activities

Soho p81, map p82
Fitness First, 59 Kingly St, W1, T020-7734 6226. £15/£10 per day, £40 per week. Gym and sauna.
The Sauna Bar, 29 Endell St, T020-7836 2236. Mon-Thu, Sun 1200-2300, Fri and Sat 24 hrs. £13. Licensed gay sauna, steam room, jacuzzi and video lounge in Covent Garden.

❶ Directory

Soho p81, map p82
Medical centres **Soho Centre for Health and Care**, 1 Frith St (off Soho Sq), W1D, T020-7534 6500. Open Mon-Fri 0800-2100, Sat, Sun 1000-2000. Walk-in NHS surgery.

West End Soho Listings

Covent Garden

Covent Garden is a tourist honeypot: a sympathetic conversion of central London's fine old covered market into a boutique shopping mall with no traffic and a hint of culture: the Royal Opera House, the Theatre Museum, and the London Transport Museum. Thankfully it's still largely free of the depressing tat peddled to visitors around Piccadilly Circus and Leicester Square.

London's largest and most famous fruit 'n' veg market moved out to Nine Elms in 1974. Now a bustling 'piazza', it still bears a faint flavour of those times thanks to its converted Victorian covered market and the crowds that flock here day and night to shop, eat, drink and enjoy a pleasant place away from all the traffic. As with Soho, people live as well as work in the surrounding streets, despite rocketing rents, and they managed to save the market from the developers when the stallholders moved out. To the east, the Royal Opera House reopened to great acclaim after its multi-million pound redevelopment. North of Long Acre, what were once narrow streets of warehouses and slums have experienced a boom in youth-orientated shops and bars, led by long-established crowd-pullers like the Donmar Warehouse theatre and Neal's Yard wholefood hippy enclave. ▸▸ *For Sleeping, Eating and other listings see pages 96-101.*

History

The area known as Covent Garden emerged as a focal point for London society in the 17th and 18th centuries. St Martin's Lane had long been the great north road from Charing Cross, but until Henry VIII seized the land during the dissolution of the monasteries, this was pasture belonging to St Peter's Convent, with narrow strips of market gardens running down what is now Long Acre. Henry granted the land to John Russell, Earl of Bedford, but it was 100 years before the area was developed, when the fourth earl commissioned Inigo Jones to build a piazza. Jones produced a courtyard of high terraced houses, with the front doors covered by vaulted arcades, and St Paul's church on one side.

Bedford had asked for the church to be little more than a barn, so Jones promised him "the handsomest barn in England". St Paul's was the first Anglican church to be built in London since the Reformation (up to 100 years earlier), and while it was damaged by fire in 1795, it is essentially still the same today. It has seen some distinguished visitors. Wesley preached here, JMW Turner and WS Gilbert (minus Sullivan) were both baptized here, while Sir Peter Lely, Grinling Gibbons, Thomas Rowlandson and Ellen Terry are among those that have never left. St Paul's columned front provides the backdrop for Eliza Doolittle's first appearance in Pygmalion.

The square was a desirable address among early 17th-century society, and the fruit, vegetable and flower market ensured a lively atmosphere. Streets built up around the square, and coffee houses such as Will's became haunts for the likes of John Dryden, Alexander Pope and Pepys, who saw Dryden there holding forth "with all the wits in town". But as the market grew, the coffee shops and taverns were supplemented by gambling dens and Turkish baths, (aka brothels), and the wealthy fled west to Mayfair, returning perhaps for a spot of theatre or opera at what is now the Royal Opera House.

The area became increasingly lively – duels were regularly fought in taverns, (Sheridan's third duel over a certain Miss Linley in the Castle Tavern on Henrietta Street resulted in such severe injuries that the pistol became the preferred duelling weapon),

Covent Garden's artistic connections

Naturally, artists and artisans were drawn by Covent Garden's vitality. Chippendale's workshop was in Goodwins Court, Boswell first met Johnson in Davies's bookshop at No 8 Russell Street, Jane Austen stayed with her brother on Henrietta Street, and Thomas De Quincey researched and wrote *Confessions of an English Opium Eater* in Tavistock Street. There was also poverty and squalor – the Seven Dials was the setting for Hogarth's *Gin Lane*, where Dickens observed its 'half-naked children that wallow in the kennels'.

press-gangs and mohocks (aristocratic gangs) roamed the streets, while *Henry's List of Covent Garden Ladies* sold out each edition. Such was the lawlessness that Henry Fielding, Bow Street magistrate and novelist, set up with his blind brother John the **Bow Street Runners**, 'thief-takers' that were precursors of the world's first Metropolitan police force.

The market steadily grew and the theatres began to flourish. The Opera House was twice rebuilt following fires, and sparked riots through its pricing policy. Meanwhile Bow Street magistrates exercised the censor's knife on DH Lawrence's *The Rainbow* – it was found to be obscene – and Oscar Wilde was charged with gross indecency here in 1895. When the market itself moved to Vauxhall in 1974, the area narrowly survived the town planners' toll, and is now a tourist trap of chic shops, restaurants and buskers, but lacks the raw energy that the market provided.

Sights ⊕ *Covent Garden, Leicester Sq.* ⊖ *See p460. www.coventgarden.org.uk.*

Covent Garden Piazza

Covent Garden tube is a popular rendezvous point, where after-work crowds gather on the corner of Long Acre and James Street before heading off for an afternoon's shopping or an evening's entertainment. Pedestrianized James Street leads directly south towards Covent Garden Piazza, one of the more pleasant and all-too-rare car-free environments in central London. Just beside the tube, Floral Street runs off to the right parallel to Long Acre, lined with the area's most fashionable clothes shops. The Piazza itself is the main event though, London's first planned square, although nothing of it remains, its Victorian covered market is very much the focal point of the area, now a dinky two-tier shopping arcade packed with tempting tourist-orientated boutiques that mostly aren't too tacky, alongside decent cafés and bars, some with balconies overlooking the courtyards on either side.

The west side is dominated by the classical portico of **St Paul's Church** ① *T020-7836 5221, Tue-Fri 0930-1630,* a 17th-century box designed by Inigo Jones that has long been known as the actors' church thanks to the plaques inside commemorating bygone stars of the stage and screen. The interior is as simple and modest as the exterior suggests, and it's reached round the back via a charming little back garden with tiny entrances off Henrietta Street, King Street and Bedford Street. The portico on the piazza forms the backdrop to regular street theatre events of widely varying quality throughout the year.

On the south side, the **Jubilee Market** is another covered market with a much lower-rent selection of clothing and jewellery stalls as well as some reasonable snack stops. Things improve here on Mondays when an antiques market sets up shop and at weekends when craftworkers arrive with their wares. The Jubilee Sports Centre (see Activities page 101) is in the same building.

‼ *See London at a glance, p19-24, for related maps.*

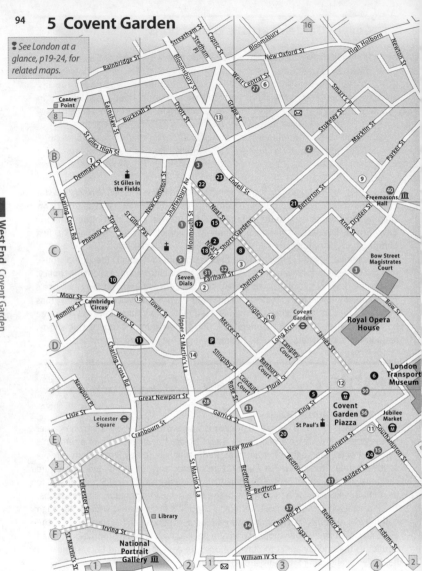

N

| 0 metres | 100 |
| 0 yards | 100 |

Sleeping 🛏
Covent Garden **1** *C2*
Fielding **3** *C4*
Radisson
 Mountbatten **5** *C2*

Travelodge in Covent
 Garden **2** *B3*

Eating 🍴
Café du Jardín **4** *D5*
Calabash at the
 Africa Centre **5** *E3*
Chez Gerrard **6** *D4*
Christopher's **7** *D5*
Food for Thought **8** *C3*
Incognito **10** *C1*
Ivy **11** *D1*
Joe Allen **12** *E5*

Livebait **14** *E5*
Maison Malinowski **15** *C2*
Mon Plaisir **17** *C2*
Neal's Yard Bakery &
 Tearoom **18** *C2*
Orso **19** *E5*
Papageno **1** *E5*
Plummers **20** *E3*
Poetry Society **21** *C3*
Punjab **22** *B2*
Rock & Sole Plaice **23** *B2*
Rules **24** *E4*
Sarastro **25** *C5*

World Food Café **2** *C2*

Pubs & bars 🍸
AKA **27** *A3*
Bar 38 **28** *E2*
Bünker **32** *C2*
Coach & Horses **29** *D5*
Crusting Pipe **30** *E4*
Detroit **31** *C2*
Freud **3** *B2*
Fuel **36** *E4*
Jewel **41** *E4*
Lamb & Flag **33** *E3*

ⓘ *T020-7379 6344, www.ltmuseum. co.uk. Mon-Thu, Sat, Sun 1000- 1800, Fri 1100-1800 (last entry 1700). Adults £5.95, concessions £4.50, free for under-16s.*

Next door, in the old flower market in the southeast corner of the piazza, the London Transport Museum is an excellent place to take the kids for free. As well as a host of antique carriages, trams, buses and tube trains, many of which can be boarded and explored, the great glass-roofed hall contains a formidable battery of hands-on exhibits, push-button panels and a cunning labyrinth of aerial walkways. Plenty of opportunities for adults to enjoy themselves too, whether coming over all nostalgic at the smell of an old railway carriage, driving a tube train simulator or discovering how designer Frank Pick arrived at the final version of his classic tube map. There's also a café here and a shop containing London Transport's distinctive and historic merchandizing: classic posters, mugs and toys.

Royal Opera House

Opposite, in the northeast corner, stands the refurbished Royal Opera House, the end result of years of controversy spiced with bitter accusations about the squandering of public funds on elitist pastimes. In fact the new development has been a huge success, open to the public throughout the day. It includes a terrace overlooking the piazza while the refurbished Floral Hall needs to be seen to be believed. The main entrance is on Bow Street. See also page 99.

Theatre Museum

ⓘ *Off Russell St, T020-7943 4700. Tue- Sun 1000-1800, last entry 1730. Free.*

Appropriately enough, given the proximity of the Royal Opera House and the Drury Lane Theatre Royal (backstage tours available, see below), the capital's theatre museum houses a cornucopia of eye-catching exhibits, antique masks, wigs, costumes and memorabilia. Special exhibitions include The Redgraves, the story of a theatrical dynasty, and The West End: a Great Night Out, charting the spectacular history of the world's most vibrant stages. There's also an impressive video archive of never-to-be-repeated performances, which can be seen on application in advance.

West End Covent Garden

★ Five of the best rooms with a view

- **Rooftop Restaurant**, National Portrait Gallery, Trafalgar Square, page 63
- **Royal Opera House Restaurant**, Covent Garden, page 99.
- **Windows Bar**, London Hilton Park Lane, Mayfair, page 108.
- **Inn the Park**, St James's Park, St James's, page 125.
- **Studio Lounge**, Waterstone's, Piccadilly, page 127.

Freemasons' Hall

ⓘ *T020-7831 9811. Museum 1000-1700 Mon-Fri, tours lasting about 1 hr at 1100, 1200, 1400, 1500 Mon-Fri unless a ceremony is in progress.*

Back on Bow Street, past **Bow Street Magistrates Court** – where the capital's first police force, the Bow Street Runners, originated – and the front of the Royal Opera House, Great Queen Street heads off to the right, continuing the line of Long Acre. The massive building at the end of Great Queen Street is the Freemasons' Hall. Constructed in the 1920s and 30s, this art deco building is the third HQ of the United Grand Lodge of Freemasonry on this site. The museum contains all kinds of Masonic regalia, clocks, watches and other artefacts, while the tours take in the Grand Master's Robing Room, the Shrine, and also the Grand Temple, a spectacular edifice boasting massive brass doors and an extraordinary mosaic ceiling.

★ Seven Dials

North of Long Acre, Covent Garden becomes considerably more intimate, a network of little streets that still retain some flavour of their dubious past. Seven Dials, a seven-arm junction marked by a restored multi-faceted sundial, provides a landmark in the western part of this area while Endell Street cuts north-south in the east. From Seven Dials, narrow little Earlham Street sneaks through to Cambridge Circus and Shaftesbury Avenue.

St Giles

Monmouth Street heads north into the area long known as St Giles, once a disease-infested slum much criticized and described by Dickens. On St Giles High Street is the church of **St Giles in the Fields**, which still looks much as it did in the 18th century. In front of it stands the Resurrection Gate, complete with a spectacular relief of the Day of Judgement carved in wood in 1687. The church has a simple interior and interesting history fully explained inside. From here, leading onto the Charing Cross Road, **Denmark Street** is London's unofficial tin-pan alley, lined with musical instrument shops.

● Sleeping

Covent Garden *p92, map p94*

L Covent Garden, 10 Monmouth St, WC2, T020-7806 1000. With 58 individually decorated rooms, this is another of the Firmdale group's boutique hotels that has proved very popular with visiting stars of screen and stage. On the ground floor, *Brasserie Max* has a styish cocktail bar to complement the reasonably priced modern British food on offer. A little over £250 for a standard double.

L Radisson Mountbatten, 20 Monmouth St, WC2, T020-7836 4300, www.radisson edwardian.com. Large, 4-star deluxe Radisson hotel with a fair amount in the way of traditional comfort and contemporary design but still lacking that special something. Still a great location though.

B Fielding, 4 Broad Court, Bow St, WC2, T020-7836 8305. Not a luxury hotel, but charming enough in its own small way (only

24 rooms) and very convenient for Covent Garden (hence popular with touring singers and dancers): £100 for a double, not including breakfast; you're paying for the location not the style or the facilities.

C Travelodge in Covent Garden, 10 Drury Lane, WC2, T020-7208 9988. Very central and convenient branch of the ubiquitous no-frills budget chain: £80 for a double, breakfast not included.

❼ Eating

Covent Garden *p92, map p94*

Covent Garden is enormously popular for dining out but has never quite fulfilled the promise of the 80s gastronomic revolution here. Now it is overshadowed by Soho, Mayfair, St James's and even Clerkenwell. That said, there are plenty of special exceptions to the complacent mediocrity all too often encouraged by tourist booms.

₸₸₸ Christopher's, 18 Wellington St, WC2, T020-7240 4222. Hasn't been around quite as long as Rules (see below) but is pretty much the American equivalent, its 1st-floor dining room reached via an impressive stone staircase making an appropriately theatrical setting for some good meat and seafood.

₸₸₸ Incognito, 117 Shaftesbury Av, WC2, T020-7836 8866. Nico Landenis' highly acclaimed new venture, doing an excellent modern French menu in a discreet and sophisticated style.

₸₸₸ The Ivy, 1 West St, WC2, T020-7836 4751. Wood panelling, stained glass, modern art, superb service and Italianate brasserie food have made this the most sought-after restaurant in London. Long popular with thespians and wealthy families, the well-deserved hype has ensured that booking weeks in advance is often the only way of enjoying a meal here in the evenings. At lunchtime it's worth having a go.

₸₸₸ Mon Plaisir, 21 Monmouth St, WC2, T020-7836 7243. A first-rate old-timer, much loved for its shabby charm and French regional cuisine. £14.50 for 3 courses on the pre-theatre menu before 2000.

₸₸₸ Rules, 35 Maiden Lane, WC2, T020-7836 5314. A world apart, this is one of the oldest English restaurants in Britain and now something of an overpriced tourist trap, but nonetheless a highly atmospheric Victorian venue for some classic game recipes.

₸₸ Joe Allen, 13 Exeter St, WC2, T020-7836 0651. Quite hard to find but definitely worth the effort. The American menu served up in this traditional basement diner never fails to please a host of theatre-going regulars as well as tourists in the know and it's open late throughout the week. Should be booked.

₸₸ Café du Jardin, 28 Wellington St, WC2, T020-7836 4123. A neat and orderly place for some reliable modern European food.

₸₸ Calabash at the Africa Centre, 38 King St, WC2, T020-7836 1976. Probably one of the best African restaurants in London, in a cosy basement which also hosts excellent African live music in a laid-back atmosphere that's not too expensive either.

₸₸ Chez Gerrard at the Opera House Terrace, 1st floor Opera Terrace, Covent Garden Central Market, WC2, T020-7379 0666. Everything its name suggests, a formulaic but successful branch of the Frenchified restaurant chain with decent enough food and views over neat box hedges towards the new Opera House.

₸₸ Livebait, 21 Wellington St, WC2, T020-7836 7161. For some decent seafood in a busy, functional environment, head to this Covent Garden branch of the Waterloo purveyors of fine fish, now owned by the Chez Gerrard chain. There's also a decent bar here.

₸₸ Orso, 27 Wellington St, WC2, T020-7240 5269. Another excellent basement venue for very good Tuscan cooking. Should be booked.

₸₸ Punjab, 80/82 Neal St, WC2, T020-7836 9787. A reliable but not cheap curry house that has been around for years in an area not blessed with a particularly wide choice of Indian restaurants.

Finding a snack in Covent Garden is no problem at all, but a cheap meal is much more difficult. Probably the best option is in one of the cafés (see below).

₸ Food For Thought, 31 Neal St, WC2, T020-7836 0239. A very good-value vegetarian. Bring your own wine.

For an explanation of sleeping and eating price codes used in this guide, see inside the front cover. Other relevant information is found in Essentials, see pages 44-46.

♥ **Papageno**, 29-31 Wellington St, T020-7836 4444. Same menu as Sarastro.

♥ **Plummers**, 33 King St, WC2, T020-7240 2534. A little more expensive, but an intimate place for good value set-price British food.

♥ **The Rock and Sole Plaice**, 47 Endell St, WC2, T020-7836 3785. Does famously good fish and chips.

♥ **Sarastro**, 126 Drury Lane, WC2, T020-7836 0101. Altogether more offbeat, this is a wacky and strange Moorish-style restaurant with a surprisingly inexpensive Turkish menu, given its location.

Cafés and sandwich bars

Covent Garden has more than enough cafés for everyone and few of them are the kind of rip-off merchants found around Leicester Square. It's pretty safe here to plump for whichever takes your fancy, although those listed below are exceptional.

Maison Malnowski, 63 Neal St, WC2, T020-7836 9779. Has tables outside, good coffee and cakes.

Poetry Society, 22 Betterton St, WC2, T020-7420 9880. The café here is an endearing little bar and wholefood place run by reliable poem-promoters.

Neal's Yard Bakery & Tearoom, 6 Neal's Yard, WC2, T020-7836 5199. Neal's Yard is a good destination for a healthy lunch provided by this vegetarian café.

World Food Café, Neal's Yard Dining Room, 1st floor, 14 Neal's Yard, WC2, T020-7379 0298. If *Neal's Yard Bakery* is too busy, this long-standing place with a self-explanatory name and basic decor, is a good destination.

❶ Pubs and bars

Covent Garden *p92, map p94*

AKA, 18 West Central St, WC2 T020-7836 0110, next door to *The End* nightclub (see page 99). Open Thu-Sat until 0300, after 2230 admission £5, has live music and DJs, one big split-level floor with a restaurant, the latest in cool.

Bünker, 41 Earlham St, WC2, T020-7240 0606. Daily 1100-2300. Underground venue, airily done out in stainless steel and pale wood, where beer is brewed on the premises and there's a separate dining area for food at reasonable prices.

Christopher's, 18 Wellington St, WC2, T020-7240 4222. A swish American-style designer bar with reasonable value cocktails. See Eating above.

Coach and Horses, 42 Wellington St, WC2, T020-7240 0553. The small Irish bar here is very cosy.

Crusting Pipe, 27 The Market, The Piazza, WC2, T020-7836 1415. In the bowels of the market, a branch of the Davy's wine bar chain, a resolutely British institution popular with the local office crowd.

Detroit, 35 Earlham St, WC2, T020-7240 2662. Open until 2400 Mon-Sat, has some character and attitude to match, a subterranean warren of alcoves providing just enough room to enjoy some excellent cocktails and decent food.

Freud, 198 Shaftesbury Av, WC2, T020-7240 9933. A more sophisticated basement cocktail bar that appeals to a rather arty crowd.

Fuel Bar, 21 The Piazza, WC2, T020-7836 2137. In the Piazza itself, one of the best bars for its views, value, hours and avoiding the crush, open until 0200 Mon-Sat, in the southwest corner with a small terrace overlooking the courtyard in front of St Paul's. At ground level it's also a coffee bar with outside seating, while the warren of rooms in the basement jumps to the latest sounds.

Jewel, 29 Maiden Lane, WC2, T020-7379 5900. Dance music bar, open until 0100 (admission charge on Fri and Sat).

Lamb & Flag, 33 Rose St, WC2, T020-7497 9504. The most famous of the old pubs, best approached down a tiny covered alley off Floral St, but its warm and woody interior and front courtyard can become impossibly busy.

Lemon Tree, tucked away behind the London Coliseum in Bedfordbury. A sweet little place adorned with operatic posters.

The Maple Leaf, 41 Maiden Lane, WC2, T020-7240 2843. One of London's few Canadian pubs.

Marquis of Granby, 51 Chandos Pl, WC2, T020-7836 7657. A characterful old-timer with its panelled partitions and glasswork intact.

RamPage, 32 Great Queen St, WC2, T020-7242 0622. A popular pub with sport on the big screen.

⊕ Entertainment

Covent Garden *p92, map p94*
Music
Classical and opera **Royal Opera House**,
Bow St, WC2, T020-7240 1200, box office
T020-7304 4000, www.royaloperahouse.org.
The redeveloped Opera House has left the
auditorium and stage almost untouched, but
front of house and backstage have had a
much-needed revamp. And what a revamp it
is: the Floral Hall is a spectacular space with a
bar and restaurant open all day, while an
escalator sweeps elegantly up to the terrace
where there are more eating and drinking
options, including a outside seating
overlooking the old market.
Rock, folk and jazz **12 Bar Club**
Denmark Pl, Denmark St, WC2, T020-7916
6989, tickets T020-7209 2248. A very
intimate and atmospheric venue for small-
scale performances of high-class folk and
rock. A bar extension and new restaurant out
front have only enhanced a club whose
reputation has soared in recent years
Pineapple Dance Studio, 7 Langley St, WC2,
T020-7836 4004. Runs regular dance classes
in a wide variety of styles catering for most
levels of ability. It also has a little café and a
gym. Day membership (approximately £4)
required and classes cost about £6 an hour.
Open 1000-2000.
Rock Garden, The Piazza, Covent Garden,
WC2, T020-7240 3961, and the **Roadhouse**,
Jubilee Hall, 35 The Piazza, WC2, T020-7240
6001. Both are probably best avoided unless
you want to let mediocre bands on the make
give you earache. Open until 0300 Mon-Sat.

Nightclubs
The End, 18 West Central St, WC2,
T020-7419 9199. One of the best clubs in
London for house and electro music.
Stringfellows, 16-19 Upper St Martin's Lane,
WC2, T020-7240 5534. Continues to draw in
older, more jaded punters with its cocktail of
flashy glamour girls on the dancefloor and a
worldwide reputation for 'good clean fun'.

Theatre
Cambridge Theatre, Earlham St, WC2,
T0870-890 1102. Erected in 1930, famous for
its offbeat musicals and drama, including

Return to the Forbidden Planet, and more
recently *Jerry Springer, the Opera*.
Donmar Warehouse, 41 Earlham St, WC2,
T0870-060 6624. The most innovative,
fashionable and exciting small-scale theatre
in the West End, once run by Sam *American
Beauty* Mendes who still directs some
productions here, as well as welcoming
top-class touring companies. Seats are
usually at a premium and need to be
booked well in advance.
Drury Lane Theatre Royal, Catherine St,
WC2, T020-7494 5000. One of London's
oldest theatres, founded in 1663,
managed by David Garrick in the 18th
century, and rebuilt in the early 19th
century after two disastrous fires. Now
usually stages large- scale musicals.
Enjoyable backstage tours, which
involve actors encouraging audience
participation, tell the history of the
theatre. Taking about 1 hr, they are at
1415, 1645 on Mon, Tue, Thu and Fri,
and at 1015 and 1200 on Wed, Sat
matinee days. £9 per person, bookable
on box office number.
Duchess, Catherine St, WC2, T0870-8901103.
Relatively small mock-Elizabethan theatre
built in 1929, often staging interesting and
intimate dramas.
Lyceum, Wellington St, WC2, T0870-
2439000. Founded in 1771 but erected on
this site in 1834, demolished in 1903 saving
the front portico, and rebuilt in 1904. After
a difficult century, it was finally fully
refurbished and re-opened in the 1990s.
Now showing *The Lion King*.
New London, 167 Drury Lane, WC2,
T0870-8900141. The most recent addition
to West End's theatreland, opened in
1973 with a Peter Ustinov production.
Currently showing *Joseph and the
Amazing Technicolor Dreamcoat*.
Shaftesbury Theatre, Shaftesbury Av,
T020- 7379 5399. Opened in 1911 and
fully reconstructed in the 1920s, this
prominent grand theatre on the edge
of 'theatreland' now usually stages
big musicals.
The Tristan Bates Studio, The Actors'
Centre, 1a Tower St, WC2, T020-7240 6283.
A small fringe theatre named in memory
of Alan Bates' son that regularly stages
promising new work.

❂ Festivals and events

Covent Garden *p92, map p94*
May Fayre and Puppet Festival, T020-7375
0441, happens on a Sun early in **May** in the
garden of St Paul's Church, celebrating the
first time Samuel Pepys saw a Punch and Judy
show in the area in 1662. Not to be confused
with the **Punch and Judy Festival** in **Oct** that
takes place in the Piazza, like various other
festivals throughout the year, some much
better than others. Some have themes like
German food, or the **Food Lover's Fair** in the
1st week of **Nov.** T020- 7836 9136 for
information on these and one-offs. The
Christmas Pudding Race has been taking
place on the 1st Sat of **Dec** for many years.

◎ Shopping

Covent Garden *p92, map p94*
Bookshops
The Banana Bookshop, 10 The Market,
Piazza, WC2, T020-7379 7475. Has a good
selection of children's books and a fairly wide
range of general-interest titles.
The Dover Bookshop, 18 Earlham St, WC2,
T020-7836 2111. Specializes in the out-of-
copyright pictorial archive of Dover
Publications for artists and designers.
Forbidden Planet, 179 Shaftesbury Av, WC1,
T020-7836 4179. Also open until 2000 Thu,
Fri, similar but much larger and more geared
to science fiction and horror, also selling
videos, games and CDs.
Mysteries, 9-11 Monmouth St, WC2, T020-
7240 3688. Titles on anything New Age.
Edward Stanford, 12-14 Long Acre, WC2,
T020-7836 1321. Exceptional map-makers and
sellers since 1900, with a comprehensive stock
of maps, travel guides and travel literature.
Waterstone's, 13-19 Garrick St, WC2, T020-
7836 6757.

Clothes
Covent Garden's main strength is its clothes
shops, ranging from a few exclusively
high-fashion outlets through to 2nd jumble.
For men Most of the big designers have
congregated on Floral St.
Kirk Originals, 29 Floral St, WC2, T020-7240
5055. Do their own-brand designer
sunglasses and specs.

Paul Smith, 40-44 Floral St, WC2, T020-7379
7133. Smart menswear and accessories.
Paul Smith Jean Shop, 7-8 Langley Ct, WC2,
T020-7379 7133, just off Floral St.
Ted Baker, 1-4 Langley Ct, WC2, T020-7497
8862. Packed full of casualwear for men.

For women Nicole Farhi, 11 Floral St,
WC2, T020-7497 8713.
Stephen Jones Millinery, 36 Great Queen St,
WC2, T020-7242 0770, beyond the market on
the other side. An excellent array of
extraordinary designer hats for every occasion.
Question Air, 38 Floral St, WC2, T020-7836
8220. Also have branches in Dulwich Village,
Wimbledon Village, and Barnes Village,
stocking eccentric lines by the likes of Shiren
Guild, Issey Miyake, Ghost, and Maria Chen.

Most of the more affordable fashion shops
can be found on the streets north of Long
Acre, especially on Neal St, Earlham St and in
Shorts Gardens. On Neal St the shops are a
little more upmarket.
Boxfresh, 2 Shorts Gardens, W1, T020-7240
4742. Own-label urban style, who also stock
Triple Five Soul.
Carhartt, 56 Neal St, WC2, T020-7836
5659. Have made a name for their trendy
men's workwear.
Diesel, 43 Earlham St, WC2, T020-7497 5543.
Throwback street styles.
Duffer of St George, 29 Shorts Gardens,
WC2, T020-7379 4666.
Hope and Glory, 30 Shorts Gardens, WC2,
T020-7240 3713.
O'Neill, 9-15 Neal St, WC2, T020-7836 7686.
Brings surfing and skiing chic off the boards
and pistes and on to the streets.
Super Lovers, 64 Neal St, WC2, T020-7240
5248. The only European outlet for the
Japanese label at the cutting-edge of
teenage fashion for boys and girls.

**Second-hand and discounted
designer clothes** With the exception of
Koh Samui, Monmouth St is the place to go
for second-hand and discounted designer
clothes, sometimes at bargain prices.
Koh Samui, 65 Monmouth St, WC2, T020-
7240 4280. Highly fashionable range of
brand new designer-label womenswear,
The Loft, 35 Monmouth St, WC2, T020-7240
3807. Good first stop.

Pop Boutique, 6 Monmouth St, WC2, T020-7497 5262. More retro.

Food and drink
Cadenheads Whisky Shop, 3 Russell St, WC2, T020-7379 4640. A connoisseur of the finest malts and blends.
Carluccio's, 28a Neal St, WC2, T020-7240 1487. Owned by an expert in his field, this is a supremely elegant and expensive Italian deli.
Neal St Restaurant, 26 Neal St, WC2, T020-7836 8368. A restaurant for fungiphiles.
Neal's Yard Dairy, 19 Shorts Gardens, WC2, T020-7240 5700. Foodies might want to check out this place for its exceptional range of home-grown British and Irish cheeses.
Tesco Metro, 21 Bedford St, WC2. Head here if you're just looking for picnic materials.

Gifts
Covent Garden is packed with individual boutiques catering for all kinds of enthusiasts and activities, making it an excellent hunting ground for gifts and quirky one-offs.
The Australia Shop, 26 Henrietta St, WC2, T020-7836 2292. Stocks all manner of items manufactured down under, including Drizabone coats, Thomas Cook clothing, and Australian chocolate and biscuits.
The Kite Store, 48 Neal St, WC2, T020-7836 1666. Has long been famous for its comprehensive stock of anything that flies high or low.
Octopus, 54 Neal St, WC2, T020-7836 2911. Stocks a range of eye-catching gifty things by the French designers Pylones.
On Show, 19 Shorts Gardens, WC2, T020-7379 4454. An Aladdin's cave of gifts from around the world, oriental lamps and Romanian shawls.
Orc's Nest, 6 Earlham St, WC2, T020-7379 4254. One of London's busiest role-playing shops, dealing in a multitude of different-sided dice and little fantasy figures.
The Tintin Shop, 34 Floral St, WC2, T020-7836 1131. The only shop in London solely dedicated to everything related to Hergé's boy detective.
The Wild Bunch, 17 Earlham St, WC2, T020-7497 1200. Has an enormous range of strange and exotic fresh flowers and potted plants.

The shops in the old Apple Market itself, in the central covered market of the Piazza, make for good browsing for gifts or clothes,

although many are fairly expensive.
Benjamin Pollock's Toy Shop, 44 The Market, WC2, T020-7379 7866. Specializes in traditional wooden toys, as well as toy theatres, pop-up books and other essentials for an old-fashioned childhood.

Music
Dress Circle, 57-59 Monmouth St, WC2, T020-7240 2227. Fans of the stage musical should head down the street where musical numbers on CD and vinyl go back over 100 years as well as posters and prints.
Eukatech, 49 Endell St, WC2, T020-7240 8060. Has 2 floors of back-catalogue CDs and vinyl and DJ mixed house, electronica and trance.

Shoes
Shoe-shoppers are unlikely to go away disappointed around here, although prices are often high.
Birkenstock, 70 Neal St, T020-7240 2783. Famous for their ergonomically sound sandals.
Camper, 39 Floral St, WC2, T020-7379 8678. Outlet for the very popular brand of Spanish casual footwear.
Natural Shoe Store, 21 Neal St, WC2, T020-7836 5254. Specializes in eccentric and comfortable footwear, good walking shoes and wide-fitters.
Sole Trader, 72 Neal St, WC2, T020-7836 6777. Stocks happening shoes, trainers and accessories.

▲ Activities

Covent Garden *p92, map p94*
Jubilee Sports Hall, 30 The Piazza, WC2 T020-7836 4835. Mon-Fri 0700-2200 (last entry 2115), Sat 0900-2100, Sun 1000-1700. Large gym, programme of exercise classes, £8 for the gym which can include an hour's induction to the machines, £6.50 for a class, or £10 for both, circuit, step, aerobics, body blast (body pump), no need for induction, plus café and sunbed.
Oasis Sports Centre, 32 Endell St, WC2 T020-7831 1804. Mon-Fri 0630-2130, Sat, Sun 0900-1730. Two swimming pools (£3.30), one of them outdoor, gym and fitness classes (£6.10).
The Sauna Bar, 29 Endell St, WC2 T020-836 2236. Men only gay sauna. Mon-Thu 1200-2400. Open all day and night from Fri-Sun.

Mayfair and Regent Street

North of Piccadilly, and south of Oxford Street, Mayfair is the West End at its most swanky. Protected from the chaos of Soho to the east by the grand swathe of Regent Street, it still earns its place as the last and most expensive stop on the Monopoly board by boasting the capital's most luxurious hotels, the hautest couture and cuisine, and some of its wealthiest residents. Unbelievably, people of more modest means do still live here, although the daytime and early evening population consists largely of itinerant office workers, business people and tourists.

Lavish and louche, Mayfair smells of money. Even if you don't happen to own a Roller yourself, there will be plenty of free opportunities to observe those that do. Recently Mayfair is supposed to have become less stuffy and more fashionable: superficially little seems to have changed, but digging a bit deeper behind those imposing façades is likely to unearth some stylish and affordable surprises. Window-shopping in the Arcades and New Bond Street, inspecting the objets d'art up for auction at Sotheby's, getting measured for a suit in Savile Row, sipping lime cordials in luxury hotel bars, and even listening for nightingales in Berkeley Square, all these cost next to nothing. » *For Sleeping, Eating and other listings see pages 108-114.*

History

Mayfair earned its name from the annual fair held in the area that is now Shepherd Market, a boisterous affair that was intermittently banned until its final demise in 1730, when residents prevented its return (see also page 108). From the 1660s building began edging northwards along Piccadilly, a reflection of the growing popularity of St James's Palace as the favoured royal residence.

By the mid-18th century almost all of the land we call Mayfair was taken up by houses, most of it owned by six estates, the largest of which was the Grosvenor estate. Three great squares of large Georgian townhouses were built – Berkeley, Hanover and Grosvenor, the largest of them all. Noblemen's residences emerged, such as Dorchester House and Grosvenor House overlooking Park Lane, then known as Tyburn Lane, into Hyde Park, and Devonshire House and Lansdowne House close by Berkeley Square. Mews of stables and coach houses were built to house the grooms and coachmen.

Old Bond Street was extended northwards to Oxford Street, and Shepherd Market emerged as a busy network of shops. St George's church in Hanover Square, where Handel was once church warden, served the wealthy residents, and became particularly popular for marriages. By 1800, tall townhouses were preferred to large piles, although the Prince Regent, later George IV, employed John Nash to develop Carlton House into the 'most perfect palace in Europe'.

He also demanded a route north to Regent's Park where he planned to build another grand residence. The result is Regent Street, also designed by Nash, which underwent several modifications in the design and building until its completion in the 1820s. It was funded by private money, and the buildings were the product of a range of architects, so there was little uniformity in the façades. The Quadrant, however, that great sweep from Piccadilly up to Oxford Circus, boasted a grand colonnade to provide cover for the shoppers, and balconies for the bachelors who took rooms above, while the stretch up to Portland Place was designed more for purely residential purposes. The elegant All Soul's church in Langham Place, another Adam product, was built to serve the growing local population.

By 1900, Regent Street had become one of society's most fashionable venues for shopping, theatres and restaurants, but the shops wanted to expand and the buildings revealed structural strains. Despite delays caused by the First World War, the Quadrant was redeveloped by the 1920s, lending the street a more uniform appearance. Meanwhile, in Mayfair itself, the price of maintaining a household forced many of the residents to sell up and move west. Embassies and hotels moved in, and as the devastation of the City during the Second World War created a shortage of office space, so businesses also arrived. More hotels and embassies followed, most notably the American Embassy in Grosvenor Square. It was first established here in 1938, and the square became unofficially known as Eisenhower Platz as American military offices took over many houses in the square during the course of the war. Mayfair retains its reputation for wealth, all the more so since it has become the playground for the global jetset.

Sights ● *Bond St, Green Park, Hyde Park Corner, Oxford Circus.* ● *See p460.*

Mayfair's traditional exclusivity has ensured that there's little of the usual 'see and do' variety. At weekends the wide streets can be almost deserted. Instead, this is a good place to take a quiet stroll around, marvelling at the Duke of Westminster's several hundred-acre Grosvenor estate (he still owns much of the area, including the land beneath the American Embassy).

Savile Row

If you want to see where the Duke and his kind might buy their suits, walk up Regent Street from Piccadilly Circus, turn left into Vigo Street and you come to Savile Row, a name that has been synonymous with high-quality bespoke tailoring since the middle of the 19th century. Many of the shops retain their old-fashioned standards of style and service: the solicitous or snobbish attentions of their staff towards potential customers have become the stuff of legend. At the northern end of the street is **Fortress House**, the home of English Heritage and hence the place to pick up information leaflets on any and every historic attraction maintained by the state throughout London and England.

Back on Vigo Street, Burlington Gardens is dominated by the back of **Burlington House** with its rows of larger-than-life statues of the great philosophers, once an outstation of the British Museum for its ethnographic collection.

Cork Street

Just up Burlington Gardens on the right is Cork Street, still one of London's most prestigious addresses for dealers in traditional and occasionally contemporary fine art. Don't be intimidated; most open during the day in the week, they're free and usually welcome browsers.

★ Burlington Arcade

Beyond Burlington House on the left, the glassy colonnade of the Burlington Arcade stretches down to Piccadilly, guarded by top-hatted beadles. These quaint anachronistic characters are supposed to ensure that no one runs, sings or whistles. Take care, because whistling would be the appropriate reaction to the price tags in some of the shops.

● *The Beatles' famous return to live performance in 1969, captured on film for Let It Be, took place on the roof of No 3 Savile Row.*

6 Mayfair & Regent St

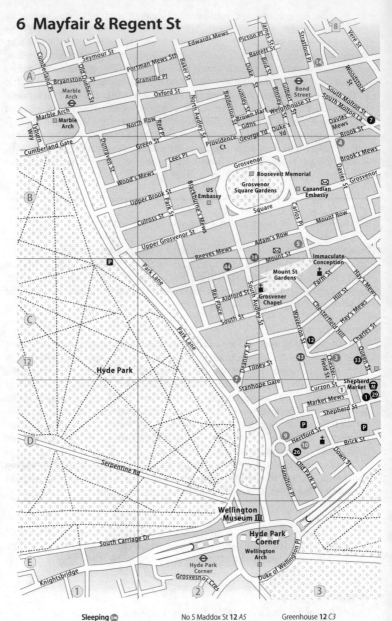

N

0 metres 100
0 yards 100

Sleeping 🛏
Brown's **2** *C4*
Claridge's & Bar **4** *B3*
Connaught **5** *B3*
Curzon Plaza **6** *C4*
Dorchester & Bar **7** *D3*
Flemings Mayfair **8** *D4*
London Hilton,
  Trader Vic's &
  Zeta Bars **9** *D3*
Metropolitan **10** *D3*

No 5 Maddox St **12** *A5*
Westbury **13** *B4*

Eating 🍴
Al Hamra **1** *D4*
Bentley's **3** *C5*
Chisou **5** *A4*
Coffee Republic **7** *A3*
Deca **10** *B4*
Destino **8** *C5*
Gaucho Grill **11** *C5*

Greenhouse **12** *C3*
Guinea Grill **13** *B4*
Kaya **16** *C4*
La Madeleine **17** *B5*
Mirabelle **21** *C4*
Mô **22** *B5*
Momo **23** *B5*
Mulligan's of
  Mayfair **24** *B5*
Nobu **26** *D3*
Rocket **27** *B4*

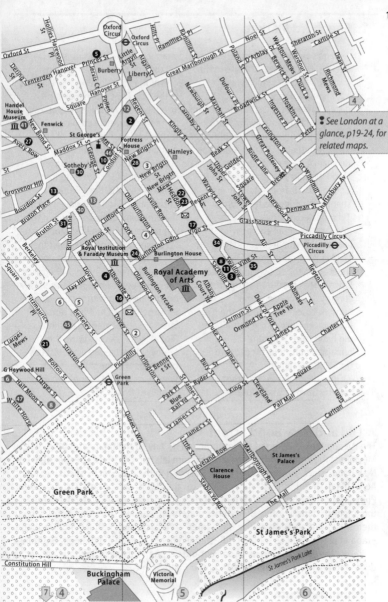

See London at a glance, p19-24, for related maps.

Sartoria **28** B5
Sofra **29** D3
Sotheby's Café **30** B4
Square **31** B4
Sketch **2** A5
Sumosan **4** C4
Tamarind **33** C3
Veeraswamy **34** B5
Yoshino **35** C6

Pubs & bars
Audley **38** B2
Chateau Bar in Radisson
 Edwardian Hotel **45** C4
Coach & Horses **40** B4
Hush **41** A4
Red Lion **43** C3
Scotts **44** C2
Windmill **46** B4
Ye Grapes **47** D4

Entertainment
Curzon Mayfair Cinema **1** D3
Dover St Wine Bar **2** C5
Embassy London **4** B5
Eve Club **3** B5
Funky Buddha **6** C4
Palm Beach Casino **5** C4

Shepherd Market

A plaque on the Al Hamra restaurant declares that this was the site of the 'historic' May Fair, which was apparently a riotous and disreputable event lasting about a fortnight, held annually for a little over half a century until the mid 1700s. Another plaque on Stanhope Row fancifully records that here stood 'Mayfair's oldest house, The Cottage, 1618, from where a shepherd tended his flock while Tyburn idled nearby'.

In fact this small and now mercifully traffic-free corner of Mayfair has nothing to do with sheep. Developed by the architect Edward Shepherd during the 18th century in response to the authorities' concern about the licentious nature of the festivities, old habits died hard and it remained notorious for prostitution until quite recently.

Once described as 'a modest little country town... small but busy... a strange survival in this most aristocratic quarter', it now boasts one of the most comfortable cinemas in the city, The Curzon Mayfair; several good pubs, like Ye Grapes; and some attractive ethnic restaurants nestling in the old mock market building itself.

On Down Street, past the front doors of various South American embassies on Hertford Street, Christchurch Mayfair is now used by the Ethiopian Orthodox Church. Look out too for Knight the fishmonger at No 8, where live lobsters await their fate in the window, and next door the old-fashioned Butwick Pharmacy. On Sundays the railings of Green Park nearby are hung with tremendously tacky paintings. On White Horse Street, once the staging post on Piccadilly for coaches west, the seamy side of the district's past has been reborn in the shape of the swanky new lap-dancing club, For Your Eyes Only.

★ Old and New Bond Street

The Arcade makes as good an introduction as any to the main shopping drag in Mayfair, at the end of Burlington Gardens: turn left into Old Bond Street or right into New Bond Street. You won't find Bond Street W1 in the A-Z. Strictly speaking, round here plain 'Bond Street' only refers to the tube station on Oxford Street. Pedestrianized South Molton Street, running south from the station, hosts probably the highest density of high-fashion outlets in London, but the Bond streets themselves are home to all the big names – Versace, Gucci, Dolce and Gabbana, Prada et al – as well as more staid establishments like the auctioneers **Sotheby's** ① *34-35 New Bond St*, with its 3600-year-old Egyptian carving of Sekhmet above the door, and the jewellers **Tiffany's** ① *25 Old Bond St*.

Faraday Museum

Slightly less grand, the Royal Arcade leads from Old Bond St into Albermarle Street near Brown's Hotel. Turn right and you can't miss the classical façade of the **Royal Institution** ① *T020-7409 2992, www.ri.ac.uk, at number 21, Mon-Fri 0900-1700, £1*, modelled on the Temple of Antoninus in Rome. The Royal Institution was established in the last year of the 18th century to 'facilitate the general introduction of useful mechanical inventions... and the application of science to the common purposes of life'. It fulfils pretty much the same role today, increasing access to scientific ideas, conducting experiments and staging an interesting programme of public lectures. It's worth looking in to check out the old-fashioned Faraday Museum in the basement. Michael Faraday was the assistant of Humphry Davy,

★ Five of the best cafés with outside seating

- **The Admiralty**, Somerset House, Strand, page 71.
- **The Garden Café**, Newburgh St, Soho, page 88.
- **Maison Malnowski**, Covent Garden, page 98.
- **Al Hamra**, Shepherd Market, Mayfair, page 110.
- **Giovanni**, James St, Oxford Street, page 131.

who invented the miners' Davy lamp, and was made a professor of the Institution in 1833 for his research into electricity. Apart from informative wall displays on Faraday's life and works, the small museum's main attraction is an evocative reconstruction of the laboratory where he discovered 'the identity of electricities', including his great electromagnet and a strange hand-operated vacuum pump.

Berkeley Square

Left at the end into Grafton Street and down Hay Hill brings you into the oldest and finest of Mayfair's three great squares. Berkeley Square is an open space preserved since 1696, although these days it's ruined by the hurtling traffic. Nightingales would now be unlikely to stop for long in any of the three dozen magnificent plane trees planted here in the 1780s. The east side of the square was completely redeveloped in the 1930s, but numbers 42-46 on the west side remain much as they would have looked 250 years ago. Number 44 was described by Pevsner as 'the finest terrace house in London'. Designed by William Kent, it now houses the Clermont Club, the private gambling club of which 'lucky' Lord Lucan was a member. Unfortunately the public aren't allowed in to see the spectacular staircase. Number 45 is where Clive of India overdosed on opium in 1774, and Winston Churchill spent time as a child in Number 47.

St George's Church

Crossing over New Bond Street into Conduit Street, St George Street heads up past St George's Church, built in the 1720s and the first London church to be graced with a portico. In the 19th century it became the most fashionable place to get married, Benjamin Disraeli and Mrs Wyndham Lewis, George Eliot and Mr Cross, among others, tied the knot here. Most fatefully, in 1814 the radical romantic poet Shelley and Harriet Westbrook confirmed the vows here that they had made three years earlier in Edinburgh. She drowned herself in the Serpentine in Hyde Park shortly afterwards and Shelley himself didn't live much longer, being lost at sea five years later.

Handel House Museum

ⓘ *T020-7495 1685, www.handelhouse.org. Tue, Wed, Fri, Sat 1000-1800, Thu 1000-2000, Sun 1200-1800. Last admission 30 mins before closing. Adult £5, concessions £4.50, children £2.*

St George Street brings you into Hanover Square, laid out in the 1720s and unremarkable today except that it has a faint buzz the others lack, probably because of the proximity of the artworld on Dering Street and the offices of Vogue in its bottom right-hand corner. Turning left leads into Brook Street where numbers 23-25 are the Handel House Museum. This is a reconstruction of the composer's home, based on his will and the inventory of the house at his death in 1759. He lived here for 35 years as composer to the courts of the Georges. Jimi Hendrix later lived briefly at number 23. It's Handel who gets the star treatment though, with displays attempting to conjure the atmosphere of his times. There's lots of interesting stuff about the man here, although not much genuinely connected with him.

Grosvenor Square and around

Brook Street runs straight into Grosvenor Square, taking its name from the family of the Dukes of Westminster. One of London's largest squares, it was the last in Mayfair to be laid out in the mid-18th century. Nothing much remains of that square today although its scale is still impressive. The west side is taken up with the massive US embassy, put up in the late 50s and topped with an enormous American eagle. Pevsner described the building's effect as 'embarrassing'. (There's a not-so-embarrassing statue of President Roosevelt on the north side.) In Carlos Place, south of the square, is **Hamilton's Gallery** ① *number 13, To20-7499 9493,* one of London's foremost photography galleries, usually holding an exhibition by one of the camera's great artists like Helmut Newton, Norman Parkinson or Cecil Beaton.

Turn left in the square and left again into South Audley Street. Just beyond Mount Street, the little **Grosvenor Chapel** ① *To20-7499 1684 for times of services,* is as old as the square and has become the favourite church of US ex-pats. It was used by American soldiers during the Second World War and is now a chapel of ease.

Behind it, Mount Street Gardens are a miniature delight full of trees and the best approach to the **Church of the Immaculate Conception** ① *To20-7493 7811, 0700-1900 daily, Latin masses sung by a world-famous choir at 1100 every Sun, bookshop Sun mornings, Tue and Fri,* a splendid neo-gothic Catholic church and the oldest Jesuit church in London: it celebrated its 150th anniversary in 2000.

The front of the church is on Farm Street. Turn right out of the door and then left down Chesterfield Hill to find Chesterfield Street, the area's least altered row of Georgian houses, giving a good idea of how Mayfair would have looked in its heyday. Somerset Maugham lived at number six. Cross Curzon Street at the end to find **Shepherd Market**.

⦿ Sleeping

Mayfair & Regent St *p102, map p104*
L The London Hilton, 22 Park Lane, W1, T020-7493 8000, www.hilton.co.uk. A towering hive of activity, with 4 different restaurants and everything an international business executive might require. Spectacular views from the top rooms and the *Windows Bar*.
L No 5 Maddox Street, 5 Maddox St, W1, T020-7647 0200, www.5maddoxstreet.com, www.living-rooms.co.uk. 12 luxurious pan-Asian style apartments in a boutique hotel fitted out with distinctive flair.
AL Brown's, 30-34 Albemarle St, W1, T020-7493 6020, www.brownshotel.com. Founded by Byron's butler, and recently completely refurbished, this Rocco Forte hotel has long been a popular place to take sumptuous English teas in calm, tinkling comfort. A family hotel that has always had a reputation for impeccable service and bags of character. 112 rooms created out of a string of grand Georgian townhouses.

AL Claridge's, Brook St, W1, T020-7629 8860, www.savoy-group.com. Mayfair's most cosmopolitan and glamorous hotel, restored to its 1920s heyday. The bar, designed by David Collins, has won awards and it's been joined by the superb Gordon Ramsay restaurant.
AL The Connaught, Carlos Pl, W1, T020-7499 7070, www.savoy-group.com. The famous restaurant has been refurbished and is run by Angela Hartnett with Mediterranean flair. A quiet country-house atmosphere prevails elsewhere, traditionally very popular with Americans. 92 rooms.
AL The Dorchester, 54 Park Lane, W1, T020-7629 8888, www.dorchesterhotel.com. One of the city's most famous hotels, refurbished in dazzling style and now once again a strong contender for the title of one of London's finest. The mirrors in the bar are a sight to behold: they even cover the piano. 250 rooms.

★ Five of the best cocktail bars

- **Lobby Bar**, One Aldwych, Strand, page 72.
- **Christopher's**, Wellington St, Covent Garden, page 97.
- **Freud**, Shaftesbury Avenue, Covent Garden, page 98.
- **Claridges Bar**, Brook St, Mayfair, page 111
- **Duke's Hotel**, St James's, page 124.

AL The Metropolitan, Old Park Lane, W1, T020-7447 1000, www.metropolitan.co.uk. Probably still the most fashionable 5-star hotel in London. Not for wallflowers, although you could always do like J-Lo who booked the whole top floor for her privacy. Nobu restaurant and Met bar complete the star-studded scene.

A Curzon Plaza, 56 Curzon St, W1, T020-7499 4121, www.curzonplaza.co.uk. Straightforward service apartments, suites for about £100 a night.

A Flemings Mayfair, 7-12 Half Moon St, W1, T020-7499 2964, www.flemings-mayfair.co.uk. Good value family-run hotel in Georgian buildings with Green Park just over the road.

A Westbury, Bond St, W1, T020-7629 7755, www.westbury-london.co.uk. More laid back than many in Mayfair. Service with a smile and excellent cocktails in the *Polo Bar*.

❶ Eating

Mayfair & Regent St *p102, map p104*
ₘₘₘ Deca, 23 Conduit St, W1, T020-7493 7070. A very reliable and more traditional destination, Nico Ladenis has long been famous for the elegance and precision of his kitchen, Deca continues that tradition in superb style although service can be brusque at times.

ₘₘₘ The Greenhouse, 27a Hay's Mews, W1, T020-7499 3331. Less posing and more cosseting goes on, does a very good value (and very busy) set lunch at £23 for 2 courses Mon-Fri. Evenings in the comfortable basement are more expensive but the modern British cuisine is worth it.

ₘₘₘ Kaya, 42 Albemarle St, W1, T020-7499 0622. Has been rated as the finest Korean restaurant in London. It specializes in table-barbecues and traditional dishes from the region of Seoul. Set menus £40 and £45.

ₘₘₘ The Mirabelle, 56 Curzon St, W1, T020-7499 4636. Marco Pierre White re-opened this classic Mayfair restaurant in the 90s to rave reviews. Everything here justifies the average £90 tab for 2, from the impeccable service to the presentation of top-notch Frenchified food. Booking in advance is strongly advised, although couples might well be found a table on spec. There's an outside seating area at the back of the elegantly designed basement space.

ₘₘₘ Nobu, 19 Old Park Lane, W1, T020-7447 4747. More expensive and probably more difficult to drop in on unless just for sushi, is Robert de Niro et al's venture at the super-fashionable *Metropolitan Hotel*. Stuff your face on some ultra-light Japanese-cum-South American food. Book up to a month in advance for 1900-2200 reservations.

ₘₘₘ Sartoria, 20 Savile Row, W1, T020-7534 7000. An Italian restaurant with similar aspirations, this is Conran's fine-dining effort in Mayfair. In summer, book a table by the large windows opening onto New Burlington St.

ₘₘₘ Sketch, 9 Conduit St, T0870 777 4488. Run by the same people as Momo (see below), and must be one of the most hyped and theatrical new restaurants to open in the city in a while, a heaving and hip complex of bars and restaurants (which certainly need to be booked) where customers can give their luxury fever full rein.

West End Mayfair & Regent St *Listings*

● *For an explanation of sleeping and eating price codes used in this guide, see inside the*
● *front cover. Other relevant information is found in Essentials, see pages 44-46.*

The Square, 6-10 Bruton St, W1, T020-7839 8787. More sophisticated, airy and popular with power lunchers during the week (closed for lunch weekends). It looks like a car showroom from the outside but the sleek interior is a stylish setting for some excellent French food majoring in fish.

Sumosan, 26b Albemarle St, W1, T020-7495 5999. One of the media set's favourite Japanese restaurants. They do modern and traditional Japanese food expertly in a busy atmosphere.

Al Hamra, 31-33 Shepherd Market, W1, T020-7493 1954. Serves very good Lebanese food in an attractive room and there are tables outside for those who want to observe the street life of this strange little corner of London.

Bentley's, 11-15 Swallow St, W1, T020-7734 4756. The haunt of old-fashioned seafood aficionados, very good fish dishes have been served here in an antique interior since 1916.

Chisou, 4 Princes St, W1, T020-7629 3931. This is one of the best Japanese restuarants in the West End, just off Regent's St near Hanover Sq. Check out the presentation of their humble spinach salad as an example of the care in the kitchen, served up in a cheerful and efficient atmosphere.

Destino, 25 Swallow St, W1, T020-7437 9895. This was once London's oldest Spanish restaurant, its sumptuous colourfully tiled interior was donated by the King of Spain in 1926. Nowadays, it does good Mexican food upstairs with a taco bar, deli and club on the top floor.

Gaucho Grill, 19 Swallow St, W1, T020-7734 4040. Strictly for voracious meat-eaters and wine-lovers: sit on cowhide-covered chairs in the cellar-like space and consume top-quality Argentine steaks, from £10, with a variety of sauces.

The Guinea Grill, 30 Bruton Pl, W1, T020-7499 1210. Tucked away behind the Young's pub of the same name and is famous for its steak and kidney pies. Cordial service, good food and a pleasant ambience have been keeping a wide cross-section of diners coming back for more since the 1950s.

Momo, 25 Heddon St, W1, T020-434 4040. Much hyped but justifiably so, a North African dining experience with a distinctly metropolitan approach to taking reservations. Pretending to be famous will guarantee a booking.

Mulligan's of Mayfair, 13 Cork St, T020-7409 1370. Attached to a very good pub, Mulligan's offers interesting dishes with an Irish twist in a woody, masculine basement that gets lively in the evenings. Last orders are unfortunately at 2045 though.

Sofra, 18 Shepherd St, W1, T020-7493 3320. A less expensive reputable Turkish restaurant.

Tamarind, 20 Queen St, W1, T020-7629 3561. A very good Indian restaurant, decorated in an opulent modern style, specializing in dishes from the Northwest Frontier that are prepared with a care that justifies their relatively high price.

Veeraswamy, Victory House, 99 Regent St (entrance on Swallow St), T020-7734 1401, www.realindianfood.com. Claims to be the first Indian restaurant in London but only moved into these beautifully clean new premises overlooking Regent St in 1998. The quality of the food certainly demonstrates their years of experience.

Yoshino, 3 Piccadilly Pl, W1, T020-7287 6622. Head here for some authentic Japanese dining. Tucked away in a corner off Piccadilly and designed by cult architect Rick Mather, the restaurant used only to print its menu in Japanese. Now there's an English translation (phew) but the food and service are still as genuine as ever.

Finding somewhere cheap to eat in Mayfair is really only for the brave. There are many places where you'll still find overpriced pub-grub, underheated pizza or soggy pasta.

Mô, 23 Heddon St, T020-7434 4040, off Regent St. An excellent Moroccan snack bar run by the people at *Momo* (see above).

Rocket, 4-5 Lancaster Ct, Brook Pl, T020-7629 2889. Good pizza can be found here.

Cafés and sandwich bars

The pick of the many coffee and sandwich shops in Mayfair include:

Coffee Republic, 2 South Molton St, W1, T020-7629 4567. Was the first, busiest and some say the best of the excellent UK coffee and cake chain.

La Madeleine, 5 Vigo St, W1, T020-7734 8353. Open until 2000 every day except Sun, a real French patisserie with a brightly lit back area for good omelettes, pasta, quiches, and grills.

Sotheby's Café, 34-35 New Bond St, W1, T020-7293 5077. A fairly expensive but very English and genteel establishment for the taking of tea in the old auction house. Last orders are at 1645 and it's closed at weekends.

---

⑪ Pubs and bars

Mayfair & Regent St *p102, map p104*
If you're looking for that perfect Martini, this is the place to start. Unsurprisingly Mayfair boasts some of the best hotel bars in the country, let alone London. None of them are cheap but some deserve the extra spend, especially these few that are outstanding.

Hotel bars

The Chateau Bar, *Radisson Edwardian Mayfair*, Stratton St, W1, T020-7629 7777. A snug New York-style piano-cocktail bar popular with sundry celebrity musos major and minor. Watch out for their famous whisky martini, the Silver Bullet.

Claridge's Bar, *Claridge's Hotel*, Brook St, W1, T020-7629 8860. For the ultimate in designer drinking, has won awards from high-chic interiors magazines while the smooth service of some delicious bar snacks is not at all condescending.

Dorchester Bar, *Dorchester Hotel*, 53 Park Lane, W1, T020-7629 8888. Nothing like as stuffy as you might expect. The charming service and a myriad of mirror tiles make drinking here a many splendoured thing.

Trader Vic's, basement of *London Hilton Hotel*, Park Lane, W1, T020-7493 8000. With its South Island Beach bar theme and glamorous oriental waitresses, this is an old-timer that still delivers a kick with its famous hot rum cocktails served in shiver-me-timbers skull mugs. Good Chinese oven-roast food too.

Zeta, ground floor of the *London Hilton Hotel*. A good-looking, health-giving fruit juice and cocktail bar that's open until 0300 Mon-Sat and offers a decently priced menu from the Pacific Rim.

Restaurant bars

Mayfair also excels in the quality of the bars attached to its smart restaurants.

Hush, 8 Lancashire Ct, Brook St, W1, T020-7659 1500. Self-conciously hip, a spacious venture that boasts a celebrity clientele and good champagne cocktails, sister bar to Shumi in St James's.

Scotts, 20 Mount St, W1, T020-7629 5248. The basement cocktail bar must be one of the most quietly sophisticated places in London to enjoy some expertly mixed concoctions. Immaculate staff glide around the Pierre Chareau sofas while a pianist plays as if she's in love.

Pubs

Surprisingly perhaps, given the area's astronomical ground rents, old-style pubs continue to thrive here.

Audley, 41-43 Mount St, W1, T020-7499 1843. Harks back to Mayfair's grand old days and indulges tourist expectations. Its historic and palatial dark red and dark wood decor is reminiscent of a rather run-down gentlemen's club.

Coach & Horses, 5 Bruton St, W1, T020-7629 4123. More of a locals' local, occupying an incongruous little timber-frame building surrounded by smart offices and boutiques. Charmingly tiny, it attracts an affable crowd of shop and office workers.

The Red Lion, tucked away at 1 Waverton St, W1, T020-7499 1307. Famously feels more like a country pub than many pubs in the country, with its snug set of panelled rooms and high-backed wooden benches. No music and an expensive but high-quality restaurant in the back room.

Windmill, 6-8 Mill St, W1, T020-7491 8050. Similar in style to *Coach & Horses* but on a larger scale, is this Young's pub with lots of character, if a bit tatty, and it does award-winning sandwiches.

Ye Grapes, 16 Shepherd Market, W1, T020-7499 1563. Quite often just as crowded as *The Red Lion*. Tiny exterior belies a louche Edwardian interior decorated with stuffed animals and plush velvet seating.

🎭 Entertainment

Mayfair & Regent St *p102, map p104*
Casinos
Palm Beach, 30 Berkeley St, W1, T020-7493 6585. Open 1230-0600 daily. Notice needed 24 hrs before you want to play for free membership on production of a passport or driving licence. Members can take up to 6 guests to try their hand at poker, roulette, ponte banco or blackjack. Also one-armed bandits, restaurant and bar. No jeans or trainers.

Cinema
Curzon Mayfair, 38 Curzon St, W1, T020-7465 8865. Probably the most comfortable cinema in London and not as expensive as you might expect for such cosseting. It generally shows middle to highbrow mainstream movies on its 1 screen.

Music
Dover Street Winebar, 8-10 Dover St, W1, T020-7629 9813. Mayfair is not a great destination for live music, with Soho so close, but this has become one of the biggest and busiest jazz restaurants in the city. It's open Mon-Thu 1200-1530 and 1730-0300, Fri 1200-1530 and 1900-0300, Sat 0700-0300. Live bands Mon-Wed 1015- 2300, 2400-0100, Thu-Sat 2230-2320; DJs Mon-Sat 0100-0300. Admission £5 Mon (free before 2130), £6 Tue, £7 Wed, £10 Thu (free before 2200 Tue-Wed); Fri, Sat diners only before 2200, and £10 after.

Nightclubs
Embassy London, 29 Old Burlington St, W1, T020-7851 0956. Another fairly long-running fashionista members club.
Eve Club, 3 New Burlington St, T020-7734 4252, info@clubeve.co.uk. Open Wed-Sat until 0300, individual nights in louche surroundings arranged by party organizers. You need to either phone, fax or email to ensure admission.

Funky Buddha, 15 Berkeley St, T020-7495 2596, guestlist@fblondon.co.uk. A lively private members club open until 0300 Thu-Sat with a variety of party nights. Get on the guest list as a prospective member by emailing.

◯ Shopping

Mayfair & Regent St *p102, map p104*
Accessories and leather
Traditional English craftwork in leather and other accessories reaches its peak in Mayfair.
Fenwick, 63 New Bond St, W1, T020-7629 9161. Much more middle of the road but also very manageable, a trip around Bond St's only department store will turn up some affordable hats, gloves or shoes.
Mulberry, 41-42 New Bond St, W1, T020-7491 3900. Make very British bags, holdalls and suitcases as well as smart gifts and clothes.
Smythson, 40 New Bond St, W1, T020-7629 8558. The last word in traditional British bespoke stationery and writing accessories.
Tanner Krolle, 3 Burlington Gardens, W1, T020-7287 5121. The place, like Mulberry, to upgrade your wallet or purse by making them about £40 lighter.

Art and auction houses
Cheek-by-jowl with the vagaries of fashion, New Bond St is home to London's two busiest auction houses.
Bonhams, 101 New Bond St, W1, T020-7629 6602. Very slightly more downmarket than *Sotheby's*, very large and very busy auction house.
The Fine Art Society, 148 New Bond St, W1, T020-7629 5116. The showroom of one of London's longest-established dealers in paintings, can also make for a rewarding browse.
Sotheby's, 34-35 New Bond St, W1, T020-7293 5000. The grandest and has been bringing the gavel down on rare and expensive objets d'art since 1744. It's open for valuations from 0900-1630 Mon-Fri, or you can pick up a catalogue (from £10) and view the current sale. Call in advance to find out what's going… going… when, before it's gone. Sotheby's Café is open 0930-1645, sometimes Sun if there's a sale on view.

Fashion

Only in Knightsbridge will you find as many high-fashion designer outlets as in Mayfair. All along Old and New Bond Sts, many of the big names' shops are gob-smacking attractions in themselves. Chances are that if you don't know what these kinds of shop are stocking, you won't want to afford them.

Chanel, 26 Old Bond St, T020-7493 5040.

Etro, 14 Old Bond St, T020-7495 5767. Less flash or intimidating than many of them.

Gucci, 33 Old Bond St, T020-7629 2716.

Donna Karan, No 19 New Bond St, T020-7495 3100.

Calvin Klein, Nos 53-55 New Bond St, T020-7491 9696.

Miu Miu, 123 New Bond St, T020-7409 0900.

Prada's, 15 Old Bond St, W1, T020-7647 5000. Gallery-style store.

Ralph Polo Lauren, 1 New Bond St, T020-7647 6510.

Versace's, 34-36 Old Bond St, T020-7499 1862. Massive over-the-top, 3-storey shopping palace. **Versace Jeans**, 113 New Bond St, T020-7355 2700.

Jewellers

Agatha, 4 South Molton St, W1, T020-7495 2779. For less expensive designer jewellery, the local branch of the famous French chain.

Asprey and Garrard, 167 New Bond St, T020-7493 6767. Similar to *Cartier* and *Tiffany* but has a few more affordable items, including stationery.

Cartier 175-176 New Bond St, T020-7408 5700. One of the most notable jewellers. Features classic, old-fashioned interiors, sky-high prices and dazzling rocks.

Electrum Gallery, 21 South Molton St, W1, T020-7629 6325. Curates a wide selection of international contemporary jewellery makers including big names like Wendy Ramshaw, Gerda Flöckinger, and Tone Vigeland. They hold four feature exhibitions a year.

Mikimoto, 179 New Bond St W1, T020-7629 5300. If it's fashionable pearls you fancy, head for this place. Gifts such as pens with a pearl stud from around £30 as well as strings of the things worth thousands.

Tiffany & Co, 25 Old Bond St, W1, T020-7409 2790. Another notable jeweller featuring classic, old-fashioned interiors, sky-high prices and dazzling rocks.

Miscellaneous

Caviar Kaspia,18 Bruton Pl, W1, T020-7493 2612. The place to seek out a variety of luxurious international foods, not just the treasured eggs of the sturgeon.

Grays Antiques Market, 58 Davies St, W1, T020-7629 7034. Always worth a browse, especially for second-hand books. Only the rare and second-hand bookshop is open on Sat.

G Heywood Hill, 10 Curzon St, W1, T020-7629 0647. A long-established upper-crust bookseller, has a good stock of rare, second-hand and new books, knowledgeable staff and charming premises.

Nelson Pharmacy, 73 Duke St, W1, T020-7629 3118. Olde-worlde, this has been purveying homeopathic medicines since 1860 and will recommend a local homeopath.

Regent Street department stores

Dickens & Jones, 224-244 Regent St, W1, T020-7734 7070. This is a huge, woman-orientated and slightly pedestrian department store.

Hamleys 188-196 Regent St, W1, T020-7494 2000. Regent St can be a risky place to take the kids. This still leads the way for toy shops the world over but can become nightmarishly busy. Its famous window displays highlight aspects of its staggering stock, none of which comes cheap.

Liberty, 210-220 Regent St, W1, T020-7734 1234. Glamorous but not intimidatingly trendy. Its mock-Tudor building on Marlborough St is a joy to wander around and home to many of the latest looks.

The Teddy Bear Shop, 153 Regent St, W1. Provides more traditional comforters, some handmade; again, at a price.

Savile Row tailors

Unless you have a spare couple of thousand, you won't want to be ordering a bespoke suit from the home of the English gentleman's tailors any time soon either. Even so, these unique and increasingly timeless institutions can be relied upon to make a visit entertaining: their staff are famous for their sense of humour.

Anderson & Shepherd, 30 Savile Row, W1, T020-7734 1420. Tailors to Prince Charles, will do you a pair of sheepskin slippers from £45.

Ozwald Boateng, 9 Vigo St, W1, T020-7734 6868. Altogether more cutting-edge and designer in style, selling snazzy off-the-peg and bespoke suits and womenswear.

Ede and Ravenscroft, 8 Burlington Gdns, W1, T020-7734 5450. Proudly displays all 4 Royal 'by appointments'. Reknowned legal and academic tailors, this shop stocks their overcoats, as well as silk hand-kerchiefs with a bird of paradise motif for about £30.

Gieves & Hawkes, 1 Savile Row, W1, T020- 7434 2001. Classic tailors that has launched a more casual range simply called 'Gieves'.

Henry Poole, 15 Savile Row, W1, T020-7734 5985. The oldest established on the Row, since 1846. Past customers include the dandy philanderer Edward VII, who changed his clothes three times a day, the Emperor Napoleon III, and more recently the Emperor of Japan. Pick up a pair of braces for £37-£47 or a silk tie for £60.

❻ Directory

Mayfair & Regent St *p102, map p104*
Medical services Gould Pharmacy, 37 North Audley St, T020-7495 6298.
Tourist offices Britain Visitor Centre, 1 Regent St, Piccadilly Circus, SW1, T020-8846 9000. Mon 0930-1830, Tue-Fri 0900-1830, Sat-Sun 1000-1600; Jun-Oct, Sat 0900-1700.

Piccadilly and St James's

Piccadilly Circus is the heart of the West End, pumping traffic and tourists round central London's party zone. Here the pomp of Piccadilly and Regent Street meets the alleyways running into Soho, the milling crowds on Coventry Street coming from Leicester Square, and theatreland's bustling Shaftesbury Avenue. The most famous sights of the Circus are the neon advertizing hoardings on its north side and the little statue of 'Eros' in the middle, but the view south down Lower Regent Street towards Westminster beats them both. Somehow the place manages to make a satisfactory fist of joining up four of the West End's most distinctive districts: Soho, Mayfair, St James's and Leicester Square's Chinatown.

Piccadilly itself goes west with considerable panache, down past Fortnum's, the Royal Academy, the Ritz and Green Park, heading for the memorials on Hyde Park Corner, and dividing the glitz of Mayfair to the north from London's most exclusive and rarefied enclave, the gentlemen's clubland of St James's. Those stately sanctuaries of affluent influence are lined up on Pall Mall (rhyming with 'gal'), trying to ignore the vulgar roar of traffic rushing out from Trafalgar Square, past the Tudor gates of St James's Palace, and up the 18th-century breadth of St James's Street. Just beyond this small quirky quarter long dedicated to keeping the English gent in shirts, shoes and headgear lies the reason for its status, Royal London: the processional splendour of The Mall, the lakeside garden tranquillity of St James's Park, and the monumental bastion of Buckingham Palace. This is London as millions of tourists expect to find it and generally they're not disappointed. ▸▸ *For Sleeping, Eating and other listings see pages 124-127.*

66 99 One explorer confessed to JM Barrie in the Travellers' Club that the most dangerous part of his latest trip to Africa had been "crossing Piccadilly Circus"...

History

The area that has become synonymous with gentlemen's clubs and fine living was built up, appropriately, around St James's Palace. Little of the original palace remains now, but it was first built by Henry VIII on the site of a leper hospital for young women, and the marshy land to the south where the lepers fed their hogs was drained and developed as a nursery for his deer.

Close to Whitehall, St James's saw many regal dramas. 'Bloody' Mary I died here, Elizabeth I hunted in the park, and James I formalized the gardens with an aviary (hence Birdcage Walk) and an orchard of 10,000 mulberry trees planted on land that is now taken up by Buckingham Palace. (One of the trees, from 1609, remains in the 45-acre garden).

Charles I's last journey to his execution took him from the palace, across the park, to Banqueting House, where his beheading was met with a groan from the crowd. Unperturbed by the area's macabre memories, however, Charles II enjoyed the palace and its grounds. He played an Italian variant of croquet, called pell-mell, on an avenue in the park, and the park was extended over what many believed to be the leper burial ground, now Green Park.

The area began to attract developers. St James's Square and St James's Street went up in the 1660s and 1670s, Buckingham House, now Buckingham Palace, was built over the River Tyburn, and Burlington House, now the Royal Academy, was one of the several grand piles stretching along Piccadilly to Hyde Park Corner. One of the earliest, dating from 1612, was built by Robert Baker, a tailor with a shop in the Strand. Nicknamed Piccadilly Hall (in reference to the source of his wealth, 'picadils' – stiff collars), the name finally won formal approval over 100 years later.

Over the next two centuries the area became a curious mix of the smart and the seedy. Fashionable shops were to be found in the grand streets – bespoke hats from James Lock, men's toiletries from perfumier Floris, or all manner of consumables from Fortnum and Mason on Piccadilly. Gentlemen's clubs blossomed, metamorphosing from coffeeshops into exclusive clubs, and in 1721 there were six dukes and seven earls living in St James's Square. But as one French visitor observed, 'it's a strange sight, in fine weather, to see the flower of the nobility and the first ladies of court mingling in confusion with the vilest populace...'. The vilest populace, as he would have it, included prostitutes in St James's Park after the gates were locked (there were thousands of keys in circulation), or seeing out the weekend in Haymarket, still a hay and straw market three days a week, but by night 'a spacious street of great Resort, full of Inns and Houses of Entertainment'.

Highwaymen and robbery were commonplace, even along Piccadilly, where you might see late-night parties returning en masse for protection from their various engagements in Kensington or Knightsbridge. Following considerable reconstruction under George IV, Buckingham Palace became Victoria's preferred residence, and the houses closed up as the rich moved to Belgravia and businesses moved in. Piccadilly

Circus, formed in 1819 to accommodate Nash's Regent Street, soon emerged as a busy intersection and a popular meeting point. One explorer confessed to JM Barrie in the Travellers' Club that the most dangerous part of his latest trip to Africa had been "crossing Piccadilly Circus".

Eros, erected in 1893, became a much-loved statue in the Circus, and until the 1940s attracted flower-girls to its base. Messrs J Lyons established their first tea-house on Piccadilly in 1894, and by 1910 neon lights shone brightly on the circus. The Mall was rebuilt as a grand avenue leading from Admiralty Arch to Buckingham Palace as part of the Victoria Memorial development; and the Ritz was constructed as the first steel-framed building in London. Although it has suffered from relentless commercialization, St James's, as David Piper noted in 1964, is where '...the embodiment, if not the spirit, of the English upper-class male persists'. Even now, a trip to St James's Park at lunchtime will be rewarded with the sight of civil servants in deep discussion, or politicians and bishops heading purposefully across the park from Whitehall for lunch at the clubs.

7 Piccadilly & St James's

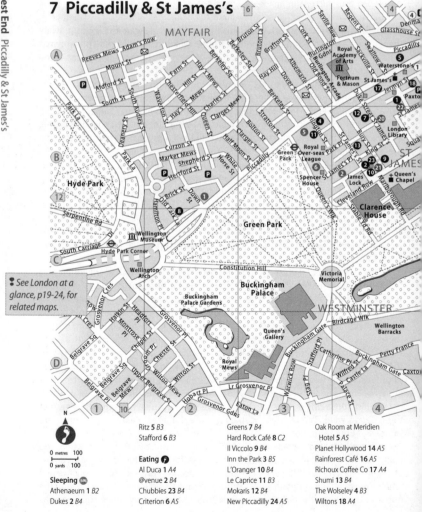

❧ See London at a glance, p19-24, for related maps.

```
N
0 metres    100
0 yards     100
```

Sleeping 🛏
Athenaeum 1 *B2*
Dukes 2 *B4*

Ritz 5 *B3*
Stafford 6 *B3*

Eating 🍴
Al Duca 1 *A4*
@venue 2 *B4*
Chubbies 23 *B4*
Criterion 6 *A5*

Greens 7 *B4*
Hard Rock Café 8 *C2*
Il Viccolo 9 *B4*
Inn the Park 3 *B5*
L'Oranger 10 *B4*
Le Caprice 11 *B3*
Mokaris 12 *B4*
New Piccadilly 24 *A5*

Oak Room at Meridien
  Hotel 5 *A5*
Planet Hollywood 14 *A5*
Rainforest Café 16 *A5*
Richoux Coffee Co 17 *A4*
Shumi 13 *B4*
The Wolseley 4 *B3*
Wiltons 18 *A4*

Sights ● *Green Park, Piccadilly Circus, St James's Park.* ● *See p460.*

Piccadilly Circus

Piccadilly Circus is usually so relentlessly busy that it's not a particularly pleasant place to linger, but thousands do, gathering around the endearing little monument representing the Angel of Christian Charity. Erected in 1893 in memory of the stern philanthropist Lord Shaftesbury, who did much to help abolish child labour, the winged boy with his bow was so unpopular that the sculptor Sir Arthur Gilbert went into retirement. Persistently taken to be the God of Love, '**Eros**', as the sculpture came to be known, was recently given loving restoration and has become one of the city's most famous landmarks. Nowadays it is dwarfed by the neon-lit logos of McDonald's, Nescafé and Coca Cola on the north side. Opposite them is the grand façade of The Criterion Restaurant. To its right, there's a strikingly beautiful view down Lower Regent Street past the Duke of York's Column and over the trees of St James's Park towards the Victoria Tower of the Palace of Westminster.

To the left of the Criterion, Coventry Street is a tasteless stretch of tourist-tat retailers and 'have a nice day' diners. Its bustling popularity can only be explained by its being the shortest, partially pedestrianized route between Piccadilly Circus and the dubious delights of Leicester Square.

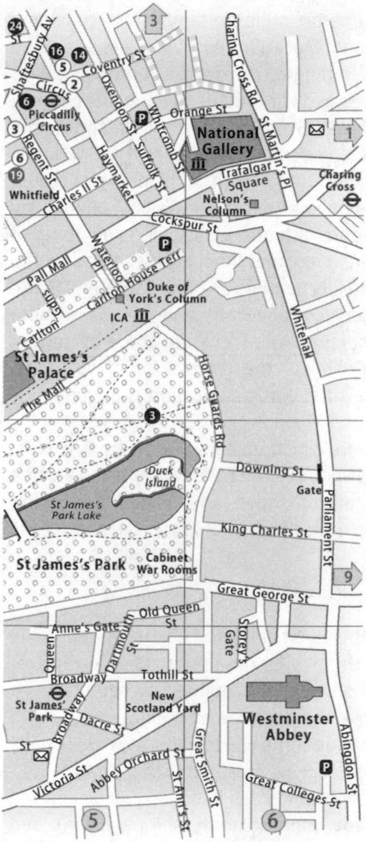

West End Piccadilly & St James's

★ Along Piccadilly

Progressing westwards for about a mile towards Hyde Park Corner, Piccadilly itself is a top-class, if frantic and congested, strip of extraordinary shops, world-class hotels, green spaces and fine architecture.

St James's Piccadilly Church
① *T020-7734 4511. 0800-1900 daily. Café, T020-7437 9419, 0800-1900 Mon-Sat, 1000-1900 Sun. Antique market Tue 1000-1730. Craft market, T020-7437 7688, Wed-Sat 1000-1730.*

One of the most beautiful churches in London is on the left a few hundred yards down from Piccadilly Circus, at 197 Piccadilly. St James's Piccadilly,

Pubs & bars 🍺
Chequers **19** *A5*
Three Crowns **20** *B4*
Red Lion (Crown Passage) **21** *B4*
Red Lion (Duke of York St) **22** *B4*

Entertainment 🎭
Café de Paris **2** *A5*
Criterion Theatre **1** *A4*
Jermyn St Theatre **3** *A5*
Piccadilly Theatre **4** *A4*
Plaza **6** *A5*
Virgin Cinema **5** *A5*

known as the 'visitors' church', was its architect Christopher Wren's personal favourite, a haven set back from the street in its own courtyard dedicated to the many Londoners who died in the Second World War, now hosting a small craft and antiques market. Completed in 1684, the church sustained severe bomb damage in the Second World War and needed extensive restoration. The interior retains delightful balance and poise, best appreciated in bright daylight, and includes a spectacular limewood altar-screen carved by Grinling Gibbons in the 17th century, who may also have been responsible for the font here in which William Blake was baptized. There's also a cinema club in the vestry (for details see Entertainment page 126).

Royal Academy of Arts

① *T020-7300 8000; bookings T020-7300 5959 or 7300 5678. 1000-1800 Mon-Thu, Sat, Sun, 1000-2030 Fri, admission to exhibitions varies.*

On the opposite side of the street, a little further along, the Albany is a Georgian mansion block tucked away behind smart iron railings, famous for providing prestigious bachelor pads for the likes of Byron, Macaulay, Aldous Huxley and more recently the late Alan Clark, MP. Next door is Burlington House, the home since 1869 of the Royal Academy of Arts, founded by George III in 1768 as the first art school in the country. A modern statue of its first president, Sir Joshua Reynolds, stands in the middle of the palatial central courtyard, which despite doubling as a car park is a pleasant enough place to escape from the traffic with a picnic. Under the directorship of Norman Rosenthal, the Academy has determinedly cast off its fusty image in the last decade by mounting popular attention-grabbing exhibitions of contemporary British art, with titles like 'Sensation' and 'Apocalypse'. Even so, the opening of its Summer Exhibition in June and July remains an important event in the social calendar, when a profusion of less controversial and generally more attractive work is selected from an open competition, including some by current Academicians. Michelangelo's *Virgin and Child with the Infant St John* (*The Taddei Tondo*) is one of only four sculptures by the artist outside Italy and is permanently on display outside the Sackler Galleries.

Guided tours of the permanent collection, which includes works by Reynolds, Turner, Constable and Stanley Spencer, are given Tuesday-Friday at 1300 and are free (be there on time). The Academy also organizes shows and hosts independent exhibitions (free admission to many of them) in the grand space vacated by the Museum of Mankind on Burlington Gardens.

Fortnum and Mason

Facing the Academy's massive portico another even older and almost as venerable institution, Fortnum and Mason, has been furnishing the upper classes with tea, fine food, glassware, clothes and antiques since it was founded by one of Queen Anne's footmen, Mr Fortnum, in 1707. Above the door, he emerges every hour to greet Mr Mason from a clock installed in the 1960s. The window displays are usually lavish artworks in themselves. ▸▸ *See Shopping, page 127 for further details.*

More window-shopping (and it's probably best to keep it to that) can be enjoyed a little further along in the **Burlington Arcade**, running north (see page 103), and through the Piccadilly Arcade's great bow windows running south, elegant spaces to gawp at unaffordable jewellery, fine art and antiques.

● *There have long been popular rumours about Green Park – not least those about*
● *the 'tree of death', a haunted tree avoided by birds, but patronized by a mysterious coated figure.*

Green Park

ⓘ *T020-7930 1793. Dawn-dusk daily.* Past Old Bond Street, St James's Street and just beyond the Ritz Hotel, the buildings on the left-hand side give way to the rolling Green Park. Laid out by Henry VIII, the 53-acre park's name is self-explanatory enough, kept free of formal flower beds out of respect for the lepers from the Hospital of St James's buried beneath. More fancifully, Charles II, who made it a Royal park, is supposed to have picked a flower to give to the next beautiful woman he saw, who happened to be a local milkmaid. Queen Katharine was so furious that she banned flower beds from the park for good. Nowadays the plane trees, crocuses, daffodils and deck chairs make it a charming spot to wile away an afternoon in the spring. Chairs can be hired from the corner of the park nearest the Ritz.

The **Queen's Walk** runs down its east side to The Mall and Buckingham Palace's ticket office, behind stately mansions like Spencer House (see next page) and the government offices of Lancaster House. The peculiar bowl of the Canadian Memorial near The Mall was erected in 1994 to commemorate the Canadian dead of the two world wars.

Hyde Park Corner

Piccadilly continues downhill to **Hyde Park Corner**. Decimus Burton's **Wellington Arch** ⓘ *T020-7930 2726, Apr-Oct Wed-Sun 1000-1700, Nov-Mar Wed-Sun 1000-1600, £3, concessions £2.30, under-16s £1.30*, erected in 1828, dominates the roundabout, celebrating Wellington's victory in the Napoleonic war. It now houses a small museum on the history of the arch and on the blue plaques that distinguish the addresses of London's famous residents. The first one was put up in 1867 on Lord Byron's house. There are fine views from the top down Constitution Hill towards the London Eye and Big Ben as well as a glimpse of the royal tennis court in the back garden of the palace.

The arch is surrounded by **war memorials**. The most recent, opened in 2001, stands at the entrance to Constitution Hill, commemorating the 5 million volunteers from the Indian subcontinent, Africa and the Caribbean who fought with Britain in the two world wars. More elaborate is the Australian war memorial, with water trickling over the carved names of the dead. On the other side of the roundabout stands the disturbing memorial to the Machine Guns Corps of the First World War, a statue of David and two gatling guns, complete with a biblical inscription referring to his slaying in his 'tens of thousands'.

The Wellington Museum

ⓘ *T020-7499 5676. Apr-Oct Tue-Sun 1100-1700, Nov-Mar Tue-Sun 1100-1600. £4.50, £3 concession, £2.30 under-16s. Guided tours on request, £30 for groups of up to 25.*

The main reason to come here and not hurry through into Hyde Park is a visit to **Apsley House**, the house that Arthur Wellesley, the Duke of Wellington, bought from his brother after Waterloo. It stands on the north side of Hyde Park corner, by the entrance to Park Lane. Known as No 1 London, for being the first house in the West End on the road from Knightsbridge, it's now The Wellington Museum, managed by English Heritage but also still the London home of the great man's descendants. The Iron Duke, so called because of the metal shutters he had fitted to his windows here to protect him from Reform Act rioters, resided here from 1817-1852. The place remains a dignified monument to the man and the post-Napoleonic era in Britain, restored in Louis XIV style, and refurbished throughout in its original colour scheme in 1995.

Of the 10 rooms open to the public, six are on the first floor, the highlight being the Waterloo Gallery, complete with a magnificent chandelier and works by Rubens, Brueghel, Van Dyck and Murillo, alongside the Duke's favourite, Correggio's *Agony in the Garden*, as well as Velázquez's *Water Seller*. The Striped Drawing Room is the most atmospheric, with its striking portraits of Wellesley's military colleagues. Most visitors are also surprised and impressed by the massive 11-ft statue of Napoleon heroically naked in the stairwell, given to Wellington in 1816 after its diminutive subject had refused it in distaste. The basement gallery displays memorabilia connected with the Duke, including 15 fine cartoons. A small shop sells books, souvenirs, postcards, and a guide, although there's also a free audio guide.

St James's

St James's is the land that time forgot, well worth exploring for its peculiar air of self-conscious restraint and an awareness that its prestige lies largely in pandering to the super rich. The layout of its streets little changed since the 17th century, it has preserved a more intimate scale than Mayfair, although the grandeur of its aspirations are forcefully expressed in St James's Square and along Pall Mall. Above all, this is the part of London that enshrines the idea of the English gentleman.

St James's Street

The smartest address for your club is St James's Street, the main thoroughfare running down from Piccadilly to St James's Palace. Try **White's** ① *Nos 37-38* (the oldest), **Brooks's** ① *No 60* (the poshest), or **Boodles** ① *No 28* (the wackiest), but you're only likely to get in to whichever one suits you anyway because you'll already know several other members. An exception are the literary, musical and artistic events organized by **ROSL Arts** at the **Royal Over-Seas League** ① *Over-Seas House, Park Pl, St James's St, SW1, T020-7408 0214 (ext 219)*. They're well worth looking into in themselves, not least to enjoy the club-like interior of Over-Seas House.

Spencer House

① *27 St James's Pl, T020-7499 8620. Feb-Jul, Sep-Dec 1030-1730 (last tour 1645), Sun only or during the week for groups by appointment in writing. £6, £5 children, guided tour obligatory, garden only £3.50.*

If you want some idea of the type of effect the interiors of these fashionable gambling houses might have hoped to imitate in their heyday, you can visit **Spencer House** the ancestral London home of Princess Diana's family from 1755 until the 1920s. The house was restored by its current owner, Lord Rothschild's bank, in 1990. Eight grand rooms are open to the public by guided tour every 15 minutes on Sundays, highlights being the views of the garden and Green Park, the ceiling of the dining room, the gilded trees in the Palm Room, and the Great Room. The garden has been returned to its late 18th-century design, complete with plants and shrubs true to the period, and can now be visited separately from the house during spring and summer. Phone for details.

Jermyn Street

Parallel to Piccadilly, off St James's Street to the left, Jermyn Street sets the tone for the shops that cater for the area's clubbable gents, passing the back door of Fortnum's (see Shopping page 127). Any street going south heads into the heart of the area. Traditional commercial art galleries line King Street, headed up by **Christie's** ① *8 King St, SW1, T020-7839 9060*, an auctioneer with a pedigree as ancient as Sotheby's. The main sale season is from September to April. Phone for details of upcoming sales or drop in and pick up a catalogue.

St James's Palace and the Queen's Chapel

At the bottom of St James's Street, where it turns sharp left into Pall Mall, two fully armed redcoats in their bearskin or busbies stand or stomp about like clockwork beneath the red-brick Tudor gatehouse of St James's Palace. Now used as offices for various Royals including Prince Charles, the palace is closed to visitors, although the **Chapel Royal** inside is open for Sunday services from October until Good Friday. Like the gatehouse, the ceiling of the Chapel is one of the last traces of the palace that Henry VIII built himself here in 1531, on the site of the Leper Hospital of St James the Less.

A little way down Marlborough Road, opposite the Ambassador's Court, its name a reminder that modern ambassadors to the UK are still received 'at the court of St James', stands the **Queen's Chapel** ⓘ *only for Sun services Easter to Jul 0830; sung Eucharist 1st Sun of the month and Great Festivals, other Suns 1115, Holy Communion on Holy Days 1230*, in the grounds of Marlborough House, the HQ of the Commonwealth. The chapel was designed by Inigo Jones for Charles I, done up by Wren, and has a classically proportioned interior that is puritan in its simplicity.

Pall Mall and St James's Square

Most of the clubs are on Pall Mall, named after the Italian Pell Mell croquet-cum-golf game beloved of Charles II, who installed his mistress Nell Gwyn in a house overlooking the pitch. Architecturally, the street is sombre, grand and restrained, with the exception of **Schomberg House** ⓘ *numbers 80-82,* in a florid red-brick Dutch style which is unique in London. Just off it is leafy **St James's Square**, until relatively recently the favourite London address of many aristocrats. The equestrian statue in the middle is that of William III, who died in a riding accident.

Today the square is home to clubs and offices. **The London Library** ⓘ *number 14, T020-7930 7705, membership applications are open to all but can take up to 1 week to process, options for membership range from full annual membership, through temporary (4-month) overseas membership (£100), to use of the reading room for 1 month for reference purposes only (£25),* in the northwest corner, was founded by Thomas Carlyle in 1841, in disgust at the poor service offered by the British Library. It's still a private members' lending library, with a wonderful 19th-century reading room and lobby.

Waterloo Place

At the bottom of Lower Regent Street, Waterloo Place crosses Pall Mall, the intersection dominated by the massive **Crimean Monument**, including a statue of Florence Nightingale and an early 19th-century street lamp. On the right-hand side of the place stands the **Athenaeum Club**, designed by Decimus Burton with a replica of the Parthenon frieze over the door, appropriate to a club popular with academics and clerics. Opposite is a matching building, also by Burton, which is now the Institute of Directors.

The most prominent monument among the several dotted around here, including a statue of Scott of the Antarctic, is the **Duke of York's Column**. Erected in 1833, it was paid for by taking one day's wages off every soldier in the army in honour of the Duke, the Grand Old one who 'had ten thousand men, marched them up to the top of the hill, and then marched them down again'. Luckily he was a popular commander.

To the right of the column, beneath a tree, is a curious little gravestone inscribed 'Giro, died 1934'. It commemorates the dog of German ambassador Leopold von Hoesch. Until the Second World War, the German Embassy was close by at numbers 7-9 Carlton House Terrace. Von Hoesch himself died two years later at the age of 55 under the strain of worsening Anglo-German relationships. From here wide steps lead down onto The Mall.

Walk down the Duke of York's steps and you are entering Toytown. Here is Royal London, with its processional road, its smart soldiers on parade, and in the distance, safe in her palace, its very own Queen. The Mall is an imposing public space, lined with trees and flagstaffs, its pink tarmac matching the forecourt of Buckingham Palace, which comes into its own for ceremonies like Trooping the Colour. Just beyond, St James's Park is the Palace's front garden, one of London's most beautiful and most popular parks.

At the bottom of the steps on the left, the **Institute of Contemporary Arts (ICA)**
ⓘ *12 Carlton House Terr, T020-7930 3647, 1200-1930 daily, day membership £1.50 Mon-Fri, £2.50 Sat, Sun*, was founded in 1948 by the anarchist Herbert Read. Nash's stately Georgian terrace seems an incongruous setting for the radical film, theatre, dance and art shown here. The gallery played an important role in launching the contemporary British art boom of the 1990s and has a theatre, two cinemas, bookshop and lively bar and café. Further up on the left, in the same building, is a more traditional exhibition space mounting temporary shows of affordable paintings and watercolours and special exhibitions.

St James's Park

ⓘ *T020-7930 1793, dawn-dusk daily.* St James's Park is the finest and most carefully laid out of the Royal parks, once again the work of the indefatigable John Nash in the early 19th century. A wander around reveals surprising but carefully orchestrated vistas at every turn. The lake teems with exotic wildfowl, including the pelicans first given to the park by a Russian ambassador in the 17th century, a tradition that has continued to increase their numbers. They're fed at 1500 daily. The view from the bridge across the lake is justly famous, looking over Duck Island towards Whitehall and Westminster. From April to September deck chairs can be hired (£1 for four hours), guided tours of the park are given by its warden, and brass bands play in the bandstand most afternoons.

★ Buckingham Palace

ⓘ *T020-7766 7300. Daily 0930-1830 Aug-Sep. £12.95, £11 OAPs and students, £6.50 under-17. Tickets bookable in advance, or on the day (subject to availability) at the Ticket Office in Green Park, 0900-1600 late July-late Sep. Free audio tour also available.*

At the opposite end of The Mall from Admiralty Arch stands the **Victoria Memorial**, a white marble monument topped with a winged figure of Victory, now best serving as a vantage point from which to view the **Changing of the Guard** on the forecourt of Buckingham Palace. This occurs at 1130 daily 1 Apr to the end of July; alternate days the rest of the year. In 1993 the Queen opened the doors of the palace for the first time to the paying public for two months to raise money for the restoration of the fire-damaged Windsor Castle. Critics scoffed at the gesture, complaining (with some justification) that tickets were too expensive, queues for entry too long, and the tour itself an anti-climax. That hasn't stopped thousands of people from all over the world lapping up the opportunity every August and September.

A maximum of 250 visitors are admitted every 15 minutes, in a fairly successful attempt to avoid overcrowding (or perhaps for fear of a rebellion) on a one-way route around 14 state rooms, including the Ballroom, shepherded by 200 extra staff in navy blue and red uniforms who are generally friendly and well-informed.

Entering via the Ambassador's entrance on the south side of the Palace, first impressions are of a place not much more opulent than many West End theatres. Emerging into Nash's central quadrangle of beautifully warm sandstone does create an impression though. 'It ain't much but it's home' was one American woman's wry comment, but then it ain't really 'home' at all. The excellent official guidebook emphasizes that this is a working palace. Even if the Royal Standard happens to be flying, indicating that Her Majesty is in residence, don't expect to bump into her.

Through the red and gold **Grand Hall** and up the Grand Staircase, which lives up to its name thanks to some Carrara marble and Samuel Parker's intricate gilt balustrade, the rooms on show are the roped-off stage set for formal state receptions. The Green Drawing Room gives onto the **Throne Room**, where the two red chairs on their podium behind a baroque proscenium arch represent the climax of royalty as pantomime.

Next comes one of the highlights of a visit, the **Picture Gallery**. The Royal Collection is the largest private collection in the world and, while it can also be enjoyed at the refurbished Queen's Gallery, it's well worth seeing the works hanging in this 50-m, toplit room purpose-built by John Nash for George IV. Look out for the likes of Vermeer's *The Music Lesson*, van Dyck's *Mystic Marriage of St Catherine*, Rubens' *The Farm at Laeken* and Rembrandt's *The Ship Builder and his Wife*, along with others by Canaletto, Guercino and Cuyp.

The gallery leads into the **Ballroom**, the first and only opportunity for a sit-down. The Ballroom looks like a very grand village hall, where state investitures take place, but it's followed, after the **State Dining Room**, by the three finest rooms on show, overlooking the back garden. The **Blue Drawing Room** looks like it belongs in a palace, a sumptuous exercise in Georgian decoration, home to the extraordinary 'Table of the Grand Commanders', commissioned by Napoleon to associate himself with Alexander the Great. The **Music Room** has a beautiful parquet floor, domed ceiling and great bow window, while Nash designed a remarkable tent-like ceiling for the **White Drawing Room** above a frieze showing *the Origin and Progress and Pleasure*. Downstairs again, the Marble Hall beneath the Picture Gallery leads into the Bow Room and the garden.

★ The Queen's Gallery
ⓘ *T020-7766 7301. Daily 1000-1730 (last admission 1630). Adult £7.50, £6 concessions, £4 under-17s.*

Next door to the visitors' entrance to the palace, and open year round, three small rooms specially designed for the Golden Jubilee in 2002 display changing selections from the Queen's collection of Old Masters and portraiture, an extraordinary array founded by Charles II. The walls of the Pennethorne and Nash galleries, rich green and red respectively, support formidable paintings, very capably described on the audio tour, hanging above some very precious furniture. The larger Chambers gallery (deep blue walls) usually contains special temporary exhibitions. An interest in their theme or fine art in general will likely prove more important to the enjoyment of a visit here than any curiosity about royalty. Fans can visit the shop, for branded mugs, tea-shirts, potted preserves and tea towels, without paying entrance to the gallery.

Royal Mews
ⓘ *T020-7766 7302. Apr-July, Oct Mon-Thu, Sat, Sun 1100-1600, Aug, Sep daily 1000- 1700 (last admission 45 mins before closing). £5.50, concessions £4.50, under-17s £3.*

Further down Buckingham Palace road towards Victoria are the Royal Mews, the working stables where all the Queen's stately transport is kept, including her gilded State coach, her Windsor grey horses and five Rolls-Royce Phantoms. If anything the array of splendid nags and carriages of state in their setting gives as good and atmospheric insight into the pageant of British sovereignty as the Palace itself.

● Sleeping

Piccadilly & St James's *p114, map 116*
L Athenaeum Hotel and Apartment, 116 Piccadilly, W1V, T020-7499 3464. *Whisky Bar, Windsor Lounge*, haute cuisine in *Bullochs* restaurant. 157 rooms, cheaper at weekend.
L Dukes, St James's Pl, SW1, T020-7491 4840, www.dukeshotel.com. With 89 very comfortable rooms and a health club, this is a very discreet luxury small hotel tucked away in a quiet backstreet with a cosy bar that mixes devastating martinis. Also very popular with families.
L The Stafford, St James's Pl, SW1, T020-7493 0111, www.thestaffordhotel. co.uk. Converted Carriage House apartments. Expensive restaurant with classic English menu, American bar festooned with hats and baseball helmets, a convivial spot popular with Americans.
AL The Ritz, 150 Piccadilly, W1J, T020-7493 8181, www.theritzlondon.com. One of the world's most famous hotels. Parisian-looking building with 133 rooms. Tea in the Palm Court for £32 and dining en plein air on the Terrace overlooking Green Park in summer.

● Eating

Piccadilly & St James's *p114, map 116*
It comes as some surprise that St James's has become one of London's gastronomic hotspots. Two of the several Italian restaurants in St James's, Al Duca and Il Viccolo, are special. The Trocadero, however, can be a nightmare at any time, and it's home to two theme restaurants at the bottom bracket of the mid-range bracket, both for price and character.
ⵑⵑⵑ @venue, 7/9 St James's St, SW1, T020-7321 2111. The huge glass frontage only narrowly denies punters a view of the Conservative party's favourite club, the Carlton. The spacious minimalist design easily soaks up the buzz of bankers young and old wolfing down schooldays' nostalgia food.
ⵑⵑⵑ The Criterion, 224 Piccadilly, on Piccadilly Circus, W1, T020-7930 0488. A grand and beautiful setting for some typically assured Marco Pierre White recipes. The interior of this old dance hall is a symphony in wood and gold, the prices are surprisingly reasonable and the atmosphere quite laid back considering the sumptuousness of the surroundings.
ⵑⵑⵑ Greens, 36 Duke St, SW1, T020-7930 4566. Similar in style to Wiltons, although with perhaps a younger clientele, this has long been one of the favourite haunts of gentlemen when not in their clubs. Serves up fresh fish and traditional British food in a congenial atmosphere.
ⵑⵑⵑ Le Caprice, Arlington House, Arlington St, SW1, T020-7629 2239, tucked away behind the Ritz. More rakish and laid back, and virtually impossible to visit without a month's notice. Looking like a London version of Rick's Bar, it's a kind of hamburger joint as it might have been in the 40s, and has proved enduringly popular with wealthy people who don't want to show off but know what they want. Worth trying to eat here just for the experience alone.
ⵑⵑⵑ L'Oranger, 5 St James's St, SW1, T020- 7839 3774. Does very fine set-price and à la carte southern French food in a much more reserved and authentically French atmosphere, closed Sun.
ⵑⵑⵑ Oak Room, 21 Piccadilly, T020-7851 3140, at the Meridien Hotel. Marco Pierre White's flagship restaurant at this rather staid (there's a dress code) and expensive place.

Shumi, 23 St James's St, SW1, T020-7747 9380. Conspicuous consumers are more likely to be found on St James's St, at joints like this: a swish, minimalist place that's caused quite a stir with an Italian-Japanese menu, but a surprisingly discreet large restaurant nonetheless, as befits its address.

Wiltons, 55 Jermyn St, SW1, T020-7629 9955. Wonderfully old-fashioned English restaurant for clubland old-timers who enjoy the top-quality seafood and game. Dress smart.

The Wolseley,160 Piccadilly, W1, T020-7499 6996. Food critics have raved about this, the most recent venture of the people responsible for the Ivy's success (see page 97), with a booking buzz to match. Smart dining in a magnificent Art Deco former bank building in the shadow of the Ritz. Careful planning is usually required to eat a full meal in the evening here, but the brasserie, coffee and drinks bar is open all day and well into the night for all and sundry.

Al Duca, 4-5 Duke of York St, SW1, T020-7839 3090. A trendy hangout where Milan meets New York in the glass and wood decor and the modern Italian menu.

The Hard Rock Café, 150 Old Park Lane, W1, T020-7629 0382. The mother of all theme restaurants, that long-playing homage to all things rock 'n' roll. It's less expensive and the burgers and Tex-Mex menu superlative. There's always a queue at the door because there's no booking, but it's worth the wait.

Inn the Park, St James's Park, SW1 T020-7451 9999. Occupies a sophisticated piece of modern architecture beside the lake 'in the park'. The modern British sit-down menu comes at a price, although this is certainly a good place for a sunny coffee and sandwich.

Planet Hollywood, Trocadero, T020-72871000, and the **Rainforest Café**, Trocadero, T020-7434 3111. The latter is more expensive, but then it comes complete with laughable animatronic animals and jungle soundtrack (tropical, not musical).

Both might appeal to hardened post-modern ironists or long-suffering parents with demanding children.

Il Viccolo, 3-4 Crown Passage, SW1, T020-7839 3960. More Neapolitan and old-style, and less expensive than Al Duca. A traditional, low-key restaurant tucked away near Pall Mall doing all the reliable staples of Italian country cooking for lunch and dinner, closed weekends.

Chubbie's, 10 Crown Passage, SW1, T020-7839 3513. A busy, popular caff serving up generous portions of English and Italian comfort food for under £5 during the day.

Mokaris, 61 Jermyn St, SW1, T020-7495 5909. The ground floor café here is a particularly good-value old-fashioned Italian restaurant, bar and café.

New Piccadilly, 8 Denman St, just off Shaftesbury Av and a stone's throw from Piccadilly Circus. Another cheap caff, setting foot in here is like visiting the 1950s.

Cafés and sandwich bars

The regular supply of office workers ensures that sandwich bars are two a penny in St James's and Piccadilly.

The ICA Café, The Mall, SW1, T020-7930 8619. £1.50 day membership required, offers imaginative meals, several vegetarian, that are exceptional value. About £4.50-7 each.

Richoux Coffee Co, 171 Piccadilly, T020- 7629 4991. Going upmarket, this does excellent value snacks in an elegant, clean and continental setting bang on Piccadilly.

○ Pubs and bars

Piccadilly & St James's *p114, map 116*
Most of the expensive restaurants (and hotels) listed above also have smart bars that don't insist you buy a meal.

Chequers, 16 Duke St, SW1, T020-7930 4007. Clubby and traditional, a wood-panelled establishment that pumps very good beer.

● *For an explanation of sleeping and eating price codes used in this guide, see inside the*
● *front cover. Other relevant information is found in Essentials, see pages 44-46.*

The ICA Bar, The Mall, SW1, T020-7930 2402. £1.50 day membership required, open Mon until 2300, Tue-Sat until 0100, Sun until 2230. A lively late-night hangout for the arts brigade.

The Red Lion, 2 Duke of York St, T020-7930 2030. A Heritage inn, with well-preserved Victorian mirrors and bar, and a more upmarket clientele than the other *Red Lion*.

The Red Lion, 23 Crown Passage, SW1, T020- 7930 4141. A bog-standard British boozer that seems to have landed in St James's from some remote provincial outpost a long time ago, and the area would be much poorer without its reassuring cosiness, as welcoming to dogs and old men as suits and bohos.

The Three Crowns, Babmaes St. Somewhere between the *Red Lion*s in its olde-worlde style and custom, and does decent enough sausages and mash for about £5.

⊕ Entertainment

Piccadilly & St James's *p114, map 116*
Cinema
ICA Cinema, Nash House, The Mall, SW1, T020-7930 6393 for recorded information, T020-7930 3647 for credit card bookings, www.ica.org.uk. The place to come if you want to see very rare or independent films.

Pepsi IMAX Theatre, Trocadero, W1, T020- 7494 4153. Huge screen but with a smaller audience capacity than the British Film Institute's IMAX in Waterloo (see page 257).

Plaza, 17-25 Lower Regent St, W1, T020- 7930 0144; recorded information and bookings T0870-603 4567.

Spiritual Cinema, in the vestry of St James's Church, T020-7381 0441 for details. An interesting independent club that takes place about once a month.

Virgin Cinema, Trocadero, T020-7434 0032. £7.50, £4.50, Mon and before 1700. Blockbuster-style mainstream cinema.

Music
Classical and opera St James's Church, T020-7381 0441. Puts on regular concerts.

Nightclubs
Café de Paris, 3 Coventry St, T020-7734 7700. A sumptuous venue for a big night out, 80 years old in 2005. Wed is *Disco Cream*, a polysexual House and Garage night popular with tourists. Last Thu of the month is *Kitsch Lounge Riot*, a popular corporate night out. Fri is *Moi*, a night of glam, and Sat always the busiest night. Book for the restaurant to guarantee entry (closed on Thu, Sat), for a meal from £24-£40.

Theatre
Criterion Theatre, Piccadilly Circus, T020-7413 1437. Currently showing the *Reduced Shakespeare Company*'s lamentable abridgements of Shakespeare and American history.

ICA Theatre, the emphasis here is firmly on the avante-garde and experimental productions.

The Jermyn St Theatre, 16b Jermyn St, SW1, T020-7287 2875. A plush little basement theatre that stages a wide variety of fringe shows, from miniature musicals to intimate stagings of the classics. Shows usually start at 1930 and cost about £15. Booking advisable.

Piccadilly Theatre, Denman St, W1, T020-7369 1734. Large and fairly modern playhouse that regularly gives space to successful productions transferred from more remote stages.

○ Shopping

Piccadilly & St James's *p114, map 116*
Heading west on Piccadilly, the shops get progressively more upmarket, especially in the arcades, relying on the custom of tourists as well as city slickers, upper-crust gents and their wives from the Shires. Jermyn Street is world famous for its shirtmakers: every Piccadilly and City gent has his favourite, from **Turnbull and Asser**, **Harvey and Hudson** to **Charles Tyrrhwit**.

Books
Books Etc, 23-26 Piccadilly, W1, T020-7437 7478. With a Starbucks café on the 1st floor.

Hatchard's, 187 Piccadilly, W1, T020-7439 9921. This is likely to be the Piccadilly gent's favourite bookshop, open 0930-1830 Mon-Sat, 1200-1800 Sun, now owned by the same company as Waterstone's, but retaining an independent choice of titles along with its old-fashioned woody and winding layout.

Waterstone's, 203 Piccadilly, T020-7851 2400. This is *the* unmissable bookshop round here. Open 1000-2300 Mon-Sat, 1200-1800 Sun. The largest bookstore in Europe, this conversion of the old Simpson's store is a bright, inspiring place to wander around, with either a café, restaurant or bar to take the book of your choice. On the lower ground floor, the *News Café*, T020-7851 2463, is a good meeting place, or there's the *Studio Lounge*, T020-7851 2433, on the fifth floor with its great views. Regular literary and celebrity events are also held here.

Clothes and accessories

Cordings, 19 Piccadilly. Classic old English tailors, friendly, reliable and remarkably affordable.

John Lobb, 9 St James's St, SW1, T020-7930 3664. Bespoke bootmakers extraordinaire, where the cobblers can be seen at work.

James Lock & Co, 6 St James's St, SW1, T020-7930 8874. Hatmakers and milliners to Royalty. A wall cabinet displays the exact shape of various famous heads, including Chaplin's and Edward VII's.

Swaine Adeney, 54 St James's St, W1, T020- 7409 7277. Saddlers to the horsey set and have also taken over the world-famous Brigg umbrellas, keeping the rain off the rich and famous since 1750. A silk brolly with a crocodile skin handle will set you back £650, or £130 for something more practical.

Food and drink

Berry Brothers and Rudd, 3 St James's St, SW1, T020-7396 9600. An old-fashioned fine wine and spirit merchant with a 19th-century interior.

Fortnum and Mason, 181 Piccadilly, W1, T020-7734 8040, www.fortnumandmason.co.uk. Most people can't resist popping in, even just for a glimpse of its theatrical way with shelf-stacking. Most famous for its own-label tea and fabulous food hall, it also sells traditional menswear, as well as china and cookware, and antiques on the 4th floor. Open 1000-1830 Mon-Sat. On the same floor, *St James's Restaurant* is the place for full English teas while the *Patio* restaurant on the mezzanine at the back of the ground floor has a less formal atmosphere and a champagne and oyster bar.

Paxton Whitfield, 93 Jermyn St, W1, T020-7930 0259. One of the city's finest cheesemongers.

Miscellaneous

D R Harris and Co, 29 St James's St, SW1, T020-7930 3915. Have long been pharmacists to Royalty.

Floris, 89 Jermyn St, SW1, T020-7930 2885. An exclusive perfumier.

Music

HMV, Trocadero, W1, T020-7439 0447. A large branch, open until 2400 Mon-Sat, 1100-1800 Sun.

Tower Records, 1 Piccadilly Circus, T020- 7439 2500. The west side of Piccadilly Circus is dominated by this massive establishment, open until 2400 Mon-Sat, 1200-1800 Sun, in the Norman Shaw building that once housed Swan and Edgar's. Four floors packed with an independent selection of all the latest CDs, DVDs, videos and a few Lps.

Oxford Street and Marble Arch

Oxford Street brings out the worst in everyone. London's longest, ugliest and most popular shopping street always gets people going: snobs scoff at its shoddy mass-market consumerism; fashion victims complain about its lack of style; day-tripping bargain hunters moan about the heaving crowds; and office workers push briskly along it without looking where they're going. Everyone objects to the pickpockets, bagsnatchers and con-artists busily dodging the CCTV. But still they keep on coming, in impossible numbers at least three times a year, for the winter and summer sales and for the Christmas season, revelling in the capital's glorified High Street.

It's extraordinary what a single-minded thoroughfare it can be, the one place in town that makes shoppers of us all because there's simply not much else to do. West of Oxford Circus, the great department stores look south to Mayfair, lined up on the north side of the street guarding their heavily scented entrance halls. East of Oxford Circus, inspired by Soho, the fly-by-night bargain-basement warehouses noisily compete in their pricing and the volume of their pumping in-store bass. There's nothing for it but to go with the flow, stay cool, hang loose, and keep an eye on your bag. ▶▶ *For Sleeping, Eating and other listings see pages 131-134.*

History

Oxford Street lies along the route of a Roman Road that linked Hampshire with Suffolk, and, along with Piccadilly, it became one of the main roads out of the city. The River Tyburn flowed south across it and fields lined its way. From the 14th century until the 18th the road remained undeveloped, but throughout this time it was also the last journey for condemned prisoners. They would be drawn in a cart

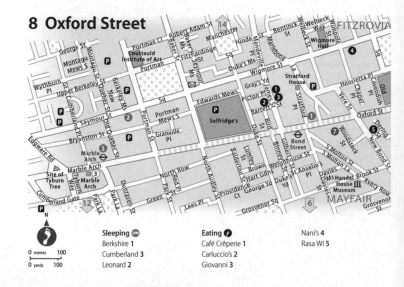

8 Oxford Street

Sleeping ⬤	Eating ❼	Nani's **4**
Berkshire **1**	Café Crêperie **1**	Rasa WI **5**
Cumberland **3**	Carluccio's **2**	
Leonard **2**	Giovanni **3**	

0 metres 100
0 yards 100

from Newgate Prison in the City, past St Giles's, where they would be offered the 'cup of charity', their last drink of ale, and on to the Tyburn Tree, a triangular gallows, near present-day Marble Arch, capable of taking 21 people at a time. The rope was attached and the cart drawn away, leaving the victim dangling – relatives would often run to pull at the body to try to ensure a swifter and less painful death.

Henry VIII legalized the sale of bodies (particularly murderers) to anatomists for dissection. Many were bought, but sales often ended in fights and riots over ownership of the body. Relatives naturally wanted a decent burial for their loved one, or to try resuscitation (it occasionally worked), while body-snatchers lurked in the graveyard further west in Bayswater (Laurence Sterne's body was snatched from here for dissection in 1768). Many people clamoured to touch the body, since it was believed to hold special powers. All this disorder did little for the decorum of the area, and after the growth of building along the street, the gallows was removed to Newgate in 1783.

The Earl of Oxford had bought land north of the Street, thereby lending his name to what was popularly known as Tyburn Way, and in the 1760s building began in earnest. It became a place of entertainment. Tiger-baiting could be seen in Mr Broughton's amphitheatre, while the Pantheon (finally replaced by Marks & Spencer in 1937) supported a magnificent rotunda and hosted masquerades, fêtes and concerts.

In 1851 the Marble Arch, which had briefly served as an entrance to Buckingham Palace, was moved to its current site, although it wasn't islanded until 1908. It was only towards the end of the 19th century, however, that Oxford Street became such a shopping mecca. DH Evans and John Lewis (with smaller outlets than at present) moved here in the 1860s and 70s, but it was the Wisconsin merchant, Harry Gordon Selfridge, who demonstrated what a department store could be (John Logie Baird gave the first public demonstration of television here). The huge block of Selfridges was begun in 1907, with Ionic columns lining its façade, (the original plans had included a massive tower), and the crowds have been flocking here ever since.

West End Oxford St & Marble Arch

Pubs & bars 🍸
Bradley's Spanish **6**
Woodstock **7**

Entertainment ♫
100 Club **1**
Costa Dorada Spanish Restaurant **2**
Odeon Marble Arch **3**

See London at a glance, p19-24, for related maps.

Sights
 ⊖ Tottenham Court Rd, Oxford Circus, Bond St, Marble Arch. ⊖ See p460.

'Don't stop, shop!' could be Oxford Street's strapline, but then there's not much worth seeing here anyway. Emerging from Tottenham Court Road tube station at the east end of the street brings you out beneath the unmistakeable honeycomb of the **Centrepoint** tower. From here Tottenham Court Road heads busily north, Charing Cross Road twists south and New Oxford Street runs east. Walking west, you have to squeeze along the street's busiest, scruffiest and most second-rate stretch. **Hanway Street**, just up on the right, a curious little alley of private drinking clubs, second-hand record shops and Spanish bars and restaurants, doubles back to Tottenham Court Road.

Apart from a few good shops and the Plaza Shopping Centre (best avoided, along with all the £1-a-slice pizza merchants), there's nothing remarkable until Oxford Circus. Any of the roads off left lead into Soho; those to the right into Fitzrovia. **Regent Hall** ① 275 Oxford St, W1, T020-7629 2766, is one of the few remaining buildings from when the street was built. It's now a West End church for the Salvation Army, thoroughly cleaned up and refurbished, with a bookshop and non-smoking café doing good value (for the area) snacks and sandwiches (open Mon-Sat 0930-1630).

Oxford Circus is a horrendously busy crossroads, although pedestrianized Argyll Street, off to the left just before it, packed with pubs, snack bars and restaurants, is a good shortcut into West Soho avoiding Regent Street. Beyond Oxford Circus, Oxford Street begins to acquire the dignity the capital's High Street deserves.

Further on to the left, **Dering Street** is sealed off by a pedestrianized area boasting a rare public convenience. This little street has also long been an exciting enclave for some of the city's leading dealers in contemporary art. Since the mid-70s **Anthony d'Offay** ① 9 Dering St, T020-7499 4100, has been seeking out rising stars as well as dealing in established names; **Anthony Reynolds** ① 5 Dering St, W1, T020-7491 0621, has been dealing in international contemporary art in all media here for almost as long, while **Annely Juda** ① 23 Dering St, T020-7629 7578, deals mainly in abstract early 20th-century art and a few upcoming artists. **Anne Faggionato** ① 4th Floor, 20 Dering St, T020-7493 6732, is well established, while **The Timothy Taylor Gallery** ① 23 and 24 Dering St, T020-7409 3344, has moved in from Bruton Place and developed a reputation for having its finger on the pulse. There's also a pleasantly ordinary pub, **The Duke of York**. The presence of these artworld impresarios is perhaps explained by their proximity to the silly money of New Bond Street, the next street off to the left.

Back on Oxford Street, a short way up on the right-hand side, opposite Bond Street tube, is Stratford Place. The grand classical building at the end is **Stratford House**, built in the 1770s, and once the home of the Earl of Derby, Secretary of War for the last years of the First World War. It is now the Oriental Club, a private club founded by members of the East India Company in the mid-19th century.

Apart from the great early 20th-century Ionic block of **Selfridges**, a sight in itself, the last sight Oxford Street has to offer is **Marble Arch**. Designed by John Nash in 1827 to stand in front of Buckingham Palace, it wasn't quite grand enough and was moved to this site 25 years later and eventually stranded in the middle of a hectic roundabout. Only senior Royals and the King's Troop Royal Horse Artillery are allowed through the arch. Nearby, on Sundays, **Speaker's Corner** has been providing a spot for any budding orator to let off steam since the middle of the 19th century. Nowadays the soap boxes are dominated by religious extremists and speakers with more passion than eloquence, but some draw surprisingly large and attentive crowds.

⋮ Shop till you drop

The Sales are a well-established retail festival every January and July and Oxford Street is guaranteed to be even more crazy during these months. In the weeks running up to Christmas, shopping hours are extended and the street puts on a high-tech light show. A celebrity switches on the lights sometime in the third week of November and brings traffic to a standstill. The crowds are often too busy to notice as they're shepherded across the major junctions by police vans with loudhailers. Retail therapy turned retail kill or cure.

● Sleeping

Oxford St & Marble Arch *p128, map p128*
L The Berkshire, 350 Oxford St, W1, T020-7629 7474, www.radissonedwardian.com. With 147 rooms recently done up in a contemporary style, the prime location of the Berkshire makes it popular with tourists as well as corporate clients. At the lower end of this price bracket.
L The Leonard, 15 Seymour St, W1, T020-7935 2010, www.theleonard.com. Only 44 rooms, and an intimate antiquey atmosphere, this is a very conveniently situated classic boutique hotel. 24-hr room service and offers that include handmade fudge complete an experience that rarely disappoints.
A Cumberland, Marble Arch, W1, T0870-400 8701. Built around Marble Arch tube, with a bustling shopping centre atmosphere at reception, this huge place with hundreds of clean, well-appointed contemporary rooms attracts all sorts.

❼ Eating

Oxford St & Marble Arch *p128, map p128*
Oxford St is not about sitting down and eating, unless you count the department store restaurants.
♩♩ **Rasa W1**, 6 Dering St, W1, T020-7629 1346. The only place within an easy distance that can be recommended. An excellent Keralan restaurant, it's not particularly cheap (£19.50 set vegetarian lunch), but some truly superb south Indian vegetarian and meat dishes are served up in a strictly non-smoking and cheerful environment.

Cafés and sandwich bars
Café Crêperie, 26 James St. Has outside tables and is reasonable value.
Carluccio's, 3-5 Barrett St, St Christopher's Pl, W1. A swanky branch of the exceptionally stylish Italian deli and café. Expensive but worth it.
Giovanni, 18 James St, W1, T020-7493 7362. Open daily 1200-2330 for cheap, filling Italian food, and also has tables outside.
Nani's, 12 Winsley St, W1, T020-7255 1928. Open Mon-Fri 0530-1730, Sat 0800-1700. A long-established, bright and cheerful Italian sandwich bar and snack stop that opens exceptionally early in the morning and represents good value for the area. There are others at 36 Albemarle St, W1, T020-7493 0821, and 8-10 Wigmore St, W1, T020-7580 7936, open the same hours.

❶ Pubs and bars

Oxford St & Marble Arch *p128, map p128*
Again, Oxford St doesn't really do pubs and bars. See also bars in Bloomsbury and Fitzrovia, page 204.
Bradley's Spanish Bar, 42-44 Hanway St, W1, T020-7636 0359. Open Mon-Sat until 2300, tapas until 2200, it is a tiny place, a media boho favourite, with a basement dive bar and excellent jukebox on the ground floor.
The Woodstock, 11 Woodstock St, W1, T020-7408 2008, just off Oxford St. An ordinary pub where you can often find a seat, even at lunchtimes. The atmosphere is pleasant and food perfectly reasonable.

West End Oxford St & Marble Arch

● *For an explanation of sleeping and eating price codes used in this guide, see inside the*
● *front cover. Other relevant information is found in Essentials, see pages 44-46.*

☺ Entertainment

Oxford St & Marble Arch *p128, map p128*
Cinema
Odeon Marble Arch, 10 Edgware Rd, W2,
National Film Line, T0870-5050 007. 5
screens, £5 before 1700, £7.50 after.

Music

100 Club, 100 Oxford St, W1, T020-7636
0933, www.the100club.co.uk. Open
Mon-Thu 1930-2400, Fri 1200-1500,
2030-0200, Sat 1930-100, Sun 1930-2330.
Famous for its nights of punk in the 70s and
before that for hosting the Stones, a
longplayer of a place that now majors in jazz
and blues, with the occasional indie rock
band. Unbeatable atmosphere though,
depending on the band, and best to arrive
early to get a good view of the stage.
Admission £7-10. Free lunchtime jazz
1130-1500 in summer. It is another name
with a healthy record in the music annals,
having staged the birth of British punk in
1976. Things have slightly changed since
then, however, and the club is now more the
home of *Take 5* than *God Save the Queen* as
traditional jazz rules the roost. The odd
obscure indie act does rear its head every
now and then, but this is largely a testament
to a decent venue which doesn't take itself
too seriously.
Costa Dorada Spanish Restaurant, 47-55
Hanway St, W1, T020-7631 5117. A very
lively, atmospheric venue for live Spanish
music and flamenco displays. It's open
Mon-Sat 1730-0300 with dance
performances at 2200 and 0030 Thu, Fri, Sat.
Regent Hall, 275 Oxford St, T020-7629 2766.
Free Fri lunchtime concerts, and a 550-seater
auditorium hired out to various musical
groups in the evenings.

◐ Shopping

Oxford St & Marble Arch *p128, map p128*
A shopping expedition is really the only
reason to spend much time on Oxford St.
Even so, apart from the department stores,
there are surprisingly few shops with any
distinctive character. Many of them are
familiar High Street chainstore branches, and
not necessarily the best value branches at

that, although here size is everything. With
the department stores, it can be worth
getting a store card for certain discounts,
and privileges during the sales. Identification
and proof of address are required but the
benefits are usually immediate. For ease of
reference, this section lists some of the more
special or interesting shops as you head west
from Tottenham Court Rd towards Marble
Arch. Addresses with even numbers are on
the right, odd numbers on the left. Late
closing for most of Oxford St is on Thu,
usually at 2000. Otherwise they tend to shut
up shop between 1800 and 1900

Tottenham Court Rd to Oxford Circus
Borders Books Music and Café, 203-207
Oxford St, W1, T020-7292 1600. London's
first book megastore, open Mon-Sat until
2300 and on Sun until 1800, holds a huge
stock of books and music, and there's a
Starbucks on the 2nd floor with big windows
overlooking the street. The regular special
events at this branch tend towards the more
middlebrow celebrity appearances, as
opposed to the literary occasions at the
Charing Cross Rd branch, which doesn't
stock music.
HMV, 150 Oxford St, W1, T020-7631 3423.
The first of the two HMV music megastores
on the street, marginally more hip than
Virgin and easier to find your way around.
Jigsaw, 9 Argyll St, W1, T020-7437 5750. Do
staple everyday wear for men and women
about town, and their sales are always
slightly later than everyone else's.
Mash, 73 Oxford St, W1, T020-7434 9609.
Worth a look for its polysexual streetwear.
Muji, 187 Oxford St, W1, T020-7437 7503.
Does a full range of excellent functionally
designed Japanese lifestyle products, from
furnishings and household goods, including
kitchenware, through health and beauty to
stationery.
Jane Norman, 262 Oxford St, W1, T020-7499
7454. One of three branches on the street of
the UK chain specializing in zippy clothes for
younger women.
Tesco Metro, 311 Oxford St. Open 24 hrs,
until 2200 Sat, is a very useful central London
branch of the UK supermarket. Grab a picnic
and head for the park before you part with
any more cash, or carry on down the street
to explore the department stores.

Top Shop/Top Man, Oxford Circus. One of the largest high-street fashion stores in the world.

Virgin Megastore,14-16 Oxford St, W1, T020- 7631 1234. Closes at 2100 most nights and sets the tone for this stretch of the street with 4 loud floors selling every multimedia music format you could wish for, as well as mini-scooters, merchandizing and computer games.

Waterstone's, 19-23 Oxford St, W1, T020-7434 9759. A small branch focusing on best-selling fiction and non-fiction.

From Oxford Circus to Bond Street

Bond's of Oxford Street, 330 Oxford St, W1, T020-7493 1025. From a different century entirely, a resolutely old-fashioned store packed with every possible accessory for smokers of pipes and cigarettes.

Niketown London, Oxford Circus, W1, T020-7612 0800. Open Mon-Wed 1000-1900, Thu 1000-2100, Fri and Sat 1000-2000, Sun 1200-1800. Landed on Oxford Circus in Jul 1999, a high-tech temple to all things Nike, the only one in the UK. In the 'launch area', a portentous inscription reads: 'To all athletes and the dreams they chase, we dedicate Niketown London'.

Waterstone's, 28 Margaret St, W1, T020-7580 2812, not far off Oxford St to the north. Another small branch of the bookshop chain, specializing in books about Christianity.

This is where the department stores begin, *John Lewis* being one of the most straightforward and dependable outfits in the country.

Debenhams, 334-348 Oxford St, W1, T020-7408 4444. Nothing special but very reliable, especially for designer bargains. The restaurant is very reasonably priced but has all the atmosphere of a motorway service station canteen. At the end of their main sales, the Blue Cross sales reduce prices even further.

House of Fraser, 318 Oxford St, T020-7529 4700, formely DH Evans. Relatively recently refurbished and now catering for youngsters as well as old-timers.

John Lewis, 278-306 Oxford St, W1, T020-7629 7711. The favourite of the middle

classes, has long been proudly claiming to be 'never knowingly undersold': if you find something here on sale for less elsewhere, they'll refund the difference. What really marks out the store though is the stake that all the staff have in the company. Service here is always polite, knowledgeable and as helpful as possible when making choices between their solid array of consumer durables.

Above and around Bond St tube station are:
HMV, T020-7514 3600, opposite the tube. Another branch of this music megastore.

West One Shopping Centre, 383 Oxford St, W1, T020-7629 3929. A bustling home for the likes of *Tie Rack*, the *Sock Shop*, *Holland and Barrett* the wholefood shop, a *Prêt* sandwich bar, and *Lego Kidswear*.

Further up on the right, James St heads into Marylebone, lined with cafés and outside seating, including a **Stockpot** and a **Café Rouge**. Just off here is St Christopher's Place, a quaint little bit of New Bond St that has slipped north of Oxford St and made itself marginally more accessible. It has a slightly precious, Parisian air, as do some of the shops, but it's a pleasant place to stop for a coffee.

Bond Street to Marble Arch

Bliss Chemist, 5-6 Marble Arch W1, T020-7723 6116. A late-night pharmacy open until midnight throughout the year.

The Body Shop, 374 Oxford St, W1, T020-7409 7868, on the corner of Duke St. The largest and busiest branch in the world of the successful cruelty-free cosmetics and bodycare company.

Books etc, 421 Oxford St, T020-7495 5850, opposite Selfridges. Another branch of this shop.

The Clarks Shop, 476 Oxford St, W1, T020-7629 9609. Almost as venerable as *M&S*, a chain that has been keeping British children well shod since 1825.

Jane and Dada, 20 St Christopher's Pl, W1, T020-7486 0977. Everyday designerwear for women aged 30 plus.

Marks & Spencer, 458 Oxford St, W1, T020- 7935 7954. The flagship store of the recently beleaguered chain. Declining profits have led to some bizarre advertising initiatives and, more damagingly, the abandonment of some of their traditional suppliers, but M&S still sets a nationwide benchmark for just-about-affordable high-quality clothes and first-rate food.

Mulberry, 11 Gees Ct, W1, T020-7493 2546. High quality handbags and accessories.

Selfridges and Co, 400 Oxford St, W1, T020-7629 1234. Across the way is the Queen of Oxford St's department stores. Nothing like as pretentious as Harrods, Selfridges does just as good a job of creating a more leisurely world behind its heavy glass doors, and its customer services are legendary. On the ground floor, beyond the inevitable perfumery (in pole position because it makes more money per square foot than any other department), you'll find fashion accessories, wines and spirits, jewellery, toiletries, a cigar shop and menswear. At the back, beyond the *Brass Rail Café* specializing in salt beef, and the fully licensed *Balcony Wine Bar*, the food hall is an extraordinary gastrodome of fresh and potted delicacies, including an oyster bar. A pint of Guinness and a dozen Irish oysters will set you back about £20. The 1st floor is given over to fashionable menswear concessions. The 2nd and 3rd floors are for womenswear. Interiors are on the 4th floor and Beauty on the 5th. All in all, even if you might not want to fulfil its founder's boast that you can 'spend the day at the Selfridges', there's more than enough here for an entertaining few hours.

Under Two Flags, 4 St Christopher's Pl, W1, T020-7935 6934. Collectable model toy soldiers (closed Sun, Mon).

▲ Activities and tours

Oxford St & Marble Arch *p128, map p128*
Centrepoint Snooker, beneath Centrepoint tower in Tottenham Court Rd tube station subway, T020-7240 6886. Open 1100-0600 daily. 7 snooker tables, 5 American pool and 6 English pool tables. £3 entrance; snooker tables £5 per hr, pool tables £7 per hr, first come first served. Bar and food.

❶ Directory

Oxford St & Marble Arch *p128, map p128*
Useful addresses Oxford Street Association, T020-7629 2738. Will give details of trading hours, Christmas lights, parking, and try to answer any other enquiries about the area.

Central London

Footprint features

Westminster and Whitehall

The seat of central government power in the Kingdom is one of the few parts of London that achieves any architectural cohesion. Parliament Square, especially viewed from the Broad Sanctuary by Westminster Abbey, manages to present a stirring picture of common purpose with its array of skybound Gothic towers. And Whitehall too makes a decent stab at Venetian grandeur as it connects Parliament with Trafalgar Square. Although the borough of Westminster encompasses most of the West End, to Brits the name really only refers to this relatively small area in the immediate vicinity of the Houses of Parliament. And even though there are easily enough places to see and things to do around here to occupy at least a whole day, the impression is very much one of being kept at arm's length.

Apart from the obvious security considerations, that's understandable. After all, the battalions of politicos and civil servants, generally prematurely bald young men and smart foxy chicks, who scurry about at lunchtime and fill the area's pubs on the dot of five, have been running the country all day. Nightlife is non-existent. In the evenings the place feels like a quiet provincial town. ▶▶ *For Sleeping, Eating and other listings see pages 146-146.*

History

As the Tyburn flowed into the Thames, it forked to create an island of marshland. It was here on Thorney Island (Isle of Brambles) that in the eighth century King Offa founded a Benedictine monastery, the West Minster, precursor to the Abbey that now graces the site. The Danes subsequently sacked the area, and it wasn't until Edward the Confessor's reign in the 11th century that the site was re-established. While the new church was being built, Edward moved his royal residence from the City to the banks of the river here in Westminster in order to supervise its construction. This move proved momentous for the political geography of London – it signalled the separation of the seat of royal power from the commercial centre of the land. The Abbey was consecrated at Christmas 1065, a few weeks before Edward's death. Nothing remains of the palace that Edward built, but Westminster Hall, which still displays its 14th-century hammerbeam roof, was part of William II's further development of the palace.

By 1265 the site further north up Whitehall was occupied by lands belonging to the Abbey of Abingdon to the west, with York Place, the Archbishop of York's London residence, sweeping down to the river to the east. The Tudors and Stuarts cemented the grandeur and power-base of the area. Wolsey developed York Place into a palace fit for a king (his wine cellar still exists under the modern Ministry of Defence) and following the fall of the cardinal in 1530 Henry VIII took over the residence. He developed the newly named Whitehall Palace further, building extensively the other side of Whitehall alongside what became St James's Park. A tilt-yard (now Horse Guards), cockpit, bowling green and tennis courts were linked to Wolsey's palace by the magnificent Holbein and King's Gate that spanned Whitehall. James I further developed the site, describing Elizabeth I's palace as an "old, rotten, slight-builded shed". All that remains of Inigo Jones's palatial vision, (and much of it was never more than a vision) is the Palladian Banqueting House, immortalized as the site of Charles I's execution.

Meanwhile, the area was swiftly becoming one of the busiest places beyond the City walls. There were respectable lodgings available for the country gentlemen who came to attend court, and Flemish milliners and stalls selling hot pies, ale and porpoise tongues lined Whitehall. Westminster Hall provided cover for an odd mix of

★ Don't miss Central London…

1. **Cabinet War Rooms** Pay your respects at the memorial to Sir Winston Churchill in the nave of Westminster Abbey before dropping into his workplace nearby, page 144.
2. **Victoria and Albert Museum** Wander around the museum in the certain knowledge that you'll see a number of extraordinary things, page 162.
3. **Bloomsbury** Browse through the bookshops after seeing and believing the world's ancient culture in the British Museum, page 192.
4. **Holborn and Clerkenwell** Absorb the architectural detail and wonder of Sir John Soane's house in Holborn before rolling into Clerkenwell to dine and dance the night away, page 206.
5. **The City** Cross the Millennium Bridge to pay a visit to St Paul's Cathedral before freely exploring the City and Museum of London, page 218.
6. **Bankside and Bermondsey** Pig out at Borough Market foodstalls and then feel remorseful at the museums of fashion or tea and coffee, page 236.
7. **South Bank** Promenade from Westminster to Tower Bridge taking your pick of the riverside's vital cavalcade of arts and entertainment, page 249.
8. **Imperial War Museum** Stomach the museum and its Holocaust exhibition in Lambeth, pausing for thought and remembrance, page 255.

Central Westminster & Whitehall

law courts (the King's Bench) on one side, and bookstalls on the other (William Caxton had set up the first printing press in a shop in the Abbey precincts). Nevertheless, crime and poverty were rife. Thieves and pickpockets roamed the area, attracted by the wealthy residents and visitors and the escape route presented by the Sanctuary tower just north of the Abbey. Slums sat within a stone's throw of the palace – Parliament Square was particularly squalid, and, due to the area's marshy origins, the people were frequently visited by plagues.

The growth of St James's as another royal residence merely reinforced Whitehall's role as the centre of political life. William III, newly arrived from Holland, chose Kensington over Whitehall as his residence on account of his asthma; Westminster, however, remained the administrative centre of Government, and under the Hanoverians residential buildings sprang up to house the growing force of bureaucrats. Queen Anne's Gate (c 1704), (Lord) North Street, Smith Square and the cul-de-sac Downing Street remain to this day, the latter built on the site of the Axe, a brewhouse that once belonged to the Abbey of Abingdon. In 1834 the whole landscape changed with a fire that razed the hotchpotch Palace of Westminster to the ground. The colossal Gothic edifice that sits there now was Charles Barry's creation, although the Commons was burned down in 1941 when hit by a German bomb (it was reconstructed).

As Britain's Empire spread so did the organs of state around Whitehall. The Treasury, Foreign Office, and War Office are all Victorian creations, the Ministry of Defence and Portcullis House are much more recent (see also architecture, page 416). The Downing Street façade, while retaining its simple street entrance, hides a network of 160 rooms linked to the Cabinet Office that looks onto Whitehall. Indeed, Westminster and Whitehall hide a series of subterranean offices built in anticipation of attack, most notably the 'Hole in the Ground' under Storey's Gate, several acres of offices protected by 17 ft of concrete. Political tentacles engulf the area – the Methodist's Central Hall hosted the inaugural meeting of the United Nations, while many of the area's residences, restaurants and pubs are permanently linked up to Parliament so MPs can mix business with pleasure without missing crucial votes.

Sights ● *Charing Cross, Embankment, St James's, Westminster.* ● *See p460.*

Westminster tube station brings you up at the foot of **Big Ben** on the western end of **Westminster Bridge**. The first bridge here was opened in 1750 and anyone caught attempting to graffiti it faced the death penalty. Wordsworth stood on it at dawn and later recollected his emotions in tranquility: 'Ne'er saw I, never felt, a calm so deep!'

Not much chance of that, even at dawn, on the cast-iron bridge of today that replaced Wordsworth's in 1862, but the view's still not bad at all, now including the full circle of the London Eye. The bridge's pavements are always busy, in winter with the hotly contested pitches for roast chestnut and caramelized peanut sellers; in summer with stalls touting for the trade from the endless stream of tourists. First thing in the morning though (or shortly after lunch during the week once the coach parties have headed off to St Paul's) is the best time to visit Westminster's main attraction, the Abbey.

★ Westminster Abbey

① *To20-7222 5152, information and tours To20-7654 4834, www.westminster-abbey.org. Mon-Fri 0930-1645 (last admission 1545), Sat 0930-1445 (last admission 1345). On Sun entry is for services only: 0800 (Holy Communion), 1000 (Matins), 1115 (Sung Eucharist), 1500 (Evensong), 1745 (Organ recital), 1830 (Evening service). Weekday services: 0730 (Matins, 0900 Sat and bank holidays), 0800 (Holy Communion), 1230 (Holy Communion, except Sat), 1700 (Evensong, 1500 Sat). Adult £8, £6 concessions, under-11s free with adult. Chapter House, Pyx Chamber and Museum: summer 1000-1700 daily. Main Cloister open same hours as Abbey. Free (from Dean's Yard). Little Cloister and College Garden: Tue-Thu summer 1030-1800, winter 1030-1600. Free.*

A surprisingly small church for one of such enormous significance in the Anglican faith and British state (especially for its monarchy), Westminster Abbey's charm lies in its age. It has also long been a well-managed tourist trap. That said, despite the milling crowds clutching the fairly patronizing audio guide and bossy 'free' floorplans, it remains a sacred building and anyone wishing to pray here (or join in a service on Sunday when the Abbey is closed to tourists) is allowed to do so free of charge. And there's plenty worth seeing for the money.

One of the better approaches to the exterior is from St James's Park tube, a short walk down Broadway and Tothill, to the west front with its twin Hawksmoor towers of 1745, the most recent additions to what from here is clearly a very tall and thin old building. Walking clockwise round to the visitors' entrance, it's easy to understand how the Abbey's architecture could be described as 'the perfect governmental report on French Gothic': it does look like a tight and proper place, lacking the majesty of some other cathedrals in England or France and all the more appropriate for that, especially in comparison to the flamboyant neo-Gothic of the Houses of Parliament across the way.

Once inside it's another story: the length and especially the height (over 100ft) of the nave are awe-inspiring. On the tourist route round from the north entrance, this impressive view is left until the end, the tour beginning in the oldest part of the main building, the central crossing built in the 13th century. Visitors then turn sharp left to skirt the sanctuary of the High Altar (where sovereigns are crowned) and the founder St Edward the Confessor's Chapel, past the tombs of Edward I and Henry III, to look at the **Coronation Chair**. Made to order for the 'Hammer of the Scots', Edward I, and used to crown every English monarch except three since 1308, the old wooden chair's most

9 Westminster & Whitehall

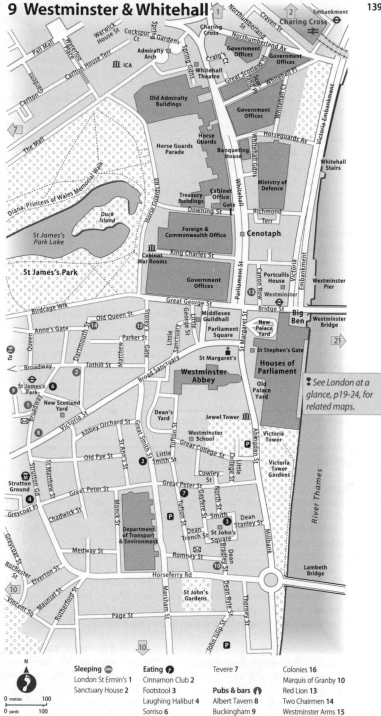

Charing Cross
Embankment
Northumberland St
Craven St
Charing Cross
Warwick House St
Cockspur Ct
Spring Gardens
Pall Mall
Wareing Place
Cockspur St
Carlton House Terr
Government Offices
Northumberland Av
Government Offices
Admiralty Arch
Craig's Ct
ICA
Whitehall Theatre
Great Scotland Yard
Scotland Pl
Whitehall Pl
Whitehall Ct
Old Admiralty Buildings
Government Offices
Carlton Gardens
Carlton
The Mall
Horse Guards Parade
Horse Guards
Horseguards Av
Banqueting House
Whitehall Gdns
Victoria Embankment
Whitehall Stairs
Diana, Princess of Wales Memorial Walk
Ministry of Defence
Horse Guards Rd
Treasury Buildings
Cabinet Office Gate
Downing St
Whitehall
Richmond Terr
Duck Island
St James's Park Lake
Foreign & Commonwealth Office
Cenotaph
Cabinet War Rooms
King Charles St
St James's Park
Government Offices
Parliament St
Cannon Row
Portcullis House
Victoria Embankment
Westminster Pier
Birdcage Wlk
Great George St
Westminster
Westminster Pier
Old Queen St
Middlesex Guildhall
Bridge St
Big Ben
Westminster Bridge
Anne's Gate
Storey's Gate
George St
New Palace Yard
Dartmouth St
Parker St
St Margaret's
Little Sanctuary
St Stephen's Gate
Queen Anne's Gate
Matthew Parker St
Broad Sanctuary
Westminster Abbey
Houses of Parliament
Broadway
Tothill St
Old Palace Yard
To 16
St James's Park
New Scotland Yard
Dean's Yard
Jewel Tower
Victoria Tower
See London at a glance, p19-24, for related maps.
Victoria St
Abbey Orchard St
St Ann's St
Great College St
Westminster School
Victoria Tower
Victoria Tower Gardens
Old Pye St
Great Smith St
Little Smith St
Cowley St
Little College St
North St
Strutton Ground
St Matthew St
Great Peter St
Tufton St
Great Peter St
Gayfere St
River Thames
Greycoat Pl
Strutton Gd
Chadwick St
Monck St
Dean Trench St
St John's Square
Smith Square
Dean Stanley St
Medway St
Department of Transport & Environment
Romney St
Dean Bradley St
Millbank
Greycoat St
Rochester St
Elverton St
Horseferry Rd
Lambeth Bridge
Vincent Sq
Maunsel St
Rutherford St
Marsham St
St John's Gardens
Dean Ryle St
Thorney St
Page St
John Islip St

N

0 metres 100
0 yards 100

Sleeping
London St Ermin's 1
Sanctuary House 2

Eating
Cinnamon Club 2
Footstool 3
Laughing Halibut 4
Sorriso 6

Tevere 7

Pubs & bars
Albert Tavern 8
Buckingham 9

Colonies 16
Marquis of Granby 10
Red Lion 13
Two Chairmen 14
Westminster Arms 15

obvious feature now is the empty space below the seat purpose-built for the Stone of Destiny. The sandstone coronation block of Scottish monarchs since the ninth century is now back home in its native land and on display in Edinburgh Castle. Beyond is **Henry VII's Chapel** (or Lady Chapel), dating from the early 16th century, an extraordinary medieval pageant of flags, stalls, and tombs below a wonderful vaulted stone roof of cobweb intricacy. On either side of this chapel are the hushed tombs of Elizabeth I and Mary Queen of Scots.

Heading back towards the Crossing, the tour passes **Poet's Corner**, decorated with sculptures and monuments to Shakespeare, Chaucer and other poets and actors, as well as scientists, architects, historians and other worthies. A memorial here is the highest posthumous honour that Queen and country can bestow.

Then it's out into the fresh air of the Cloisters of the 11th-century monastery, past the Chapter House, Pyx Chamber and Museum. These three less busy rooms are well worth a look. In the octagonal **Chapter House**, where the House of Commons sat from the mid-14th-16th centuries, the medieval wall paintings of the Last Judgement and the Apocalypse, and remarkable tiled floor, decorated with griffins, lions, and mythical beasts, have a faded splendour. The dark little **Pyx Chamber** was the monastery's strongroom and is the oldest building on site. And the **museum** in the monks' common room contains some weird royal funeral effigies from the Middle Ages as well as a more recent and peculiar effigy of the Duke of Buckingham. He died of tuberculosis in Rome in 1735 aged 19 and his waxwork image lies dressed up in his peer's robes, wearing his own wig, in a glass case scratched with 19th-century graffiti.

From Tuesday to Thursday, the **Little Cloisters** and **College Garden** are also well worth seeking out. The Little Cloisters are reached through an old whitewashed stone tunnel off the main cloisters, giving a striking view of the Victoria Tower of the Houses of Parliament rearing up above a small fountain enclosed by the quiet stone arches. After time in the peace of the College Garden beyond (where concerts are sometimes given at lunchtimes on Thursdays in July and August), the busy tour route back in the main cloisters may seem like a distant memory. It returns though into the Abbey at the 14th-century part of that great Nave near the tombs of the Unknown Soldier and Sir Winston Churchill and ends outside the west front by the Abbey Bookshop.

Around Westminster Abbey

Church of St Margaret's

① *T020-7222 5152. 0930-1630 Mon-Fri, Sun service 1100. Free.* The early 16th-century Church of St Margaret's stands next to the Abbey to the north on Parliament Square. The House of Commons' local place of worship and a popular venue for society weddings, it was founded by the Abbey's monks in the late 11th century as a refuge from the crowds. The church's east window depicting the Crucifixion is famously one of the most beautiful arrays of pre-Reformation stained glass in London while the 19th-century west window celebrates the life of Sir Walter Raleigh, the Elizabethan courtier who helped found Virginia, introduced the potato to Europe and was buried in the Chancel here after his execution for treason. The modern stained-glass window in the south aisle was designed by the John Piper in the 60s.

The small archway by the Abbey's west front leads into **Dean's Yard**, the large quadrangle from which the cloisters and College Garden of the Abbey can be accessed and also the front entrance of **Westminster School** ① *Little Dean's Yard, T020-7963 1000*, one of the country's oldest and most prestigious public (ie fee-paying) schools. Tours of some of its Elizabethan buildings are available by arrangement during the school holidays.

⦂ How to act like a Londoner on the tube

After the incredibly annoying London Underground tannoy warning to 'Mind the Gap', which is repeated ad nauseum by equally annoying tourists, should be added, 'and do not, under any circumstances, talk to, or even look at, the natives'. Visitors please take note: that broadsheet newspaper is not for reading. It is the London tube traveller's shield against the outside world. London can be a tough place, full of highly undesirable and dangerous people, and those precious few millimetres of newsprint are all that stands between the London commuter and the excrutiating pain and social embarrassment of human interaction with a perfect stranger in a crowded place. So, please, dear visitor, be sensitive. Do not engage your neighbour in conversation – even if it's to tell them their hair's on fire – and do not attempt to read their newspaper. This can result in a severe bout of tut-tutting or, worse still, a filthy look. Just head straight for the nearest seat, open your copy of the *Financial Times*, and ignore everything and everyone around you – especially if it's someone asking if this train stops at Buckingham Palace.

The gate at the far corner of Dean's Yard gives onto **Tufton Street** at its meeting with the old ragstone wall of Great College Street, near Church House, the administrative centre of the Church of England. Look out for the sumptuous window display of clerical garb in the old shopfront of *J Wippell & Co* at 11 Tufton Street.

Around Smith Square

The quiet streets between here and Millbank are the place to explore the secluded heart of British political life and make the perfect introduction to the pomp and circumstance of the Houses of Parliament.

It comes as something of a shock on entering Smith Square to be confronted by the massive baroque shape of **St John's Hall** ① *T020-7222 1061, www.sjss.org.uk, see also page 146*, in the middle. Completed in 1728 it was much mocked a century later by the Victorians, including Dickens who said it looked like 'some petrified monster, frightful and gigantic, on its back with its legs in the air'. In fact the design had long been attributed to the short-tempered Queen Anne kicking a four-legged footstool over to demonstrate how she wanted the new church to look. Repeatedly gutted by fire, it was deconsecrated after the Second World War and has become one of the city's best classical music concert halls, with superb acoustics and its own resident Academy of Ancient Music.

The atmospheric **Footstool Restaurant** ① *T020-7222 2779, Mon-Fri 1000-1700 or until 30 mins after concerts start, and also 1 hr before concerts start on Sat, Sun or Bank Holidays*, in the crypt is managed by Digby Trout, also responsible for the well-prepared and fairly reasonably priced modern European food at many other major London sights like the Science Museum, Royal Court Theatre and Dulwich Picture Gallery.

On the north side of Smith Square, the parallel 18th-century terraces of Gayfere Street and North Street are worth comparing, Gayfere Street clearly designed for the tradesfolk catering for the wealthier inhabitants of North Street. Both lead onto Great Peter Street where a right turn heads for Millbank and the **Victoria Tower Gardens**. This is the most pleasant riverside spot around here. Monuments in the small triangular park include a copy of Rodin's *Six Burghers of Calais*, a Gothic drinking fountain celebrating the abolition of slavery in the Empire, and a statue of the campaigner for votes for women, suffragette Emmeline Pankhurst.

ⓘ *T020-7222 2219. Summer 1000-1800, Oct 1000-1800 (last admission 1730) or dusk if earlier, winter 1000-1600 (last admission 1530). Adults £2.60, concessions £2, under-15s £1.30.*

Opposite the gardens, on Abingdon Street over the road from the Houses of Parliament and often overlooked, stands the little Jewel Tower, one of the last vestiges of the medieval Palace of Westminster. Surrounded by a dry moat, and emphatically not where the crown jewels are kept, this was a fortified wardrobe for Edward III built in 1365 and now contains a small exhibition on Parliament Past and Present along with a few other interesting things, including, in the ground floor shop, a rusted Rhineland sword of about 800 AD dug up in Victoria Tower Gardens.

Up the narrow winding stair, the exhibition displays some Speakers' robes, contemporary china caricatures of prime ministers Gladstone and Disraeli, amid a series of explanatory wall texts. Also on display are a stack of the 19th-century Board of Trade's working standards. From 1869 to 1935 the Jewel Tower's thick walls and constant temperature suited its use as the nationwide centre for the accurate calibration of weights and measures. The brass barrels for converting gills, pints, and gallons into pecks, bushels and chaldrons were in use until 1962.

Houses of Parliament

ⓘ *Commons Information Line T020-7219 4272; Lords Information Line T020-7219 3107; www.parliament.uk. Parliament usually in session mid-Oct to Christmas, Jan to Easter, Jun and Jul: Mon 1430-2200, Tue-Thu 1130-1900, Thu until 1800 approximately.*

The exhibition in the Jewel Tower just might stoke up an appetite to see Parliament doing its thing over the road in the **Palace of Westminster**, better known as the Houses of Parliament. The government of England has met on this spot since the reign of Edward III in the 14th century, when the King and his court of barons and bishops would meet in St Stephen's Chapel. The chapel and surrounding palace were almost completely razed to the ground by a dramatic fire in 1834, resulting in the building of the golden Gothic glory in use today. Looking at the building from Parliament Square, the House of Commons is on the left and the House of Lords on the right. Parliament in session is indicated by a light on Big Ben and a Union Jack flying from the Victoria Tower.

Its most famous feature is **Big Ben**, the clock tower overlooking Westminster Bridge. Remarkably accurate for such a big timepiece, the clock strikes the hour on the 13-ton bell that gives the tower its name, and which can be heard up to 4 ½ miles away, and sounds the quarters on four smaller bells to a tune from Handel's *Messiah*.

The oldest part of the building is **Westminster Hall**, which survived the fire, behind the statue of the victor in the Civil War, Lord Protector Oliver Cromwell, standing proudly with the British lion at his feet. For about 25 years after his death though, the southern gable of the Hall was adorned with his head until, in 1686, it was blown off in a storm and hidden away. The ancient interior of the Hall with its great hammerbeam roof and the beautifully decorated **St Stephen's Crypt** can only be seen on a guided tour.

When Parliament is in session the public are admitted (after a thorough security check) to the **'Strangers' Galleries'** of either House through St Stephen's Gate, just beyond Cromwell's statue. The queue for the Commons is on the left and the Lords on

● *The recently retired Big Ben guide, who took visitors to the top and back, is reckoned to*
● *have climbed the equivalent of 76 Mount Everests.*

⁞ Demonstration London

The Peasants' Revolt in 1381 started the trend. London has long been the destination of choice for dissenters and protesters of all kinds. Thankfully they haven't all resorted to the wholesale slaughter of resident foreigners, the burning of palaces and the beheading of the Archbishop of Canterbury. The place in Hampstead where Jack Straw rallied his medieval Essex revolutionaries is now a luxury condominium. Although London has seen more than its fair share of violent protests – the most recent being the Poll Tax riots in 1990 – modern demonstrations have either been much larger, more peaceful or more imaginative. The single most popular mass protest recorded in the city's history took place in February 2003, when more than a million marched into Hyde Park against the war in Iraq. Three months earlier, almost half a million had strolled along the river Thames to Trafalgar Square to make their voices heard against the ban on fox-hunting. The same issue prompted Brian Ferry's son Otis to

storm the debating chamber of the House of Commons with seven friends in September 2004. Protests by individuals in London have become increasingly imaginative in an attempt to grab headlines. In the same month, Jason Hatch dressed up as Batman and clambered onto a balcony at Buckingham Palace to publicize the Fathers 4 Justice campaign. Unfortunately, as with Otis Ferry's stunt, the media focused more on the security breach than on the issue of divorced dads' access to their children. The same group staged more successful high-profile protests by scaling the London Eye and strapping themselves onto a crane in Docklands. Back in the mid 15th century, when Jack Cade wanted to express his anger at Henry IV's high taxes, he kicked the symbolic London Stone, the ancient rock now embedded in the wall of a Cannon St bank. Doing that might be unlikely to make the papers today, but maybe the spirit in which it was done wasn't that different after all.

Central Westminster & Whitehall

the right. Anyone is welcome to wait in line although whether or not you make it inside depends on the business of the day. If any debate of national interest is going on, the chances are slight.

Generally it's easier and quicker gaining access to the **House of Lords**, a very grand and gilded debating chamber with its benches of red morocco. In front of the thrones is the woolsack, a cushioned ottoman for the land's senior judge the Lord Chancellor. By contrast, the **House of Commons** seems small and business-like, with its green leather benches and safety glass in the gallery. The Government sit to the Speaker's right and the Opposition to the left with the front benches reserved for Cabinet Ministers and ex-Ministers.

⁞ *The simplest way of identifying all the different buildings around the square is to take a look at the Jubilee Walkway information board on the corner of the square nearest Great George St.*

Apart from during Prime Minister's Question Time on Wednesdays at 1500, which can only be seen on application well in advance to your MP or embassy, both houses are often half-empty or half-asleep. Guided historical tours of both houses are available during August and September and sometimes sell out well in advance. Check with the Information lines.

Anyone genuinely interested in seeing the sharp end of the law in action can sit in on a case at the **Middlesex Guildhall Crown Courts** ① *on the west side of Parliament Square, 7 criminal courts usually in session Mon-Fri 1030-1300, 1400-1600*. Parliament Square was laid out by Sir Charles Barry, the designer of the Palace of Westminster, and since becoming the world's first roundabout in 1926 – dubbed the 'new gyratory system' – it has gradually been dotted with worthy statuary, most prominently **Winston Churchill** looking sturdy and combative, and also Abraham Lincoln, just risen to his feet from his chair to hold forth on democracy.

★ Cabinet War Rooms

① *To20-7930 6961, http://cwr.iwm.org.uk. Winter 1000-1800 winter, summer 0930-1800 (last admission 1700). Adults £10, concessions £8, under-16s free.*

More on Churchill and his achievement can be found at the Cabinet War Rooms, round the corner up Horse Guards Road on the right, at the foot of the Clive Steps on King Charles Street. During the Blitz these underground rooms in the only steel framed building in Whitehall became the nerve centre of Churchill's morale-boosting war effort. In the claustrophobic cabinet war room itself the U-shaped table laden with ashtrays encircles three hot seats for the Chiefs of staff of army, air force and navy. A sufferer from depression himself, which he called the 'black dog', Churchill propped a personal note against their water decanter: 'Please understand there is no depression in this house and we are not interested in the possibilities of defeat: they do not exist.'

Most of the rooms are off one long gloomy corridor, including his tiny bedroom, the cramped typing pool, the map room, and his office hotline to the US president, all echoing with ringing telephones and the sound of his famous speeches. Also on display is the original map used to hang the Iron Curtain at Yalta. The entertaining audio guide (included in the ticket price and taking about an hour and a half) features personal memories of the people who worked here, like the trainee typist tested by the great man's cigar-chewing speech impediment. Overall the place remains a testament to the dogged forbearance of a charismatic leader and his government with their backs against the wall. A new state-of-the-art Churchill Museum, almost doubling the rooms on view, opened in February 2005 and takes visitors through the whole life of the man many still consider Britain's finest, hence the elevated admission fee (also down to fact that the war rooms receive no government arts grant).

Diana Princess of Wales Memorial Walk

① *To20-7298 2000*. From outside the Cabinet War Rooms, **St James's Park** (see page 122) stretches dreamily off into the distance, the start of an almost unbroken tract of green from here to **Kensington Palace** (see page 323), a fact that has been officially recognized by the circular Diana Princess of Wales Memorial Walk that can be joined here. The seven-mile route through St James's Park, Green Park, Hyde Park and Kensington Gardens is marked with 90 rose-emblem plaques in the ground and was formally opened on 30 June 2000, the day before the 39th anniversary of Diana's birth. It now includes the controversial memorial water feature in Hyde Park. Halfway up Birdcage Walk on the left is Queen Anne's Gate, a rare survival from the early 18th century, and number two is the United Kingdom Office of the European Parliament.

Whitehall

① T020-7930 4179, www.hrp.org.uk. 1000-1700 (last entry 1630) Mon-Sat. Adults £4, concessions £3, under 16s £2.60, under 5s free.

Back by Westminster tube, on the left **Portcullis House** contains brand new and very expensive offices for MPs opposite the Houses of Parliament, the latest in the series of palatial government buildings that make up Whitehall. With its black ventilation stacks and deferential mock-Gothic design it makes interesting comparison with the huge Edwardian block on the corner of Parliament Square and Parliament Street. These 'New Government Offices' of 1898 now house some departments of the Treasury. A short way up Parliament Street on the left, through the triple arch of King Charles Street, is the **Foreign and Commonwealth Office** ① T020-7270 1500, www.fco.gov.uk, which occasionally arranges guided tours round its old building.

In the middle of the road, where Parliament Street becomes Whitehall, stands the **Cenotaph**, a simple block of Portland Stone designed rapidly by Lutyens for the peace celebrations in July 1919, it has become the focus for national remembrance of the dead of the two World Wars, where a service is held annually on the Sunday nearest November 11, the date of the Armistice in 1918.

Just further down on the left, behind guarded gates in **Downing Street**, number 10 is the deceptively small-looking home and offices of the Prime Minister, recognizable by the policeman standing outside. Next door, number 11 is the Chancellor of the Exchequer's home and offices.

Whitehall then continues its wide progress up to Trafalgar Square, lined with the offices of the Cabinet and the Treasury, and the Scottish Office. Opposite stands the massive **Ministry of Defence** (MOD) ① www.mod.uk, towering over a little statue of Sir Water Raleigh and big statues of Field Marshalls Montgomery (of Alamein) and Slim. The front entrance of the MOD on Horse Guards Avenue is flanked by enormous stone women representing Earth and Water.

On the corner of Horse Guards Avenue and Whitehall stands the last survivor from the original Whitehall Palace, Inigo Jones's **Banqueting House**. Completed in 1622, the building is the only Government property on Whitehall that welcomes uninvited visitors (although it, too, occasionally closes for private receptions). A 20-minute audio guide describes the splendidly proportioned Banqueting Hall itself. Apart from its historical associations – the beheading of Charles I that took place here is marked annually on 31 January with a small ceremony and service – the main attraction is the ceiling, decorated with nine canvasses by Rubens including the extraordinary *Apotheosis of James I*, aka Union Jack, in the middle, complete with a couple of mirror-table trolleys to save admirers from cricked necks. Lunchtime concerts are held here on the first Monday of every month except August.

Across the road another Palladian edifice built a century later, **Horse Guards**, is the HQ of the Household Division. The **Changing of the Queen's Life Guard** ① Mon-Sat 1100, Sun 1000, guard parading dismounted at 1600 daily, takes place here amid a strong smell of horse dung. The guard is drawn from the squadrons of the Household Cavalry stationed at Hyde Park Barracks, alternating daily between Life Guards (red tunics and white helmet plumes) and the Blues and Royals (blue tunics and red plumes). When the Queen is in London, the guard is commanded by an officer with standard and a trumpeter on a grey horse. When she's not, by an NCO without standard or trumpeter, inspected by an officer at 1600. The main purpose of the guard now seems to be to entertain tourists and stop people driving or bicycling through the arch without a special ivory pass from her Maj.

It's worth walking through to have a look at the **Parade Ground** facing St James's Park. From here the Duke of York's column on the Mall is often confused by visitors with Nelson's in Trafalgar Square to disorientating effect. On the right, the Old

Admiralty Buildings stand next to the bomb-proof ivy-clad Citadel with its overgrown grass roof supposed to make aerial spotters think it a part of the park. On the left of the arch is the Chinese dragon mortar given in gratitude by the Spanish for the Duke of Wellington's relief of the siege of Salamanca by the French. It was ridiculed when it was erected. The parade ground itself is romantically lit at night by gas lamps

😑 Sleeping

Westminster & Whitehall *p136, map p139*
A London St Ermin's, Caxton St, SW1, T020-7222 7888, www.jollyhotels.com. Erstwhile Edwardian splendour in a baroque fantasy of a building in an exceptional location, where the first pan-African conference in history was held. Has 85 rooms and breakfast is usually included in price.
A Sanctuary House, 33 Tothill St, SW1, T020-7799 4044, www.sanctuaryhouse hotel.com. A very serviceable option, with 34 clean rooms above a Fuller's Ale and Pie House, cheaper at weekends. Breakfast not included.

😮 Eating

Westminster & Whitehall *p136, map p139*
¶¶¶ The Cinnamon Club, The Old Westminster Library, Great Smith St, SW1, T020-7517 9898. A smart 200-seat Indian restaurant in the shell of the old library opposite Little Smith St. Much enjoyed, quite deservedly, by paunchy politicos, civil servants and their clients on expense accounts.
¶¶ Sorriso, 10a The Broadway, SW1, T020-7222 3338. Reached down a strange free-standing spiral staircase in the shadow of New Scotland Yard which leads down to an a/c cellar where there's a well-regarded and roomy ristorante Italiano, closed weekends.

Cafés and sandwiches
Strutton Ground is lined with sandwich shops and cafés for the local office workers, many only open Mon-Fri.
¶ The Laughing Halibut, Strutton Ground, T020-7799 2844. Open 1115-2000, perfectly decent fish and chips to eat in or take away.
¶ Tevere Restaurant, St Ann's St. Open 1130-1500, a characterful panelled corner café seemingly unchanged since the 50s, an excellent venue for the likes of double

poached eggs on toast for £1.80 or Italian and basic British hot meals for about £7.

😮 Pubs and bars

Westminster *p136, map p139*
Government pen-pushers get thirsty, and they keep a variety of oases very lively.
Albert Tavern, 52 Victoria St, SW1, T020-7222 5577. All creamy walls and tched glass.
Buckingham, 62 Petty France, SW1, T020-7222 3386, close to the Passport Office. A Young's pub opposite the barracks of the Scots Guards that, like many of the pubs in the area, looks grand on the outside but is not that special within.
The Colonies, Wilfred St, SW1, T020-7834 1407. Smoky confines.
Marquis of Granby, 41 Romney St, SW1, T020-7227 0941. Popular with nostalgic Tory MPs, once the closest watering hole to the former Conservative HQ in Smith Square.
Red Lion, 48 Parliament St, SW1, T020-7930 5826. A splendid Victorian place.
Two Chairmen, 39 Dartmouth St, SW1, T020-7222 8694, near St James's Park. Worth seeking out for its quaint location in Queen Anne's Gate but not much else.
Westminster Arms, 9 Storeys Gate, nearer Parliament Sq, SW1, T020-7222 8520. Has tables outside and is fairly expensive but the wood-panelled *Storeys Winebar* in the basement is a cosy and usually convivial spot.

😮 Entertainment

Westminster *p136, map p139*
Music
Classical and opera St John's Hall, Smith Sq, T020-7222 1061. Grand but spartan concert hall staging a variety of choral, orchestral, and chamber performances both amateur and professional. Tickets £5-£35.

● *For an explanation of sleeping and eating price codes used in this guide, see inside the* ● *front cover. Other relevant information is found in Essentials, see pages 44-46.*

Victoria, Belgravia and Pimlico

One of central London's busiest transport hubs, the scrum at Victoria round the train and coach stations does much to enliven the almost deserted splendour of Belgravia – the poshest address in town – and Pimlico, its proper little neighbour. The grandeur of Belgravia's Eaton Square continues the line of Chelsea's King's Road up to the back door of Buckingham Palace, crossed before it gets there by the Belgrave Road striding up through Pimlico from the river to end in some style at Belgrave Square.

Meanwhile, down by the river on Millbank, the heavy classical portico of Tate Britain belies the energy and imagination within, its collection of contemporary and British art still reeling from the excitement of coming into much more space to play with downstream on Bankside. The old gallery has bravely managed to keep its head above the tide of attention turning towards the new arrival and stays in the swim, most notoriously with the annual award of the Turner Prize each autumn. ⇥ *For Sleeping, Eating and other listings see pages 152-154.*

History

While Westminster had created its own community outside of the City, the land beyond was largely left to pasture. In the 17th century, a large field stretched west behind Buckingham House. Criss-crossed by paths, earning it the name Five Fields, sheep and donkeys grazed on the treeless expanse that was to become Belgravia. A bridge over the Westbourne River became known as Bloody Bridge on account of the highwaymen who swooped here, and it was a favoured duelling spot. Ebury Farm, an estate of 430 acres, spread out across Pimlico and the swamps and creeks of Victoria, although the Reverend James Palmer's village of alms houses sat south of modern Victoria Street, and an annual fair, bull-baiting and a pleasure garden occupied the current site of Westminster Cathedral nearby.

Over the river, Vauxhall, named after Fulkes Hall, a house built there in the 13th century, was a mere village. It wasn't until the 18th century, and notably in the wake of George III's move to Buckingham House (later Buckingham Palace) in 1762, that the area began to show life. New Spring Gardens in Vauxhall and Ranelagh Gardens in Chelsea drew the crowds at the weekends. These "pretty contrived" plantations held firework displays and orchestral performances in among the rotundas, grottoes, statues and pavilions. In 1749 an orchestra played to a crowd of 12,000 in New Spring Gardens, and in 1786, 61,000 attended a fancy-dress party, although Horace Walpole argued that Ranelagh "has totally beat Vauxhall". Nearby, the Chelsea Bun House would attract queues of 50,000 on Good Fridays, a ridiculous claim, no doubt, but clearly popular.

Five Fields, now a patchwork of market gardens, still drew people to shoot duck and to watch bull-baiting and cock-fighting. Lanesborough House became a hospital, the Grosvenor Canal (some of it ran under the current Victoria Station) opened in 1725, and a row of houses in Grosvenor Place emerged to accommodate the royal household. When the Grosvenor estate, the owners of the land, came to an agreement with developer Thomas Cubitt in the early 19th century, building began in earnest.

The stuccoed houses of Belgravia drew the nobles from Mayfair, with Belgrave Square (the bricks were made on site from its own damp clay) the gleaming torch for new fashionable addresses. Cubitt then turned his attention to Pimlico (probably

Central Victoria, Belgravia & Pimlico

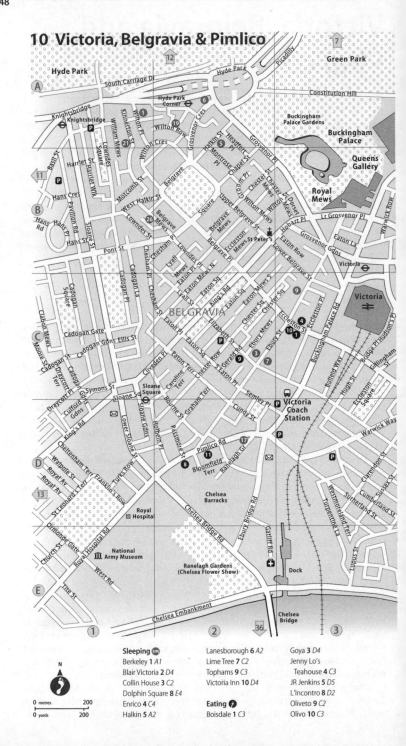

10 Victoria, Belgravia & Pimlico

Sleeping 🛏
Berkeley **1** *A1*
Blair Victoria **2** *D4*
Collin House **3** *C2*
Dolphin Square **8** *E4*
Enrico **4** *C4*
Halkin **5** *A2*

Lanesborough **6** *A2*
Lime Tree **7** *C2*
Tophams **9** *C3*
Victoria Inn **10** *D4*

Eating 🍴
Boisdale **1** *C3*

Goya **3** *D4*
Jenny Lo's
Teahouse **4** *C3*
JR Jenkins **5** *D5*
L'Incontro **8** *D2*
Oliveto **9** *C2*
Olivo **10** *C3*

N

0 metres   200
0 yards   200

Central Victoria, Belgravia & Pimlico

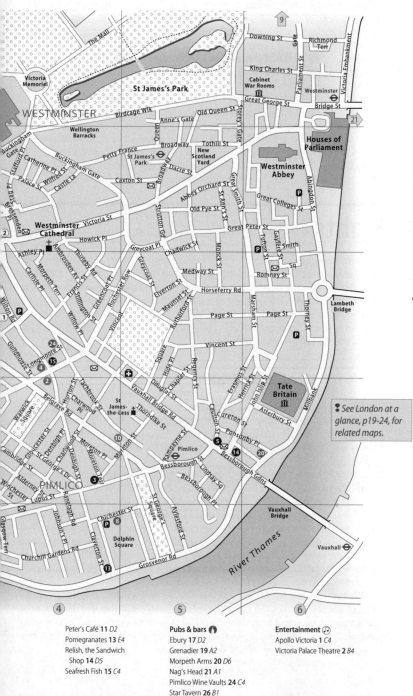

Peter's Café **11** *D2*
Pomegranates **13** *E4*
Relish, the Sandwich
Shop **14** *D5*
Seafresh Fish **15** *C4*

Pubs & bars 🍸
Ebury **17** *D2*
Grenadier **19** *A2*
Morpeth Arms **20** *D6*
Nag's Head **21** *A1*
Pimlico Wine Vaults **24** *C4*
Star Tavern **26** *B1*

Entertainment 🎵
Apollo Victoria **1** *C4*
Victoria Palace Theatre **2** *B4*

📍 See London at a
glance, p19-24, for
related maps.

after a local drink), the poorer relation to Belgravia, uprooting agricultural leaseholders to create a grid of stuccoed Italianate houses around Warwick and Eccleston squares. On its eastern riverbank lay the Millbank Penitentiary. Inmates in this star-shaped prison awaited transportation or referral, although many died in the scurvy and cholera that flourished in its marshy setting. At the turn of the century it was replaced with the Tate Gallery.

Victoria grew in the 1840s and 50s, most significantly with Victoria Street cutting through the slums in 1851, and the opening of the railway station in 1862. Victoria Station served most of the channel ports, so most troops left for the carnage of the First World War from this terminus. The building of Vauxhall Bridge Road in 1816 signalled the stirrings of Vauxhall, which grew steadily through the century as Lambeth and Kennington expanded. In more recent years, Belgravia and Pimlico have become popular among diplomatic and commercial concerns, while much of Victoria has been rebuilt. At the turn of the last century it was remarkable for holding some of London's earliest mansion blocks, and although some still survive, Victoria Street, for example, is now lined with post Second World War edifices.

Sights ⊖ *Pimlico, St James's Park, Vauxhall, Victoria.* 🚇 *See p460.*

Pretty well everyone visiting London finds themselves in Victoria sooner or later, even though its status as the gateway to the continent has diminished since the opening of the Eurostar terminal in Waterloo. Even so, the combined impact of the trains serving Gatwick, Brighton and the southeast, and the National Express Coach station on Buckingham Palace Road still creates considerable foot pressure in the area. But most don't hang about here much. It's not hard to see why, with other more enticing parts of the city being so close at hand.

Westminster Cathedral

① *T020-7798 9055. 0645-1900 Mon-Fri, 0800-1900 Sat, 0800-2000 Sun; Campanile Thu-Sun in winter, daily in summer 0900-1700. Adult £2, child £1. Audio guide. Sun services 0800, 0900, solemn sung Mass, 1030, 1200, 1730 and 1900; Mon-Fri sung Mass 1730; Sat sung Mass 1030, vigil Mass 1800.*

The one sight worth a special trip is Westminster Cathedral on Victoria Street, the senior Catholic church in London. A vast edifice of stripy red brick and grey stone in a Byzantine style, the building was begun in 1895. The first worshippers passed through its doors in 1903 but the place wasn't consecrated for another seven years, church law forbidding the ceremony until the fabric of the building was complete. The echoing interior is still being decorated bit by bit, eventually to be lined throughout with the extremely expensive marble and mosaic that the architect JF Bentley envisaged. Currently it reaches about a third of the way up the columns marching down the widest nave in England.

The cathedral's most famous decorations are on the walls, the elegant stone reliefs by Eric Gill depicting the 14 Stations of the Cross. Gill also carved the statues of Saints Thomas More and John Fisher in the St George's Chapel. From Thursdays to Sundays, it's also possible to take the lift up the 273-ft campanile (or St Edward's Tower) for some broad views across central London.

Around Pimlico

Victoria Street continues its unprepossessing way down to Parliament Square while, even less inspiring, from Victoria Station Vauxhall Bridge Road makes a busy and almost featureless beeline for the river. A little way down on the right though it's met by Warwick Way, the main shopping street in Pimlico with several interesting shops and some good places to eat. Tachbrook Street on the left hosts a rather forlorn local fruit 'n' veg street market overlooked by more tempting shops. After a short distance Warwick Way crosses the wide stuccoed pomp of Belgrave Road and cuts between Eccleston and Warwick Squares. These two grand squares are the heart of Pimlico, both with beautiful gardens for the use of keyholders only. The residential streets around here are a pleasant enough place to explore even though the uniformity of their creamy whiteness can be disorientating.

Belgrave Road runs parallel to Vauxhall Bridge Road down towards Pimlico tube. Between the two, off Moreton Street, stands the remarkable **Church of St-James-the-Less** ① *To20-7630 6282, www.sjtl.org, 1200-1500 Mon-Fri, Sun services: 0930 Communion, also 1100, 1800 and 1915*, an amazing Victorian flight of fancy in red brick and grey slate fenced in with some impressive cast-iron work and more recently by a competition-winning 1970s council estate.

Tate Britain

① *To20-7887 8000/8008, www.tate.org.uk/britain. 1000-1750 daily. Free, but special exhibitions £10, £8 concession. Audio guide, guided tours, gallery talks, lectures and events. Café 1030-1730 daily, Tate Restaurant, To20-7887 8825, 1200-1500 Mon-Sat, 1200-1600 Sun. A boat runs between the two Tate galleries, see page 238.*

A five-minute walk from Pimlico tube, left out of the station past Paolozzi's strange industrial sculpture, and left off Vauxhall Bridge Road just before the bridge, leads onto Millbank and the area's main attraction, Tate Britain. The home of the national collection of British and modern art dramatically expanded at the end of the last millennium into Tate Modern downriver on Bankside, but this was only the latest and most impressive of a series of expansions – not least in Liverpool and Cornwall – since it opened here in 1897. On this site, the Lindbury galleries recently opened to great acclaim, providing even more space for British art down the centuries downstairs, as well as providing more room for the temporary exhibitions and the country's contemporary art scene, one of its key events being the award and exhibition of the Turner Prize each December. The extra space on Bankside prompted a rethink of the gallery's remit here and now it is nominally dedicated to British art both ancient and contemporary. In fact the boundaries between the collections on display in the two places are blurred: several continental or American works are still quite likely to be found here.

The gallery is arranged chronologically. There is every chance that the displays will include works by the visionary **William Blake**, the satirist **William Hogarth**, and the **Pre-Raphaelites**, among others. Tate Britain also remains the best place in the country to admire the work of arguably its greatest artist, **JMW Turner**, in the Clore Gallery to the right of the Millbank entrance. These purpose-built rooms opened in 1987 display the entire development of Turner's remarkable skill in handling the drama of natural scenes, atmosphere and the effects of light. From *Snow Storm: Hannibal and his Army Crossing the Alps*, painted in 1812, through his first brush with Mediterranean light on his regular visits to Italy, to *Snow Storm: Steam Boat off a Harbour's Mouth*, in 1842, the magic of his work hardly ever fails to delight. Several rooms are also dedicated to the great landscape painter John Constable and there are regular special temporary exhibitions.

Turning right and right again out of the gallery's front entrance, Atterbury Street leads past the old Royal Army Medical College and Millbank Barracks, recently taken over and redeveloped by the **Chelsea College of Art**. A **gallery space** ① *T020-7514 7751, for programme details/opening times*, opened to the public in February 2005, complements a trip to the Tate with a look into the future of art, taking an experimental, sidelong view of art and design.

Turning left, Millbank rushes round to Lambeth Bridge and the Houses of Parliament. Directly opposite the gallery though, usually hidden by lines of tourist coaches, there's a small riverside terrace adorned with **Henry Moore**'s *Locking Pieces* and a view of Terry Farrell's high-tech ziggurat for the secret service **MI6** on the south bank of the river by Vauxhall Bridge.

Belgravia

North of Victoria Station, over Buckingham Palace Road, stretch the stately white-stuccoed squares and terraces of Belgravia, named after a small village on one of the Grosvenor family's country estates. Its centre is **Belgrave Square**, now almost entirely occupied by embassies and consulates, although many of the residences in the surrounding streets, and especially **Eaton Square**, still represent the pinnacle to which every self-respecting social climber aspires. That leaves little room around here for the general public to enjoy themselves much, other than by wondering what kind of baroque powerplays might be being acted out behind all the closed doors, although the area does boast some exceptional old-fashioned public houses and at least three of London's most luxurious hotels. **Elizabeth Street** is the main shopping drag while to the west of Belgrave Square, **Chesham Place** and **Pont Street** slide seamlessly via Cadogan Place into Knightsbridge.

● Sleeping

Victoria & Belgravia *p147, map p148*
L Dolphin Square, Chichester St, SW1
T020-7834 3800, www.dolphinsquarehotel.
co.uk. At the lower end of this bracket, a large,
comfortable and fairly informal hideaway near
the river with its own gardens, swimming
pool and fine-dining restaurant Allium.
AL The Berkeley, Wilton Pl, SW1, T020-7235
6000, www.savoy-group.com. Recently
renovated in a traditional English country-
house-in-the-city kind of a way (frosted
glass, modern materials), this is probably the
most fashionable of the Savoy group of
hotels. With 214 rooms, it's also the home of
the design classics Boxwood Café (T020-
7235 1010) and Blue Bar. Another of the last
words in swish jet-set accommodation.
AL Halkin, 5-6 Halkin St, SW1, T020-7333
1000, www.halkin.como.bz. With its ultra-
contemporary design, a fusion of Asian and
Italian, and owned by a Singaporean

company, this very elegant and discreet hotel
has 41 rooms in a prime Belgravia location
also boasting the top-class Thai restaurant
Nam (T020-7333 1234) with 1 Michelin star.
AL The Lanesborough, Hyde Park Corner,
SW1, T020-7259 5599, www.lanesborough.
com. Once the St George's Hospital although
you'd never know it, with 95 rooms now done
up in restrained Regency style incorporating
the discreet pleasures of the Library Bar.
A Lime Tree, 135 Ebury St, SW1, T020-7730
8191, www.limetreehotel.com. Small neat and
very popular little B&B guest house with 37
rooms, with comfortable old-fashioned style.
Breakfast included. Bottom end of this bracket
and very convenient for Victoria station.
A Topham's Belgravia, 28 Ebury St, SW1,
T020-7730 8147, www.tophams.co.uk.
Slightly grander and more formal, a charming
small country house-style hotel with 37
rooms, family-run, friendly, £110 a double.

B **Collin House**, 104 Ebury St, SW1, T020-7730 8031, www.collinhouse.co.uk. Small, clean B&B with 12 rooms at surprisingly reasonable rates considering its location. Even cheaper rooms are available with shared baths (£68 per night). Breakfast included.

C **The Blair Victoria**, 78-84 Warwick Way, SW1, T020-7828 8603, sales@blairvictoria. 62 rooms with showers en suite and internet access. One of the better examples of the area's countless small hotels, rated for its warm welcome and efficient service. Full English breakfast included.

C **The Victoria Inn**, 65-67 Belgrave Rd, SW1, T020-7834 6721, www.victoriainn.co.uk. 43 rooms. No-nonsense, functional place popular with business travellers and tourists on the busy Belgrave Rd.

D **Enrico**, 79 Warwick Way, SW1, T020-7834 9538, www.enricohotel.com. Tiny and basic with only 25 rooms on bustling Warwick Way, some quieter than others. Very friendly and very good value even so, including the full English breakfast.

● Eating

Belgravia p152, map p148
Apart from the restaurants in the Halkin and Berkeley hotels (see above), gourmet dining experiences are surprisingly thin on the ground in Belgravia.

♥♥♥ **Boisdale**, 15 Eccleston St, SW1, T020- 7730 6922. One of London's very few specifically Scottish restaurants (although with a French twist) and its old-school whisky and cigar room at the back beyond the courtyard is a treat, along with the Macdonald Bar, at the back of the main green, red and tartan restaurant (open Mon-Sat until 0100). The whole creaking complex can become impossibly busy with shirt-sleeved bonhomie but then again it is a cheerful place.

♥♥ **Oliveto**, 49 Elizabeth St, SW1, T020-7730 0074. A swish spot in Belgravia for some top-class and reasonably priced pizzas and pastas.

♥♥ **Olivo**, 21 Eccleston St, SW1, T020-7730 2505. Oliveto's grown-up sibling serves a wider variety of Sardinian dishes, closed for lunch at weekends.

♥ **Jenny Lo's Teahouse**, 14 Eccleston St, SW1, T020-7823 6331. Open Mon-Fri 1130-1500, 1800-2200, Sat 1200-1500, 1800-1000. An excellent Chinese noodle bar (eat in or takeaway) run by the daughter of celebrity chef Ken Lo. Marginally more expensive than some elsewhere that have followed in its wake, the quality of the ingredients and fine vegetarian options keep it a cut above.

Pimlico p147, map p148
♥♥♥ **L'Incontro**, 87 Pimlico Rd, SW1, T020-7730 6327. For the refined appreciation of some modern Italian cuisine in a sleek environment (set lunch £16.50 for 2 courses).

♥♥♥ **Pomegranates**, 94 Grosvenor Rd, SW1, T020-7828 6560. Rather similar in style to Boisdale, even more clubby and old-fashioned, with an excellent wine list to accompany its rich, accomplished and eclectic fare. At the lower end of this price bracket (set lunches £15 for 2 courses).

♥ **Goya**, 32 Lupus St, SW1, T020-7976 5309. A Spanish tapas bar and restaurant that's very popular with locals (and usually needs to be booked); ask for a table upstairs if possible.

♥ **Peter's Café**, 59 Pimlico Rd, SW1, T020-7730 5991. The cabbie's favourite local for its large platefuls of comfort food at sensible prices, open until 2200.

♥ **Seafresh Fish Restaurant**, 80 Wilton Rd, SW1, T020-7828 0747. A typically no-nonsense and unfussy haven for some good quality fish and chips to eat in or take-away.

Cafés and sandwich bars
JR Jenkins Café, 10a Vauxhall Bridge Rd, SW1, T020-7821 8849, near Tate Britain. Excellent and tiny bog-standard café for full-sized hot meals and teas, closes 1530, Mon-Fri only.
Relish, the Sandwich Shop, 8 John Islip St, T020-7828 0628. Makes very good fresh sandwiches much appreciated by local office workers, closes 1530, Mon-Fri only.

● Pubs and bars

Victoria & Belgravia p147, map p148
Three pubs tucked away in Belgravia stand out for their traditional atmosphere, beer, interesting clientele and affable bar staff:

Central Victoria, Belgravia & Pimlico *Listings*

● *For an explanation of sleeping and eating price codes used in this guide, see inside the*
● *front cover. Other relevant information is found in Essentials, see pages 44-46.*

The Grenadier, 18 Wilton Row, SW1, T020-7235 3074. Honest-to-goodness old-soldiering associations and often overcrowded.
The Nag's Head, 53 Kinnerton St, SW1, T020-7235 1135. A free house with excellent beers, the largest and most rambling of the three.
Star Tavern, 6 Belgrave Mews West, SW1, T020-7235 3019. A rewarding find, a cosy wood-panelled place for some reasonable food, through an arch in its own little mews.
Ebury, 139 Ebury St, SW1, T020-7730 5447. Further west than *The Nag's Head*, a buzzy bar with pretty good food. With a quieter modern European restaurant upstairs, a busy and convivial atmosphere prevails among drinkers and diners on the ground floor.

Pimlico *p147, map p148*
Morpeth Arms, 58 Millbank, SW1, T020-7834 6442, near Tate Britain. Quite touristy but has some outside seating on pleasant Ponsonby Pl.
Pimlico Wine Vaults, 12-22 Upper Tachbrook St, T020-7233 5801. Take their wine seriously and stock some top-quality clarets.

● Entertainment

Victoria *p147, map p148*
Theatre
Apollo Victoria, Wilton Rd, T0870-4000870. Was purpose-built for musicals in 1901 and has returned to its roots in some style, currently hosting 'Saturday Night Fever'
Victoria Palace Theatre, Victoria St, SW1, T0870-1611977. Opposite Little Ben, it was built as a music hall in 1911 and now stages big musicals.

● Shopping

Belgravia *p152, map p148*
In Belgravia, Elizabeth, Eccleston and Ebury streets are the best destinations for a more expensive, style-hunting jaunt.
Ben de Lisi, 40 Elizabeth St, SW1, T020-7730 2994. The flagship store of this American fashion designer.
The Chocolate Society, 36 Elizabeth St, SW1, T020-7259 9222. Rare sweets and very fine cocoa solids.
Jeroboams, 51 Elizabeth St, SW1, T020-7823 5623. Fine wine and cheese.

Pimlico *p147, map p148*
Warwick Way and especially Tachbrook St, with its food market and curious little shops, are likely to be the most fertile ground for a successful shopping trip in the area. The market, which closes around 1630, and doesn't operate on Sun, mainly sells fruit and veg to locals although occasionally other stalls turn up.
Bonne Bouche, 40 Tachbrook St, T020-7630 1626. The patisserie here can provide some delicious French cakes.
Cornucopia, 12 Upper Tachbrook St, SW1, T020-7828 5752, on the other side of Warwick Way. Second-hand classic clothes (mainly for women) from past eras at bargain prices.
Ivano's Deli, 38 Tachbrook St, T020-7630 6977. The place to assemble a fine southern Italian picnic from a variety of his specialities and excellent value takeaway snacks.
Rippon Cheese Stores, 26 Upper Tachbrook St, SW1, T020-7931 0628, on the other side of Warwick Way. Have a pungent and mouthwatering array of produce from all over Europe, including Scotland and Ireland.
Wilton Cycle and Wireless Co, 28 Upper Tachbrook St, SW1, T020-7834 1367. Not for bikes or radios but for Hornby train-sets and several other model manufacturers.

▲▲ Activities

Victoria, Belgravia & Pimlico *p147, map p148*
Queen Mother Sports Centre, 323 Vauxhall Bridge Rd, SW1, T020-7630 5522. Opening hours 0630-2000 Mon-Fri; Sat, Sun 0800-2000. Large council-run swimming pool £3.40 a session. Also has a gym, squash, basketball, badminton, martial arts, and scuba diving.

● Directory

Victoria, Belgravia & Pimlico *p147, map p148*
Tourist information Victoria Station Forecourt, SW1. Open Easter-31 May Mon-Sat 0800-2000, Sun 0800-1800; 1 Jun-30 Sep Mon-Sat 0800- 2100, Sun 0800-1800; 1 Oct-Easter daily 0800-1800.

Knightsbridge, South Kensington and Hyde Park

Like Mayfair and neighbouring Belgravia, Knightsbridge and South Ken is one of the wealthiest areas in central London. Favoured by cosmopolitan jetsetters, wayward little rich girls and anyone dressed up and on the pull, the multicultural cake mixed here has a noticeable Middle Eastern, Far Eastern and American flavour with some distinct French, Italian and Polish notes.

Knightsbridge especially is pretty much the exclusive playground of the super-rich, with fashion labels, deluxe hotels, expensive restaurants and private clubs to match. Three tremendous exceptions are the great museums: the Victoria and Albert (V&A), Natural History, and Science Museums each deserve at least a day of anyone's time. Each of them has long been bending over backwards to make their vast collections as accessible and rewarding as possible. Although such a short distance apart, the temptation to 'do' all three in one visit should definitely be resisted. Even two could prove too rich a treat. To the south, Chelsea merges seamlessly with South Ken via Brompton and the Fulham Road. At the top of Exhibition Road, protecting the area from Bayswater to the north, the delightful green acres of Kensington Gardens and Hyde Park harbour grand or whimsical memorials and the world-famous little Serpentine Gallery. ▸▸ *For Sleeping, Eating and other listings see pages 165-168.*

History

In the Middle Ages the road from Piccadilly ran through a small village called Knightsbridge on the route to the village of Kensington. To the north, three manors occupied the land up to the Tyburn Way (Oxford Street) and stretched west of the Tyburn Lane (Park Lane). The River Westbourne flowed south across the land, with a crossing at the Knight's Bridge (It may have been King's Bridge), and deer, boar and wild bulls roamed the woods and pasture.

At the Dissolution of the Monasteries, Henry VIII sold two of the manors, but kept Hyde as a hunting ground. Knightsbridge boasted several taverns (Elizabeth I frequently stopped at the *Fox & Bull* en route to visiting her chief adviser Lord Burleigh in Brompton Hall), while Kensington further west had grown around the church founded in the 12th century, now St Mary Abbots. Market gardens and nurseries surrounded Knightsbridge, most notably the Brompton Park Nursery that flourished in the 18th century.

When William of Orange opted for Nottingham House, later Kensington Palace, as his main residence (he moved from Westminster on account of his asthma), Rotten Row, the *route du roi* from Kensington to St James's, became the first illuminated road in England when 300 oil lamps were hung from the trees lining the route.

In 1730 work began in the park. The Westbourne was dammed to create the Serpentine, the Broad Walk was laid out, and the Round Pond was created as a centrepiece of formal gardens. The gardens were largely closed to the public until George III took up residence in Buckingham Palace in the 1760s, when they were open to the respectably dressed. The Serpentine, although carrying much of the local area's sewage, was a popular swimming and boating venue and a grand fair in 1814 celebrated the triumph of Trafalgar by re-enacting the battle on the lake. A large enclosure, the Ring, hosted carriage racing.

But the park's high point, and the spark for the growth and development of Knightsbridge and South Kensington, was the **Great Exhibition** of 1851. The brainchild of Victoria's beloved Prince Albert, this display of national confidence was housed in a magnificent Crystal Palace. It was such a success (in just five months, six million visitors enjoyed the 19,000 exhibits and refreshments supplied by Messrs Schweppe), that the whole glass construction was transplanted to Sydenham, where it enjoyed continued popularity until it burnt down in 1936.

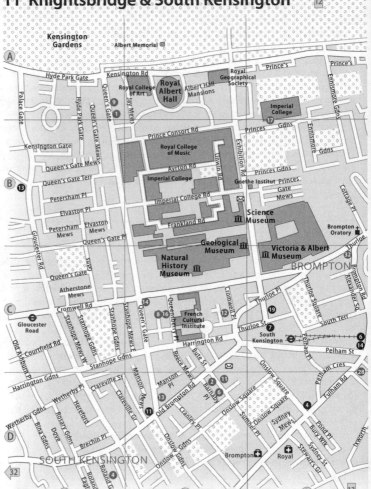

11 Knightsbridge & South Kensington

Sleeping
Albert **1** A1
Aster House **2** D2
Basil Street **3** A5
Blakes **4** D1
Claverley **15** B4
Diplomat **5** C6
Five Sumner Place **6** D2
Franklin **7** B4
Gallery **8** C2
Gainsborough **16** C2
Gore **9** A1
Linstead Hall **17** B3
Mandarin Oriental
  Hyde Park **10** A5
Number Sixteen **11** D2
Pelham & Kemps
  Restaurant **12** C2
Regency **13** D2
YHA South
  Kensington **14** C2

Eating
Bibendum **2** C4
Cactus Blue **4** D3
Café Monpelliano **5** B4
Collection **6** C3

N

0 metres 100
0 yards 100

Although the likes of Onslow Square and Gardens, Pelham Crescent and Thurloe Place had all emerged before the 1850s, and hospitals such as the Royal Marsden and the Brompton reflected the area's reputation as being "remarkable for the salubrity of its air", it was the profits from the Great Exhibition that transformed South Kensington. The area was still largely market gardens and nurseries, with the occasional modest mansions, such as Gore House, Brompton Hall, Cromwell House and Gloucester Lodge, but the whole area was bought and transformed into a mix of museums, academic institutes and Italianate stuccoed terraces for the well-to-do.

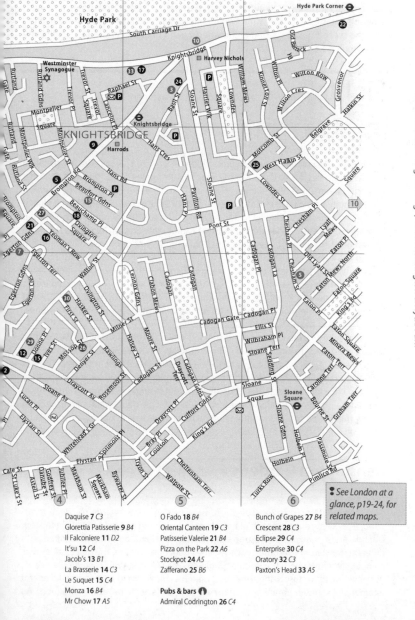

Central Knightsbridge, South Kensington & Hyde Park

Daquise **7** *C3*
Glorettia Patisserie **9** *B4*
Il Falconiere **11** *D2*
It'su **12** *C4*
Jacob's **13** *B1*
La Brasserie **14** *C3*
Le Suquet **15** *C4*
Monza **16** *B4*
Mr Chow **17** *A5*

O Fado **18** *B4*
Oriental Canteen **19** *C3*
Patisserie Valerie **21** *B4*
Pizza on the Park **22** *A6*
Stockpot **24** *A5*
Zafferano **25** *B6*

Pubs & bars 🍸
Admiral Codrington **26** *C4*

Bunch of Grapes **27** *B4*
Crescent **28** *C3*
Eclipse **29** *C4*
Enterprise **30** *C4*
Oratory **32** *C3*
Paxton's Head **33** *A5*

📍 See London at a glance, p19-24, for related maps.

Queen's Gate, Cromwell Road, and Exhibition Road framed a centre of learning in the High Victorian tradition, with the Natural History Museum and Victoria and Albert Museums among the most architecturally resplendent. The Royal Albert Hall, home to Sir Henry Wood's Promenade Concerts, held all kinds of events, from the Shakespeare Ball in 1911 attended by 80 visiting royals, to Oswald Moseley's fascist rallies or a psychic's public attempt to reunite Conan Doyle with 10,000 of his admirers one week after the author's death. The Albert Memorial overlooking the site testifies to Prince Albert's influence in these massive changes.

The last century's rebuilding has for the most part reflected the wealth of its residents – Harrods was rebuilt in 1905, and Knightsbridge now boasts many of London's smartest shops – while South Kensington continues to be 'Museumland', with the Lycée Charles de Gaulle and the French Cultural Institute in Queensberry Place lending a Gallic air to the area.

Sights ⊖ *Hyde Park Corner, Knightsbridge, South Kensington.* ⊖ *See p460.*

Hyde Park

① *General information from Rangers Lodge, T020-7298 2100.* The road called Knightsbridge begins at Hyde Park Corner, where Apsley Gate, Decimus Burton's classical screen, provides the most impressive entrance to the park. Just beyond is a colossal statue of Achilles erected in honour of the Duke of Wellington, like the plan of Hyde Park Corner itself. Parallel to Knightsbridge, the soft horse-riding track of **Rotten Row** heads west, once the site of the Great Exhibition's Crystal Palace. To the north along **Park Lane** stand huge hotels, car showrooms and mansion blocks hidden behind the trees.

The wide open stretch of grass between here and the Serpentine often seems deserted, even in summer, except during the regular open-air concerts, demonstrations and Royal occasions. A little further on, a tiny information centre selling official guidebooks and postcards can be found in the grand Old Police House, headquarters of the Royal Parks.

From here the Meadow and the Dell roll down to the shore of the **Serpentine Lake**, a good place to hire a boat or swim in summer on the opposite bank at the **Lido** ① *T020-7706 3422, Jul and Aug*, and take a snack in the more attractive of the two café-restaurants in the park (reached across the bridge that divides the Serpentine from the Long Water and hence Hyde Park from Kensington Gardens). The path in Hyde Park along the north side of the Long Water, past the **Henry Moore Arch**, ends up among the fish ponds and fountains of the Italian Gardens at Lancaster Gate. Look out here for the classical arch known as **Queen Anne's Alcove**, designed by Wren.

Kensington Gardens → *See page 323 for Kensington Palace.*

Over the Long Bridge, towards the Lido, is Kensington Gardens' prize asset, the **Serpentine Gallery** ① *T020-7402 6075, www.serpentinegallery.org.uk, daily 1000-1800, free*, a little square 1930s tea pavilion with a lantern and golden ball on the top. Outside are a semi-circle of stone benches by Ian Hamilton Finlay, inscribed with different translations of some evocative lines from Virgil. Inside, the quiet gallery was completely refurbished in 1998, confirming a reputation steadily acquired since its opening in 1970 for being one of London's most exciting small spaces for international contemporary art, charmingly at odds with its dinky situation. An

⁞ Harrods' Hall of Fame

Harrods is hard to miss: well signposted at Knightsbridge tube, its famous terracotta building, picked out like a fairground at night, has dominated the Brompton Road for almost a hundred years. Founded by Charles Harrod in 1849, this small perfume and cosmetics store became the largest general shop in the world, boasting the first escalator in London and employing thousands of staff. Its seven floors remain a sumptuous five- star shopping experience, featuring the marble chiller cabinets of the legendary Food Halls, acres of designerwear and an alarmingly tidy toy shop.

Since the 1980s though it has become almost as famous for the notoriety of its current owner, Mohammed Al Fayed. A controversial character who loves the limelight, he has stamped his personality all over the store, sadly all the more so since the death of his son Dodi with Princess Diana. Whatever they may be looking to purchase upstairs, most tourists don't want to miss the Diana and Dodi Memorial in the basement at the foot of one of the Egyptian escalators. Portrait photos of the tragic pair are sentimentally enshrined on a sort of funereal ivy-bedecked wishing-well, a fairly second-rate exhibition of the window dresser's art sandwiched between the Harrods marketing shop and the lost property department. Its most macabre feature is an actual wine glass supposedly in use on that fateful night at the Paris Ritz. As everybody knows, the couple were killed in a car accident pursued by paparazzi, making it all the more ironic that this is the only part of the whole store were photography is permitted.

exciting new initiative has been the annual commissioning of inspiring temporary pavilions by outstanding contemporary archtiects.

Tree-filled Kensington Gardens spread out behind the gallery, criss-crossed with signposted paths leading to the Round Pond, the Peter Pan statue beside Long Water, and the Broad Walk in front of Kensington Palace. The latest suggested route is the seven-mile **Diana Princess of Wales Memorial Walk** ① *for more information, To20-7298 2000, or call into the Old Police House information centre,* through four of central London's Royal parks (see also page 144).

Albert Hall

Beyond the gallery on the right looms the Gothic spire and canopy of the Albert Memorial, designed by Sir George Gilbert Scott and finished in 1872. On closer inspection a 14-ft gilded bronze statue of Prince Albert can be found keeping his finger in the place where he's just left off reading the catalogue of his Great Exhibition. Much against his own wishes, Victoria's far-from-pompous or grandiose consort is commemorated by an excess of ardently imperialist statuary and fancy stonework. Across the road is his much more fitting memorial, the great domed oval of the Royal Albert Hall. Queen Victoria unexpectedly christened the building as she laid the foundation stone in 1867, six years after Albert's death, and she was still too overcome with grief to attend the opening four years later.

Around Albert Hall

To the right of the Albert Hall is the **Royal College of Art** ① *To20-7590 4444*, one of the city's most prestigious and accomplished art schools, mounting regular exhibitions of student's work. Left of the Hall, on the corner of Exhibition Road, is the mid-19th century red-brick home of the **Royal Geographical Society** ① *T020-7591 3000, Mon-Fri 0930-1730*, adorned with sculptures of Shackleton and Livingstone, two of the explorers that the Society dispatched in its heyday. Exhibitions of photography and on geographical themes are mounted in the new annexe next door. Off Exhibition Road are **Imperial College** and the **Royal College of Music** (see page 167) and also **The Polish Institute and Sikorski Museum** ① *20 Princes Gate, T020-7589 9249, Mon-Fri 1400-1600, free*, a very traditional military memorabilia museum on three floors in memory of the Polish forces that fought in the Second World War. Nearby, the **Polish Hearth Club** ① *55 Princes Gate, T020-7589 4635*, is a smart Polish restaurant. Next up on Exhibition Road is the first of the area's main events.

Science Museum

① *T020-7942 4455, booking and information T0870-8704868, www.sciencemuseum.org.uk. 1000-1800 daily. Free, charges for combinations of IMAX and Virtual Voyage (£2.50 extra), screenings in IMAX Cinema (T0870-8704771, £7.50, £6 concessions and children): at 1045 (Sat, Sun only), 1145, 1245, 1345, 1445, 1545, 1645 daily, free 20-min guided tours on the hour every hour, as well as 1 50-min tour of the whole museum usually at 1400.*

The Science Museum prides itself on being one of the most forward-thinking, interactive and accessible museums in the country, a claim fairly recently enhanced with the opening of the new Wellcome Wing: four floors dedicated to displaying cutting-edge science and technology incorporating an Imax cinema and the first Virtual Voyage simulator in Europe. With origins similar to the V&A's, the emphasis here has always been on education. One of the best things about the Science Museum is that guidebooks or guided tours are hardly necessary: most of the exhibits either speak for themselves or are thoroughly labelled.

Strictly speaking it's more a museum of technology or applied science than science itself, with the wonders of technology artfully employed to make their own story entertaining. The Post Office at the main entrance sets the everyday tone, where the Barclays cashpoint and Bureau de Change could almost be exhibits in themselves, next to the enormous wheels and landing gear of an Airbus. The museum

12 Hyde Park & Kensington Gardens

is more open plan than most, its six long floors divided by broad themes and subjects rather than rooms, and with more than enough absorbing activities to keep children amused for hours. In the basement is Launch Pad, a very popular hands-on gallery of educational scientific games.

Immediately beyond the high-tech ticket desks and the Information Point on the ground floor, the pioneers of the Industrial Revolution are celebrated in *Power* and *Synopsis*, beautifully engineered steam engines alongside a reconstruction of James Watt's workshop and Foucault's Pendulum demonstrating that the earth spins on its axis. Leaping into the 20th century, the **Space Gallery** features a replica of the Apollo 11 lunar lander and explores rocket science in general.

See-through glass lifts glide up and down from here between all floors. The main body of the ground floor is then taken up with **Making the Modern World**, a series of important 'firsts' from 1750 to 2000. These include: *Puffing Billy* from 1815; the oldest surviving steam engine in the world, Stephenson's *Rocket*; the streamlined powerboat *Miss England* from 1929; aircraft like the Lockheed *10A Electra* hanging from the ceiling; a stack of Volkswagen *Beetles* on the wall; the *Apollo 10* Command Module; and a copy of the spiral model for DNA. At the far end glows the weird blue light of the new Wellcome Wing. The space age **Deep Blue Café** with its spooky underlit tabletops provides a spot to one side where the future can be discussed over coffee and rotisserie chicken.

The **Wellcome Wing** brings the museum bang up to date with the latest advances in digital technology and biomedical science. On the ground floor, along with the gigantic **Imax Cinema** and a theme-park ride to Mars in the **Virtual Voyage Simulator**, the slickly designed displays of *Antenna* include Rapid Exhibitions based on scientific news changing weekly; features covering specific issues in more depth, changing every six months; and *Newsflash*, a digital information system on hot topics updated hourly.

Three overhanging floors then take the debate upstairs: on the first floor, largest and most interesting, **Who am I?** looks at the Human Animal and what separates us from other species, charts the Family Tree growing in our genes, tests individuals with computers psychologically and physically in Identity Parade, and more radically, involves visitors in on-going research projects in Live Science. **Digitopolis** on the second floor is divided into five 'warps' exploring the impact of digital technology on our daily lives. The third floor encourages playful discussion with some specially designed computerized board games called **In Future** that seem to be rather temperamental.

If time is limited, don't miss the third floor of the main museum, home to the **Gallery of Flight** including Amy Johnson's Gipsy Moth, other antique and modern aircraft, and the Flight Lab of interactive exhibits and models exploring how we get airborne, as well as **Health Matters**, a newish high-tech gallery dedicated to advances in modern medicine.

On the first floor, **Time Measurement** includes almost 1,000 different historic timepieces of all types, while **Food for Thought** looks at the social history and science of food and how we've arrived at the supermarket (Sainsbury's to be precise).

The second floor is the most technical, including displays on computing, nuclear physics, chemistry and printing, as well as an extraordinary collection of model ships. The top two floors are dedicated to medical and veterinary history, art and science.

Central Knightsbridge, South Kensington & Hyde Park

Natural History Museum

① To20-7942 5000, www.nhm.ac.uk. Mon-Sat 1000-1750, Sun 1100-1750. Free.

Behind the Science Museum, on Cromwell Road, stands the extraordinary old orange and blue terracotta building of the Natural History Museum. Until 1963 part of the British Museum, and since then also gobbling up the Geological Museum, this is a serious academic research institution that has become seriously fun-packed. Divided into Life Galleries and Earth Galleries, it tells the history of our animated planet with a not entirely successful combination of venerable artefacts and playschool attractions. Occasionally it feels as if the museum had been entrusted to an over-excited and over-budget biology teacher. Even so, it never disappoints children, and adults are sure to learn something about the natural world whether they want to or not. The whole building has a fundamentally serious point, effectively made, about the threat that humanity currently poses to the balance of nature.

Greeting visitors in the impressive central hall behind the majestic main entrance on Cromwell Road is the famous skeletal cast of the large herbivorous dinosaur Diplodocus. Beyond, Waterhouse Way (named after the designer of the spectacular building) is the main spine of the **Life Galleries**. (The front entrance of the Earth Galleries is on Exhibition Road down from the Science Museum.)

Left and left again on Waterhouse Way leads to the main **Dinosaur Exhibition**, its animatronic models inevitably suffering by comparison with Spielberg's special effects, but great fun for kids. Nearby are the **Mammal Galleries,** including the giant model of a blue whale and the skeleton of a woolly mammoth. Upstairs are rooms full of stuffed animals demonstrating biodiversity and a model of natural history's totem thinker, Charles Darwin in his study, as well as a collection minerals and meteorites. A right turn on Waterhouse Way passes **Creepy Crawlies** and a very worthy **Ecology Exhibition** with a weird balloon-filled 'leaf factory' demonstrating photosynthesis. The new Darwin centre displays part of the museum's massive collection of pickled lifef orms.

The **Earth Galleries** can be reached from Life Gallery 50 but it's best to take the escalator ride through the earth's core, reached through the Exhibition Road entrance. At the top, there's the opportunity to 'experience' the Kyoto earthquake in a Japanese supermarket, appreciate the span of geological time by touching a 3,850 million-year-old rock from Greenland, and ogle at some beautiful gemstones while exploring three floors of interactive questionnaires, touch-screen tellies and illuminated information panels.

★ Victoria and Albert Museum

① To20 7942 2000, exhibition booking line To870 906 3883. 1000-1745 daily, till 2200 Wed and the last Fri of the month. Free.

Better known as the V&A, the Victoria and Albert Museum is one of the world's greatest museums. Surprisingly, considering its grand façade on Cromwell Road, it wears that greatness lightly. Originally called the Museum of Manufactures, and then the South Kensington Museum, it was founded in 1857 with the intention of educating the populace in the appreciation of decorative art and design by exhibiting superb examples of what could be achieved in that field: the object lesson equivalent to the exemplary lives held up for emulation at the National Portrait Gallery (see page 62).

like the British Museum's from all corners of the globe. The overall impression it makes, though, is much more human and domestic than the British Museum (BM), despite its equally astonishing scale. Many of the objects on display around its seven miles-worth of galleries would once have decorated or been in everyday use in people's homes – very wealthy and powerful people's homes for the most part – as well as in magnificent places of worship. And most are nothing like as ancient and remote as the antiquities in the BM. On making first acquaintance with the V&A, instead of trying to see as much as possible with a limited amount of time, a better bet is simply to wander slowly around in the certain knowledge that you'll find a rewarding number of amazing things.

Broadly speaking the galleries are arranged on six different levels either by area and/or period of origin or by type of material and/or object. At the front entrance and ticket desks, beneath the impressive dome of the Central Hall, a small army of staff attempt to orientate visitors with a formidable combination of ground plans, audioguides, leaflets and polite concern.

Ground floor: Level A

Immediately inside the front door, staircases lead down on the right to **19th-century Europe and America**, and on the left to **Europe from 1600 to 1800**: illuminated books, medieval ship-shaped salt cellars, stained glass, wooden carvings, Renaissance ceramics, silverware, tapestries, dinner plates, and furniture among a horde of other things. Straight ahead on the ground floor (Level A) leads into **The Medieval Treasury**: early artefacts such as the carved ivory Veroli Casket made in 11th-century Constantinople, the 12th-century Eltenburg Reliquary, the Gloucester Candlestick cast in molten coins, a spiralling contortion of men and monsters decorating its medieval shaft, or velvet priests' robes woven with silk and silver thread. Beyond is the **Pirelli Garden**, an open-air sculpture court giving onto rooms full of graceful Renaissance sculptures from Italy. Behind these are the **Morris, Poynter and Gamble Rooms**, the V&A's original 19th-century refreshment rooms: William Morris's leafy-branched Green Dining Room, James Gamble's golden-arched and ceramic-tiled central room and Edward Poynter's Grill Room or Dutch Kitchen. The rooms were in use until the Second World War.

To the left of the information desks are rooms dedicated to the **Arts of the Islamic World** (closed for refurbishment until 2006), **India**, the **Dress Collection** (also closed until 2006) and the **Raphael Gallery**. Carpets, crystal decanters, brass basins, and an extraordinary tiled fireplace grace the Islamic Gallery; The **Nehru Gallery of Indian Art** displays sculptures based on temple dances, Mughal miniatures and jades, painted cotton coverlets, turban jewels, the golden throne of Maharaja Ranjit Singh, and Tipu's tiger. One of the museum's most popular exhibits, this strange model of a tiger attacking a redcoat, complete with an internal organ to provide sound effects, was commissioned by Tipu Sultan, ruler of Mysore and scourge of the British East India Company until his defeat at Seringapatam in 1799.

In the **Raphael Gallery** on the left are the great Renaissance artist's paper cartoons – or preliminary designs – for the Sistine Chapel tapestries depicting the lives of St Peter and St Paul. Opposite is another of the museum's favourite attractions, the **Dress Collection** from 1600 to the present: the extremity and vagaries of fashion down the ages conclusively prove that the contemporary catwalk is no more bizarre than it's ever been. In the circular room above is a selection of the museum's collection of historic musical instruments.

To the right of the information desks are Chinese, Japanese and Korean art, plaster casts and the Canon Photography Gallery. Among the wealth of exhibits dating from 3000 BC to the present in the **TT Tsui Gallery of Chinese Art** are earthenware sculptures, beautiful bodhisattvas, and the lacquer throne of Emperor Chien Lung. Next door, in the **Toshiba Gallery of Japanese Art**, are lacquer screens, silk kimonos, and ceremonial swords. On the left the monumental **Cast Courts** contain full-size plaster casts of European architecture and sculpture including Trajan's Column (in two halves) and Michelangelo's David. Beyond, the **Canon Photography Gallery** mounts regular themed exhibitions on issues in photography and retrospectives of great photographers' work.

Level Lower B

Between the ground and first floors, on Lower B, up the staircase immediately to left and right of the front entrance, are the **British Galleries**. These 15 rooms have been transformed by a £31 million project to tell the history of British design from 1500 to 1900 chronologically with the help of four themes: *Style, Who Led Taste?* , *What Was New?* and *Fashionable Living*. It features big names like Robert Adam, Thomas Chippendale and William Morris along with the Great Bed of Ware, the Melville Bed, James II's wedding togs and furniture by Charles Rennie Mackintosh.

First Floor: Level B

On the first floor (Level B) are the Ironwork Galleries, the Jewellery Gallery, the Silver Gallery, Tapestries and the 20th-Century Gallery. The **Jewellery Gallery** (closed until 2008), its precious exhibits dating from 2000 BC to the present day, includes the Armada Jewel given by Queen Elizabeth I to her favourite vice-chamberlain; the finest **Tapestries** are the Devonshire Hunting Tapestries, wool-woven in the early 1400s, portraying the medieval chase both sporting and amorous. The intriguing **20th-Century Gallery** exhibits modern landmarks in design and applied art: a Bauhaus table lamp, mass-produced Eames furniture, Kandinsky's book of painted music *Klänge*, and the work of contemporary potters.

Second floor: Level C

On the second floor (Level C) the **Glass Gallery** displays a sparkling array of the stuff dating back 4000 years, one highlight being the *Luck of Edenhall*, a beautiful Syrian beaker that has managed to avoid being broken since it was brought back to England from the Crusades.

Third floor: Level D

On the third Floor (Level D), the **Ceramics Gallery** displays the most comprehensive collection of pottery in the world, including a very rare Medici porcelain bottle which was Europe's first attempt to copy the Chinese potters, and a vase by Picasso.

Henry Cole Wing

The Henry Cole Wing, named after the museum's first director, is devoted to the largest single collection of the great landscape painter **John Constable**'s oils and watercolours, donated by his daughter, as well as **Rodin** sculptures (both on level 6); marvellous 16th-century portrait miniatures by **Nicholas Hilliard** (level 4); the **European Ornament Gallery**; and the **Frank Lloyd Wright Gallery**.

Brompton Oratory

ⓘ *T020-7808 0900. 0630-2000 daily. Free.* Next door to the V&A, on Thurloe Place, stands the Brompton Oratory, the most flamboyant Catholic church in London, built in 1884 and a very English take on the Italian and French church builders. With its marbles, candles and 17th-century statuary, it provides a grand and peaceful haven off the busy Brompton Road.

● Sleeping

Knightsbridge, South Kensington & Hyde Park *p155, maps p156 & 160*

L Basil Street, 8 Basil St, SW3, T020-7581 3311, www.thebasil.com. 87 rooms. A nostalgic piece of the Algonquin in old Edwardian Knightsbridge, very traditionally English and great for quiet afternoon teas in the lounge.

L Pelham, 15 Cromwell Pl, SW7, T020-7589 8288, www.firmdale.com. 50 rooms. Genuinely warm and effortlessly gracious staff, a decent rival to Blakes with untrendy but delicately tasteful rooms, 2 lobbies and nestling spots just for visitors. In the same group as the Charlotte Street and Covent Garden hotels, and also Number 16.

AL Blakes, 33 Roland Gdns, SW7, T020-7370 6701, www.blakeshotels.com. 47 rooms. Another Anoushka Hempel concern and a celebrity and honeymooner favourite without self-consiousness, a place to be pampered. Private, recherché and cramped. Each room is different.

AL Mandarin Oriental Hyde Park, 66 Knightsbridge, SW1, T020-7235 2000, www.mandarinoriental.com. 200 rooms. Underrated luxury hotel, good for genteel teas, with an excellent restaurant called Foliage doing very competent contemporary fusion food.

A Aster House, 3 Sumner Pl, SW7, T020-7581 5888, www.asterhouse.com. Sweet little guest house with 14 rooms, a garden and conservatory tea room.

A The Claverley, 13-14 Beaufort Gdns, SW3, T020-7589 8541, www.claverleyhotel.co.uk. Comfortable and classy small hotel (8 double rooms out of a total of 30). All rooms different, with marble bathrooms, decorated in a romantic English way. Breakfast included.

A Diplomat, 2 Chesham St, SW1, T020-7235 1544, www.btinternet.com/~diplomat.hotel. An old building with a beautiful staircase, 26 rooms, near Harrods; large quiet rooms at the back.

A Five Sumner Place, 5 Sumner Pl, SW7, T020-7584 7586, www.sumnerplace.com. Another cosy, chintzy and award-winning hideaway.

A Franklin, 28 Egerton Gdns, SW3, T020-7584 5533, www.franklinhotel.co.uk. 46 rooms, quiet, other-worldly but also very 'English' hotel out of the way just off

Brompton Rd. Dining room mainly for guests and their friends.

A The Gainsborough, 7-11 Queensberry Pl, T020-7957 0000. Over the road from, and part of the same group as, the Gallery (see below), equally comfortable but slightly less expensive (with only showers en suite).

A The Gallery, 10 Queensberry Pl, South Kensington, SW7, T020-7915 0000, www.eeh.co.uk. Four diamonds (ie no restaurant) but very smart bar and lobby, breakfast included in price.

A The Gore, 189 Queen's Gate, SW7, T020-7584 6601, www.gorehotel.com. 53 rooms, a classic hotel, wood-panelled, and with that certain something for special occasions, family-run by the same people as Hazlitt's in Soho. Now with the added attraction of the Bistro 190 bar and restaurant.

A Number Sixteen, 16 Sumner Pl, SW7, T020- 7589 5232, www.numbersixteenhotel.co.uk. 42 rooms in 4 small townhouses. Elegant privacy and the most salubrious (and expensive) of the set in this dainty little stucco street. Another of the successful Firmdale group's operations.

B The Regency, 100 Queen's Gate, SW7, T020-7373 7878, www.regency-london.co.uk. 210 rooms. Efficient, clean, corporate, ready-and-waiting but in a fine old building.

D Linstead Hall, on Imperial College Campus (Accommodation Link), Watts Way, Prince's Gdns, SW7, T020-7594 9507, www.imperialcollege-accommodationlink. co.uk. Student hall of residence in pole position for museum visits.

E Albert, 191 Queen's Gate, SW7, T020-7584 3019, www.thealberthotel.uk.com. Student halls let in the summer holiday, 70 beds, 10-bed dorms £15 a night, all including breakfast. Book well ahead.

E South Kensington YHA, 65-67 Queen's Gate, SW7, T0870 770 6132, outside UK T+44-207-584 7031, bph.hostel@ scout.org.uk. Open Feb-22 Dec daily, reception 0700-2200, £30.50, under-18s £20.00. 180 beds in Baden Powell House, home of the international Scout movement, popular with educational groups.

❼ Eating

Knightsbridge, South Kensington & Hyde Park p155, maps p156 & 160

Bibendum, 81 Fulham Rd, SW3, T020-7581 5817. Conran's great big gastrodome above a stylish oyster and champagne bar, on the first floor of the old Michelin building, still happening after all these years.

The Collection, 264 Brompton Rd, SW3, T020-7225 1212. For poseurs with less style but more balls this is a DJ-driven music bar and restaurant approached by a corridor catwalk, the sort of place where Posh might have met Becks, choosing confidently from the global menu.

Fifth Floor, Harvey Nichols, 109-125 Knightsbridge, SW1, T020-7235 5250. *The Collection*'s low-rise equivalent, the penthouse joint atop London's most fashionable department store adored by fans of *Sex and the City* enjoying the light, bright atmosphere and each other as much as the global menu, closed Sun nights.

Zafferano, 15 Lowndes St, SW1, T020-7235 5800. Of the many celebrity Italian restaurants this is easily the best value (it only just scrapes into this bracket), not at all intimidating and worth every penny.

La Brasserie, 272 Brompton Rd, SW3, T020-7581 3089. One of the most delightful restaurants in this price bracket, a proper Parisian all-day nosherie that shows up some of its chain competitors, best for an evening rendezvous at the bar or a sit down with your shopping for a late brunch or high tea.

Cactus Blue, 86 Fulham Rd, SW3, T020-7823 7858. A beautifully designed and hip restaurant and bar where the surprisingly wide-ranging menu from New Mexico rarely disappoints.

Mr Chow, 151 Knightsbridge, SW1, T020-7589 7347. For top-quality Chinese cuisine this is something of a Knightsbridge institution, making no concession to passing fashions in its interior design but sticking to the delivery of highly accomplished recipes from Beijing.

O Fado, 45-50 Beauchamp Pl, SW3, T020-7589 3002. An old Portuguese restaurant with bags of character, never afraid to let the joint start jumping to live music.

It'su, 118 Draycott Av, SW3, T020-7584 5522. Younger and more upbeat than *Mr Chow*, this is one of the most fashionable conveyor belt sushi operations in London. Not bookable.

Kemps, 15 Cromwell Pl, SW1, T020-7589 8288, near South Ken tube, in *The Pelham Hotel*. Another reliable option with a sense of occasion, for some good modern British food in a genteel environment.

Monza, 6 Yeoman's Row, SW3, T020-7591 0210. Has a casual and home-baked Italian atmosphere that belies the quality of the food.

Le Suquet, 104 Draycott Av, SW3, T020-7581 1785. An intimate and reliable little French seafood restaurant.

More difficult to find is an inexpensive treat in this area, although the cafés below are all of a superior standard.

Daquise, 20 Thurloe St, SW7, T020-7589 6117. This is the one charming place that tourists and Londoners agree can't be bettered, a perennially fading but stubborn survivor, a Polish restaurant that sums up the spirit of old South Ken.

Il Falconiere, 84 Old Brompton Rd, SW7, T020-7589 2401. For a traditional family-style Italian meal at a leisurely pace, this place is a bargain.

Jacob's, 20 Gloucester Rd, SW7, T020-7581 9292. A quirky little Armenian 'wysiwyg' restaurant (ie, you can't understand the menu): order food direct from the display trolleys.

Oriental Canteen, 2a Exhibition Rd, SW7, T020-7581 8831. Does good noodle soups and rice dishes in an even more basic and no-nonsense atmosphere, a favourite with the local Cantonese.

The Pizza on the Park, 11 Knightsbridge, SW5, T020-7235 5273. One of the better branches of Pizza Express with live jazz (£10-18) downstairs every night.

Stockpot, 6 Basil St, SW3, T020-7589 8627. The other long-standing old-timer, beloved for its no-nonsense approach to basic hot meals.

● *For an explanation of sleeping and eating price codes used in this guide, see inside the* ● *front cover. Other relevant information is found in Essentials, see pages 44-46.*

Cafés and sandwich bars

Café Monpelliano, 144 Brompton Rd, SW3, T020-7225 2926. Another busy, bustling Knightsbridge Italian institution.

Fifth Floor Café, Harvey Nichols, Knightsbridge, T020-7235 5000 (see above). This has to be top of the fashion pack, not cheap but then that's not the point.

Glorietta Patisserie, 128 Brompton Rd, SW3, T020-7589 4750. A sweet little Viennese cake shop opposite Harrods.

Patisserie Valerîe, 215 Brompton Rd, SW3, T020-7823 9971. A little further down from Glorietta Patisserie this is another fine branch of the delicious and sophisticated patisserie chain.

Pubs and bars

Knightsbridge, South Kensington & Hyde Park *p155, maps p156 & 160*
Many of the area's old locals have been converted into restaurants or private houses, leaving the remainder to the tourists and language students. However, there are some notable exceptions.

Admiral Codrington, 17 Mossop St, SW3, T020-7581 0005. One pub that has remained very popular with locals, despite refurbishment, confidently crossing the divide between pub and bar.

Bunch of Grapes, 207 Brompton Rd, SW3, T020-7589 4944. A cosy Victorian place.

The Crescent, 99 Fulham Rd, SW3, T020-7225 2244. A little designer surprise, also with fine wines, wonderful bar snacks and room upstairs.

The Eclipse, 113 Walton St, SW3, T020-7581 0123. A cocktail bar that may prove to have caught the pulse of the area with its combination of understated beige interior and enthusiastic staff. Then again, most of the area's smart restaurants (see above) offer drinking experiences of a similar style.

The Enterprise, 35 Walton St, SW3, T020-7584 3148. Has been turned into a swanky gastrobar with a considerable reputation for the quality of its expensive food.

Oratory, 232 Brompton Rd, SW3, T020-7584 3493. A little more grown-up than the Enterprise or Eclipse, this is an unpretentious winebar in an old building with seats outside and amazing toilets in the bowels of the Brompton Oratory itself,

very convenient for the V&A.

Paxton's Head, 153 Knightsbridge, SW1, T020-7589 6627. A splendid Edwardian place.

Entertainment

Knightsbridge, South Kensington & Hyde Park *p155, maps p156 & 160*
Cinema
Cine Lumière, 17 Queensberry Pl, SW7, T020-7073 1350. The well-appointed cinema in the French Institute shows European classics and recent releases, most with English subtitles.

Goethe Institut, 50 Princes Gate, SW7, T020-7596 4000. Has undergone a major refurbishment and shows mainly German films with subtitles or surtitles. There's a German film festival in conjuction with the NFT at the end of Nov.

Music
Classical and opera Royal Albert Hall, Kensington Gore, SW7, T020-7589 8212. Grand setting for just about any and every type of entertainment spectacular from high- to lowbrow. The BBC Henry Wood Promenade Concerts, aka The Proms, are a huge and ever-popular classical music festival with a jingoistic 'last night', taking place at the Albert Hall every year between Jul and Sep. £3 for a promenading ticket on sale 1 hr before each concert.

Royal College of Music, Prince Consort Rd, SW7, T020-7589 3643, www.rcm.ac.uk. Lunchtime concerts Tue and Thu at 1305 and on Fri term-time in St Mary Abbots Church, South Kensington. Prestigious concerts in the evenings.

Rock, folk and jazz The Pizza on the Park, 11 Knightsbridge, SW5, T020-7235 5273. Has live jazz (£10-18) downstairs every night, often with top names, best booked well in advance.

Shopping

Knightsbridge, South Kensington & Hyde Park *p155, maps p156 & 160*
Lots of people go to Knightsbridge and South Ken solely for the shops, and very brave they are too. The chances are slim of escaping from an expedition down Sloane St, Brompton Rd, Beauchamp

Pl, Walton St or Draycott Av without being forced to phone an independent financial adviser.

Passing Harrods on the right, near Knightsbridge tube is Basil Street, one of the best little secret streets in Knightsbridge linking the area's topping shopping attractions, Harrods and Harvey Nichols.

Brompton Road and Knightsbridge
Brompton Rd is the generally more accessible place for fashion victims under 35.
Emporio Armani, 191 Brompton Rd, SW3, T020-7823 8818. The flagship store.
Harrods, 87-135 Brompton Rd, SW1, T020-7730 1234, www.harrods.com. Top of the heap of course, open Mon-Sat 1000-1900 (Nov-Jan also Sun 1200-1800). The smartest and most famous department store in the city, possibly the world, now blessed with a mawkish shrine to the owner's son Dodi Fayed and his girlfriend Princess Diana. Dodge the gawpers and head boldly into what is undoubtedly the most lavish and disorientating temple to retail sales in the UK, not just for its palatial food hall but for any kind of consumer durable. Many staff have perfected the exquisite supercilious tone of voice that the immortal sit-com enquiry 'Are you being served?' really deserves. Their stock is still admirable too but considering the mark-up is generally better left on the peg or shelf where it always looks as if it belongs. Service goes out of the window during the sales every Jan and Jul, when the initial scrum beggars belief.
Betty Jackson, 311 Brompton Rd, SW3, T020-7589 7884. For wearable designs 'aimed at 20-60-year-old' women.
The Library, 268 Brompton Rd, SW3, T020-7589 6569. Kind of Issy Miyake meets gay combat gear.
Issy Miyake, 270 Brompton Rd, SW1, T020-7581 3760. The man himself, for the more sombre classic lines.
Harvey Nichols, 109-125 Knightsbridge, SW1, T020-7235 5000, www.harveynichols.com. Knightsbridge's shrine to haute couture, open Mon-Fri 1000-2000, Sat 1000-1900, Sun 1200-1800. 'Harvey Nicks' to the darlings who would simply die if this department store did not exist. It too has unseemly sales every Jan and Jul.

Janet Reger, 2 Beauchamp Pl, SW3, T020-7584 9360. Beauchamp Pl (pronounced *Beecham*) is lined with upmarket boutiques, including this world-famous women's lingerie designer.
Whistles, 303 Brompton Rd, SW3, T020-7823 9134. For own-label and left-field women's designerwear.

Sloane Street
Generally speaking the high fashion outlets and designer jewellery concerns around here are less concentrated but even more numerous than in Mayfair. On Sloane St can be found the likes of Chanel, Dior, D&G, Gucci, Hermes, Valentino and Starewski.
Joseph, 16 Sloane St, SW1, T020-7235 1991 (for women), 74 Sloane Av, T020-7591 0808 (for men). Marginally more affordable and youth-orientated.

Sloane and Draycott Avenues
Where the Brompton Rd becomes the Fulham Rd, heading south for the King's Rd are Sloane Av and Draycott Av, the home of outlets for:
Gallery Gautier, 171 Draycott Av, SW3, T020-7584 4648.
Betsey Johnson, 106 Draycott Av, SW3, T020-7591 0005. Originals, very feminine dresses, cute cardigans and matching skirts.
Paul Smith, 84-86 Sloane Av, SW3, T020-7589 9139.

Fulham Road
On the Fulham Rd designer jewellery and furnishings tend to take over from fashion, at places like:
Conran Shop, Michelin House, 81 Fulham Rd, SW3, T020-7589 7401.
Divertimenti, 139-141 Fulham Rd, SW3, T020-7581 8065. An upmarket chain specializing in groovy kitchen- and homeware.
Oggetti, 135 and 143 Fulham Rd, SW3, T020-7581 8088. For stylish household goods that partly explain why Brits take jobs in Milan.

Near South Kensington tube
Tridias, 25 Bute St, SW7, T020-7584 2330. Wooden toys, some made by independent toymakers.

Chelsea

Chelsea is a very comfortable, stylish part of town with an impeccable bohemian pedigree, occasionally displaying bursts of real street cred. Its High Street, the King's Road, became one of the pivots of 'swinging London' in the 1960s and outraged middle England again a decade later by spawning the Sex Pistols, the shock troops of punk.

Nowadays much quieter and more expensive, freighted with designer boutiques and the sleek Chelsea boys and babes they attract, the well-heeled King's Road heads southwest between the Fulham Road and the river, threading its way through smart residential squares and quaint cobbled mews. The most interesting streets to explore lie on its south side, towards the river, along Royal Hospital Road and the Chelsea Embankment up to the Albert Bridge. Apart from the Royal Hospital itself, very grand almshouses from another era for retired soldiers, this pretty area conceals the peaceful delights of the Chelsea Physic Garden, the pickled Victoriana of Carlyle's House and some very genteel pubs. Further down the King's Road, around the World's End, Chelsea loosens up a little to become fertile browsing ground for offbeat fashions and better-value restaurants. ▸▸ *For Sleeping, Eating and other listings see pages 174-177.*

▸▸ For Sleeping, Eating and other listings see pages 174-177.

History

Chelsea, or 'chelchythe', Isle of Shingles, was cut off from the spread of London by marshy fields and creeks around modern Victoria Station. The Domesday book describes it as a village in Middlesex, but when Chelsea Bridge was built in the 1850s workers uncovered Roman and British weapons and bones suggesting that a battle was fought hereabouts. Under the Tudors and Stuarts, it became known as the 'Village of Palaces' – Henry VIII built Chelsea Manor House, the Earl of Shrewsbury and Duke of Norfolk moved here, as did Sir Thomas More. At Beaufort House More welcomed distinguished visitors such as Erasmus and Holbein, and is said to have flogged heretics against trees in the substantial orchard.

All Saints' church sat down by the river, so by the late 17th century a number of isolated houses were scattered across arable fields and pasture, orchards, gardens and riverside meadows. Chelsea Common provided grazing land and also held a gravel pit. The King's Highway (modern Fulham Road), notorious for its footpads, sped carriages to Portsmouth, while Charles II would use his private road (modern King's Road) to travel to Hampton Court. In 1687 Sir Christopher Wren built Chelsea Royal Hospital for veteran soldiers – Wellington lay in state here in 1852 and two people died in the crush – and the Physic Garden was set up by the Apothecaries Company. It exhibited the country's first rock garden and the first greenhouse, and sent cotton seed to America.

In the reign of Queen Anne townhouses appeared in Cheyne Walk and Cheyne Row, while Sloane Square and Sloane Street took shape in the 1770s and 1780s, but by 1801 the population was still only 12,000. By 1901, however, it had risen almost eightfold. The area developed a reputation for its artistic community – the formation of the Chelsea Arts Club emerged from regular meetings of the likes of Whistler and Sickert in the *Six Bells* on the King's Road. George Eliot died in number 4 Cheyne Walk, and JMW Turner lived out his life under the pseudonym of Admiral or 'Puggy' Booth at number 119.

Central Chelsea

13 Chelsea

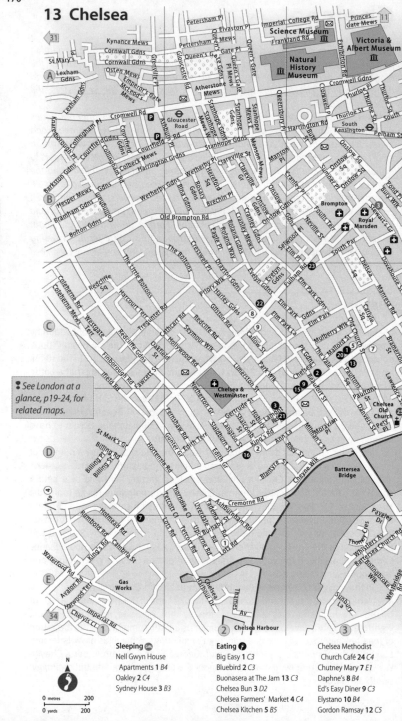

Central Chelsea

❗ *See London at a glance, p19-24, for related maps.*

N
0 metres 200
0 yards 200

Sleeping 🛏
Nell Gwyn House
 Apartments **1** *B4*
Oakley **2** *C4*
Sydney House **3** *B3*

Eating 🍴
Big Easy **1** *C3*
Bluebird **2** *C3*
Buonasera at The Jam **13** *C3*
Chelsea Bun **3** *D2*
Chelsea Farmers' Market **4** *C4*
Chelsea Kitchen **5** *B5*

Chelsea Methodist
 Church Café **24** *C4*
Chutney Mary **7** *E1*
Daphne's **8** *B4*
Ed's Easy Diner **9** *C3*
Elystano **10** *B4*
Gordon Ramsay **12** *C5*

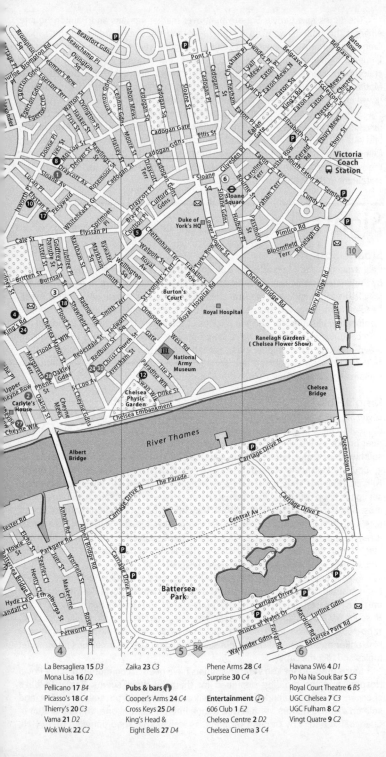

La Bersagliera **15** *D3*	Zaika **23** *C3*	Phene Arms **28** *C4*	Havana SW6 **4** *D1*
Mona Lisa **16** *D2*		Surprise **30** *C4*	Po Na Na Souk Bar **5** *C3*
Pellicano **17** *B4*	**Pubs & bars** 🍷		Royal Court Theatre **6** *B5*
Picasso's **18** *C4*	Cooper's Arms **24** *C4*	**Entertainment** 🎭	UGC Chelsea **7** *C3*
Thierry's **20** *C3*	Cross Keys **25** *D4*	606 Club **1** *E2*	UGC Fulham **8** *C2*
Vama **21** *D2*	King's Head &	Chelsea Centre **2** *D2*	Vingt Quatre **9** *C2*
Wok Wok **22** *C2*	Eight Bells **27** *D4*	Chelsea Cinema **3** *C4*	

The 1830s saw Carlyle Square built over market gardens and Paulton Square emerge, The Boltons went up in the 1850s and Cadogan Gardens in the 1890s. Cremorne Gardens, meanwhile, became a popular venue. As with other pleasure gardens, it held a banqueting hall, grottoes and bowers, and hosted a bizarre collection of events, from the re-enactment of the storming of the fort in Sebastopol to Madame Genevieve crossing the Thames from here on a tightrope. By the 1880s, however, it was considered a "nursery of every kind of vice".

By the early 1900s, the site still held market gardens, (in 1977 a large council development known as World's End swallowed up the area), and Sloane Avenue was laid out in the 1920s. The football stadium was built in 1905 next to Brompton Cemetery, and the Michelin building on the Fulham Road produced tyres until it went the way of much of the rest of Chelsea and was turned into a fashion store and restaurant in the 1980s.

Sights ⊖ *Sloane Square, South Kensington.* ⊖ *See p460.*

See p460.

Sloane Square

Belgravia ends and Chelsea begins at Sloane Square, quite an attractive spot spoilt by the endless traffic but romantic and European in atmosphere at night when the fairy lights are twinkling in the branches of its trees. The Square and Sloane Street, heading north up to Knightsbridge, take their names from Sir Hans Sloane, whose 'cabinet of curiosities' formed the nucleus of the British Museum's collection in the 18th century. Since then they have more famously given their names to a particular breed of young upper-middle class English society: 'Sloane Rangers' turn up their shirt collars, wear pearls and live according to a regimented set of social rules in Fulham and Parsons Green.

King's Road

Lower Sloane Street heads south towards Chelsea Bridge, but it was the King's Road, the real spine of Chelsea, that became famous in the 1970s for what is now a much rarer breed: punks, and their arch enemies, the hippies. The King's Road weaves southwest for a mile before jinking sharp left and then right at the Moravian burial ground and *Man in the Moon* pub, and then carrying on down past the World's End to Fulham. Near this kink, at number 430, Malcolm Maclaren and Vivienne Westwood set up the shop called *Sex* that gave its name in 1976 to their brainchild, punk rock's most notorious band, the **Sex Pistols**. They briefly became the epicentre of one of rock's most anarchic, disaffected and influential new departures. Nowadays anarchy is hardly uppermost in the minds of the road's well-groomed shoppers. Number 430 King's Road has become the *World's End Shop*, a pricey outlet for Vivienne Westwood's wacky and ground-breaking designerwear.

Almost any left turn off the King's Road shortly after Sloane Square passes through small Georgian streets, squares and mews towards Royal Hospital Road and the river. Here lives another of Chelsea's rare breeds, the **Chelsea Pensioners** ① *Royal Hospital Rd, T020 7730 5282, www.chelsea-pensioners.org.uk, Mon-Sat 1000-1200, 1400-1600, Sun 1400-1600 (not Oct-Apr), free*, easily recognizable in their smart navy blue uniforms and peaked caps, or in summer and on special occasions their scarlet tunics and tricorne caps.

Since 1689, about 400 veteran soldiers have been accommodated in the Royal Hospital and the building designed for them by Wren seems hardly to have changed. Its three splendid neoclassical courtyards still possess a stirring and solemn dignity. Visitors are allowed a look into the central one, with its statue of Charles II in a toga by Grinling Gibbons, as well as the wood-panelled Great Hall, containing an impressive portrait by Verrio of that dissipated monarch on horseback, and the Chapel, adorned with some French eagle standards captured at Waterloo. The Hospital's museum tells the story of the pensioners, a familiar sight in the area, in their navy blue uniforms and peaked caps. The **Chelsea Flower Show** takes place in the grounds every May (see page 47).

National Army Museum
① T020-7730 0717 www.national-army-museum.ac.uk. 1000-1730 daily. Free.

Appropriately enough, the National Army Museum is next door to the Royal Hospital. Established here in 1971, the museum is an efficient public relations exercise as well as an important academic resource. 'The Modern Army', exhibiting many of the latest military gizmos in use today, is the most recent addition to the displays on the history of the British army since the reign of Henry VII, told through uniforms, memorabilia and antique oddities such as the skeleton of Napoleon's horse and a scale model of the Battle of Waterloo complete with flashing lights and cottonwool smoke. In fact, far from being triumphalist, the sobering impression made by the series of darkened rooms is that organized armed conflict has been a necessary even if occasionally glamorous evil down the ages. An exhibition on the modern army displays some of the gizmos used recently in the Gulf.

Chelsea Physic Garden
① Swan Walk, T020-7352 5646, www.chelseaphysicgarden.co.uk. Apr-Oct Wed 1200-1700, Sun 1400-1800 (as well as daily throughout the Chelsea Flower Show and Chelsea Festival), winter openings on 2 Sun in Feb. Adults £5, under-16s £3.

A little further down Royal Hospital Road, Swan Walk on the left leads to the entrance (No 66) of one of the area's most enchanting places, the Chelsea Physic Garden. This walled garden is at least as old as the Royal Hospital and still plays an important role in botanical research, hence the restricted opening hours. One concession to its increasing popularity is the special snowdrop openings on two Sundays in early February.

Apart from the riverside location, the garden's attraction lies in its small scale and the care that has clearly been lavished on the wide variety of rare and interesting plants within its walls. Here, as well as the world's first rockery and some very old trees and shrubs, are borders and flowerbeds neatly divided up and laid out according to their occupants' classification and taste for light or shade. Along with the flowers and vegetables in the greenhouses, these are just some of the plants that have given us painkillers, contraceptives and expensive perfumes. A statue of 1723 commemorates Sir Hans Sloane who bought the garden around that time and gave it to the Society of Apothecaries 'so that apprentices may better distinguish good and useful plants from those that bear resemblance to them and yet are hurtful'.

Carlyle's House
① 24 Cheyne Row, T020-7352 7087, www.nationaltrust.org.uk. Apr-Oct Wed-Fri 1400-1700, Sat, Sun 1100-1700. Aults £3.70, concessions £1.80.

Beyond the **Albert Bridge**, built in 1873 and prettily lit at night, at No 24 Cheyne Row off to the right, can be found Carlyle's House, where the 'awesome sage of Chelsea', the historian and writer Thomas Carlyle and his spirited wife Jane lived from 1834. Bought by popular public subscription in the late 19th century the house is now run by the National Trust and has been kept much as it was during the couple's tempestuous cohabitation. From 1866 Carlyle lived on here alone after Jane's untimely death from a heart attack brought on by an accident involving a close friend's dog in Hyde Park. Even though his florid works are little read these days, his writing room at the top of the house, the cosy parlour, kitchen and the little back garden are all highly evocative of middle-class Victorian domesticity and mores.

Around the corner in **Glebe Place**, No 51 has long been supposed to be the oldest house in Chelsea, believed to have been a hunting lodge built for Henry VIII, although some doubt has been cast on whether it actually was. It's worth seeing, though, even if just for the extraordinary art deco house next door. Nearby, on **Lawrence Street**, where Chelsea China was once made, the novelists Henry Fielding and Tobias Smollett lived in Monmouth House.

Back on Cheyne Walk, **Chelsea Old Church** ① *T020-7352 5627, Mon-Fri 1200-1600, all day Sun,* is aptly named, dating from the early 14th century, although so badly bombed during the war that only parts of the original remain, including the More Chapel, rededicated by Thomas 'Man for all Seasons' More, the Catholic martyr, in 1528.

At the end of the Cheyne Walk, after it has moved onto the Chelsea Embankment and passed Battersea Bridge, Lots Road leads off on the left to **Chelsea Harbour**, ultra desirable condos for the very rich with a landmark tower topped by a ball that rises and falls with the tide.

● Sleeping

Chelsea *p169, map p170*
A Sydney House, 9-11 Sydney St, SW3, T020-7376 7711, www.sydneyhousechelsea.com. A luxurious boutique hotel with 21 delightful rooms, recently renovated in a wonderfully elegant style. The top room (£250 a night) has a roof terrace, well worth the extra spend.
C Oakley, 73 Oakley St, SW3, T020-7352 5599. 12 rooms, small, clean, friendly and excellent value on the approach to Albert Bridge (£45 including breakfast with shared bathrooms, £59 with en suite bathroom).
Nell Gwynn House Apartments, Sloane Av, SW3, T020-7589 1105, www.ngh apartments.co.uk. From £545-£700 per week for decent self-catering studio apartments in Nell Gwynn House on Sloane Av.

● Eating

Chelsea *p169, map p170*
Ⅲ Bluebird, 350 King's Rd, SW3, T020-7559 1000. Less expensive than Restaurant Gordon Ramsay, Terence Conran's is also an experience, a successful conversion of an old garage into a café with outside seating, a food market and, upstairs, a large and bustling restaurant doing reliable seafood and modern European dishes.
Ⅲ Daphne's, 112 Draycott Av, SW3, T020-7584 6883. Glamour-pusses, jetsetters and flashy businessmen have

long enjoyed basking in the brisk Italian atmosphere here.
Ⅲ Restaurant Gordon Ramsay, 68 Royal Hospital Rd, SW3, T020-7352 4441. The most celebrated gourmet and Michelin-starred restaurant in Chelsea, run by the famously bad-tempered celebrity chef and named after himself (closed weekends).
Ⅲ Ristorante La Bersagliera, 372 King's Rd, SW3, T020-7352 5993. A traditional Italian doing fine pizza and pasta.
Ⅲ Wok Wok, 140 Fulham Rd, SW10, T020-7370 5355. A smallish branch of the modern Chinese chain where standards are high and the atmosphere lively.

Most of the less pricey options on the King's Rd are beyond the World's End.
Ⅱ The Big Easy, 332-334 Kings Rd, SW3, T020-7352 4071. A loud party atmosphere, tries to imitate an American Bar-B-Q diner and Crabshack. Whether or not it succeeds, it remains very popular.
Ⅱ Chutney Mary, 535 King's Rd, SW10, T020-7351 3113, just off Lots Rd. A top-quality, fairly formal Indian restaurant in a swish modern building.
Ⅱ Elystano Restaurant, 25-27 Elystan St, SW3, T020-7584 5248. Another good modern Italian restaurant popular with the locals.
Ⅱ Pellicano, 19 Elystan St, SW3, T020-7589 3718, nearer Sloane Sq, between the King's Rd

and the Fulham Rd. A minimalist place to enjoy some very good modern Italian food with a Sardinian accent.

♥♥ **Thierry's**, 342 King's Rd, SW3, T020-7352 3365. Has been around for years, a thoroughly cosy and welcoming venue for some classic French recipes.

♥♥ **Vama**, 438 King's Rd, SW10, T020-7351 4118, on the corner of Limerston St. Less expensive and less formal than Chutney Mary, this modern Indian restaurant specializes in food from the northwestern frontier.

♥♥ **Zaika**, 257 Fulham Rd, SW3, T020-7351 7823. A sumptuously decorated Indian restaurant that is justifiably more expensive than many.

There are a surprising number of decent places in Chelsea where it's possible to eat a full meal (usually of Italian food) for not much more than a tenner. Most of the cheaper options are on the King's Rd itself.

♥ **Buona Sera at The Jam**, 289 King's Rd, SW3, T020-7352 8827. Has signature bunk-bed-style tables for fairly cheap and very cheerful platefuls of Italian food (just before Bluebird on the opposite side of the street).

♥ **Chelsea Bun**, 9a Limerston St, SW10, T020-7352 3635, round the corner from Ed's Easy Diner. Another Chelsea institution, almost but not quite as popular as its 19th-century namesake (see page 147), offering over 200 different straightforward meals like pasta or filled baked potatoes.

♥ **Chelsea Farmers' Market**, Sydney St. Good fresh soups can be found in the basement.

♥ **The Chelsea Kitchen**, 98 King's Rd, SW3, T020-7589 1330, nearest to Sloane Sq. Once a branch of the Stockpot chain and still doing basic meals at rock-bottom prices for this part of London.

♥ **Ed's Easy Diner**, 362 King's Rd, SW3, T020-7352 1952, nearer the World's End. Big, satisfying burgers in a buzzy atmosphere.

♥ **Picasso's**, 127 King's Rd, SW3, T020-7352 4921. Part of the Dino's chain, has also long been a King's Rd institution, more expensive but with a lively atmosphere in which to enjoy Italian and British staples.

Cafés and sandwich bars

Coffee and sandwich chains proliferate on the King's Rd.

Chelsea Methodist Church, 155a King's Rd, SW3, T020-7352 9305, next door to the Old Town Hall opposite *Habitat*. The best-value freshly made sandwiches on the King's Rd can be found in the café here, 1000-1400 Mon-Fri.

Mona Lisa, 417 King's Rd, SW1, T020-7376 5447, near the World's End. A very friendly one-off, run by Italians (surprise, surprise) doing good value hot meals and snacks.

⊙ Pubs and bars

Chelsea *p169, map p170*
Chelsea thrives on its pub life and it shows in their quality. The loudest and busiest drinking establishments, such as *Chelsea Potter*, are on the King's Rd, but it's the genial popularity of those tucked away in the side streets that marks the area out as ideal territory for an enjoyable crawl.

The Cooper's Arms, 87 Flood St, SW3, T020-7376 3120. Young's pub boasting good newspapers, a stuffed bear and more big tables.

Cross Keys, 1 Lawrence St, SW3, T020-7349 9111, heading back inland. Has a real fire. Some may find the decor over-designed, but it's good for a lively drink.

King's Head and Eight Bells, 50 Cheyne Walk (at the junction with Cheyne Row), SW3, T020-7352 1820, down by the river, with a great view of the Albert Bridge. On the tourist coach trail but that doesn't detract from the quality of the real ales or the location.

The Phene Arms, 9 Phene St, T020-7352 3294. Long a favourite with the area's gilded youth, a modern bar in an old pub with outside seating and a good but quite expensive menu.

The Surprise, 6 Christchurch Terr, T020-7349 1821. A roomy place with bare floorboards, large tables and pleasant atmosphere.

⊙ Entertainment

Chelsea *p169, map p170*
Cinema
Chelsea Cinema, 206 King's Rd, SW3, T020-7351 3742, next to *Habitat*. Has 1 screen usually showing the kind of new releases the

Central Chelsea Listings

⬤ *For an explanation of sleeping and eating price codes used in this guide, see inside the*
⬤ *front cover. Other relevant information is found in Essentials, see pages 44-46.*

good burghers of Chelsea might enjoy. **UGC Chelsea**, 279 King's Rd, SW3, T0871-2002000. 4 screens of major new releases, screens 3 and 4 the smaller pair. **UGC Fulham Rd**, 142 Fulham Rd, SW10, T0871- 2002000. 6 screens of new releases, and greater capacity than the one on the King's Rd.

Music
Rock, folk and jazz **606 Club**, 90 Lots Rd, SW10, T020-7352 5953, www.606club.co.uk. Open Mon-Wed 1930-0100, Thu 2000-0130, Fri, Sat 2000-0200, Sun 2000-2400. Admission: Mon-Thu £7, Fri, Sat £9, Sun £8. Always book at weekends. A basement jazz and blues bar that had a long and illustrious beatnik history in its old premises on the King's Rd. Now it's more plush and mainstream and requires drinking punters to eat a full, fairly reasonably priced meal. **Havana SW6**, 490 Fulham Rd, SW6, T020-7381 5005. Open 1700-0200, Salsa classes Mon, Tue, Wed, Thu at 1930. Smaller and more intimate branch of the Hanover Square Latin music cocktail bar.

Nightclubs
Most of the late-night drinking in Chelsea happens behind closed doors in private members' clubs.
Po Na Na Souk Bar, 316 King's Rd, SW3, T020-7352 7127. A loud, late and lively venue. **Vingt-Quatre**, 325 Fulham Rd, SW10, T020-7376 7224. Not really a club, but a 24-hr café bar (alcohol served till midnight) that's a long-standing late-night institution in the area doing decent continental cuisine.

Theatre
Chelsea Centre, World's End Pl, SW10, T020-7352 1967. Quite a large fringe theatre with an eclectic mix of shows.
Royal Court Theatre, Sloane Square, SW1, T020-7565 5000. Most famous for starting the 'kitchen sink' school of drama under George Devine in the 50s with plays like Osborne's *Look Back in Anger* (although it had already carved out a reputation for radicalism by staging the first productions of many of GB Shaw's plays). It has fairly recently been fully refurbished and still pursues an adventurous policy of commissioning new writing. The refurbishment includes an atmospheric and

happening restaurant and bar in the basement (T020-7565 5061).
Royal Court Theatre Upstairs, stages experimental small-scale work (same box office as main theatre).

O Shopping

Chelsea *p169, map p170*
Heal's, 234 King's Rd, SW3, T020-7349 8411. Heading down the King's Rd, most of the big-name clothes and fashion shops are lined up on the stretch before the Old Town Hall, where a change in emphasis towards interior design, antiques and homewares is marked by this branch of the furniture shop, the gateway to an area that has increasingly been branded 'Little Chelsea'. **Peter Jones**, T020-7730 3434, standing on the gateway to the King's Rd in Sloane Sq. The area's major department store (a branch of *John Lewis*), stunningly refurbished and still the favoured repository of wedding present lists for the Sloaney set.

In 'Big' Chelsea then, shops worth investigating might include:
After Noah, 261 King's Rd, SW3, T020-7351 2610, beyond *Heal's*. Specialists in contemporary and vintage 'furniture and furniment', bric-a-brac and objets d'art largely inspired by the arts and crafts movement.
Arrogant Cat, 311 King's Rd, SW3, T020-7349 9070, nearer the World's End. There are more restaurants and arty clothes shops here, like this.
Daisy and Tom, 181 King's Rd, T020-7352 5000. Stocking tasteful toys and clothes for little Jeremies and Lucindas.
Hudson and Heaton, 319 King's Rd, SW3, T020-7352 7710. Make some interesting silver jewellery.
R Soles, 109a King's Rd, SW3, T020-7351 5520. Inimitable for their way-out selection of cowboy boots and 'western' footwear.
Rococo Chocolates, 321 King's Rd, SW3, T020- 7352 5857. Make their own amazing 'artisan' bars, and also stock delights by Valrhona.
World's End Shop, 430 Kings Rd, SW10, T020-352 6551. The turquoise number with the clock going backwards, once Vivienne Westwood's shop *Sex* is still hers, now stocking a wide variety of her designer clothes.

Other designer outlets in the area include:
Agnes B, 111 Fulham Rd, SW3, T020- 7225
3477. Womenswear shop.
Patrick Cox, 129 Sloane St, SW1, T020-7730
8886. Ultra chic footwear for men and women.
World's End Bookshop, 357 King's Rd, SW3,
T020-7352 9376. An exception to all the clothes shops with a good stock of mainly second-
hand biographies and humanities titles.

▲▲ Activities

Chelsea *p169, map p170*
Chelsea Sports Centre, Manor St (next door

to the Old Town Hall), T020-7352 6985.
Swimming pool (£3), gym, classes. Open
Mon-Fri 0700-2130. **Chelsea Football Club**,
Stamford Bridge, Fulham Rd, SW6, T020-
7385 5545, near Fulham Broadway tube.

❻ Directory

Chelsea *p169, map p170*
Libraries   Chelsea Library, in the Old Town
Hall, SW3, T020-7352 6056. Open 1000-2000
Mon, Tue, Thu, 1000-1300 Wed, 1000-1700
Fri, Sat. Has a good reference section and is an
excellent source of local information.

Marylebone and Regent's Park

A discreet Georgian and Victorian backwater just to the north of the busiest street in the West End, much to its own surprise Marylebone has become distinctly fashionable. Marylebone Lane twists up from Oxford Street, an old-timer defying the regular gridiron of severe streets like Wigmore, Wimpole and Harley, and broadens out to become Marylebone High Street, still refusing to follow a straight path up to the traffic jam on the massive Marylebone Road.

Over the last decade, the High Street has been steadily colonized by upmarket fashion boutiques and a few gourmet restaurants, while Marylebone's hidden treasure, the Wallace Collection of 18th-century French paintings in Hertford House, has had a centennial overhaul courtesy of the National Lottery Heritage Fund. Along with the Wigmore Hall, one of London's most endearing venues for chamber music and song, the Wallace Collection continues to conjure the ghost of 19th-century and Edwardian London. In many of the streets and mews around, it doesn't take much imagination to hear the clatter of carriage wheels carrying Sherlock Holmes back to his Baker Street home after his latest adventure.

The crowds imitating the traffic as they queue outside Madame Tussaud's might have been a familiar sight to him, although it's difficult to say what he would have made of the story of space exploration at the revamped Planetarium. Certainly he would still recognize much of Regent's Park, just to the north, still the most delightful place in central London to escape the crush of the West End. And if hell has become other people, here's the chance to get close to some of the protected wildlife in London Zoo. ➤➤ *For Sleeping, Eating and other listings see pages 184-186.*

History

Marylebone, sitting north of the Tyburn Road was until the 18th century a series of fields and isolated houses. In 1066 the western part was the Manor of Lileston (Lisson) and the Manor of Tyburn owned the land to the east. In the 14th century parishioners moved their church from near the Tyburn gallows – "the lurking place of cut-throats" – to alongside the river Tyburn, hence the name 'St Mary-by-the- bourne'. Henry VIII appropriated both manors, and sold much of the land to, among others, the Portman and Portland estates. He did, however, keep the northern part of the Tyburn Manor lands for his hunting pursuits, enclosing Marylebone Park (later Regent's Park) with a ditch, rampart and fence to ensure good sport, and converting Marylebone Manor into a hunting lodge.

A survey of 1649 reported over 16,000 trees, including oak, ash, elm, whitehorn and maple, but by 1800, thousands of trees had been felled to be replaced by smallholdings that supplied London with dairy products and hay. Meanwhile, housing had grown north from Oxford Street. The two estates, Portland slightly ahead of Portman, built up the east and west respectively with streets named after members of their family or their country estates – Henrietta, Margaret, Harley, Holles, Wigmore, Wimpole. Cavendish Square, built in 1717, started the boom. St Peter Street, Vere Street and the Oxford Market (meat, fish and vegetables) were built to support and encourage a growing community.

By the 1770s, a suburban development had grown up around Cavendish Square. Great Portland Street, Portland Place and Baker Street ran north-south, while Wigmore and New (now Marylebone) Road ran east-west. Marylebone Gardens attracted gamblers and sharpers to its dog- and cockfights, its bear-and-bull-baitings, and to their human equivalent, boxing.

Later in the century, activities were more refined, with assembly rooms built for balls and concerts, and the discovery of medicinal waters providing for a spa. Indeed, the attraction of the *rus in urbe* ('the Country in the City') was growing. Sheep were imported to graze in Cavendish Square, and the likes of Portman Square were carefully landscaped.

The new vogue was not lost on the architect, John Nash, who developed the idea in his great project for his patron, the Regent's Park. This estate was to be the epitome of the *rus in urbe*, the "attraction of open space, free air and the scenery of Nature" as Nash put it. Surrounding the park, he planned grand stuccoed terraces, a scattering of some 56 villas, and a further residence for the Prince Regent. By 1828, when the building was largely done, the reality was somewhat scaled down, (only eight villas were built), but the effect was still magnificent.

To the northwest, market gardens and dairy farms gave way to increasing development along Wellington Street towards St John's Wood and the border with Hampstead, and building continued throughout the century such that when Marylebone Station opened in 1899, the Great Central Railway carved out 70 acres of picturesque suburbs. The area suffered heavy bombing in the middle of the last century – at least 300 bombs hit Regent's Park, which had been taken over for military encampments – and since then the properties have steadily been utilized as business premises.

Sights

⊖ *Baker St, Bond St, Great Portland Street, Oxford Circus, Regent's Park.* ⊕ *See p460.*

Marylebone Lane or James Street, both best reached by crossing Oxford Street from Bond Street tube, provide the most charming routes into deepest Marylebone. The winding path of Marylebone Lane, as its name suggests, is still just about recognizably the old village main street, before it turns into the grander breadth of modern-day Marylebone High Street. James Street (and parallel St Christopher's Place, see page 133) is lined with pleasant enough cafés. Both cross the wide progress of Wigmore Street as it rises from the gentle valley of the hidden river Tybourne.

Wallace Collection
ⓘ *T020-7935 0687, www.the-wallace-collection.org.uk. 1000-1700 daily. Free (£3 donation requested).*

Over Wigmore Street and left up Hinde Street leads into the relative quiet of Manchester Square, dominated on its north side by the Georgian mansion of Hertford

House, home of the Wallace Collection and a Marylebone must-see. In 2000 the Collection celebrated the centenary of its opening with the completion of architect Rick Mather's glass roof over the central courtyard of the old house, creating a sculpture garden and room for an expensive restaurant (**Café Bagatelle** ① *To20-7563 9505, open same hours as the Collection*), as well as the redevelopment of the basement to provide a library, lecture theatre and three new galleries.

That said, the peculiar pleasure of a visit here has not been diminished: as well as the masterpieces on the walls – some of which are superb, including **Hals'** *The Laughing Cavalier*, **Rembrandt**'s portrait of his son Titus, **Velazquez**'s *Lady with a Fan* and **Delacroix**'s *Execution of the Doge Marino Faliero* – the best thing about the Wallace Collection remains the way that is has preserved intact the particular tastes, in fine art, furniture, and, more bizarrely, medieval armour and weaponry, of a succession of 18th- and 19th-century grandees, the Marquess of Hertford and his illegitimate heir Sir Richard Wallace. The house and its extraordinary collection of 18th-century French paintings were bequeathed to the nation in 1897 by Lady Wallace.

The most inspiring purpose-built gallery (**Gallery 22**) is at the back of the house on the first floor, reached by a sweeping staircase with a spectacular early 18th-century French balustrade. Turning right at the top of the stairs takes you through the room that was once Lady Wallace's boudoir – now hung with paintings from the 18th-century 'cult of sensibility' and home to a pair of Boulard chairs intended for Louis XVI's card room at Fontainebleau – and then a series of rooms displaying more pre- and post-Revolutionary French furniture and art.

The beautiful **great gallery** lies at the end, full of remarkable 17th-century European masterpieces, by the likes of Titian, Rubens, Poussin and Van Dyck, all vying for space with the famous works mentioned above.

Continuing clockwise round the house are galleries devoted to Dutch and Flemish paintings, and just before arriving back on the landing, a gallery with six mid-to-late 18th-century views of Venice, two by Canaletto and four by Guardi, above a Riesener roll-top desk from 1769.

Back on the ground floor by the front entrance, **Gallery 5** (and the Hallway) was restored in 1995 to its former glory as the front state room and decorated with portraits of types like George IV as the Prince of Wales who would have visited the house in its heyday. Beyond it, going anti-clockwise round the courtyard, are galleries reflecting Sir Richard Wallace's enthusiasm for strange medieval and baroque objets d'art. Next are rooms packed full of a staggering array of Renaissance and medieval European and 200-year-old Oriental weapons and armour, including the sword of Ranjit Singh 'Lion of the Punjab', a fully-armoured warhorse and a pair of jousting gauntlets from the Middle Ages inscribed 'amor'.

RIBA Architecture Gallery

① *Ticket line, To20-7307 3792, programme details on To20-7307 3770, www.architecture.com. Mon-Fri 0800-1800, Sat 0800-1730. Bookshop and café.*

Up Portland Place, at No 66, is the RIBA Architecture Gallery. There are three galleries in the building, a large, airy and inviting space for exhibitions of architectural competitions, new projects, and architectural subjects of more general interest. The Florence Hall contains a decent café.

Regent's Park

① *Information Office, The Store Yard, Inner Circle, To20-7486 7905. 0500 until dusk daily. Boating on main lake from Apr-Sep, rowing and electric launches. Also Children's Boating Lake: rowing, canoeing and pedalos (To20-7724 4069).*

14 Marylebone & Regent's Park

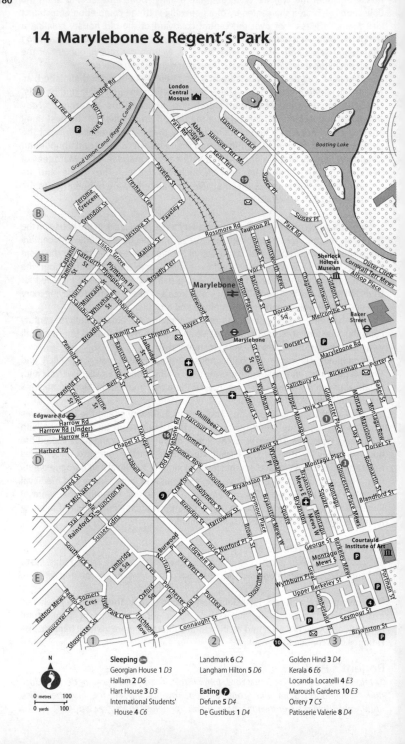

London Central Mosque

Boating Lake

Grand Union Canal (Regent's Canal)

Oak Tree Rd

Lodge Rd

North Bank

Lodge Rd

Park Rd

Hanover Terrace

Hanover Terr Ms

Abbey Lodge

Kent Terr

Sussex Pl

Jerome Crescent

Grendon St

Tresham Cres

Paveley St

Paveley St

Rossmore Rd

Taunton Pl

Sussex Pl

Lisson Grove

Litstone St

Mallory St

Broadly Terr

Lilestone St

Capland St

Samford St

Gateforth St

Plympton Pl

Plympton St

Church St

Salisbury St

Mulready St

Whitehaven St

Ashbridge St

Broadley St

Penfold St

Ashmill St

Ranston St

Daventry St

Skalbrade St

Shroton St

Hayes Pl

Harewood Av

Limerove Rd

Lisson St

Bell St

Penfold Pl

Cosel St

Bunc St

Edgware Rd

Harrow Rd

Harrow Rd (Under)

Harrow Rd

Harbed Rd

Praed St

St Michael's St

Star St

Rainsford St

Junction Ms

Sussex Gdns

Radnor Mews

Radnor Pl

Somers Cres

Gloucester Sq

Southwick St

Cambridge Sq

Hyde Park Cres

Titchborne Row

Gloucester Sq

Oxford Sq

Kendal Pl

Connaught St

Burwood Pl

Norfolk Cres

Park West Pl

Edgware Rd

Forset St

Nutford Pl

Brown St

Cato St

Harrowby St

Molyneux St

Brendon St

Crawford Pl

Thoulttah St

Homer Row

Homer St

Harcourt St

Shillibeer Pl

Chapel St

Cabbell St

Transept St

Old Marylebone Rd

Crawford St

Salisbury Pl

Enford St

Wyndham St

York St

Seymour Pl

Bryanston Pla

Wyndham Pl

Upper Montagu St

Montagu Place

Montagu Sq

Bryanston Mews E

Bryanston Mews W

Bryanston Sq

Montagu Mews W

Montagu Mews S

George St

Seymour St

Wythburn Pl

Upper Berkeley St

Cumberland Pl

Bryanston St

Berkeley Mews

Portman St

Marylebone

Marylebone Rd

Boston Pl

Balcombe St

Ivor Pl

Huntsworth Mews

Linhope St

Park Rd

Dorset Sq

Gt Central St

Dorset Cl

Glentworth St

Siddons La

Melcombe St

Chagford St

Baker Street

Bickenhall St

Gloucester Place

Montagu Row

Montagu Mansions

Clay St

Dorset St

Rodmarton St

Blandford St

Gloucester Place Mews

Sherlock Holmes Museum

Cornwall Terr Mews

Outer Circle

Allsop Place

Baker Street

Porter St

Baker St

Courtauld Institute of Art

N

0 metres 100
0 yards 100

Sleeping	**Landmark** 6 *C2*	**Golden Hind** 3 *D4*
Georgian House 1 *D3*	Langham Hilton 5 *D6*	Kerala 6 *E6*
Hallam 2 *D6*		Locanda Locatelli 4 *E3*
Hart House 3 *D3*	**Eating**	Maroush Gardens 10 *E3*
International Students'	Defune 5 *D4*	Orrery 7 *C5*
House 4 *C6*	De Gustibus 1 *D4*	Patisserie Valerie 8 *D4*

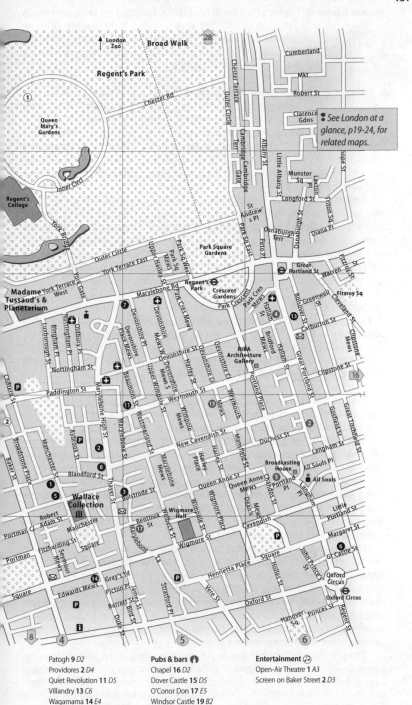

❖ See London at a glance, p19–24, for related maps.

Patogh 9 D2	Pubs & bars 🍸	Entertainment 🎵
Providores 2 D4	Chapel 16 D2	Open-Air Theatre 1 A3
Quiet Revolution 11 D5	Dover Castle 15 D5	Screen on Baker Street 2 D3
Villandry 13 C6	O'Conor Don 17 E5	
Wagamama 14 E4	Windsor Castle 19 B2	

Portland Place ends up in Nash's beautiful **Park Crescent**, the perfect introduction to his masterpiece, Regent's Park itself. The highlights of the park today are London Zoo (see below), the rose gardens, rockeries and Open-Air Theatre in Queen Mary's Gardens, and the Boating Lake, but the scale of its rolling, carefully planned layout makes the whole place a joy to explore.

❧ *In summer, the Chester Gate Lodge, off Chester Road, serves drinks and snacks in a little cottage, the oldest building in the park.*

In **Queen Mary's Gardens**, there's a small ornamental lake, set among alpine rockeries and a cascade, as well as extraordinary rose gardens at their best in June although flowering well into the autumn.

The **Open-Air Theatre** stages enchanting plays during the summer (see page 185) and the **Park Café** ① *To20-7935 5729*, is the largest of the park's 10 refreshment points, a self-service canteen with plenty of outside seating. During winter, only this one and the **Broadwalk Park Café** ① *To20-7224 3872*, a strange little chalet further north, are open.

Behind Queen Mary's Gardens lies the **Boating Lake**, and further round, the Boathouse for the hire of rowing boats and electric launches. The lake abounds in wild and domesticated waterfowl, the number of herons a good sign of healthy fish stocks, and it's an officially recognized inland bird observatory. There's an identification board near the stage door of the Open-Air Theatre. Near the northeastern arm of the lake, by the Children's Boating Lake, can be seen the distinctive domes of the London Central Mosque at Hanover Gate.

London Zoo

① *To20-7722 3333, www.zsl.org. Daily 1000-1730 summer, 1000-1630 winter (last admission 1 hr before closing). Adults £14, 3-15 year olds £10.75, under 3s free, concessions £12. NB: nearest tube is Camden Town, see map page , but is best reached either by a walk through the park, or by the waterbus service along the Regent's Canal from Camden Lock or Little Venice (see page 43).*

London Zoo first opened to the public in 1828 and rapidly became a fashionable freak show. Monkeys, kangaroos, zebras and emus were some of the animals that people flocked to gawp at and prod. Mercifully all that's changed, and the top priorities now for the Zoololgical Society of London's gardens are research and conservation. As well as nurturing a particularly important collection of Golden Lion Tamarin monkeys, of which only about 500 are believed still to exist in the wild, all the animals have been given more space, and those not threatened with extinction or especially unsuited to confinement have been sent elsewhere. While this may lead to some disappointment for children – Bear Mountain is now home to only a couple of reclusive bears and there are no large hippos, polar bears or pandas – it makes a visit here much less harrowing for animal lovers.

Over 35 acres of winding paths, tunnels and bridges, the zoo still manages to care for an extraordinary variety of animals, from dwarf mongooses and pigmy marmosets, looking like a cross between a chimp and a small bird, to black rhinos, gorillas and Asian elephants, lions, tigers and Mexican red-knee spiders. Highlights of a day here include feeding the penguins at 1430, and at the same time on Fridays only the snakes, and elephant bath-time at 1530. Every day at 1700 visitors can meet the one-eared giraffe called Achilles. Like the rest of his kind, he can never lie down because of the blood pressure in his brain.

Many of the buildings and enclosures are interesting in themselves, from the clapperboard aquarium to the graceful shape of the penguin pool and the soaring cage of Snowdon's aviary. The Web of Life Biodiversity Centre was opened in 1999, constructed to the latest high-tech energy-saving design, home to over 100 different species including a giant clam, giant anteaters and jellyfish. The Fountain Court in the

Sherlock Holmes Museum

ⓘ *To20-7935 8866, www.sherlock-holmes.co.uk. 0930-1800 daily. Adults £6,
under-16s £4.*

Leaving Regent's Park from the opposite corner to the Zoo, at Clarence Gate, leads
onto Baker Street. Look out for the statue of Sherlock Holmes outside Baker St tube
station. Just down from here, the Sherlock Holmes Museum, is actually at 239 Baker
Street, but has battled it out with the Post Office and Abbey National Building Society
at 221 to claim the sleuth's fictional address. A passable reconstruction of his
Georgian townhouse on four levels as described in the books, the place pleases fans
but may seem expensive to the merely curious.

The Showdome

ⓘ *To870-400 3000. 1030-1700. 1st show: summer 1030 daily, winter weekends
1030, weekdays 1230, not bookable in advance. Adult £6.75, under-16s £4.65,
concessions £5.30. Not recommended for under-5s, see below for combined entry
tickets with Madam Tussauds.*

Left onto the Marylebone Road at Baker Street tube and it's impossible to miss the
dome of the former London Planetarium and next door, Madame Tussaud's. Now
called the Showdome and much more sci-fi, movie music and projections onto the
darkened roof of the dome whizz through the history of the cosmos and make some
attempt to explain astronomy. The refurbished exhibition on discovering the
universe, including a full scale model of a moon rover, has been made more
interactive. Even so, it's probably still only worth seeing if visiting the much more
famous attraction next door.

Madame Tussaud's

ⓘ *Marylebone Rd, To870-400 3000, www.madame-tussauds.com. 0930-1730 Mon-
Fri, 0900-1800 Sat, Sun, 1000-1630 bookable in 30-min timeslots, booking fee £1 per
ticket. Adults £13-£22.99 depending on time, under 16s £8-18, under-5s free. Price
includes entry to Showdome.*

The popularity of Madame Tussaud's continues unabated, a surefire hit with tourists
since shortly after the French Revolution when the aristocratic French woman
exhibited the waxwork portraits of some of her friends who had lost their heads. In
those days it may have been understandable, when people had little chance to see
what the rich and famous looked like. Nowadays it panders effectively enough to the
cult of celebrity – Jennifer Lopez and Britney Spears are among the latest to join the
array of immaculately modelled dummies.

    The likenesses are fairly hit and miss, although some do look as if they might
just turn round and shake your hand. Here David Beckham joins screen superstars
like Sean Connery, Morgan Freeman and Samuel L Jackson. In the Grand Hall,
monarchs and politicians rub shoulders, while the Chamber of Horrors remains the
most crowded of the rooms, a gruesome celebration of goriness in very dubious
taste that children adore. Finally, the Spirit of London dark ride speeds comically
through London's history in five minutes, concluding appropriately with the
lascivious comedian Benny Hill. The whole moderately entertaining visit should
take about an hour and a half, after which the unfamiliarity of strangers' faces on
the streets comes as a real relief.

● Sleeping

Marylebone and Regent's Park *p177, map p180*

AL Landmark Hotel, 222 Marylebone Rd, NW1, T020-7631 8000, www.landmark london.co.uk. 299 rooms, about 100 years old, recently refurbished with individually furnished rooms and increasingly popular with A-list celebrities, overnighting perhaps from their palaces in Buckinghamshire (Marylebone station is across the road).

A Langham Hilton, 1 Portland Pl, W1, T020-7636 1000, www.langham.hilton.com. 429 rooms, one of the oldest large hotels in London, in pole position near Oxford Circus, fully refurbished in the 90s and now a corporate favourite but pretty good value for tourists too.

B Georgian House Hotel, 87 Gloucester Pl, W1, T020-7935 2211/7486 3151, www.londoncentralhotel.com. 19 reasonably large rooms with bathrooms in an attractive townhouse, breakfast included.

B Hart House Hotel, 51 Gloucester Pl, Portman Sq, W1, T020-7935 2288, www.harthouse.co.uk. 15 spacious rooms with shower in an attractively converted townhouse. Book at least 2 weeks in advance. Full English breakfast included.

C Hallam Hotel, 12 Hallam St, Portland Pl, W1, T020-7580 1166, www.hallamhotel.com. Another small townhouse with 25 rooms, all with en suite bathroom, and pretty good value for the area.

D International Students' House, 229 Great Portland St, W1, T020-7631 8300, www.ish.org.uk. Not necessary to be a student to stay here, 275 rooms, open to public throughout, but very full at all other times. Restaurant with international food in the basement, refurbished bar open late to residents. Laundry, cybercafé, microwave.

● Eating

Marylebone and Regent's Park *p177, map p180*

♥♥♥♥ Defune 34 George St, W1, T020-7935 8311. One of the better and more expensive Japanese restaurants in the area, with a wonderfully lit cavernous basement and some very good softshell crab on the menu.

♥♥♥♥ Locanda Locatelli, 8 Seymour St, W1, T020-7935 9088. Italian cooking is elevated to new heights (and prices) in stylish and comfortable surroundings.

♥♥♥♥ The Orrery, 55 Marylebone High St, W1, T020-7616 8000. One of the smaller additions to Terence Conran's gastronomic empire, complete with all his trademark designer trimmings and serving the freshest modern European food in a swish atmosphere.

♥♥♥♥ Providores, 109 Marylebone High St, T020-7935 6175. One of the best destinations for a smart meal out in Marylebone, a small tapas bar and diner downstairs, with some seriously accomplished New Zealand fusion recipes upstairs. Hugely popular, booking essential.

♥♥♥♥ Villandry, 170 Great Portland St, W1, T020-7631 3131. Occupies minimalist premises fronted by an amazing deli and laid-back bar.

♥♥ Maroush Gardens, 21 Edgware Rd, W2, T020-7723 0773. A very comfortable branch of the Arabic chain with 'exotic' entertainment at the weekends and reliable food.

♥♥ O'Conor Don, on Marylebone Lane (see Pubs below). The Irish restaurant above is popular with lunching suits.

♥ The Golden Hind, 73 Marylebone Lane, W1, T020-7486 3644. An old-school eat-in or take away fish and chip shop done up in a timeless style. Perhaps more expensive than you might expect.

♥ Kerala, 15 Great Castle St, W1, T020-7580 2125. A busy south Indian restaurant near Oxford Circus.

♥ Patogh, 8 Crawford Pl, W1, T020-7262 4015, nearer the Edgware Rd. Unfussy and unlicensed (BYOB), Persian food can be enjoyed here.

♥ Wagamama, 101a Wigmore St, T020-7409 0111. A branch of the popular Japanese canteen, unbookable and sometimes with queues at lunchtimes but always worth the wait.

Cafés and sandwich bars

De Gustibus, 53 Blandford St, W1, T020-7486 6608. For a simple but expertly constructed sandwich made from a wide choice of breads, smaller than the one in Borough, non-smoking but with a few tables outside.

Patisserie Valerie, 105 Marylebone High St, T020-7935 6240. An unmissable destination and excellent outpost of the patisserie française, less arty but more sophisticated than the one in Soho.

Quiet Revolution, 62 Weymouth St, W1, T020-7487 5683. Specializes in 100% organic soups and delicious stews for about £6 to eat in or take away.

♦ Pubs and bars

Marylebone and Regent's Park *p177, map p180*

The Chapel, 48 Chapel St, NW1, T020-7402 9220, in the far west of Marylebone, nearer Edgware. A large gastropub popular with local office workers.

The Dover Castle, 43 Weymouth Mews, W1, T020-7580 4412. A fine and cheery Samuel Smith's pub hidden away in a small mews off Portland Pl.

O'Conor Don, 88 Marylebone Lane, W1, T020-7935 9311. An Irish original, tatty and informal, and serving good food at the bar all day and in the restaurant upstairs for lunch and supper (closed weekends).

Windsor Castle, 98 Park Rd, NW1, T020-7723 9262, near Regent's Park. A grand and busy old place with a pool table.

♦ Entertainment

Marylebone and Regent's Park *p177, map p180*

Cinemas

Screen on Baker St, 96 Baker St, NW1, T020-7935 2772. 2 screens showing first-run films from the artier side of the spectrum.

Music

Classical and opera Wigmore Hall, 36 Wigmore St, W1, T020-7935 2141, www.wigmore-hall.org.uk. One of London's premier small concert halls, purpose-built in 1901 by the piano-maker Bechstein. Stages a huge variety of world-class performances of chamber music and song, lunchtimes at 1300 and evenings at 1930 Mon-Sat, 1600 and 1900 Sun, and popular hour-long coffee concerts at 1130 on Sun. Tickets £8-30.

Theatres

Open Air Theatre, Queen Mary's Gdns, Regent's Park, NW1, T020-7486 2431 (summer only). Shakespeare's comedies and pastorals have been performed here since 1933, although recently the seasonal repertoire has also included modern musicals. The more than 1000-seat auditorium, exposed to the elements, along with a good restaurant and bar, always generates a sense of occasion. Booking well in advance is advisable.

♦ Shopping

Marylebone and Regent's Park *p177, map p180*

Marylebone Lane and High St are the main shopping streets in Marylebone itself. The High St in particular has gone steadily upmarket. A little further afield in Lisson Grove, Church St is also well worth exploring for a less expensive and more offbeat expedition.

Alfie's Antique Market, 13-25 Church St, NW8, T020-7723 6066, northwest of the Marylebone Rd, in Lisson Grove. One of London's lesser-known but still lively fruit 'n' veg and clothes markets, at its best on Sat, is a rambling place with countless stalls and everything under the sun on sale at reasonable prices, open Tue-Sat.

Button Queen, 19 Marylebone Lane, W1, T020-7935 1505. A quirky shop, stocks a huge variety of old and modern buttons, buckles and cufflinks made from buttons.

Daunt's Books for Travellers, 83 Marylebone High St, W1, T020-7224 2295, www.dauntbooks.com. Half way down the High St. One of London's most charming travel bookshops, its galleried Edwardian space stacked with just about every conceivable new title to do with travel as well as carrying an excellent second-hand stock.

Gallery of Antique Costume and Textiles, 2 Church St, NW8, T020-7723 9981. Stocks yards and yards of antique cloth of a very high quality.

Talking Books, 11 Wigmore St, W1, T020-7491 4117. Probably the largest stockist in Europe of talking books, cassettes and CDs, mostly in English but a few in French.

🔻 *For an explanation of sleeping and eating price codes used in this guide, see inside the*
⬤ *front cover. Other relevant information is found in Essentials, see pages 44-46.*

▲ Activities

Marylebone and Regent's Park *p177, map p180*

Seymour Leisure Centre, Seymour Pl, W1, T020-7723 8019, bookings T020-7238 0019, www.courtneys.co.uk. Open 0700- 2000 Mon-Tue, Fri Sat, 0700-2100; Wed, Thu; 0800-2000 Sun. Large and well-appointed public swimming pool and leisure centre. **Regent's Park Tennis Centre**, York Bridge, NW1, T020-7486 4216. 12 courts. Non-members £9 an hour, open throughout the year 0800-2100. **Regent's Park Golf and Tennis School**, Outer Circle, Regent's Park, NW1, T020-7724 0643. Golf lessons on driving range, tennis, throughout the year. Open 0800-2100.

Euston, St Pancras and King's Cross

Euston, St Pancras and King's Cross have long had the worst of all worlds, sandwiched between more attractive parts of town like Regent's Park, Bloomsbury, Clerkenwell, Islington and Camden. The rail gateways to the north, cut off by the constant traffic on the east-west artery of Euston Road, once had a bad reputation for prostitution, drugs and street crime. Still far from salubrious, the whole area is in the process of being transformed by the construction of the Eurostar terminal at St Pancras. Perhaps this long-neglected and rundown district will get the break it deserves. Even the unlovely Euston Road has cleaned up its act in recent years. The opening of the state-of-the-art British Library here represented the first bold public statement of government confidence in an area that looks set to boom. Meanwhile on Friday and Saturday nights the Scala and the marshalling yards north of the stations are still a Mecca for clubbers, injecting a welcome dose of wide-eyed nightlife into one of the city's more desolate backyards.▸▸ *For Sleeping, Eating and other listings see pages 190-191.*

History

Until the development of the New Road (modern Marylebone, Euston and Pentonville Roads) in the mid-18th century, the area north of Bloomsbury and Fitzrovia was largely fields, with the River Fleet running alongside an ancient track (modern Pancras Road) up to Old St Pancras Church. There was a small village called Battle Bridge, but none of the settlement or manored estates to be found in neighbouring Marylebone.

The furthest north most people ventured was to visit St Chad's Well at the top of the Gray's Inn Road for its medicinal waters, or to seek sanctuary in the smallpox hospital located at King's Cross. Nursery gardens grew in modern Euston Square, while cattle were driven along the New Road on their way to Smithfield Market. But the laying of the road, and the arrival of the Regent's Canal in 1820 further north sparked a hotchpotch of development.

Somers Town began to grow from 1786, but remained an isolated suburb and later suffered at the hands of the railways. Much of the area became an industrial suburb fed by the canal. Gasworks, timber and building trades, factories and workshops dotted the wasteland and brick fields, and St Pancras developed a reputation for furniture and piano manufacturing businesses. Agar Town, a shanty town dubbed 'Ague Town' whose stench Dickens claimed "is enough to knock down a bullock", grew up almost overnight in 1851 on fields that later became the site of St Pancras Station.

The Fig Mead scheme, the Duke of Bedford's attempt to develop a model middle-class suburb on land now occupied by Mornington Crescent, was also felled by the railway. The Duke's interest in the area, however, didn't extend to establishing links with his Bloomsbury estate. With the development of Seymour Street and Caledonian Road, and the dark courts and backyard industries springing up on Chalton and Ossulton Streets, he blocked off Seymour Street with gates in order to preserve the superior tone of Bloomsbury.

The advent of the railways ensured that when Nash built Albany Street on the eastern edge of Regent's Park it was to serve as a boundary between the wealthier west and the inferior east. **Euston Station** was the first railway station (1838), where an enormous Doric arch welcomed travellers into a magnificent great hall. Railway carriages would be drawn up the hill to Camden on a winch, and on their return ran downhill under the control of a brakeman. As was to become the fashion, the Adelaide and Victoria Hotels partially covered the grand screen of the station, but the structure's demolition for its current building in 1963 lost London one of its more dramatic architecural sights.

King's Cross, an altogether plainer affair, was built in the 1850s, but **St Pancras** (1863-1872) earned the critic's approval. "It stands without rival for palatial beauty, comfort and convenience" wrote one Victorian admirer, although the architect himself observed that the Midland Grand Hotel that was built around the train shed was "possibly too good for its purpose". Development continued to be patchy throughout the 20th century. **The Friends' House**, headquarters for the Quakers, was built in 1927, the St Pancras (now Camden) Town Hall in 1937 – it's flown the Red Flag in its time – and the new **British Library** opened to the public in 1998. In 1924 the vicar of St Mary's Somers Town observed: "Overcrowding and poverty are here being used by the Devil in order to steal from the children of God the health and happiness which are their right". Housing estates and blocks of flats were built between Euston and St Pancras, and warehouses and factories still share space with the railways.

Sights ⊖ *Euston, Euston Sq, King's Cross.* ⊖ *See p460.*

King's Cross and the Euston Road are not obvious destinations for a sightseeing trip, but both have enough places of interest to wile away more than a couple of hours. Across Pancras Road to the west is the magnificent red-brick neo-Gothic palace of **St Pancras Station**, formerly the Midland Grand Hotel. Its architect, Sir George Gilbert Scott, had hoped to build something similar in Whitehall but later wrote that he was 'glad to be able to erect one building in that style in London'. And most people passing the place today are glad that he was too. The whole building is set to be given a new lease of life with the opening of the St Pancras Channel Tunnel rail terminal for Eurostar.

Camley Street Natural Park ① *To20-7833 2311, Mon-Thu 0900-1700, Sat 1100-1700, Sun 1000-1600, free, near the junction with Goods Way*, is a sweet little community nature reserve run by the London Wildlife Trust. A place to watch dragonflies, herons, and even the occasional kingfisher in late autumn, these two wildflower acres beside the canal with their quiet reed-whispering pools are an unexpected inner city oasis.

Another small local initiative can be found by continuing up Goods Way and crossing York Way to the **London Canal Museum** ① *12-13 New Wharf Rd, To20-7713 0836, www.canalmuseum.org.uk, Tue-Sun 1000-1630, £3, £2 concession, under 15s £1.50, under 5s free*. The museum tells the story of the Regent's Canal and the boats that worked it, especially those that supplied the ice house which the museum has preserved. Moored in the canal alongside is a renovated 1940s' tugboat.

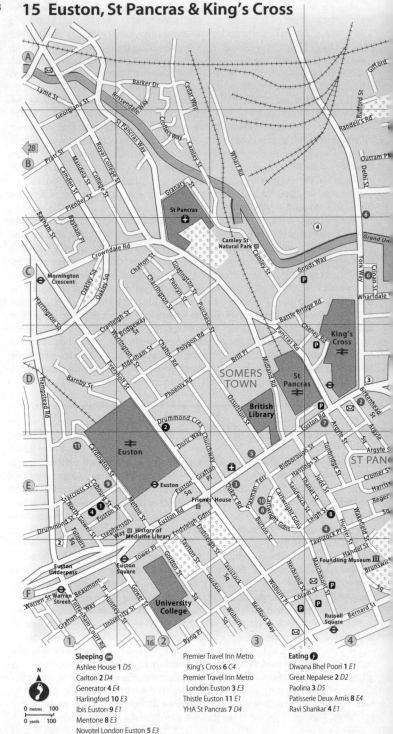

Sleeping

Ashlee House **1** *D5*
Carlton **2** *D4*
Generator **4** *E4*
Harlingford **10** *E3*
Ibis Euston **9** *E1*
Mentone **8** *E3*
Novotel London Euston **5** *E3*

Premier Travel Inn Metro
King's Cross **6** *C4*
Premier Travel Inn Metro
London Euston **3** *E3*
Thistle Euston **11** *E1*
YHA St Pancras **7** *D4*

Eating

Diwana Bhel Poori **1** *E1*
Great Nepalese **2** *D2*
Paolina **3** *D5*
Patisserie Deux Amis **8** *E4*
Ravi Shankar **4** *E1*

N

0 metres 100
0 yards 100

See London at a glance, p19-24, for related maps.

Pubs & bars 🍺
Babushka 5 *C5*
Backpacker 6 *B4*
Islington Bar 9 *A5*
Sahara Nights 7 *D5*

Entertainment 🎵
Camden People's
  Theatre 2 *F1*
Courtyard
  Theatre 3 *D4*
Cross 4 *C4*
Scala 5 *D4*
Water Rats 6 *D5*

Southeast of King's Cross station, an indication of the area's potential can be found at the **Gagosian Gallery** ① *6-24 Britannia St, T020-7841 9960, Tue-Sat 1000-1800, free*, tucked off the Gray's Inn Rd behind the Scala. A massive converted garage, it's the latest venture of the flamboyant New York art dealer Larry Gagosian, mounting consistently high-profile exhibitions of contemporary art.

Back by St Pancras Station over Midland Road, stands the **British Library** ① *96 Euston Rd, T020-7412 7332, www.bl.uk, 0930-1800 Mon, Wed, Thu, Fri, 0930-2000 Tue, 0930-1700 Sat, 1100-1700 Sun, free*, the best reason to visit the Euston Rd on purpose on foot. A decade behind schedule, the building was finally completed in 1997 to the usual chorus of dismay and disapproval. Whatever people have made of the exterior, with its straight lines of plain red brick and dark green trim offset by its splendid Victorian neighbour (see also architecture, page 416), the interior has provoked few complaints. Cool acres of white stone and careful attention to details, such as the handrails, the spacing of the steps and the diffusion of light, all combine to make the building a joy to use. Anyone engaged in research can apply for free membership to gain access to the reading rooms and some 18 million volumes, as well as maps, manuscripts, the national sound archive and the newspaper library in Colindale, while the two permanent exhibitions (which can be seen without a pass) are well worth a visit in themselves. The library also has a good restaurant and two cafés.

The **Treasures Gallery** is a beautiful and carefully explained display of precious books and manuscripts: the illuminated Lindisfarne Gospel from around 700 AD; a copy of the Magna Carta of 1215 – the document that laid the foundations for Parliamentary democracy, the Sherborne Missal – the only painted book in England to have survived the Reformation, Shakespeare's first folio from 1623, and the manuscripts of great authors such as Jane Austen, Thomas Hardy, Charles Dickens and Lewis Carroll.

In **The Workshop** there are regular demos of bookbinding, calligraphy and printing, a reconstruction of a 15th-century illuminator's workshop and an exhibition on the history of recorded sound. Another space is reserved for special temporary exhibitions generally of a high standard.

A walk down Judd Street opposite the Library leads to Brunswick Square and **Coram's Fields** where Captain Thomas Coram persuaded the gentry to build a hospital for destitute children in the middle of the 18th century. He was a great friend of Hogarth, who did a very sympathetic portrait of him (and persuaded other artists such as Reynolds and Gainsborough to contribute paintings, creating 'Britain's first art gallery'), and also of Handel, whose organ recitals made the hospital's chapel popular with the likes of Dickens. Coram's Foundation still exists in Berkhamsted.

The art collection can still be seen in a reconstruction of its original setting at **The Foundling Museum** ① *40 Brunswick Sq, WC1, T020-7841 3600, Tue-Sat 1000-1800, Sun 1200-1800, £5, concessions £3, under-16s free*, along with displays on the history of the hospital and its eminent supporters.

St George's Gardens, the first graveyard in the world to be turned into a pleasure garden, to the north of the children's playground in Coram's Fields, are a delightful place for a picnic and a good starting point for an exploration of this often overlooked corner of Bloomsbury.

Beyond Euston Station, on the same side of the road, The Wellcome Trust at 210 Euston Road, puts on small foyer exhibitions, and it's also possible here to visit the **History of Medicine Library** ① *183 Euston Rd, NW1 (information line, T020-7611 8888), www.wellcome.ac.uk/library, Mon, Wed, Fri 0945-1715, Tue, Thu 0945-1915, Sat 0945-1300, free, personal ID required for 1st visit which must be made Mon-Fri 0900-1700,* a new exhibition and museum on biomedical reasearch is set to open in 2006.

● Sleeping

Euston, St Pancras & King's Cross
p186, map p188

A Novotel London Euston, 100-110 Euston Rd, T020-7666 9000, www.novotel.com. 312 rooms with a panoramic elevator. A 4-star hotel on the site of the once radical *Shaw Theatre*, which has been preserved inside, and where interesting shows are still occasionally staged.

B Harlingford, 61-63 Cartwright Gdns, WC1, T020-7387 1551, www.harlingfordhotel.com. 43-room B&B, the most contemporary in this popular location, a thorough refurbishment has given it a colourful edge over the competition; friendly staff.

B-C Mentone Hotel, 54-56 Cartwright Gdns, WC1, T020-7387 3927. En suite bathrooms, tastefully decorated, a good value family-run B&B.

B-C Premier Travel Inn Metro Kings Cross, York Way, King's Cross, T0870-990 6414. Similar to the above: around £83 Mon-Thu, £75 Fri-Sun.

B-C Premier Travel Inn Metro London Euston, 1 Duke's Rd, WC1, T0870-238 3301, www.premiertravelinn.com. 220 rooms, clean, safe, modern and impersonal budget chain.

C The Carlton Hotel, Birkenhead St, WC1, T020-7916 9697, www.smoothound.co.uk/hotels/Carlton5. 32 clean rooms in what was once a NatWest bank.

D-E The Generator, 37 Tavistock Pl, WC1, T020-7388 7666, www.generatorhostels. com. With 217 funky cell-like twin bunk rooms £26.50 per person, 8-bed dorm £15 a night, 4-bed dorms £17 a night, including continental breakfast, busy bar in an old police station.

D-F Ashlee House, 261-265 Gray's Inn Rd, WC1, T020-7833 9400. Clean, secure and bright designer budget backpackers' hostel, twin room £44, 4-6 bedded dorm £17, 8-10 bed dorm £15, 16-bed dorm £13.

E YHA St Pancras , 79-81 Euston Road, NW1, opposite St Pancras station, T0870-770 6044 (within UK), T+44 20-7388 9998 (outside UK), stpancras@yha.org.uk.

Reception open 0700-2300 daily, £24.60, under-18 £20.50, 152 beds in a 4-star hostel, no groups. Premium rooms available.

🍴 Eating

Euston, St Pancras & King's Cross
p186, map p188

Not a hot destination for gourmets, King's Cross is surrounded by fast-food joints and dodgy cafés. Euston doesn't fare much better, although behind the station Drummond St is a famous destination for fans of bargain vegetarian south Indian food.

Ÿ Diwana Bhel Poori House, 121 Drummond St, NW1, T020-7387 5556. Very basic and also unlicensed, so diners can bring their own booze.

Ÿ Great Nepalese, 48 Eversholt St, NW1, T020-7388 6737, on the other side of the station. A quirky little restaurant, specializing entirely in Nepalese dishes, quite different from Indian food, especially their famous starter, momo, thin pastry-based snacks that started life as street food but here have been raised to greater heights.

Ÿ Ravi Shankar, 133-135 Drummond St, NW1, T020-7388 6458. The most mellow and comfortable place.

Cafés and sandwich bars

Again, the area is packed with places catering badly for the passing trade.

Paolina, 181 King's Cross Rd, WC1, T020-7278 8176. A BYOB Thai café that is a reliable bargain, only open for lunch and supper.

Patisserie Deux Amis, 63 Judd St, WC1, T020-7383 7029. A good place for tempting cakes and baguettes with tables outdoors. Try also the cafés in the British Library.

🍺 Pubs and bars

Euston, St Pancras & King's Cross
p186, map p188

Sahara Nights, 257-259 Pentonville Rd, N1 T020-7278 7223, close to King's Cross station. A Moroccan-themed bar that serves decent Turkish food and holds Egyptian dance classes on Tue and Thu. Live music and late opening at the weekends and a roof terrace too.

Two bars near King's Cross are very popular for pre-club warm-ups:

Backpacker, 126 York Way, N1, T020-7278 8318. Even more crazy, open Fri and Sat 1900-0200, Sun 1530-2300, with sawdust floor, clinical 'shots chair', very loud music and bumper all-you-can-drink offers, dedicated to drunkeness in the way only Aussies do well.

Islington Bar, 342 Caledonian Rd, N1, T020-7609 4917. Open until 2400 Mon-Thu, until 0200 Fri, Sat £3, a way-out and wild venue for DJ-driven dance nights.

🎭 Entertainment

Euston, St Pancras & King's Cross
p186, map p188
Music
Rock, folk and jazz The Water Rats, 328 Gray's Inn Rd, WC1, T020-7837 7269. A basic boozer with an even more basic back bar that hosts 3 bands a night 6 nights a week, 1st set at about 2000. £5 admission.

Nightclubs

Clubnights are the area's strong point at weekends.

The Cross, The Arches, 27-131 King's Cross Goods Yard, off York Way, N1, T020-7837 0828, www.the-cross.co.uk. The megaclubs in the area are the Ibiza of North London, check this one out.

The Scala, 278 Pentonville Rd, N1, T020-7833 2022, www.scala-london.co.uk. The old cinema here now hosts the regular Fri mixed gay night *Popstarz* (£3 before 2300, more after), its 4 different rooms dedicated to indie music, sounds of the 60s and 70s, and pop trash. During the week and on Sat there are one-off clubnights and live bands.

Theatre
The Camden People's Theatre, 58-60 Hampstead Rd, NW1, T020-7916 5878. Another small community fringe theatre which quite often turns up interesting plays.

The Courtyard Theatre, 10 York Way, N1, T020-7833 0870. A small fringe theatre in a quaint old courtyard that sometimes stages good productions of contemporary classics.

Bloomsbury and Fitzrovia

Bloomsbury is the academic heart of London, the home of the acronym, full of august institutions better known as SOAS, UCL, RADA and ULU than by their full names, most of them part of the sprawling University of London. North of High Holborn, south of the Euston Road and west of Judd Street, its long straight streets of Georgian and Victorian brick can be gloomy in winter, but in bright sunshine the area's severe little squares with their flower- and tree-filled gardens are a delight. Then again it's no coincidence that this is also the place to find three of the city's most rewarding museums, all free, and each defying expectations in their different ways: the revitalized and monumental British Museum obviously, but also the serene and quiet beauty of the Chinese ceramics in the Percival David Foundation and the intriguing collection of ancient Egyptian artefacts in the Petrie Museum.

The student population ensures that the area is packed with reasonable places to eat and sleep, surrounded by lively pubs and excellent bookshops. To the west, over Tottenham Court Road, that ugly northbound arm of Oxford Street, 'Fitzrovia' is the name that has been given to the blocks south of Fitzroy Square from here to Portland Place. Something like an upmarket version of Soho, on Charlotte Street and Goodge Street it boasts some of its southern neighbour's media buzz. ➤➤ For Sleeping, Eating and other listings see pages 202-206.

History

Bloomsbury and Fitzrovia have long acted as magnets for London's intellectual and medical communities. Hospitals and university buildings dominate the area, scattered in and around Georgian squares and modern developments. Once upon a time though it was a series of fields, interspersed with buildings such as Tottenham Court (on modern Grafton Way), and tributaries from the River Fleet crossing its eastern edge. By the early 18th century, there was still little by way of suburban development, although the Republic and then the Restoration had seen the building of a few grand residences. Southampton House (whose gardens lay along modern Southampton Row), Montague House (later the British Museum) and Thanet House sat alongside each other on modern Great Russell Street, but the view north was still over pasture and meadows to the villages of Hampstead and Highgate on the distant hills.

In the 1660s The Earl of Southampton, in a shrewd series of deals worthy of any modern property tycoon, began to develop the area. He built a square (now Bloomsbury Square) south of his house, in the process launching a new style for town houses. These narrow-fronted terraces, four stories high with accommodation for the servants in the loft and their workspace in the basement, were so celebrated that foreign Princes were brought to see them. (The square drew more visitors in the 1960s when the country's deepest car park was excavated under the gardens – seven levels fed by a twin helix of ramps devised to avoid damaging the plane trees' roots.) Other streets were laid, particularly Queen Square, where George III was to stay with his doctor, Dr Willis, while suffering the tempests of his illness, and Great Ormond Street, where the Hospital for Sick Children was to open in the 1850s.

The area's association with sick children had begun 100 years earlier with Thomas Coram's Foundling Hospital for the care of sick infants. It sat, isolated, near Coram Fields (see page 190), and its work was aided by fundraising by Hogarth and Handel, an act repeated in 1929 by JM Barrie when he bequeathed the copyright for *Peter Pan* to the Great Ormond Street Hospital. Over the Tottenham Court Road, the Middlesex Hospital emerged on a site next to a pond on Windmill Street, and Goodge

Street, laid out in Crab Tree Field in the 1740s, followed the emergence of Berners, Newman and Hanway Streets 20 years earlier. When the estate passed to the Dukes of Bedford in the 18th century, development began in earnest.

From 1775 when work began on Bedford Square, through to the late 1820s, terraces and squares spread northwards up to New Road (modern Euston Road). Six hundred houses were built on the Foundling Hospital estate, Brunswick, Mecklenburgh and Russell Squares were laid out, and Thomas Cubbitt, the architect behind Belgravia and Pimlico, set to on Gordon and Woburn Squares which were still forming by the 1860s. (Some were protected as private enclaves by gates, which were only removed in 1893.)

The University of London, from small beginnings in 1836, stamped its mark on the area in 1932 with Senate House, a "bleak, blank, hideous" (Max Beerbohm) creation that was the model for the Ministry of Truth in Orwell's *1984*, having been the real Ministry of Information during the Second World War.

Throughout this period, Bloomsbury and Fitzrovia (the term is a 1930s creation) were popular with lawyers for its proximity to the Inns of Court but also among London's most lively artistic, literary, and intellectual community. William Morris, Charles Dickens, Charles Darwin and later WB Yeats and GB Shaw all lived hereabouts, while the British Museum's Reading Room witnessed Karl Marx and Lenin poring over books. The Bloomsbury Group (which included Virginia Woolf, EM Forster and Roger Fry) formed in the belief that an appreciation of art and beauty are essential to progress, earned much public disapproval and scorn through their openly risqué behaviour (love triangles and lesbianism, for instance).

A slightly later generation – Dylan Thomas, Augustus John, as well as the nation's hangman, Albert Pierrepoint – frequented the pubs of Fitzrovia in the 1940s, most notably the Fitzroy Tavern.

After some damage during both wars (a Zeppelin bomb exploded in Queen Square in 1915) development continued, with Brunswick Square and the British Telecom Tower both examples of 1960s modernization (see architecture, page 416), and the artists moved to Soho. The area's medical traditions have remained. With no less than eight hospitals, the area's reputation for being 'very healthful' is well founded.

Sights ⊖ *Goodge St, Russell Sq, Tottenham Ct Rd, Warren St.* ⊕ *See p460.*

★ British Museum

ⓘ *T020-7323 8000, disabled information T020-7636 7384, minicom T020-7323 8920, Reading Room T020-7323 8162, www.thebritishmuseum.ac.uk. 1000-1730 Sat-Wed, 1000-2030 Thu, Fri (late view of main floor and some upper floor galleries only), Great Court 0900-2100 Mon-Wed, 0900-2300 Thu-Sat, 0900-1800 Sun. Free (donations appreciated), prices of temporary exhibitions vary. Guided tours: Highlights tour (90 mins) £7, £4 concession 1030, 1300 Mon-Sat, 1230, 1330, 1430, 1600 Sun; Focus tour (60 mins) at 1515 Mon-Sat, 1630 Sun, £5, £3 concession; EyeOpener gallery talks, free.*

Most people visit Bloomsbury for the British Museum. With its new slogan 'illuminating world cultures', it now comes closer to that ideal in spectacular style. Architect Norman Foster's redevelopment of the central Great Court, opened in December 2000, turned the museum's long-hidden central quadrangle into the largest covered square in Europe, rechristened the Elizabeth II Great Court (see also architecture, page 416).

A beautiful canopy made up of a latticework of 3312 unique panes of glass now wraps itself around the dome of the round Reading Room, free-standing once again at the heart of the museum. From beneath the grand old front portico on Great Russell Street, through the tall front doors, visitors pass straight into a vast creamy space to be confronted by the Reading Room, freshly clad in white stone like a huge post box in the middle of the indoor square. The four classical porticos on each side have also been revealed again. The overall impression of light and space created by the new design is impressive. And the museum is now much more accessible to London's working population, with late openings for the major galleries on Thursday and Friday while The Great Court's restaurant, shops and gallery are open in the evenings throughout the week (see details below).

On entering the Great Court from the south, the information desk is on the left and the box office for special exhibitions and audio guides on the right, the places to pick up floorplans and get your bearings. Within the square itself there are now two cafés, two shops and, up the wide staircases round the outside of the reading room, a temporary exhibition area and a restaurant. Twelve sculptures are set around the place at ground level making up the Great Court Concourse Gallery, introducing the museum's collections.

Reading Room

Straight ahead as you enter is the little door into the Reading Room. Designed by Robert Smirke in 1823, the Round Reading Room was first opened in 1857 and its original colour scheme of light blue, cream and gold leaf has been restored. A host of famous (mainly male) thinkers, writers, politicians and idlers have studied, mused or snoozed beneath the lofty dome at one of the 35 long tables fanning out from the central enquiry desk.

Once the pride of the British Library (now in new premises at St Pancras) and then only for the use of card-holders, anyone can now soak up the room's resonant atmosphere and imagine the likes of Marx (presumed to have sat near row L), Lenin, Shaw, Carlyle, Elgar or Yeats hunched over their books. The reopening as the British Museum Reading Room includes an exhibition on the Reading Room's history, with sample books by famous and infamous readers, the use of the Paul Hamlyn Library of reference books relevant to the museum's collection and of colour and black and white photocopiers (coin or smart card), and the Walter and Leonore Annenberg Centre, 50 computer terminals comprising COMPASS (Collections Multimedia Public Access System) where you can plan a visit to the museum, take a virtual tour, find information on artefacts, or print out images (with smart cards, £2 from Central Enquiry Desk).

Around the museum

A first visit to the British Museum galleries themselves is likely to both inspire and bewilder. That said, the new developments mean that the arrangement of several million objects from all over the world of every shape, size, and age laid out for inspection in over 90 rooms now seems much more straightforward.

The main part of the museum is on the ground floor in the **west wing**, through the left-hand wall of the Great Court after entering from the main southern entrance. The galleries stretching the length of this wing are devoted to Ancient Egyptian sculpture, the Ancient Near East (including art from the palaces of Nimrud and Nineveh, and Assyrian sculpture), and Ancient Greece (including the sculptures from the Parthenon, the Nereid Monument and the Mausoleum of Halikarnassos). These collections also spill downstairs onto the lower floors of this wing.

On the right-hand side of the Great Court is the **Enlightenment Gallery**. The most recent major addition to the museum, this celebration of the dawn of the age of reason (and hence the museum itself) is housed in the magnificent neo-classical room purpose-built for the King's Library in 1823. Divided into seven sections (Trade and Discovery, Religion and Ritual, Ancient Scripts, Classifying the World, Art and Civilisation, The Birth of Archaeology and The Natural World), the gallery displays an absorbing variety of artefacts of the kind that first fuelled Europe's new hunger for knowledge: ammonites, sculptures, drawings, books and Sir Hans Sloane's original 'cabinet of curiosities'.

Straight ahead past the Reading Room leads into the **north wing**, another temporary exhibition space and rooms devoted to artefacts from China, Southeast Asia, India and the Americas, with the African collection housed on the lower floors: remarkable displays of drums, knives, masks, art and pottery. Look out for the 16th-century Benin plaques.

On the **upper floors**, above the galleries in the west wing – best reached up the south stairs on the left just before entering the Great Court from the front entrance – are more objects from Ancient Greece and also from the Roman Empire. Straight ahead at the top of these stairs leads into the rooms in the east wing devoted to Europe from the Middle Ages to modern times. Beyond these, on the upper floors of the east wing, can be found Roman Britain, Prehistory, and more monuments and treasures from the Ancient Near East which continue round into the north wing, also home to the museum's extraordinary collection of early Egyptian funerary objects – including mummies – as well as the Korean and Japanese collections.

Central Bloomsbury & Fitzrovia

British Museum - lower floors

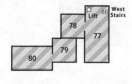

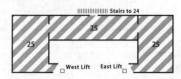

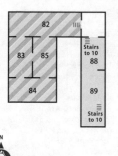

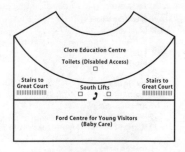

Not to scale

N

World cultures	82 Ephesus
25 *The Sainsbury African Galleries*	83 Roman sculpture
	84 Townley sculptures
Greece & Rome	85 Portrait sculpture
77 Greek & Roman architecture	
The Wolfson Galleries: 78-85	**Ancient Near East**
78 Classical inscriptions	88 Archaeology and the New Testament
79-80 Early Greek sculpture	89 Assyrian art

British Museum - main floor

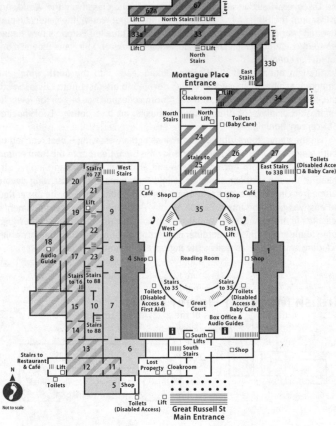

Enlightenment Gallery

1 Enlightenment: Discovering the World
   in the 18th century

Special Exhibitions

5, 35 Exhibitions

Egypt

4 Egyptian sculpture

Ancient Near East

6 Assyrian sculpture

7, 8 Nimrud Palace reliefs

9 Nineveh Palace reliefs

10 Khorsabad Palace reliefs & Assyrian sculpture

Greece & Rome

11 The Cyclades in the Bronze Age

12 *The Arthur I Fleischman Gallery*
   Greek Bronze Age

13-14 Geometric & Archaic Greece

15 Greece: 5th century BC

16 Bassae sculptures (mezzanine)

17 Nereid Monument

18 The Parthenon Galleries

19 Greece: The Acropolis & the late
   5th century BC

20 Greece: 4th century BC &
   the Payava Tomb

21 Mausoleum of Halikarnassos

22 The Hellenistic World

23 Greek & Roman sculpture

World cultures

24 *Wellcome Trust Gallery*
   Living and dying

26 *The JP Morgan Chase Gallery*
   North America

27 Mexico

Asia

33 *The Joseph E Hotung Gallery*
   China, South & Southeast Asia

33a *The Asahi Shimbun Gallery*
   Amaravati sculpture

33b *The Selwyn & Ellie Alleyne Gallery*
   Chinese jade

34 *The John Addis Gallery*
   Islamic Art

67 The Korea Foundation Gallery

It would be quite impossible to see everything in one day: apart from the guided and audio tours, it's well worth finding out from the Information desk when and where the free 50-minute 'EyeOpener' Gallery Talks are taking place (the first usually at about 1100 and the last at about 1500). Every day many of the museum's main areas are covered, with enthusiastic and well-informed volunteers describing the contents of a particular room in fascinating detail.

Main floor (Rooms 1-35)

In the west wing, in Room 4, (on the left through the Great Court) among the sculptures from Egypt stands the **Rosetta Stone**, discovered by Napoleon's troops on the banks of the Nile. The three types of script on the block, each describing the same decree passed by priests gathered at Memphis, enabled the decoding of Egyptian hieroglyphs in the mid-19th century. In Rooms 6-10 look out for the fifth-century BC Assyrian relief of Ashurbanipal's garden party from the Palace of Nineveh, with the head of the defeated Elamite Teumann hanging from a tree.

The sculptures of the Parthenon, aka the **Elgin Marbles** (in Room 18), are fragments from a fifth-century BC processional frieze that decorated the temple on the Acropolis in Athens dedicated to Athena. Two-thirds of it have survived, just over half of it looked after by the British Museum. Far from being 'stolen', they were bought off Lord Elgin by the British Government for considerably less than he himself had paid to have them removed and preserved, after receiving permission to do so from occupying Turkish forces in the early 1800s. A free audio guide in the room tells the full story.

The **Nereid Monument** (in Room 17) is a spectacular Ionic burial tomb dating from 390 BC from Xanthos in Turkey, featuring three sea nymphs in extraordinary graceful robes. In Room 22 the carved column from the **Temple of Artemis at Ephesus**, which was one of the seven wonders of the ancient world, shows the figures of Hermes, Thanatos and a woman who is likely to be either Iphigenia, Alcestis or Eurydice. In Room 21, more fragments from one of the wonders of the world include a 9-ft high statue and a frieze depicting the Greeks at war with the Amazons, both from **The Mausoleum of Helikarnassos** that once stood in modern-day Bodrum.

In the north wing (straight ahead), in Rooms 33-34, the **Amaravati sculptures** come from a Buddhist stupa in Andhra Pradesh, southeastern India, including carved slabs portraying the birth and life of Prince Siddartha.

Upper floors (Rooms 36-73, 90-94)

In the southeast wing (double back on yourself up the stairs in the south entrance) highlights of the **European rooms** (40-48) include the Sutton Hoo Ship Burial (Room 41), an amazing Anglo-Saxon Royal grave hoard of ornate shoulder clasps, drinking bowls, and cauldrons, as well as a shield, sword and helmet. Discovered in Suffolk in 1939, the entire find was generously given to the museum by the landowner Mrs Edith Pretty. Next door in Room 42 are the Lewis chess men, part of four sets of chess pieces of mysterious origin carved from walrus tusks, dating from the 12th century and found on the wild and remote Outer Hebridean island of Lewis.

In Room 49, for **Romano-British finds**, it may still be possible to see one of the oldest representations in the world of the face of Christ, set into the roundel of a mosaic from Hinton St Mary in Dorset. Round in the east wing on this level, Room 50 is full of prehistoric British artefacts, and the home of **Lindow Man**, aka 'Pete Marsh' after the peat that preserved his body for almost two millennia. Sliced in half by a bog-cutting machine in Cheshire in 1984, these freeze-dried remains of a 25-year-old sacrificial or murder victim from the first century AD look as if they had been buried last year. Look out too for the Sweet Track, a section of neolithic pre-fab wooden plank walk from the Somerset Levels, dated about 3807 BC. It could be erected in the course of a day across marshy ground over a distance of about two miles.

British Museum - upper floors

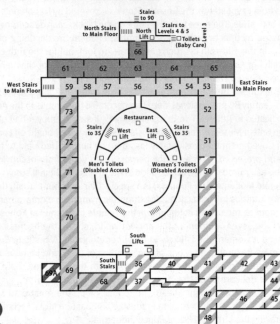

N
Not to scale

Britain & Europe
- **36,37** Prehistory
- **41** Sutton Hoo & Early Medieval
- **42** Medieval
- **43** Medieval tiles & pottery
- **44** Clocks & watches
- **45** The Waddesdon Bequest
- **46** Europe: 15th-18th centuries
- **47** Europe: 19th century
- **48** Europe & America: 20th century
- **49** Weston Gallery of Roman Britain
- **50** Later Bronze Age & Celtic Europe

Ancient Near East
- **51** Palmyra/South Arabia
- **52** Ancient Iran
  The Raymond & Beverly Sackler Galleries: 53-59
- **53-54** Ancient Anatolia
- **55** Later Mesopotamia
- **56** Early Mesopotamia
- **57-59** The Ancient Levant

Egypt
- **61** Ancient Egyptian culture

- **62-63** *The Roxie Walker Galleries*
  Egyptian funerary archaeology
  The Raymond & Beverly Sackler Galleries: 64-65
- **64** Early Egypt
- **65** Egypt & Africa
- **66** Coptic Egypt

Money
- **68** *HSBC Money Gallery*

Greece & Rome
- **69** Daily Life
- **70** *The Wolfson Gallery*
  Rome: City & Empire
- **71** Italy before the Roman Empire
- **72** *The A G Leventis Gallery*
  Ancient Cyprus
- **73** The Greeks in Southern Italy

Changing displays
- **69a** Money & medals
- **90** Prints & drawings
- **91** Asia
- **92-94** Japan

The rest of the east wing (Rooms 53-59) contains objects from the ancient near east that include the **Oxus Treasure**, the most important single collection of Ancient Persian (5th-4th century BC) gold and silverwork in the world. Continuing round into the north wing (above the Montague Place entrance), in Rooms 60-66, highlights include an astonishing array of Egyptian funerary archaeological finds – mummies, masks, sarcophagi and canopic boxes and jars for preserving the internal organs of the deceased.

In Room 56, there's an extraordinary collection of objects from the ancient Mesopotamian city of Ur, including the **'Ram in the Thicket'**, an 18-inch furniture support from around 2600 BC in the shape of a goat made from lapis lazuli, white shell and gold leaf, and the 'Royal Standard of Ur', a box decorated with the first known pictures of wheeled transport.

The upper floors of the west wing (Rooms 69-73) contain more exhibits from Greece and Rome, including the beautiful deep-blue Portland vase (Room 70), from the first century AD, invisibly mended many times since, and an inspiration to British potters since it came into the possession of the Dukes of Portland in 1785.

Around Bloomsbury

Turning right out of the back entrance of the British Museum on Montague Street leads into **Russell Square**, the largest, most famous and freshly renovated of Bloomsbury's famous squares. The formal gardens and fountains in the middle are surrouned by magnificent plane trees, with a pleasant and straightfoward Italian café in one corner (outside seating available).

In the northwest corner of the square, on Thornhaugh Street, **The Brunei Gallery** ① To2o-7898 4915, daily 1030-1700, free, gallery talks Thu 1330, free, is a newish exhibition space for London University's School of Oriental and African Studies (SOAS), putting on four temporary exhibitions a year of African and Asian art or anything else to do with those continents. Their resources and scholarly support usually ensure that the exhibitions are outstanding.

Bedford Square is the least altered of the squares and one that gives the best idea of how many of them would have looked in their heyday. The leafy gardens are private and locked (unless you happen to meet a friendly keyholder) but the **Architectural Association** ① To2o-7636 0974, on the north side at Nos 34-36 welcomes visitors. Energetic and avant-garde, as well as training architects, the Association puts on thought-provoking exhibitions about contemporary architecture and has a select bookshop and licensed café doing good food at lunchtimes. It becomes a pleasant enough bar in the early evenings.

The dark-brick Georgian terraces of **Gower Street** head north from the square's west side, home to the refurbished **Royal Academy of Dramatic Art** and also a substantial percentage of Bloomsbury's temporary population in a succession of guest house hotels. A little way up on the right on Keppel Street, the **London School of Hygiene and Tropical Medicine** is decorated with the names of pioneers in the ongoing fight against infectious diseases alongside stone carvings of some of the bugs that have been blamed for them.

Almost opposite Keppel Street, can be found the **Political Cartoon Gallery** ① 32 Store St, WC1, To2o-7580 1114, Mon-Fri 0900-1730, Sat 1100-1730, where satirical caricature has found a permanent home, displaying deft skits on national and international politicians from the scabrous pens of a variety of successful newspaper cartoonists.

A walk northwards up Malet Street takes you past the back door of RADA (Royal Academy of Dramatic Art), and the front entrance of its theatre, past Birkbeck College for extramural studies and mature students, and at the junction with Torrington Place, brings you to the University of London Union (ULU) which hosts cheap and cheerful club nights with occasional live bands on the up (see page 205).

16 Bloomsbury & Fitzrovia

N

0 metres 100
0 yards 100

Sleeping
Academy 1 C4
Carr-Saunders 12 C2
Charlotte Street 3 D3
County 14 A4
Grange Blooms 2 D5
Harlingford 6 A4
Indian Students
  YMCA 15 C2
Jesmond 7 C3
Mentone 8 A4
Morgan 9 D5
MyHotel 10 D4
Principal Russell 11 C5
Ruskin 13 D5

Eating
Abeno 1 D5
Alara Wholefoods 2 B5
Back to Basics 3 D1
Bam-Bou 4 D3
Bar Centrale 5 B5
Café Deco 6 D4
Café Rive Gauche 7 B2
Eagle Bar Diner 22 E3
Elena's L'Etoile 9 D3
Hakkasan 8 E4
Hare & Tortoise 11 B6
Ikkyu 12 D3
Marino's 13 E3
Mash 14 E1
North Sea Fish 15 A5
Pied-à-Terre 16 D3
Pizza Express 17 D5
Rasa Samudra 18 D3
RK Stanley 19 E1
Roka 10 D3
Sardo 24 B2
Savoir Faire 20 E5
Thai Garden Café 21 D5
Wagamama 23 E5

Pubs & bars
Champion 25 E2
Duke of York 26 D3
Grafton Arms 28 B2
Jamie's 29 C2
Jerusalem 30 E3
King & Queen 31 D2

ⓘ *Malet Pl, To20-7679 2000 (Ext 2884). Tue-Fri 1300-1700, Sat 1000-1300. Free (donations appreciated).*

Directly opposite Waterstone's bookshop on Torrington Street, the Petrie Museum of Egyptian Archaeology is bound to delight anyone whose appetite for all things Ancient Egyptian has been whetted by the British Museum. Donated by Sir Flinders

Petrie to University College London (UCL) in 1933, this old-fashioned academic museum is a glass-cased treasure trove of amulets, beads, ornaments, instruments and decorative art. The museum's quiet rooms contain a huge variety of things strongly evocative of how lives in the Nile valley were led (and corpses interred), from the dawn of time through to more recent history. The collection ranges from the oldest dress in the world (2800 BC), discovered in 1977 amongst a pile of rags excavated by Petrie in 1912, with sweat stains showing in its armpits, down to weird things that might have helped Cleopatra with her make-up. Cat lovers should check out the small Langton Collection of miniature cat figures, donated by N&B Langton, authors of *The Cat in Ancient Egypt*. The Museum is due to be moved into a new gallery in the near future, so catch it here while you can.

University College London ⓘ *Gower St, To20-7679 2000, Mon-Sat 0900-1700*, is itself well worth a look, for its architecture, library, and not least the fully-clothed skeleton of its founder Jeremy Bentham. His 'Auto-Icon', dressed in his original clothing topped by a wax copy of his head, can be seen sitting in a cupboard in the South Cloisters. In the same building, the **Flaxman Gallery** ⓘ *To20-7679 2540, Wed-Fri 1300-1700 in term time*, an impressive round room beneath the college's central dome, displays changing selections of art and literature from UCL's extensive collection.

Round the corner is **Gordon Square**, once the centre of literary Bloomsbury, as its numerous blue plaques testify, and still the square with the most attractive public gardens, its winding paths and borders home to a surprising variety of wildlife, including hedgehogs. Nos 31-34 are UCL's **Institute of Archaeology** ⓘ *with temporary displays viewable Mon-Fri 0900-1700.*

Lord John Russell 32 *A5*
Museum Tavern 33 *D5*
One Tun 34 *D2*
Plough 36 *D5*
Roxy 35 *E3*
Sevilla Mia 38 *E4*
Social 39 *E2*
Truckles of Pied Bull Yard 40 *D5*

Drill Hall 4 *C3*
Odeon Tottenham Court Rd 5 *D3*
Renoir 6 *B6*
The Place 7 *A4*
ULU 8 *C4*

✿ *See London at a glance, p19-24, for related maps.*

Entertainment ♫
Bloomsbury Theatre 1 *B3*
Dominion Theatre 3 *E4*

Central Bloomsbury & Fitzrovia

Percival David Foundation of Chinese Art

ⓘ T020-7387 3909. Mon-Fri 1030-1700. Free (donations appreciated). Under-14s must be accompanied by an adult.

In the southeastern corner of Gordon Square (No 53), the Percival David Foundation of Chinese Art consists of a series of quiet, serene rooms containing a large collection of exquisite Chinese ceramics from the 10th-18th centuries: Ming, Qing, Song and Tang vases, dishes, pots, incense burners and water droppers, many of which were previously owned by Chinese emperors. The cumulative effect of such an absorbing wealth of fine detail is memorable.

Around Fitzrovia

Heading back west again and crossing over Gower Street, Torrington Place hits the middle of Tottenham Court Road just above Goodge Street Station at one of the most appealing stretches of this otherwise characterless northbound thoroughfare. Left from here begins the succession of competing cut-price computer and hi-fi shops for which the Tottenham Court Road has become famous. Goodge Street is a busy shopping street and one of the gateways to Fitzrovia. There's not much in the way of 'sights' as such but the area's tight little network of streets and alleyways makes for some rewarding browsing.

A little way down it on the right, **Pollock's Toy Museum** ⓘ No 1 Scala St, T020-7636 3452, Mon-Sat 1000-1700, £3, child £1.50, looks like it belongs in another century, a quaint little place packed with olde-worlde toys, most famously the carboard cut-out theatres last made by Benjamin Pollock in Hoxton. The museum features a reconstruction of his shop and some of his original creations. The shop beneath the museum sells the modern equivalents and other new-old toys.

Charlotte Street, Fitzrovia's main artery, heads north-south close by, leading northwards to the **Fitzroy Square**. Originally planned by the Adams brothers, No 29 was the home of both GB Shaw and Virginia Woolf (at different times). Nearby, the British Telecom Tower is Fitzrovia's most prominent landmark, reminiscent of the space race. The revolving restaurant at the top has sadly been closed to the public since a bombscare in the 1970s.

● Sleeping

Bloomsbury & Fitzrovia p192, map p200
L Charlotte Street Hotel, 15-17 Charlotte St, W1, T020-7907 4000, www.firmdale.com. Super-fashionable, with 52 stylish and very comfortable rooms, a decent restaurant and buzzy bar Oscar, popular with movie industry players and people in advertising.
L MyHotel Bloomsbury, 11-13 Bayley St, WC1, T020-7667 6000. With 76 freshly Conran-decorated rooms, utilizing the latest in feng shui principles, it's still mainly the location that you're paying for here, functional, efficient but fun too.
A Academy, 21 Gower St, WC1, T020-7631 4115, www.theetoncollection.com. Unpretentious Georgian townhouse, library and conservatory, charming staff, full English

breakfast, and a bar open to non-residents. By the same people as the new Glasshouse hotel in Edinburgh.
A Grange Blooms, 7 Montague St, WC1, T020-7323 1717, www.grangehotels.com. Behind the British Museum, an aspirational 18th-century country house atmosphere with imitation furniture to match and a quiet walled garden. The cosiest of the group of Grange hotels in the area.
A Hotel Principal Russell, Russell Sq, WC1, T020-7837 6470, www.principalhotels .co.uk. Massive terracotta building on Russell Sq, with 336 rooms, many of them, including the Edwardian bar made famous by some of the Bloombury set, recently completely revamped.

B Morgan, 24 Bloomsbury St, WC1, T020-7636 3735. Marginally more expensive but similar in style, more central though, with 20 rooms. Breakfast included.

B Ruskin Hotel, 23-24 Montague St, WC1, T020-7636 7388, www.ruskinhotellondon.com. Much more old-fashioned, a typical small London guest house, with a certain faded charm, small but fairly comfortable rooms. £84 for double (plus en suite), £67 without.

C County Hotel, Upper Woburn Pl, WC1, T020-7387 5544, www.imperialhotels.co.uk. Large, old-fashioned, unreconstructed hotel near the Euston Rd. All rooms, which are defiantly basic, share bathrooms but do have TVs. Somewhere from another much less fussy era. £52 a night for a double.

C The Jesmond, 63 Gower St, WC1, T020-7636 3199, F020-7323 4373, www.jesmondhotel.org.uk. 16 rooms, excellent value small hotel, with a garden and quieter rooms at the back away from thundering Gower St.

D Carr-Saunders Hall, 18 Fitzroy St, W1, T020-7580 6338, www.lse.ac.uk/vacations. LSE hall of residence just beneath Telecom Tower. 10 twin rooms available during Easter and summer holidays. Book as early as possible.

D Indian Students YMCA, 41 Fitzroy Sq, WC1, T020-7387 0411, www.indianymca.org. Anyone can stay here, you don't have to be Indian or a student. 109 rooms, clean and efficient, with dinner and breakfast included in an Indian canteen.

❼ Eating

Bloomsbury & Fitzrovia *p192, map p200*
Bloomsbury's largely academic and student population don't really encourage gourmet dining options whereas Fitzrovia's advertising execs and their clients certainly do.

Bam-Bou, 1 Percy St, W1, T020-7323 9130. One of the media set's favourite places, a modern Southeast Asian restaurant with an airy wooden interior and high-style quotient.

Elena's L'Etoile, 30 Charlotte St, W1, T020-7636 1496. Very traditionally French in both its menu and clientele, closed Sat lunch and Sun.

Hakkasan, 8 Hanway Pl, W1 T020-7907 1888. Mon-Sat 1200-1500, 1900-2300, Sun. Probably the funkiest basement Chinese in the capital, with its blue-lit banquettes and stylish decor and a Michelin star for the food to boot. Expensive but worth it.

Pied-à-Terre, 34 Charlotte St, W1, T020-7636 1178. Much more traditional atmosphere, a small 2 Michelin-starred French restaurant, expert at nouvelle cuisine. Closed Sun.

Roka, 37 Charlotte St, W1 T020-7580 6464. Another relatively recent arrival, a very sophisticated Japanese restaurant.

Fitzrovia is also the best place to head for in the mid-range price bracket.

Back To Basics, 21a Foley St, W1, T020-7436 2181. Another good destination for seafood, a cheerful restaurant at the lower end of this bracket. Closed Sat, Sun.

Eagle Bar Diner, 3-5 Rathbone Pl, W1 T020-7637 1418. Possibly inspired by the success of RK Stanley, a fairly pricey but pretty cool cod-American diner doing big burgers and chips by day and excellent cocktails by night.

Mash, 19-21 Great Portland St, W1, T020-7637 5555. Another media favourite, a 90's take on the 70s in the own-brew bar (open until 0200 Wed-Sat) and good food in the busy restaurant upstairs until 2300.

Rasa Samudra, 5 Charlotte St, W1, T020-7637 0222. The most laid-back branch of the excellent Rasa chain, distinguished from the others by doing seafood alongside the famously fragrant south Indian vegetarian dishes and having a smoking section. Closed Sun.

RK Stanley, 6 Little Portland St, W1, T020-7462 0099. Very good purveyors of fine sausages and real ale in a stylish modern British take on American diner-style eating and drinking. Open until 2400 Mon-Sat.

Sardo, 45 Grafton Way, W1 T020-7387 2521. In the northern part of Fitrzrovia, is a reasonably priced and very popular little Sardinian restaurant.

Bloomsbury comes into its own in the cheap food department. Museum St is a good destination for an inexpensive meal

Abeno, 47 Museum St, WC1, T020-7405 3211. A smallish Japanese restaurant doing teppanyaki and okonomiyaki (little stuffed doughballs fried at the table).

Hare and Tortoise, 15-17 Brunswick Shopping Centre, Brunswick Sq, WC1, T020-7278 4945. A spacious and very cheap non-smoking Japanese dumpling and noodle bar.

Ikkyu, 67a Tottenham Court Rd, W1, T020-7636 9280. Another good basic and inexpensive Japanese restaurant.

North Sea Fish Restaurant, 7-8 Leigh St, WC1, T020-7387 5892, on the other side of Bloomsbury, near Russell Sq. Top-quality sit-down fish and chips in timeless style at lunch and dinner. Next door is a take-away chippie.

Pizza Express, Coptic St. A splendid tiled branch of this chain.

Savoir Faire, 42 New Oxford St, WC1, T020-7436 0707. More old-fashioned and intimate, doing a reasonable 2-course lunch for about £8, and a 2-course dinner for about £14, with friendly service.

Thai Garden Café, 32 Museum St, WC1, T020-7323 1494. Capable little Thai restaurant.

Wagamama, 4 Streatham St, WC1, T020-7323 9223. The brightly lit Japanese basement canteen that has been wowing diners for some time with its brusque efficiency and the quality of its noodle soups. Queues still sometimes form for lunch and supper.

Cafés and sandwich bars

Museum St is a reliable destination for coffee and sandwiches, although the cafés along here can get very busy at lunchtime.

Alara Wholefoods, 58-60 Marchmont St, WC1, T020-7837 1172. Very good value hot veggie and organic meals to take away or eat outside.

Bar Centrale, 4 Bernard St, WC1, T020-7278 5249, near Russell Sq tube. A very popular 70s-style Italian café/sandwich shop, with a restaurant next door, doing a wide range of fillings and breads.

Café Deco 43 Store St, WC1, T020-7323 4501. A little further afield, an interesting range of Italian sandwiches and home-made pasta.

Café Rive Gauche, 20-21 Warren St, W1, T020-7387 8232. A sweet little French place for good salads and light meals. Opens early in the morning during the week (closed weekends) and closes at 1500.

Marino's, 31 Rathbone Pl, W1, T020-7636 8965. An excellent down-to-earth and cheerful Italian café, if a bit smoky, doing great platefuls of inexpensive comfort food.

Pubs and bars

Bloomsbury & Fitzrovia *p192, map p200*
No surprise that Bloomsbury's large student population keeps a wide variety of pubs doing very good business.

Plough, 27 Museum St, WC1, T020-7636 7964, near the British Museum. Larger and often less packed than the famous Museum Tavern at the end of the street. It too has a refurbished Victorian interior and serves reasonable food throughout the day.

Lord John Russell, on bustling little Marchmont St. A pleasant 1-roomed local with a wooden interior and benches outside, a favourite with students and their tutors.

Truckles of Pied Bull Yard, off Bury Pl, WC1, T020-7404 5338. More popular with suits than students, this is a good wine bar (part of the Davy's chain) hidden away in its own little courtyard among a clutch of expensive art shops. It has an atmospheric basement as well as tables outside in summer.

More vibrant drinking can be found in several bars, many of them late-night, scattered around Fitzrovia.

Champion, 12-13 Wells St, W1, T020-7323 1228. Good old-style pubs in Fitzrovia include this beautifully decorated place, its tiled and stained-glass interior is an antique homage to winning sportsmen of all kinds.

Duke of York, 47 Rathbone St, W1, T020-7636 7065. A cosy little Greene King pub on the corner of the chi-chi shopping mews of Charlotte Pl.

Grafton Arms, Grafton Way, W1, T020-7387 7923. Specializes in 1st-class real ales and has a tiny little roof terrace, popular with students and local office workers during the summer.

Jamie's, 74 Charlotte St, W1, T020-7636 7556. A fashionable wine bar on 2 levels popular with the local media set.

Jerusalem 33-34 Rathbone Pl, W1, T020-7255 1120. A roomy basement bar with great solid tables and vaguely dungeon-like feel. Despite its size, it often gets loud and busy. Open Mon-Wed 1200-0100, Thu-Sat 1200-0100 (admission charge after 2130 Fri, Sat £5).

King & Queen, 1 Foley St, W1, T020-7636 5619. A resolutely unreconstructed old boozer with friendly bar staff, behind Middlesex Hospital.

The One Tun, 58 Goodge St, W1, T020-7209 0559. A lively Young's pub with a well-established clientele of local office workers.
Roxy, 3-5 Rathbone Pl, W1, T020-7636 1598. Catering for a younger crowd, open Mon-Fri 1700-0300, Fri 1700-0330, Sat 2130-0330; admission usually charged after 2030, another large basement bar, funkily lit and always jumping late in the week.
Sevilla Mia, 22 Hanway St, W1, T020-7637 3756. Very different in style, open Mon-Sat 1900-0100, Sun 1900-2400, a scruffy, cosy little basement tapas bar that often has live Spanish guitar music and flamenco.
The Social, 5 Little Portland St, W1, T020-7636 4992. Open Mon-Sat 1200-2400, Sun 1700-2300, an industrialized music bar serving food upstairs, hardcore sounds and demon cocktails in the basement, popular with 20-somethings on pre-club warm-ups.

● Entertainment

Bloomsbury & Fitzrovia *p192, map p200*
Cinema
Odeon, Tottenham Court Rd, W1, T0871-2244007. 3 first-run screens, one often given to more offbeat releases.
Renoir, Brunswick Centre, Brunswick Sq, WC1, T020-7837 8402. Usually foreign films, 4 screenings a day on 2 screens.

Dance
The Place, 17 Duke's Rd, WC1, T020-7380 1268. London's premier small-scale contemporary dance venue has been given a hefty refurbishment with new restaurant and reception.

Music
St George's Bloomsbury, Bloomsbury Way, T020-7405 3044. An interesting church design-ed by Nicholas Hawksmoor, its stepped steeple modelled on the Mausoleum of Halicarnassus (see British Museum above) and surmounted with an unusual statue of George I in a Roman toga. The airy interior is an enchanting place to hear a free lunchtime concert in summer. Open Mon-Fri 0930-1730, Sun 0900-1700.
ULU, University of London Union, Manning Hall, Malet St, WC1, T020-7664 2000. Open 2030-2300, nights vary. Admission £5-10. Student bashes and upcoming bands. Non-students may need to be signed in after 1900.

Theatre
Bloomsbury Theatre, 15 Gordon St, WC1, T020-7388 8822. Middle-scale fringe theatre, part of UCL, often hosts good touring productions.
Dominion, Tottenham Court Rd, W1, T020-7413 1713. Large West End theatre almost exclusively devoted to blockbusting musicals.
Drill Hall, 16 Chenies St, WC1, T020-7637 8270. London's foremost gay and lesbian theatre and cabaret venue. Vibrant bar.

● Shopping

Bloomsbury & Fitzrovia *p192, map p200*
Books
Like the Charing Cross Rd, when it comes to shopping Bloomsbury means books, mainly antiquarian, out of print, second-hand and remaindered.
Waterstone's, 82 Gower St, WC1, T020-7636 1577. The main seller of new books in the area, open until 2000 Mon-Fri, unitl 1900 Sat, 1200-1800 Sun, the university bookshop, formerly Dillons, with a wide range of academic titles and a good second-hand section too.

Antiquarian, second-hand & specialist
Great Russell St and Museum St are home to several good specialist, second-hand and antiquarian bookshops.
Atlantis Bookshop, 49a Museum St, WC1, T020-7405 2120. Stocks any and every esoteric and occult title, embracing mysticism, mythology and folklore, both new and second-hand.
Bookmarks, 1 Bloomsbury St, WC1, T020-7637 1848. Specializes in new socialist material.
Cinema Bookshop, 13-14 Great Russell St WC1, T020-7637 0206. Has a vast range of new and out-of-print books on the movies.
Samuel French's Theatre Bookshop, 52 Fitzroy St, W1, T020-7387 9373. The destination par excellence for theatrical bibliophiles, and stocks just about every new play in print.
Robert Frew, 106 Great Russell St, WC1, T020-7580 2311. An antiquarian bookshop specializing in travel, illustrated books and library sets.
Gay's the Word, 66 Marchmont St, WC1, T020-7278 7654. One of London's premier gay and lesbian bookshops.

Gosh!, 39 Great Russell St, WC1, T020-7636 1011. Open to 1900 Thu, Fri, sells comics and cartoons.

Judd Books, 82 Marchmont St WC1, T020-7387 5333. Have lots of low-price second-hand academic titles, especially on philosophy, architecture, and film.

London Review Bookshop, 14 Bury Pl, WC1, T020 7269 9030. Emphasises fiction, biography, poetry, history, politics and philosophy with a selection informed by the prestigious literary magazine of the same name.

The Marchmont Bookshop, 39 Burton St, WC1, T020-7387 7989. An endearing little second-hand bookshop specializing in poetry.

Museum Bookshop, 36 Great Russell St, WC1, T020-7580 4086. A charming and scruffy establishment, stocking new and out-of-print books, with archaeology, ancient history and conservation as strong points.

Arthur Probsthain Oriental & African Bookseller, 41 Great Russell St, WC1, T020-7636 1096. Caters comprehensively for the graduates and students of SOAS, the School of Oriental and African Studies.

Unsworth's, 12 Bloomsbury St, WC1, T020-7436 9836. Open until 2000 Thu-Sat, popular with students for second-hand and remaindered humanities titles.

Miscellaneous

Heal's, 196 Tottenham Court Rd, W1, T020-7636 1666. For furniture, gifts, homeware, magnificent beds and accessories with a certain flair, open until 2000 Thu, usually a good but fairly expensive bet.

James Smith & Sons, 53 New Oxford St, WC1, T020-7836 4731. Other than books this is one of the best places in London to buy a good umbrella, or a walking- shooting- or sword-stick, with a long-established and extraordinary range of stick-related things on display.

▲ Activities

Bloomsbury & Fitzrovia *p192, map p200*

YMCA Health and Fitness Centre, 112 Great Russell St, WC1, T020-7343 1700. £45 a week associate membership, £10 for a day. Swimming pool, gym and sauna.

University of London Students Union, open until 1900, associate membership for gym, pool, sports hall, squash court, and the choice of 3 bars: The Venue, Bar 101, and the Duck and Dive.

Holborn and Clerkenwell

East of the West End and west of the City, Holborn, long colonized by lawyers, the press and intermediaries of all kinds, falls between two stools. Twenty years ago, though, the media and its journos moved out east to Wapping and Docklands and the buzz of the latest news being churned on Fleet Street died down. Without the newspapers to leaven the lump, the district is now dominated by the atmosphere of the ancient Inns of Court, neat and officious places founded on discretion and class-ridden legal traditions: don't be caught pronouncing the silent L – for litigation – in Holborn. It's pronounced 'Ho-bon'. That said, the quiet lawns, secret alleyways and collegiate architecture of the barristers' stamping grounds are peaceful havens for outsiders to explore, and Lincoln's Inn Fields houses two of the city's most unusual museums, the Hunterian Museum of the Royal College of Surgeons and the spellbinding curiosity of Georgian architect Sir John Soane's home.

Over the same period Clerkenwell, on the other hand, northeast of the City and Holborn beyond the Gray's Inn Road, has become one of the most vibrant and creative parts of London, the fashionable home of design consultancies, independent media groups and sassy restaurants. Although it's beginning to look as though the party might already be over, with some tenants feeling the pinch of City property prices, the old streets north of Smithfield Market are still a top place to paint the town red. ▶▶ *For Sleeping, Eating and other listings see pages 215-217.*

History

At the end of the 14th century, Holborn and Clerkenwell were still separated by fields, with the 'Holebourne', a tributary of the River Fleet, running across it. The track running east carried carts loaded with wool, corn, cheese and wood, and ended at the Holborn Bar, where tolls were exacted and rogues and lepers refused entry to the City. A hamlet had grown up around the Bar, and further west there were the inns of court, Lincoln's Inn, and Gray's Inn. The latter included a windmill, dovecots and lakes and occupied the site of the manor house of Purpoole alongside the ancient road to the north, now Gray's Inn Road.

There was little else but fields to the west until St Giles-in-the-Fields. Clerkenwell, just outside the city walls and set in meadowlands rich in springs, was a hamlet that evolved to serve the two 12th-century monastic foundations, St Mary's Nunnery (the Clerk's well supplied the nunnery) and the Priory of St John of Jerusalem. Closer to the City walls lay Charterhouse, a Carthusian monastery built on burial ground set aside for victims of the Black Death, and a ten-acre field surrounded by ponds and trees.

'Smoothfield' (later Smithfield) was well known for its horse market (although other livestock was also traded), and, for over 700 years, as the venue for the annual Bartholomew Fair until it was suspended in 1855 for rowdiness and debauchery. It also served as a medieval sports field where archery, wrestling, athletics, jousting and royal tournaments could be seen.

Following the Reformation, and the redistribution of monastic lands, a 'better qualitie' of resident arrived in the several mansions erected by the nobility. When General Monck rode down the Gray's Inn Road into the City to proclaim the Restoration of Charles II, it also signalled a change of gear in Clerkenwell's development. Since the court was now settling further west, and its acolytes following suit, so the great houses were sold on to merchants and craftsmen. Townhouses sprang up in modern Britton Street, and 'a little towne', Hatton Garden, was built alongside the Bishop of Ely's London palace. Gardens opened up, spurred on by the area's 'medicinal waters'. English Grotto, Merlin's Cave, London Spa (behind modern Exmouth market) and Sadler's Wells drew enthusiastic crowds through much of the 18th century, while Mohocks (gangs of aristocratic thugs) roamed around Snow Hill looking for old ladies to sieze and roll down the hill in a barrel.

Artisans and craftsmen, many foreign, moved in, as the area earned a reputation for its jewellers (particularly in Hatton Garden) and watchmakers. The good waters attracted brewers (Whitbread) and gin distillers such as Gordon's and Booth's. During the 19th century, as the local population rocketed, so both Holborn and Clerkenwell earned notoriety for their slums. The Fleet River was a virtual sewer, Smithfield Market continued to trade in live animals (blood and entrails in the gutters, and stray cattle hid in houses and shops), and once pleasant streets saw urban squalor for the first time.

Despite the large slum clearances that made way for the Clerkenwell and Farringdon Roads, Holborn Circus and Viaduct, and later the Metropolitan Railway, the area still presented a horrifying spectacle for the Prince of Wales when he visited in 1884. The poverty ensured it became a lively centre of radicalism. In the Gordon Riots of 1780 a mob attacked and set alight Clerkenwell's two prisons and Orator Hunt launched his assault on the Tower from Spa Fields (1816). Clerkenwell Green has instigated many a subversive act, whether Chartist meetings in the mid-1800s, the Socialists setting off to Trafalgar Square on Bloody Sunday in 1887, or Lenin producing several editions of *Iskra* from what is now the Marx Memorial Library. The last century, however, has seen a gradual change in fortunes. Businesses have moved back into Holborn after the area suffered severe bombing in the Second World War, and Clerkenwell has more recently become a fashionable residential district, while still supporting a cottage industry of craftsmen.

17 Holborn & Clerkenwell

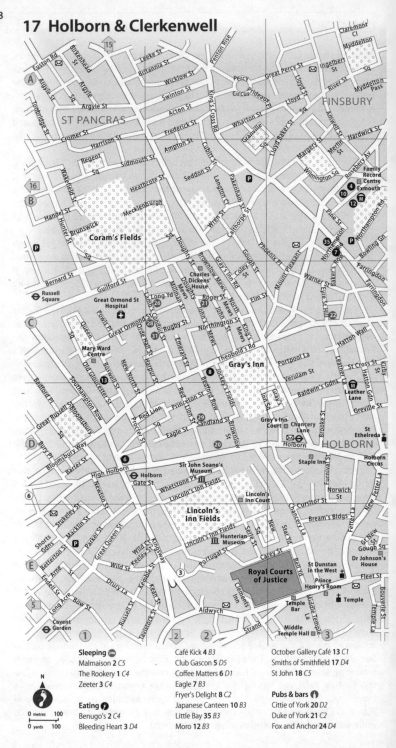

Sleeping 🛏
Malmaison **2** *C5*
The Rookery **1** *C4*
Zeeter **3** *C4*

Eating 🍴
Benugo's **2** *C4*
Bleeding Heart **3** *D4*

Café Kick **4** *B3*
Club Gascon **5** *D5*
Coffee Matters **6** *D1*
Eagle **7** *B3*
Fryer's Delight **8** *C2*
Japanese Canteen **10** *B3*
Little Bay **35** *B3*
Moro **12** *B3*

October Gallery Café **13** *C1*
Smiths of Smithfield **17** *D4*
St John **18** *C5*

Pubs & bars 🍺
Cittie of York **20** *D2*
Duke of York **21** *C2*
Fox and Anchor **24** *D4*

N
0 metres 100
0 yards 100

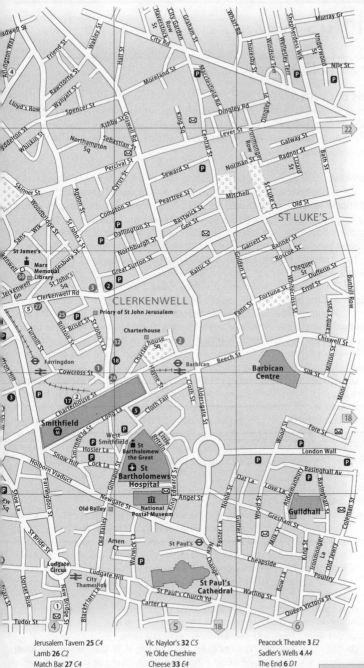

Jerusalem Tavern **25** *C4*
Lamb **26** *C2*
Match Bar **27** *C4*
Perseverance **28** *C2*
Portenckih **22** *C3*
Three Cups **29** *D2*
Three Kings **30** *C4*
VATS Winebar **31** *C2*

Vic Naylor's **32** *C5*
Ye Olde Cheshire
  Cheese **33** *E4*
Ye Olde Mitre **34** *D4*

Entertainment 🎵
Bridewell Theatre **1** *E4*
Fabric **2** *D4*

Peacock Theatre **3** *E2*
Sadler's Wells **4** *A4*
The End **6** *D1*
Turnmills **5** *C4*

❧ See London at a glance, p19-24, for related maps.

Sights ● *Barbican, Chancery Lane, Farringdon, Holborn, Temple.* ● *See p460.*

Around Holborn

Inns of Court

① *Hall To20-7427 4800. Temple Church To20-7797 8241, To20-7353 3470, Wed-Sun 1100-1600. Phone ahead to check opening hours and for guided morning tours that include Inner Temple Hall (£10). Middle Temple Mon-Fri 1000-1130, 1445-1600, free.*

The Victoria Embankment sweeps round to Blackfriars Bridge from the riverside frontage of Somerset House, passing Temple tube and the old gardens of the **Inner and Middle Temple Inns of Courts**. These ancient alleyways and courtyards stuffed with lawyers' offices and barristers hustling about their business take their name from the crusading Knights Templar, the Inner Temple being the one nearest the City, the Outer Temple long gone. The warren of streets around the four venerable Inns of Court are a peculiar place to explore, still very much alive but also pickled in the aspic of legal tradition.

The Templars built their distinctive little round church here in 1185, the most important of the nine in the UK and the only one in London. Like the others dotted about the country, the design of **Temple Church** was based on the Church of the Holy Sepulchre in Jerusalem. Only one doorway is original, the building having been badly damaged in the Second World War, but its mixture of Romanesque and Gothic, already much tinkered with by Wren and Decimus Burton in the 18th century, was beautifully restored in the early 1960s.

Located in the Inner Temple, the Church is shared with the **Middle Temple**, which boasts a magnificent old wooden hall dating from 1573. Thanks to its great hammerbeam roof, crested screens of oak and a high table hewn from one solid trunk donated by Queen Elizabeth I, it's not that difficult to picture the first ever performance of *Twelfth Night* that was staged here with Shakespeare himself quite probably taking part. The little table was supposedly made from the timbers of Francis Drake's globe-trotting ship the *Golden Hinde*, of which you can see a replica on Bankside.

Fleet Street and around

Above the Inner Temple Gate opposite Chancery Lane, at 17 Fleet Street, is another period piece from roughly the same era, **Prince Henry's Room** ① *To20-7936 4004, 1100-1400 Mon-Sat, free*, so named because it was used by lawyers acting on behalf of James I's oldest son. Oak panelled, with its fine moulded plaster ceiling dating from 1610, it narrowly escaped the Great Fire of 1666. On display here are some artefacts relating to the room's history and the diarist of the Great Fire, Samuel Pepys.

Fleet Street was once the main artery of the 'fourth estate', when it was lined with publishing houses, newspaper offices and printing works, and its pubs and restaurants were packed with journalists scratching a living.

On the other side of Chancery Lane, the **Church of St Dunstan in the West** ① *To20-7242 6027, Tue 1000-1600, Sat 1400-1800, Sun 0900-1500*, is easily recognizable by its strange clock, apparently the first in London with minute marks, and featuring a pair of muscle-bound gong-beaters said to represent Gog and Magog. The clock was installed in 1671 in gratitude for the church being spared from the flames.

66 99 The warren of streets around the four venerable Inns of Court are a peculiar place to explore, still very much alive but also pickled in the aspic of legal tradition...

On the right of the church through a heavy iron gate into the forecourt stand the statues of King Lud and his children (the pre-Roman rulers of London) and of Queen Elizabeth I, all originally from the Ludgate, demolished like other City gates in 1760. Towards the bottom of the street, near the old smoked-glass Art Deco building of the Express newspapers (now in Southwark), there's a fine view of St Paul's standing on the top of Ludgate Hill.

Dr Johnson's House ⓘ *T020-7353 3745. Mon-Sat winter 1100-1700 (last admission 1645); summer Mon-Sat 1100-1730 (last admission 1715). £4.50, concession £3.50.* Just to the north of Fleet Street, at 17 Gough Square, can be found the home from 1748-59 of one of the street's most fearsome, productive and engaging characters, 'Dictionary' Johnson, aka Ursa Major to his friends. Dr Johnson's House sensibly does not attempt a full period reconstruction of the chaotic squalor in which the awesome man of letters and his six amenuenses compiled his great dictionary. Instead this is a fine place to browse around, with plenty to read and a facsimile of the big book itself, particularly influential in its use of literary precedents but also famous for its sense of humour, defining lexicographer as 'a compiler of dictionaries, a harmless drudge'. The work went on in the top room of the narrow house and all four floors have been furnished in an appropriate style with displays on a variety of Johnsonia, the one on his women friends introducing the original blue-stocking, the frighteningly learned Elizabeth Carter who could speak seven languages, as well as a rather whimsical 25-minute video drama-doc of Johnson showing his indefatigable biographer Boswell round the house. Recently refurbished, hands-on activities for children include the opportunity to try on some replica Georgian costumes.

Back at the top of Fleet Street near the Strand stands a bronze griffin, the adopted emblem of the City of London, marking the site of the **Temple Bar**, a Wren building that controlled and eventually fatally restricted the flow of traffic into the City. It was removed in 1878 and rebuilt at Theobald's Park in Hertfordshire. There's a long-running campaign to return the remarkable gateway to London, possibly siting it somewhere near St Paul's.

From here it's impossible to mistake the great red-brick Gothic edifice that holds the **Royal Courts of Justice** ⓘ *T020-7947 6000, Mon-Fri 0930-1200, 1300-1630, free.* Designed by aspiring cathedral builder GE Street, it was completed in 1882, its high moral, religious and national purpose emphasized with statues of Solomon, Jesus and Alfred the Great. This High Court is where civil cases are heard: divorces, bankruptcy hearings, building disputes, tribunals, custody battles and endless others, as well as criminal cases that have been referred to the Court of Appeal. Through the front entrance, the massive Great Hall (where a list of current cases is posted; the curious can ask an usher what they're about) is a suitably intimidating space, hardly much enlivened by a little exhibition of lawyers' regalia to one side.

Behind the Royal Courts of Justice, between Kingsway and Chancery Lane, lies **Lincoln's Inn Fields**, the largest square in London and home to two of its most unusual museums.

Hunterian Museum of the Royal College of Surgeons
ⓘ *T020-7869 6560, www.rcseng.ac.uk/services/museums. Mon-Sat 1000-1700. Free.*
On the south side of the square, at 35-43, is the Hunterian Museum of the Royal
College of Surgeons. In the 18th century John Hunter amassed a huge collection of
pathological specimens, human and animal, in the course of his anatomical studies.
With the addition of thousands more in the 19th century, the museum once held a
world-beating variety of pickled body parts and dissected animal exhibits. Reopened
after major refurbishment in February 2005, as well as the more ghoulish attractions,
the museum holds a famous portrait of a rhinoceros by George Stubbs, and
odontological displays of old teeth, including some gathered on the battlefield of
Waterloo and others strung together on a necklace brought back from the Congo by
Stanley the explorer.

★ Sir John Soane's Museum

ⓘ *T020-7405 2107, www.soane.org. Tue-Sat 1000-1700, 1st Tue of month also
1800-2100. Free. Guided tour on Sat at 1430, £3, concessions free.*

On the opposite side of the square, at Nos 12-14 Lincoln's Inn Fields, Sir John Soane's
Museum is a remarkable memorial to the imagination of one of Georgian London's
greatest architects, and today one of the city's most extraordinary sights. Most
famous for designing the Bank of England, Sir John Soane left his treasured project of
a lifetime to the nation on his death in 1837. The eight or so rooms in No 13 that can
now be seen are a purpose-built showcase for his highly idiosyncratic and eclectic
collection of antiquities, artworks and objets d'art, as well as being a successful and
much admired manipulation of architectural space. At its most atmospheric
(although often also most crowded) during the late openings on the first Tuesday of
every month, an hour spent here is usually enough to persuade most people that they
need to come again with more time. There are far too many surprising effects and
curious or beautiful things to take in or understand on a single visit.

Unmissable are: the rooms specially constructed for Hogarth's series of
paintings, *The Rake's Progress* (from inherited wealth to the madhouse) and *The
Election* (a satire on political ambition), the hieroglyphic sarcophagus of Pharaoh Seti
I from around 1200BC, the bogus monk's parlour, the breakfast room and the
comparatively airy drawing room on the first floor with Soane's answer to Nash's
ideas on urban planning. The museum also holds regular temporary exhibitions on
other great architects.

Lincoln's Inn Court and around

ⓘ *T020- 7405 6360.* Lincoln's Inn Court itself, although largely closed to the public,
can be seen through its gates from the square. A very pleasant way to enjoy its
collegiate gardens, however, is to take in one of the open-air Shakespeare
productions that are usually staged there in the summer. On Chancery Lane, the Inn's
Tudor gatehouse was where Oliver Cromwell lodged as a young law student.

A few steps to the east towards Chancery Lane tube, **Staple Inn**, one of the nine
Inns of Chancery and now occupied by the Institute of Actuaries, is a remarkable
refurbished survival of a Tudor courtyard; again, it too was severely blitzed but has
since been renovated.

At the foot of Gray's Inn Road, High Holborn and its massive office blocks become
plain Holborn before reaching Holborn Circus. On the left beyond the Gray's Inn Road,
Leather Lane Market runs north, one of London's better street markets. Worth the
scrum, Cockney barrowboys selling all sorts of quality and tat lord it over a curious
mixture of customers, very busy at midday, and good for bargain clothes for women.
Parallel to Leather Lane, **Hatton Garden** has long been the centre of London's
diamond trade, which partly explains the market's wide variety of customers.

Nearby the little Gothic **Church of St Etheldreda** ① *Ely Place, EC1, T020-7405 1061, 0830-1830 daily*, is the only Catholic church in the City to have survived from the reign of Edward I (after being bought back from the reforming Anglicans in the 18th century). The 'Strawberry Fayre' held here in Ely Place on a day in mid to late June is a charity street party commemorating the old episcopal palace's famous strawberry fields.

Gray's Inn Court

① *T020-7458 7800. The walks are in summer 1230-1400 Mon-Fri.* In the angle of Gray's Inn Road and Holborn lies Gray's Inn Court itself, founded in the 14th century but badly damaged during the Second World War. Most famously associated with its 16th-century treasurer, the great natural philosopher Francis Bacon, its now much renovated hall was where Shakespeare's Comedy of Errors was first performed. A walk through these hushed courtyards and their expansive gardens can lead appropriately enough up to Charles Dickens' House, the novelist who memorably described the punishing effect of the law's interminable delays in *Bleak House*.

Charles Dickens' House

① *48 Doughty St, T020-7405 2127. Mon-Sat 1000-1700, Sun 1100-1700. Adults £4, £3 concession.*

Charles Dickens' House is a smart four-storey Georgian terraced house where Dickens lived for two years while writing *Oliver Twist* and *Nicholas Nickleby*, between 1837 and 1839. The drawing room, wash house and wine cellar have been recreated as they were in his day, with the drawing room in particular using much of his original furniture; indeed all the rooms are packed with Dickens memorabilia sure to delight fans of the troubled storyteller.

As well as manuscripts of his works on display, and lots of Dickensia for sale in the shop, a half-hour video runs through the high and low points of Dickens' life, while in June and July on Wednesdays at 1930, *The Sparkler of Albion* is a two-hour theatre show doing much the same but with more gusto (£12.50).

A short walk left along Guilford Street from here leads to Guilford Place at the top of **Lamb's Conduit Street**, a quiet pedestrianized street with its original gas lamps still in place and several pubs and shops of real character. The conduit was a dam in one of the tributaries of the Fleet river in Elizabethan times, hence the elegant statue of the water carrier in Guilford Place.

West of the street lies Bloomsbury, and beyond Great Ormond Street Hospital for Children, the peaceful haven of Queen Square, home to several other specialist hospitals. Here also is the **Mary Ward Centre** ① *Queen Square, T020-7831 7711, excellent value vegetarian café Mon-Thu 0930-2100, Fri 0930-2030, Sat 0930-1600*, named after the best-selling 19th-century novelist known as Mrs Humphrey Ward, who in 1899 founded the first school for physically handicapped children in England. Evening classes and various courses now take place in its fine red-brick, black-and-white tiled building.

Clerkenwell

Clerkenwell is one of the more exciting parts of London to wander around, not simply because of the clutch of new shops, restaurants, clubs and bars that have opened up here in the last decade, but also because it's an old part of town still visibly in a state of fashionable flux.

❖ *Clerkenwell.org, 53 Clerkenwell Cl, EC1, T020-7251 6311, is a local history information point and outlet for local crafts.*

A good place to start is in the south of the area around Smithfield Market, London's meat distribution centre. Unlike the other wholesale fish and fruit and veg markets at Billingsgate and Covent Garden, the market has managed to cling on to its ancient site in the city centre. Especially late at night and at dawn, when the area round about is partying hard or fast asleep, the comings and goings of huge articulated and refrigerated lorries unloading endless fresh carcasses into its grand late 19th-century building can take on a surreal quality.

Just to the northeast of the market is **Charterhouse Square** ① *To20-7253 9503, guided tours Apr-Jul, Wed 1415, £3, otherwise by appointment*, named after the Tudor manor house on its north side. The Charterhouse is a set of beautiful 16th-century almshouses on the site of a 14th-century Carthusian monastery which later became a top public school that moved out to Surrey in the 19th century. It's long been the Anglican church's venerable equivalent of the Royal Hospital at Chelsea, providing peaceful accommodation for gentleman pensioners. The tour includes the gardens, medieval buildings and 17th-century chapel as well as the manor house.

Nearby in West Smithfield is the oldest parish church in London, **St Bartholomew the Great** ① *To20-7606 5171, Mon-Fri 0830-1600, Sat 1030-1330, Sun 1400-1700*. Not much of the 12th-century priory church remains, but the Norman nave has featured in several major films including *Shakespeare in Love*, *The End of the Affair*, and *Robin Hood Prince of Thieves*.

St John Street

In the 12th century, St John Street was already the main road north from Smithfield Market to the Angel Islington. Its wiggling pack-pony trail is now one of Clerkenwell's most happening street at night. Just off to its west, tucked away down St John's Lane, stands the early 16th-century gatehouse of the **Priory of St John of Jerusalem**, the impressive remains of the medieval home of the Knights Hospitaller. In the 19th century the place was taken over by the Order of St John, a Victorian chivalric society that founded the St John's Ambulance Brigade which provides voluntary ambulances and first aid at a huge number of public events around the country.

The **Museum of the Order of St John** ① *To20-7324 4070, Mon-Fri 1000-1700, Sat 1000-1600, free, guided tours (£5 lasting about 1 ½ hrs) Tue, Fri, Sat 1100, 1430, include the Church and Crypt*, in the gatehouse, has a small exhibition divided between the stories of the Order and its Brigade and the armour of the Knights Hospitaller.

Clerkenwell Green and Exmouth Market

A left turn at the end of St John's Lane onto the Clerkenwell Road leads to Clerkenwell Green. Here the classical poise of the late 18th-century **Church of St James** ① *To20-7251 1190, 1000-1800 Mon-Fri, Sun service 1100*, contributes to the charming atmosphere of one of the area's most subversive corners, a centre for its artisan associations with several interesting crafts designers and the place to find the **Marx Memorial Library** ① *37a Clerkenwell Green, To20-7251 4706, www.marxlibrary.net, Mon-Thu 1300-1400 for casual enquirers, and Mon, Tue, Thu 1300-1800, Wed 1300-2000, Sat 1000-1300 for members, free*. Built as a Welsh Charity School in the early 18th century, in 1933 it became a members' lending library for socialist and working-class literature in honour of the great economist, having been the offices from 1892-1922 of the radical Twentieth Century Press supported by William Morris. There's a genuine fresco by Lord Hastings from the 1930s depicting the overthrow of capitalism and Lenin edited *Iskra* in a little room here that has hardly been changed since 1903. The lending library is available to members upstairs and anyone is welcome at weekday lunchtimes to have a look around. Marx is even reckoned to have taken coffee on the Green, still not a bad idea today.

⁝ Blood and guts

The blood and entrails of the livestock slaughtered in Smithfield ran in the streets' gutters, and rogue bulls sought sanctuary in the houses and shops around – hence the phrase 'bull in a china shop'.

But it wasn't only animals who were butchered at Smithfield Market. Until the gallows moved west to Tyburn (modern Marble Arch), this was also a place of execution. Burnings, roastings and boilings were visited on witches and heretics in front of enthusiastic crowds, and Wat Tyler, leader of the Peasants' Revolt of 1381, was stabbed here before being beheaded in front of St Bartholomew's Hospital.

Clerkenwell Green joins up with Farringdon Lane, where at No 16 the lid of the Clerk's Well that gives the area its name can be seen through a window. Closer inspections can be arranged through **Finsbury Lending Library** ① *T020-7527 7960*.

Farringdon Lane joins the traffic-choked Farringdon Road opposite the offices of the Guardian newspaper that contributes so much to the left-wing vogue of the area. Their Newsroom exhibition space here gives a flavour of the month. At the top of the hill, where Farringdon Road meets Rosebery Avenue, is **Exmouth Market**, a pedestrianized old street where the market had died on its feet before being revitalized by a wave of hip eateries and street fashion boutiques.

At the end of the street the **Family Record Centre** ① *1 Myddelton St, T020-8392 5300, www.familyrecords.gov.uk, Mon, Wed, Fri, 0900-1700, Tue 1000-1900, Thu 0900-1900, Sat 0930-1700, free,* is the branch of the National Archive where births, deaths, marriages and adoptions can be traced as far back as July 1837. On the first floor there's an exhibition on the first national census taken in the 19th century, and anyone is welcome to browse the indexes for documents (facsimiles available) on their friends, family or ancestors.

● Sleeping

Clerkenwell *p206, map p208*
A Malmaison, 18-21 Charterhouse Sq, EC1, T020-7012 3700, www.malmaison.com. Marginally cheaper, with 97 differently shaped rooms, this is the latest in the successful lifestyle brand of UK hotels, comfortable, easygoing but quite flash.
A The Rookery, Peter's Lane, Cowcross St, EC1, T020-7336 0931, www.rookeryhotel.com. A renovated old-fashioned townhouse hotel with 33 rooms in an antique building with a crow's nest of a penthouse and wooden toilet seats in all bathrooms. Owned by the same people as Hazlitt's and the Gore. Top end of this bracket.
A The Zetter, 86-88 Clerkenwell Rd, EC1, T020-7324 4444, www.thezetter.com. A new 'restaurant with rooms', 59 of them in fact, designed in some style around a superb Italian restaurant. Best of all are the rooftop studios, with balconies and fabulous views, which range from £280-£305 per night.

● Eating

Holborn *p206, map p208*
♥♥♥ Bleeding Heart Bistro and Restaurant, Bleeding Heart Yard, off Greville St, EC1, T020-7242 2056. A bustling old-fashioned place for some superior French and Kiwi cooking, closed weekends.
♥ The Fryer's Delight, 19 Theobald's Rd, WC1, T020-7405 4114. A traditional fish and chip shop beloved by cabbies.
♥ October Gallery Café, 24 Old Gloucester St, T020-7242 7367. In summer, the secret garden comes into its own at lunchtimes.

Cafés and sandwich bars
Coffee Matters, 4 Southampton Row, WC1, T020-7242 9090, specialize in Fair Trade coffee, organic yoghurt, and delicious salads.

Clerkenwell *p206, map p208*
For discerning carnivores, Clerkenwell is a top destination.

¶¶¶¶ Club Gascon, 57 West Smithfield, EC1, T020-7796 0600. Specializes in the regional produce of Gascony, foie gras of course, exquisite (and expensive) gastronomic delights served plate by plate in a gentle, slightly fey and appreciative atmosphere.

¶¶¶¶ Moro, 34-36 Exmouth Market, EC1, T020-7833 8336. A large modern Spanish restaurant that has been wowing the area's hipsters, movers and shakers for some time with its artful way with super-fresh ingredients. So successful that one of its main suppliers, Brindisa Spanish Food Importers, have opened a deli next door.

¶¶¶ The Eagle, 159 Farringdon Rd, T020- 7837 1353. Was one of the first pubs to go gastro, cooking up excellent modern European food right behind the bar.

¶¶¶ St John, 26 St John St, T020-7251 0848. Especially good, offal and freshly baked bread are served up in a stark former smokery celebrating 'nose to tail' eating.

¶¶¶ Smiths of Smithfield, 67-77 Charterhouse St, EC1, T020-7236 6666 www.smithsofsmith field.co.uk. Another meat-market restaurant, a loud busy place playing club music with different moods on each of its 4 levels.

¶ Japanese Canteen, 21 Exmouth Market, EC1, T020-7833 3521. A busy branch of the basic Japanese chain.

¶ Little Bay, 171 Faringdon Rd, EC1, T020- 7278 1234. A very good value little place with a no-nonsense approach to good European food all day every day, main courses about £5 before 1900 and not much more than that until 2300.

Cafés and sandwich bars

Benugo's Sandwich and Juice Bar, T020- 7253 3499, on the junction of St John St and Clerkenwell Rd. A hip place for healthy drinks and good breads.

Café Kick, 43 Exmouth Market, EC1, T020- 7837 8077. Is as much a bar as a café, a shrine to table football that does a huge variety of different coffees and decent food.

❶ Pubs and bars

Holborn *p206, map p208*

It doesn't come as much of a surprise that Holborn has plenty of antique drinking holes. The famous 3 are below and are old hands at serving boozy office workers and tourists.

Cittie of York, 22 High Holborn, WC1, T020-7242 7670. With an extra long bar, cubby holes for lawyers and crude wallpaintings of famous tipplers.

Ye Olde Cheshire Cheese, 145 Fleet St, EC4, T020-7353 6170. A warren of historic wooden rooms.

Ye Olde Mitre Tavern, Ely Court, Ely Pl, EC1, T020-7405 4751. Tucked away up a tiny alleyway, the last word in cosy and quaint.

A quieter and in some ways more satisfying destination is the area around Lamb's Conduit St.

Duke of York, 7 Roger St, WC1, T020- 7242 7230, near the Dickens' House Museum. Does good real ales, has tables outside and serves up scrummy but expensive food.

The Lamb, 94 Lamb's Conduit St, WC1, T020-7405 0713. A cosy old-timer that hasn't changed in years and keeps a loyal and mixed crowd of fans happily in their pints of Young's Special.

The Perseverance, 63 Lamb's Conduit St, WC1, T020-7405 8278. A proper London freehouse popular with a younger crowd, with tapas at the bar and a modern British restaurant upstairs.

The Three Cups, 21 Sandland St, WC1, T020-7831 4302. A very pleasant old-school Young's pub with tables outside in summer.

VATS Winebar, 51 Lamb's Conduit St, WC1, T020-7242 8963. Even more local and also inimitable, genially stuck in the 1950s with a loyal troupe of affable middle-aged bon viveurs.

Clerkenwell *p206, map p208*

3 pubs are especially well worth seeking out:

Fox and Anchor, 115 Charterhouse St, EC1, T020-7253 4838, near Smithfield Market. Has Victorian correctness and very full breakfasts served up to meat market porters from 0700.

The Jerusalem Tavern, 55 Britton St, T020-7490 4281. Scruffy wood-panelled place with Georgian charm, the sole London outlet for St Peter's Ale from Bungay in Suffolk.

The Three Kings, 7 Clerkenwell Cl, EC1, T020-7253 0483. Check out the colourful old interior of Clerkenwell Green's local. It's the bars rather than the pubs that lead the way in Clerkenwell, most staying open at least until midnight, and many until later on Fri and Sat. Lastest arrival is the **Green**.

Match Bar, 45-47 Clerkenwell Rd, T020-7450 4002. Typical of the area, does excellent food and cocktails in a sleek and happy atmosphere.

Vic Naylor's, 38-40 St John St, EC1, T020-7608 2181. Old-style, but equally typical, loud and cheerful, the restaurant and bar was used as a location for Sting's bar in Guy Ritchie's hit movie *Lock, Stock and Two Smoking Barrels*, open until midnight Mon-Thu, till 0100 Fri and Sat.

Potemkin, 144 Clerkenwell Rd, EC1 T020-7278 6661. Vodka drinkers should seek out this place, a tiny and convivial style bar with lots of flavoured distillations of the grain and a restaurant downstairs.

⊕ Entertainment

Holborn & Clerkenwell *p206, map p208*
Dance
Sadler's Wells, Rosebery Av, EC1, T020-7863 8000, nearest tube Angel Islington. Superb state-of-the-art new North London base for large-scale dance and opera, sadly struggling financially. Also houses the **Lilian Baylis Theatre**, a smaller studio space for adventurous new work, and **The Peacock Theatre**, Portugal St, WC2, a smaller theatre for the same sort of thing.

Music
Sadler's Wells (see Dance above).
St James's, Clerkenwell Cl, EC1, T020-7251 1190. Bach organ recitals on the 3rd Thu of the month at 1310.

Nightclubs
The End, 18a West Central St, WC1, T020-7419 9199. Mon 2200-0300 *Trash* for indie £4, Thu 2100-0330, *Atelier* for house £5, Fri 2200-0600, Sat 2200-0600, *End Saturdays* tech house, £10-15. Owned by Mr C of the Shaman and Leo. Techno-driven lounge and main room are the last words in cool.
Fabric, 77a Charterhouse St, EC1, T020-7336 8898. Fri 2200-0500; Sat 2200-0700; Sun

2200-late. Still one of the most cutting-edge clubs in London.
Turnmills, 63 Clerkenwell Rd, EC1, T020-7250 3409. Long queues form at this long-player after 2100.

Theatre
The Bridewell, Bride Lane, Fleet St, EC4, T020-7936 3456. A wonderful old converted swimming baths housing a fringe theatre that maintains a pretty high standard, especially on the musical front.

❀ Festivals and events

Clerkenwell *p206, map p208*
Clerkenwell Festival, **mid-Jul**, community festival focused on Clerkenwell Green with a big Fri music night at Smithfield Market and a Sun event on the Green, a celebration of local history. Organized by Clerkenwell.org, 53 Clerkenwell Cl, T020-7251 6311. **Clerkenwell Literary Festival**, usually some time in **late Jul** or **early Aug**, at the Tardis, Turnmill St, T020-7336 6366, and other venues.

O Shopping

Holborn & Clerkenwell *p206, map p208*
In **Clerkenwell Green**, the name of the game is still arts and crafts.
Clerkenwell Green Association, Pennybank Chambers, 33-35 St John's Sq, EC1, T020-7251 0276. Represents and provides space for craftworkers, stages exhibitions of their work and can point the curious towards the likes of Lesley Craze or Dominic Walmsley for jewellery, or fresco painter Sarah Hocombe.

Exmouth Market is the best spot for fashion.
Antoni and Alison, 43 Rosebery Av, T020-7833 2002. T-shirt supremos.
North 2, 31 Exmouth Market, T020-7837 5822. Men and women's designer clothes by Kenzo, Geoffrey West shoes, and an emphasis on the cutting edge.
Space EC1, 25 Exmouth Market, T020-7837 1344. Stock an inspired range of gifts, from bags and cushions to mugs.

⬤ *For an explanation of sleeping and eating price codes used in this guide, see inside the*
● *front cover. Other relevant information is found in Essentials, see pages 44-46.*

The City

The City is where London began, and judging from the harried look of its working population, it ain't over yet. Nowhere is the contrast stronger between weekday and weekend, or even between lunch and supper. During the week thousands storm into the Square Mile to deal with billions of other people's money, fortunes are made or broken with a few megabytes in massive offices, and then come Saturday it all might never have happened: the place is left to the coach parties and tourists, a gigantic modern ghost town sprinkled with beautiful and empty little churches.

The grand exception is St Paul's Cathedral, its great stone interior always echoing with sightseers or worshippers, its dome one of the most beautiful, symbolic landmarks in London and a spectacular view point. Some idea of what has being going down as well as up all around its prime position over the centuries can be discovered at the excellent Museum of London, while next door the Barbican Centre provides another cultural oasis for live performances of a consistently high standard. Like Wren's churches though, all three seem sadly and oddly isolated from their local situation: with its guilds, livery companies and all-powerful Corporation, its banks, brokers and beadles, its secrecy and greed, the City has become a formidable but finally rather characterless money market and global betting shop. ►► *For Sleeping, Eating and other listings see pages 227-229.*

History

The Square Mile has always been the pulsating business end of London, around which the rest of the city has grown. Although Celtic settlements dotted the banks of the Thames, Roman Londinium, occupying a smaller area than the later medieval City, was the first substantial settlement here. Following Boudicca's destruction of the city in AD 61 it was fortified by a wall three miles long, 8 ft thick and up to 20 ft high. The commercial heart was a giant basilica on Cornhill, public baths lay by formidable city gates (recalled in the current names Ludgate, Newgate, Bishopsgate and Aldgate) and a fort was erected near Cripplegate.

The richer merchants built villas along the eastern banks of the Walbrook, and the Thames shoreline was lined with jetties and wharves laden with goods. A wooden bridge spanned the Thames to a small settlement that became Southwark. Tacitus, in about AD 67, described Londinium as 'a celebrated centre of commerce', and towards the end of Roman rule in 410, it boasted a population of at least 50,000.

There is no record of City life until the seventh century, when the Christian King of Kent, Sebert, founded St Paul's and built a palace at Aldermanbury that served successive Saxon kings until Edward the Confessor moved to Westminster in 1060 to supervise the building of the Abbey. Following the sacking of the city by the Danes, King Alfred re-established the trading prowess of London, and when another Viking invasion saw Canute take the throne in the early 11th century, London replaced Alfred's Winchester as the capital of England.

The Norman invasion brought further consolidation of the City's political and economic status. The White Tower was built just outside the city walls, and a couple of further forts within the city itself, Baynard's Castle and Montfichet's Tower, served to control the Saxon subjects as much as to defend the city. Medieval London flourished, despite the fact that two thirds of its people died painfully during the Black Death of 1347-1348.

London's independence was granted in a charter from King John, entitling the City to elect its own Mayor who was answerable to none but the sovereign. Guilds (or later the City Livery Companies) formed to represent their members' interests, and built fine halls in which to meet. Mercers, grocers, drapers, fishmongers, ironmongers, clothworkers... there were 80 of them in all and they governed the city from the Guildhall, a legacy of Mayor Richard 'Dick' Whittington.

London Bridge was rebuilt in stone, a ditch was dug around the city, and the markets flourished. Poultry could be found at Leadenhall; fish, corn and salt at Billingsgate; old clothes on Petticoat Lane; while Bread (John Milton was born here) Milk, and Wood Streets speak for themselves. Lombard Street was where one sought financial expertise, the Lombards having arrived from Italy following the expulsion of the Jews in 1290, who had themselves occupied the area around Old Jewry (Cromwell welcomed them back in the 17th century).

Market gardens and orchards spread out by the north wall. Violence was rife. Cheapside, the largest market, witnessed bloody battles between the skinners and the fishmongers, and an explosion of xenophobia against foreign merchants in 1517. The companies of guilds were always at each others throats, sometimes literally, especially the spicers and the pepperers, or the tailors and the drapers. Religious houses dotted the landscape – Austin friars, Crossed (Crutched) Friars, Dominicans at Blackfriars (the site of Baynard's Castle).

By the 16th century, the city was overcrowded, and the hamlets beyond the gates and Bars (Temple, Holborn and others) began to grow. Henry VIII freed up a good deal of building land within the City with the Dissolution of the Monasteries, and London's central position in European trade was aided by the Royal Exchange, built as a meeting place for City merchants. Stock companies such as the Levant Company emerged to benefit from Britain's expansion to the New World and the East. But again, in 1665 and 1666, the City and its residents were virtually destroyed by two apocalyptic events.

The **Great Plague** was brought by Norwegian brown rats, but its rapid spread was aided by the close, cramped, overhanging houses and filthy streets (Houndsditch is so called because it's where the dead dogs were thrown.) The close, wooden housing also meant that, following a hot, dry summer and aided by an easterly wind, the **Great Fire** swept through the streets for four days, destroying four-fifths of the City. Despite rebuilding plans of grand design being submitted by the likes of Sir Christopher Wren, the merchants couldn't afford to wait, so the rebuilding followed the medieval street plan, but this time using stone and brick.

Wren's **St Paul's** emerged as intended – a Protestant rival to the Catholic St Peter's in Rome – and he supervised a further 51 churches erected within the City. The Bank of England was founded to finance war with France, and the Mansion House to house the Mayor. The Roman Wall and old city gates were demolished, the houses and shops lining the bridge were removed and in 1769 Blackfriars became the first new bridge out of the City since the first London Bridge built by the Romans. Nevertheless, slums also emerged, like those around Smithfield (see page 214).

With the Industrial Revolution the City changed rapidly. A new system of sewers was built following cholera epidemics in the 1830s and 40s; new roads and surfaces were laid to accommodate the Omnibus Company; railways ploughed into Cannon Street, Liverpool Street and Blackfriars; and the first underground (the Metropolitan Line) was opened in 1863. Edwardian and modern structures continued to rise up in the course of the last century – *The Daily Telegraph* and *Daily Express* moved to Fleet Street, and Leadenhall and Bishopsgate saw several office blocks in the 1920s.

Further upheaval was caused following the Second World War, when the City was heavily bombed. Twenty of the City's churches and 18 of its livery halls were destroyed, and while the subsequent rebuilding has not always been of great architectural merit there are some notable exceptions, such as the Lloyd's Building in 1986 and more recently, the Gherkin at St Mary Axe. The 1970s Barbican estate, reviled by some, is now

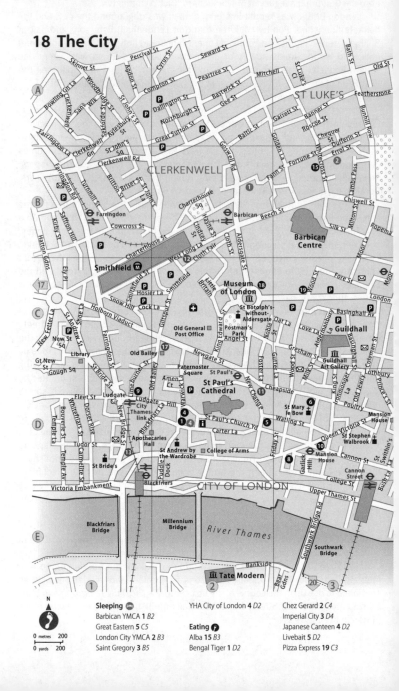

18 The City

N

0 metres 200
0 yards 200

Sleeping	YHA City of London 4 *D2*	Chez Gerard 2 *C4*
Barbican YMCA 1 *B2*		Imperial City 3 *D4*
Great Eastern 5 *C5*	Eating	Japanese Canteen 4 *D2*
London City YMCA 2 *B3*	Alba 15 *B3*	Livebait 5 *D2*
Saint Gregory 3 *B5*	Bengal Tiger 1 *D2*	Pizza Express 19 *C3*

the only large residential centre within the Square Mile (the residential population is only about 5000, although over 250,000 commute in every weekday). The City is now almost exclusively home to financial institutions, with more foreign banks than any other city in the world, and as such is seen as the economic pillar of the state, as the IRA chose to demonstrate by bombing the Baltic Exchange in 1992.

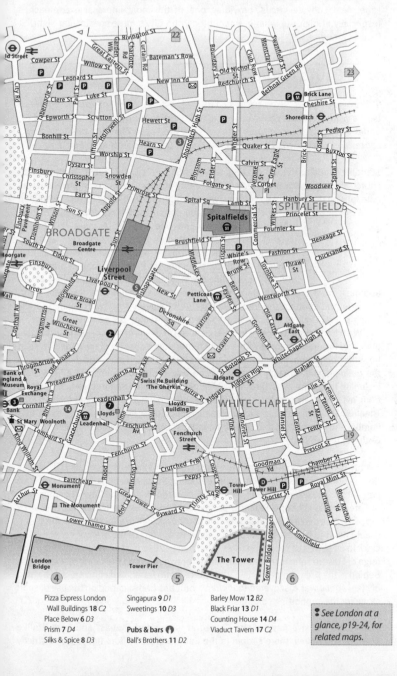

Pizza Express London
  Wall Buildings **18** *C2*
Place Below **6** *D3*
Prism **7** *D4*
Silks & Spice **8** *D3*

Singapura **9** *D1*
Sweetings **10** *D3*

Pubs & bars
Ball's Brothers **11** *D2*

Barley Mow **12** *B2*
Black Friar **13** *D1*
Counting House **14** *D4*
Viaduct Tavern **17** *C2*

See London at a glance, p19-24, for related maps.

Sights ● *Bank, Barbican, Monument, St Paul's.* ● *See p460.*

The City proper begins in the west at the site of the old Temple Bar on Fleet Street (see page 210). Fleet Street heads down into the valley of the Fleet River at Fetter Lane, near Ludgate Circus, providing one of the most impressive approaches (especially at night) to what is undoubtedly the City's most spectacular sight, St Paul's Cathedral.

★ St Paul's Cathedral

① *T020-7236 4128, www.stpauls.co.uk. 0830-1600 Mon-Sat (phone to check before visiting). Adults £8 including Cathedral Crypt and Galleries, concessions £7, under 16s £3.50. Guided tours 1100, 1130, 1330, 1400 Mon-Sat, adult £2.50, £2 concessions, under-16s £1, audio guide £3.50. Organ recitals 1700 Sun. Free.*

Standing proud at the top of Ludgate Hill is St Paul's Cathedral. At least the fifth church on the site, it was started in 1675, taking about 35 years to complete and was paid for with taxes raised on coal and wine coming into the Port of London. Hemmed in on all sides over the centuries, Wren's relatively colossal church still inspires awe and wonder. A massive cleaning project inside and out has been undertaken and the redevelopment of Paternoster Square has opened up new views of the place, reflecting its Portland stone in plate-glass office blocks, while the Millennium Bridge now provides a neat approach from the South Bank riverside and Tate Modern. At the west front, compare and contrast the imperialist statue of Queen Anne with sculptor Emily Young's semi-circle of neo-classical stone heads fronting the new development.

❗ *During the summer, the crowds can be avoided by arriving first thing in the morning during the week.*

Wren had originally hoped to build a church in the form of a Greek cross, but this plan, and his desire to top it with a dome rather than a steeple, were vetoed. Instead he settled on the more traditional Latin cross for the ground plan, and then carried on the building work in such secrecy that no one could complain before his vision, including the dome, was substantially in place. He could see the work in progress from his house across the river (still standing next to the reconstructed Globe Theatre). The final result is a kind of mini version of St Peter's in Rome, much less flamboyantly decorated, and one of the most successful classical interpretations of Gothic in the world.

Twenty-two wide steps lead up to the West Front, looking down Ludgate Hill, with its double portico containing a bas-relief depicting the conversion of the tax-collector Paul. At the apex stands St Paul himself, the patron saint of the City of London, with St Peter on his right and St James on his left, flanked by the two belltowers, each topped with a decorative pineapple. The southern clock tower is home to the 17-ton Great Paul, the biggest bell in Britain, used to announce the start of services. The clock itself strikes the hours on three other bells, the largest of which was cast in the reign of Edward I and is traditionally tolled for two hours on the death of a monarch. Behind is the Great Dome, invisibly supported with reinforced concrete and a chain of steel after it was discovered that Wren's builders had skimped on the use of solid stone for the supporting columns.

Inside, the massive nave of the Cathedral is wonderfully vast and bare. Unlike Westminster Abbey, there's room in the Cathedral for visitors not to be so strictly regimented in what they see. In fact most of the decoration was only added in the late 19th and early 20th centuries, and not very well at that. It's definitely well worth climbing up the long, gentle, wide wooden spiral staircase to the **Whispering Gallery**, around the base of the inner dome, decorated with statues of early church fathers and painted scenes from the life of St Paul. People press their ears to the wall here hoping to catch what their friends are whispering on the other side. Unfortunately the hubbub from far below often drowns out the famous effect.

Several steep and narrow flights of stone steps with regular resting places then lead up to the **Stone Gallery** outside, where the views through the balustrade are quite spectacular. In order to look west from here, though, it's necessary to brave the extraordinary series of vertiginous cast-iron spiral stairways heading up to the **Golden Gallery**. The tremendous wrap-around open-air views from the cramped little balcony up here easily rival those from the London Eye. And they're not even from the very top of the building.

Back in the main body of the Cathedral, unmissable sights include the **choir**, gorgeously carved by Grinling Gibbons, **Henry Moore's sculpture** of Mother and Child in the north choir aisle, the copy of Holman Hunt's *The Light of the World* in the north transept, a small display on the firewatch that saved the building during the Blitz and the **American Memorial Chapel** at the very east end of the church in the apse, consecrated to the memory of over 28,000 US servicemen based in Britain who died in the Second World War.

Downstairs, 'the largest crypt in Europe' contains the OBE Chapel, monuments to Wellington, Nelson and many others, and more interestingly, Wren's original models for the Cathedral and the Treasury of the Diocese of London. There's also a shop, expensive café and a restaurant.

Around St Paul's

South of St Paul's Churchyard, beyond the **City Information Centre** ① *T020-7332 1456, 0930-1700 Mon-Fri, 0930-1200 Sat*, the streets around Carter Lane have kept much of their medieval layout, leading down to the 17th-century **Apothecaries Hall** ① *Blackfriars Lane, T020-7236 1180, open for group tours of 10-25 people, £3 each*, and the plain brick church of **St Andrew by the Wardrobe**, the last that Wren built in the City.

Nearby is the beautiful 17th-century home of the **College of Arms** ① *130 Queen Victoria St, T020-7248 2762, Mon-Fri 1000-1600*, the place to find out whether a family is qualified to carry a heraldic coat of arms. Three kings of arms (Garter, Clarenceux and Norroy), six heralds, and four pursuivants regulate the bearing of arms and trace pedigrees. Visitors can see the Court of the Earl Marshal (always the Duke of Norfolk), who organizes most of the state ceremonies involving the monarchy, and evening tours are given by arrangement.

Old Bailey
① *Newgate St, T020-7248 3277. 1030-1300, 1400-1630 Mon-Fri.*
West of St Paul's stands the Old Bailey, or Central Criminal Court, topped by its copper dome and famous statue of Justice balancing a sword and a pair of scales, on the site of the notoriously brutal Newgate Prison. The prison was finally pulled down in 1902 after countless people had literally rotted away there, forcing the judges to stop their noses with scented posies. Much of the front of the new building used stones from the old prison. Nowadays the famous British justice system, tarnished in the past by a series of flawed convictions in the fight against terrorism, can be seen in action from the public galleries of any of the 18 modern courtrooms here.

Postman's Park

North of St Paul's, beyond Paternoster Square, King Edward Street heads past the old General Post Office into Little Britain. On the right is the tiny **Postman's Park**, behind the church of **St Botolph's-without-Aldersgate**, where the wall of Commemoration of Heroic Sacrifice overlooks a fountain and fish pond in the garden where the founder of Methodism, John Wesley, once preached. Porcelain memorials describe the heroic deeds, such as 'PC Percy Edwin Cook who voluntarily descended into a high tension chamber at Kensington to rescue two workmen overcome by poisonous gas, 7 October 1927', or 'Mary Rogers, Stewardess of the *Stella*, self-sacrificed by giving up her lifebelt and voluntarily going down with sinking ship, March 30 1899', or 'Edmund Emery of 272 King's Rd Chelsea who leapt from a steamboat to rescue a child and was drowned 31 July 1874'.

St Bride's Church

① *To20-7427 0133. 0900-1600 Mon-Fri and Sun services 1100, 1830.*

Close to Ludgate Circus is another Wren masterpiece, St Bride's Church, known as the 'Cathedral of Fleet Street', and one of the finest specimens of the Italian style in England. With its wonderful wedding cake spire, it's believed that here the 6th-century Irish St Bridget (who shares her feast day with Brigit, the Celtic goddess of fertility) founded a church near the holy Bride Well. The church is also the burial place of the printer Wynkyn de Worde, the apprentice to Caxton who set up shop on Shoe Lane, establishing Fleet Street's traditional trade. The excavated crypt exposed by bombing in the Blitz houses a small museum on the street's associations with the press.

★ Museum of London

① *To20-7600 3699, events To20-7814 5777, www.museumoflondon.org.uk. Mon-Sat 1000-1750, Sun 1200-1750. Free. Café Mon-Sat 1000-1730, Sun 1130-1730.*

Just round the corner, at 150 London Wall, bang in the middle of a busy roundabout on the site of a Roman fort, is the excellent, purpose-built Museum of London, one the city's liveliest. Opened in 1976, it has a refreshing visual approach to the social history of the city, illustrating the daily lives led here down the ages with a combination of genuine artefacts, reconstructions and some canny design.

On the first level, along with the temporary exhibition galleries, the museum plunges back into prehistory with some recently renovated galleries displaying a variety of Iron Age objects, many dredged up from the river, some accompanied by an evocative soundtrack. Further on, Roman London features a reconstruction of a wealthy Roman's house and one of the museum's most exciting recent addition: a cache of 43 gold coins dating from AD 65-170 discovered in the autumn of 2000 buried in a hole in the floor of Plantation House, just off Eastcheap. Many are in almost mint condition, the Emperors' profiles still remarkably vivid. Eight of these coins could have bought a boy slave, or maybe about 23 acres of Kentish woodland.

The Dark Age and Saxon galleries are inevitably quite scant in artefacts, but the Medieval and Tudor galleries beyond make up the deficit with carvings, astonishing jewellery, armour and more coins set amid excellent scale models of how a few important buildings may have looked before that defining event, the disastrous Great Fire.

Downstairs the story of the city's rebuilding, expansion and growth continues around the Garden court and the sumptuously decorated Lord Mayor's Coach, still used annually for the Lord Mayor's Show. The late Stuart and 18th-century London galleries include a reconstructed late 17th-century room, the door of a cell from Newgate Prison, and some gorgeous dresses. In the 19th-century and Imperial Capital galleries the contrast between the city's architectural grandeur and the prevailing squalor becomes acute. A beautiful art deco lift from Selfridges is a highlight of the transition into the early 20th century, the Second World War and London Now room.

Barbican Centre ▸ *See also architecture, p414*

Close by the Museum between Aldersgate and London Wall rears the immense, famously disorientating and surprisingly popular 1970s housing complex called the Barbican, one of the City's very few residential enclaves. Somewhere in here it's usually an enjoyable challenge looking for the Barbican Centre, with its vibrant galleries, cinemas, music halls and theatres. Be sure to allow plenty of 'ticket time'.

The **Barbican Art Gallery** ⓘ *Level 3 of the Barbican Centre, box office T020-7638 8891, general enquiries T020-7638 4141, 1000-1800 Mon, Tue, Thu-Sat; 1000-2000 Wed, 1200-1800 Sun, adults £8, £6 under-16s,* mounts a wide variety of exhibitions, usually lasting two or three months, with a reputation for taking interesting angles on all kinds of different aspects of art and design: centenary celebrations, fine art retrospectives, furniture making and jewellery as well as much more.

The Guildhall

ⓘ *Details on tours of the crypt from the Remembrances department, T020-7332 1313, general enquiries, T020-7606 3030. Mon-Sat 0930-1700. Free.*

Just southeast of the Barbican off Gresham Street is the City of London's town hall, the Guildhall, the 500-year-old home of the city council aka the Corporation of London. The fully restored 15th-century Great Hall with its bizarre cod-Indian façade is festooned with flags and arms of the 12 major livery companies. Above the gallery at the west end stand the statues of Gog and Magog, replacing the 14-ft versions carved in 1708 that were destroyed in the Blitz. Wickerwork models of these two characters were traditionally carried in the Lord Mayor's procession.

According to legend Gog and Magog were more accustomed to doing the carrying themselves as porters at the royal palace of the mythical English King Brute, the captive and sole survivors of his triumph over their sibling giants, all bastard offspring of some demons and the 33 husband-murdering daughters of the Emperor Diocletian. Now they look down each year on the keynote Prime Minister's speech at the Lord Mayor's Banquet, held in the hall on the Monday after his annual Show. The crypt below contains a forest of columns, a spectacular vaulted ceiling and some remarkable stained glass.

Guildhall Art Gallery and Roman Amphitheatre
ⓘ *T020-7332 1632, recorded info T020-7332 3700, www.guildhall-art-gallery.org.uk. Mon-Sat 1000-1700, Sun 1200-1600. Adults £2.50, concessions £1, under 16s free.*

The Guildhall Art Gallery does a fine job of displaying the Corporation of London's large art collection – several of local topographical interest – in purpose-built premises next to the ancient Guildhall. Beneath the gallery, a Roman amphitheatre from the second century AD was unearthed during construction of the gallery and has been preserved for public perusal.

Opposite is **St Lawrence Jewry** ⓘ *T020-7600 9478, Mon-Fri 0700-1300,* founded in the 12th century and topped with a gridiron weathervane, a reminder that the Saint's martyrdom involved being roasted alive. Only the walls and tower of this neo-classical Wren church were left standing after the Second World War. Fully rebuilt and now rather soulless, it's the Corporation's grand official place of worship and also the official church of the New Zealand Society.

Guildhall Library and Clockmakers' Museum

① *T020-7332 1868, Mon-Sat 0930-1700. Clockmakers' Museum 0930-1630 Mon-Sat (often closed Mon morning). Free.*

In the Guildhall's modern west wing is the Library and the Clockmakers' Museum. The oldest collection of its kind in the world, the chief attraction of this one-room museum run by the Clockmakers' Company is the overall aesthetic appeal of the hundreds of ancient watches and grandfather clocks on display. Individual timepieces of interest include Harrison's chronometer, made famous by Dava Sobel's *Longitude*, which first allowed navigators to calculate their distance east or west from the meridian, a clock in the shape of a skull that supposedly belonged to Mary Queen of Scots, and the first watch to reach the summit of Everest, on the wrist of Sir Edmund Hillary in 1953. In the same building there's the extensive public reference library on London history and an excellent bookshop specializing in the city.

Bank

Gresham Street runs eastwards from here down to the corner of Lothbury and Prince's Street which leads past the 19th-century Grocers' (or Pepperers') Hall to where seven roads converge at Bank. If anywhere can really claim to be the hub of the City of London, this is it. The hectic junction is dominated by the Bank of England, the Royal Exchange and Mansion House, three neoclassical monuments to the City's former Imperial power.

The Bank of England Museum

① *T020-7601 4878. 1000-1700 Mon-Fri. Free.* The Bank of England occupies the entire north side between Prince's Street, Lothbury, Threadneedle Street (hence its nickname 'the old lady of Threadneedle Street') and Bartholomew Lane where visitors are welcomed free of charge into the museum. The only time the public are allowed into the high-security vaults of the Bank itself is on the Open House day each year in late September (see page 48). The centrepiece is a reconstruction of Sir John Soane's original stock office, with six other rooms telling the history of the Bank since 1694 entertainingly enough, including a couple of real gold bars and a pyramid of replicas. There's also the opportunity to chance your arm with a three-minute spot of simulated foreign exchange trading. Here the Great Motivator gets all the respect it deserves.

Royal Exchange and around

① *www.theroyalexchange.co.uk. Mon-Wed, Fri 1000-1800, Thu 1000-1900.* Opposite the bank, the 19th-century Royal Exchange building stands on the site of London's original 'bourse', founded by Sir Thomas Gresham in 1565. The fine quadrangle and arcades at its heart now provide shop space for a wide variety of super-luxury retailers and a few quirky one-offs.

The **Church of St Mary Woolnoth** ① *on the corner of Lombard St and King William St, T020-7626 9701, 0930-1630 Mon-Fri*, was rebuilt by Hawksmoor for Queen Anne and boasts one of the architect's most beautiful interiors.

King William Street leads down to Monument tube at the north end of London Bridge. **The Monument** ① *T020-7626 2717, Apr-Oct 1000-1730, Nov-Mar 0930-1700* daily, £2, £1 under-16s, is a venerable 320-year-old column designed by Wren to commemorate the Great Fire, with 311 steps up a steep spiral stairway that takes 13 turns to reach a height that equals the distance from the base of the column to the place in Pudding Lane where the fire started. Breathless if not breathtaking riverside views from the top.

Further down Walbrook is the **Church of St Stephen Walbrook** ① *39 Walbrook, T020-7283 4444*, Wren's rehearsal for St Paul's. Badly damaged in the Second World War, the property developer Peter Palumbo paid for its restoration, including an altar by Henry Moore that has affectionately been called 'the Camembert'.

Poultry and Cheapside head back to St Paul's from here, passing the **Church of St Mary-le-Bow** ① *on Cheapside, T020-7248 5139, 0630-1730 Mon-Thu, 0630-1600 Fri*, famous for the bells that confer true Cockney status on anyone born within earshot. Rebuilt by Wren in the 1670s, it was destroyed in the Blitz, but its beautiful spire was restored in the 1950s.

Heading east from Bank, Cornhill leads up to Gracechurch Street. Tucked away to the left off Gracechurch Street is the **Leadenhall Market**, a superb Victorian cast-iron covered market. Not really a street market any more, it now houses some fine food shops and cafés that are always packed at lunchtimes. North and east from here towards Liverpool Street the City really means business. Beyond the gleaming Lloyd's Building and Tower 42 (the former Nat West tower), behind Liverpool Street Station, stands the enormous **Broadgate Centre**. In its massive scale, snappy shops and American confidence it makes interesting comparison with the quaint old Leadenhall Market. Nearby on St Mary Axe, on the site of the old Baltic Exchange, badly damaged by an IRA bomb in 1992, the latest major alteration to the City's skyline looks like a giant glass artillery shell but has been fairly affectionately nicknamed **'the gherkin'** ① *www.30stmaryaxe.com*. Designed by Sir Norman Foster, and occupied by the insurance company Swiss Re, it makes the marginally taller Tower 42 look positively dowdy and old-fashioned.

● **Sleeping**

The City *p218, map p220*
AL Great Eastern Hotel, 40 Liverpool St, EC2, T020-7618 5000, www.great-eastern-hotel.co.uk. 267 rooms, Sir Terence Conran's first hotel, right on top of Liverpool St Station, with several excellent restaurants (Terminus brasserie, Aurora fine dining, Fishmarket and Miyabi) and tranquil bars.
A Saint Gregory, 100 Shoreditch High St, E1, T020-7613 9800, www.saintgregoryhotel. com. Fairly new hotel with 196 rooms done up in a contemporary style, about 10 mins walk from Liverpool St station.
D Barbican YMCA, 2 Fann St, EC2, T020-7628 0697, F020-7638 2420, admin@barbican.ymca.org.uk. Single and double rooms for 240 people, £56 including breakfast.
D London City YMCA, 8 Errol St, EC1, T020-7628 8832. Breakfast included, 4 twin rooms only, 101 capacity, £33 per night for a single room, £55 for a double including breakfast.

E YHA City of London, 36 Carter Lane, EC4, T0870 770 5764 (within UK), T+44 20 7236 4965 (outside UK), city@yha.org.uk. £24.60 per night, under-18s £20.50. Open every day including Christmas and New Year. Reception is open 24 hrs. With 190 beds, this 3-star hostel is right opposite St Paul's in the old choir school. There's no self-catering kitchen and groups are not accepted. Lockers and internet access.

● **Eating**

The City *p218, map p220*
Almost every restaurant apart from Pizza Express is closed on Sat and Sun when the only signs of life are usually to be found around Liverpool St Station.
₩₩₩ **Aurora**, T020-7618 7000, ground floor of the *Great Eastern Hotel*, Liverpool St Station. This Conran restaurant is a reliable option similar in its prices and modern European cooking to the Orrery in Marylebone (see p184).

¶¶ **Chez Gerard Bishopsgate**, 64 Bishopsgate, EC2, T020-7588 1200. The French
brasserie food here is perfectly serviceable.

¶¶ **Imperial City**, Royal Exchange, Cornhill,
EC3, T020-7626 3437. A Cantonese restaurant
in a very grand vaulted room beneath the old
Royal Exchange, closes at 2030.

¶¶ **Livebait St Paul's**, 1 Watling St, EC4,
T020-7213 0540. From the same chain as
Chez Gerard Bishopsgate, the seafood here is
perfectly serviceable.

¶¶ **Prism**, 147 Leadenhall St, EC3, T020- 7256
3888. The only restaurant run by Harvey
Nichols' in the City, for brasserie-style food can
be enjoyed in chic designer surroundings.

¶¶ **Ristorante Alba**, 107 Whitecross St, EC1
T020-7588 1798. Very convenient if visiting
the Barbican, a first-rate modern Italian
restaurant on the northern edge of the City.

¶¶ **Silks and Spice**, Temple Court, 11 Queen
Victoria St, EC4, T020- 7248 7878. A pricey
and sophisticated Thai restaurant.

¶¶ **Singapura**, 1 Limeburner Lane, EC4,
T020-7329 1133, www.singapura-
restaurants.co.uk. Runs the gamut of Malay,
Indonesian, Thai and Singaporean recipes in
a busy and friendly atmosphere.

¶¶ **Sweeting's**, 39 Queen Victoria St, T020-
7248 3062. A very down-to-earth fish restaurant that makes no concessions to passing fads
and doesn't take bookings. A City institution.
Recommended. Open 1130-1500 Mon-Fri.

¶ **Bengal Tiger**, 62-66 Carter Lane, EC4,
T020-7248 6361, www.bengaltiger.co.uk.
Open Mon-Fri 1130-2330, a modern tiger-
print Indian restaurant and bar.

¶ **Japanese Canteen**, Ludgate Broadway,
T020-7329 3555, round the corner from
Bengal Tiger. A small branch of the excellent
noodle bar chain. Open 1130-2000 Mon-Fri.

¶ **Pizza Express**, 125 Alban Gate, London Wall,
T020-7600 8880, beneath Chase Manhattan
Bank, and also at their new branch nearer
Finsbury Circus, 150 London Wall Buildings.
Reliable savoury Italian flatbreads, open 1130-
2300 Mon-Fri, 1200-2100 Sat, 1200-2000 Sun.

¶ **The Place Below**, St Mary-le-Bow,
Cheapside, EC2, T020-7329 0789, in the crypt
of the church on Cheapside. Bargain
vegetarian breakfasts and lunches can be
found here. Open 0730- 1430 Mon-Fri.

◗ Pubs and bars

The City *p218, map p220*

There's no shortage of drinking dens in the
City but some can become pretty obnoxious
once the suits are well in their cups. Many of
the pubs and bars are closed at the weekend
and some close early during the week.

Balls Brothers, 6-8 Cheapside, EC2, T020-
7248 2708. Fine wines and a genteel
atmosphere as well as outside seating with
views of St Paul's are the highlights. Open
1130-2130 Mon-Fri.

The Barley Mow, 50 Long Lane, EC1, T020-
7606 6591, near Smithfield. Open 1100-2300
Mon-Fri, a surprisingly laid-back Hogshead
pub pulling some good real ales.

Black Friar, 74 Queen Victoria St, EC4, T020-
7236 5474, near Blackfriars Bridge. Famous for
its extraordinary carved interior and outdoor
drinking area. Open Sat 1200-1500.

Counting House, 50 Cornhill, EC3, T020-
7283 7123. Another pub with exceptionally
grand decor. A loud and busy Fuller's outfit
in a former bank. Open 1100-2300 Mon-Fri.

George Bar, Great Eastern Hotel, 40
Liverpool St, EC2, T020-7618 7400,
www.terminus-restaurant.co.uk. Worth
knowing about for its food and the fact that
it's open at weekends, but not much else.
Open 1100-2300 Mon-Sat, 1200-2030 Sun.

Viaduct Tavern, 126 Newgate St, EC1,
T020-7606 8476, close to the Old Bailey. Come
here for some quiet Victorian splendour,
although the beers are nothing special. Open
Mon-Fri 1100-2300, Sat 1200-1500.

Weatherspoon, Hamilton Hall, Liverpool St
Station, T020-7247 3579, in the station. Worth
knowing about for its food and opening times.
Open 1100-2300 Mon-Sat, 1200-2030 Sun.

◗ Entertainment

The City *p218, map p220*

Barbican Centre, T020-7638 8891,
www.barbican.org.uk. Apart from the lunchtime concerts during the week in many of the
City churches (contact the City Information line
for details), this bewildering centre is just about
the only place around to see an art show, listen

to live music or catch a film or play. The **Barbican Theatre** stages a mixture of touring productions and classic revivals, and there's also the **Pit**, a subterranean studio theatre that sometimes stages more adventurous work. Shows often sell out well in advance and usually begin at 1915. Tickets £5-29. The **Barbican Cinema** has 2 screens showing first-run and arthouse films, often with excellent special seasons and themed weekends, and a Sat children's cinema club. Tickets £6.50, £4 on Mon. The **Barbican Hall** is one of London's major middle-scale live music venues hosting a huge variety of different orchestras, bands and choirs. Tickets £6.50-35. The centre stages outdoor theatre festivals and events in summer. **Guildhall School of Music and Drama**, Silk St, EC2, T020-7628 2571, box office T020-7382 7192, next door to the Barbican. Has a theatre and concert hall for regular student performances, often of a very high calibre.

⊛ Festivals and events

The City *p218, map p220*
City of London Festival, T020-7377 0540, www.colf.org, **Jun** and **Jul**, within the Square Mile, and also at The Spitz in Spitalfields Market, box office Barbican, T020-7638 8891, a classical music, jazz, gospel and world music festival in a variety of City churches including St Paul's, livery halls and office buildings. The Lord Mayor's Show takes place on the **2nd Sat in Nov**, usually taking a theme chosen by the Lord Mayor to raise funds for charity, with floats, bands and formal receptions at Mansion House, T020-7332 1456.

⊙ Shopping

The City *p218, map p220*
The City shops in the West End but there are a couple of old-timers worth a look if you happen to be passing.
Thresher and Glenny, 50 Gresham St, EC2, T020-7606 7451. Tailors and shirtmakers to City gents, with the oldest Royal warrant of them, and they also do shoes by Harry B Hart.

▲▲ Activities

The City *p218, map p220*
Broadgate Ice Rink, Broadgate Circus, Eldon St, EC2, T020-7505 4068. Winter only Mon-Fri 1200-1430, 1530-1800, Fri also 1900-2200, Sat 1100-1300, 1400-1600 Sun 1100-1300, 1400-1600, 1700-1900. £8 adults, £5 under-16s. Open-air skating in the Broadgate Centre.

⊙ Directory

The City *p218, map p220*
Tourist information Corporation of London Information St Paul's Churchyard, south side of the Cathedral, T020-7332 1456.

The Tower and around

Londoners traditionally dislike the Tower of London. After all, it wasn't built 900 years ago to protect them, but to subdue them, a role it played until the mid-19th century when it was freshly fortified against the Chartist rioters. Nowadays many have their revenge by either ignoring the place or dismissing it as a tourist trap. In fact it's less a trap than a treat, making an enormous effort to elucidate its wealth of historical associations and bring the old buildings to life for their two and a half million or so visitors each year. Inevitably the gate pressure means that the castle and its grim story come across a bit like a sanitized medieval theme park, but the central place it occupies in the Royal heritage and history of Britain and its capital is impossible to deny.

It may be no coincidence that the Tower has ended up lonely and isolated, wide busy roads cutting it off from the City although the entertaining neo-Gothic extravagance of Tower Bridge keeps it company. Next door, St Katharine's Dock may not be quite the fashionable playground of the super-rich that it would like to be, but remains a tranquil and rather chi-chi waterside development. Downstream, deserted Wapping introduces Docklands. ►► *For Sleeping, Eating and other listings see pages 235-236.*

History

In 1076, William the Conqueror commissioned a certain Gundulf to build him a stone keep in the eastern wall of the City. Fifteen feet deep at the base, with four floors rising to 90 feet high, the White Tower has been besieged and attacked several times in its long history, but never captured. It was designed to secure the Norman hold on the crown of England. Steps, which could be removed, rose to the only entrance on the south side, 15 feet above ground level. The ground floor held the stores (and later the infamous dungeons), the first floor was for soldiers and servants, the next the nobility, the banqueting hall and St John's Chapel, and the top floor provided the royal bedrooms and council chamber.

Used as a royal residence until the beginning of the 17th century, it has been constantly added to by successive monarchs, but has always served as a garrison, armoury, jewel house and, even, a museum. From 1235, when the Holy Roman Emperor gave Henry III three leopards, the Tower held a menagerie that was open to the public. A polar bear and elephant followed (gifts from Louis IX), until in 1609 an inventory listed 11 lions, three eagles, two mountain cats, two leopards, two owls, a jackal and, briefly, a bear, which having killed a small child, was torn apart by baiting dogs.

James I staged animal fights (such as lions against mastiffs), but when the number of species had grown to over 50 in 1835, and a lion attacked some members of the garrison, the collection was moved to the recently opened zoo in Regent's Park.

Under Charles II the public were invited to peer at the inmates in the dungeons and watch new arrivals pass through Traitor's Gate. Executions at the Tower were either conducted outside the walls on Tower Hill, or in the relative privacy of Tower Green – like beheading, a privilege granted only to a distinguished few. The list of those executed here is impressive – Anne Boleyn, Catherine Howard and Lady Jane Grey share the accolade with countless heretics, rebels, traitors and, in the case of the Princes in the Tower, victims of regicide. Prior to their expulsion from the country in 1290, 600 Jews were held in St John's Chapel – 267 were subsequently executed for coin clipping, and several of the crowd died when a stand collapsed at what turned out to be the last beheading in England in 1747. The Tower served as a prison until well into the 20th century – Rudolph Hess was held here for four days during the Second World War.

Other than a few hamlets in service to the Tower (hence Tower Hamlets), the area around the Tower was largely fields until the 16th century. To the north, the Minories, an abbey of nuns, was taken over by Henry VIII and replaced by a mansion, an armoury and workhouses. Until the late 19th century, it was noted for its gunsmiths. To the east, the Foundation of St Katharine, located at a creek, gave shelter to many foreigners refused entry to the city. A hospital, brewery and glassworks emerged until the whole area was cleared for St Katharine's Dock in 1828. Nearby a ghetto of up to 10,000 freed or abandoned slaves settled over the course of the 18th century.

Further east, wharves and boatyards emerged, and with it a settlement called Wapping-in-the-Wose that was hemmed in from the north by the Wapping marshes until it was drained in the 16th century. It became a popular place of entertainment for sailors (in 1750 there were 36 taverns on Wapping High Street, and many of the more squalid brothels), but in the 19th century warehouses replaced the "alleys of small tenements and cottages". Execution Dock, the graveyard of pirates, still saw corpses chained to the riverbank and pecked by passing birds. Tower Bridge, the first bridge down river from London Bridge, opened in 1894. During the 20th century St Katharine's Dock became a coveted residential and office area, sited around a marina developed by Taylor Woodrow. Wapping, having suffered badly from the Blitz, witnessed industrial disputes following the arrival of News International (publishers of *The Sun* and *The Times* newspapers), but has been redeveloped with flats, gardens and offices.

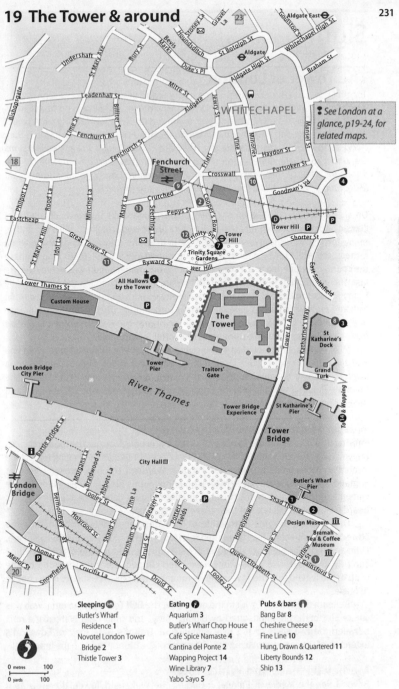

See London at a glance, p19-24, for related maps.

Sleeping 🛏	Eating 🍴	Pubs & bars 🍸
Butler's Wharf Residence **1**	Aquarium **3**	Bang Bar **8**
Novotel London Tower Bridge **2**	Butler's Wharf Chop House **1**	Cheshire Cheese **9**
Thistle Tower **3**	Café Spice Namaste **4**	Fine Line **10**
	Cantina del Ponte **2**	Hung, Drawn & Quartered **11**
	Wapping Project **14**	Liberty Bounds **12**
	Wine Library **7**	Ship **13**
	Yabo Sayo **5**	

N

0 metres 100
0 yards 100

Sights ⊖ *London Bridge, Tower Gateway (DLR), Tower Hill, Wapping.* ⊖ *See p460.*

The Tower of London

① *Recorded information T0870-7566060, advance booking T0870-7567070, switchboard T0870-7515177, www.tower-of-london.org.uk, www.hrp.org.uk. Mar-Oct 0900-1800 Tue-Sat, 1000-1800 Mon-Sun; Nov-Feb 1000-1600 Mon, Sun, 0900-1600 Tue-Sat. Last admission 1 hr before closing. Adult £14.50, concessions £11, under 16s £9.50, under 5s free. (Also various combined, group and family prices, phone for details.) Free Yeoman Warder tours (60 mins) every 30 mins from 0925, (Sun, Mon from 1000), last tour 1530 (summer), 1500 (winter).*

Outside Tower Hill tube station a viewing platform overlooks The Tower of London, a classic photo-opportunity for an overall picture of the layout of the fortification and its many towers, with the river in the background. In the middle stands the original fortress, the White Tower, one of the first, largest and most complete Norman keeps in the country, surrounded at a respectful distance by smaller buildings erected over the last 900 years, all protected by the 13th-century inner wall and ten towers added by Henry III. His son Edward I had the whole lot ringed with an impressive outer curtain wall and moat which was drained in the mid-19th century. The main public entrance and ticket office is round to the right, near the river in the western corner, accessed from here via an informative underpass beneath the busy road.

With some justification, the Tower claims to be several tourist attractions in one and for clarity's sake divides itself into seven colour-coded areas, each taking a suggested 20 or 30 minutes to see: the Western Entrance and Water Lane, the Medieval Palace, the Wall Walk, the Crown Jewels, Tower Green, the White Tower, and the Fusiliers' Museum.

Western Entrance and Water Lane
Passing through the **Middle Tower** and over a stone bridge across the moat, chances are you'll be greeted by one of the castle's most celebrated and engaging features, a Beefeater. More properly known as Yeoman Warders, the first standing army in England, these genial old coves in their quaint uniforms display an allegiance to the Queen and the Tower that no museum attendant could hope to match, all eager to beard visitors with tall tales of their home's grisly past.

One of them delights in the title of Ravenmaster, charged with feeding the Tower's six flesh-eating feathered friends: Hardey, Cedric, Gwyllum, Munin, Hugine, Odin and Thor. The big black birds patrol four territories around the White Tower and can't fly away because their wings have been clipped, stacking the odds on the truth of the legend that the Tower and its monarch will collapse should they choose to leave.

Beneath the Byward Tower in the outer wall, the **Bell Tower** on the inner wall was where Elizabeth was imprisoned by Bloody Mary, and from here Water Lane runs between the two walls to the river entrance at **Traitor's Gate**, part of Edward I's extension of the castle, replacing the water gate of the Bloody Tower in the inner wall.

Medieval Palace and White Tower
Beyond lies the Medieval Palace, including the Wakefield Tower, done up as it might have been in the reign of Edward I and occasionally enlivened by costumed guides. The Lanthorn Tower further on is the starting point for the entertaining Yeoman Warder talks.

A small gate leads through the inner wall to a souvenir shop and café and the main event, the White Tower. Up its wooden outside staircase and narrow winding stair, the most extraordinary place in here comes first: the small Chapel of St John the Evangelist. With its heavy round columns, tiny arched windows and surrounding gallery, the Chapel conjures up the Middle Ages more surely than any of the reconstructed rooms elsewhere. The bare Norman stonework adds to the ancient atmosphere, although apparently it would once have been brightly painted. A leap back into the 21st century is then made next door with a three-dimensional virtual tour of the Tower's construction projected onto the wall. In the next room is Henry VIII's armour as both a young man on a horse and in the fullness of his old age. Compare and weep.

Downstairs, the other floors are given over to exhibitions from the Royal Armouries, displaying the line of Kings, muskets and pistols, and the Spanish Armoury, with breastplates, wooden model horses, canons and the axeman's chopping block.

Crown Jewels

Behind the White Tower, the **Waterloo Barracks** contain the Jewel House, its entrance hall lined with the crested pews of English monarchs down the ages, although strangely there only seems to be room for two more. Roped crowd-controllers then wind through several large, loud projected videos of Queen Elizabeth II's coronation and other royal ceremonies and displays of maces, bugles, and swords. Finally, through a pair of massive metal doors glitter the glass-encased crown jewels themselves, flanked by two slow travelators that can be ridden as often as the crowds permit. The right-hand travelator affords a view of the legendary Koh-i-Noor diamond set in the crown of Queen Elizabeth the Queen Mother. The Imperial State Crown contains more than 3000 precious gems, with the oblong diamond second Star of Africa beneath its encrusted cross, while in the head of the Sceptre sits the largest top-quality cut diamond in the world, the first Star of Africa, estimated to be worth a cool £350 million.

On emerging behind the barracks, the **Martin Tower** is the end of the Wall Walk along the Tower Bridge side of the castle from the Salt Tower. The Martin Tower also contains a small exhibition on the history and making of the crowns and their jewels.

Tower Green

West of the Waterloo Barracks lies Tower Green, site of the scaffold where the privileged were executed away from the crowds on Tower Hill. Most of its victims are buried in the crypt of the adjacent Tudor Chapel of St Peter ad Vincula, of which the historian Macaulay wrote that "there is no sadder spot on earth". Behind the chapel, but closed to the public, Devereux Tower is the most strongly fortified of all the towers on the inner wall, facing the City to the northwest and named after its prisoner Robert Devereux, Earl of Essex, the popular hero and favourite of Elizabeth I who was forced to order him to be beheaded here. The first floor of the Beauchamp Tower on the west side contains the engraved signatures of many other noble prisoners. These have recently been enhanced with hands-on activities and information panels.

The south side of the green is overlooked by the **Queen's House**, traditionally the Lieutenant's lodgings, where Guy Fawkes was interrogated and from which Lord Nithsdale, a supporter of the Old Pretender, escaped in drag in 1716. Next door is the **Bloody Tower**, where the rooms have been decorated as they might have looked during the days and nights of its most famous prisoner, Sir Walter Raleigh. The room above is supposedly where the child Princes were murdered, and where Sir Thomas Overbury was slowly poisoned to death with sweetmeats sent in by the Countess of Somerset.

By applying in writing at least two months in advance, the public are admitted free to the seven-minute **Ceremony of the Keys** at 2200 every night (atmospherically floodlit in winter), when the Tower is locked and the keys handed over to the Governor. The Chief Warder cries 'God preserve Queen Elizabeth' and the Guard responds 'Amen' followed by the sounding of the Last Post.

Around Tower Hill

Back beside Tower Hill tube, to the left stands one of the best-preserved and most impressive parts of the Roman wall that once encircled Londinium, originally almost 6½ metres high. Running right down to the river, it once protected the White Tower too. Look out for the statue of the Emperor Trajan donated by the vicar of All Hallows (see below). A right turn out of the tube leads into Trinity Square Gardens, with its memorial to 12,000 merchant seamen and the site of the Tower Hill scaffold (a plaque in the gardens marks the Martyrs' Memorial). **Trinity House** (closed to the public) on the north side of the square is the headquarters of the organization founded in 1515 that maintains the automated lighthouses strung around the coast of the UK. Next door are the enormous former headquarters of the Port of London Authority until 1970, opened in 1922 and surmounted by a mighty statue of Father Thames.

Across the road, on Byward Street, more reminders of the Romans can be found in the peculiar undercroft of the church of **All Hallows by the Tower** ① *To20-7481 2928, Mon-Fri 0900-1645, Sat, Sun 1000-1700, crypt Mon-Sat 1100-1600 (except during services).* As well as a beautifully preserved tesselated Roman pavement and a dusty model of the extent of Roman London, there's also the crow's nest barrel from Sir Ernest Shackleton's last Antarctic expedition in the good ship *Quest*, a 14th-century alabaster relief of St Hubert, patron saint of huntsmen, and a medieval chapel supposed to contain the heart of Richard I, Coeur de Lion. On the ground floor, the Saxon arch exposed by the Second World War bombing is also worth a look, proof that there has been a church on this site for at least 1300 years. Famous names associated with this venerable place of worship include William Penn, Lancelot Andrewes, Albert Schweitzer and the founder of Toc H, the charity celebrating the commradeship born in the First World War trenches, the Rev Philip 'Tubby' Clayton. The diarist Samuel Pepys watched London go up in smoke from the church tower.

Tower Bridge

① *To20-7403 3761, recorded information To20-7940 3985, bridge lift recorded information line To20-7940 3984, www.towerbridge.org.uk. Daily Apr-Oct 1000-1830, Nov-Mar 0930-1800 (last entry 1 hr before closing). Adults £5.50, concessions £4.25, under-16s £3, under-5s free.*

Best approached from the riverside, London's most famous bridge was first opened in 1894, and until the completion of the Dartford Crossing remained the only bridge downriver of London Bridge. Designed by Wolfe Barry, son of the architect responsible for the Houses of Parliament, it now houses the **Tower Bridge Exhibition**, run by the Corporation of London, capitalizing on this impressive relic of the Victorian imagination, its wonderful views and the antique heavy engineering in the basement that once raised the massive bascules. This is an impressive free show when it happens, a few times on most days, best viewed from the riverbank upstream by the Tower or City Hall. Half a century ago the bridge needed to be raised and lowered at least 15 times a day. Visitors can take a lift up the four storeys of the north tower to the enclosed east walkway between the towers. (There are great views from here of Docklands, with the wind whistling through the girders.) After the west walkway, which gives superb views of the Tower, St Paul's, the London Eye and Big Ben, accompanied by piped seagull sounds, there's a walk across the bridge itself into the basement of the south tower. Here perhaps are the most interesting parts of the museum: the cast-iron boilers, flywheels, accumulator tanks and 'Billy the stoker', who falls asleep on the job after getting overexcited about a royal visit.

St Katharine's Dock

The Pool of London Tourist Zone continues along the north bank of the river past K2, a brand new office development by Richard Rogers, into St Katharine's Dock, an expensive marina full of flashy yachts and some charming old Thames barges. Free lunchtime concerts are given here in summer on Marble Quay. Commodity Quay is now shared by Reuters and the International Petroleum Exchange. In the middle stands the Ivory House, where shameful quantities of elephant tusks were once unloaded and stored, now adapted into a smart waterside shopping arcade.

Other sights around the dock include the old swing bridges, a plaque commemorating 300 years of Anglo-Dutch maritime friendship, and lock gates designed to cope with the Thames' 10-metre tides, the dockmaster's house surrounded by views of Tower Bridge and around, weeping willows (introduced to this country from the Middle East, like all others, from cuttings taken by the poet Alexander Pope in his garden at Twickenham). For information on berthing your boat here, contact **St Katharine's Haven** ① T020-7264 5312.

Further east on the north bank of the river, **Wapping High Street** makes a good introduction to Docklands, with its vast converted warehouses, smart riverside condos and old south-facing waterside pubs. Unfortunately, apart from a few oases, it remains fairly soulless and deserted except on Friday nights. Two places merit a special trip during the day: on the High St, the **River Police Museum** ① T020-7275 4421, by appointment only, free, is on the site of the old Execution Dock (where pirates were dispatched and then displayed). Guided tours by working police officers tell the interesting history of policing the river over the last 200 years (making them the oldest force in the UK). And then there's the **Wapping Project** ① Wapping Wall, E1, T020-7680 2080, Mon-Fri 1200-2300, Sat 1000-2300, Sun 1000-1800, a superior organic restaurant and bar alongside an impressive art space located in the old Wapping Hydraulic Power Station, a kind of fringe version of Tate Modern (without any government or lottery funding). A registered charity, it regularly stages hip new contemporary art shows and events as well as being a beacon of designer cool (cf the colourful Jasper Morrison Sim chairs by Vitra). The building itself is worth a look in itself, with plenty of disused heavy machinery still in place.

● Sleeping

A Novotel London Tower Bridge, 10 Pepys St, EC3, T020-7265 6000. Good example of the chain with 203 rooms, *Pepys Bar*, garden brasserie and fitness centre.

A Thistle Tower, St Katharine's Way, E1W, T020-7481 2575, www.thistlehotels.com. 801 a/c rooms in a formidable 70s riverside block beside Tower Bridge. Wonderful westward views from some of the rooms, their dimensions reminiscent of ships' cabins.

● Eating

††† The Aquarium, Ivory House, E1, T020-7480 6116. An upmarket fish restaurant in St Katharine's Dock. Simple grilled fish or more complicated piscine delicacies can be enjoyed overlooking the water, outside too in summer.

††† Wapping Project, Wapping Wall, E1, T020-7680 2080. Marginally less expensive than The Aquarium, serves well-hung organic meat and free-range poultry in hip and arty surroundings (mains about £16, starters £7).

†† Café Spice Namaste, 16 Prescot St, E1, T020-7488 9242, close to Tower Hill tube. Superior Indian cuisine in a colourful and loud great big warehouse conversion.

†† Il Bordello, 75-81 Wapping High St, E1, T020-7481 9950. A well-known superior pizzeria with a lively atmosphere.

†† Wine Library, 43 Trinity Sq, EC3, T020-7481 0415. An oenophile curiosity, a well-stocked

Central The Tower & around Listings

● *For an explanation of sleeping and eating price codes used in this guide, see inside the*
● *front cover. Other relevant information is found in Essentials, see pages 44-46.*

cellar where a £15 cheese and cold buffet lunch can be enjoyed with a bottle of off-licence wine (£4.50 corkage) selected from the racks around. Open lunch Mon-Fri 1130-1500, evening Tue-Fri 1730-2000.

Yabo Sayo, All Hallows by the Tower, EC3, T020-7488 1777. A good bet for a mid-afternoon light meal close to the Tower. A variety of well-made Korean and Japanese dishes majoring on fish are served up in an airy glass room (starters about £5, mains £9-12). Open 1130-2000 Mon-Sat.

✿ Pubs and bars

Captain Kidd, Wapping High St. The least expensive pub of the lot round here, also with fine views and a stirring tale to tell.

Cheshire Cheese, 48 Crutched Friars, EC3, T020-7265 5141. A decidedly no-nonsense City pub beneath the railway. Closed weekends.

Hung Drawn and Quartered, 26/27 Great Tower St, EC3, T020-7626 6123. The nearest decent pub to the Tower of London and All Hallows. A Fuller's pub with many of its Edwardian fittings intact.

The Liberty Bounds, 15 Trinity Sq, EC3. The local Weatherspoon operation, a huge multi-level boozer with all the usual JD hallmarks: cheap beer, a reasonable and basic menu, no smoking and no music.

Prospect of Whitby, 57 Wapping Wall, E1, T020-7481 1095. The most famous (and touristy) but charming of the Wapping riverside pubs, a short walk from the tube.

The Ship, 3 Hart St (off Mark Lane), EC3, T020-7481 1871, deeper into the City. A tiny little local pub with a spectacular frontage and considerable character. Closed weekends.

Town of Ramsgate, 62 Wapping High St, E1, T020-7264 0001. If Prospect of Whitby is too busy for its own good, this is a reliable local Wapping alternative with just as much history but not quite as old-fashioned.

More sophisticated but not quite as convivial drinking can be found at the **Samuel Pepys Bar** in the Novotel, or at **The Fine Line**, 124-127 Minories, EC3. **The Bang Bar**, Ivory House, St Katharine's Dock, E1, T020-7480 7781, near Tower Bridge, above the *Aquarium* fish restaurant. One of this quiet area's louder and more lively venues for some well-mixed cocktails and designer lagers.

Southwark, Bankside, Borough and Bermondsey

Over the last 15 years or so the south bank of the river between Blackfriars and Tower Bridge has been transformed into one of the most happening areas of town for visitors. The conversion of the old Bankside Power Station into a world class modern art gallery at Tate Modern and the Millennium Footbridge over the river to St Paul's have only been the most recent and spectacular confirmations of the area's new-found success. They have joined a wide variety of other attractions already well-established and continuing to thrive. A superb riverside walk downstream from the gallery passes Shakespeare's Globe, the Golden Hinde, Borough Market, Southwark Cathedral and, beyond London Bridge, the Old Operating Theatre and HMS Belfast, before fetching up beyond City Hall and Tower Bridge at the Design Museum and Shad Thames. A little further 'inland' south of London Bridge, Southwark and the Borough have rediscovered some of the energy that has long characterized their remarkable history, with thriving markets, pubs, cafés and streetlife. Bound to reward adventurous visitors are unusual one-offs like the peculiarly English Bramah Tea and Coffee Museum on Southwark St or areas like booming Bermondsey, now home to Zandra Rhodes' ambitious Fashion Museum.
▶▶ For Sleeping, Eating and other listings see pages 246-248.

66 99 An evening out in Southwark offered the lot – drink, sex and entertainment, with possible absolution or incarceration just down the track...

History

Sitting just over the river from the City, there has been a settlement at 'South Warke' since the Roman occupation. Archaeological evidence suggests a wooden bridge spanned the river (east of the current London Bridge) and a hamlet grew up around the bridgehead with two Roman roads (modern Newington Causeway and Old Kent Road) meeting in Borough High Street. A settlement survived the vacillations of Danish and Saxon rule (a church has existed on the site of Southwark Cathedral since the seventh century), so that by the end of the Middle Ages Southwark was the most significant community (after Westminster) outside of the City.

Far to the west, Lambeth Palace, London residence for the Archbishop of Canterbury, was surrounded by marsh, meadows and woodland, the Bishop of Winchester's house and lands stretched around Clink Street, and St Thomas's Hospital emerged in the grounds of the Augustinian monastery centered around St Saviour and St Mary Overie, now Southwark Cathedral. Indeed, partly because the area could escape the jurisdiction of the City, Southwark served a strange mix of people. Several prelates had their London residences here – the Bishops of Winchester and Rochester, the Abbots of Lewes and Battle on modern Tooley Street, and Bermondsey Abbey sat further to the east, but the area was also swimming in taverns and brothels.

Bankside, particularly, was the centre for the 'stewes', a series of brothels that were regulated by, and provided revenue for, successive Bishops of Winchester, earning the prostitutes the name 'Winchester Geese'. Taverns (and some breweries) lined the streets, such as the Tabard, where Chaucer's pilgrims met before starting on the road to Canterbury, and the Queen's Head was finally sold by a certain John Harvard to help found a university across the Atlantic.

In the 16th century, theatres (the Rose, Swan, Hope and, of course, the Globe) sat alongside bear-, bull-, dog- and cock-fighting and baiting pits – there were even gladiatorial contests in which men slashed at each other before baying crowds. Such dissipation warranted some sense of control, and over the years several prisons emerged in the area, notably Marshalsea and the Clink (hence the expression 'in the clink'), a presence oddly complemented by the sanctuary at St Saviour's that attracted fleeing criminals. The gatehouse to London Bridge (houses, stores and a chapel were built along it) displayed the boiled and tarred heads of criminals and traitors (William Wallace and Sir Thomas More among them), sometimes 30 at a time. An evening out in Southwark offered the lot – drink, sex and entertainment, with possible absolution or incarceration just down the track.

By the start of the 19th century wet docks had been excavated in Rotherhithe, wharves, warehouses and timber yards lined the river, while building had rapidly developed along Borough High Street, partly in the wake of a fire that swept Southwark in 1676. Elephant and Castle emerged as a coaching, and later tram, terminus, while the coaching inns of Borough High Street were the destination of the traffic from the southeast. Breweries, tanneries, foundries, glassmakers and print machinery manufacturers provided the local small industry, while the fruit and veg market that first appeared in the 13th century continued to thrive.

Over the next hundred years the population more than trebled to over 200,000. Blackfriars (1769) and Southwark (1819) bridges encouraged expansion, as did a new London Bridge further upstream (1831) and the arrival of a railway terminal nearby, but the area became suffused with slums and lodging houses for ex-convicts. Guy's Hospital continued to expand, but St Thomas's moved to Lambeth. The market sought a new site, and towards the end of the century a new nave at St Saviour's helped create Southwark Cathedral. Hay's Wharf continued to invite river traffic, and pioneered cold storage for butter and cheese from New Zealand. More recently, the railway's growth has cut swathes through the area, but the reconstruction of the Globe and the conversion of Bankside Power Station into a modern art gallery maintains Southwark's traditional association with entertainment.

Sights ⊖ *Blackfriars, Borough, London Bridge, Southwark.* ⊖ *See p460.*

Tate Modern

① *T020-7887 8000; ticket bookings T020-7887 8888; information T020-7887 8008, www.tate.org.uk. Sun-Thu 1000-1800, Fri and Sat 1000-2200 (last admission 45 mins before closing). Free (charges for special exhibitions around £7).*

Tate Modern has been one of the most spectacular and popular new additions to London in years. Opened in May 2000, the converted Bankside Power Station now houses the Tate's collection of international modern art from 1900 to the present. An extraordinary great solid box of brick with a single free-standing square chimney front centre, the power station was designed by Sir Giles Gilbert Scott to be a striking landmark, responding architecturally to its position across the river from St Paul's Cathedral. The building was begun in 1937 but didn't start generating electricity until 1963. Decommissioned in 1986, it was left desolate and empty for a decade. Swiss architects Herzog and de Meuron were finally appointed to adapt the building to its new role. Typically, the praise for their work has not been entirely unqualified but the hype surrounding the project as a whole now seems to be completely justified. See also architecture, page 413.

> ⦂ *The Tate Boat runs backwards and forwards between Tate Britain and Tate Modern every 40 mins. Single: adult £4, under 16s £2. Return: adult £7, under 16s £3.50.*

The main entrance is through the west, right-hand side of the building (turn right, away from the river, just beyond the riverside pub the Founder's Arms). A wide sloping ramp of brick leads down into the immense **Turbine Hall**, an astonishing space for artworks on a grand scale. In here, towering up through seven storeys on the north side of the building facing the river, linked by central escalators and stairways, are the galleries themselves, standing proud as illuminated boxes of light.

In a much-publicized break with traditional historical and chronological hangings, the collection is permanently arranged around four themes suggested by the four genres of fine art laid down by the French Academy in the 17th century: Still Life, Landscape, the Nude and History.

On **level 3**, Still Life/Object/Real Life covers the contents of the 14 exhibition spaces on the east side of the building, while Landscape/Matter/Environment covers those on the west side. **Level 4** is taken up with temporary exhibitions, while on **level 5**, the Nude/Action/Body galleries are on the east side, and History/Memory/Society on the west. Under these headings the galleries are devoted to selections from the collection that are changed every six months or so, often arranged as monographs to single artists, or under themes like *Inner Worlds* or *Autonomous Objects*. The method is designed to ensure that the gallery as a whole can respond to changing currents in **239** contemporary art as well as commenting on how the traditional subjects of artistic activity have been interpreted throughout the modern era.

Because of the mission and layout of the gallery, it's impossible to say exactly what can be seen or heard where and when, but a visit to the website in the **Clore Study Room on level 1** enables the location of specific works or of artists room by room. The collection (which even in this vast building cannot be permanently on display in its entirety) contains examples of work by most of the big names of 20th-century art, from Duchamp, Matisse and Picasso through to Bacon, Beuys and Warhol, whose pieces are likely to be found in striking juxtaposition to those of lesser-known or more contemporary artists.

Gallery tours

From the Turbine Hall information desk and also on level 3, **hand-held audio tours** (£2) in several languages are available, including the **Collection Tour**, with illuminating commentaries by artists and curators explaining the galleries' themes (each room also has an explanatory panel), specific works and artists, and the **Highlights Tour**. Free audio points are also available in some of the rooms and **free guided tours** leave from level 5 at 1100 around Nude, at 1200 around History, from level 3 at 1400 around Still Life, and at 1500 around Landscape. The Starr Auditorium incorporates a cinema showing free films throughout the day and special seasons by art directors in the evenings.

Overall, the gallery's popularity is the strongest testament to its success in making modern art more accessible: each of the rooms evokes a different atmosphere, but few the hushed reverence traditionally associated with art galleries. The place has an industrial impersonality, and yet comfortable armchairs and sofas overlook the Turbine Hall on several of the levels; on level 4, the espresso bar has an outside terrace, while the Reading Points on level 5 provide another chill-out zone with great views and some relevant reading matter. And then there are the views: the East Room on level 7 hosts special events and provides an impressive panoramic view over the thatched circular roof of the Globe Theatre towards the City. Friends of the Tate (annual membership £49) can use the members' tearoom and terrace on level 6, a considerable privilege when the gallery is at its busiest. Of the three shops, the one on the ground floor is the largest, those at the north entrance and on level 4 the quietest, each stocking stacks of Tate merchandizing (like desk tidies, shoulder bags, umbrellas and rainjackets), postcards and books on modern art.

Central Southwark, Bankside, Borough & Bermondsey

★ Around Tate Modern

Back by the river, those with healthy bank balances inspired to own a piece of contemporary art for themselves might want to look into **Purdy Hicks** ① *65 Hopton St, SE1, T020-7401 9229*. For traditionalists, or for anyone who paints, the **Bankside Gallery** ① *48 Hopton St, SE1, T020-7928 7521 (admission £3.50, £2 concession)*, is the answer, the home of the **Royal Watercolour Society** and the **Royal Society of Painter-Printmakers**, it also has a shop selling artists' materials.

Opposite Tate Modern, the new **Millennium Bridge** – a footbridge designed by architect Norman Foster with the sculptor Anthony Caro and engineered by Ove Arup (see also page 414) – arcs gracefully over the river to St Paul's. Unfortunately when it opened in the summer of 2000 its experimental design caused an alarming wobble. Some thought it an exciting feature of the new crossing – the London Evening Standard even launched a campaign to 'Save the Wobble' – but safety concerns prevailed and the engineers were called back to limit the swaying of the bridge. It still provides exhilarating views either way between the City and Bankside.

A short walk downstream brings you to Bankside pier and **Shakespeare's Globe Theatre** ⓘ *box office T020-74019919, Exhibition T020-7902 1500, www.shakespeares-globe.org, May-Sep, 0900-1200 daily, Oct-Apr, 1000-1700 daily, adult £8.50, £6 child, £7 concession, family £25*. The brainchild of American film-maker Sam Wanamaker, who sadly didn't live to see its completion, this sweet little open-air Elizabethan playhouse – Shakespeare's 'wooden O' – was reconstructed using original techniques and materials. It has been an enormous success: under the inspired ten-year directorship of Mark Rylance, summer seasons of four productions played in rep, some in period dress, often sell out well in advance. Cheap standing room for 'groundlings' is usually available in the yard, aka 'the pit'. It's typical of the spirit of Bankside that the open-air view through the thatched roof from the hard benches now frames the purple light box on the top of Tate Modern's chimney. The theatre's balustraded balconies and gorgeously decorated stage can be viewed throughout the year on guided tours and there's also a bookshop, restaurant and café with river views.

20 Southwark: Bankside, Borough & Bermondsey

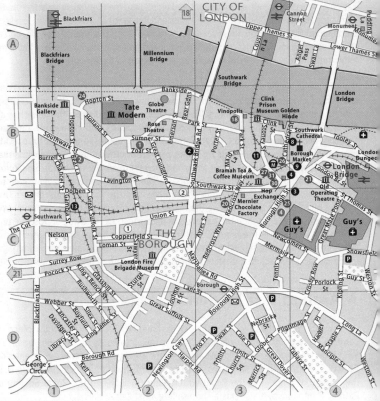

N

| 0 metres | 200 |
| 0 yards | 200 |

❗ See London at a glance, p19-24, for related maps.

Sleeping 🛏
Bankside House **1** *B2*
Holiday Inn Express **2** *B1*
London Tower Bridge
  Travel Inn **5** *D6*
Mercure City Bankside **3** *B2*
St Christopher's Inn **4** *C3*

Eating 🍴
Balls Brothers **1** *B5*

Bankside **2** *B2*
Conti's **3** *C4*
De Gustibus **4** *B4*
Delfina Studio Café **5** *C5*
Fina Estampa **7** *C5*
Fish! **8** *B4*
Garrison **6** *D5*
Konditor & Cook **11** *B3*
Leather Exchange **12** *D5*
M Manze **10** *D5*

Mar i Terra **13** *C1*
Tapas Brindisa **9** *B4*

Pubs & bars 🍺
Anchor Bankside **18** *B3*
Boot & Flogger **20** *C3*
Bunch of Grapes **21** *B4*
Founders Arms **24** *A1*
George Inn **25** *C3*
Globe **26** *B3*

From the Globe east to Southwark Cathedral

The actual site of the original Globe Theatre was a short walk from where the theatre now stands and is visible from Park Street outside the backdoor of the offices of the Financial Times beneath Southwark Bridge. An information panel and preservation area mark the spot.

Rose Theatre

ⓘ *56 Park St, SE1, T020-7593 0026, www.rosetheatre.org.uk.* On the way, you pass the site of another Elizabethan theatre, the Rose, where the foundations, in the process of being preserved, are marked out with illuminated light pads, and there's an exhibition on the theatrical and social history of the area.

Continuing the walk along the riverbank towards London Bridge takes you past the historic and frequently overcrowded Anchor pub and into one of the most evocative and distinctive parts of Bankside, hidden away beneath giant road and railway arches.

Clink Prison Museum

ⓘ *T020-7378 1558, www.clink.co.uk, 1000-1800 daily, £5, £3.50 child and concession.* Just round the corner, at 1 Clink Street, beneath the arch of the railway, the Clink Prison Museum is a small exhibition, with wall displays of a standard familiar from junior school classrooms, in a blackened breeze-block building on the site of the old jail that provides the excuse for the museum. Some of the torture instruments are moderately interesting though, and stories are told inside about various connections with gaols overseas.

Golden Hinde

ⓘ *St Mary Overie Dock, in Cathedral St, bookings and information T020-7403 0123, www.goldenhinde.co.uk. 1000-1700 daily (phone to check for weekends). Adults £3.50, children £2.50, concessions £3, guided group (minimum 15) tours bookable in advance £4.50, child £3.50.*

Just down the road, past an extraordinary ruined rose window surviving from the Bishop of Winchester's 16th-century palace, demolished in the civil war, is another excellent reconstruction of a thing in wood from the Elizabethan era, the **Golden Hinde**. It's an exact replica of the type of square-rigged galleon in which Sir Francis Drake sailed around the world from 1577 to 1580. Launched in 1973, it spent two decades circumnavigating the world before docking

Market Porter 27 *B3*
Southwark Tavern 30 *B3*
Wheatsheaf 31 *B3*

Entertainment ☺
Jerwood Space 1 *C2*
Southwark
 Playhouse 2 *C2*

here and becoming an educational museum. Self-guided tours of the little ship's five decks can be made during the day, or tours complete with entertaining costumed 'crew' can be booked. Anyone with children and more time should consider one of the very popular overnight stays, provided complete with period food, activities, dress and bedding (£40 per person).

Southwark Cathedral

① *To20-7367 6700, www.dswark.org. 0900-1800 daily (closing times vary on religious holidays). 3 services each day throughout the week. Free (donations appreciated).*

Round the corner, in Montague Close, is Southwark Cathedral, a beautiful place of worship dating back to the seventh century. It may be small in comparison to other cathedrals in the country, but its place in the heart of a crowded inner-city community makes it distinctive. Both the new London Bridge and the railway nearly ploughed straight over it. The tower was completed in the late 17th century, still standing over the fourth nave that was constructed for the church in the late 19th century, and refurbishment still continues.

Inside, notable monuments include the tomb of John Gower, a friend of Chaucer's and, like him, one of the fathers of English poetry; a monument to Shakespeare, the cathedral having been his parish church and the supposed burial place of his brother Edmund; and a rare wooden effigy of an unknown 13th-century knight. In the north transept, which dates from the same era, a chapel has been dedicated to John Harvard, founder of the American university, who was baptized here in 1607. The retro-choir, the oldest part of the cathedral, behind the high altar and its 16th-century great screen, is currently being restored. It should still be possible to see the Nonesuch Chest, a beautiful wooden box given to the church in 1588 for the safe-keeping of parish records.

★ Borough Market

Nestling beneath the cathedral, Borough Market is a wholesale fruit 'n' veg market that has probably been trading near this spot since the Middle Ages and certainly on this spot since the middle of the 18th century. Nowadays it shelters beneath a great cast-iron Victorian canopy but like other old buildings around here is under threat from the proposed widening of the railway viaduct above. The market itself caters mainly to the restaurant trade and other fruit 'n' veg stallholders, and is at its busiest at dawn. The retail food market on Fridays 1200-1800 and Saturdays 0900-1600 is famous for the superb variety of high-quality organic, traceable and seasonal produce peddled by specialists. This is the place to find some of the finest bread, meat, fish, fruit, nuts and veg in the capital.

London Bridge

From the market, steps lead up onto London Bridge. Built 1967-1972, this is the third stone bridge called London Bridge to have crossed the river near this point. The first, a little further downstream, stood for over 600 years, crowded with houses, a chapel in the middle, and almost damming the river with its 19 arches. There's an impressive model of the bridge in the Museum of Docklands (see page 273). For several centuries it was the only bridge in London, and Southwark's position at its southern end, beyond the jurisdiction of the City fathers, was responsible for the area's importance to trade, as well as its heavy drinking, gambling, prostitution and lawlessness. The approach from the south was dominated by the famous drawbridge and gate adorned with an array of traitors' heads pickled in tar and stuck on stakes, a tradition that continued up to the 17th century, and included in its time those of the Scottish freedom fighter William Wallace, the rebel Jack Cade and the Catholic martyr Thomas More. The second bridge, built 1823-1831, was sold and rebuilt in Lake Havasu City, Arizona.

South from London Bridge

South of the bridge, Borough High Street rushes towards Elephant and Castle. Just down here on the right, at the junction with Southwark Street, stands **The Hop Exchange** ① *24 Southwark St*, once the biggest and busiest of all the exchanges in the area, trading in brewers' hops from the fields of Kent for most of the 19th century. Its central courtyard surounded by cast-iron galleries is a unique survival from the era. Now run as office space for about 20 small businesses, the doorman is usually happy to let visitors have a quick look inside.

★ Bramah Tea and Coffee Museum

① *40 Southwark St, T020-7403 5650, www.bramahmuseum.co.uk. 1000-1800 daily. Adults £4, children and concessions £3.50. Lectures are usually given Wed and Fri at 1400.*

Almost next door is the Bramah Tea and Coffee Museum, a lively one-man crusade against the tea-bag. Edward Bramah has amassed an extraordinary collection of teapots, percolators, coffee machines, and teasmades, pressing them entertainingly into service on his mission to remind the British how they once enjoyed their tea: by taking the time to warm the pot, allowing the delicate leaves to infuse for five minutes, and avoiding skimmed milk. The idiosyncratic displays provide an entertaining insight into the history of the tea trade, involving the Opium Wars with China, racing clipper ships and the Russian samovar, as well as the history of tea gardens and coffee houses in London and beyond. The busy tearoom and café adjoining the museum (free to enter, along with the giftshop) does real justice to the brews and Mr Bramah's regular lectures on the subject are bound to provoke a thirst for the stuff.

Menier Chocolate Factory

① *T020-7378 1712, 1200-1500, 1800-2300.* Further down Southwark Street on the opposite side of the road, the remarkable 19th-century building that was once Menier's chocolate factory has been turned into an alternative art gallery, fringe theatre, buzzy bar and decent restaurant by David Babani and his partner Danielle. They proudly boast of two West End transfers for productions staged here within the first seven months of their opening.

London Fire Brigade Museum

① *94a Southwark Bridge Rd, T020-7587 2894. Entry by advance booking only for 1½-hr guided tours at 1030 or 1430, Mon-Fri. Adults £3, children and concessions £2, under-7s free.*

The London Fire Brigade Museum occupies part of the Brigade's Training Centre at Winchester House, formerly the HQ and home of the Brigade's Chief Fire Officers. Tours explain the history of firefighting in the capital since 1666, the year of the Great Fire. Several original fire engines can be seen, before visitors are taken through a series of old-fashioned museum rooms in the main house, an opportunity to learn about the insurance companies that were the original blaze-busters (more interested in property than people) and the naval origins of the first government-funded firefighting service in the world. In the light of 9/11 and successive waves of industrial action in the UK, the museum provides ample fuel for thought on fire and those that fight it, if not that much to entertain the kids.

Central Southwark, Bankside, Borough & Bermondsey

Old Operating Theatre, Museum and Herb Garret
① To20-7955 4791. 1000-1600 Tue-Sun, most Mon (phone to check). Adults £4.25, concessions £3.25, children £2.50.

Heading east down St Thomas Street, there's an even more extraordinary survival from the 19th century at No 9a. The Old Operating Theatre, Museum and Herb Garret is a remarkably well-preserved surgeons' demonstration theatre dating from 1822, discovered in the roof-space of St Thomas' Church in 1957. A narrow and steep winding staircase leads up to the theatre and museum, both highly evocative and atmospheric reminders of the advances that have been made in medicine over the last 150 years. Centre stage in the little U-shaped attic lined with tiers of standing stalls for students and spectators, the battered operating table stands above a sawdust box that stopped the blood dripping through the floorboards into the church below.

The herb garret next door was used by the apothecary to store and cure herbs in medicinal compounds and there's a chance to try your own hand at pill making. The museum displays surgical instruments for amputation, bleeding, cupping and scarification as well as pickled specimens of the results: lungs, brains, hips, etc and an exhibition on medieval monastic health care. Special events, talks and demonstrations (thankfully not of the period) are included in admission price. Not for the faint-hearted, over-sensitive or infirm, but genuinely educational and entertaining.

East from London Bridge

London Dungeon
① 28-34 Tooley St, To20-7403 7221, www.thedungeons.com. Oct-Mar 1030-1700 daily, Apr-Sep 0930-1730 daily (late night openings until 1930 Jul-Sep). Adults £16.50, children £12.95, concessions £13.95.

Not far away the blood and guts theme continues, but in a much less authentic way, at the London Dungeon. Waxwork animatronic models, reconstructed instruments of torture, and sensationalist light effects on a variety of 'dark rides' are intended to scare the living daylights out of visitors. Themes include a medieval siege, the Jack the Ripper Experience, the Great Plague and the Great Fire of London, and most recently, Traitor's Boat Ride to Hell. Children enjoy it, judging from the attraction's enduring popularity (although very small saucepan lids – kids – may find it too scary).

Winston Churchill's Britain at War Experience
① 64-66 Tooley St, To20-7403 3171, www.britainatwar.co.uk. Apr-Sep 1000-1800 daily, Oct-Mar 1000-1700 daily (last admissions 1 hr before closing). Adults £8.50, concessions £5.50, children £4.50.

On the same street, Winston Churchill's Britain at War Experience is another, less high-tech tourist attraction, probably also worth avoiding unless with children. It does at least treat history with more respect, including a mock-up underground station, exhibitions on women at war, bomb disposal and the home front, and a recreation of a blitzed street. If the Second World War is your thing, remember that HMS Belfast is moored only a short walk away.

HMS Belfast
① To20-7940 6300, www.hmsbelfast.org.uk. Mar-Oct 1000-1800 daily (last entry 1715), Nov-Feb 1000-1700 daily (last entry 1615). Adults £8, concessons £5, under-16s free.

From anywhere along the riverside here it's difficult to miss the great grey bulk of *HMS Belfast*, the Second World War cruiser now in the care of the Imperial War Museum and permanently moored opposite the Tower of London. Launched in 1938, it saw active service protecting the Arctic convoys to Russia, at the D-Day landings, and supported the UN in Korea before being retired in 1965. The cramped conditions on its eight decks, including the amazing engine room, make for quite an exhausting visit, likely to take at least an hour and a half, especially if accompanied by children, who find the ship much easier to get around. Most of the rooms are clearly marked up with informative wall panels about the difficulties and dangers of life on board and there are regular temporary exhibitions on aspects of the ship's history. With its guns now trained on Scratchwood service station on the M1, it is a remarkable insight into the war at sea.

Further downriver, along the Queen's Walk and before Tower Bridge, stands **City Hall** ① *T020-7983 4100, Mon-Fri 0800-2000*, the headquarters of the Greater London Assemby. A leaning glass globe designed by Sir Norman Foster, it opened in 2002 to the usual chorus of derision, rapidly dubbed the 'glass testicle'. A temple to political correctitude, it has been forced to cope with far more than the 400 occupants originally envisaged. Interesting exhibitions are mounted on its spiral walkway; there's a café and unhelpful information desk in the basement. Next door is the massive More London development, promising to draw more businesses and their clients into this otherwise neglected stretch of the river.

Design Museum

① *T0870-909 9009, information T0870-833 9955, www.designmuseum.org. (See map page 231). 1000-1745 daily (last entry 1715). Adults £6, concessions £4, children under 12 free.*

To the east beyond Tower Bridge the south bank riverside walk continues along Shad Thames past Butler's Wharf to the Design Museum. Housed in a cunningly converted white-clad 1950s banana warehouse, since 1989 the museum has made a stylish stab at illustrating, demonstrating and describing the designs we meet with every day, but might not know as such. That said, exhibitions aimed at widening the museum's appeal – such as Constance Spry's flower arrangements – led recently to the resignation of one of its founding fathers, design sophisticate Stephen Bayley. Expect to find illuminating and exciting displays on any subject – from film titles, brand recognition, and video games, to cars, architects and industrial appliances – that has something to do with design.

★ Borough and Bermondsey

Southeast of London Bridge, the Borough and Bermondsey have become a vibrant extension of the Bankside boom. Long famous for its antiques market (see Shopping below), where stolen goods were once legitimately sold during the hours of darkness, Bermondsey has since benefited from City overspill and the Jubilee line, now boasting at least a couple of very worthwhile visitor destinations.

A short walk south of Tooley Street, the river and HMS Belfast, the **Fashion and Textile Museum** ① *83 Bermondsey St, T020-7407 8664, www.ftmlondon.org, 1000-1645 (last entry 1600) Tue-Sun, £5, £3 under-16s, concessions, free under- 5s*, is unique in the UK, the brainchild of fashion designer Zandra Rhodes, who aims to provide 'a home for the fashion industry'. Bright orange on the outside, pink within, and very popular with Japanese tourists, this is a funky one-stop injection of fashion awareness. In one large room with a balcony gallery, regular themed exhibitions explore the changing faces and forms of contemporary haberdashery. Well worth a look, fashion victim or no.

Nearby, in Leathermarket, is the **London Glassblowing Workshop** ① *7 The Leathermarket, SE1, T020-7403 2800, www.londonglassblowing.co.uk, 1000-1700 Mon-Fri, free.* This workshop and gallery, occasionally open at weekends, incongruously situated in a warehouse office development, is one of the few places in central London where glassblowers can be seen at their fiercely hot and enthralling work. Exhibitions are mounted here of their own and others' work. Great for kids too.

● Sleeping

Southwark, Bankside, Borough & Bermondsey *p236, map p240*

A Holiday Inn Express, 103-109 Southwark St, SE1, T020-7401 2525, T0800-434040, www.hiexpress.com/ lon-southwark. Continental breakfast included. 88 rooms, internet access, small bar, book several weeks in advance. Busy chain hotel. Around £115 per night, including breakfast.

A Mercure London City Bankside, 75-79 Southwark St, SE1, T020-7902 0800. Newish '3-star deluxe', 144 rooms part of the Novotel chain, £12 breakfast, mainly corporate custom, halfway down Southwark St.

C Bankside House, 24 Sumner St, SE1, T020-7633 9877, bankside-reservation @lse.ac.uk. LSE hall of residence behind Tate Modern, beds in 4-bed rooms for £55 double including breakfast, own shower, 30 Jun-21 Sep only, book as early as possible.

C London Tower Bridge Travel Inn, Tower Bridge Rd, SE1, T0870 238 3303. Functional and efficient budget chain hotel, Mon-Thu £80 or Fri-Sun £70.

D Butler's Wharf Residence, Gainsford St, SE1, T020-7407 7164. For self-catering flats next to Design Museum, another LSE property, approx £22.50 per person per night, each flat for 6/7 people, own room, not right on the river, needs booking well in advance. (See map, page 231.)

F St Christopher's Inn Backpackers' Village, 161-163, 121 and 57 Borough High St, SE1, T020-7407 1856. 160 beds; £10 beds in 4 12-bed dorms, internet access, laundry, sauna £1 a day, no kitchen, remember to book a week in advance for staying on weekends. Sweaty discos downstairs on Fri and Sat, about £5 admission.

● Eating

Southwark, Bankside, Borough & Bermondsey *p236, map p240*

On Shad Thames, the 3 just-about-affordable Conran restaurants each reward holding out for a window seat with river views.

♥♥♥ Blue Print Café, Shad Thames, SE1, T020-7378 7031, in the Design Museum. The original and with the best vantage point overlooking the river, inspired modern British cuisine. (See map page 231.)

♥♥♥ Butler's Wharf Chop House, Butler's Wharf Building, 36e Shad Thames, SE1, T020-7403 3403. Has an excellent view of Tower Bridge illuminated at night and specializes in some thoroughly well-sourced, home-grown British recipes. (See map page 231.)

♥♥♥ Cantina del Ponte, Butler's Wharf, Shad Thames, SE1, T020-7403 5403. Less pricey, playing delicious variations on Italian peasant cooking. (See map page 231.)

♥♥ Balls Brothers, Hay's Galleria, Tooley St, SE1, T020-7407 4301. A new-old-fashioned wine bar doing decent food, also majoring on fish, popular with local office workers, and they run the free Pétanque Terrain in the middle of the Galleria open in the summer if you feel like imitating old Frenchmen.

♥♥ Bankside Restaurant, 32 Southwark Bridge Rd, entrance on Sumner St, SE1, T020-7633 0011. A large modern international restaurant, 170 covers, zippily designed by Dalziel and Pow, with art on the walls. Cheaper food in the brasserie, away from corporate atmosphere at lunchtimes.

♥♥ Fina Estampa, 150 Tooley St, SE1, T020-7403 1342, on the other side of Borough High St. Probably the UK's only specifically Peruvian restaurant with a healthy emphasis on seafood and live music on Mon, quite romantic and smart, closed Sun.

● *For an explanation of sleeping and eating price codes used in this guide, see inside the front cover. Other relevant information is found in Essentials, see pages 44-46.*

fish!, Cathedral St, SE1, T020-7407 3803, in a spacious glass and metal pavilion in Borough Market. The original, now one and only, branch of the once ubiquitous absolutely fresh fish chain, at the lower end of this price bracket, the place for piscivores who know how they want them, with a choice of simple sauces.

Delfina Studio Café, 50 Bermondsey St, SE1, T020-7357 0244. Away from the river, and much more gastronomically ambitious (and also more expensive), open for lunch only, closed weekends. The name belies the quality of the food but declares the place's affiliation to one of the first of the wave of fashionable galleries still opening up in Bermondsey. Booking is advisable for some imaginative fusion or Pacific-rim dishes using top-quality ingredients.

Garrison Public House , 99-101 Bermondsey St, T020-7089 9355, just down the road from the Fashion Museum. Not really a pub, more a rococo gastropub with hip sounds playing behind the bar and its very own private cinema. Very popular, so booking advised.

The Leather Exchange 15 Leather Market St, SE1 T020-7407 0295. A good upmarket wine bar and brasserie with an affordable menu.

Tate Cafés, T020-7401 5020, on levels 2 and 7 of the Tate Modern. Open throughout the week for lunch (expect to queue) and in the evenings on Fri and Sat, last orders at 2130 but open until 2300, both offering excellent brasserie-style modern European food, sandwiches and snacks. Tables can be reserved to guarantee a window seat on level 7, which has the extraordinary views and a full wine list, while the one on level 2 (T020-7401 5014) is bigger and a bit more buzz. Both are at the lower end of this price bracket.

M. Manze, 87 Tower Bridge Rd, SE1, T020-7407 2985. Good for lunch if not supper, is one of the few remaining 'eel and pie' houses, a peculiarly East End phenomenon: delicious eels, smoked, hot and jellied, as well as pies, mash and 'liquor' (pea soup) in antique surroundings.

Mar i Terra, Gambia St, T020-7928 7628, tucked away off Union St, a short walk from Tate Modern. Open 1200-2330, closed Sun, is a very good authentic Catalan tapas bar and restaurant. The food is great value and prepared from the finest ingredients direct from Spain, served up in a jolly atmosphere.

Tapas Brindisa, 18-20 Southwark St, SE1, T020-7357 8880. Different in style, more designer, but equally good for tapas, as its name suggests, very busy at lunch and supper. No booking, so turn up and hope; it only scrapes into this price bracket.

Cafés and sandwich bars

Conti's, 53 Borough High St, SE1, T020-7407 2002, and 53-57 Southwark Bridge Rd, SE1, T020-7234 0218. More straightforward and less expensive, offering a full range of well-filled sandwiches.

De Gustibus, on Borough High St, T020-7407 3625, opposite London Bridge tube. The place to go for high-quality sandwiches, featuring a choice of 19 varieties of bread, also hot food and soups.

Konditor and Cook, 10 Stoney St, SE1, T020-7407 5100, next to Borough Market. The local branch of the exceptional Waterloo outfit, the home of luxury cakes, sandwiches, biscuits, teas and top-notch natural ingredients.

Pubs and bars

Southwark, Bankside, Borough & Bermondsey *p236, map p240*

Anchor Bankside, 34 Park St, SE1, T020-7407 1577. Almost too famous for its own good, a much older, very busy warren of rooms, very touristy and also with a riverside terrace tucked beneath the railway line into Cannon St.

Bunch of Grapes, 2 St Thomas St, SE1, T020-7403 2070, near the Old Operating Theatre. A fine Young's pub with wooden floors and pews, popular at lunchtimes but not excessively so.

The Boot and Flogger, Redcross St, hidden away off Union St, T020-7407 1116. Local office workers favour this for a glass of exceptionally good wine at lunchtime or early evening, leather armchairs and woody furnishings give it the appreciative atmosphere of a gentleman's club. Closed Sat-Sun.

Founders Arms, 52 Hopton St, SE1, T020-7928 1899, on the river. An excellent Young's pub that must be laughing all the way to the bank since the opening of Tate Modern. That said, its combination of large riverside terrace with outside seating and efficient, friendly service of decent food all day and everyday deserves to be a success.

The Globe, 8 Bedale St, T020-7407 0043. A scruffy, good-natured pub with a pool table and a bunch of affable regulars.

George Inn, 77 Borough High St, SE1, T020-7407 2056. Most famously this is London's last remaining coaching inn, its galleried design the inspiration for Elizabethan theatres, and now a convivial low-ceilinged series of rooms much enjoyed by both local office workers and tourists.

The Market Porter, 9 Stoney St, SE1, T020-7407 2495. Another masculine kind of place, pumping excellent real ales in a dark woody atmosphere and opening to thirsty market traders at 0600 in the morning on weekdays.

The Southwark Tavern, on the corner of Stoney St and Southwark St. Opens at 0630 on weekdays.

Wheatsheaf, 6 Stoney St, SE1. An unreconstructed working men's pub with decent food at lunchtime and bags of character.

◐ Entertainment

Southwark, Bankside, Borough & Bermondsey *p236, map p240*
Theatre
Globe Theatre, see page 240.
The Jerwood Space, 171 Union St, SE1, T020-7654 0171. A newish contemporary art gallery, with decent café (open 0930-1800) attached, alongside rehearsal rooms for top theatre companies.

Southwark Playhouse, 62 Southwark Bridge Rd, SE1, T020-7620 3494, www.southwark-playhouse.co.uk. A cosy fringe theatre with a strong track record of innovative and challenging productions, its stage designs often making startling transformations to the limited space at its disposal.

❀ Festivals and events

Southwark *p236, map p240*
The Southwark Festival usually takes place in the first 3 weeks of **Oct**, an interesting array of community fringe events – plays, poetry, art,

food, and music in Southwark Cathedral, Borough Market, Hays Galleria, and Guy's Hospital Chapel. In 2000, for the first time there was also a **Southwark Literary Festival** in **late Oct** and **Nov**, also administrated by the *Southwark Festival Association*, 16 Winchester Walk, SE1, T020-7403 7474, www.southwarkfestival.org.uk.

◑ Shopping

Southwark, Bankside, Borough & Bermondsey *p236, map p240*
Bermondsey Market, in Bermondsey Sq, T020-7351 5353, further south but well worth the trek early on a Fri morning, a professional antiques market that gets going as early as 0330 in the morning and winds down around mid-morning, this is the place to find an astonishing array of Victorian furniture, jewellery, kitchenware and oddments. Not necessarily cheap, it's one of the most authentic of London's antiques markets, supposedly not a haven for tacky bric-a-brac.

Borough Market, see page 242.

Neal's Yard Dairy, 6 Park St, SE1, T020-7645 3550, near Borough Market. Open throughout the week providing a comprehensive range of cheeses from around the British Isles.

◉ Directory

Southwark, Bankside, Borough & Bermondsey *p236, map p240*
Internet **Backspace Internet Providers**, Winchester Wharf, Clink St, T020-7234 0804. **Medical services** **St Thomas's Hospital**, 2 Lambeth Palace Rd, SE1, T020-7928 9292. **Tourist information** **London Bridge**, T020-403 8299. Open Easter-Oct Mon-Sat 1000-1800, Sun 1030-1730, Nov-Easter Mon-Sat 1000-1600, 1100-1600. **Vinopolis**, 1 Bank End, SE1, T020-7357 9168. Open Tue- Sun 1000-1800. **Pool of London and Southwark Heritage Centre**, 12a Lower Ground Floor, Hays Galleria, Tooley St, SE1, T020-7357 9294. **South Bank Events 'from Vauxhall Bridge to St Saviour's Dock'**: www.London-SE1.co.uk. **Bankside Walks**: meet at Bankside pier (opposite the Globe), bookings: T01689-838410.

South Bank and Waterloo

Londoners have rediscoverered their river and the South Bank is booming. As the architecture critic Ian Nairn noted way back in the 1960s, the area is 'a real skeleton key. London is bent around the Thames: however much the north bank might wish to forget it, the south holds the centre of gravity.' That's never been more true than now. On the map, this is the centre of the city. A crow flying from Westminster Abbey to St Paul's Cathedral would have to dodge the vast white frame of the London Eye, cast its shadow over the concrete slabs of the largest arts complex in Europe, and then swoop past the red neon-lit noughts and crosses of the Oxo Tower.

Further south, the 18th-century obelisk in St George's Circus, Lambeth, records the fact that this is the only spot exactly one mile from Westminster, Fleet Street (once the home of 'the fourth estate'), and the City. Even so, it comes as some surprise that the riverside walk from County Hall to London Bridge has become a must for every visitor with a day or more to spare. Only 10 years ago the faceless grey blocks of the South Bank Centre and the National Theatre were accused of being a dirty, graffiti-stained and inaccessible ghetto for culture vultures. Nowadays, especially on sunny summer weekends, the riverside teems with Londoners and others from across the globe enjoying the breezy traffic-free views of the River Thames. ▸▸ *For Sleeping, Eating and other listings see pages 256-258.*

History

With the exception of the Archbishop of Canterbury's London residence at Lambeth Palace, which first appeared in the 13th century, marshland and fields covered much of this area until the early years of the 18th century. St George's Fields, a large open space between Lambeth and Southwark, drew crowds through the centuries, either for Sunday leisure, or as a place of execution. As late as 1780 it was the gathering point for the Protestant Association before they embarked on their protest that became the Gordon Riots.

Following the building of Westminster and Blackfriars bridges in the mid-18th century, modern Blackfriars Road and Westminster Bridge Road saw ribbon development along their length, meeting at an obelisk at St George's Circus. Once the marshy land was drained, one Charles Bascom built Belvedere House on the reclaimed land, eventually turning its grounds into a pleasure garden, one of many that emerged in the area over the next century.

Wharves and light industry sprang up (timber yards lined the curve of the Thames), the largest concerns being the Lambeth waterworks and Coade's Artificial Stone Manufactory which used a secret mixture of terracotta, quartz and other materials to produce a revolutionary hard-wearing 'stone'. In 1837 the material was used for the figurehead on top of the Lion Brewery that replaced the waterworks. The lion now stands in pride of place at the southern end of Westminster Bridge, alongside St Thomas's Hospital from Southwark which, when it first moved here in 1871, was a magnificent Victorian edifice, a worthy companion to the Palace of Westminster opposite. It was here that Florence Nightingale introduced her radical overhaul of nursing training that raised its status as a profession.

During the First World War, County Hall was erected as the seat of London's local government, and during the Second World War, the old Waterloo Bridge was replaced by the beautiful five-span reinforced concrete one of today. Designed by Sir Giles Gilbert Scott, it was nicknamed 'the women's bridge' after the women that helped build it when the war caused a shortage of manpower.

But it wasn't until after the Second World War that the area really came into its own, with the Festival of Britain in 1951. Mooted two years earlier by the Labour government as a morale booster after the war, the Festival included a Dome of Discovery, a Ferris Wheel (precursors of the Dome in Greenwich and the London Eye), and most importantly, the construction of the Royal Festival Hall. Other concert halls and the Hayward Gallery were added in the 60s, followed by the National Theatre, the National Film Theatre and the BFI's IMAX cinema. With the opening in 1993 of the Eurostar terminal, designed by Nicholas Grimshaw, the seal was set on the strategic importance of the South Bank and Waterloo.

Sights

🚇 *Embankment or Westminster (then cross the river), Lambeth North, Waterloo.* 🚉 *See p460.*

The riverside promenade between Westminster and Blackfriars bridges has become central London's multicultural playground. Crowds wander down from the Eye and County Hall, past the Royal Festival Hall and the Royal National Theatre, towards Tate Modern and the Millennium Bridge on Bankside. In some ways the most typical, central spot is the open-air second-hand book market sheltering beneath the arches of Waterloo Bridge, surrounded by buskers, skateboarders and coffee-drinkers perusing their programmes in the National Film Theatre's café. Overhead, the graceful sweep of the bridge provides the best approach to the area from the north and Covent Garden, famously offering one of the finest views of the city.

As you emerge from the main entrance of Waterloo Station (see also page 413), you're greeted by the great glass cylinder of the British Film Institute's latest venture, a purpose-built **IMAX Cinema**. Standing in the middle of the roundabout at the southern end of Waterloo Bridge, the building swept away Waterloo's notorious 'cardboard city', the squalid semi-permanent home of countless down-and-outs in the pedestrian area beneath the road known as 'the bullring'. The exterior of the building is an extraordinary blow-up of a Howard Hodgkin painting.

London Eye ‣ *See also architecture, p413*

① *To870-5000600, www.ba-londoneye.com. May-Sep Mon-Thu 0930-2000 Fri-Sun 0930-2100, Jun Mon-Thu 0930-2100 Fri-Sun 0930-2200, Jul-Aug daily 0930-2200, Oct-Dec daily 0930-2000. Adults £12.50, under-15s £6.50, under-5s free, private capsule £375 (advance booking available on the web, prices subject to change).*

The British Airways London Eye is the vast spoked white observation wheel beside Westminster Bridge that has already become one of the most welcome additions to the London skyline in years. Well over 100 m in diameter, the largest structure of its kind in the world, it's visible from unexpected places all around the city. There's no denying its novelty value, or even perhaps its beauty.

The half-hour 'flight' in one of its surprisingly roomy glass 'capsules', moving at a quarter-metre a second, provides superb 25-mile views over the city, and is neither vertiginous nor at all boring. On a clear day you can see all of London and beyond, including Guildford Cathedral and Windsor Castle. If the weather is less fine, and there's no banking on it if you've booked in advance (or even stood in the queue for an hour), you're at least guaranteed the peculiar sensation of looking down on the top of Big Ben and overlooking Nelson on his column.

County Hall

251

Built just before the First World War for the London County Council, the fate of this magisterial building, which became the seat of the left-wing Greater London Council (GLC), is one of London's odder ironies. It now houses the London Aquarium, the Saatchi Gallery, a 24-hour health club, and a Chinese restaurant, as well as a five-star Marriot Hotel and a budget Travel Inn. Ken Livingstone, leader of the GLC in 1986, might have difficulty finding his way around it. As the freshly re-elected Mayor of

21 South Bank & Waterloo

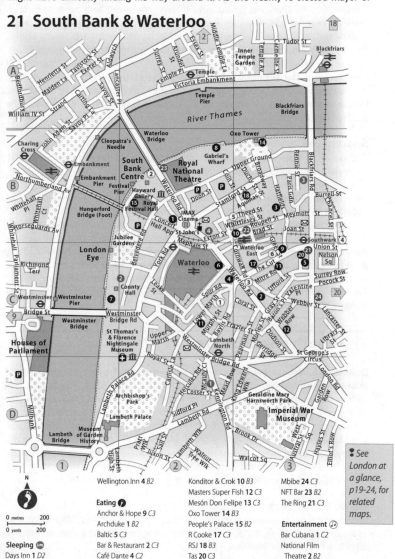

Central South Bank & Waterloo

❣ See London at a glance, p19-24, for related maps.

Sleeping 🛏
Days Inn **1** *D2*
London Marriot County
  Hall & London County
  Hall Travel Inn **2** *C2*
Mad Hatter **3** *B3*

Wellington Inn **4** *B2*

Eating 🍴
Anchor & Hope **9** *C3*
Archduke **1** *B2*
Baltic **5** *C3*
Bar & Restaurant **2** *C3*
Café Dante **4** *C2*
Casse Croute **11** *C2*
Fire Station **6** *C2*
Four Regions **7** *C1*
Gourmet Pizza Co **8** *B2*

Konditor & Crok **10** *B3*
Masters Super Fish **12** *C3*
Mesón Don Felipe **13** *C3*
Oxo Tower **14** *B3*
People's Palace **15** *B2*
R Cooke **17** *C3*
RSJ **18** *B3*
Tas **20** *C3*
Waterloo Café **3** *B3*

Pubs & bars 🍺
King's Arms **22** *B3*

Mbibe **24** *C3*
NFT Bar **23** *B2*
The Ring **21** *C3*

Entertainment 🎭
Bar Cubana **1** *C2*
National Film
  Theatre **2** *B2*
Old Vic **3** *C3*
Union Theatre **4** *B3*
Warehouse **5** *B2*
Young Vic **6** *C3*

0 metres 200
0 yards 200

London, he and his Greater London Assembly are now housed in brand new purpose-built offices near Tower Bridge (see page 245).

London Aquarium

① *To20-7967 8000, www.londonaquarium.co.uk, daily 1000-1800 (last admission 1700). Adult £9.75, concessions £7.50, under-14s £6.25.*

The London Aquarium was opened to great acclaim in the late 1990s, thanks In part to the wackiness of the idea of lots of exotic fish swimming about so close to the humble Thames. That said, its success is largely deserved: you descend through three darkened floors of aquaria cunningly designed around two huge tanks, Atlantic and Pacific, home to small sharks, stingrays and conger eels among others. The favourite attractions for children of all ages are the open-top 'touch pools' downstairs: a rock pool alive with crabs and anemones, and the beach pool full of thornback rays. Not as prickly as their name suggests, these personable rays seem to enjoy performing aquabatic feats and allow themselves to be stroked and petted. On the way out, there's a display on the threat mankind's activities pose to the marine environment.

Saatchi Gallery

① *County Hall, To20-7823 2363, www.saatchi-gallery.co.uk, Sun-Thu 1000-1800, Fri, Sat 1000-2200, adult £9, £6.75 under-16s.*

The new kid in the block is advertising guru Charles Saatchi's contemporary art collection, so influential in launching the careers of the YBAs (Young British Artists) of the late-80s and 90s. Much has been made of the disparity between the cut-and-thrust of the attention-grabbing artworks themselves and their serious official setting, a reminder of the effect of the 'Sensation' show at the Royal Academy in 1997. Probably the single most famous exhibit is Damien Hirst's pickled shark, entitled 'The Physical Impossibility of Death in the Mind of Someone Living' but it's the sheer variety and accessibility of the sculptures (mainly) and also paintings that makes a visit here wonderfully provoking.

The South Bank Centre

Downstream from County Hall and Jubilee Gardens, just beyond the Hungerford railway and footbridge, stands the South Bank Centre (SBC). The largest arts complex of its kind in Europe, it grew up around the **Royal Festival Hall**, the centrepiece of the Festival of Britain, see also architecture, page 413. Apart from the main concert hall, the Grade I listed building also houses an exhibition space, a good bookshop, the Poetry Library, and the high-class People's Palace restaurant. Nearby, connected by concrete terraces overlooking the river, are more concert halls, the Purcell Room and Queen Elizabeth Hall, as well as the cutting-edge Hayward Gallery. ➹ *See also page 257.*

Hayward Gallery ➹ *See also architecture, p413*
① *To20-7928 3144, www.hayward.org.uk. Mon, Thu, Sat, Sun 1000-1800, Tue, Wed 1000-2000, Fri 1000-2100. Adults £9 approximately, concessions £5/6, under 16s £3, all tickets half price on Mondays.*

The Hayward Gallery was opened in 1968 and is now one of the few remaining examples of 'brutalist' architecture in London. It will probably survive the planned alterations to the South Bank Centre. The cantilevered tower of neon tubes on its

⚡ Local action keeping the riverside alive

That the riverside around the Oxo Tower is even accessible to visitors is thanks largely to the concerted efforts of a small group of local residents who resisted the big property developers in the 70s and early 80s. Oxo Tower Wharf itself, which at that time was reduced to producing the extended tubular eggs for the middle of pork pies, was to be demolished and replaced with a skyscraper hotel and 20-storey office block designed by Richard Rogers. As had happened in Covent Garden a few years earlier, an action group was formed to protect the interests of residents, proposing instead a new park, a riverside walkway, room for shops, and most importantly, affordable housing. Remarkably enough, the success of their proposals can now be appreciated today.

The campaign lasted seven years, including two public inquiries, the second of which granted planning permission to both the community and the office developers. Ownership of the land then became the key issue. Thankfully the Greater London Council stepped in to support a small not-for-profit organization set up by local community groups. Eight plots of wasteland and warehousing were bought around Coin Street. Most remarkable of all, Coin Street Community Builders, as the organization was called, is still going strong. They are now responsible for Gabriel's Wharf, Bernie Spain Gardens, named after Bernadette Spain, one of the members of the original action group, the Oxo Tower development, including the Bargehouse and Museum of…, and the Coin Street Festival. Plans for the future include the Thames Lido, an Olympic-sized swimming pool floating on the river, and a River Thames Discovery Centre in the Barge-house. It's heartening that these projects are being proposed and managed by people living here by the river. The Coin Street Information Centre (see page 254) is a good place to find out more about their story.

roof, a kinetic sculpture controlled by the windspeed, has become a familiar, very 70s landmark. This is the place to come for major state-subsidized temporary exhibitions of contemporary art. They tend to focus on four main areas: single artists, historical themes or artistic movements, other cultures, and contemporary art. It will be interesting to see how its curatorial policy will respond to the Tate Modern's existence.

Also managed by SBC, but beneath the arches of Hungerford Bridge, **Feliks Topolski, Memoir of the Century** ① *Mon-Sat 1700-2000, free*, is one artist's highly idiosyncratic take on his travels around the world throughout the 20th century. Opened in 1984, the comic and nightmarish quality of the late Feliks Topolski's disturbing, atmospheric walk-in installation makes it one of the South Bank's more peculiar institutions.

National Film Theatre ▸▸ *See also architecture, p413*
① *T020-7928 3232 box office, www.bfi.org.uk*. Next up on the riverside, beneath the arches of Waterloo Bridge, is the National Film Theatre. Its restaurant and bar have become one of chattering London's favourite meeting places. Major relocation of the cinema to Jubilee Gardens is still planned in the near future, although it will hopefully still be possible to take some refreshment, and shelter from the weather, beneath the bridge. ▸▸ *See also page 257.*

National Theatre

Next door is the Royal National Theatre. The foundation stone was laid for the Festival in 1951, but architect Denys Lasdun's terraced concrete ziggurat didn't open until 1976, the new home for the National Theatre Company. Its grey blocks suit its position next to Waterloo Bridge, although Lasdun apparently hoped they would turn interesting shades of green once lichen and algae had bloomed on the textured walls. Air pollution has so far put paid to the desired effect. Recent developments have created Theatre Square, an open-air performance space for street entertainers and occasional showcase events. The views of Somerset House across the river still give some idea of how things looked from here more than 200 years ago. ▶▶ *See also page 258.*

Gabriel's Wharf

Continuing downriver, past the National Theatre, beyond the offices of IBM and the distinctive black and white stack of the London Weekend Television tower, Gabriel's Wharf is a quirky little riverside area. Another initiative of the Coin Street Community Builders (see page 253), this small square with its pavilion in the middle, craft shops and restaurants, looks slightly twee but is full of surprises, not the least of which is its popularity. Busy with weekend shoppers and afterwork drinkers and diners, a village feel has been conjured out of nothing. Next door are Bernie Spain Gardens, named after the campaigning founder of Coin Street Action Group in the 1970s, before you arrive at the Community Builders proudest achievement, the redeveloped **Oxo Tower Wharf**.

The Oxo Tower became a trademark landmark in the 1920s when the famous stock cube manufacturers got round local advertising regulations by putting a light inside their logo on top of their warehouse. The distinctive noughts and cross are now picked out in red neon, shining out above the successful redevelopment. The striking redesign by Lifschutz Davidson turned it into affordable flats for locals, with showcase applied art workshops on the second floor and a swish bar, brasserie and restaurant run by the stylish Knightsbridge store Harvey Nichols at the top (see Eating below). The views of the river, the City and St Paul's from here are superb, although unfortunately the bar and brasserie can't allow seating outside if there's the slightest wind.

★ Lambeth and Waterloo

Staying with the river, heading upstream from County Hall along the Albert Embankment is as good a place to start an exploration of Lambeth as any, behind St Thomas's Hospital, providing the most-photographed view of the Houses of Parliament across the water.

A short walk 'inland', south of the river, takes you away from the mainstream into a district that still retains a strong sense of its own identity. This is Lambeth, childhood home of Charlie Chaplin, site of the 'Lambeth Walk' from *Me and My Girl*, and also the largest, most mixed-up borough in London.

Florence Nightingale Museum

ⓘ *St Thomas's Hospital, 2 Lambeth Palace Rd, T020-7620 0374. 1000-1700 Mon-Fri (last admission 1600), 1000-1630 Sat and Sun (last admission 1530). Adults £5.80, concessions £4.20, 20-min tour daily at 1400 and 1500.*

The Florence Nightingale Museum is where the 'lady with the lamp' opened the world's first nursing school in 1860. The Hospital has recently relocated to its present site in order to be nearer the new Waterloo Station. The small exhibition includes a 20-minute video on her life and displays explaining her experiences in the Crimean War, her influence in the British Army and the primitive hospital conditions of her era. A fuller understanding of her life and times is provided by the tours.

Museum of Garden History

ⓘ *T020-7401 8865, www.museumgardenhistory.org. Daily 1030-1700 (phone to check), £3, concessions £2.50.*

At the southern end of Lambeth Bridge, at St Mary-at-Lambeth on Lambeth Palace Road, the Museum of Garden History is a small display in a converted church on the history of gardening. A quirky enough place, it's not really aimed at amateurs, appealing mainly to real horticultural historians, honouring the great Elizabethan and Jacobean gardeners, the Tradescants. Their original collection of exotic animals and plants was expanded by Elias Ashmole, founder of the Ashmolean in Oxford. It included the pineapple, hence the exotic fruit's presence on Lambeth Bridge over the road. There's a memorial to Ashmole in the church, which was restored in the 19th century, although the tower is 14th-century, while in the graveyard you'll find the tomb of John Tradescant, next to that of Captain Bligh of the mutinous *Bounty*. The museum includes a reconstruction of a 17th-century knot garden in the little churchyard.

The museum stands next door to the gate of **Lambeth Palace**, the London home of Archbishops of Canterbury since the early 13th century. It experimented with opening to the public in 2000, although may not do so again. The **Library** ⓘ *T020-7898 1200*, in the 17th-century Great Hall is viewable by appointment; group bookings only.

★ Imperial War Museum

ⓘ *T020-7416 5000, www.iwm.org.uk. Daily 1000-1800. Free.* Heading away from the river down Lambeth Road brings you to The Imperial War Museum, founded in 1917 to record the British Empire's involvement in the First World War. Since then it has dedicated itself to the history and consequences of all 20th-century warfare. Just before the Second World War it was relocated from its original site in Crystal Palace to be housed, appropriately enough, in the 19th-century lunatic asylum known as Bedlam, the Bethlem Royal Hospital. Its grounds now include the Tibetan Peace Garden, opened by the Dalai Lama in 1999, symbolizing understanding between cultures. The bronze cast of the Kalachakra Mandala, associated with world peace, is a good object of contemplation in juxtaposition with the grand entrance to the museum, guarded by a pair of the largest naval guns ever built. Depending on your sensibilities, you may only be able to cope with a couple of hours here.

On the ground floor you'll find an even more fearsome collection of military hardware, all quiet, cleaned up and cut away for easy viewing: tanks, mini-subs, aeroplanes and more peculiar equipment like the little observer's pod that was dangled beneath zeppelins hidden in the clouds. Downstairs the museum expertly explains and illustrates its horrific subject matter without over-exploiting its dubious entertainment value. A reconstructed First World War trench, 'The Trench Experience', is genuinely unpleasant, although thankfully nothing like as awful as the original must have been. 'The Blitz Experience' is more dramatic, but oddly less effective. These two are part of walk-through static displays explaining a mass of memorabilia, backed up by informative touch tellies explaining the historical contexts and some harrowing films. An immensely informative and disturbing exhibition on the Holocaust also puts the whole bloody business in perspective, while the top floor houses a harrowing presentation on war crimes and genocide up to the present day. A visit to the museum, however brief, is likely to be memorable and sobering.

● Sleeping

South Bank & Waterloo *p249, map p251*
L London Marriott County Hall, T020-7928
5200. 5-star, 200 rooms, majority with river
views, from £245 excluding VAT, up to £750
for the Westminster suite. *County Hall
Restaurant*, cocktail area, *Leader's Bar*, open
to the public.
B The Mad Hatter, 3-7 Stamford St, SE1,
T020-7401 9222, Madhatter@fullers.
demon.co.uk. Bright new rooms above a
Fuller's pub in an old hat factory, largish,
double-glazed against noise from the busy
road junction outside.
C Days Inn, 54 Kennington Rd, SE1, T020-
7922 1331, freephone UK reservations
T0800-0280 400, www.daysinn.com. 162
rooms, limited free parking. Another busy
chain hotel.
C London County Hall Travel Inn,
Belvedere Rd, SE1, T0870-2383300,
www.travelinn.com. 313 surprisingly large
rooms, basic, secure and very central,
Mon-Thu £87 or Fri-Sun £85.
C Wellington Inn, 81-83 Waterloo Rd, SE1,
T020-7928 6083. Small, clean rooms above a
busy refurbished pub, quite noisy, right next
to the railway, but very convenient location,
4 double rooms, 2 twins and 6 singles.
booking at least 2 weeks ahead is advisable,
good for singles and business travellers,
breakfast not included.

● Eating

South Bank & Waterloo *p249, map p251*
♥♥♥ Anchor and Hope, 36 The Cut, T020-7928
9898. Does exceptionally fine modern European food with a very lively bar next door, no
booking, so best to arrive early or late for
supper on spec. Closed lunch Mon, and Sun.
♥♥♥ The Baltic, 74 Blackfriars Rd (on the
corner of the Cut), SE1 T020-7928 1111. A
superb Russo-Polish-Scandinavian restaurant
and bar in an immaculately converted
warehouse.
♥♥♥ Four Regions, County Hall, SE1,
T020-7928 0988. A relatively expensive but
unusually grand Chinese restaurant with
tremendous views of floodlit Big Ben.

♥♥♥ Oxo Tower Restaurant, 8th Floor, Oxo
Tower Wharf, Barge House St, SE1, T020-
7803 3888. Still the smartest restaurant
in the area, it's a busy, costly, corporate
favourite run by Harvey Nichol's Fifth-Floor
team serving up some excellent modern
European food with the best views over
the river.
♥♥♥ The People's Palace, Level 3, Royal
Festival Hall, SE1, T020-7928 9999. Has
superb views onto the river through the
huge plate-glass windows of the Festival
Hall. Solicitous staff serve upmarket
French food in the spacious Soviet-style
dining room.
♥♥♥ RSJ, 13a Coin St, T020-7928 4554.
A very good French restaurant tucked
away off Stamford St. Ask for a table
upstairs if available, where the atmosphere
is more romantic.
♥♥ Bar and Restaurant, 131 Waterloo Rd,
T020-7928 5086, just behind the Old Vic
Theatre. A quieter and smarter alternative to
the Fire Station below.
♥♥ The Fire Station, 150 Waterloo Rd, SE1,
T020-7620 2226. A varied and interesting
global menu is served up at the restaurant
part of this place. Service can be erratic,
and the large bar area at the front gets
very loud, but the reliable food is
excellent value.
♥♥ Mesón Don Felipe, The Cut, T020-7928
3237. For some high-quality tapas in a very
lively atmosphere (tables are bookable
before 2030, it's always packed after that),
complete with live Spanish guitar.
♥ The Archduke (under the arches), Concert
Hall Approach, South Bank, SE1, T020-7928
9370. The place to go for a lively
atmosphere in a bar/restaurant. Upper end
of this price category.
♥ R Cooke, 84 The Cut, SE1, T020-7928 5931.
Traditional pie and mash and eels.
♥ Gourmet Pizza Company, Gabriel's Wharf,
56 Upper Ground, SE1, T020-7928 3188, right
on the river.
♥ Masters Super Fish, 191 Waterloo Rd,
T020-7928 6924. Top-quality fish and chips,
possibly the best in London.

● *For an explanation of sleeping and eating price codes used in this guide, see inside the*
● *front cover. Other relevant information is found in Essentials, see pages 44-46.*

Tas, 33 The Cut, SE1, T020-7928 1444. Turkish restaurant, probably the best value, fixed-price mezes, decent main courses, friendly staff and cheerful, modern decor set Tas apart.

Cafés and sandwich bars

There are lots of cafés and sandwich bars catering for the local office workers.

Café Dante, 6 Baylis Rd, SE1, T020-7928 5225. A traditional Italian café doing enormous platefuls of comfort food in a smoky atmosphere at very reasonable prices.

Konditor and Cook Bespoke Bakery and Fine Food Shop, 22 Cornwall Rd, SE1, T020-7261 0456. At the opposite end of the spectrum this makes some of London's most superb pastries and cakes as well as providing sandwiches and soup.

Casse Croute, 19 Lower Marsh, T020-7928 4700. Another almost gourmet sandwich bar.

Waterloo Cafe, 4-5 Hatfields. One of the best traditional 'greasy spoons' in London, doing the likes of ham, egg and chips at bargain prices, closes early in the afternoon and doesn't open at weekends.

🟠 Pubs and bars

South Bank & Waterloo *p249, map p251*

The King's Arms, Roupell St. Best of all with its wooden public and saloon bars, and strange 'conservatory' at the back, stands out in the Lambeth Conservation Area of Roupell St. It pulls a good pint, is very lively and does reasonable Thai food.

Mbibe, 173 Blackfriars Rd, SE1, T020-7928 3693. A funky modern bar/restaurant with DJs on Fri and Sat and decently priced British food.

NFT bar (see below), a good rendezvous, with long tables in the shelter of Waterloo Bridge.

The Ring, 72 Blackfriars Rd, SE1, T020-7928 2589, on the corner of the Cut and Blackfriars Rd. A straightforward boozer distinctive for being decked out with tributes to the area's boxing history.

🟠 Entertainment

South Bank & Waterloo *p249, map p251*

South Bank Centre, T020-7960 4242. Dominates the entertainment scene here. Together with the National Film Theatre and the Royal National Theatre, it adds up to a complex comparable with the Lincoln Center in New York, with the Kennedy Center in Washington, and perhaps most of all with the South Bank Centre in Melbourne. By no means solely the preserve of 'high art', the complex has established itself as one of the liveliest concentration of arts venues in the city.

Cinema

British Film Institute IMAX cinema/ theatre (see also page 250), T020-7902 1234. Quite tricky to reach, marooned in the middle of a busy roundabout. It's best approached from Belvedere Rd through a tunnel studded with blue stars. Inside, the IMAX screen is the size of a large house and quite mind-blowing. Unfortunately few proper dramatic movies have yet been made in the format. Daily showings from 1210 onwards. £8.50, concession £6.50.

National Film Theatre (NFT), South Bank, T020-7928 3535. London's flagship repertory cinema, showing a truly international selection of rare, first-run and classic films on its 3 screens. Every Nov it forms the focal point of the increasingly prestigious **London Film Festival**.

Music

Several restaurants in the area also have live music but otherwise the South Bank Centre is once again the best bet.

Classical and opera The 3 concert halls of the South Bank Centre (SBC), the **Royal Festival Hall**, **Purcell Room**, and **Queen Elizabeth Hall**, are without doubt the first stop for classical music lovers in London. Their programme manages to embrace an astonishingly wide range of different musical styles, often played by world-beating orchestras, ensembles, bands, groups and soloists.

St John's Church, at the top of Waterloo Rd, T020-7366 9279. Runs a good programme of free lunchtime concerts.

The Warehouse, 13 Theed St, T020-7928 9251, www.lfo.co.uk. A small, new, fairly trendy concert venue. The brainchild of the London Festival Orchestra. Concerts open to the public are usually given about twice a month.

Rock, folk and jazz **Bar Cubana**, Lower Marsh, T020-7928 8778. Sometimes has live Latin music.

Nightclubs

Ministry of Sound, 103 Gaunt St, Elephant and Castle, SE1, T020-7378 6528, Elephant and Castle tube. The mother of all mega- clubs, once the hippest night in the city. Relentless.

Theatre

Old Vic, The Cut, SE1, T020-7928 7616. Built in 1817 as Royal Coburg Theatre, and later known as the 'Bucket of Blood' because of the cheap melodramas staged here, the Old Victoria theatre was taken over for 25 years from 1912 by Lilian Bayliss, the founder of Sadler's Wells. In 1962, it became the birthplace of the National Theatre Company under the directorship of Laurence Olivier. It recently narrowly avoided being turned into a lap-dancing venue and is now run by a board of affectionate trustees that includes Kevin Spacey.

Royal National Theatre, South Bank, T020-7452 3000. The foundation stone was laid in 1951, but Denys Lasdun's terraced concrete ziggurat only opened in 1976, the new home for the National Theatre Company under the directorship of Peter Hall. It has 3 stages: the *Olivier*, the largest, with an open stage, steeply raked auditorium, and massive revolve. For some productions, the theatre has been brilliantly converted into a vast theatre in the round. The *Lyttelton*, slightly smaller, is the most traditional, with the option of a proscenium arch. The *Cottesloe*, round the side, is a much more intimate studio theatre for experimental productions. Director Trevor Nunn has continued the successful mix of popular classics, a summer musical, and more offbeat productions pioneered by his predecessor Richard Eyre.

Union Theatre, 204 Union St, SE1, T020-7261 9876. A small fringe theatre under the arches that occasionally shows interesting new work.

Young Vic, 66 The Cut, SE1, T020-7928 6363. The best middle-scale experimental theatre in the country, at time of writing currently being redeveloped.

⊛ Festivals and events

South Bank & Waterloo *p249, map p251*
For details, T020-7401 2255, or visit the Coin St Information Centre in Oxo Tower Wharf. Almost every Sun from **May to Sep**, and often during the week as well, the area around the Oxo Tower Wharf is given a shot in the arm by the annual **Coin Street Festival**. Billed as the largest free festival in the city, it's an invigorating multicultural jamboree of food, music, theatre and dance, usually taking place around Bernie Spain Gardens and along the river. The festival culminates in the enormously popular **Thames Festival**, on a Sun in the middle of **Sep**, with an illuminated procession, river-related events and shows, finishing up with a spectacular firework display. The **Waterloo Festival**, T020-7633 9819, www.stjohnswaterloo.ukf.net, in the middle of **May** is centred around the Church of St John, presenting a week of music and drama.

O Shopping

South Bank & Waterloo *p249, map p251*
Lower Marsh Street Market is all that remains that of the huge New Cut market that once stretched all the way to Blackfriars Rd along The Cut. At its best on a Fri, the stalls are mostly laden with cheap new goods, with a couple of second-hand clothes dealers and fruit and veg at the Westminster Bridge Rd end.

Behind the market though are some interesting shops:

Gramex, 25 Lower Marsh, SE1, T020-7401 3839. Open 1230-1800 Tue-Sat, offering a wide range of second-hand classical CDs and LPs complete with guarantees.

Radio Days, 87 Lower Marsh, T020-7928 0800. Excellent beatnik second-hand shop stuffed with collectables, vintage clothing and accessories.

Twice the Siren, 28 Lower Marsh, T020-7261 0025. For Caroline Scott's colourful, casual designerwear.

● Directory

South Bank & Waterloo *p249, map p251*
See Bankside Directory, page 248.

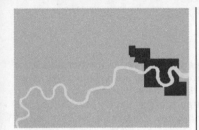

East End

The East End has long been forced to make the best of a bad lot. North and east of the wealth in the City of London, there's little room here for complacency about cheery cockneys weathering the worst of it with their colourful rhyming slang and robust attitude to a fair deal. In particular, many parts of East London have always had a nasty track record when it comes to race relations. Resentment still festers all too easily here, of strangers, of the government and of change. That said, the small area round Shoreditch, Spitalfields and Whitechapel has changed considerably in recent years, now attracting a large number of outsiders and boasting the most vibrant nightlife in the city beyond Soho. The spectacular boom in late-night clubs, bars and restaurants here has made the area one of the most exciting afterwork destinations in town later in the week. On Sunday mornings, the markets on Brick Lane, Columbia Road and Petticoat Lane continue to thrive. One attraction in the East End that should definitely not be missed is the antique splendour of the Geffrye Museum, providing a peaceful and faintly unlikely insight into well-to-do domestic interiors down the ages. ➤➤ *For Sleeping, Eating and other listings see pages 267-271.*

History

The East End has over the centuries earned a reputation as 'the dark continent beyond Aldgate', for as the City has expanded east, the cockney's 'sturdy optimism' has been an essential attitude for survival in the poverty and squalor that has plagued the area. But this was a problem that reached its peak in the 1800s – up until the 17th century, development in the East End was sporadic.

Spitalfields was a mass of sprawling monastic lands, bricks were manufactured in kilns in fields along Brick Lane, and the village of Bethnal Green huddled around modern Bethnal Green Gardens, with mansions nearby for the likes of the Bishop of London. Hackney presented a similar scene, with nobles', merchants' and academics' mansions (Sutton House still survives; the Astronomer Royal, Edmund Halley, lived in Haggerston) dotting the pleasant open countryside around a sprawling village. In Mile End, the common land was a popular recreation and meeting place (in 1381 the peasants met Richard II here to demand an end to serfdom), although by 1600 cottages and enclosures had arrived.

A milling industry built up around the River Lea, where grain from Hertfordshire was unloaded around a bow-shaped stone bridge – Bow was busy enough to earn its own chapel as early as 1311. Whitechapel, close to the City, had begun to grow in the 14th century (a chapel was built here in 1338), around the road east to Essex. Trades considered to be a nuisance were expelled by the City, so the likes of metalwork moved out to Whitechapel (the Bell Foundry moved here from Houndsditch in 1583).

Although there were wealthy residents in the area during this time, they moved west as cottages, alleys, and yards spread during the 17th century. Huguenot refugees arrived in huge numbers after 1685, boosting the weaving industry in Spitalfields and Bethnal Green, and establishing a chapel in Fournier Street. Sephardic Jews set up around the modern Leman Road, and bought land for a burial ground in Brady Street. Wealthy silk merchants moved into Fournier Street, and by 1724 there were 'close-built and well inhabited' houses stretching from Spitalfields to Brick Lane.

★ Don't miss East London...

Whitechapel High Street was lined by coaching inns, choked with cattle, sheep and tradesmen with their carts, but when the London Hospital moved to its current site in 1750, fields still spread east. Mile End New Town grew as an expansion of Spitalfields, housing labourers for the dyehouse, metalworks, refineries and the Truman Brewery. Nevertheless, it still had its more pleasant open areas, and Captain Cook ('discoverer' of Australia) lived here in the 1760s.

By the middle of the 18th century, Bethnal Green had a population of 15,000 (weavers, mariners and manufacturers), but market gardens still spread out on its eastern side. Hackney was still largely rural until the 19th century, when the plight of the East End slums attracted attention. Cholera was a recurrent problem (there was no public drainage), juvenile thieves prowled the maze of alleys, and 'purefinders' would collect dog-shit (used to dress leather) rather than face the workhouse.

The Whitechapel murders, committed by Jack the Ripper against local prostitutes, gave the area national coverage. The East End was variously described as 'an evil plexus of slums that hide human, creeping things', or 'ancient, dirty and degraded', with slum districts such as Jago notorious for their crime and poverty. Such deprivation couldn't go unnoticed, not least among the Victorian philanthropists and clergy. Several initiatives were introduced. Slum clearances made way for the likes of Commercial Street and Bethnal Green Road, and educational colleges such as the People's Palace, Toynbee Hall (Arnold Toynbee would tell East Enders that "we have sinned against you grievously") and Oxford House emerged in the 1880s. Both The Salvation Army and Dr Barnardo's were first established in Mile End, and George Peabody built his first artisan dwellings on Commercial Street in 1864.

Towards the turn of the century, a large influx of Jewish refugees from Eastern Europe ensured that the one time Huguenot Chapel on Fournier Street became a synagogue. When the fascist Oswald Mosley planned a march through the East End in 1936, radicals and residents barricaded Cable Street to prevent its progress. They clashed with the police, and Mosley was persuaded to cancel the march. A week later, however, all the Jewish shops along Mile End Road were smashed, and a year later the fascist candidate earned 23% in the local election. Since the Second World War, when the East End suffered extensive destruction, the Georgian and Victorian terraces have been replaced with municipal housing estates. Refugees from Bangladesh are among the latest arrivals in the area, and the Fournier Street Synagogue is now the Jamme Masjid Mosque.

Sights

⊖ *Aldgate East, Bethnal Green, Liverpool St, Old St, Whitechapel.* ⊜ *See p460.*

★ Old Street, Hoxton and Shoreditch

Old Street tube surfaces on a large and unfriendly roundabout that spins traffic around just north of the City. From this frantic crossroads Old Street itself runs west back to Clerkenwell and east into Shoreditch, while the City Road heads south to the Square Mile and Moorgate, and northwest to the Angel Islington.

To the right on the southbound arm of the City Road lies the non-conformist burial ground of **Bunhill Fields**, aka 'the cemetery of Puritan England' and the last

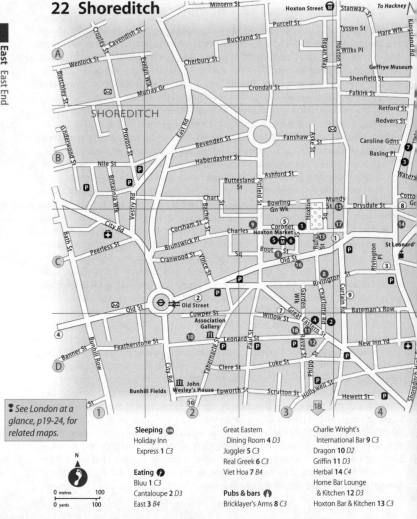

22 Shoreditch

‼ See London at a glance, p19-24, for related maps.

Sleeping 🛏
Holiday Inn
Express **1** *C3*

Eating 🍴
Bluu **1** *C3*
Cantaloupe **2** *D3*
East **3** *B4*

Great Eastern
Dining Room **4** *D3*
Juggler **5** *C3*
Real Greek **6** *C3*
Viet Hoa **7** *B4*

Pubs & bars 🍺
Bricklayer's Arms **8** *C3*

Charlie Wright's
International Bar **9** *C3*
Dragon **10** *D2*
Griffin **11** *D3*
Herbal **14** *C4*
Home Bar Lounge
& Kitchen **12** *D3*
Hoxton Bar & Kitchen **13** *C3*

East End

resting place of many of London's dissenters and freethinkers. The shady graveyard contains memorials to John 'Pilgrim's Progress' Bunyan, as well as Cromwell's son-in-law General Fleetwood, Daniel Defoe and William Blake. Also buried here is Susannah Wesley, the mother of John Wesley, the founder of Methodism who lived across the road.

John Wesley's House ① *49 City Rd, EC1, T020- 7253 2262, 1000-1600 Mon-Sat, 1200-1345 Sun, free (donations requested)*, now a museum, is next door to the chapel that he had built in 1778, known today as the Cathedral of World Methodism. Wesley lived in the fine 18th-century house for the last 11 years of his life, and it has been restored to look as it might have done in his day. The museum in the atmospheric crypt of the chapel contains an extensive collection of Methodist memorabilia, including a moving portrait of the great preacher on his death bed.

Next to Bunhill Fields stands **Armoury House**, the little mock-medieval castle of the Honourable Artillery Company. It's the grand 19th-century home of an organization that claims to be the oldest military unit in Britain, dating back to a fraternity of crossbowmen who were granted a charter by Henry VIII. The HAC still performs ceremonial duties around London and takes part in the Lord Mayor's Show.

Left off the City Road before Armoury House down **Leonard Street** leads into the heart of an area dubbed 'Sosho' (south Shoreditch) by estate agents keen to capitalize on an arty district's fashionable cachet. Look out here for the **Association Gallery** ① *81 Leonard St, T020-7739 6669*, a contemporary photography space that was one of the first kids on the block.

Leonard Street meets the massive Great Eastern Street at its junction with northbound Curtain Road, the name a reminder that it was on this spot that the first playhouse in London was opened by James Burbage in 1576. Called simply 'The Theatre', it was dismantled 22 years later and its timbers were used to construct the original Globe Theatre on Bankside. Memorials to many of Shakespeare's contemporaries, including James Burbage, can be found in the restored 18th-century **Church of St Leonard's**, in the centre of Shoreditch nearby. A whipping post and village stocks can also be found in the churchyard. Next door to the church, the Clerk's House, at 118 Shoreditch High Street, fared less badly in the Blitz than many and is the oldest house in the area, dating from 1735.

At the top end of Curtain Road, at its junction with Old Street, Hoxton Street continues north. On the left, **Hoxton Square** was the epicentre of Shoreditch's rebirth as

East East End

the most happening place in the East End. The square itself is a gloomy little spot but then that adds to its offbeat appeal. By contrast **Hoxton Market** next door has had a thorough makeover, is now a smart pedestrianized area, and not to be confused with **Hoxton Street Market** further up the eponymous street on Saturdays, one of the most welcoming and laid-back of London's local street markets. Halfway down is **Hoxton Hall** ① *130 Hoxton St, N1, T020-7684 0060, visits can be arranged Mon-Wed*, the last surviving Victorian music hall.

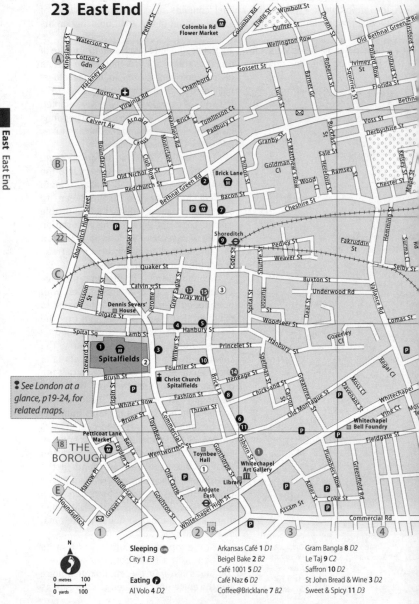

23 East End

See London at a glance, p19-24, for related maps.

Sleeping	Arkansas Café **1** *D1*	Gram Bangla **8** *D2*
City **1** *E3*	Beigel Bake **2** *B2*	Le Taj **9** *C2*
	Café 1001 **5** *D2*	Saffron **10** *D2*
Eating	Café Naz **6** *D2*	St John Bread & Wine **3** *D2*
Al Volo **4** *D2*	Coffee@Bricklane **7** *B2*	Sweet & Spicy **11** *D3*

N

0 metres 100
0 yards 100

Northbound, Shoreditch High Street becomes the Kingsland Road, following the course of the Roman road, Ermine Street, dead straight north all the way through Dalston, Stoke Newington, Stamford Hill and out towards Cambridgeshire.

★ Geffrye Museum

ⓘ *Kingsland Rd, T020-7739 9893, recorded information T020-7739 8543, www.geffrye-museum.org.uk. Tue-Sat 1000-1700, Sun 1200-1700. Free.*

On the right a few hundred yards up from St Leonard's church, are the peaceful 18th-century almshouses of the Ironmongers' Company that have housed the

Geffrye Museum since 1913. A beautifully laid out history of furniture and interior design is told here, a series of period rooms along the front of the old building decorated as they might have been at various times between 1600 and the late Victorian age. Most of the furniture and fittings in each are original, the atmosphere in a few enhanced by music of the time. Apart from the aesthetic value of the decor, the details reminiscent of the social history of the different eras – for example the stuffed armadillo in the 17th-century room a reminder of the period's excitement about natural history – make the museum much more than a dry lecture on different ways to furnish a small room. Capitalizing on the TV-driven enthusiasm for home decorating, the museum has been extended to include a purpose-built 20th-century gallery, with four rooms dating from the Edwardian era, the 1930s, 1960s, and a fairly flash 1990s loft conversion. The extension also includes a good-value non-smoking café, a shop and a wacky wooden spiral staircase leading down to an interesting temporary exhibition space for contemporary design. At the back of the building, plots have been divided up into a series of period 'garden rooms', including a lovely walled herb garden, open in the summer only.

Spitalfields, Brick Lane and Bethnal Green

★ Spitalfields Market

Southbound Shoreditch High Street heads into the City via Bishopsgate. Off to the left just before Liverpool Street Station stands the green cast-iron and brick spectacle of the old Spitalfields Market. The wholesale fruit 'n' veg market here was closed down in 1992, and since then the building has been the subject of local concern about its future,

Pubs & bars 🍷
Approach Tavern **16** *A6*
Big Chill **13** *C2*
Pride of Spitalfields **14** *D2*
Vibe Bar **15** *C2*

Entertainment 🎦
93 Feet East **3** *C2*
Arts Café **1** *E2*
Genesis Cinema **4** *D6*
Spitz **2** *D2*

East East End

a campaign being rallied under the acronym SMUT. It now looks as if half will inevitably soon be replaced by a new development, while the Victorian eastern part will be preserved. Catch the ramshackle whole while you can, at its best during the Farmers' and Crafts Market on Sundays.

Petticoat Lane Market

Also on Sundays, many of the streets south of here are taken up by the huge and infamous Petticoat Lane Market. Masses of new leather jackets, fake designer labels and gold jewellery among other goods of questionable provenance are flogged here with serious enthusiasm. Although there's always the chance of discovering an exception, the average quality of the merchandise is low. Then again many of the punters look as though they have come for the event itself and have no intention of parting with much cash.

Christ Church Spitalfields

ⓘ *To20-7247 7202. Tue 1100-1600, Sun 1300-1600.*

Back behind Spitalfields Market, on Commercial Street, rears the huge Hawksmoor creation of Christ Church Spitalfields. The full restoration of the exterior of this striking local landmark was completed in late 2000, and the vast interior has also recently been renovated and restored in quite spectacular style. Every year the **Spitalfields Festival of Music** ⓘ *To20-7377 0287 www.spitalfieldsfestival.org.uk*, takes place here in June and during the two weeks before Christmas, with concerts of mainly baroque music, as well as some by new composers.

Beyond the church the mid-18th-century streets, like Fournier and Princelet, running towards the aptly named Brick Lane are some of the most atmospheric and evocative in London. Still gaslit at night, the old brick terraces adapted for weavers have not yet been over-restored, while a few have been converted into galleries and shops. Most are still private homes in various states of genteel dilapidation or refined refurbishment.

Dennis Severs' House

ⓘ *To20-7247 4013 (0930-1500), www.dennissevershouse.co.uk. 'The Experience' on 1st and 3rd Sun of month 1400-1700 (£8, no booking required) and the Mon after 1200-1400 (£5), and 'Silent Night' by candlelight every Mon evening (£12), booking essential, or by appointment.*

The desire to slip back into the past was taken to an artistic extreme by the late Dennis Severs, who ran an eccentric 'living museum' nearby at his home, No 18 Folgate Street. His life's work, an extravagantly camp recreation of a master silkweaver's house from the mid-18th century to early 20th can now be explored on 'The Experience'. Half-eaten meals, strange smells, sound-effects (bells, birdsong and babies crying) and admonitory notices ('the late 20th century is an interesting place to visit, but who'd want to live in it?') encourage visitors to reassess their attitudes to their own thoughts and feelings about past, present and future. Dennis Severs' obsessive attention to detail and the different moods in each room certainly make this one of the oddest visitor attractions in London, the current caretakers discourage anyone not prepared to enter into the spirit of their friend's vision.

★ Brick Lane

Running roughly parallel to Commercial Street, Brick Lane is the main artery of 'Bangla Town', famous for its Bengali and Bangladeshi curry houses and warehouses, and also for the extraordinary market held at its top end every Sunday morning (see Shopping page 271). The long narrow street has recently become almost too hip and 'regenerated' for its own good. By and large the Balti houses still manage to draw people in and the old Truman Brewery building has been successfully converted into fashionable retail outlets and bars as well as a cutting-edge performance and contemporary art space. At the bottom end, Osborn Street comes out near Aldgate East tube and Whitechapel.

To the north Brick Lane hits Bethnal Green Road. The hard-bitten and tenacious fruit and vegetable market that sets up shop on this street every day except Sunday, just north of Bethnal Green itself, could reasonably claim to be the heart of the East End.

Bethnal Green Museum of Childhood

ⓘ T020-8983 5200, recorded information T020-8980 2415, www.vam.ac.uk. 1000-1750 Mon-Thu, Sat, Sun. Free.

There may be no room for sentiment at the Bethnal Green Road market, but plenty nearby at the Bethnal Green Museum of Childhood, on Cambridge Heath Road. Part of the Victorians' urban renewal scheme, it was established as a local museum for the East End in 1872 (the building a direct descendant of the Great Exhibition of 1851) and only became the Museum of Childhood in 1974. This delightful offshoot of the V&A houses an extensive, superior and priceless collection of antique doll's houses, old puppets, model trains and just about anything else that has been manufactured in the last few centuries to keep the nippers amused. Kids today are less likely than adults to be particularly taken with the displays, although the museum organizes a variety of special events at weekends and during the school holidays in an attempt to redress the balance.

★ Aldgate and Whitechapel

At the southern end of Commercial Street, Aldgate is a frantic road junction on the site of one of the old gates into the City, its name a corruption of All-gate (or open to all). Next door to Aldgate East tube station is the old **Whitechapel Library** ⓘ 77 Whitechapel High St, E1, and also, at No 80-82, the **Whitechapel Art Gallery** ⓘ T020-7522 7888, recorded information T020-7522 7878, 1100-1800 Tue, Wed, Fri-Sun; 1100-2100 Thu, free, one of London's most innovative and exciting public spaces for contemporary art, opened in 1901. Its art nouveau façade belies the radical edge to many of its shows.

Further up towards Whitechapel tube is the **Whitechapel Bell Foundry** ⓘ 32-34 Whitechapel Rd, T020-7247 2599, www.whitechapelbellfoundry.co.uk, a small foyer display is open during office hours, and on Sat at 1000 and 1400 guided tours are given by appointment (£8; no under-14s), that usually need booking at least a couple of weeks in advance. Founded in 1570, the firm has cast bells for Westminster Abbey since 1583. The premises are too small and dangerous to be operational during the tour, which nonetheless provides a fascinating insight into an ancient manufacturing process. Here you can see the original mould for Big Ben.

🛏 Sleeping

East End p260, maps p262 & 264
B Holiday Inn Express London-City, 275 Old St, EC1, T020-7300 4300, www.hiexpress.com. Over 200 rooms, functional and efficient branch of the hotel chain.

C City Hotel, 12 Osborn St, E1, T020-7247 3313, www.rcahotels.co.uk. Clean and well-run hotel near Brick Lane, with 50 rooms, all of which are ensuite. Makes a decent base for exploring the East End.

East End *p260, maps p262 & 264*

Bluu, 1 Hoxton Sq, N1, T020-7613 2793, www.bluu.co.uk. A music gastrobar that does a good homely menu (fish fingers and chips £8) in comfortably fashion-conscious surroundings in the building that was once the ground-breaking *Blue Note* club.

The Cantaloupe, 35-42 Charlotte Rd, EC2, T020-7613 4411. One of the first restaurant-bar combinations to establish Shoreditch's reputation as a hip destination for a dinner out and it continues to provide good-value modern European food in a surprisingly intimate dining area raised above a heaving bar.

Great Eastern Dining Room, 54-56 Great Eastern St, EC2, T020-7613 4545. Decent Pan-Asian dishes are rustled up at speed next to a busy bar with a loud City buzz. Open until 0100 Thu-Sat.

St John Bread and Wine, 94-96 Commercial St, E1, T020-7247 8724, nearer Brick Lane and Spitalfields. A newish outpost of the excellent Clerkenwell meat appreciation diner. Grab a bowl of lamb broth and barley for about £6, or an Old Spot chop and chutney for £15. They also do vegetarian options.

The Real Greek, 15 Hoxton Market, T020-7739 8212. This is the restaurant that had just about every food critic reaching for superlatives when it opened, bright blue on the outside and mellow yellow within, a very successful pub conversion where Greek staples reach new culinary heights. Mezes and small dishes are about £8.

Brick Lane is still the best destination in the East End for an inexpensive meal as long as you fancy a curry. The sheer number of options on Brick Lane itself is bewildering and competition is fierce.

Café Naz, 46-48 Brick Lane, E1, T020-7247 0234. One of the first to take the traditional curry house in a more contemporary direction.

Saffron, 53 Brick Lane, E1, T020-7247 2633. Stands out for the quality of service and kitchens.

Le Taj, 134 Brick Lane, E1, T020-7247 4210. A reliable old-timer, slightly more expensive than most but worth the extra spend.

If you don't want curry, the best bets are the cafés or bars listed below or you could try:

Al Volo, 15 Hanbury St, E1 T020-7377 0808. Excellent pasta and salads on the go (for about £6) for lunch and supper (not Fri) and on Sun.

East, 58 Kingsland Rd, E2, T020-7729 5544. If *Viet Hoa Café* (below) is too busy, this place next door has an extensive Chinese and Vietnamese menu served up in expansive and smart surroundings.

Viet Hoa Café, 70-72 Kingsland Rd, Shoreditch, E2, T020-7729 8293. Serves excellent Vietnamese food.

Cafés and sandwich bars

Arkansas Café, Unit 12, Old Spitalfields Market, E1, T020-7377 6999. For lunch in Spitalfields Market try this place, good for meat-eaters, an inimitable American barbecue shack that's excellent value, closed Sat.

Beigel Bake, 159 Brick Lane, E1, T020-7729 0616. Has long been doshing out well-filled beigels to all and sundry 24-hrs 7 days a week.

Café 1001, Dray Walk, 91 Brick Lane, E1, T020-7247 9679. A funky sandwich bar in fashionable Dray Walk, the place for jacket potatoes and salads.

Coffee@brick lane, 154 Brick Lane, E1, T020-7247 6735. The best place for a damn fine brew, a hip joint on the corner of Cheshire St, open 0700-2000 daily.

Gram Bangla, 68 Brick Lane, E1, T020-7377 6116. A clean, basic café specializing in fish and curries from Sylhet.

The Juggler, 5 Hoxton Market, N1, T020-7729 7292. Open until 1830, a stylish café attached to the Shoreditch Art Gallery.

Sweet and Spicy, 40 Brick Lane, E1, T020-7247 1081. Very cheap and popular with locals, no alcohol here, closes 2230.

● *For an explanation of sleeping and eating price codes used in this guide, see inside the front cover. Other relevant information is found in Essentials, see pages 44-46.*

☉ Pubs and bars

East End *p260, maps p262 & 264*
City workers, tourists and bohos flock into Shoreditch at the end of each week to enjoy any number of stylish music bars confidently blurring the difference between diners and drinkers. Most have kitchens attached serving up fairly reasonably priced food either at the bar or in separate rooms.

The Approach Tavern, 47 Approach Rd, Bethnal Green, E2, T020-8980 2321. Combines an art gallery with a characterful old boozer and serves good food.

Big Chill Bar, Dray Walk, off Brick Lane, E1 T020-7392 9080. A happening DJ bar open until midnight with a serious music policy, lots of cocktails and a designer boho atmosphere.

Bricklayers Arms, 60 Charlotte St, EC2, T020- 7739 5245. Raucous pubby delights for a youngish crowd. An old-timer of the Shoreditch scene. Also has an upstairs dining room.

Charlie Wright's International Bar, 45 Pitfield St, N1, T020-7490 8345. A legendary latenight spot (until 0100 during the week, later at weekends) owned by a formidable weightlifter, that attracts a lively mix of locals and visitors.

The Dragon, 5 Leonard St, EC2, nearer the City Rd, T020-7490 7110. A wacky unmarked pub conversion with thumping house music on the ground floor and a chill-out zone in the basement, more popular with afterwork drinkers than its tatty bohemian atmosphere might suggest.

The Griffin, 93 Leonard St, EC2, T020-7739 6719. An ordinary freehouse pub with a pool table that makes a refreshing alternative to some of the area's more self-conscious designer excesses, serving up very reasonably priced pub grub.

Herbal, 10-14 Kingsland Rd, Shoreditch, T020 7613 4462, www.herbaluk.com. It's nothing but a green door on the outside, but inside there are 2 floors, 1 DJ-driven and both usually open until 0200 most nights. Admission charged Fri and Sat.

Home Bar Lounge and Kitchen, 100 Leonard St, Sosho, T020-7684 8618, www.homebar.co.uk. Still the most typical designer drinking and eating venue in the area, with its smartish restaurant upstairs and laid-back, surprisingly large lounge bar downstairs.

Hoxton Bar and Kitchen, 2 Hoxton Sq, T020-7613 0709. A bricky, low-lit cavern that's a more serious music bar than other places like the *Electricity Showrooms*.

Pride of Spitalfields, 3 Heneage St, E1, T020-7247 8933. Much more of a locals' local and something of a Brick Lane institution, a friendly boozer that has become popular with the art crowd.

Red Lion, Hoxton St, N1. The pub that has found most favour with young local artists. A scruffy little DJ-driven place pulling a superior pint of Guinness.

The Reliance, 336 Old St, EC1, T020-7729 6888, www.thereliance.co.uk. Traditional pub with upstairs dining room and a warm welcome.

Shoreditch Electricity Showrooms, 39a Hoxton St, N1, T020-7739 6934. Originally helped to set the tone for the area, with battered sofas and rickety tables offset by sparse designer decor and witty touches like the idyllic Alpine scene on one wall.

Smersh, 5 Ravey St, T0961-869876. Hard to locate and generally much less busy, a strange red-painted vodka divebar, with a cramped music bar and a coffee bar on the ground floor.

Vibe Bar, Truman Brewery, 95 Brick Lane, T020-7377 2899. Still the busiest destination, has a free internet terminal, a large courtyard drinking area, sofas, big tables and the latest dance tracks.

☉ Entertainment

East End *p260, maps p262 & 264*
East London, like the South, is afflicted by a paucity of good live venues. It does, however, possess the **London Arena** (see also page 277), an increasingly prominent venue. Situated in the heart of the Docklands developments, the colossal Arena has started to play host to more and more of the better known bands, fans of whom unfortunately fall victim to

exorbitant ticket and concession prices in what is an acoustically barren cultural wasteland. Slightly more accessible (and a whole lot more fun) is **Spitz** (see below) which houses a restaurant and bar as well as live music. It is also notable for its free 'live classic jazz' shows every Fri night.

Cinema

Genesis Cinema, 93-95 Mile End Rd, T020-7780 2000, www.genesiscinema.co.uk. 5-screen independent multiscreen.
Rio Cinema, 107 Kingsland High St, Hackney, E8, T020-7241 9410 (Dalston Kingsland BR). 1-screen repertory and mainstream.
Stratford East Picture House, Gerry Raffles Sq, T020-8555 3311 for information. Multiscreen mainstream.

Music

Classical and opera Ocean, 270 Mare St, Hackney, E8, T020-8986 5336, www.ocean. org.uk. Brand new large-scale live music venue with 3 stages dedicated to all types of music, especially classical, jazz and rock.
Rock, folk and jazz 93 Feet East, 150 Brick Lane, T020 -7247 3293. This place has established itself as firm favourite with locals. Good for just a drink during the week or for one of its well known club nights, live acts and Rock 'n' Roll cinema (screenings of short films from Future Shorts www.futureshorts.com, on the first Sun afternoon of every month).
Arts Café, 28 Commercial St, E1, T020-7247 5681. Live indie and electronic sounds generally on Fri at this pizza and pasta joint.
Central Bar, 58 Old St, EC1, T020-7490 0080. Jazz every Tue and Thu, £4 before 2030, £5 after. Mon-Thu open till 2445, Fri, Sat 0145. Hectic cocktail bar.
Spitz, Old Spitalfields Market, 109 Commercial St, E1, T020-7392 9032. Live jazz in bistro on Fri nights, as well as a variety of other music and art events.
Vibe Bar, Truman's Brewery, Brick Lane, E1, T020-7377 2899. Occasionally showcases live bands, has regular sound system sessions.

Nightclubs

333, 333 Old St, EC1, T020-7739 5949. Fri 2200-0500, Sat 2200-0500, Sun £5 before 2300, £10 after. 3 floors for various enormously popular and hip dance nights. The *Mother Bar* above is open until 0300 most nights.
Cargo, Rivington St, EC2, T020-7739 3440, www.cargo-london.co.uk. Large, happening and very popular Latin house, jazzy house bar and club.
Club Aquarium, 256 Old St, EC1, T020-7251 6136, www.clubaquarium.co.uk. Large dance bar and club. Thu night Russian night £8, Fri US house and disco, Sat night is Carwash (a long-running 70s disco night) £15, 2 dance areas, a swimming pool and jacuzzi.
The Medicine Bar, 89 Great Eastern St, EC2 T020-7739 5173, www.medicinebar.net. Large bar-club, formerly *Katabatic*, now plays party house tunes on Fri and Sat. Open until 0200 on Thu-Sat. Admission Thu free, Fri non-members £4, Sat non-members £6.
Plastic People, 147 Curtain Rd, EC1, T020-7739 6471. Disco nights Mon, Thu, Fri-Sat.
Soshomatch, 2a Tabernacle St, EC2, T020-7920 0701. Nu-jazz, deep house, funk and soul, very hip. Open Thu, Fri, Sat until 0200. Admission £5 after 2200 Sat, after 2100 Fri.

Theatre

Chat's Palace, 42-44 Brooksbys Walk, E9, T020-8986 6714. Music, physical theatre, dance and comedy on the fringe in deepest Homerton.
The Circus Space, Coronet St, N1, T020-7613 4141, www.thecircusspace.co.uk. London's only circus school, doing a 2-year degree course, based in a training centre with occasional shows.
Hackney Empire, 291 Mare St, E8, T020- 8985 2424. Superbly restored Victorian theatre staging a vibrant mix of community theatre, panto, touring productions and comedy.

✿ Festivals and events

East End *p260, maps p262 & 264*
Shoreditch Festival local community festival held in **Jul**, especially on Hoxton St on Sun 15. Details from 182 Hoxton St, N1, T020-7613 2727. *Brick Lane Festival* in **Sep**, weekend festival of Bangladeshi culture.

☉ Shopping

East End *p260, maps p262 & 264*
The best way to fully appreciate the character of the East End is to pay a visit to its markets.

★ **Brick Lane Market**, easily the most vital and varied market on Sun mornings. The action takes place north of Buxton St and south of Bethnal Green, with traders arriving as early 0500 to grab a pitch. Cheshire St is one of the best spots to look for retro clothing and furniture, while second-hand toys, bikes, books and a whole lot of other bargains and junk clutter the pounds off Sclater St and the stalls along Brick Lane itself. Cygnet St is where the patter- merchants can be heard winding up their audience to purchasing-pitch for a variety of cut-price consumer durables. Things become even more desperate on the Bethnal Green Rd.

★ **Columbia Road Flower Market**, a little to the north and very different in atmosphere, also on Sun mornings, where wholesale flower traders and florists fill a polite Victorian terrace with a magnificent array of blooms and bushes, a weekly flower fest that is quite a sight in itself.

Beyond Retro, 110-112 Cheshire St, E2, T020-7613 3636, www.beyondretro.com. The rest of the week, look out for warehouse shops like this one, a huge jumble of second- hand clothes from the 60s and 70s.

A Butcher of Distinction, 11 Dray Walk, T020-7770 6111. The Truman Brewery lets out large amounts of space to retails like this one, doing distinctive designerwear for men.

Junky, 12 Dray Walk, T020-7247 1883. Stocks an interesting array of 'recycled' clothes, with 'originality stitched into every garment'.

Nudge Records, 20 Hanbury St, T020-7655 4823. Enthusiastic purveyors of soul, funk and reggae.

Sh!, 39 Coronet St, N1, T020-7613 5458, www.sh-womenstore.com. Anyone who thinks the British are still prudish should pay a visit to this place, a bright and cheerful shop selling erotic playthings for women, like dildos and furry handcuffs. Male browsers here have to be accompanied by a woman. Open 1000-2000.

Story Space Ltd, 4 Wilkes St, Spitalfields, E1, T020-7377 0313. A little further afield, this is an unusual craft and art gallery-shop in an old weaver's house.

Docklands

The London Docklands Development Corporation (LDDC) was set up in 1981 to regenerate the abandoned docks on the Isle of Dogs. Ah, the docklands ... such a romantic sound to the name, with its promise of the open seas, adventure and precious goods from far and wide coming and going within this wide meander of the Thames. Twenty years on, the result is a teeming money-driven futuristic cityscape plonked on one of the most deprived parts of town. Resident streetlife and visitors have followed in the wake of the office workers. Where once the masts of tall ships dominated the skyline, the massive obelisk of Canary Wharf now towers over gleaming office blocks and swish apartments, winking across lots of landlocked riverwater. The peculiar history of the place still makes it an intriguing destination and the views from Island Gardens are compensation enough for the architectural eyesores. The new Museum of Docklands does a thorough job of telling the area's story and that of London as a whole. Now fully linked up by rail to Greenwich and beyond just south of the river, there seems to be plenty of life in the Isle of Dogs yet. To the north, you're back in the East End proper at Limehouse. ➤➤ For Sleeping, Eating and other listings see pages 276-278.

History

London's water trade meant busy quays and wharves lining the bank from London Bridge to east of the Tower. Remnants of Roman quays have been found near Customs House, but the first wet dock was built at Blackwall in the early 16th century. Although places such as Billingsgate, the Tower, and Wapping offered further unloading space, most ships anchored in the river itself and unloaded their cargo onto lighters. River traffic was therefore busy, plentiful and chaotic, and to ensure that smuggling was kept to a minimum, Elizabeth ordered that goods should be unloaded at only the 'legal quays' between London Bridge and the Tower.

Although some quays existed beyond Wapping, by the 17th century there was still little development inland. The fields of Limehouse held lime kilns producing thin tile-like bricks, and were a popular residential area among distinguished Elizabethan explorers and seafarers. Shadwell was a hamlet with a tide mill where a few wealthy families had also settled. The Isle of Dogs, probably so-called because the royal kennels resided here, was marshland until the 13th century, and thereafter was barely populated until the 18th century, despite its windmills and cornfields.

The 1700s saw a burgeoning in the river's activity. Limehouse became London's foremost shipbuilding centre – Hawksmoor's fine church to St Anne was erected to serve a growing population – and in Shadwell ropemakers, tanners and brewers mixed with the regular turnover of seamen, watermen and lightermen. London's trade increased fivefold, and with it the need for an overhaul of the docks.

In the first decade of the 1800s, and then steadily over the next hundred years or more, huge docks were built along the north bank. East of Wapping were the London Dock for coffee, cocoa, fruit and wine, the West India for rum and hardwood, and later the Royal Victoria and Royal Albert Docks, where the warehouses were "filled to overflowing with interminable stores of every kind of foreign and colonial products", while to the west of Wapping was St Katharine's for sugar and rum. Cubitt Town on the Isle of Dogs was built to house the workers in the nearby shipyards and factories.

❖ *The purpose-built driverless Docklands Light Railway (DLR) is easily the most efficient way of reaching the area. Alternatively, there is a fast riverboat commuter service morning and evenings from the West End and the City.*

Predictably, slum areas soon developed. Shadwell was said to have "homes and workshops [that] will not bear description" and Limehouse grew a reputation for its brothels, gambling and opium dens, the latter aided by a sizeable Chinese population that had grown here in the 1890s, but which later gravitated to Soho as the docks' fortunes declined.

Following severe damage caused by regular raids during the Second World War, the docks mustered a brief revival, but by the 1960s business was in decline. Competition from Rotterdam hurt a dwindling industry as the Empire was dismantled, and the huge modern ships needed deeper water in which to dock.

By 1980, most of the docks were undergoing some form of development, the most high profile of which was the office tower at Canary Wharf, at 500 m the tallest building in Britain. Developers were encouraged by favourable tax breaks, but limited public investment in the transport links meant the Docklands Light Railway and Jubilee extension have been slow to finish, and the early 1990s recession left investors struggling with empty premises. Docklands is currently undergoing a new lease of life, but the waters are now part of a landscape of offices and expensive apartments, and rarely see any significant river traffic at all.

Sights ⊸ *Canary Wharf, Shadwell (East London line).*

Canary Wharf and the Isle of Dogs » *See also p415*

Arriving on the DLR at Canary Wharf, or emerging from Norman Foster's fairly awe-inspiring new station for the Jubilee line, a modern architectural wonder in itself, it's impossible to miss the **Canary Wharf Tower** ① *1 Canada Sq, E14*, the beacon at the heart of Docklands. Fear of a terrorist attack means no public access to Europe's second tallest building, but standing at the bottom of Cesar Pelli's tower looking up is almost as daunting.

On the other side of the tube, in Cabot Square, the best place for taxis, signs of halfway normal human existence have returned after several years of cultural dearth. The Square boasts an impressive array of high street shops, whilst **Cabot Hall** ① *Cabot Pl West, E14, T020-7418 2783*, is starting to host some serious music events and theatre.

A little to the north, the new **Museum of Docklands** ① *Warehouse No 1, West India Quay, Hertsmere Rd, E14, T020-7515 1162, recorded information T0870-444 3856, switchboard T0870-444 3857, www.museumindocklands.org.uk, daily 1000-1800 (last admission 1730), Wed 1000-2000, adult £5 (free after 1830 on Wed), concessions £3, under-16s free*, takes the themes of 'River', 'Port' and 'People' to tell the story of the area from the Romans and salty seafarers via desolation to corporate hospitality. The full history of Docklands and the river is covered in considerable depth at this state-of-the-art outpost of the Museum of London, going some way towards recapturing the spirit of the area's exciting past in a remarkable old wooden warehouse. Highlights include a model of the original London Bridge, ship's figureheads, the gibbet from Execution Dock, skiffs and wherries, paintings from the Port of London collection and a disturbing display on slavery featuring abolitionist Thomas Buxton's library table. Sailor Town, a recreation of a local 19th-century street, is the mandatory walk-through see-hear-and-smell show, fun for the kids. In fact the whole museum is a fairly full-on audio-visual experience. Fortunately quiet areas are provided for anyone suffering from strident information overload.

Beyond the Enterprise Business Park and the London Arena on Millwall Inner Dock, a strange anomaly in the area is the **Mudchute City Farm** ① *Pier St, E14, T020-7515 5901, Mudchute Equestrian Centre T020-7515 0749, 1000-1600, free but donations appreciated*, Britain's largest city farm. Always a big hit with the kids, its location also offers superb and slightly surreal views back up the Isle of Dogs to the Canary Wharf developments, and also away up the Thames to the City. Riding lessons are available at the Equestrian Centre (booking essential) on the same site morning and lunchtimes.

Over the playing fields from here, the **Island History Trust** ① *197 East Ferry Rd, E14, T020-7987 6041, Tue, Wed 1330-1630, free*, holds at least 5,000 photos depicting the Isle of Dogs in the 20th century. Along with the new museum, a visit to this venerable old institution is a must to fully appreciate the changes, good and bad, the area has undergone in recent times. Located in a working community centre, the photographs are all neatly packed into boxes by themes such as docks, rivers, streets, works, war and hopping.

Nestling at the tip of the Isle of Dogs, **Island Gardens** is a small park that makes an ideal place to sit and admire the glorious view of maritime Greenwich and the Cutty Sark. Look over your shoulder, and you're back in the 21st century with a bang, Canary Wharf still oddly close though more than a mile away. From Island Gardens, the Greenwich foot tunnel, constructed in 1902 for the West India dockers, sneaks under the river and back in time.

East Docklands

Limehouse and Poplar

North of the Isle of Dogs, smacking more of the East End than the river or the sea, **Narrow Street**, Limehouse's sleepy main thoroughfare, gives an idea of what

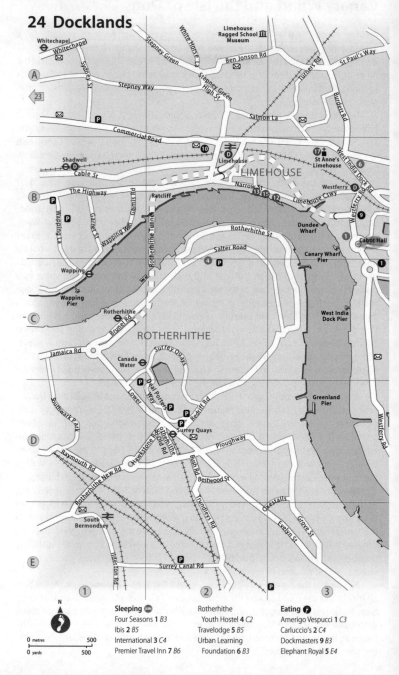

24 Docklands

East Docklands

0 metres 500
0 yards 500

Docklands could yet become. The old has been renovated and preserved in riverside warehouses and pubs (see below), while the newer flats and hous sensitively designed than the space pods around Canary Wharf, are beg weather and mellow into their surroundings.

See London at a glance, p19-24, for related maps.

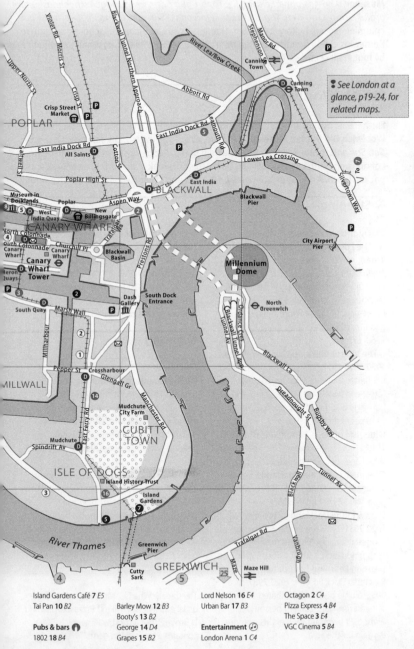

Island Gardens Café **7** *E5*
Tai Pan **10** *B2*

Pubs & bars 🍸
1802 **18** *B4*

Barley Mow **12** *B3*
Booty's **13** *B2*
George **14** *D4*
Grapes **15** *B2*

Lord Nelson **16** *E4*
Urban Bar **17** *B3*

Entertainment 🎭
London Arena **1** *C4*

Octagon **2** *C4*
Pizza Express **4** *B4*
The Space **3** *E4*
VGC Cinema **5** *B4*

St Anne's, Limehouse ① *3 Colt St, E14, 1400-1600, Mon-Fri, 1400-1700 Sat, and 1430-1730 Sun*, Hawksmoor's grand creation, with its leaning framework and eroding pyramid in the churchyard, is a reminder of the area's former importance and gives a glimpse of an older, more ramshackle Limehouse. Built in 1714, it also boasts London's second highest clock tower after Big Ben.

A walk up the Grand Union Canal from the station is **Limehouse Ragged School Museum** ① *46-50 Copperfield Rd, E3, T020-8980 6405, www.raggedschoolmuseum. org.uk, 1000-1700 Wed, Thu, and 1400-1700 on 1st Sun of each month, free*, a tiny but charming social history of Tower Hamlets, with a Victorian schoolroom where Barnardos children were educated from 1877 to 1908. With Canary Wharf just minutes by foot, it all seems so far away.

North Woolwich

Further east beside the City Airport and the riverside Royal Victoria Gardens, the **North Woolwich Old Station Museum** ① *Pier Rd, E16, T020-7474 7244, Jan-Nov 1300-1700 Sat, Sun and school holidays, free*, is a train buff's Mecca paying tribute to the defunct London and North Eastern Railway. Take a flask of weak lemon drink, an anorak and a packed lunch. A miniature train runs on the first and second weekend of each month.

● Sleeping

Docklands *p271, map p274*
AL The Four Seasons Hotel, Canary Wharf, 46 Westferry Circus, E14, T020-7510 1999. Giant space-age structure for the wheeler-dealers of Canary Wharf. In-room facilities include multiline telephones and CD players, in-house hydrotherapy centre and fitness suite. Doubles range from £250-£355.
A The International, 163 Marsh Wall, E14, T020-7515 1551. Clean and modern, part of the Brittania Group, with superb views of the tower and waterfront. 3 restaurants and in-house gym and swimming pool. Around £110 per night, room only.
C Ibis, Isle of Dogs, Prestons Rd, E14, T020-7517 1100. Standard chain fare, near Canary Wharf and shopping complex.
C Premier Travel Inn Docklands, Royal Victoria Dock, London, E16, T0870-238 3322. Mon-Thu £73 or Fri-Sun £55.
C Travelodge Docklands, Coriander Av, E14, T020-7531 9705. Not as spicy as the address suggests but good budget chain accommodation. £60 Mon-Thu, £50 Fri-Sun
D Urban Learning Foundation, 56 East India Dock Rd, E14, T020-7987 0033. Single beds only in shared self-catering flats. £30 per person per night, £25 per night for 2 nights or more. Bargain for the area.

D YHA Rotherhithe, 20 Salter Rd, SE16, T0870 770 6010, outside UK T+44-20 7232 2114, rotherhithe@yha.org.uk. Open daily, reception 0700-2300, £24.60, under-18s £20.50, large, 320-bed 2-star hostel, some way out east, popular with groups and families. Breakfast included in price.

● Eating

Docklands *p271, map p274*
††† The Quadrato Restaurant, Four Seasons Hotel, 46 Westferry Circus, E14, T020-7510 1999. Docklands' only truly world-class restaurant, with a southern Italian chef serving up international delicacies from an open-plan kitchen amid the diners.
†† Dockmaster's, The Dockmaster's House, West India Dock Gate, 1 Hertsmere Rd, E14, T020-7345 0345. A smartish Indian restaurant in a historic Georgian house. Excellently spiced and very good value food, even if more expensive than the average (about £8.50 for a main). Closes Sat lunch and Sun.

The Canary Wharf Complex contains all the usual quality chains like **†† Pizza Express** and **†† Browns**, but a short walk away the area contains a few hidden gems.

¶¶ Amerigo Vespucci, 25 MacKenzie Walk, E14, T020-7513 0288. Does above-average Italian cuisine for the English palate. Decent wine list.

¶¶ The Elephant Royal, Locke Wharf, Ferry Rd, E14, T020-7987 7999. A modern Oriental at a gorgeous location on the river opposite Greenwich with a cocktail bar that's lively at weekends. Set meal for 1 comprises 6 courses for £26.50.

¶¶ Tai Pan, 665 Commercial Rd, T020-7791 0118. An honest family-run Cantonese, oyster sauce et al.

Cafés and sandwich bars

Carluccio's, Nash Court, Canary Wharf, E14 T020-7513 1197. A very busy, fairly expensive but very tempting outlet of the superior Covent Garden Italian deli.

Island Gardens Café, Island Gardens, E14, T020-7515 4532. Overlooking the Royal Naval College at Greenwich this is a garden shed with a view. Standard snacks like chilli and baked potatoes for around £4.

Also worth checking out is the café at the Space Arts Centre (see below).

¶ Pubs and bars

Docklands *p271, map p274*
In Docklands itself, a proliferation of chain pubs and bars cater for the afterwork crowds.

The 1802 Bar, Museum in Docklands, No. 1 Warehouse, West India Quay, Hertsmere Rd, E14 T020-7537 1149. Fairly typical, run by Searcy's. Loud and lively, with uniformed staff serving up decent enough grub.

More characterful drinking holes can be found to the north in Limehouse.

The Barley Mow, 44 Narrow St, E14, T020-7265 8931. Riverside vistas without the history and attendant tourists.

Booty's 92a Narrow St, E14, T020-7987 8343. When *The Grapes* gets overcrowded this place is worth trying.

The George, 114 Glengall Rd, E14, T020- 7987 2954. A rare historic boozer next to the DLR at Crossharbour. Real ales, quiet conversation and definitely no cocktails. Apparently the back of the building contains an area consecrated to a covert Masonic lodge.

The Grapes, 76 Narrow St, E14, T020-7987 4396. Allegedly an inspiration for Dickens' *Our Mutual Friend*, this oak-panelled boozer has seen centuries of satisfied drinkers gaze out onto the Thames and has won awards for its fish suppers.

The Lord Nelson, 1 Manchester Rd, E14, T020-7987 1976. A quiet, relaxed family pub, ideal for a refreshing pint if you've just popped through the tunnel from Greenwich.

The Urban Bar, 27 Three Colt St, T020-7537 1601, in the shadow of St Anne's Limehouse. A refreshing blast of Soho chic in an area where most water-holes have the atmosphere of an airport departure lounge after an IKEA makeover. A zebra-skin paintjob outside and very low sofas, antelope skins and snake tanks inside ensure a funky crowd at weekends. Nice food too.

✪ Entertainment

Docklands *p271, map p274*
Cinema
UGC Cinema, Hertesmere Rd, E14, T0870-9070722. Standard Multiplex.

Music
Rock, folk and jazz Cabot Hall, Cabot Pl West, E14, T020-7481 2783. This concert hall is beginning to attract some big names.
London Arena, Limeharbour, E14, T020-7538 1212. Tends toward trashy mainstream pop and rock.
Pizza Express, Floor 2, Cabot Pl, E14, T020-7513 0513. Specializes in occasional jazz, check listings for time.
The Space, 269 Westferry Rd, T020-7515 7799. Ballroom and tango. Weekly jazz night on Mon.

Nightclubs
The Space, 269 Westferry Rd, E14, T020-7515 7799. Live music and DJs at weekends.

Theatre
Cabot Hall, Cabot Pl West, E14, T020-7481 2783. Diverse but mainstream dance, comedy, music and live bands.

For an explanation of sleeping and eating price codes used in this guide, see inside the front cover. Other relevant information is found in Essentials, see pages 44-46.

London Arena, Limeharbour, E14, T020-7538 1212. Large-scale shows and concerts.
The Octagon, 1 Harbour Exchange Sq, E14, T020-7410 0770. A smaller independent theatre.
The Space, 268 Westferry Rd, T020-7515 7799. One of Docklands' few fringe venues. Features small-scale theatre and variety. Convenient restaurant for a pre-show bite.

○ Shopping

Docklands p271, map p274
Cabot Place is the only place in Docklands for standard high street shops. A decent array of stores, especially clothing for professionals, are on offer, such as

Phase Eight, T020-7513 0808 and **Austin Reed**, T020-7513 0146.

Overall you'll being doing well to find anything out of the ordinary, but a few of the more interesting places to look are **Pepper St**, a pleasant pedestrian precinct by the water with clothes, jewellery and boutiques amongst the grocers' stores.
Crisp Street Market, E14, near All Saints DLR. Tue, Thu, Sat, a pleasant but unremarkable local market featuring food, clothes and bric-a-brac.
New Billingsgate Market, Trafalgar Way, E14, just off the A13 behind Canary Wharf. London's 900-year-old fish market is now at modern new premises. Get there early, it shuts at 0830.

Greenwich

Greenwich has been attracting visitors for centuries. Initially a few were far from welcome, like the Danes who arrived and murdered the bishop in the 11th century. But about 1000 years later the town was the obvious focus for the nation's millennium celebrations. As well as being the home of Greenwich Mean Time, the area's ancient royal and naval associations made it seem an appropriate spot to wave goodbye to the lost empire of the 20th century and welcome in the era of 'New Britain'. Unfortunately the Millennium Dome and its contents got such bad press that far fewer than expected bothered to turn up. Its future hangs in the balance, but meanwhile the old town is still a favourite weekend destination for Londoners and very popular with visitors to the city. It's not hard to see why: a fairly short river trip from Westminster past many of London's most famous sights, Greenwich rewards the journey with a convenient cluster of top attractions, most especially the National Maritime Museum, but also the Royal Observatory, Greenwich Park and the 18th-century grandeur of the Royal Naval College. The town itself is also pleasant to explore, packed with antiques, artists and idiosyncratic Greenwich villagers. Nearby are the even quainter sloping streets of fashionable Blackheath, while downstream the dockyard and arsenal at Woolwich, along with the state-of-the-art 1930s house and medieval hall at Eltham Palace, are revamped and offbeat attractions hidden away to the southeast. ▶▶ *For Sleeping, Eating and other listings see pages 284-286.*

History

Greenwich, or 'green port' as the Saxons called it, only really emerged in the life of London in the 15th century when Humphrey, Duke of Gloucester and brother to King Henry V, built himself Bella Court, a grand residence on the riverside. Until then, Greenwich had seen the Danish fleet anchor offshore in the 11th century, and there is evidence of a Roman settlement in what is now the park. But in early medieval times its manor was merely the sub-manor to Lewisham, with the Greenwich marshes spread out to the east.

Henry VII rebuilt the house, and it soon became popular with the Tudor monarchs, so much so that for a while under Henry VIII it became the political and diplomatic focal point for the country. He built a tiltyard and armouries, went hawking and hunting, and visited his warships anchored nearby. England's first masquerade was performed here in 1516, and it was at a May Day tournament that Anne Boleyn allegedly dropped a hanky as a signal to a lover. She was in the Tower the next day.

Later in the century Shakespeare is said to have performed in his plays here before Elizabeth I. James I walled in the park, and his wife, Anne of Denmark, commissioned Inigo Jones to build the Palladian Queen's House. When the Parliamentarians took control following the Civil War, having emptied it of much of its treasures (Charles I was an extensive art collector), it spent time as both a biscuit factory and a holding house for Dutch prisoners of war.

Following the Restoration, Charles II had designs on a new palace, but money and enthusiasm dried up, leaving only the west wing of the Naval Hospital, later the Royal Naval College. The parks were laid out though, inspired by the French designer, Le Notre, and in 1675 the Royal Observatory was built on the site of Humphrey's watchtower, an event that led, almost literally, to Greenwich's unique relationship with Father Time. Some 200 years later, at Washington in America, it was agreed that the Greenwich Meridian should define 0° longitude. The Royal Observatory's fine reputation (Edmond Halley was Astronomer Royal, and its Nautical Almanac of 1767 became the navigator's bible the world over), earned it this special status.

Meanwhile, Greenwich as a settlement grew little. In the 18th century some grand houses were erected, such as the Ranger's House and Vanburgh's Castle, but by the mid-19th century it was more a venue for Londoners to visit on steamers, gigs and hackney-coaches. London's first railway line ran to Greenwich, a much-celebrated affair with orchestras at the stations. The population grew with the spread of the Docklands, music halls and theatres opened up, and Goddard's Eel and Pie House (only recently closed down) gained a sizeable reputation. In 1902, the Greenwich Foot Tunnel opened, giving the dockers easier access to the West India Docks, and by 1905 the houses stretched all the way south to Blackheath and Lewisham. The building of the Dome at the end of the 20th century may have been ridiculed, but it has provided employment and hope of some much needed regeneration in the area.

East Greenwich

Sights

   Cutty Sark or overland train from Charing Cross or London Bridge to Greenwich train station.

Cutty Sark
ⓘ *King William Walk, SE10, T020-8858 3445, www.cuttysark.org.uk. Daily 1000-1700 (last admission 1630). Adult £4.50, concessions £3.75, under-16s £3.20.*

Appropriately enough, visitors to Greenwich arriving by boat land right next to the Cutty Sark. This is the only surviving tea clipper of the kind that raced around the world under sail for the Empire, laden with tea or opium and displaying a turn of speed that could cover about 350 miles in a day. Built in 1869 in Dumbarton on the River Clyde, and named after the skimpy nightie on a dancing witch admired by Tam O'Shanter in Burns' poem, she made her last commercial voyage in 1922, and was dry-docked in Greenwich in 1954. Three decks can be explored, including the Captain's cabin, as well as a large collection of figureheads from other tall ships. Unfortunately the ship is still steadily succumbing to the weather, in danger of crumbling away completely, and has become the worthy subject of an urgent fund-raising appeal.

❢ *Greenwich is best approached by boat (see page 456) for the views of the Cutty Sark, the Royal Naval College and Queen's House from the river; or by the foot tunnel from Island Gardens.*

Close by is the distinctive domed entrance to the eerie **Greenwich foot tunnel** under the Thames to the Isle of Dogs. In Cutty Sark Gardens is the **Greenwich Tourist Information Centre** ① *T020-8858 6376, 1000-1700 daily*, a mine of local information where accommodation can also be booked (£2 fee).

Heading inland, Greenwich Church Street leads up to the centre of the town which is dominated by **St Alphege's Church** ① *T020-8858 6828, 1000-1600 Mon-Sat, 1300-1600 Sun*, named after Greenwich's patron saint, the bishop murdered on this spot by the Danes in the 11th century. Hawksmoor designed its impressive exterior in 1712.

Royal Naval College

① *T020-8269 4747, tours T020-8269 4791, www.greenwichfoundation.org.uk. Daily 1000-1700 (last admission 1615). Free, guided tours £4 (children free).*

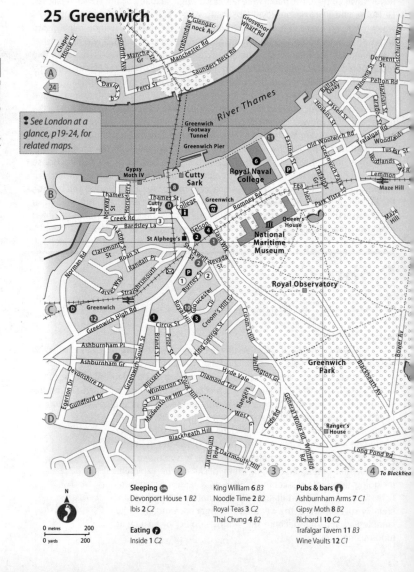

25 Greenwich

❢ See London at a glance, p19-24, for related maps.

Sleeping 🛏	Eating 🍴		Pubs & bars 🍺
Devonport House 1 *B2*	Inside 1 *C2*	King William 6 *B3*	Ashburnham Arms 7 *C1*
Ibis 2 *C2*		Noodle Time 2 *B2*	Gipsy Moth 8 *B2*
		Royal Teas 3 *C2*	Richard I 10 *C2*
		Thai Chung 4 *B2*	Trafalgar Tavern 11 *B3*
			Wine Vaults 12 *C1*

N

0 metres 200
0 yards 200

Greenwich High Road rounds the corner towards the train station and New Cross, while Romney Road leads off to the left past Greenwich market towards the main event, the National Maritime Museum (see below) on the right in Greenwich Park and the Royal Naval College on the left beside the water. Designed by Royal command not to obstruct the view from the river of the Queen's House at the centre of the museum, the College represents English architecture at its grandest and most formal. Three of the most celebrated 18th-century British architects had a hand in the design – Wren, Hawksmoor and Vanbrugh – and its twin domes and columns still make a stunning picture when seen from the water or from the hills of Greenwich Park.

Now used by Greenwich University, visitors can wander its great riverside quads and see the Painted Hall, beneath the southwestern cupola, an extraordinary and theatrical room, busy with murals beneath a magnificent ceiling, all painted by

Thornhill over a period of 19 years. In the Undercroft beneath the hall, temporary exhibitions are displayed in Queen Mary's anteroom. The Chapel of St Peter and St Paul, in St Mary Court, was designed by Wren but gutted by fire in 1779. The airy neoclassical interior by 'Athenian' Stuart features a remarkable altar painting by Benjamin West of *The Preservation of St Paul after the Shipwreck at Malta*. The Ward Room in the Undercroft is a smart new lunch place (see Eating below), and the Tilt Yard Café is in the Greenwich gateway furthest from the river.

Queen's House

ⓘ *Romney Rd, SE10, T020-8858 4422, information T020-8312 6565, www.nmm.ac.uk. Daily 1000-1700 (last admission 1630). Free.*
The Queen's House was the first truly Renaissance house constructed in England, and a beautiful piece of architecture: the Great Hall is a perfect cube, while the 'tulip staircase' named after the designs on its bannisters is beautiful too. Look out for **Canaletto**'s view of the Royal Hospital and Greenwich from the Isle of Dogs, little changed today.

★ National Maritime Museum

ⓘ *T020-8858 4422, recorded information T020-8312 6565, www.nmm.ac.uk. Daily 1000-1700 (last admission 1630). Free.*
A covered colonnade connects Queen's House on either side to the National Maritime Museum, with its three levels pretty much doing justice to their enthralling subject, the sea. This is one of the most engaging museums in London.

East Greenwich

Entertainment ♫
Greenwich Cinema **1** C2
Greenwich Theatre **2** C2
Up the Creek **3** B2

The ground floor here contains a exhibition on Maritime London, including the original façade of Lloyd's Coffee House and is divided into five themes: Shipping and Shipbuilding, Pageantry and Pleasure, Bridges and Buildings, Companies and Cargoes, and London Lives. The west wing covers explorers, from the Vikings and Phoenicians to the Polar expeditions, one highlight being a fragment of Sir John Franklin's last message, written in 1847, on his way to his death searching for the Northwest Passage.

In the Neptune Court, an adjunct to these displays covers the history of underwater exploration and the discovery of the Titanic. 'Passengers' in the south wing looks at emigration, and life on board the great ocean liners. The extraordinary glass roof designed by Rick Mather over the Neptune Court was manufactured by the company that built the Eiffel Tower.

First floor

On the first floor (Level 2), the Upper Court, is flooded with natural light from the glass roof, 'Your Ocean' next to the café contains the Museum's brave attempt to explain the ecology of the sea.

The east wing on this level is the picture gallery, hung with a selection from the Museum's vast collection of maritime paintings, from **Eric Ravilious'** *Submarine Dream* to **Whistler's** *Black Lion Wharf*. Overlooking Greenwich Park, 'Trade and Empire' covers the touchy matter of the British Empire's global expansion across the billowing ocean wave, with displays on slavery, the missionaries and white settlement of the colonies. Among the objects providing ample food for thought here are the figurehead of *HMS Seringapatam* carved to represent Tipu Sultan, the Indian ruler defeated in 1798.

Level 3

On Level 3, one of the Museum's most popular rooms is still the Nelson Gallery, containing plenty of memorabilia relating to the flawed hero, the man and the myth, including the blood-stained tourniquet for his wound and a computer animated Battle of Trafalgar. On the same level, two hands-on galleries for kids are 'The Bridge', where a ferry needs to be steered out of Dover and a Viking ship docked, and 'All Hands', with interactive exhibits on diving, gunnery and cargo handling. The south wing is given over to temporary exhibitions.

★ Royal Observatory

① *T020-8858 4422, information T020-8312 6565, www.rog.nmm.ac.uk. Daily 1000-1700 (last admission 1630). Free.*

A steep walk up the hill through the park behind the Museum leads to the Royal Observatory. Most prominent of the buildings is **Flamsteed House** which looks and sounds like something out of Harry Potter but is in fact the 17th-century home of the Astronomer Royal. On its roof, the red Time Ball, put up in 1833 to give an exact time signal to the docks in the distance, drops on the dot of one o'clock every day.

A visit to the Observatory starts in the **Meridian Courtyard**, where it's possible to straddle the dividing line between eastern and western hemispheres, and then takes in Flamsteed House, with its four reconstructed period rooms and Wren's Octagon Room for watching celestial events; the Harrison Gallery containing four of the revolutionary clocks that allowed sailors to find longitude accurately for the first time in 1735; the Meridian Building and the instruments used down the centuries to determine the meridian; and next door the Airy Transit Circle, the telescope that pinpointed the current meridian in 1851 and now the source of the green laser beamed exactly due north every evening. A spiral staircase then leads up to the large 28-inch telescope, housed in its distinctive dome and in use until 1957 to examine the orbits of binary stars. Beyond is the **Altazimuth Pavilion**, named after a type of telescope that plotted the co-ordinates of a planet or star by measuring their altitude above the horizon and their azimuth, or position east along the horizon. The building now houses a photoheliograph used to look at an image of the sun projected onto a flat plate.

Greenwich Park

① *To20-8858 2608. Open 0700-dusk daily.* Famous for its wide views over Docklands, the City, Tower Bridge and round to the London Eye and Big Ben, and best appreciated from near the Observatory or from One Tree Hill, Greenwich Park is a relatively high rolling expanse of green, criss-crossed by tree-lined avenues embracing a lakeside flower garden, deer park and some Roman remains.

In fact it's surrounded on all sides by old buildings of considerable interest. **Croom's Hill** on the west is a sloping row of very fine Georgian houses leading up to the red-brick 18th-century **Ranger's House** ① *Chesterfield Walk, To20-8853 0035, www.english-heritage.org.uk, 24 Mar-30 Sep Wed-Sun 1000-1700, other times by pre-booked guided tour only, £5.30, concessions £4, under-16s £2.70*, now the home of the Wernher Collection of medieval and Renaissance works of art. As well as about 700 paintings including several Dutch old masters, the panelled rooms contain a sumptuous variety of antique furniture and silver, the fruits of diamond magnate Sir Julius Wernher's late 19th-century collecting hobby.

Beyond Ranger's House lie the Dell and the Blackheath Gate, the usual starting point for the London Marathon every April, and in the park's often-deserted eastern corner, woodland walks and another viewpoint. At the bottom of Maze Hill stands **Vanbrugh's Castle**, a mock-medieval folly, the first of its kind in the country, designed and lived in by Sir John Vanbrugh. On summer weekends, the park is always crowded with visitors and Londoners picnicking and taking the air.

Further south, the almost featureless expanse of Blackheath stretches down to Greenwich's smart little neighbour, **Blackheath Village**. Also unmistakable from most viewpoints in the park is the huge **Millennium Dome** in North Greenwich. At the time of writing, this great white elephantine structure is being overhauled by Anschutz Entertainment, the American group heading a £1 billion project to turn it into a sports and entertainment complex. The revamped venue will hold 23,000 people and is being heralded as a potential Olympic venue if London wins the 2012 Games bid. See also architecture, page 415.

Beyond Greenwich

Downriver past the Millennium Dome, and best viewed by boat, the **Thames Barrier** ① *1 Unity Way, SE18, To20-8305 4188, Visitor Centre 1100-1530 daily, £1, 50p concession and children, 75p OAP (tickets from café)*, is the world's largest movable flood barrier, completed in 1982 after seven years under construction. An impressive sight in itself, with its rank of shining steel 'sails', the barrier has often been raised in emergencies. Alarmingly enough, it has already been suggested that even this formidable barrier will be incapable of preventing central London from flooding as a result of a surge tide within the next two decades.

The Visitor Centre on the southern bank explains the hydraulics that operate the massive paddles and also explains the threat the river presents. Ideally a visit should be timed to coincide with one of the monthly testings, phone for details.

● *There are rumours that a film is to be made of the foiled diamond heist at the Millennium Dome, starring Brad Pitt. When the chief superintendent who caught the gang heard, he apparently joked that they should find someone better looking to play the part.*

① T020-8855 7755 www.firepower.org.uk. Apr-Oct Wed-Sun 1030-1700, Nov-Mar Fri-Sun 1030-1700, £5, concessions £4.50, under-16s £2.50.

A mile further downstream is Woolwich, a top destination for fans of gunnery, being home to the Museum of Artillery, recently relocated to the old buildings of the Royal Arsenal, re-christened 'Firepower'. The new revamped interactive displays combine the collections of the Royal Artillery Regimental Museum, the Rotunda Museum and the Medal Collection, ranging from pieces of 14th-century ordinance to nuclear Lance missiles. A new Cold War gallery takes the story up to 2003. Outside there are howitzers as well as Chinese and Russian-made guns captured in the Gulf War, and a unique 18-inch British railway gun guarding the gate on Repository Road, built in 1917 to defend the coast during the First World War, not actually fired until 1921.

Eltham Palace

① T020-8294 2548. Apr-Oct Sun-Wed 1000-1700, Nov-Dec and Feb-Mar Sun-Wed 1000-1600. Adults £7.30, concessions £5.50, under-16s £3.70. Best reached from Charing Cross Station, taking either the Dartford line via Bexley Heath to Eltham, or Sidcup line to Mottingham, then a 15-min walk, or No 161 bus, or take bus 286 from Greenwich beside Cutty Sark, about 20 mins.

Further to the southeast, Eltham Palace was the 1930s home of millionaire Stephen Courtauld which he had purposebuilt around the Great Hall of a medieval palace. Most impressive is the entrance hall, a spectacular reception room for Virginia Courtauld's glamorous parties. Like the rest of the house, it has been lavishly restored to its art deco heyday, but some may be disappointed by the absence of original paintings. The garden has also recently been returned to its former glory.

● Sleeping

Greenwich p278, map p280

A Devonport House Hotel and Conference Centre , King William Walk, SE10, T020-8269 5400, www.devonport-isc.co.uk. With 94 rooms in a fully renovated old building close to the National Maritime Museum. Popular with corporate clients, as the name suggests, but a reasonable option in the heart of Greenwich for tourists too.

C Ibis Hotel, 30 Stockwell St, SE10, T020-8305 1177, www.ibishotel.com. 82 rooms all with en suite bathrooms in standard, clean and newish branch of the budget chain, breakfast £4.25 extra.

♥♥ The King William, Royal Naval College, SE10, T020-8858 4143. A decent enough lunchtime restaurant in the Undercroft beneath the Painted Hall, with high standards of service, a friendly place in a historic building (mains about £10), closed on Sat.

♥ Noodle Time, 10-11 Nelson Rd, SE10, T020-8293 5263. This is the best budget option, roomy, cheap and cheerful, where a generous bowl of noodles costs about £5. Open 7 days all day and evenings.

♥ Thai Chung, 8 Nelson Rd, SE10, T020-8858 8588. If Noodle Time is impossibly busy, this place is just next door, also doing Thai food, noodles, pad thai and Ho Fun. Open all day until 2330.

● Eating

Greenwich p278, map p280

♥♥ Inside, 19 Greenwich South St, T020- 8265 5060. A good bet for its acclaimed modern European fusion food in an unpromising location, lively and fun. The Sun brunch here is good value for £8-9.

Cafés and sandwich bars

Royal Teas, 76 Royal Hill, SE10, T020-8691 7240. From the places that open up specifically at the weekends, this place does excellent home-made meals, tea and coffee on a boutique-lined strip that's popular with the local intelligentsia.

Blackheath *p283*

¶¶ **Chapter Two**, 43/45 Montpelier Vale, Blackheath Village, SE3, T020-8333 2666, does imaginative modern British food in comfortable surroundings (for dinner £16.95 for two courses).

Cafés and sandwich bars

Village Delicatessen, 1/3 Tranquil Vale, SE3, T020-8852 2015. A local deli and café with superb freshly baked bread.

❶ Pubs and bars

Greenwich *p278, map p280*

Ashburnham Arms, 25 Ashburnham Grove, SE10, T020-8692 2007, off Greenwich South St. Slightly off the beaten tourist track and much more popular with the locals, good beer, bar billiards and a good-natured atmosphere.

Gipsy Moth, T020-8858 0786. Right on the dockfront near the Cutty Sark, and consequently usually heaving with tourists.

Richard I, 52 Royal Hill, SE10, T020-8692 2996. A good Young's pub with a beer garden, decent food lunchtimes and evenings and a largely appreciative local crowd.

Trafalgar Tavern, Park Row, SE10, T020- 8858 2909. Downstream, next to the Royal Naval College, a large historic pub with river views, often loud and busy on Fri and Sat, but a traditional retreat serving reasonable grub (especially good on fish) at other times.

The Wine Vaults, 165 Greenwich High Rd, SE10, T020-8858 7204. May be part of the Davy's chain, but are nonetheless authentic cellars with loyal staff and reasonable food.

The Yacht, 5 Crane St, SE10, T020-8858 0175. Rival to Trafalgar Tavern, tucked down an alleyway, the cosy old back bar overlooking the river and good guest ales.

Blackheath *p283*

Cave Austin, 79 Montpelier Vale, SE3, T020-8852 0492. A typical Blackheath-style bar.

The Hare and Billet, Hare and Billet Rd, SE3, T020-8852 2352. A very busy and popular local on the heath with pub grub.

Zerodegrees, 29-31 Montpelier Vale, SE3, T020-8852 5619. A microbrewery, light and modern, with a straightfoward modern European menu and long wine list.

❸ Entertainment

Greenwich *p278, map p280*

Southeast London has spawned some of the greatest music talent to have come out of the city – David Bowie was born in Bromley, the Rolling Stones grew up in the southeast and Dire Straits first came together there as a band. Strangely though, it lacks any really noteworthy venues.

Amersham Arms, 388 New Cross. Hosts a number of student bands, mainly of the punk and indie variety, benefiting from its proximity to Goldsmith's College.

Blackheath Concert Halls, 23 Lee Rd, SE3, T020 8463 0100. Stage the occasional show – politico folk legend Billy Bragg and top saxophonist Courtney Pine have played there in recent times – though such performances are infrequent.

Trafalgar Tavern (see above). The pub holds regular gigs for aspiring local acts (indie upstairs, jazz downstairs).

Cinema

Greenwich Cinema, 180 Greenwich High Rd, SE10, T01426-919020. 3-screen mainstream new releases.

Music

Classical and opera Blackheath Concert Halls (see above). Resident Orchestra of St John's. Very fashionable and lively concert halls.

Nightclubs

Up the Creek, 302 Creek Rd, SE10, T020-8858 4581. Quality comedy, dodgy cabaret and disco dancing till 0200 as well as very cheap food Fri-Sun. Tickets about £14.

Theatre

Greenwich Theatre, Croom's Hill, SE10, T020-8858 7755. Old-fashioned and much-loved theatre in a modern building that has

🍷 *For an explanation of sleeping and eating price codes used in this guide, see inside the* ● *front cover. Other relevant information is found in Essentials, see pages 44-46.*

been struggling to stave off closure, so far with some success. Hosts middle-scale touring productions.

⊛ Festivals and events

Greenwich *p278, map p280*
Greenwich Artists' Open Studios, on 2 weekends in **Jun**, T020-8692 3239

○ Shopping

Greenwich *p278, map p280*
Bullfrogs, 22 Greenwich Church St, T020-8305 2404. On the main drag, specializes in urban unisex clubwear and casual clothes, shoes and sunglasses.
Cheeseboard, 26 Royal Hill, Greenwich, SE10, T020-8305 0401. Award-winning cheeses and breads along with excellent service – an immaculate deli.
Church St Market, in the old covered market, full of craftsfolk peddling their handywork.
La Fleur, 18 Royal Hill, SE10, T020-8305 1772. A flower and gift shop with a tea garden.
Greenwich High Rd Market, where people flog their surplus consumer durables.
Greenwich Market, T020-7639 8659. Open at weekends, no longer excellent for antiques, riddled as it is with a fair amount of tat, but the odd gem may show up.
Halcyon Books, 1 Greenwich South St, T020-8305 2675. A large and rambling second-hand bookshop complete with small stools for weary browsers.

Spread Eagle Antiques, 9 Nevada St, SE10, T020-8305 1666. A reliable and long-standing destination.

Spread Eagle Books, 8 Nevada St. A junk shop on Greenwich South St.
The Village Market, on Stockwell St. Has the most jumble, junk and the odd rare record.

⚠ Activities

Greenwich *p278, map p280*
Docklands Sailing and Watersports Centre, Millwall Dock, Westferry Road, E14, T020-7537 2626. Open 0930-1130 Mon-Fri, 0930-1700 Sat and Sun. Dragon boat racing, sailing, rowing, canoeing.
Docklands Watersports Club, Gate 14, King George V Dock, Woolwich Manor Way, E16, T020- 7511 7000. Jet-skiing.
F1 City Racing, 199 Connaught Bridge, Royal Victoria, E16, T020-7476 5678. Open-air go-karting.
London Arena, Limeharbour, E14, T020-7538 8880. If it's spectator sport you're after then major London ice hockey and basket ball teams play their home games here.

❶ Directory

Greenwich *p278, map p280*
Greenwich Tourist Information Centre, 2 Cutty Sark Gardens, Greenwich, SE10, T0870-6082000.

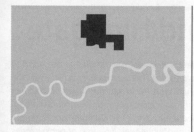

Hampstead and Highgate

Hampstead is a London high point. An affluent town astride the hills to the north, it competes in both elevation, social status and antique authenticity with the neighbouring hilltop village of Highgate. Although no longer the liberal, bohemian enclaves they once were, both remain strongly associated with their literary and cultural heritage. Blue plaques adorn many of the beautifully preserved Georgian and Victorian buildings, some of which are open to the public, while their labyrinth of narrow lanes and leafy picturesque streets are a joy to explore. Virginia Woolf, Andrew Marvell, Wordsworth, Coleridge, Dickens, DH Lawrence, John Constable, Gerard Manley Hopkins and Sigmund Freud are just a few of the greats who settled here.

Both places are also deservedly famous for the 800 or so acres of rolling grassland, lakes, meadows and woodland of Hampstead Heath that divides them. There's a distinctive 'villagey' feel to the area, passionately protected by the locals. Hampstead's two cinemas and clutch of theatres cater for the well-to-do artistic community that has long been at home here, while more recently it has also been adopted by a younger handful of celebrities and fashionable emigrants from West London. Highgate is often seen as the poor relation, but its famous cemetery and village atmosphere make it a rewarding destination on the more attractive eastern side of the heath. ▸▸ *For Sleeping, Eating and other listings see pages 294-296.*

History

Hampstead and Highgate, with commanding views over the Thames valley, have long been popular sites for human settlement. Tribes lived here in prehistoric times (they left a barrow on Parliament Hill), and the Roman road to St Albans ran across the heath through woodland brimming with deer, boars, wild cattle and wolves. By medieval times, the land was in the possession of the church.

Highgate grew around the gate to the Bishop of London's Hornsey Estate, and the Abbot of Westminster came to the heath to escape (unsuccessfully) the Black Death. Hampstead regularly featured as a place of refuge, with Londoners fleeing to its hillsides from real or imagined catastrophes – in 1524 to escape the predicted great floods, in the 1660s from the Great Plague and the Great Fire, and in 1736 for the end of the world.

When in 1700 its spring water was being sold in London's taverns, Hampstead's reputation for health and safety was confirmed. The village boomed – new lodging houses and taverns were built, bun and teashops lined the High Street, and Keats and Byron were part of a distinguished political and literary world. William Blake (who was imprisoned for debt following a well-intentioned attempt to establish a hospital for orphaned children in Highgate), was not so taken by the village, describing a "journey to Hampstead without due consideration" as "only for a soldier of Satan to perform."

He may have had a point. Until it was drained in 1777, the Vale of Health was a malarial swamp, known as Hatches Bottom. Highgate, on the other hand, was "a most pleasant dwelling" and also popular.

Aristocrats built huge piles (Arundel, Cromwell, Fitzroy and Lauderdale houses), merchants erected elegant townhouses, and morris-dancing and fairs were held on the green. Nevertheless, development was slow and by 1835 Hampstead was still little more than a large village. The Caen Wood (later Kenwood) Estate sprawled to the north, beyond the isolated Vale of Health, and Church Row was a genteel "avenue of Dutch red-faced houses" with St John's church at the end.

★ **Don't miss North London...**

1. **Hampstead Heath** Head up for a breezy walk on the heath: spectacular views from Parliament Hill and a great house to visit at Kenwood, page 289.
2. **Camden market** Have a rummage for a bargain: it's less expensive before the magic mushrooms take effect, page 299.
3. **Primrose Hill** Admire the cityscape before enjoying the shops and cafés of Regent's Park Road or a pub lunch on Gloucester Avenue, page 301.
4. **Islington** Clock into a play at one of the area's adventurous theatres, page 309.

A footpath over the fields and past the ponds led to Highgate, a smaller village radiating from the church. It was soon to open the cemetery which became a tourist attraction initially for its architecture and views over London, and latterly also for its residents (Karl Marx and Tom Sawyer, the last of the bare-fisted fighters whose funeral in 1865 drew 100,000 mourners). Urban expansion arrived in the 1880s, but the villages' "august respectability" remained. Highgate's grand houses became convalescence homes, and Hampstead drew more and more literary and political figures: including, over the years, Katherine Mansfield and Ramsay MacDonald, DH Lawrence and Harold Wilson, Mohammed Jinnah and Rabindranath Tagore. Sigmund Freud spent his last years in Hampstead, adding another element to its reputation. In the 1960s Doris Lessing described Hampstead as a world of "political intellectuals, reformers, therapists, feminists", a situation not wholly unrecognizable today.

North Hampstead & Highgate

Sights ⊖ *Belsize Park, Hampstead, Highgate.*

Hampstead Heath

From Hampstead tube, Heath Street heads sharply uphill towards Hampstead Heath, an oasis of uncultivated land where it is easy to forget the urban mayhem as one wanders leafy avenues, open fields and shaded woods. Divided roughly into **West Heath** and **East Heath**, West Heath stretches down towards Golders Green, while East Heath comprises the main body of the heath reaching towards Highgate. West Heath is notorious for its gay cruising scene but is also home to the lovely **Hill Garden**, which has a magical landscaped walkway through the woods. East Heath is more traversable, with walks to suit all ages. An especially good one is to **Kenwood House** near Highgate (see below) which is best begun from the avenue at the end of Well Walk and then through Kenwood Woods (between 30 minutes and an hour).

❣ *Highgate is best reached by bus. The tube is some way down the hill from the village near the Queen's Wood.*

Spectacular views of London can be found from the top of Parliament Hill, which is also a very popular place to fly kites. At the bottom of the hill, near the running track, is an Italian family-run café serving hot dishes and light snacks. There are three swimming ponds; mixed, ladies and men's, as well as an open-air **swimming pool** ① *T020-7485 4491, 0700 till dusk daily, free.* Die-hard aficionados swim here all year round, cracking the ice in winter for their daily dips. In the 18th century, the water in Hampstead was declared medicinal and a spa and bathhouse were built in Well Walk where there is still a fountain of drinking water. The Vale of Health is a secret cluster of highly desirable houses on the fringes of the Heath.

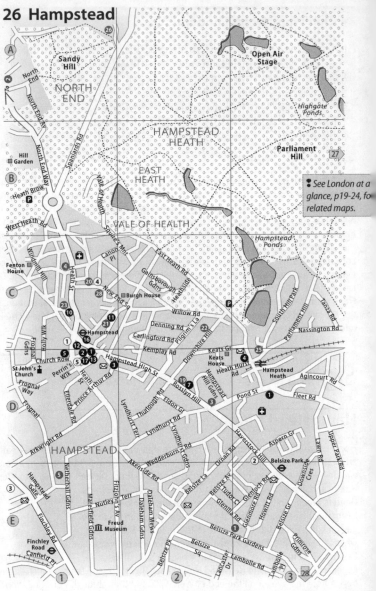

♣ See London at a glance, p19-24, fo related maps.

North Hampstead & Highgate

N

0 metres   200
0 yards   200

Sleeping 🛏
Belsize **1** E3
House **3** D2
La Gaffe **4** C1
Langorf **5** E1

YHA Hampstead **2** A1

Eating 🍴
Base **1** D1
Café Bianco **2** D1
Coffee Cup **3** D1
Cucina **4** D3
Dim T Café **5** D1
Giraffe **7** D2
Jin Kichi **10** C1
Le Cage Imaginaire **11** C1
Louis Patisserie **12** C1

Maison Blanc **13** D1
Toast **16** C1
Villa Bianca **17** D1
Zamoyski **1** D3

Pubs & bars 🍸
Bar Room Bar **19** D2
Duke of Hamilton **20** C1
Flask **21** C1
Freemasons' Arms **22** C2
Holly Bush **23** C1
Magdala **25** D3

Spaniards Inn **26** A1
Ye Olde White Bear **28** C1

Entertainment 🎭
Everyman **1** C1
Finchley Road
  Warner Village **3** E1
New End Theatre **4** C1
Pentameters **5** D1
Screen on the Hill **2** D3

Around Hampstead

Burgh House
ⓘ *New End Sq, NW3, T020-7431 0144. 1200-1700 Wed-Sun, free*. This genteel Queen Anne house was saved from the developers by local support. It now contains a small museum of local Hampstead history as well as changing exhibitions with a local flavour. Evening concerts and talks by famous residents are also often given here. The buttery in the basement serves light meals when the house is open.

Keats House
ⓘ *Wentworth Pl, Keats Grove, NW3, T020-7435 2062, Apr-Oct 1300-1700 Tue-Sun, Nov-Mar 1300-1600 Tue-Sun; adults £3, concessions £1.50, under-16s free but donations gratefully accepted.*
This is the little Regency house and garden where Keats penned his most famous poem, *Ode to a Nightingale*, under a plum tree while staying there in 1819. The house was saved and opened to the public in the 1920s largely thanks to the poet's American fans, and since being taken over by the Corporation of London in 1997 has undergone an extensive and ongoing refurbishment. Rooms display various items of Keats memorabilia, manuscripts and letters, while in the garden a mulberry tree survives from the Romantic poet's day.

Fenton House
ⓘ *Windmill Hill, Hampstead Grove, NW3, T020-7435 3471, Mar Sat, Sun 1400-1700, Apr-Oct Wed-Fri 1400-1700, Sat, Sun 1100-1700, adults £4.50, under-16s £2.25.*
This late 17th-century Merchant residence is a beautiful example of the smart houses once typical of Hampstead, containing a collection of early keyboard instruments (concerts are sometimes given) and porcelain with a lovely walled flower garden to stroll around. It's run by the National Trust.

2 Willow Road
ⓘ *T020-7435 6166, Apr-Oct Thu-Sat 1200-1630, Mar, Nov Sat 1200-1630, admission by guided tour only every hr, £4.50.*
This is a very fine example of modern domestic architecture designed and lived in by Erno Goldfinger from 1939, complete with artwork by Moore, Max Ernst, and Bridget Riley. Call for tour details, which include illuminating explanations of the architect's methods and rationale.

The Freud Museum
ⓘ *20 Maresfield Gardens, NW3, T020-7435 2002, Wed-Sun 1200-1700, adults £5, concessions £2, under-12s free.*
This is the Arts and Crafts house where the great psychoanalyst spent the last years of his life. The house has been preserved for posterity, now including a reconstruction of his study and consulting room, complete with the famous couch, and a surprising number of classical antiquities testifying to Freud's passionate interest in the ancient world. Upstairs there's a gallery devoted to exhibitions with some relevance to the great shrink as well as a display centred around his wife Anna's handloom and child therapy work.

St John's Churchyard
St John's Church, in Church Row, is the site of Constable's tomb. The churchyard offers a shady retreat if in need of relief from too much shopping or walking, with a peaceful secluded view over London. Church Row itself is one of the most beautiful avenues of elegant Georgian houses in the area, once home to the likes of HG Wells, and it remains a good spot for some nostalgic time travelling.

North Hampstead & Highgate

Around Highgate

Highgate Hill runs up from Archway and becomes the High Street of the old village. A left turn into South Grove leads to the top of the steep slope of Swain's Lane which runs downhill between Highgate Cemetery and Waterlow Park.

27 Highgate & Hampstead Heath

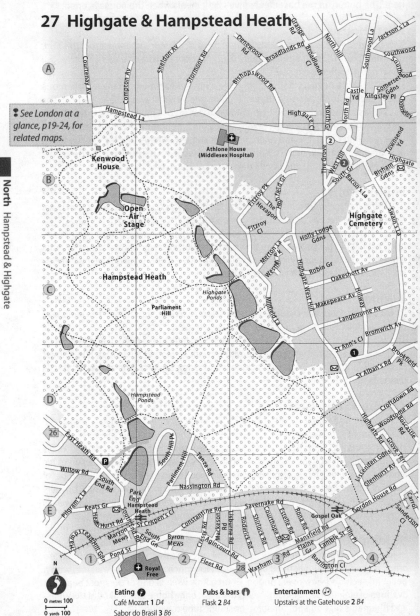

See London at a glance, p19-24, for related maps.

Eating 🍴
Café Mozart **1** *D4*
Sabor do Brasil **3** *B6*

Pubs & bars 🍺
Flask **2** *B4*

Entertainment 🎭
Upstairs at the Gatehouse **2** *B4*

North Hampstead & Highgate

Highgate Cemetery

① T020-8340 1834, Eastern cemetery: 1000-1600 Mon-Fri, 1100-1600 Sat, Sun; Western cemetery: Sat, Sun tours at 1100, 1200, 1300, 1400, 1500, Mar-Oct Mon-Fri also at 1400, tours cost £3.

Highgate Cemetery is most famous for being the burial place of **Karl Marx**, in the more modern eastern part of the cemetery; on its western side is also one of London's most extraordinary and atmospheric burial grounds. The western part is the most overgrown and now carefully protected by a society of friends who offer informative guided tours taking in the remarkable Egyptian catacombs, famous graves, monuments and an abundance of wild flowers. Both parts are sometimes closed to the public during funerals.

Waterlow Park

① T020-8348 8716, Tue-Sun 1100-1600.

Waterlow Park is one of the most attractive of north London's green spaces, with wooded walks, ponds and splendid views of London. In a secluded corner of the park stands **Lauderdale House**, a mid-17th century house that stages regular concerts, art exhibitions and theatre shows.

★ Kenwood House

① T020-8348 1286, Apr-Oct daily 1000-1700, Nov-Mar daily 1000-1600, free.

Highgate High Street ends at the top of the hill near the Gatehouse pub, from where Hampstead Lane leads round the north side of Hampstead Heath to Kenwood House. This 17th-century mansion renovated in 1760 by the architect Robert Adam, stands in the middle of the Heath in a glorious sweep of landscaped grounds looking down on a wide lake. The house and its delightful Adam rooms are open free to the public and hold a permanent display of European Art, bequeathed by its last owner, Lord Iveagh Guinness, including Gainsboroughs, Reynolds, Vermeers and van Dycks, as well as mounting temporary exhibitions (admission charged) on a variety of themes. The gardens and grounds are at their best in May when the explosion of colour from the rhododendron blossoms rivals a Las Vegas chorus line. Sculptures by the likes of Henry Moore and Barbara Hepworth are dotted around the park. The Brew House café and restaurant attached to the house offers delicious breakfasts, lunches and teas in the old coach house as well as outside in a peaceful walled garden. In the summer months delightful open-air concerts are given in the Kenwood Bowl to one side of the lake. Paid entrance guarantees a view of the orchestra but anyone can bring a picnic and settle on the meadow to enjoy the sound of the strings drifting across the lawns on a summer's evening, often finishing up with a firework display.

⊜ Sleeping

Hampstead *p288, maps p290 & 292*
A The House Hotel, 2 Rosslyn Hill, NW3, T020-7431 8000, www.thehousehotel.com. Refurbished small hotel at the foot of Rosslyn Hill, top of Haverstock Hill, near South End Green, with 27 quite large and very comfortable rooms, and a salubrious lounge, popular with artists recording at Air Studios over the road.
B La Gaffe, 107-111 Heath St, NW3, T020-7435 8965, www.lagaffe.co.uk. A small family-run hotel offering 18 cosy rooms in a period house with its own locally favoured Italian restaurant, AA and RAC graded.
B The Langorf Hotel and Self-Catering Apartments, 20-22 Frognal, NW3, T020-7794 4483. The hotel offers a variety of singles and doubles with an executive range available too. Given a 2-crown commendation. The apartments range from 1-2 beds at nightly and weekly rates.
D Belsize, 40 Belsize Park Gdns, NW3, T020-7722 8131, www.londonhostels.co.uk. Group rooms and doubles available at varying rates, just north of Camden and Primrose Hill.
E YHA Hampstead, 4 Wellgarth Rd, Golders Green, NW11, T0870 770 5846 (within UK), T+44-20 8458 9054 (outside UK), hampstead@yha.org.uk. £21, under-18s £18.50, a 3-star, 199-bed hostel just to the north of Hampstead Heath, popular with groups and anyone who wants to escape the crush in town.

❷ Eating

Hampstead *p288, maps p290 & 292*
♈ Le Cage Imaginaire, 16 Flask Walk, NW3, T020-7794 6674. An intimate cosy French restaurant tucked away in a little lane off the High St.
♈ Cucina, 45a South End Green, NW3, T020-7435 7814, south of the Heath. Has a champagne bar out front and a modern Italian menu served up behind in bright designer surrounds. Understandably very popular with locals.

♈ Jin Kichi, 73 Heath St, NW3, T020-7794 6158. This could well be the most esteemed Japanese restaurant in Hampstead, always busy with a varied and lively crowd. The walls here are decorated with autographs and praise for the place from famous customers that have dropped in for some reasonably priced delicacies, although all the tempting little treats inevitably add up.
♈ Toast, 50 Hampstead High St, NW3, T020-7431 2244. An unusually hip (for the area) restaurant and bar right above the tube station, with a brasserie menu featuring a mixture of modern British and Mediterranean dishes with an emphasis on fish. The fashionable set have already departed, but it remains popular with a young Hampstead crowd who don't baulk at the Mayfair tariff.
♈ Villa Bianca, 1 Perrins Court, NW3, T020-7435 3131. A long-established Italian restaurant with a small outside terrace for al fresco dining in the summer months.
♈ Zamoyski, 85 Fleet Rd, NW3, T020-7794 4792, in South End Green. A very different option, a lively but also charming Polish vodka bar and restaurant.
♈ Base, 71 Hampstead High St, NW3, T020-7431 2224. Offers a Mediterranean menu of a high standard in a tastefully decorated small dining room. At the front there is more of a deli/sandwich bar operation with outside pavement seating.
♈ Dim T Café, 3 Heath St, NW3, T020-7435 0024. A trendy dim sum café-style restaurant serving a variety of noodle-`based dishes and changing specials, its bright and cheerful design with Mao-emblazoned cushions encourage a laid-back atmosphere.
♈ Giraffe, 46 Rosslyn Hill, NW3, T020-7435 0348. A cheerful kid-friendly café/restaurant which serves great breakfasts, fresh juices and an interesting mix of dishes for lunch and dinner canteen style – long communal tables with a few more intimate tables for 2-4 people.

★ Five of the best cheap eats

- **Dim T Café**, Heath St, Hampstead, page 294.
- **Mango Rooms**, Kentish Town Rd, Camden, page 301.
- **Wagamama Camden**, Jamestown Rd, Camden, page 302.
- **The Afghan Kitchen**, Islington Green, Islington, page 308.
- **Gallipoli**, Upper St, Islington, page 308.

Cafés and sandwich bars

Café Bianco, 12 Perrins Ct, NW3, T020-7431 0363. Generously filled sandwiches in a tiny café with tables outside on a pleasant pedestrian walkway between the High St and Heath St. They also claim to do the best breakfasts in town.

The Coffee Cup, 74 Hampstead High St, NW3, T020-7435 7565. Another Hampstead institution that has staved off numerous threats of closure thanks to tireless petitions from local residents. The loyalty of its eccentric local clientele must be due more to nostalgia than the particularly good quality of the food or drink, although they do a mean hot chocolate. A people-watcher's haven with a good view of the High St poseurs from within its dark rather gloomy interior, or from the seats outside.

Louis Patisserie, 32 Heath St, NW3, T020-7435 9908. A distinctly Hampstead atmosphere prevails in Hungarian tea rooms where delicious cakes and patisseries are served in a genteel olde worlde style in elegant surroundings – at a price.

Maison Blanc, 62 Hampstead High St, NW3, T020-7431 8338. A superior French patisserie selling cakes, breads, sandwiches, quiches and an array of tempting confectionery with a tiny seating area.

Highgate *p292, map p292*

♦ **Sabor do Brasil**, 36 Highgate Hill, N19, T020-7263 9066. Run by an Englishman and his flamboyant Brazilian wife, a place that's a real pleasure to visit and where you get a warm welcome.

Cafés and sandwich bars

Café Mozart, Swains Lane. Great cakes although the staff could do with a spell at charm school.

Oshobasho, near the tube in Queens' Wood, T020-8444 1505. Excellent café, does decent veggie food and has a pleasant outside seating area.

♦ Pubs and bars

Hampstead *p288, maps p290 & 292*
A more rounded impression of Hampstead life can be found in its pubs.

Bar Room Bar, 48 Rosslyn Hill, NW3, T020-7431 8802. Part of a chain but a popular and busy hangout for the local youth that also does coffees, bar snacks and light lunches.

The Duke of Hamilton, New End, NW3, next door to the little New End Theatre. Caters to the pre- and post-show audience in a more sedate atmosphere.

The Flask, 14 Flask Walk, NW3, T020-7435 4580. One of the old peculiars hidden away in the backstreets, a characterful pub with a strong local flavour.

The Freemasons' Arms, Downshire Hill, NW3, T020-7433 6811, near the Heath. Large and impersonal, its huge garden comes into its own in the summer after a walk on the Heath.

The Holly Bush, 22 Holly Mt, NW3, T020-7435 2892. A timeless old pub with a real coal fire, much beloved by locals and visitors alike and beautifully maintained, in its own little square perched above Heath St. It can best be reached on foot up a flight of stone steps between 73 and 75 Heath St opposite the tube.

For an explanation of sleeping and eating price codes used in this guide, see inside the front cover. Other relevant information is found in Essentials, see pages 44-46.

Magdala, 2a South Hill Park, NW3, T020-7435 2503, near South End Green. An old pub which has been revamped with stripped pine and boasts an accomplished kitchen; food is their strong point.

Spaniard's Inn, perched on the edge of West Heath near Kenwood. A landmark highwayman's pub and the most famous pub in Hampstead with little dark rooms, a large beer garden and reasonable food.

Toast, 50 Hampstead High St, NW3, T020-7431 2244 (see above). Sometimes operates a door policy after 1800, aspires towards exclusivity but often admits anyone suitably dressed up. Oriental-style bar snacks are available here.

Ye Olde White Bear, New End, NW3, T020-7435 3758. A small and friendly old-fashioned establishment with a few tables outside on a narrow pavement strip and some superior pub grub.

Highgate *p292, map p292*
Flask, 77 Highgate West Hill, N6, T020-8340 7260. The warren of rooms and heated front garden overflows with a lively crowd every weekend.

❻ Entertainment

Hampstead *p288, maps p290 & 292*
Cinema
The Everyman Hampstead, 1 Hollybush Vale, Hampstead, NW3, T020-7431 1777. Famous local cinema that offers a mix of mainstream and repertory films in a luxurious space. Standard, deluxe and 'love seats' available. Bar and Sat morning kids' club.

Screen on the Hill, 203 Haverstock Hill, NW3, T020-7435 3366 (Belsize Park tube). Part of a small cinema group offering mainly arthouse films and often arranging talks by the director. Comfortable cinema with small bar area.

Music
Classical and opera Lauderdale House, T020-8348 8716. Regular concerts are given throughout the year.
Music on a Summer's Evening, at Kenwood Lakeside, T020-8233 5892 for details. Concert series on Sat during Jul and Aug.

Theatre
Hampstead Theatre, Avenue Rd, NW3, T020-7722 9301. Near Swiss Cottage tube, this recently revamped middle-scale theatre still has a strong reputation.

New End Theatre, 27 New End, NW3, T020-7794 0022. Small, intimate theatre with an interesting repertoire of new and established plays and attracting loyal audiences.

The Pentameters, Three Horseshoes Pub, 28 Heath St, NW3, T020-7435 3648. Small theatre space above the pub, well deserving of notice.

Upstairs at the Gatehouse, Hampstead Lane, N6, T020-8340 3488. Relatively large pub theatre with an interesting variety of visiting productions.

❺ Shopping

Hampstead *p288, maps p290 & 292*
The 2 main thoroughfares in Hampstead (the High St and Heath St) are lined with familiar stores and brand names. More interesting is **Flask Walk**, a small pedestrian alley off Hampstead High St (near the tube station) which preserves a quaint, timeless feel in all the shop fronts and has a wonderful second-hand bookshop.

Keith Fawkes, stuffed with books and infused with the aroma of musty pages.
Villa Fern, opposite. Established around 30 years ago, sells freshly ground coffees and a variety of interesting grocery gift items including a nostalgic selection of old- fashioned sweets still served out of glass jars.

Continuing down Flask Walk all the way to the bottom, you come to Well Walk.
Community Market, Hampstead High St, in the hall near the post office, at the weekend sells locally produced crafts as well as antiques and bric-a-brac. Tea and coffee, homemade cakes and snacks available.
Linea, in Perrins Court, sells designer clothes.
Well Walk Pottery, on the corner. Sells imaginative pottery and stained-glass items made by the owner who also runs short and long courses in both arts.

There are also a couple of second-hand designer clothes shops on the High St.

Camden

Camden is the axis around which north London spins. And a strange mixed-up place it is too, with its music and markets, its dirt, drugs, hard drinking and organic juice bars. The scruffy High Street teems with grungy indie kids, stylish bohos, raving drunks and bright young tourists, becoming almost impassable every weekend thanks to the crowds cramming into the markets. Meanwhile the Chalk Farm Road carries the High Street on northwest past the genteel slopes of Primrose Hill, a chichi celebrity hideout.

The markets are obviously Camden Town's main attraction, the city's weekly street festival, but the dubious charm of the area lies in the messy and animated job it makes of tying up all of north London's loose ends before they head into the centre of the city. It manages this with a formidable combination of loud music, Irish accents, plenty of booze and late opening hours. Take your courage in both hands and go with the flow. ►► *For Sleeping, Eating and other listings see pages 301-304.*

History

When the canons of St Paul's visited their manor at 'Cantelowes' in the 11th century, the nearby Primrose Hill was brimming with stags, bucks, boars and wild bulls; Elizabeth I cleared it for meadowland, and the abundance of primroses that subsequently grew here probably accounts for the hill's name. Cows grazed on the fine pastureland to the east around the manor, where the heavy clay soil prevented the sinking of wells or effective drainage. As a result, it wasn't until the end of the 18th century when the First Earl of Camden leased land for 1,400 houses that Camden Town began to show any signs of life. In the same year, 1791, the Veterinary College on College Street was the country's first training college in the field.

In 1804, however, little more than Camden itself was built up, and rural lanes criss-crossed hedged-in fields. Thomas Cubitt lent some time to building here before turning his attention to Belgravia in the 1820s, and Mornington Crescent went up in 1821. But it was the arrival of the Regent's Canal in the 1820s, and the railways after 1830 that sparked speedier changes.

Coal wharves and small industry sprang up along the canal, and a huge depot was built for the railway. For a while, carriages were hauled up and down the Camden Incline to Euston by cable, having been uncoupled at the depot, and used the Round House for turning. A tunnel was drilled through Primrose Hill to link up with Chalk Farm. Businesses moved in, and the area gained a reputation for manufacturing musical, astronomical and scientific instruments. Dickens, who lived briefly as a child in Bayham Street, observed in *Dombey & Son*: "Everywhere were bridges that led nowhere; Babel towers of chimney..., temporary wooden houses and ragged tenements".

In 1846, riots broke out between Irish and English navvies. Nevertheless, when Miss Frances Buss set up her school for girls in 1851 (later Camden School for Girls), despite finding the limits of their general knowledge to be "beyond belief", the area was still "thickly inhabited by professional men".

In time, the professionals moved out, and the new householders turned to renting out rooms to lodgers. The area earned a reputation as a haven for artists and writers that it retains to this day, most notably the Fitzroy Group (now known as the Camden Town Group), formed in 1911 by Walter Sickert from rented studios around Mornington Crescent. In the 1950s Dylan and Caitlin Thomas used to have rows in their caravan parked in a friend's garden (neighbours used to gather to listen), while

Primrose Hill is currently home to writers such as Martin Amis, Alan Bennett and Ian McEwan. A Greek Cypriot community settled here after the Second World War, during which a huge anti-aircraft battery sat on Primrose Hill.

Camden went down in the world in the 1960s, but its bohemian reputation earned it a revival that has seen a return of the professionals to the restored Victorian terraces, while the media and music industry continue to mythologize its new-found status.

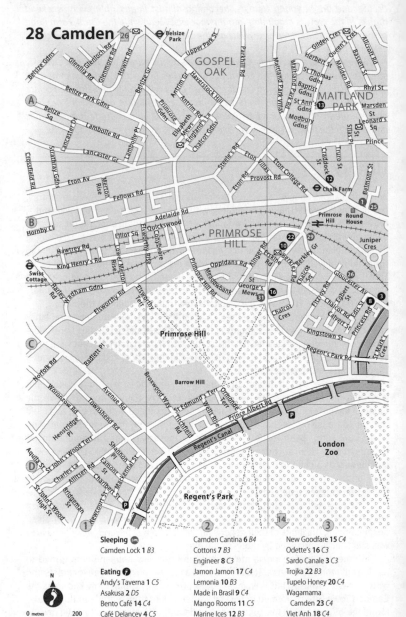

28 Camden

Sleeping 🛏
Camden Lock 1 *B3*

Eating 🍴
Andy's Taverna 1 *C5*
Asakusa 2 *D5*
Bento Café 14 *C4*
Café Delancey 4 *C5*
Camden Brasserie 5 *C4*

Camden Cantina 6 *B4*
Cottons 7 *B3*
Engineer 8 *C3*
Jamon Jamon 17 *C4*
Lemonia 10 *B3*
Made in Brasil 9 *C4*
Mango Rooms 11 *C5*
Marine Ices 12 *B3*
Monkey Chews 13 *A3*

New Goodfare 15 *C4*
Odette's 16 *C3*
Sardo Canale 3 *C3*
Trojka 22 *B3*
Tupelo Honey 20 *C4*
Wagamama
  Camden 23 *C4*
Viet Anh 18 *C4*

0 metres 200
0 yards 200

Sights ● *Camden Town, Chalk Farm, Mornington Crescent.* ● *See p460.*

★ Camden Market

ⓘ *T020-7284 2084, www.camdenlockmarket.com; Camden Market, High St, daily 0900-1730; Electric Ballroom, High St, 0900-1730 Sun; Camden Lock Market, Camden Lock Pl, off Chalk Farm Rd, daily 1000-1800 and indoor stalls Tue-Sat.*

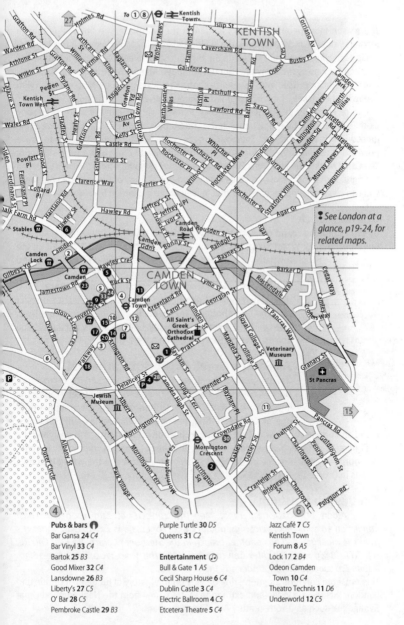

: See London at a glance, p19-24, for related maps.

North Camden

Pubs & bars ●
Bar Gansa **24** *C4*
Bar Vinyl **33** *C4*
Bartok **25** *B3*
Good Mixer **32** *C4*
Lansdowne **26** *B3*
Liberty's **27** *C5*
O' Bar **28** *C5*
Pembroke Castle **29** *B3*

Purple Turtle **30** *D5*
Queens **31** *C2*

Entertainment ●
Bull & Gate **1** *A5*
Cecil Sharp House **6** *C4*
Dublin Castle **3** *C4*
Electric Ballroom **4** *C5*
Etcetera Theatre **5** *C4*

Jazz Café **7** *C5*
Kentish Town
  Forum **8** *A5*
Lock 17 **2** *B4*
Odeon Camden
  Town **10** *C4*
Theatro Technis **11** *D6*
Underworld **12** *C5*

66 99 Walk along the canal towpath for a minute and you'll see the kind of mix of old and new, rich and poor, public and private that London specializes in...

The reason most people come to Camden in the first place, the 'market' (although markets would be more accurate), has ballooned from lowly beginnings into a series of stalls occupying any vacant space on the High Street between Camden Town tube and Camden Lock every Saturday and Sunday. Camden Market and the Electric Ballroom, and the High Street itself, with its outsize shop signs, are a pop kids' Mecca, awash with cheap leather jackets, brashly sloganed T-shirts and hectic drinking holes.

In recent years though, **Camden Lock Market**, with its array of more interesting clothes, jewellery, books and handicrafts, and **Stables Market** ① *Chalk Farm Rd, at the junction with Hartland Rd, T020-7485 5511*, with furniture and bric-a-brac, have provided satisfying browsing for those who do not wish to dress as if it were still 1966. The **Canal Market** runs off Chalk Farm Road, just over the bridge from the High Street on the right, with a mish-mash of stalls inside and out. If none of these tickle your fancy you can always plump for plain old fruit 'n' veg at the market on **Inverness Street**.

Camden Lock

By the High Road stand many of the original Grand Union buildings alongside the huge new Suffolk Wharf shop, restaurant and office development. Walk along the towpath for a minute and you'll see the kind of mix of old and new, rich and poor, public and private that London specializes in. Ridiculously expensive waterside condos back onto dilapidated railway bridges, and the area's gentrification doesn't stop the odd shopping trolley disfiguring the canal. From here, **The London Riverboat Company** operates trips regular via the Zoo as far as Little Venice (see page 43).

‡ Camden Town tube station becomes one-way into the area on Sat and Sun. To get out of the mayhem go to Chalk Farm or Mornington Crescent tubes, or take a very slow bus. Alternatively, there's Camden Rd train station on the North London Link.

All Saint's Greek Orthodox Cathedral

① *T020-7485 2149, 1000-1700 daily, Sun service 0930-1300.* On the corner of Camden Street and Pratt Street stands the imposing All Saint's Greek Orthodox Cathedral, a reminder of one of Camden's first immigrant communities. This charming grand and ornate church was built in 1822 by Inwood and son who also designed the St Pancras New Church. It was taken over by the Greek Orthodox community in 1948, appropriately enough since its design displays the influence of the young Inwood's travels in Greece.

The Jewish Museum

① *129 Albert St, T020-7284 1997, Mon-Thu 1000-1600, Sun 1000-1700 (last admission 30 mins before closing), adults £3.50, concessions £2.50/1.50, under 16s free. The museum also has another branch in the Sternberg Centre, 80 East End Rd, N3, T020-8349 1143, (Finchley Central tube), Mon-Thu 1030-1700, Sun 1030-16.30. Adults £2, concessions £1, under 16s free.*
This museum contains an interesting display on the history of Judaism in Britain and London, including a video and extraordinary treasures from the Nazi-bombed Great Synagogue such as a 16th-century Arc of the Covenant.

⁑ A bit of rough

Camden Town has long had an attraction for artists and bohemian types, due to its rough and ready image and the availability of cheap housing and spacious commercial premises.

The reason Camden was cheap was the large Irish immigrant population, who had something of an undesirable reputation for drunk and disorderly behaviour. The old saying, 'Camden Town for the rough lie down' is a reference to their supposed habit of sleeping in the streets after the pubs closed and the fighting stopped.

★ Primrose Hill

A few minutes' walk from the High Street, or best reached directly over the railway bridge from Chalk Farm tube, the pretty village here could hardly be more different from its raving eastern neighbour. The hill itself affords magnificent vistas over central London, Essex and Kent beyond. The London Eye in the distance makes a striking addition to one of the city's greatest views, which was much marred in the 1960s by a series of thoughtless housing projects.

◉ Sleeping

Camden *p297, map p298*

A Thistle Euston, Cardinton St, NW1, T020-7387 4400, www.thistlehotels.com (see map p188). A lack of accommodation in this bracket might tempt the comfort-hungry nearer to Euston, with all the big-chain perks.

C The Camden Lock Hotel, 89 Chalk Farm Rd, NW1, T020-7267 3912, www.camdenlockhotel.co.uk. Despite looking like a motel somewhere off a motorway in the Midlands, this is a safe, clean bet for those wishing to stay in the middle of Camden.

C Ibis Euston, 3 Cardington St, NW1, T020-7388 7777, www.ibishotel.com (see map p188). Cheap(ish) and cheerful branch of the budget chain convenient for the delights of Camden High Rd.

❼ Eating

Camden *p297, map p298*

₮₮₮ Café Delancey, 3 Delancey St, NW1, T020-7387 1985. An old-timer still delivering the goods, with tables outside and inside. The kind of place where just about anyone can feel at ease.

₮₮ Bento Café, 9 Parkway, NW1 T020-7482 3990. Nearer the tube and a surprisingly cosy example of its type, this is a good value Japanese noodle and sushi restaurant.

₮₮ Camden Brasserie, 216 Camden High St, NW1, T020-7482 2114. The other old-timer, has changed little since 1983, when it was one of the newly fashionable area's first brasserie-style eateries; a 3-course Frenchified meal with good wine can be had here for little over £20, in busy and convivial surroundings (needs to be booked Fri and Sat).

₮₮ Camden Cantina, 34 Chalk Farm Rd, T020-7267 2780. Offers fairly cheap and cheerful but very tasty Tex-Mex in garish and lively premises near Camden Lock

₮₮ Cottons, 55 Chalk Farm Rd, NW1, T020-7485 8388. Smaller, louder, more laid-back and less expensive than *Mango Rooms*, this is another more thoroughly Jamaican rum shop and restaurant, goat curry a speciality.

₮₮ Mango Rooms, 10 Kentish Town Rd, NW1, T020-7482 5065. A super-cool and very popular venue for some West Indian tucker in low-lit surroundings, serving up some excellent fish recipes.

₮ Andy's Taverna, 81 Bayham St, NW1, T020-7485 9718. A Greek Cypriot taverna with a jolly atmosphere and a fine way with its fresh ingredients.

₮ Asakusa, 256 Eversholt St, NW1, T020-7388 8533, near Mornington Cres. Another very good value Japanese restaurant and always needs to be booked at weekends, its low prices and lively atmosphere ensuring its continuing popularity.

Jamon Jamon, 38 Parkway, NW1, T020-7284 0606. Some fairly reliable Spanish food and tapas can be found here, each dish costs between £3 and £5.

Made in Brasil, 12 Inverness St, NW1, T020-7482 0777. Features a live parrot, cachacaria cocktail bar, a cheerful atmosphere and the likes of fish stew with a coconut sauce for about £12.50 (starters £5).

Marine Ices, 8 Haverstock Hill, NW3, T020-7485 3132. An utterly genuine Italian restaurant and ice-cream parlour that has been serving up the very best sweet and savoury dishes since 1946; a North London institution.

Viet Anh, 41 Parkway, NW1, T020-7284 4082. A very popular and superbly competent Vietnamese joint.

Wagamama Camden, 11 Jamestown Rd, NW1, T020-7428 0800, in the new Glass House development. Provides the kind of efficient Japanese canteen food that helped kick start the cuisine's reputation in London.

Cafés and sandwich bars
New Goodfare Restaurant, 26 Parkway, NW1, T020-7485 2230. A defiantly traditional café that serves up good, simple Italian and British snacks and light meals at low prices.
Tupelo Honey, Parkway, NW1, T020-7284 2989, over the road. Very different in style, named after a Van Morrison song and with similar charm, candlelit in the evenings. A laid-back and contemporary haven on 2 floors for some fine homebaked recipes (£8 vegetarian, £9 meat, including salad).

★ **Primrose Hill** *p301*
Odette's, 130 Regent's Park Rd, NW1, T020-7586 5486. This is the star, a locally patronized shrine to modern British cookery that definitely needs to be booked. Three different rooms of varying sizes create different moods (the French mirrored one is wonderful), while impeccable service promotes an appreciative atmosphere.
Sardo Canale, 42 Gloucester Av, NW1, T020-7722 2800. A newish branch of the excellent Warren St Sardinian restaurant,

occupying a swish new development on the canal. Worth booking for some elegantly prepared and presented rustic Italian specialities.

The Engineer, 65 Gloucester Av, NW1, T020-7722 0950. This popular gastropub is a labyrinthine establishment with an outside dining yard offering superior versions of global cuisine (check out the very meaty burgers). In the evenings the food is more adventurous, blending various Mediterranean styles.

The Lansdowne (see Pubs below). As much of a pub as a restaurant but the food is superb and the place has a lively buzz. The restaurant upstairs is marginally quieter and more formal.

Lemonia, 89 Regent's Park Rd, NW1, T020-7586 7454, also on Primrose Hill's charming main street. A Greek version of an American diner offering an extensive range of Aegean classics in bustling and convivial surroundings.

Monkey Chews, 2 Queen's Cres, NW5, T020-7267 6406. Further afield, cheaper and considerably more offbeat than either *The Lansdowne* or *Lemonia*, this is a bizarre mixture of arty pub, decent fish restaurant and music bar, worth seeking out for its independent spirit.

Cafés and sandwich bars
Trojka 101 Regent's Park Rd, NW1, T020-7483 3765. Reasonable value and also worth checking out for being one of London's few Russian and Polish tea rooms.

♦ Pubs and bars

Camden *p297, map p298*
Camden boasts a bewildering range of drinking options. Every evening the whole place seems to be loudly drowning its sorrows with a vengeance. Many of the older pubs are better avoided later in the night, but thankfully there are plenty of alternatives.
Bar Gansa, 2 Inverness St, NW1, T020-7267 8909. A self-consciously cool drinking-den still favoured by the young and beautiful, but not by those who want to talk over a quiet beer: the music in the evenings can be deafening.

● *For an explanation of sleeping and eating price codes used in this guide, see inside the*
● *front cover. Other relevant information is found in Essentials, see pages 44-46.*

★ Five of the best pubs for outdoor drinking

- **The Flask**, Highgate West Hill, Highgate, page 295.
- **The Engineer**, Gloucester Avenue, Camden, page 302.
- **Camden Head**, Camden Walk, Islington, page 309.
- **The Albion**, Thornhill Rd, Islington, page 309.
- **Duke of Cambridge**, St Peter's St, Islington, page 309.

Bar Vinyl, 6 Inverness St, NW1, T020-7681 7898. One of the pioneers of the concept of DJ-driven drinking.

Bartok, 78-79 Chalk Farm Rd, NW1, T020-7916 0595. Marginally more civilized, its 30-something Ikea-style décor just about forgiveable because it specializes in modern classical music, a rare treat in Camden. A chilled place to sit and talk to friends.

The Good Mixer, 30 Inverness St, NW1, T020-7916 7929. Usually lives up to its name, originally a down-beat Irish boozer that gained international fame during the mid-90s Britpop explosion. Those heady days are over, and now it's a marginally quieter place.

Liberty's, 100 Camden High St, NW1, T020-7485 4019. Features the stripped wooden floors of modern Camden, but has retained just enough custom from its previous incarnation as an Irish boozer to provide a mixed and interesting crowd.

O'Bar, 111-113 Camden High St, NW1, T020-7911 0667. A good place to go with a large group at weekends and enjoy cheap and cheerful cocktail fun.

The Purple Turtle, 61/65 Crowndale Rd, NW1, T020-7383 4976. An expansive joint that, like its nation-wide counterparts, caters for a boisterous crowd of students and other committed drinkers.

Primrose Hill *p301*

Lansdowne, 90 Gloucester Av, NW1, T020-7483 0409. A genteel gastropub that provides a welcome break from all the loud music and shouting on Camden High St.

Pembroke Castle, 150 Gloucester Av, NW1, T020-7483 2927. A large and relatively lively pub for the area, favoured by younger locals.

Queens, 49 Regent's Park Rd, NW1, T020-7586 0408. A friendly Aussie-run corner pub on Primrose Hill's main street with a balcony giving onto the park and a thoroughly competent kitchen.

⊙ Entertainment

Camden *p297, map p298*

Cinema

Odeon Camden Town, Parkway, NW1, T0870-5050007. Mainstream multiscreen.

Phoenix, High Rd, East Finchley, N2, T020-8883 2233, bookings T020-8444 6789. Nearest tube East Finchley, a short haul from Camden. One of London's last remaining single-screen reps.

Music

Rock, folk and jazz The Camden scene was especially potent throughout the early 80s and 90s when it gained its reputation as the hangout of the likes of Madness (who often played at the Dublin Castle), and then a decade later as the creative centre of the Britpop explosion. Britpop has long been dead, but Camden retains its reputation for being a launchpad for undiscovered talent, though still mainly of the Indie variety.

The Bull & Gate, 389 Kentish Town Rd, NW5, T020-7485 5358. Gigs 2030-2300 Mon-Sat, 2030-2230 Sun, £2-5. One of the city's top pub venues and regularly presents 3 bands at a time for a very modest sum. The chances of ever having heard of/hearing of any of them again is, of course, minimal, though it is a renowned haunt of the A&R industry.

Cecil Sharp House, 2 Regent's Park Rd, NW1, T020-7485 2206. Open at 1900, nights vary, £3-6. Traditional folk, undiluted, the Cecil Sharp is a leader in an otherwise under-represented field and involves nigh-on mandatory audience participation.

Dublin Castle, 94 Parkway, NW1, T020-7485 1773. In many ways the epitome of the Camden pub scene. Dim and dingy, the Castle gives a platform to aspiring bands who all tend to churn out raucous indie rock. Admission is on the door and the back room is in no way large, so be prepared to be

North Camden Listings

disappointed if one of the acts has conned all its mates into turning up.

The Electric Ballroom, 184 Camden High St, NW1, T020-7485 9006. Long-established venue for young folk with guitars on the verge of greatness.

The Jazz Café, 3 Parkway, NW1, T020-79166060. Well-established venue specializing in modern jazz, with a hint of blues, soul and hip-hop, world, funk and folk music, as well as its jazz staple, and the acts are always of a decent standard. It often pulls in the big names and the atmosphere is relaxed and enjoyable. Slightly awkward positioning of the bar can make it a hassle to gain refreshment while an act is on stage but this is a minor quibble about a fine venue providing first-rate entertainment.

Kentish Town Forum, 9-17 Highgate Rd, NW5, T020-7344 0044. Excellent mid-sized rock venue, and flagship of the Mean Fiddler chain. Undoubtedly one of the best venues in London. Despite its size, the demarcation between the front and back of the hall makes for an intimate connection between band and audience. The bar facilities are excellent and should hunger get the better of you there is even a small food counter. Most now-famous bands (Radiohead, Blur, etc) have played here before hitting the really big time. Good acoustics and an enthusiastic crowd.

Lock 17, Middle Yard, off Camden Lock, NW1, T020-7267 1577. Tables and seating can prove obstructive and it is more at home hosting the Jongleurs comedy nights at the weekend. You can get very close to the performers though, who are more often than not largish indie bands.

Theatre

The Etcetera Theatre Club, Camden High St, NW1, T020-7482 4857. Located above a busy pub with a beer garden (the Oxford Arms), the productions here frequently showcase new writing with its finger on the pulse.

Theatro Technis, 26 Crowndale Rd, NW1, T020-7387 6617. A surprisingly roomy fringe theatre specializing in Greek classics and contemporary political issues.

○ Shopping

Camden *p297, map p298*

It goes without saying that the markets are the thing here, but if you want to avoid the standard second-hand and cheap clothing stalls, it's best to head for **Camden Lock** which is choc-full of jewellers, antiques, boutiques and ethnocraft.

Afghan, Persian and Turkman Rugs, East Yard, T020-7482 4355. Open Tue-Sun 1000-1800, has a better quality range than many of the stalls.

Blackgull Bookshop and Bindery, East Yard, T020-8740 0713. Open Tue-Sun 1000-1800, is an excellent place to pick up a cheap fictional or academic read.

Kaleido, East Yard. Open Tue-Sun, 1000-1800, for exciting modern jewellery among much of the prevailing tat.

Stables Market, at the junction of Chalk Farm and Hartland rds. Open weekends, 0800-1800, offers an array of household accessories and furniture for those who like a bit of kitsch in their abode.

Elsewhere

LA1, 17 Chalk Farm Rd, NW1, T020-7267 2228. Designer labels for the young, beautiful and not too short of cash.

GB, 61 Parkway, NW1, T020-7485 5354. Walks the tightrope between cool and traditional, a well-established gentleman's clothier for every soon-to-be-dad in North London.

Music & Video, 281 Camden High St, NW1, T020-7267 0123. Stock some decent soul, funk and jazz but their main shop is over the road at **Music & Video Exchange**, 229 Camden High St, T020-7267 1898, open daily 1000-2000, both being branches of the Notting Hill-based store, good for vintage vinyl as well as cheap CDs and vids.

Walden Books, 38 Harmood St, NW1, T020-7267 8146. An excellent second-hand bookshop away from the crowds.

Islington

Sitting on a low hilltop northwest of the City and east of King's Cross, Islington likes to think of itself – with some justification – as the left-wing Notting Hill of north London. Its transformation over the last 20 years into the fashionable stamping ground of the liberal middle classes has not always been entirely happy though. It remains one of London's most socially deprived and densely populated boroughs, although either side of Upper Street, among the genteel Georgian and Victorian estates of Canonbury and Barnsbury – formerly home to Prime Minister Tony Blair – you'd hardly know it. More confident than ever now since being credited with nurturing the political ideals of New Labour, Islington rewards visitors not with its sights but with a welcoming attitude (although surprisingly few hotels or guest houses), a wide array of ethnic restaurants, old pubs and fashionable bars, a thriving theatre and music scene, and two excellent small markets. The antique shops in Camden Passage have long been a major attraction, while Chapel Market is a thriving local street market and increasingly hot nightspot. Friday and Saturday night excitement in Islington can be just as mad, bad and dangerous-to-know as anywhere in the West End. ▶▶ *For Sleeping, Eating and other listings see pages 308-310.*

History

Although it wasn't until the late 18th century that Islington began to show signs of developing as a suburb of London, a church has stood here since the 14th century. The manors of Barnsbury, Canonbury and Highbury lie to the north, set among fields and fine grazing meadows, where young bucks would come to the fields to practice archery. Henry VIII kept mistresses in Newington Green and hunted nearby, while elegant mansions with fine gardens and orchards dotted the landscape (Sir Walter Raleigh lived on Upper Street). Canonbury Tower stood proudly by the Priory, the manor house surrounded by rich dairy fields, and with Barnsbury Manor up on the hill.

Although Londoners took refuge in the fields around Islington during the turbulent years of the Great Plague and the Great Fire, it was only during the 18th century that it became popular. It earned a reputation for its duck shooting, cakes and cream (there were several dairies in the area) and its tea-gardens and spa. Pleasant walks were taken to Canonbury at the weekend, or trips to see 'Bruising Peg', the female boxer, do battle at Mr Stokes' Amphitheatre. Further north, at the Highbury Barn, Willoughby's bowling green and tea-garden attracted large crowds. Closer to the city, Copenhagen House began as a ninepins and skittles venue, but turned to bulldog fights and bull-baiting when a certain Mr Tooth became the landlord. Proprietors of pleasure gardens employed foot guards to escort visitors back to London from the Angel Inn, where reputedly Thomas Paine penned some of the *Rights of Man*.

The developers followed the crowds. Upper Street was lined by houses by 1735, Colebrooke Row 30 years later, Liverpool Street grew from a short terrace after 1790s, and Canonbury Square and Compton Terrace around the turn of the 19th century. Landowners established brickfields on their estates. Developments along Liverpool Street into Barnsbury went up in the 1820s (Cubitt built Manchester Terrace), and the London Fever Hospital moved here in 1848. Canonbury displayed fine villas, and was earning a reputation as a pretty suburb.

Nevertheless, by the 1830s, all the roads out of Islington still opened onto fields, nurseries and market gardens. When the Regent's Canal ducked under Islington through a long tunnel, its arrival, and that of the railway, attracted some small industries, but smart shops still lined the High Street, and theatres and music halls,

29 Islington

See London at a glance, p19-24, for related maps.

North Islington

0 metres 100
0 yards 100

N

Sleeping 🛏

Hilton London
 Islington 1 *D2*
Jurys London Inn 2 *E1*
Kandara Guest
 House 3 *C3*

Eating 🍴

Afghan Kitchen 1 *D2*
Casale Franco 4 *C2*
Gallipoli 6 *D2*
Gallipoli Again 7 *D2*
La Porchetta 10 *C2*
Le Mercury 11 *C2*
Lola's 2 *E2*
Pasha 13 *C2*
Portofino 14 *D2*
Strada 16 *D2*
Trattoria Aquitino 17 *D2*

Pubs & bars 🍺

Albion 19 *C1*
Bierodrome 20 *C2*
Camden Head 21 *D2*
Cuba Libre 24 *D2*
Duke of Cambridge 25 *E3*
Island Queen 26 *E3*
Medicine Bar 28 *C2*

Entertainment 🎭

Almeida 1 *C2*
Elbow Room 3 *E1*
Electrowerkz 2 *E2*

Garage 4 *B2*
Hen & Chickens 5 *B2*
Holloway Odeon 11 *A1*
Hope 6 *B2*
King's Head 7 *D2*
Little Angel 8 *D2*
Old Red Lion 9 *E2*
Pleasance
 Theatre 14 *A1*
Rosemary Branch 10 *C3*
Screen on the
 Green 12 *D2*
Tower Theatre 13 *B3*

such as the Collin's, drew the crowds. The'Leviathan' at Highbury Barns could boast the gymnast Leotard, the highwire artist Blondin, and the original Siamese Twins. Slums also developed and by the beginning of the 20th century, Barnsbury and Islington were declining in popularity. Absentee landlords and small tenancies meant that the fabric decayed, and after it suffered severe damage during the the Second World War, many streets gave way to modern council housing estates. Islington regained popularity with the media and entertainment set in the 1960s, a desirability that remains intact in and around areas such as the Cloudesley Estate and Canonbury.

Sights ⊖ *Angel, Highbury and Islington.* ● *See p460.*

Angel tube deposits passengers on Upper Street, Islington's main drag, at the junction of St John Street coming all the way up from Clerkenwell, the City Road from Shoreditch, and the Pentonville Road coming up from King's Cross. Most of the action in Islington takes place here and in the streets immediately around, including Chapel Market. Take a right turn out of the tube station and Upper Street forks almost immediately where the toll gate of the Great North Road once stood. Liverpool Road heads off left, and Upper Street carries on for almost a mile to Highbury Corner and Highbury and Islington tube. Islington High Street is no more than a quaint pedestrianized stretch off Duncan Street. On the right, just beyond the Duke of York pub, the little High Street ends up in **Camden Passage**, running parallel to Upper Street for a short distance, lined with enticing antique shops and restaurants and hosting a bric-a-brac market on Wednesdays (see Shopping on page 310). At the end, where the Essex Road meets Upper Street, **Islington Green** is a triangular garden that only really comes into its own during the Islington Festival when it often provides space for stalls and a fairground. The statue on the junction commemorates Hugh Myddelton, a Welsh goldsmith who brought fresh water into the city with his construction of the New River in 1613.

On the other side of Upper Street stands the **Business Design Centre** ① *To20-7359 3535*, on the site of the old Royal Agricultural Hall built in the mid-19th century. The enormous 'Aggie' became North London's most prestigious exhibition hall and Royal ballroom before winding up as a Royal Mail parcel office by 1971. Some of its former glory can still be appreciated from the Liverpool Road. The mock-crystal palace of the Business Design Centre now also holds huge trade fairs and art shows.

Further along Upper Street, the 18th-century tower of **St Mary's** survived the Second World War bombing and now stands opposite the crumbly old **King's Head Theatre Pub**, where Dan Crawford almost single-handedly established North London's booming fringe theatre scene in the 1970s and still insists that his till tells its prices in pounds, shillings and pence.

Behind the church is the **Little Angel Puppet Theatre**, and on the left beyond the pub, the **Almeida**, London's most star-studded medium-scale theatre, freshly refurbished, occupies the old Islington Literary and Scientific Institute built in 1837.

Past Islington Town Hall on the right, home to the **Islington Museum Gallery** ① *To20-7354 9442*, a small local museum, the imposing presence of Cubitt's **Union Chapel** ① *To20-7226 3750, recorded information line To20-7226 1686*, dominates the east side of the street. Formerly a Congregational chapel containing a fragment of the rock on which the Pilgrim Fathers landed, it has been semi-converted into a performance venue for all manner of different events, including a flamenco club, theatre, art shows and music in its echoing auditorium and studio theatre. Opposite is the **Hope and Anchor pub**, one of the places that punk rock was born and still a thriving live indie music venue.

North Islington

East of Upper Street lies Canonbury, best appreciated by a visit to the **Estorick Collection of Modern Italian Art** ① *39 Canonbury Sq (entrance on Canonbury Rd), T020-7704 9522, www.estorickcollection.com, Wed-Sat 1100-1800, Sun 1200-1700, adults £3.50, concessions £2.50*, not least for a good opportunity to take a look inside a fine Georgian house and enjoy some good food from the café indoors or out. The intriguing permanent collection of Italian art here, featuring an especially strong selection of Futurist work, is often complemented by contemporary exhibitions.

Nearby, **Canonbury Tower** ① *Canonbury Pl*, is an Elizabethan building dating back to Roman times, supposedly on a site of considerable pagan significance. Famous tenants down the ages have included Sir Francis Bacon, Oliver Goldsmith and Washington Irving, and since 1952 the amateur Tavistock Rep theatre company have been staging plays in the little theatre.

Stoke Newington

Essex Road leads on to Newington Green and eventually to Stoke Newington, where 18th-century Church Street is still recognizably a village high street. Daniel 'Robinson Crusoe' Defoe was educated here, and today the street is lined with a surprising number of good-value restaurants, shops and lively pubs, including the original south Indian vegetarian **Rasa** (now also in the West End), a popular Thai restaurant called **Yum Yums**, and the **Anglo-Anatolian**, a cosy Turkish barbecue restaurant.

◉ Sleeping

Islington *p305, map p306*

A **Hilton London Islington**, 53 Upper St, N1, T020-7354 7700, www.islington.hilton.com. Large chain hotel bang next to the Business Design Centre. About £160 for a double room.

A **Jurys London Inn**, 60 Pentonville Rd, N1, T020-7282 5500, www.jurys-london-hotels. com. Another large chain hotel, clean and safe, at the top of the hill above King's Cross, close to Angel tube. About £110 for a double.

C **Kandara Guest House**, 68 Ockenden Rd, N1, T020-7226 5721, www.kandara.co.uk. 11 rooms with shared bathrooms, basic but clean and quiet, full English breakfast included, non-smoking. £59 per night.

❶ Eating

Islington *p305, map p306*

¶¶¶ **Lola's**, 359 Upper St, N1, T020-7359 1932, above the smart Mall antiques arcade. An exceptionally assured modern British and continental menu, from steak and chips to liver and chestnut squeak, in a very Islington atmosphere, at a fair price.

¶¶ **Casale Franco**, 134-137 Upper St, N1, T020-7226 8994. A popular and bustling ristorante pizzeria tucked away off Upper St.

¶¶ **Pasha**, 301 Upper St, N1, T020-7226 1454. Does superior Turkish cuisine in a restrained

and formal atmosphere and can be excellent value for money.

¶¶ **Ristorante Portofino**, 39 Camden Passage, T020-7226 0884. A favourite with Italian ex-pats and locals alike.

¶ **The Afghan Kitchen**, 35 Islington Green, N1, T020-7359 8019. A fine little place for some café-style Afghan home cooking. Items such as *Suhzi Gosht* (lamb with spinach), or *Bonjan-e-Barani* (aubergines with yoghurt), both for £5 and also some good value French wine. Closed Sun and Mon.

¶ **Gallipoli**, 102 Upper St, N1, T020-7359 0630. A Turkish café-restaurant that has braved its unfortunate name to the extent that it has also opened **Gallipoli Again**, 120 Upper St, N1, T020-7359 1578, both good-value venues for salads and some meaty Turkish staples, the former with tables outside, the latter more cosy.

¶ **Le Mercury**, 140a Upper St, N1, T020-7354 4088. An Islington institution on the corner of Almeida St, a French restaurant where the low prices and busy atmosphere are more important than any kind of French food snobbery.

¶ **La Porchetta**, 141-142 Upper St, N1, T020-7288 2488. A very popular branch of the phenomenally successful Stroud Green pizzeria with a clean-cut, bright look.

¶ **Strada**, 105-106 Upper St, N1, T020-7226 9742. This branch of the sleek modern Italian pizzeria chain doesn't accept reservations but offers a pager service to let diners know when a table is free (it's not always that packed out though) for the enjoyment of their wood-fired flatbreads.

¶ **Trattoria Aquilino**, 31 Camden Passage, T020-7226 5454. This is a much more traditional little restaurant where regulars and visitors alike are fussed over until they feel at home with the straightforward presentation of some hearty Italian staples.

Stoke Newington *p308*
¶¶ **Mesclun**, Stoke Newington Church St, T020-7249 5029. A small Anglo-French restaurant that always requires booking at the weekends, such is its reputation.

⊕ Pubs and bars

Islington *p305, map p306*
At weekends, the pubs and bars on Upper St are most people's reason for being there; quite a few stay open after 2300. The more vibrant places tend to be a little way away from Angel tube, either on Upper St beyond the Business Design Centre or on Chapel Market.

Bierodrome, 173-174 Upper St, N1, T020-7226 5835, www.belgo-restaurants.com. A much-hyped and seriously designer bar concept. Part of the Belgo group, and regularly jumps until midnight.

Camden Head, Camden Walk, N1, T020-7359 0851. One of the few regular old pubs worth checking out near Upper St, has a pleasant outside drinking area and almost unreconstructed Victorian interior. The Kinks made a name for themselves here.

Cuba Libre, 72 Upper St, N1, T020-7354 9998. A loud, cheery and late-night restaurant and bar with a vaguely Cuban theme (£3 on the door after 2230 on Fri, Sat).

The Medicine Bar, 181 Upper St, N1, T020-7704 9536. £4 after 2200 on Fri and Sat, dark, has scruffy and comfortable decor, a refreshing change from over-designed music bars.

Just about within walking distance of Upper St, several pubs rather than bars are particularly worth seeking out.

The Albion, 10 Thornhill Rd, N1, T020-7607 7450. Flower-bedecked frontage, benches outside and cosy country-pub interior, a favourite, very Barnsbury local.

Island Queen, 87 Noel Rd, N1, T020-7704 7631. Nautical decor, excellent little pool room and hot food at lunchtimes. Was once one of playwright Joe Orton's favourites.

A pleasant walk can be taken back towards the Angel tube along the Regent's Canal towpath, past the City Rd Basin.

Duke of Cambridge, 30 St Peter's St, N1, T020-7359 3066. An excellent quite expensive organic (even the wines and beers) gastropub that has become very popular with the locals, partly because of its outdoor drinking and dining opportunities in a quiet part of the area.

☺ Entertainment

Islington *p305, map p306*
Cinema
Holloway Odeon, 417 Holloway Rd, N7, T0870-5050 007. Mainstream multiscreen.

Screen on the Green, 83 Upper St, N1, T020-7226 3520. Single-screen fashionable arthouse and mainstream.

Music
Rock, folk and jazz **Electrowerkz**, 7 Torrens St, Islington, N1 T020-7837 6419. Fairly spacious warehouse place that's popular with Goths but not exclusively so.

The Garage, 20-22 Highbury Corner, N5, T020-8963 0940. Mean Fiddler outfit: live bands famous, infamous and unknown almost every night.

The Hope, 207 Upper St, N1, T020-7354 1312. Live bands in a bricky basement almost every night beneath an animated old pub.

Nightclubs
Elbow Room, Chapel Market, N1, T020-7278 3244. Open noon until 0200 Fri, Sat, 10 pool tables £9 per hr. Very lively and late pool hall and dance club.

★ Theatre
Almeida, Almeida St, N1, T020-7359 4404, www.almeida.co.uk. The most star-studded

middle-scale theatre in London, in a freshly refurbished theatre with fashionable bar.

Hen and Chickens, 109 St Paul's Rd, N1, T020-7704 2001. Lively drama and comedy pub theatre on Highbury Corner.

King's Head, 115 Upper St, N1, T020-7226 1916. Solid and adventurous trooper that pioneered the concept of dinner theatre in its amazingly uncomfortable back room. Productions are often of a high standard.

Little Angel Theatre, 14 Dagmar Passage, N1, T020-7226 1787, www.littleangel theatre.com. Old-time puppet theatre with shows for kids at weekends, termtime. Also has occasional adult puppetry shows.

Old Red Lion, 418 St John St, EC1, T020- 7837 7816. Long-standing small theatre with a very good reputation above a busy drinking hole.

Pleasance Theatre, 41 North Rd, N7, T020-7609 1800. Large and very well-appointed fringe theatre in converted warehouse near Caledonian Rd tube that often mounts exciting touring productions, located above a bustling bar and brasserie called *Shillibeers*.

Rosemary Branch, 2 Shepperton Rd, N1, T020-7704 6665. Tiny theatre above an arty pub near the canal.

Tower Theatre, Canonbury Pl, N7, T020- 7226 3633. Box office 1400-2000. Plays by the resident amateur Tavistock Rep Company, a mixture of mainstream classic and contemporary drama in a historic building. Shows Jun, Jul and Sep.

⊛ Festivals and events

Jun Islington International Festival.
Jul Stoke Newington Festival.
Sep Angel Canal Festival.

⊘ Shopping

Islington *p305, map p306*
Apart from bars and restaurants, Upper St is packed with Estate Agents, jostling for space with some interesting gift, home furnishing and designerwear shops. Less expensive options can be found on Cross St cluminating in the extraordinary **Get Stuffed**. Fans of retro are well catered for in Islington.

After Noah, 121 Upper St, N1, T020-7359 4281. The North London branch of the King's Rd art nouveau and deco furniture shop.

Angel Bookshop, 102 Islington High St, N1, T020-7226 2904. An excellent little independent bookseller.

Annie's Vintage Costume and Textiles, 10 Camden Passage, T020-7359 0796. Fine vintage clothes for women.

Camden Passage Market. An antiques and bric-a-brac market (second-hand book market Thu, farmers' market on Sun) in a covered area at the end of a street full of superior antique shops that make for intriguing browsing. Open Wed and Sat 0800-1600, most of the shops are closed on Mon.

Chapel Market, one of London's less well-known, and still very busy, old street markets. For well over a century stalls have lined this scruffy street laden with the fruit 'n' veg and comestibles of all kinds as well as a good deal of not very durable tat. Open 0900- 1600 Tue, Wed, Fri, Sat; 0900-1300 Thu, Sun.

Clarks Factory Shop, 67-83 Seven Sisters Rd (nearest tube Finsbury Park), T020-7281 9364. Considerably further afield, try this for cheap Clarks shoes. Open Mon-Sat 0930-1730.

Cloud Cuckoo Land, 6 Charlton Pl, T020-7354 3141. Stock fine vintage clothes for women.

Flashback, 61 Essex Rd, N1, T020-7354 9356. Stocks a huge selection of clothes from the 1950s to the present, with the emphasis on the 1970s. Lots of bargains to be had for keen-eyed browsers. Over the road at No 50 is their music outlet, which boasts an excellent collection of second-hand vinyl and CDs covering just about every type of music.

Get Stuffed, 105 Essex Rd, N1, T020-7226 1364. One of London's most famous taxidermists: pick up a stuffed chaffinch for £75, or a stuffed lion for £5000. The glass domes and display cases on sale are also unique.

The Hart Gallery, 113 Upper St, N1, T020-7704 1131. Sells just about affordable contemporary art for the living room.

Planet Bazaar, 397 St John St, EC1, T020-7278 7793. 1960 and 70s furniture, lighting, telephones, mirrors and artwork.

Reckless Records, 79 Upper St, T020-7359 7105. Sells second-hand CDs and vinyl. It's mostly mainstream but has comprehensive soul and dance sections.

Segunda Mano, 111 Upper St, N1, T020-7359 5284. Stock a good range of used and new designer clothes.

Twenty Twenty One, 274 Upper St, N1, T020-7288 1996. Contemporary interiors shop.

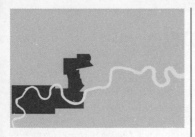

❗Footprint features

★ Five of the best

Notting Hill and Holland Park

It's hard to know what greater heights of fashionability Notting Hill can reach. Here TV presenters and rockstars have sacrificed their lives; politicians have gambled their careers for houses; and Hollywood has made the movie. Notting Hill basks in celebrity status, even if sometimes for all the wrong reasons. One of London's original and more successful gentrified multicultural districts, its sloping terraces may not be the most attractive in town but the fashionable types patrolling its boutiques, galleries, cafés and bars may well be. Most famously, once a year at the Carnival these media darlings give way to the wildest and most uninhibited street party in Europe. A full-on two-day festival of Afro-Caribbean and urban youth culture packs into W11's narrow streets but has divided the community: some would like to see it moved to Hyde Park. The rest of the year, Portobello Road Market continues to pull in the punters every Saturday for its antiques, groovy second-hand clothes and bric-a-brac. Close by but a world apart, the houses on Campden Hill and around Holland Park are some of the most expensive and sought after in London, but the park itself is a delightful place to explore and one of the best approaches to the exotic splendours of Leighton House.

➤➤ *For Sleeping, Eating and other listings see pages 316-322.*

History

The explosion in the development of Notting Hill and Holland Park took place in the 19th century. Until then, Notting Hill (and its northwestern extremities in Notting Dale) was largely farmland, with piggeries scattered across the fields, and Portobello and Notting Barns providing the main farm settlements. A hamlet had developed around the Kensington Gravel Pits at the northern end of Kensington Church Street, and a gate had been built to regulate the Uxbridge turnpike during the 18th century.

To the south, the hill now known as Holland Park was one of the four manors in the Kensington Estate, and from 1606 was crowned by the majestic Jacobean mansion of Cope's Castle, or Holland House. Further mansions were built, such as Campden House in 1612, and Aubrey House (over a medicinal spring) some 80 years later, while the surrounding fields supplied hay for the city. When the Parliamentarians confiscated Holland House during the Civil War, Cromwell is reputed to have taken his deaf son-in-law, General Ireton, into the fields so he could 'shout' tactics and still avoid being overheard.

Further south, the village of Kensington grew at the foot of the hill around St Mary Abbots, with nurseries and market gardens to the south. In the late 18th and early 19th century, Lady Holland hosted lavish parties (albeit with indifferent food apparently) for Whig politicians like Earl Grey, George Canning, Lord Palmerston, and even Talleyrand, as well as London aesthetes and writers like Lord Byron, William Wordsworth, Charles Dickens and Sir Walter Scott. In 1802 the Earl and his wife met Napoleon, and became his firm supporter thereafter – they sent him a fridge while he was in exile in Elba.

In the 19th century, however, the area was developed massively. Campden Hill was laid out to give access to grand lodges that had been built along its length – though Thorpe, Moray and Bedford have since been replaced by Holland Park Comprehensive School and the Queen Elizabeth College. Campden Hill Square emerged in the 1820s and 30s (JMW Turner used to frequently paint sunsets from beside a tree in the gardens), the Phillimore Estate began to build on their land to the west of St Mary

★ Don't miss West London...

1. **Leighton House** Exploring the park and seek out this Edwardian Arabesque fantasy, page 315.
2. **Portobello Road** Potter down from Notting Hill to the market, at its best on Saturdays but somewhere to be seen throughout the week, page 321.
3. **Kensington Gardens** Visit Kensington Palace then stroll through the gardens past the Round Pond to the Serpentine Gallery, pages 158 and 323.
4. **Kew Gardens** Steam upriver or take the train to some world-class glasshouses, botanics and horticulture, page 341.
5. **Hampton Court** The palace of King Henry VIII and later William and Mary, page 350.

Abbots, and land south of the Bayswater Road was sold for development in the 1860s, with building extending as far west as Holland Villas Road by the 1870s.

Further north, the Norland Estate (between Norland and Portland Roads) was under construction by the 1840s and the Ladbroke Estate, following the failure of the Hippodrome racecourse (commemorated in Hippodrome Place) in the 1830s, embarked on developing their land with paired villas set in picturesque crescents around St John's church. Chepstow and Pembridge Villas were up by the 1860s, and the Greek Cathedral of St Sophia emerged to cater for the growing Greek population in Bayswater. Later still, the wealthy began building grand residences in Holland Park – Lord Leighton's pile still features his magnificent Arab Hall, while 'Peacock House' on Addison Road, with its glorious tiled façade, was built for Sir Earnest Debenham in 1906.

But it wasn't simply a tale of grand mansions for grand personages. At the turn of the last century infant mortality in the northern estates of Notting Hill reached 50%, and the influx of West Indian immigrants in the 1950's was met with racial intolerance that resulted in race riots in the 1958 when West Indian homes were systematically attacked around the Pembridge Road. The Westway, completed in 1970, cut a swathe over and through the area, but the Notting Hill Carnival, an annual celebration masterminded by the West Indian community that has grown to be the largest in Europe, now passes through streets lived in by wealthy residents in an increasingly desirable neighbourhood.

Sights ⊖ *Holland Park, Ladbroke Grove, Notting Hill.*

Notting Hill

The relatively unprepossessing main road called Notting Hill Gate continues the westward thrust of Oxford Street and the Bayswater Road towards Holland Park Avenue. The tube station straddles the street at the point where Kensington Church Street dips south to High Street Kensington and Pembridge Road heads north to the Portobello Road and Westbourne Grove. Notting Hill itself is at the top of Ladbroke Grove, ringed with grand crescents and squares around the church of St John, but most of the action in the area day or night can be found either on the Gate itself or along **Portobello**. Near the tube are the area's cinemas and high street shops, while the Portobello Road gradually gets marginally more downmarket as it approaches the Westway flyover. This is the end to look for most of Notting Hill's more happening retailers and restaurants. Bear in mind that it's less of a walk to this end from Ladbroke Grove tube.

West Notting Hill & Holland Park

30 Notting Hill

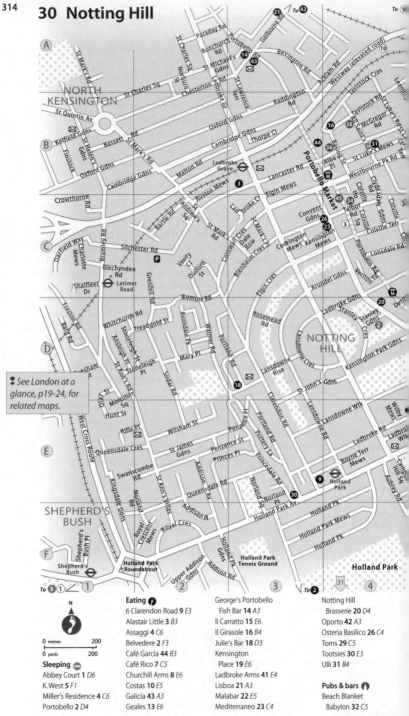

West Notting Hill & Holland Park

❧ See London at a glance, p19–24, for related maps.

Holland Park

N

0 metres 200
0 yards 200

Sleeping 🛏
Abbey Court **1** D6
K. West **5** F1
Miller's Residence **4** C6
Portobello **2** D4

Eating 🍴
6 Clarendon Road **9** E3
Alastair Little **3** B3
Assaggi **4** C6
Belvedere **2** F3
Café García **44** B3
Café Rico **7** C5
Churchill Arms **8** E6
Costas **10** E5
Galicia **43** A3
Geales **13** E6

George's Portobello
Fish Bar **14** A3
Il Carratto **15** E6
Il Girasole **16** B4
Julie's Bar **18** D3
Kensington
Place **19** E6
Ladbroke Arms **41** E4
Lisboa **21** A3
Malabar **22** E5
Mediterraneo **23** C4

Notting Hill
Brasserie **20** D4
Oporto **42** A3
Osteria Basilico **26** C4
Toms **29** C5
Tootsies **30** E3
Ulli **31** B4

Pubs & bars 🍸
Beach Blanket
Babylon **32** C5

Holland Park

ⓘ *Dawn (0700) to dusk throughout the year.*
South of Notting Hill Gate to the west, the pretty white stuccoed terraces on the slopes of Campden Hill provide an attractive backdrop for a walk up to Holland Park. In the grounds of the former Holland House – this is one of the most charming and individual of central London's parks. From fine hilly woods to wide-open sports fields busy with local dog walkers, joggers, nannies and babies – Holland Park has something for everyone. The walled exterior makes it feel like a private garden at the Holland Park entrance and yet once you've meandered through each different flowered garden, rose garden and the meditational Japanese garden, there are wooded walks, little duck ponds and sculpture trails as well as hidden adventure playgrounds and bustling coffee shops, ice-cream kiosks, resounding tennis courts and an open-air theatre beside the wide greensward sweep down to Kensington High Street. The peacocks, the wild rabbits and squirrels complete the semi-rural idyll.

★ Leighton House

ⓘ *12 Holland Park Rd, W14, T020-7602 3316, www.rbkc.gov.uk/leightonhouse museum. Open Mon, Wed-Sun 1100-1730. Adults £3, concessions and under-16s £1.*

This is an exquisite, pre-Edwardian, red-brick treat – despite being Victorian – with its extensive pre-Raphaelite collection of Millais, Burne-Jones and of course, Lord Leighton's own paintings. The private house was built between 1864-79 by the Royal Academy President – his salon conjours up the heady whirl of Arabian spice and Oscar Wilde salaciousness. The central fountain in the Arab Hall with its opulent gilt mosaic frieze and intricate Isnik tiles are a thrilling miniature Alhambra, despite now being run by the local council and as far from the magic of the Moors as leafy Holland Park can be. The househosts regular events including drawing classes, special exhibitions and classical concerts – with a strong emphasis on the arts and crafts and a few events for children. **The Orangerie** and the **Ice House** are two other small galleries in the park run by Leighton House.

🚇 Sleeping

Notting Hill *p312, map p314*

L Miller's Residence, 111a Westbourne Gr, W2, T020-7243 1024, www.millersuk.com. Popular with the likes of Hugh Grant, it's eccentric, camp and very old English London townhouse in style, with an antique-stuffed living room, wooden toilet seats and log fires, and just 8 individually furnished rooms named after great poets, from £170-£250 including a free cocktail bar, no restaurant.

A The Abbey Court Hotel, 20 Pembridge Gdns, W11, T020-7221 7518, www.abbeycourthotel.co.uk. The cleanest and most luxurious of this street packed with modest hotels, the breakfast is served ad lib in the conservatory in its quiet garden, breakfast included in price.

A Portobello Hotel, 22 Stanley Gdns, W11, T020-7727 2777, www.portobello-hotel.co.uk. Internationally trendy hotel to the stars, where Johnny Depp and Kate

Moss allegedly bathed in champagne. All the usual treats you'd expect if you were an internationally famous celebrity (including 24 restaurant and bar) or just someone willing to cough up the basic £170 a night for a double room.

Holland Park *p312, map p316*

A K-West, Richmond Way, W14, T0870-0274343, www.k-west.co.uk. 224 4-star rooms, £158 a standard room, in a refurbished modern designer hotel near Shepherd's Bush, with spa, sauna and gym. Popular with middle-rank musicians performing at the Carling Hammersmith Apollo.

B Holland Court Hotel, 31-33 Holland Rd, W14, T020-7371 1133. Clean, friendly and cheap (for the area) hotel close to Olympia, and the far end of Kensington High St (with its wealth of Persian cafés). Buffet breakfast included.

West Notting Hill & Holland Park *Listings*

31 Kensington High Street & Holland Park

N

0 metres 100
0 yards 100

Sleeping 🚇
Holland Court **2** *C3*
London Visitors **3** *C3*
Royal Garden **4** *A6*
YHA Holland House **1** *B3*

Eating 🍴
Abingdon **1** *C5*
Alounak **2** *C2*
Arcadia **3** *B6*
Bellini **4** *B6*

Cibo **5** *B2*
Holland Park
Café **6** *B4*
Il Portico **7** *C4*
Le Monde **8** *C5*

Maggie Jones **9** *A6*
Muffin Man **10** *B6*
Patisserie
Valerie **11** *A6*
Scoffs **13** *C4*

C London Visitors Hotel, 42-44 Holland Rd, W14, T020-7602 1282. Big double-fronted, cheap hotel, round corner from Olympia and nearby Holland Park.

E YHA Holland House, Holland Walk, Kensington, W8, T0870-770 5866 (within UK), T+44 20 7937 0748 (outside UK), hollandhouse@yha.org.uk. £21.60, under-18s £19.30, a 3-star, 201-bed hostel in a superb position in Holland Park, partly Jacobean and of considerable historical interest.

🍴 Eating

Notting Hill *p312, map p314*

ᵀᵀᵀ Assaggi, 39 Chepstow Pl, W2, T020-7792 5501. The chef is the toast of other London chefs. The finest Italian food in London – although the space isn't great – it's tucked away and not easy to find. Booking essential (weeks in advance).

ᵀᵀᵀ Kensington Place, 201 Kensington Church St, W8, T020-7727 3184. Was Lady Diana's former favourite lunch spot, west of the Ivy. Its long windows and simple chic has never changed. Its contemporary European menu is reliable and delicious.

ᵀᵀᵀ Notting Hill Brasserie, 92 Kensington Park Rd, T020-7229 4481. A mega fashionable media hangout for lunch and supper, for some very fine French brasserie food in surprisingly romantic surroundings (main courses £20). The bar is open all day.

ᵀᵀ Alastair Little, 136a Lancaster Rd, W11, T020-7243 2220. Slightly off the beaten track, a very fine spin off of the ground-breaking chef's flagship Soho branch. The food is consistently inventive and the set menu makes it an affordable date for funky media types.

ᵀᵀ Ladbroke Arms, 54 Ladbroke Rd, T020-7727 6648. Restaurant serving up possibly the best modern European cuisine in this part of London, still masquerading as the old-fashioned boozer that is once was.

ᵀᵀ Malabar, 27 Uxbridge St, W8, T020-7727 8800, behind the Coronet cinema. A chic Indian restaurant high on style, spice and price but an established local favourite that does a good-value buffet lunch on Sun.

ᵀᵀ Mediterraneo, 37 Kensington Park Rd, W11, T020-7792 3131. Another Italian with less rustic décor the Osteria Basilico (below) and equally fine recipes, at the top of this bracket (main courses £12-£15).

ᵀᵀ Osteria Basilico, 29 Kensington Park Rd, W11, T020-7727 9372. Rated by many locals the best Italian pizza parlour in London – definitely needs booking (and try for a table upstairs), at the top of this bracket (main courses £12-£15).

Hidden away behind Notting Hill tube are 3 popular, and cheap, old-timers:

ᵀ Il Carratto Ristorante, 20 Hillgate St, W8, T020-7229 9988. A lively and reasonably priced Italian local.

ᵀ Costas Grill, 14 Hillgate St, W8, T020-7229 3794. An inimitably cheap and cheery Greek taverna, also doing excellent fish dishes.

ᵀ Geales, 2 Farmer St, W8, T020-7727 7528. A sort of old seaside stalwart fish restaurant.

ᵀ Churchill Arms, 119 Kensington Church St, W8, T020-7792 1246. For some surprisingly good Thai food at ridiculously cheap pub prices (£5-6 per main course), you can't beat this place, open Mon-Sat 1200-2130, Sun 1200-2000. The restaurant is through the back in the indoor 'beer garden' and in the evenings you must book.

Pubs & bars 🍸
Bar Cuba **14** *B6*
Scarsdale **16** *C4*

Entertainment 🎭
Holland Park Open-
  Air Theatre **1** *A4*
Odeon Kensington **2** *C4*
St Mary Abbots **3** *B6*

¶ **Galicia**, 323 Portobello Rd, T020-8969 3539. Spanish family restaurant that's an old favourite with the local Iberian community around Golbourne Rd. Authenically brusque service and some very munchable tapas as well as acceptable and very good value mains. Hard to beat in the cheap and cheerful category. Closed Mon.

¶ **Ulli**, 16 All Saint's Rd, W11, T020-7727 7511. Further afield and more of a Portobello scene, does a good mixture of Chinese, Malaysian and Thai food.

Cafés and sandwich bars

Notting Hill (and the Portobello Road in particular) is café heaven. It's almost as if the place exisits solely to supply the needs of caffe latte-deprived locals and tourists. But there are also some excellent rougher round the edges Portugese places further up the Portobello Road and on Golbourne Road, at the northern end of Portobello, that are well worth a visit.

Café Rico, 118 Westbourne Grove, W11, T020-7792 2112. If Toms is too hectic, this is an airy and delicious patisserie nearby.

Café Garcia, 250 Portobello Rd, T020-7221 6119. An excellent new addition to the burgening café scene, this place is attached to a Spanish deli that has been here for years. Serves up tapas and hearty chorizo stews as well as hot chocolate and churros.

George's Portobello Fish Bar, 329 Portobello Rd, W10, T020-8969 7895. Established in 1961 by George and Eve and remains the cleanest and most fun chippie in the locale, stays open until just before midnight.

Il Girasole, 78 Tavistock Rd, W11, T020-7243 8518. An Italian coffee shop and takeaway that's very down to earth. Tables outside in the paved cul-de-sac make this a happy spot.

Lisboa, 57 Golborne Rd, W10, T020-8968 5242. Top of the heap. Rough and ready, it does the best 'galao' and immediately whisks you off to Lisbon (the locals gossiping inside and out help the dream).

Oporto, if there's no spare corner at *Lisboa*, wander over to this place or further down – the whole street is rich in Portuguese groceries and bakers.

Toms, 226 Westbourne Grove, W11, T020-7221 8818. Terence Conran's son's

fashionable hit. The café is the place to sit and sip, the front shop the place to take out. Over the top in price but delicious in stock. High in local celebs: every other customer wearing jeans and shades is likely to be a star.

Holland Park *p312, map p316*

¶¶¶ **The Belvedere**, Holland House, Holland Park, W8, T020-7602 1238. A magical location in the heart of the park where diners look out over the orangerie and the rose gardens and can stroll around the exhibitions, hear peacocks cry or the opera waft through the vast windows as they eat.

¶¶ **6 Clarendon Road**, at 6 Clarendon Rd (where else?) W11, T020-7727 3330. Dinner only Tue-Sat, lunch Wed-Sun, is upmarket but informal. Very simple and small – standard white walls and tablecloths – with an excellent wine list to accompany some fine euro-dining (2 courses for £15 at lunchtimes).

¶¶ **Cibo**, 3 Russell Gdns, W14, T020-7371 6271, off Holland Rd. A fine Italian local, with big paintings on the walls and excellent lobster dishes on the tables (main courses £10-£18).

¶¶ **Julie's Bar and Restaurant**, Holland Park Village, 137 Portland Rd, W11, T020-7229 8331 (restaurant), T020-7727 7985 (bar). A 1960s survivor, many-chambered and multifarious, a must for any visitor in one of the prettiest corners of the area. The food varies wildly but book in at different times and experience the difference between Sun brunch, dinner and the everyday team.

¶ **Alounak**, 10 Russell Gdns, W14, T020-7603 7645, off Holland Rd. This is like an Iranian caravan canteen that has put down roots. Its huge open oven provides endless hot pitta-type bread to wrap around fresh handfuls of mint and cheese. Dish of the day is always the best bet (usually a lamb stew). Persian food may not be for vegetarians but its BYOB – pile in with your own crate of red wine and soak up the souk.

¶ **Tootsies**, Holland Park Av, W11, T020-7229 8567. A West London hamburger chain, where the meat sandwiches are meaty, juicy, and fun for all the family. This branch is very friendly, does takeaways, and also real banana milkshakes.

● *For an explanation of sleeping and eating price codes used in this guide, see inside the front cover. Other relevant information is found in Essentials, see pages 44-46.*

Cafés and sandwich bars

Holland Park Cafeteria, a local favourite, full of mums, tourists, dog-wakers and locals all rubbing shoulders under the beautiful tiled arches in the ruins of the old Holland House. Take away or eat in (come rain or shine), it's dirt cheap and hits the spot (soups and main lunches as well as sandwiches and cakes to order).

Pubs and bars

Notting Hill *p312, map p314*
Pubs and bars come and go like boy bands in Notting Hill.

Beach Blanket Babylon, 45 Ledbury Rd, W11, T020-7229 2907. A long-player. A camp place always heaving with the pre-club scene. The restaurant's pricey but good, spread about in strange little nooks, serving surprisingly accomplished grub in opulent portions – great for brunch when the bar is quiet and the weird furniture holds sway – all wrought iron and vulgar vast cushions.

The Bed Bar, Portobello Rd, W10, T020-8969 4500, www.seriously.com. Dark Moroccan-style bar, complete with bed, that has now been around for a while. Djs most nights.

Ground Floor Bar, 186 Portobello Rd, W11, T020-7243 8701, beneath the *First Floor*. Muted tones, sensible menu and huge glass windows on the corner has become a firm favourite with the local schmoozers.

The Market Bar, 240a Portobello Rd, W11, T020-7229 6472. Formerly the hang-out of Rastas and Trustas selling and buying weed, this place still feels quite naughty but has a more suave finish these days, with a decent Thai restaurant upstairs and DJs in the bar at weekends when it gets jumping.

Mau Mau Bar, 265 Portobello Rd, W11, T020-7229 8528. Busy with bright young things this place has a more laid-back feel than some of the others, live jazz on Wed and Djs at other times.

As well as designer bars, Notting Hill does a fine line in pub-restaurant conversions.

The Cow, 89 Westbourne Park Rd, W2, T020-7221 5400. Leading the herd is Tom Conran's Oirish hit. As well as the posh separate restaurant upstairs, there's a cosy nook at the back, and summer or winter it's a local favourite because it has remained an old-fashioned, if quite expensive, pub.

The Hillgate, 24 Hillgate St, W8, T020-7727 8543. A good eccentric local with tables outside beneath flowerbaskets and traditional panelled pub décor.

Pelican, All Saints Rd, T020-7792 3073. Less modish than The Cow or The Westbourne but very popular with a young crowd for its music and laid-back attitude, a happening big-windowed corner pub just up from the Portobello Rd.

The Westbourne, 101 Westbourne Park Villas, W2, T020-7221 1332. The Cow's rival, busier and more sexy. This joint is just as popular, if less relaxing if you're without a posse. Most of the hip circuit may be knocking back cocktails and pretending to be quickly on the move, but hours later they're still there, as if standing about were an end in itself. Dress down but groovy. In the long spring and summer evenings the big front benches can barely hold the revellers.

The Windsor Castle, 114 Campden Hill Rd, W8, T020-7243 9551. Very old and snug. The Tudor-style interior is a hit with old Etonians, while wintry mulled wines, panelled seating and nooks make it more authentic when autumn sets in. In summer the big walled garden has a char-grilled barbecue.

Entertainment

Notting Hill *p312, map p314*
Cinema
The Coronet, Notting Hill Gate, W11, T020-7727 6705. The best complement to the Gate (see below) – only a few doors down and not at all arty – offering a mainstream Hollywood diet but its old musical hall seating and proscenium arch screen, as well as its star turn in the movie *Notting Hill* make it a popular dating spot and even quite Cinema Paradiso in atmosphere. Worth travelling to find.

The Electric Cinema, Portobello Rd, T020-7229 8688. The lovely old art deco cinema on the Portobello Rd has been fully restored once again, redesigned by the Soho House team and programmed by Cityscreen, owners of the Gate, The Ritzy, Clapham Picture House and Stratford Picture House (T020-7734 4342, www.picturehouses.co.uk).

The Gate Cinema, 87 Notting Hill Gate, W11, T020-7727 4043. Late night shows at 2300 on Fri and Sat. An excellent arthouse cinema

– uncomfortable but worth it – with delicious ice-cream and snacks – special old screenings at the weekend through Video City. Cult and popular programmes. Book up quick – but they'll try and find you a chair even in the first weekend if you hit the late-night screening.

Music
Classical and opera Holland Park Open-Air Opera, annually every Jul-Aug. London's answer to Glyndebourne. Mixed excellence – but always very ambitious … stroll and picnic outside with the dogwalkers and hear the wafting arias for free during the dusk instead. Makes visitors to the YHA even luckier (unless they prefer techno).
Rock, folk and jazz Shepherd's Bush Empire, Shepherd's Bush Green, W12, T0870-771 2000. Box office open Mon-Fri 1000-1800, Sat 1200-1800. One of the best venues in London for rock acts – everything from Iggy Pop to Beck. Admission £5-20.

Nightclubs
Neighbourhood, 119 Westbourne Studios, 12 Acklam Rd, W10, T020-7524 7979. House, funk and elektro sounds in the old Subterrania club under the Westway. Taken over in late 2003 by the owners of Cherry Jam in Royal Oak (see p333) with a very mixed crowd throwing shapes.
Notting Hill Arts Club, 21 Notting Hill Gate, W11, T020-7460 4459. Very lively and late post-industrial basement club, regularly sweaty and packed. Expect to queue even on a Wed. Closed Mon.
Woodys, 41-43 Woodfield Rd, W9, T020-7266 3030, www.woodysclub.com. A little way off the beaten track but possibly even more fashionable.

Theatre
The Bush Theatre, Shepherd's Bush Green, W12, T020-7610 4224. One of London's more exciting small-scale studio theatres, much more comfortable since being re-upholstered and cushioned.
The Gate Theatre, 11 Pembridge Rd, W11, T020-7229 5387. Long narrow fringe theatre above a busy pub with a strong reputation for innovative takes on the classics as well as new writing.

The Tabernacle Community and Arts Centre, Powis Sq, W11, T020-7565 7800, www.tabernacle.org.uk. Open Fri, Sat until 0100. Temporary art shows and events.

☸ Festivals and events

Notting Hill *p312, map p314*
Portobello Film Festival, 3 weeks where over 400 brand new, 'lo- and no-' budget short British and international films are shown at **end of Jul beginning of Aug**, www.portobellofilmfestival.com. **Notting Hill Carnival**, **Aug bank holiday**, see page .

◯ Shopping

Notting Hill *p312, map p314*
One of the most rewarding shopping areas in London, Notting Hill boasts an extraordinary array of independents and one-offs.

Antiques
Apart from the stalls in the **Portobello Road** market on Saturday, antique and bric-a-brac shops open throughout the week around here and those worth a look include:
Bazar, 82 Golborne Rd, W10, T020-8969 6262. French antique and period country furniture – great for nestbuilding and original presents.
MAC, 86 Golborne Rd, W10, T020-8960 3736. A treasure trove of architectural and decorative antiques – many from France and the west country.

Books
Books for Cooks, 4 Blenheim Cres, W11, T020-7221 1992, www.booksforcooks.com. Blenheim Cres has a little series of rival specialist bookshops – from gardening to cooking, offering shop-made lunches, coffee and cakes from the Test Kitchen, cookery demos and even cookery holidays in Tuscany, as well as a cornucopia of recipe reads.
Notting Hill Books, 132 Palace Gardens Terr, W8, T020-7727 5988. Do bargain paperbacks, publishers remainders and discounted press edition hardbacks. Popular with everyone from bishops to backpackers, this little bookstore is well frequented and refuses credit cards. Notting Hill Gate may be slowly yielding to the mass-market high street chains but this place is typical of the area's wealth of second-hand and exchange stores ribboning

the main road. Closed Thu afternoons.

Simon Finch Rare Books, 61a Ledbury Rd, W11, T020-7792 3303. Specialize in modern literature, photography, art and design – pretentious high design mostly.

The Travel Bookshop, 13-15 Blenheim Cres, W11, T020-7229 5260. One of the best travel bookshops in the city, and yes, Hugh Grant was the manager here in the movie.

Fashion

Apple Tree, 230 Portobello Rd, T020-72436424. Affordable and pretty street clothes for women.

The Cross, 141 Portland Rd, W11, T020-7727 6760. Stock very expensive, must-have designer womenswear, popular with the likes of Nicole Kidman.

Emma Hope's Shoes, 207 Westbourne Grove, W11, T020-7313 7493. The shoes to buy when Cinderella is invited to the ball – individual, gorgeous and the fave of policewomen to princesses (may be best visited in the sales).

London Beach Store, 23 Kensington Park Rd, T020-7243 2772. Has been selling urban fashion, skateboards and kites and the like for many years now. Well worth a look. There's more here for boys than girls.

Paul Smith, Westbourne House, 122 Kensington Park Rd, W11, T020-7727 3553. The British designer's gear is eloquently presented in Westbourne House, a 19th century villa renovated by the architect Sophie Hicks. Men and women's clothes and accessories.

Food and drink

Mr Christian's Delicatessen, 11 Elgin Cres, W11, T020-7229 0501. For commendable comestibles, stocks a wide selection of fine foods from around the Med. On Sat – their breads, sandwiches and pastries spill onto the street stall outside, they are so popular – it saves the crowds pushing inside.

Coffee Plant, 180 Portobello Rd, T020-7221 8137. Probably the coolest place for an espresso on this strip of the Portobello Rd, this is really a retail outlet selling organic, fairtrade tea and coffee from all over the world.

R Garcia & Son, 248-250 Portobello Rd, W11, T020-7221 6119. Tue-Sat 0830-1830, is an excellent Spanish grocery – very authentic and comprehensive, deli and other comestibles.

Portobello Road market on Saturday is the destination for antiques, fruit 'n' veg and all kinds of second-hand gear. Most of the superior antique stalls are at the top (southern) end of the street, giving way to food and clothes halfway down, before finishing up beneath the flyover with jumble stalls and second-hand clothes where many a bargain is likely to lurk. Also on Saturday mornings, the **Farmers' Market** in Hillgate Village (behind Kensington Church St) is a quirky event where the Hillbillies like to pretend they know their onions.

Miscellaneous

Graham & Green, 4, 7 and 10 Elgin Cres, W11, T020-7727 4594. Something of a Notting Hill institution, this is a funky, chic shop selling everything from fun, quirky toys, presents, and arty household nick-nacks to stationery, fabrics, clothes and jewellery – their stock is very influenced by the Big Apple and the Milan precincts.

"Turquoise Island", 222 Westbourne Grove, W11, T020-7727 3095. A famous tiled folly, is part clock, part toilet and mainly a flower stall run by Wild at Heart – spilling out onto the pavement in this ultra fashionable corner. It's bold modern architecture won wide acclaim when it was created; the flowers are lovely, too.

Music and video

Music & Video Exchange, another Notting Hill institution. Their sprawling chain of scruffy shops on Notting Hill Gate stock a vast selection of vinyl and CDs. For general rock, pop and modern jazz head for No 38; for classical go to No 36; and for blues, folk and trad jazz No 42. All branches are open daily 1000-2000.

Rough Trade, 130 Talbot Rd, W11, T020-7229 8541. Another classic independent that is its own label and sells an eclectic collection of music (mainly indie rock, folk, blues and all manner of house, techno and electro) on CD and vynyl.

Video City, 117 Notting Hill Gate, W11, T020-7221 7029. "The best little video store in the world", they assure us – don't forget to ring and say you need it for an extra night for nothing, and they'll agree.

Holland Park Avenue is a good spot to compile a pricey but very special picnic. **Jeroboams**, 96 Holland Park Av, W11, T020-7727 9359. Excellent cheeses, cider, charcuterie, oil and sandwiches as well as wine. **Lidgates**, T020-7727 8243. One of London's finest organic butchers. Much lauded with queues round the corner for Christmas turkeys – its prices reflect its upmarket appeal.

Maison Blanc, 102 Holland Park Av, T020-7221 2494. The fine French bread and cake mini-chain finishes off any picnic (or you can stand and munch on the premises). French fêtes demand they supply epiphany cakes and chocolate logs as if you're there. **Speck**, 2 Holland Park Terr, Portland Rd, T020-7229 7005. An excellent Italian deli, with everything from lasagne to pickles (open til 2000). Expensive but worth the indulgence.

Kensington High Street and Earl's Court

Sandwiched between the slopes of Holland Park and South Kensington, Kensington Road and Kensington High Street continue Knightsbridge west of Hyde Park and Museumland. North of High Street Ken, as it's usually abbreviated, antiquey Kensington Church Street twists up to Notting Hill, while to the south, either side of the Earl's Court Road, peaceful squares and tall Victorian terraces contain some very expensive addresses indeed. The High Street once bustled with some of the buzz of the King's Road in Chelsea, but since the 1980s it too has become considerably more wealthy and more staid, dominated now by chain stores and multinational clothing brands. To the east, in the west end of Kensington Gardens, stands the traditional explanation for the area's cachet, Kensington Palace, former home of Princess Diana and still the second most important Royal residence in London after Buckingham Palace. Some 20 splendid rooms here are open to the public throughout the year, housing the faintly ridiculous and genuinely priceless Royal Dress Collection. To the southwest, Earl's Court is the Kensingtons' embarrassing neighbour, a lively, fairly dodgy district long colonized by hard-partying Antipodeans and South Africans and more recently by the gay scene. The wide range of mid-price hotels boosts the transient population. ⮞ *For Sleeping, Eating and other listings see pages 324-327.*

History

Since at least the 12th century, the little hamlet of 'Chenesit' nestled at the foot of the hill, around a church that lay on the site of St Mary Abbots. It had grown little by the time William III moved into Nottingham House on the western edge of Hyde Park, and set Wren the task of transforming it into Kensington Palace. In the previous hundred years Holland House and Campden House had been built in extensive grounds overlooking Kensington, while Earl's Court remained as a hamlet of farms to the south. Meadowland, fruit gardens and nurseries lay in between, and although Kensington Square went up in 1685, it was still surrounded by fields some 30 years later.

During the 1700s, Kensington grew as society followed royalty to settle close to the court at Kensington Palace. Villas sprang up along the hillside north of the High Street, the Phillimore Estate sold their land for building, and by the early 19th century buildings extended as far Edwardes Square. There was such significant evening traffic between Kensington and Piccadilly that horse patrols were introduced to protect travellers from marauding highwaymen (George II himself was robbed, with 'much deference', within the grounds of Kensington Palace).

Kensington's population had risen eightfold in the 18th century to 8000, yet by 1901 it was some 175,000. Street after street spread west, swallowing up the market gardens and the hamlets of Earl's Court and Walham Green on the way towards Hammersmith and Fulham. Further impetus was provided by the arrival of the railways.

In the 1860s Earl's Court was still largely market gardens employing a significant Irish workforce for whom the Roman Catholic St Thomas' had been built in 1848. Nevertheless, a farm was cleared to make way for a station, and development grew in earnest from the 1880s. Spectacular arenas of entertainment emerged nearby. Olympia opened in 1884 and hosted the circus troupes of Bertram Mills and Barnum. The 'Paris Hippodrome' of 1886 displayed chariot racing and stag hunting. Further south the Earl's Court Pleasure Ground offered the Great Wheel and annual spectaculars such as 'Buffalo Bill's Wild West Show'.

When the Exhibition Hall was built on the site in 1937, however, it was soon in use as an internment camp. By then, Earl's Court tube station had been honoured as the first station to boast an escalator. Attempts to allay public anxiety extended to employing the one-legged 'Bumper' Harris to ride up and down the contraption throughout the opening day.

Houses were divided up into several lodgings or converted to hotels as the area gained a growing, but transient, population. In Kensington, Barker's continued to expand into new buildings (there were 400 staff as early as the 1880s), and the Georgian terraces in Kensington were largely replaced by flats in the 1930s.

As the century progressed Earl's Court earned the nickname 'Kangaroo Valley' as a largely young Australian community populated the bedsit jungle. Since the 1960s and 70s, Earl's Court has also drawn a gay community (Brompton Cemetery has long been a famed venue for trysts), while Kensington has retained some of the grandeur it first experienced in the 1700s.

Sights ⊖ *Earl's Court, High St Kensington, West Brompton.* ⊖ *See p460.*

High Street Kensington tube emerges via a shopping arcade onto Kensington High Street's western end. A right turn heads past Kensington Church Street, Barkers department store, and the Royal Garden Hotel to Kensington Palace and Gardens.

Kensington Palace

ⓘ *T020-7937 9561, www.hrp.org.uk. Daily Nov-Feb 1000-1700 (last admission 1500), Mar-Oct 1000-1800 (last admission 1600). Adult £11, concession £8.30, under 16s £7.20, under 5s free, price includes audio guide, cheaper tickets available if booked in advance on the website.*

Queen Victoria's birthplace is one of the most significant and evocative of the Royal palaces, unfortunately all the more so since the death of Princess Diana, who lived here after her separation from Prince Charles.

The Palace itself has been open to the public for at least a century, the 20 or so rooms on the one and a half hour audio-guided tour including the antique-stuffed King's State Apartments, William Kent's trompe l'oeil ceilings and staircases, a considerable selection of old master paintings from the Royal Collection in the Long Gallery and some fine views over the lakes and gardens. Also on display is the Royal Ceremonial Dress Collection, which now rather ghoulishly contains some of the dresses that Diana wore on state occasions, as well as the gilded pageantry of the 19th century. As the Palace is keen to point out, everything that can be seen is the genuine article. What any of it really represents is more of a mystery.

Kensington High Street *p322, map p316*
L The Royal Garden Hotel, 2-24 Kensington High St, W8, T020-7937 8000. This huge modern monstrosity next to Diana's old Kensington Palace is a popular international stopover with all the usual business facilities, as well as spectacular views from the bar on the 10th floor.

Earl's Court *p322, map p324*
B Best Western Burns Hotel, 18-26 Bark-ston Gdns, SW5, T020-7373 3151. Nearest the corner with the main Earl's Court Rd, this is the biggest and briskest of a long row of perfectly pleasant hotels, all of which seem individual, clean and welcoming, prices here usually includes breakfast

C Barkston Gardens Hotel, 34-44 Barkston Gdns, SW5, T020-7373 7851. Less fancy,

cheaper and more businesslike, conference facilities, breakfast included.

C Henley House Hotel, 30 Barkston Gdns, SW5, T020-7370 4111, henleyhse@aol.com. With bookshelves and tartan sofas, this hotel appeals to the olde-worlde visitor, more ind-ividual and charming than the rest of the row.

C Kensington Travel Inn, 11 Knaresborough Pl, SW5 T0870 238 3304. Standard bugdet chain fare. Mon-Thu £80 or Fri-Sun £70 per night.

C Maranton House Hotel, 14 Barkston Gdns, SW5, T020-7373 5782. Single, double and triple rooms available, breakfast included.

D The Court Hotel, 194-196 Earl's Court Rd, SW5, T020-7373 0027, www.lgh-hotels.com. Right beside the tube station tucked above the newsagents, this must be the bargain of the century,

32 Earl's Court

🛏 *See London at a glance, p19-24, for related maps.*

WEST KENSINGTON

Earl's Court Exhibition Centre

N

0 metres 100
0 yards 100

Sleeping 🛏
Albany **1** *B3*
Barkston Gardens **2** *B3*
Best Western Burns **3** *B3*
Court **4** *B3*
Henley House **5** *B3*
Kensington Travel Inn **8** *A3*

Maranton House **6** *B3*
YHA Earl's Court **9** *C3*

Eating 🍴
Dall'Artista **3** *C3*
Langans' Coq d'Or **5** *C3*
La Pappardella **6** *C3*
Little French **7** *B3*

Lou Pescadou **8** *C3*
Mohsen **9** *A1*
Mr Wing **10** *B3*
Troubador Café **12** *C3*

Pubs & bars 🍺
Balans West **13** *C3*
Colherne **14** *C3*

frequented by Ozzie backpackers, offering 15 rooms with TV, a kitchen and a microwave to share. £35 a double.

D-F Albany Hotel, 4-12 Barkston Gdns, SW5, T020-7370 6116, www.hostelworld.com. Youth hostel with rooms for 1-4 people in this popular strip of hotels, £40 a double room per night.

E YHA Earl's Court, 38 Bolton Gdns, SW5 T0870-770 5804, outside UK T(+44)20-7373 7083, earlscourt@yha.org.uk. £19.50, under-18s £17.20, reception open 24 hrs, a 3-star 180-bedded hostel in the thick of the action around Earls Court, close to the Museums, with a small courtyard garden.

⑦ Eating

Kensington High Street *p322, map p316*
† † † The Abingdon, 54 Abingdon Rd, W8, T020-7937 3339. A good example of the rash of corner pubs which are no longer pubs but fancy brasserie/restaurants with fine wine lists. A light, airy, luxurious yet informal place. Locals choose to dine in the long bench-like conservatory. Booking essential, but high tables or bar seats serve expensive beers and snacks – less satisfying but unhurried (and cheaper).

† † † Maggie Jones, 6 Old Court Pl, Kensington Church St, W8, T020-7937 6462. Sister act to the marvellous Belgravia 'La Poule Au Pot' this is a more sombre Kensington hideaway. Always packed, it serves delicious hearty British fayre – especially recommended for a Sun lunch and then a stroll through the passage to the back entrance of Kensington Gardens to walk off the feast (mains £11-£17).

† † Arcadia, Kensington Ct, 35 Kensington High St, W8, T020-7937 4294. A rather wonderful crisp-clothed dining place in a little cobbled yard providing respite from the Ken High St noise. It offers a fine gourmand Italian menu with a live parrot and individualistic decor (main courses about £12).

† † Bellini, 47 Kensington Court, W8, T020-7937 5520, next to Arcadia. Much more trendy, with a long bar and cocktails, modern and unpretentious in a Soho kind of way.

† Il Portico, 277 Kensington High St, W8, T020-7602 6262. Another classic Italian restaurant –

as authentic and as old as its next-door neighbour *Scoffs* – (mains £8-£15) but this is the white tableclothed, more expensive version and demands more time and a bit of luck with a table in order to savour the food.

† Scoffs, 267 Kensington High St, W8, T020-7602 6777. Open daily. Italian trattoria and the cinema stalwart, the place to grab a cappuccino out of dining hours, or hungry bowl of pasta anytime all day or just before or after you've popcorned at the Odeon next door. Unchanged in decades because it works.

Cafés and sandwich bars

Le Monde, 56 Earl's Court Rd, W8, T020-7938 1206, at the other end of the shopping strip. A fresh, all-window French café – good for lunch and closes at 1900– similar to all the coffee shops across London – but being a one-off has its own charm.

The Muffin Man, 12 Wrights Lane, W8, T020-7937 6652. An old-fashioned sit-down, doilly and teacup tearoom, round the corner from the tube, closes at 2000.

Patisserie Valerie, 27 Kensington Church St, W8, T020-7937 9574. One of the more reliable French gâteaux takeaway and sit-down chain – a slice of unchanged continental sipping, closes at 1900.

Earl's Court *p322, map p324*
† † † Langans' Coq d'Or, 254-260 Old Brompton Rd, SW5, T020-7259 2599. A modern European brasserie option, £17.50 for 2 courses.

† † † Lou Pescadou, 241 Old Brompton Rd, SW5, T020-7370 1057. An excellent local seafood restaurant. Blue paint and white linen, fresh, French and real with 3-course weekday lunches for about £11.

† † Mr Wing, 242 Old Brompton Rd, SW5, T020-7370 4450. At the lower end of this bracket. A curious nightspot – a Chinese restaurant offering live jazz ever Fri, Sat, tacky and fun. Open daily 1200-2400, all performances 2015-2345, £2 cover charge.

† Dall'Artista, 243 Old Brompton Rd, SW5, T020-7373 1659. A friendly, cheap pizzeria-pasta place for lunch or supper.

† The Little French Restaurant, 18 Hogarth Pl, SW5, T020-7370 0366. Romantic and very

French – little white tables and fresh handwritten menu.

♥ **Mohsen**, 152 Warwick Rd, W14, T020-7603 9888. A surprising find on the otherwise rather bleak Warwick Rd – an authentic friendly, open-ovened Persian treat, open all day until midnight.

♥ **La Pappardella**, 253 Old Brompton Rd, SW5, T020-7373 7777. Open 7 days, is another, offering home-made pasta and tempting pizzas, open all day.

Cafés and sandwich bars

Troubadour Café, 265 Old Brompton Rd, SW5, T020-7370 1434, www.troubador.co.uk. Best of all is this inimitable place, a dark and atmospheric brasserie/bar/café open all day until late and with a small garden. A very individualistic place – a old-time slice of Paris in an otherwise unprepossessing area – with regular poetry events (every 2nd Mon), short film shows once a month and in-house music most other nights since way back when.

❶ Pubs and bars

Kensington High Street *p322, map p316*
Bar Cuba, 11-13 Kensington High St, W8, T020-7938 4137. Great fun – running regular excellent Samba classes on Thu nights – a hugely popular Latin bar which downstairs offers one of the tiniest, liveliest slices of honest raunch in London. Not remotely sleazy, a holiday atmosphere prevails. Open until 0200 Mon-Sat.

The Scarsdale, 23a Edwardes Square, W8, T020- 7937 1811. Hidden away in this lovely Georgian secret square, right behind the cinema – like a lively seaside inn with proper tables outside for the summer and gas fires for the winter, charming bar staff and all-day dining.

Earl's Court *p322, map p324*
Balans West, 239 Old Brompton Rd, SW5, T020-7244 8838. Nearer Earl's Court, this is the sister act to the one in Soho, a very hip corner spot where the locals and the gay crowd love to cool their heels with some sexy cocktails (open until 0200 on Fri, Sat, until 0100 every other night).

The Colherne, 261 Old Brompton Rd, SW5, T020-7244 5951. A big, dark, throbbing gay pub with a disco-lit pool table.

⊕ Entertainment

Kensington High Street & Earl's Court
p322, map p316 & p324
Cinema
Odeon Kensington, Kensington High St, opposite The Commonwealth Institute. Mainstream refurbished multiscreen. T0870-5050 007.

Music
Classical St Mary Abbots Church, Kensington Church St, W8. Fri lunchtime concerts 1310-1350 given by students of Royal College of Music, admission free.

Theatre
The Finborough Theatre, 118 Finborough Rd, SW10, T020-7373 3842, above a busy Irish pub. This small fringe theatre has an excellent reputation for promising new work.

❍ Shopping

Kensington High Street *p322, map p316*
Kensington is not what it used to be – if you remember its 1960s heyday then Biba was an ephemeral moment. Worse still, the indoor market stalls that gave the street some much-needed offbeat appeal have also been closed. For three decades these were the place to find antique clothing, avant garde high-fashion, punk and leatherwear, making Ken High St the must-stop shop above Camden.

Ken High St no longer offers the unique, so much as a select trail of all the best high street chains. They're all here including a reasonably good department store:
Barkers, 63 Ken High St, W8, T020-7937 5432. Open Mon-Wed 1000-1900, Thu 1000-2000, Fri 1000-1900, Sat 0930-1900, Sun 1200-1800. 4 floors and part of House of Fraser.

The only individual shops that hint at the old boutique style crawl up Kensington Church Rd, lead you up to Notting Hill and turn into a string of specialist fine antique shops. Down the other end by the cinema there is a cluster at the top of the Earl's Court Rd. The long High St now boasts everything from **Safeways**, **M&S**, **Boots** to all the other necessities near the tube station. There's also a mini mall in **Barkers** with **Morgans**, **Karen Millen** and other trendy chain stores.

Children Books Centre, 237 Ken High St, T020-7937 7497, www.childrensbookcentre .co.uk. A superb kiddy specialist shop – always full of enthusiastic admirers – close by Gap Kids.
Designer Bargains, 29 Kensington Church St, T020-7795 6777. Stock some excellent women's second-hand finds – from Gucci to Chanel, Jigssaw to Katherine Hamnett.
Non Stop Party Shop, 214/216 Ken High St, T020-7937 7200. Full of party ideas and little gifts and an unlimited choice of personal printing and other miscellaneous services.
Orsini, 76 Earl's Court Rd, W8, T020-7937 2903. Go bargain-hunting for vintage ladies clothing and pick some period wonders from the 20s to the 60s here at the other end of the High, Tue-Sat 1200-1800 only, with a mass of classic prints and satin feathery shoes, frocks and suits; a real treat.

Earl's Court *p322, map p324*
There's not a lot in Earl's Court really. The main purchase made here is an international phone card. Along the main drag are the odd second-hand charity shop, a string of newsagents and travel agents and bakeries up and down the Earl's Court Rd. Gloucester Rd has a Waitrose and a small Partridges (the fine speciality food shop on Sloane Street),

otherwise the area lacks boutiques and only caters for snackers and news.

▲ Activities

Kensington High Street & Earls Court
p322, map p316 & p324
Earl's Court Gym, 254 Earl's Court Rd, T020-7370 1402. 'Urban fitness' very efficient and seemingly very gay. Day membership £9. **The Phillimore Club**, 45 Phillimore Walk, Kensington, W8, T020-7937 2882, www.phillimoreclub.com. "Quietly celebrating the privilege of being a woman" this place offers steam rooms, beauty salon, gym and dance studio as well as treatments such as enzymatic sea mud wraps and Ayurvedic Indian head and face massages.

❶ Directory

Kensington High Street *p322, map p316*
Libraries **Kensington Central Library & Town Hall** Philimore Walk W8, T020-7937 2542. Behind Kensington High Street – the big borough-wide resource – all information from the usual multi-media lending faciltes to jobs, arts, fashion and antique fairs in their portals.

Bayswater, Paddington and Little Venice

From Marble Arch, the Edgware Road pushes busily plumb straight northwest towards Maida Vale, Kilburn and Cricklewood, while the leafy Bayswater Road sidles along the northern edge of Hyde Park, taking the line of Oxford Street out west to Notting Hill. The wedge on the map between these two main roads is one of London's most contradictory areas. At its tip, Sussex Gardens isolates an exclusive enclave of stately mansions and expensive squares from the scruffy chaos around Paddington Station. Further north, beyond the Westway flyover and the rundown Harrow Road, the area called Little Venice overstates its case but is nevertheless a watery and genteel haven on the Grand Union Canal, its Paddington arm recently given a facelift. Meanwhile, west of Lancaster Gate, which is one of the most attractive entrances to Kensington Gardens via the Italian gardens, Bayswater is an almost uniform stretch of crumbling stucco and porticos labouring under the weight of a population continually on the move. Queensway is the tacky hub of the area, so glitzy and gawdy that it's really quite good, always buzzing with passing trade. At its north end, home to the first ever coin-op launderette in the UK, opened in 1949, Westbourne Grove goes steadily upmarket on the approach to Notting Hill. ⏵⏵ *For Sleeping, Eating and other listings see pages 331-334.*

History

Followers of the Anglo-Saxon chieftain 'Padda' probably gave Paddington its name, as they settled around modern Paddington Green. The Edgware and Bayswater Roads were ancient Roman routes north and west respectively, but development was limited, not least because from the 14th century the Tyburn gallows (at modern Marble Arch) ensured 'Tyburnia' retained a notorious reputation. In Westbourne Park (the River Westbourne ran south through here) a farm existed until the mid-19th century, and there were reservoirs where Sussex and Talbot Squares now sit.

33 Bayswater, Paddington & Little Venice

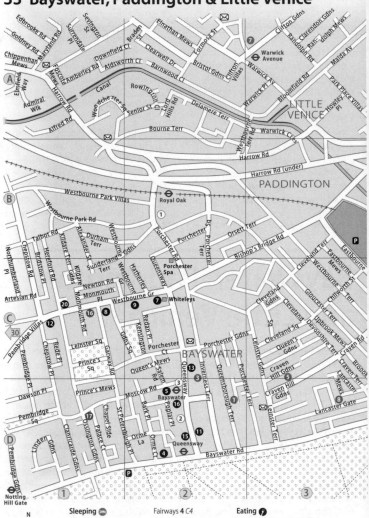

West Bayswater, Paddington & Little Venice

N

0 metres 100
0 yards 100

Sleeping	Fairways 4 *C4*	Eating
Byron 1 *D2*	Hempel 5 *C3*	Baghdad Restaurant 20 *C1*
Border 2 *C4*	Lancaster Hall 6 *D4*	Bottega del Gelato 4 *D2*
Colonnade 7 *A3*	Royal Lancaster 7 *D4*	Byzantium 5 *D2*
Columbia 8 *D3*		Khans 7 *C2*
Dean Court 3 *C2*		L'Accento 8 *C1*

From the 15th century the Bayswater conduit supplied the city with water (Bayswater is named after Bayard's Spring, situated near Queensway), but until it was diverted in 1834, the Westbourne became so polluted that the Serpentine, which it also fed, became a cesspit. Although the village of Paddington grew following an influx of Huguenots in the 18th century, and small farms and taverns (in which Shakespeare is reputed to have performed) lined the Edgware Road, it was the removal of the gallows in 1783 that enabled the settlement to expand.

A further impetus for development followed the opening in 1801 of a section of the Grand Junction Canal between Uxbridge and the Paddington Basin, and later with the arrival of the railways. Expansion spread to the north and west –

West Bayswater, Paddington & Little Venice

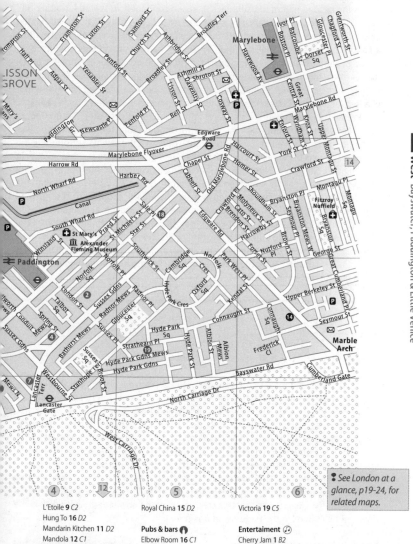

⁑ See London at a glance, p19-24, for related maps.

L'Etoile **9** *C2*
Hung To **16** *D2*
Mandarin Kitchen **11** *D2*
Mandola **12** *C1*
Pierre Pechon **13** *C2*
Renoush Juice Bar **14** *C6*

Royal China **15** *D2*

Pubs & bars 🍺
Elbow Room **16** *C1*
Leinster **17** *D1*
Rob Roy **18** *B5*

Victoria **19** *C5*

Entertainment 🎭
Cherry Jam **1** *B2*
Gala Casino **3** *D2*
Queen's Ice Bowl **2** *D2*

Tomlin's Town housed canal workers, and Connaught Place signalled plans to create a rival to Belgravia.

For a while, Bayswater did indeed become a much coveted address. Stuccoed mansions in Westbourne Terrace earned it the description as 'the finest street in London', Westbourne Grove became a popular shopping street, especially for fashionable drapers, and in the 1850s large houses went up in Lancaster Gate, Leinster and Princes squares. Military officers returned from India to settle here, as did a range of distinguished writers and entrepreneurs. WH Smith moved in to Sussex Square, Thomas Hardy wrote his (rejected) first novel, *The Poor Man and the Lady*, from Westbourne Park Villas, Aubrey Beardsley and Oscar Wilde lived in Palace Court, while later JM Barrie wrote Peter Pan while living on the corner of Bayswater Road and Leinster Terrace.

In the second half of the century expansion continued westwards: Notting Hill, Kensal Town and Queen's Park all grew through to the 1870s. Meanwhile, Paddington underwent its own transport revolution. Following the completion of the canal in 1801, a link to the Regent's Canal was built in 1820. A railway station was built in 1838, although the current station was designed by Isembard Kingdom Brunel a touch further east. Queen Victoria arrived at the original wooden station following her first railway journey, although perhaps the most internationally acclaimed arrival was that of a lost (and fictional) bear from Peru to launch a popular children's book series.

In 1861 horse-drawn trams were introduced on Bayswater Road, George Shillibeer's Omnibus ran from the Green to the City, and the new Metropolitan underground line arrived in 1863. Predictably, perhaps, the streets surrounding the canal and railway became slums, such that soon 'rags and riches eyed each other in Paddington'. St Mary's Hospital on Praed Street (where Sir Alexander Fleming discovered penicillin in 1929) and Paddington Green Children's Hospital (its building destroyed the last thatched house in London) catered for the growing population, a task made all the more important as more and more Victorian terraced streets turned to slums. Unscrupulous landlords such as Rachman exploited the squalid housing and the growing immigrant population in the 1950s (there is still a large Arab population along the Edgware Road), and the area became notorious for crime and prostitution. It is only just beginning to restore its reputation to that of its heyday in the mid-19th century.

Sights

⬗ *Bayswater, Lancaster Gate, Paddington, Queensway, Royal Oak.* ⬗ *See p460.*

Apart from delayed trains, there's not much to keep anyone for long in Paddington. The revamped Paddington Station for tubes and trains greets the Heathrow Express. Queensway tube is at the main drag's southern end, near Hyde Park; Bayswater tube is halfway down. If you happen to have time to kill in the area, then the **Alexander Fleming Museum** ① *in St Mary's Hospital, Praed St, T020-7886 6528, Mon-Thu 1000-1300, £2 adults, £1 concessions*, is worth a quick look. It contains the actual laboratory in which the great man accidentally discovered penicillin and hence invented antibiotics, a video on the history of his research and its wide-reaching benefits, and an exhibition on the history of the pills that were once hailed as cure-alls. Boffins like to joke that this celebration of the power of the petri dish is the one spot of 'culture' in the Paddington Basin.

Warwick Avenue and **Little Venice** are a short distance north of the station, but reached with difficulty from here because of the hectic road systems around the

Marylebone flyover. It's easier, and certainly safer, to take the tube one stop to Warwick Avenue. **Blomfield Road** is the most attractive of the canalside streets of this quiet residential area. The best reason for a visit are the narrowboat trips up to the Zoo, Regent's Park and Camden Lock (see page 43).

On **Bayswater Road**, the strangest thing is the regular market of terrible paintings hung on the railings of Hyde Park every Sunday. They make a good introduction to the fiercely unfashionable and cheesy main drag of Queensway heading up to Westbourne Grove. The **Queen's Ice Rink**, the shopping mall of **Whiteleys**, and the **Porchester Spa** (see Activities below) nevertheless make an impressive trio of attractions along with any number of cheap restaurants and cafés.

⬤ Sleeping

Bayswater, Paddington & Little Venice *p327, map p328*

L The Colonnade, 2 Wellington Cres, Little Venice, W9, T020-7286 1052, www.theetoncollection.com. £173 not including breakfast, 43 rooms, bar and restaurant. Restored Victorian townhouse tucked away in Little Venice.

L The Hempel, 31-35 Craven Hill Gdns, W2, T020-7298 9000, www.the-hempel.co.uk. 41 rooms, 6 apartments, the smartest hotel in the area is still this elegant extravagance designed by the Queen Bee of designer hotels – former model Anouska Hempel aka Lady Weinberger. Very different from her own hotel, Blakes, although it too occupies one whole side of a white stucco square. The minimalist Japanese design with its exquisite interiors defies the Regency architecture outside – every wall, window and portal is different and chic, the central garden holds a pool amongst the shaken-but-never-stirred bay trees amid lots of pebbles, the 'Oriental' restaurant and a new bar, the H Bar, are open to non-residents.

L Royal Lancaster Hotel, Lancaster Terr, W2, T020-7262 6737, www.royallancaster.com. Has 416 rooms at the lower end of this price bracket, as well as the famous Nipa restaurant, doing immaculate Thai cuisine in authentic surroundings.

B Columbia Hotel, 95-99 Lancaster Gate, W2, T020-7402 0021, www.columbiahotel. co.uk. Grand-looking hotel just off the Bayswater Rd, popular with visiting rockers and musos and hence often a very lively post-gig late bar. £83 a double including VAT and breakfast.

B-C Fairways Hotel, 186 Sussex Gdns, W2, T020-7723 4871, www.fairways-hotel.co.uk.

Typical guest house for the area, clean but fairly basic, the Mitre hotel next door (same details) is run by the same family, marginally more expensive but includes breakfast.

C Border Hotel, 14 Norfolk Sq, W2, T020-7723 2968, www.stdavidshotels.co.uk. 74 rooms, English breakfast included.

C Byron Hotel, 36-38 Queensborough Terr, W2, T020-7243 0987, www.capricornhotels. co.uk. 45 rooms, 3-star, also pretty typical of the area, with full English breakfast included.

C Lancaster Hall Hotel, 35 Craven Terr, W2, T020-7723 9276, www.lancaster-hotel.co.uk. 103 rooms, tucked away, this large, concrete block is surprisingly quiet in the heart of Bayswater backstreets, between the hub of Queensway and Paddington, only a stone's throw from Lancester Gate entrance to the park, very pleasant despite its 60s concrete exterior and being a corporate favourite, only twin-bedded rooms.

D-E Dean Court Hotel, 57 Inverness Terr, W2, T020-7229 2961. Australian-managed, 3-4 to a room, £17 a night, £79 a week, including breakfast, single sex, double £45, dorm room bookable only for a minimum of 2 nights.

⬤ Eating

Bayswater, Paddington & Little Venice *p327, map p328*

The avenue of Queensway is a busy strip of cheap eateries – all the world's flavours are on offer – a well-known draw for oriental, Greek and Middle East muncheries and pastry shops.

⫙⫙ Royal China, 13 Queensway, W2, T020-7221 2535. Apart from the restaurant in the Hempel Hotel, this is the place to treat yourself. It is the glamorous and cavernous Chinese highspot of the area. It's like walking into a dark, 1970s disco, where large round tables feed gangs of those who like their Peking Duck flown in fresh and the dim sum are legendary (filling and considerably less expensive than a full meal). Delicious and definitely worth travelling to find.

♥♥ L'Accento, 16 Garway Rd, W2, T020-7243 2664. A little way off the beaten track, a very fine and quiet modern Italian restaurant open for lunch and dinner only.

♥♥ Mandarin Kitchen, 14-16 Queensway, W2, T020-7727 9012. Among the other Chinese restaurants on Queensway, this is famous for its lobster noodles, which put it squarely in this price bracket. More simple and still pretty delicious food can also be had here for half the price.

Queensway and Westbourne Grove are classic destinations for a cheap meal out although many are best avoided.

♥ The Baghdad Restaurant, 107 Westbourne Grove, W2, T020-7229 3048. Head here or Arabic cuisine and a charcoal grill. Charming service in a pretty tiled room offering the full range of Middle Eastern eats. Cleaner and brighter than the ubiquitous doner kebab fare that dominates the area. Open daily 1700-2330 and also at lunchtimes during weekends.

♥ Hung To, 51 Queensway, W2, T020-7727 5753. A busy Chinese, full of locals tucking in and an authentic piece of Chinatown.

♥ Khans, 13-15 Westbourne Grove, W2, T020-7727 5420. Probably one of the biggest and most popular curry houses in London. The bustle and cheapness make it London's answer to Paris's 'Chartier'. Don't count on friendliness from the busy staff – it's the speed with which the Delhi grub arrives that makes people rendezvous and return here. Open 1200-1500, 1800-1200.

♥ Mandola, Westbourne Grove, W2, T020-7229 4734. A local Sudanese favourite that has expanded into the next door room. Sit for hours over an authentic North African feast. Their mezze and the pot of the day is always reliable. The Sudanese coffee is an

Arabian treat while the staff are as unaffectedly beautiful as ebony statues in their natural woven wraps. Best to book.

Cafés and sandwich bars

Bottega del Gelato, 127 Bayswater Rd, W2, T020-7243 2443. Do an astonishing array of delightful fresh home-made ice creams.

Byzantium, 31 Moscow Rd, W2, T020-7229 9367. One of the best cafés in an area full of them. The food and cakes may not beat the French ones, but this fuggy backwater is the one where the locals stay and gossip and read their papers. The owner is so cheerful that your stay is welcome however little you sip. Open until 2100 daily.

L'Etoile, 73 Westbourne Grove, W2, T020-7229 0380. Another popular French patisserie.

Pierre Pechon, 127 Queensway, W2, T020-7229 0746. Has been Queenway's foremost Patisserie Française since 1925. It's still a lively spot, good for hot coffees and all the usual comfort foods. Takeaway cakes and breads are perfect for Sun brunch.

Ranoush Juice Bar, 43 Edgware Rd, W2, T020-7723 5929, www.ranoush.com. Open until 0300 daily, an Arabian juice bar with impeccable style.

☻ Pubs and bars

Bayswater, Paddington & Little Venice *p327, map p328*

Most of the pubs in Bayswater are tourist traps.

Elbow Room, 103 Westbourne Grove, W2, T020-7221 5211, www.theelbowroom.co.uk. Has perfected a popular and trendy 90s concept of making pool, lounge, groove and bar all come together. The coolest place to hang, shoot pool and have a meaty snack over a long, slow cocktail. The original one of a chain of three where the tables aren't green and the players only sport designer anoraks.

Leinster, 57 Ossington St, W2, T020-7243 9541. A pub that pulls in the locals with its recent refurbishment, another opportunity to drown your sorrows while your smalls are spinning in the Central Wash launderette next door. No frills but the natives are friendly.

● *For an explanation of sleeping and eating price codes used in this guide, see inside the front cover. Other relevant information is found in Essentials, see pages 44-46.*

Rob Roy, 8 Sale Pl, T020-7262 6403. One of London's few Scottish boozers.
Victoria, 10a Strathearn Pl, W2, nearer Paddington, T020-7724 1191. A posh old Victorian pub with a lovely upstairs bar.

● Entertainment

Bayswater, Paddington & Little Venice *p327, map p328*
Casinos
Gala Casino, 79-81 Queensway, W2, T020-7221 8788. Daily 1330-0600. Cheesy and swanky gambling den, one of a chain of five. The pictures make it look more like Butlins than Monte Carlo or Las Vegas. "The sheer size of the gaming room will impress" they declare. Membership required 24 hrs in advance. Casino Restuarant open 1900 or a good late-night fix is the £5 breakfast available from midnight to 0200. There is also Sky TV, car jockey and free parking. Presumably you pay more to get out than you pay to get in...

Cinema
UCI Whiteleys, top floor of the Shopping Centre, T08700-102030. 8-screen mainstream multiplex.

Nightclubs
Cherry Jam, 58 Porchester Rd, W2, T020-7727 9950, www.cherryjam.net. Unusual and stylish cocktail bar and club playing live sounds from around the world – 'Outernational' – Wed-Sat. Also has a trailblazing 'Book Slam' spoken word night once a month. Open til 0200.
Ice Disco, Queens Ice Bowl, 17 Queensway, W2, T020-7229 0172. Admission £7 including skate hire. Fri and Sat 1930-2300 with Live DJs, giveaways and more, also every Sun 2000-2200.

● Shopping

Bayswater, Paddington & Little Venice *p327, map p328*
Whiteleys. Bayswater is known for this central shopping mall which was once one of the first and most successful wonderful old department stores. Its founder was shot in his office by his bastard son who received widespread sympathy, resulting in his death sentence being commuted to hard labour.

The transformation into major mall emphasizes its origins, retaining the original white stucco pillars and high inner arches. Apparently Whiteleys was targeted by Hitler as his preferred HQ in London and spared by the Luftwaffe. All the usual stores offer the shopper long hours and delights from M&S. The central fountains with coloured lights and regular mini 'events' prove popular with the waiting dads and pushchairs. At night, the teenagers gather in the top floor bars and fake boulevards where the brasseries and bars spill onto the 'pavement', actually a vinyl extension of the escalator. The mini-multiplex cinema is the big draw – with all the latest Hollywood releases on show.

On Queensway itself the cheap boutiques and shops are many – mainly brisk, pile-em-high, hi-fi, electronic and lugguage shops. You can find most things here – cheaper than Oxford St.
Archie, 14 Moscow Rd, W2, nearer Notting Hill, T020-7229 2275. An English, Continental, Middle Eastern deli, veg, groceries – a useful authentic corner shop (before you hit Hyde Park for a picnic).
Athenian Grocery, 16a Moscow Rd, W2, T020-7229 6280. Specializes in Greek Cypriot wines and foods with even more fruit and veg than their neighbour.
Capital News, Queensway, T020-7229 8007. Open daily until 2230, is the oldest and liveliest of the strip's newsagents – all the world's papers and magazines, telephone cards and sweeties – clearly a favourite gossip spot for all the locals from far-flung places.
Nickoldeon Video, 53 Queensway, W2, T020-7229 1333. Open 7 days 1030-2300, is the best of the string of video stores (stocks the lot and is an independent). Everything at £1.50 only per night. Staff have the shifty, edgy look of Tarantino before he was famous.
Planet Organic, 42 Westbourne Grove, W2, T020-7221 7171. The original large, and ludicrously expensive must-have organic supermarket. The mecca for the must-do betters. Full of Holland Park-Hoxton trustifarians and lonely merchant bankers seeking out a fly-free beetroot. Great if you want to prove your veggie cred. Anyone sensible supports the locals and picks out the best from the butchers and Portobello greengrocers for a fifth of the price.

▲ Activities

Bayswater, Paddington & Little Venice *p327, map p328*

Porchester Spa, 225 Queensway, W2, T020-7792 3980, ladies only Tue, Thu, Fri 1000-2200 (last entry 2000), men only Mon, Wed, Sat 1000-2200 (last entry 2000), Sun women only 1000-1600, mixed couples 1600-2200 (last entry 2000). £19.45 non-members. A treat in the area; old Turkish, Russian steam rooms, cold plunge pool, jacuzzi, showers, therapy rooms and swimming pool. Café open daily 1100-1930. Towel and wrap provided, bring your own shower stuff and swimming costume.

Queen's Ice Bowl, 17 Queensway, W2, T020-7229 0172. Mon-Sun 1000-1345, 1400-1645, 1700-1845, and also Mon-Thu 1600-2300. Adults and children £7 including skate hire. The 50,000-ft ice rink is a real gem. It's always been there and it's got to be the most fun ice rink in London. Since refurbishment it now also offers 12 lanes of fullsize tenpin bowling, 50 hi-tech video games, amusements, a bar and a Wimpy restaurant.

Fulham, Hammersmith and Putney

Beyond the glamour of Chelsea and the passing trade of Earl's Court, densely residential Fulham stretches down to the river. Once a solidly working-class area, the regular terraces of little houses here have long since become some of the most sought after in West London, where the idea of village London has become enshrined. Half the population apparently heads off at the weekends for the real thing in the country and regards the rest of London as 'up town'. Around Parsons Green and down by the river at the Bishop's Palace, this is Middle England in the big smoke. Apart from a small area around Fulham Broadway, the evenings are quiet in Fulham. That's not the case in Hammersmith, a little further upstream. Here a couple of big music venues, the lively Riverside Studios and the innovative Lyric Theatre boost the cultural life of an area almost overwhelmed by massive roads and streaming traffic. Most visitors wisely escape to the riverside, where a popular promenade lined with a variety of pubs does brisk business summer and winter. Across the river, Barnes is a peaceful backwater, now blessed with its very own waterfowl sanctuary at the Wetland Centre, while a walk back downstream towards Fulham takes in the little town of Putney. ▶▶ For Eating and other listings see pages 339-340.

History

By the 14th century, small riverside settlements such as Fulham, Hammersmith and Putney were common features along the banks of the Thames. Further inland, isolated hamlets such as Parsons Green, Walham Green and Earl's Court were surrounded by fields, market gardens and nurseries. Fulham Palace, on the river's edge, was the residence for Bishops of London from 704 to 1973, and it is thought that the huge moat (it was finally filled in 1921) followed the line of a Roman defensive earthwork.

Putney, where there was also once a Roman settlement and maybe even a bridge, was a riverside village concentrated on fishing and farming. Under the Tudors, it became a popular site for Tudor mansions (Thomas Cromwell, chief architect of the Dissolution of the Monasteries, lived here), and a wooden bridge was built in 1729 (from which Mary Wollstonecraft threw herself in an attempt to commit suicide) for the Fulham Road and the busy coaching route to Portsmouth and the southwest.

By the 18th century, traffic was busy enough for highwaymen to patrol the heath and several further houses had been built as merchants sought out purer air than the City. Hurlingham House (it didn't turn to sports until the mid-1860s, when pigeon shooting, skittles, croquet and polo were introduced), Brandenburgh House (with a theatre in the grounds), Chiswick and Sandford Manor House were among the grander residences.

In Hammersmith the Lower Mall, Upper Mall (William Morris lived and died here) and Hammersmith Terrace were fashionable riverside addresses, commanding privileged views of the Thames Regatta, and London's first suspension bridge opened at Hammersmith in 1827. At Parson's Green the grand houses surrounding the green were inhabited by 'Gentry and Persons of Quality'. Walham Green, later to become part of Fulham Broadway, housed a green, pond and whipping post, but was yet to earn a church.

Expansion continued sporadically until after the mid-19th century (both Fulham and Hammersmith were still renowned for their spinach and strawberries in the 1840s) when the tide of expansion from Kensington finally swallowed up the area. Now a range of industries, from distilleries to mills to boatyards was being established. The Fulham Hospital opened to serve the workhouses, and Irish labourers drawn by the railways moved into cottages set on boggy land around Brook Green. Shops opened along Putney High Street, and the tentacles of housing spread into Fulham, such that it became 'a portion of the outer fringe of the great city'.

Over the last century Fulham has become increasingly fashionable, while Hammersmith has suffered somewhat from road building programmes such as the flyover and Great West Road. Putney has not had to endure much rebuilding since the Victorian and Edwardian era, and retains its popularity as a smart residential retreat.

Sights ⊖ *Fulham Broadway, Hammersmith, Parsons Green, Putney.*

It's generally accepted that Chelsea ends and Fulham begins at the railway line running through West Brompton past Chelsea FC's Stamford Bridge football stadium, crossing first the Fulham Road and then the King's Road. Both roads head southwest for Putney Bridge roughly parallel to each other, but the difference between the two says a lot about Fulham's divided nature. The King's Road is the more polite, and its stretch as the New King's Road around Parsons Green is the most desirable part of the area. The Fulham Road on the other hand takes in Fulham Broadway, where the area's nightlife is concentrated, and then weaves for about a mile through row upon row of gentrified workers' cottages down to the river and Fulham's main visitor attraction: the Bishop's Palace. Fulham is famous for its antique shops, especially along the Fulham Road south of Fulham Broadway, while the New King's Rd boast a few just-about-affordable designer boutiques, superior off-licences and delicatessens.

Bishop's Palace
ⓘ *To20-7736 3233. Mar-Oct Wed-Sun 1400-1700, Nov-Feb Thu-Sun 1300-1600. Free (donations requested).*
The home of the Bishop of London until 1973, this doesn't look like much of a palace at all, but instead is a beautiful, partly early 16th-century diamond-patterned red-brick house with an 18th century bell-turret set in an attractive gardens (that are open dawn to dusk daily). There's a small two-room museum on the history of the palace and guided tours (£4) of the building are given on Sundays twice a month, and every third Wednesday. The riverside walk shaded with huge plane trees in Bishop's Park provides fine views towards Putney.

34 Fulham & Putney

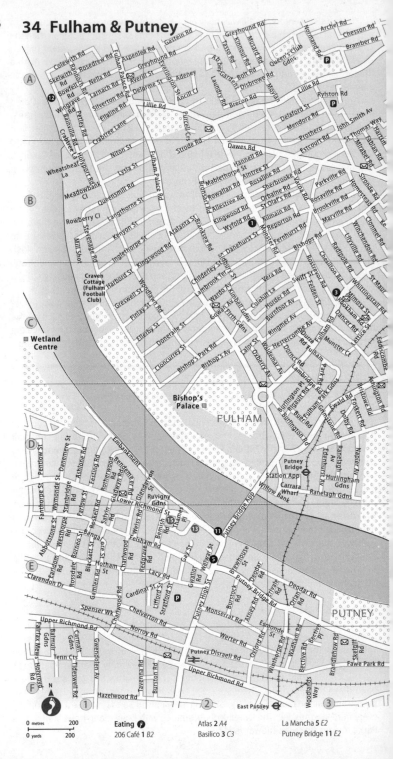

West Fulham, Hammersmith & Putney

| 0 metres | 200 |
| 0 yards | 200 |

Eating 🍴
206 Café **1** *B2*

Atlas **2** *A4*
Basilico **3** *C3*

La Mancha **5** *E2*
Putney Bridge **11** *E2*

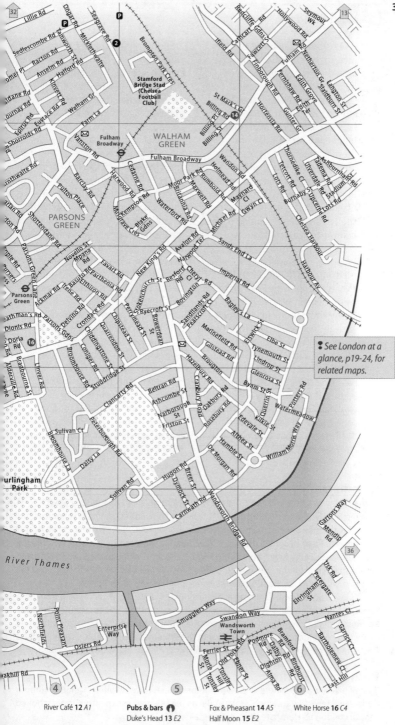

See London at a glance, p19-24, for related maps.

River Café **12** *A1*

Pubs & bars
Duke's Head **13** *E2*

Fox & Pheasant **14** *A5*
Half Moon **15** *E2*

White Horse **16** *C4*

⁘ Wild London

Few European capital cities are as green as London, making it a top location for city-dwelling tree-huggers, urban twitchers and more casual nature lovers looking to stretch their legs. As well as its famous parks, the capital contains hundreds of smaller patches of green and substantial tracts of managed open space, all teeming with unexpected wildlife. Even the River Thames receives surprising marine visitors: seals have been spotted between Richmond Bridge and Westminster; bottlenose dolphins venture up as far as Wapping and Blackfriars. At Isleworth Ait (T020-8392 9135) a river island nature reserve managed by the London Wildlife Trust (www.wildlondon.org.uk), rare birds such as treecreeper, heron and even kingfisher can occasionally be glimpsed from the riverbank.

Of the Trust's two dozen or so nature reserves, perhaps their most unusual is the inner-city wildlife refuge at Camley St, King's Cross (see page 187), a metropolitan oasis on the Regent's Canal, alive with birds, bees and amphibians.

Further north, the most accessible wide open space from central London is the high ground of Hampstead Heath (see page 289). Several different habitats here – ponds, grassland, wood and scrub among others – support a huge variety of flora and fauna: waterfowl, fungi, strange lichens, mosses and small mammals, including bats. In the air, magpies, crows, jays and pigeons just about leave room for smaller species: thrushes, blackbirds, bluetits, robins, sparrows and wrens are the most likely to be seen. On or under the ground, badgers, hedgehogs, voles and moles might be spotted if you're lucky or prepared to stay very still and quiet in the early hours. Foxes are increasingly common. No prizes for seeing a squirrel or a rabbit.

In the southwest, Richmond Park (see page 346) is home to as many species as Hampstead Heath, with the added attraction of its grazing domesticated deer. On the way southwest, in Barnes, the London Wetland Centre is well worth a look for rare sightings of migratory duck, geese, waders and warblers.

Hammersmith

To the northwest, up the Fulham Palace Road, Hammersmith and its arty associations have been badly mauled in the 20th century by road building schemes. First impressions on leaving the tube are that the place is one big roundabout. At the Hammersmith flyover the Cromwell Road becomes the Great West Road rushing out to Chiswick towards the M4 motorway. Scruffy King Street is the heart of the area, home to the Lyric Theatre and the Polish Cultural Centre. Most visitors quite sensibly head for the river though, and the strip of pubs lining Lower and Upper Malls west of Hammersmith Bridge.

A very pleasant walk leads all the way along the north bank of the river from here to pretty Chiswick Mall and beyond. Just to the east of the bridge are the **Riverside Studios**, with their art gallery, cinema, theatre and TV studios. The bridge links Barnes to the rest of London. It crosses the river to the Wildfowl and Wetland's Trust Wetland Centre in the converted Barn Elms Water Works a mile to the south (see below).

Putney and Barnes

Putney has the atmosphere of a riverside provincial town, while its quiet neighbour Barnes still feels like a village. Both make as pleasant an escape from traffic-choked central London as Hampstead in the north.

From Putney Bridge, a walk west along the south bank for about a mile along the Embankment, past Putney Boat House and the spooky old Harrod's repository looking across the river to Bishop's Park, leads eventually to the **London Wetland Centre** ① *Queen Elizabeth's Walk, T020-8409 4400, www.wwt.org.uk, daily summer 0930-1800 (last admission 1700), winter 0930-1700 (last admission 1600), £6.75, concessions £5.50; under-16s £4.* Converted from four Victorian water-work reservoirs, the reed-filled ponds look surprisingly natural. After a look round the Discovery centre, with its AV displays on wetland habitats, visitors stroll around the perimeter of the 105-acre site, viewing the entire area and the waterbirds from a three-storey hide and also via hidden cameras dotted about the birds' feeding ground.

⦿ Eating

Fulham *p334, map p336*
₩₩₩ **Putney Bridge**, The Embankment, SW15, T020-8780 1811. Very refined modern French food is served up in designer surroundings in a plum location. The river views, if not perhaps the food, are better than the River Café.
₩₩₩ **River Café**, Thames Wharf, Rainville Rd, W6, T020-7386 4200. For some time now the celebrated TV chefs and cookery writers Ruth and Rosie have been wowing this 'new establishment' with their Tuscan recipes (main courses £25-30). The restaurant was designed by Ruth's husband Richard Rogers, and it's airy and light, and it often needs to be booked a week in advance.
₩₩ **The Gate**, 51 Queen Caroline St, W6, T020-8748 6932, close to the Riverside Studios. Rich and satisfying vegetarian treat in an old church building very popular with locals and theatre-goers.
₩ **206 Café**, 206 Munster Rd, SW6. Some way from the action and considerably less expensive, very popular with BYOB Fulhamites, a tiny Thai restaurant full of personality, not least that of its owner, Joy.
₩ **The Atlas**, 16 Seagrave Rd, SW6, T020-7385 9129. A vibrant and woody gastropub with an excellent daily changing Mediterranean menu, no bookings, lunch and supper, tucked away behind the Earl's Court Exhibition Centre but reachable from Fulham Broadway.
₩ **Basilico**, 690 Fulham Rd, SW6, T020-7384 2633, the southern end of the Fulham Rd, www.basilico.freeserve.co.uk. The place to look for top-quality but fairly expensive thin crust pizzas to eat in at tiny designer tables or to take away.

Hammersmith *p338*
₩ **Lowiczanka**, 238-246 King St, W6, T020-8741 3225. A friendly and traditional Polish café-restaurant on the 1st floor of the Polish Cultural Centre.

Putney *p338, map p336*
₩ **La Mancha**, 32 Putney High St, SW15, T020-8780 1022. A buzzing Spanish tapas bar and restaurant, a superior paella factory, open 7 days.

⦿ Pubs and bars

Fulham *p334, map p336*
Fox and Pheasant, 1 Billing Rd, SW10, T020-7352 2943. A straightforward and very small old boozer near Chelsea FC that almost stands alone in the area against the tide of chain bars and ropey theme pubs.
White Horse, 1-3 Parsons Green, SW6, T020-7736 2115. Known by some as the 'Sloaney Pony', this is a heaving real ale pub right on the green with a small restaurant in the converted coach house at the back, the place to take the pulse of this wealthy area.

Hammersmith *p338*
Blue Anchor, 13 Lower Mall, W6, T020-8748 5774. The friendliest and most cosy of the pubs on the strip along the river.
Dove, 19 Upper Mall, W6, T020-8748 5405. Further along, the most famous place on the river here. Does food too and purportedly has the smallest bar in London, which doesn't help with the overcrowding.
Old Ship, 25 Upper Mall, W6, T020-8748 2593. The least pretentious and most family-friendly.

⬤ *For an explanation of sleeping and eating price codes used in this guide, see inside the* ⬤ *front cover. Other relevant information is found in Essentials, see pages 44-46.*

Bar M, T020-8788 0345, next door to the Duke's Head. Has regular live music.

Duke's Head, 8 Lower Richmond Rd, SW15, T020-8788 2552. Overlooking the Thames, this is a huge party pub that does reasonable food at lunch and dinner.

Half Moon, 93 Lower Richmond Rd, SW15, T020-8780 9383, www.halfmooon.co.uk. The best pub near (but not on) the river, where Young's ales are pumped amid antiques and bric-a-brac, and there's regular good live music.

The Putney Bridge, Embankment, 2 Lower Richmond Rd, SW15, T020-8780 1811. Has river views, an expensive designer bar attached to the French restaurant (see above).

---

❸ Entertainment

Fulham, Hammersmith & Putney *p335*

Cinema

Riverside Studios, Crisp Rd, W6, T020-8237 1111. Excellent single-screen repertory arthouse.

Dance

Dance Attic, 368 North End Rd, SW6, T020-7610 2055. Dance classes as well as Sat night entertainment 1845-2030, free admission to the cabaret and theatre bar.

Music

Rock, folk and jazz Hammersmith & **Fulham Irish Centre**, Blacks Rd, W6, T020-8563 8232. Modern Irish and country music gigs from 2000 usually Fri and Sat, nights vary, £5-£10. Also holds film and poetry nights.

London Apollo, Queen Caroline St, W6, T0870-606 3400. For medium scale live pop concerts.

Nightclubs

Hammersmith Palais, 242 Shepherd's Bush Rd, W6, T020-8600 2300. Mainstream dance club with occasional live events.

Havana, 490 Fulham Rd, SW6, T020-7381 5005. Very loud, lively and late (until 0200 Fri, Sat) salsa.

Theatre

The Baron's Court, 28A Comeragh Rd, W14, T020-8932 4747. A quirky little dive for experimental productions beneath a loud Irish pub.

The Lyric Theatre, King St, W6, T08700-500 511, and **Lyric Studio Theatre**, 2 of London's most exciting stages, housed in the unpromising looking King's Mall.

The Riverside Studios, Crisp Rd, W6, T020-8237 1111. Have a tiny studio stage and also a larger main theatre for interesting touring productions.

Richmond and Kew

A visit to Kew or Richmond, upriver southwest of Putney, is likely to take up a whole day, but with fine weather the two-hour riverboat or half-hour train journey will be well rewarded. The varying seasonal delights of the Royal Botanical Gardens at Kew are world famous, while the town of Richmond with its tree-lined riverside walk, views from the hill and rolling deer park are the most rural places within easy reach of the city. Here in the buckle of Surrey's stockbroker belt, the English dream of house and garden – rus in urbe – reaches its most complete expression. As well as the more obvious attractions such as Kew Gardens and Richmond Hill, many of the area's old mansions are also worth travelling to find, especially the early 17th-century Ham House, just over the river by foot ferry from Marble Hill House, the Orleans House Gallery and Twickenham. Children love exploring the London Butterfly House and its strange insects in the grounds of stately Syon Park. Closer to London, Chiswick House and Hogarth's House make a fine 18th-century destination near the flower-filled riverside along Chiswick Mall. ▶▶ *For Eating and other listings see pages 347-349.*

The old palace of Shene was a popular royal residence in the 14th century (it is said that Richard II entertained 10,000 guests here over the summer months), but by Henry VII's accession it was a relatively unspectacular manor house next to a hamlet of fishermen's cottages. When the house burnt down, however, Henry elected to build a palace on its site. Named Rychemond after his earldom in Yorkshire, the palace spawned craftsmen's cottages and taverns.

Pageants shared the green with grazing sheep, a spectacle that could be seen from a number of Elizabethan houses built nearby, and the hill was dotted with wealthy men's houses overlooking the Thames. Courtiers moved into Kew, either to serve Richmond Palace itself, or the various nobles and royalty established in houses around. The Dutch House (later to become Kew Palace) was built by a Dutch merchant, while Charles I enclosed the park with an 8-mile wall taking common land and estates from his subjects in the process. There were grumbles, but the compensation was considered fair.

Towards the end of the 17th century, Richmond Wells opened in the grounds of Cadigan House on Richmond Hill. Such was the attraction of dancing in the summer season that the two sisters who lived opposite bought it in order to close it down. Further fine houses emerged, such as those on Maids of Honour Row, and Richmond's increasing popularity saw the introduction of public buildings such as the Theatre Royal or the Star and Garter Inn, 'more like the mansion of a noblemen' which held grand parties for grand guests.

But as Richmond Palace decayed, so the focus shifted to Kew. Frederick, Prince of Wales, built a pleasure garden here, his wife later set out a nine-acre botanical garden and in the 1770s Lancelot 'Capability' Brown laid out new grounds. The Isabella Plantation was enclosed within the park in 1831, and Queen Victoria lent Pembroke Lodge to the then Prime Minister, Lord John Russell (his grandson Bertrand Russell, the philosopher, must have done much of his early thinking here). The ferry to Twickenham had been replaced by a bridge in 1777, and a railway bridge was added in 1848, but the railway brought little in the way of industry or rapid development. Richmond remained a quiet, healthy and genteel suburb. Fishing was still a popular pastime, and the Star and Garter, now rebuilt and considered 'a great disfiguring wart or wen on the face of Richmond' served as a home for disabled soldiers during the First World War.

Virginia Woolf came here to recuperate from a mental breakdown. With her husband, she formed the Hogarth Press in their flat, from which TS Eliot's *The Wasteland* was first published. Electric trams reached Kew in 1901, inevitably drawing more residents; the area remains a much-favoured suburb, despite the heavy flow of people passing through to visit the The Royal Botanical Gardens.

West Richmond & Kew

Sights ❂ *Kew Gardens, Richmond.*

★ Kew Gardens

ⓘ *To20-8940 1171, www.kew.org.uk. Apr-Aug Mon-Fri 0930-1830, last admission 1800: Sat, Sun 0930-1930 (last admission 1900); Sep-Oct 0930-1800 (last admission 1730); Nov-Mar 0930-1615 (last admission 1545). Adults £10, concesssions £7, under-16s free.*

In an area rich in parkland, gorgeous scenery, antique architecture and oodles of stereotypical English charm – somewhat disturbed by the airliners roaring overhead every two minutes into Heathrow – the Royal Botanical Gardens (Kew Gardens for short) are the jewel in the crown and a World Heritage Site. Originally founded as a private garden in the grounds of what became Kew Palace by Prince Frederick, the ill-fated heir to George II, in 1731, Kew has evolved into a 300-acre site containing more than one in eight of all flowering species grown in plantations, borders and glasshouses and is a world-renowned centre for horticultural research.

The first ports of call for most visitors are the **Palm House** and the **Princess of Wales Conservatory** (nearby, a grand new Alpine glasshouse should be open some time in

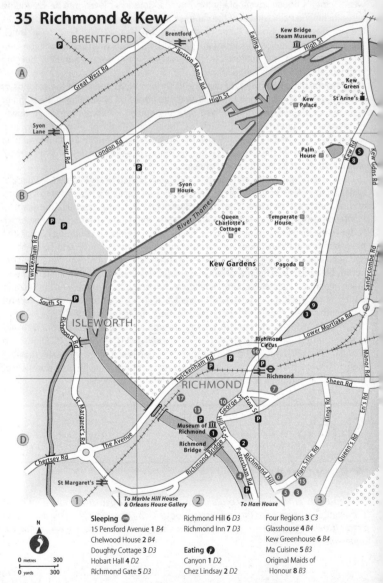

35 Richmond & Kew

West Richmond & Kew

N
0 metres 300
0 yards 300

Sleeping 🛏️
15 Pensford Avenue **1** *B4*
Chelwood House **2** *B4*
Doughty Cottage **3** *D3*
Hobart Hall **4** *D2*
Richmond Gate **5** *D3*

Richmond Hill **6** *D3*
Richmond Inn **7** *D3*

Eating 🍴
Canyon **1** *D2*
Chez Lindsay **2** *D2*

Four Regions **3** *C3*
Glasshouse **4** *B4*
Kew Greenhouse **6** *B4*
Ma Cuisine **5** *B3*
Original Maids of
Honour **8** *B3*

late 2005). The former was the first and is still most magnificent of the glasshouses, fully restored, tropical in both content and humidity, while a rather fine exotic aquarium lurks underneath. The latter houses 10 different zones of computer-maintained climates, complete with foliage, carnivorous and otherwise.

The **Temperate House** is awe-inspiring, if not in content at least in size. The most outstanding feature among the representatives of each of the world's continents is the Chilean Wine Palm, which now measures around 60 ft and is one of the largest indoor palms in the world. Just behind the Temperate House lies the **Evolution House**, though while the subject is fascinating, the hi-tech sound and light approach is patronizing.

Outside, the 18th-century gardens are an attraction in themselves. Originally designed in the 1760s, the later work of Capability Brown (possibly the greatest of

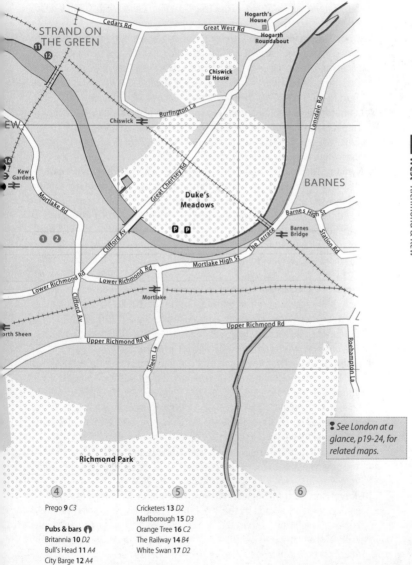

See London at a glance, p19-24, for related maps.

West Richmond & Kew

Prego **9** *C3*

Pubs & bars
Britannia **10** *D2*
Bull's Head **11** *A4*
City Barge **12** *A4*

Cricketers **13** *D2*
Marlborough **15** *D3*
Orange Tree **16** *C2*
The Railway **14** *B4*
White Swan **17** *D2*

⁝ Ten other gardens near London

1. **Bedgebury Pinetum** Superb 150-acre Forestry Commission plot containing the most comprehensive collection of conifers in the world. Also lillies on the lake, wild flowers in late summer, and an extraordinary Leylandiae hedge that you can climb inside. ① *T01580-211044. Adults £4, under 16s £2. Train from Charing Cross to Tunbridge Wells, then bus to Goudhurst and 2-mile walk/bike ride.*

2. **Great Dixter** Eminent gardening writer Christopher Lloyd's experimental garden blooms all year round with meadow flowers, beautiful ponds and an 'exotic' garden. ① *T01797-252878. Closed Mon. House and garden £6.50, under 16s £2, garden only £5, under 16s £1.50. Train from Charing Cross/Waterloo to Ashford, then bus to Tenterden, then Northiam.*

3. **Groombridge Place** The 17th-century formal and topiary gardens here are now part of a well-packaged visitor attraction, its highlight being the Enchanted Forest. Once the secret location for Peter Greenaway's *Draughtsman's Contract*. ① *T01892-863999. Adults £8.50, under 12s £7. Charing Cross to Tunbridge Wells, then bus or steam train to Groombridge.*

4. **Leonardslee** Extraordinary azaleas and hydrangeas in a quite magical landscape and woodland garden laid out around seven hammer ponds. ① *T01403-891212. Adults £6-8, under 16s £4. Train from Victoria to Horsham, then 5-mile bus ride towards Brighton.*

5. **Nymans** National Trust garden, designed by Ludwig Messel covering more than 30 acres around a grand old house. Especially beautiful (in late summer) are the white Eucryphia Nymansis. ① *T01444-400321. Closed Mon, Tue. Adults £6.70, under 16s £3.30. Train from Victoria to Balcombe then 4-mile taxi ride.*

6. **Painshill Landscape Gardens** Landscape garden laid out in the mid-18th century by Charles Hamilton, now carefully restored complete with Turkish tent, Gothic tower and ruined abbey. ① *T01932- 868113. Closed Mon. Adults £6, £3.50 under 16s. Waterloo to Stoke D'Abernon, then 1.25-mile walk/taxi ride.*

7. **Sheffield Park Garden** Laid out by Capability Brown and developed in the early 20th century by Arthur Soames, this is a spectacular landscape garden set around four large lakes with acers and waterlilies. ① *T01825-790231. Closed Mon. Adults £5.50, under 16s £2.75. Victoria to East Grinstead, then bus 473 for Kingscote and the Bluebell Railway (T01825-720800).*

8. **Sissinghurst Castle** The famous horticultural creation of Vita Sackville-West and Harold Nicholson. A staggering variety of plantings burst into bloom throughout the season. ① *T01580-710700. Closed Wed, Thu. Adult £7.50, £3.50 under 16s. Train from Charing Cross to Staplehurst. A bus connects with the 1030 on Sun and 1130 on Tue otherwise bus to Sissinghurst village, and a mile's walk.*

9. **Wakehurst Place** An outstation of Kew Gardens, Wakehurst Place is an Elizabethan mansion and National Trust property surrounded by acres of wild and ornamental gardens. ① *T01444-892701. Adults £8, under 16s free. Train from Victoria to Haywards Heath, then bus 81 or 82.*

10. **Royal Horticultural Society, Wisley** Two hundred and forty acres of gardens expertly tended by the RHS, bursting with an astonishing variety of apples and soft fruit, herbaceous borders and roses, as well as ornamental walks and greenhouses. ① *T01483-224234. Adult £7, under 16s £2, under 6s free. Train from Waterloo to Woking, then 4.5 mile taxi ride.*

British romantic landscapers) can be appreciated in the lake dominating the Syon Vista. Original features punctuate a wide expanse of flowerbeds and woodland: the **Orangery**, once a notable hothouse, is now a decent restaurant, though the **Pagoda**, at 163 ft, is the most noticeable and impressive thing in the gardens. A number of 18th-century neoclassical temples can be found near the Victoria Gate (now the major entrance). For utter seclusion, check out **Queen Charlotte's Cottage** to the distant southwest, too far for the crowds to trek.

Kew Palace (closed for restoration until 2006) is Britain's smallest Royal residence and only George III ever actually lived here, even then only at the peak of his illness. The exterior is worth a quick view. If nothing else, have a glance before exiting the gardens at the **Main Gate** which is still impressive despite being superceded in its original role by the Victoria Gate.

Around Kew

Having exited the gardens via the Main Gate you step into the country idyll that is **Kew Green**. Surrounded by Georgian architecture and with a cricket pitch in the centre, nothing could be more quintessentially English. At the end of the Green, **St Anne's Church** dates from 1714 and is the secluded resting place of the painters Gainsborough and Zoffany, so secluded in fact that finding them takes some time and effort.

Kew Bridge Steam Museum

ⓘ *To20-8568 4757. Daily 1100-1700. Weekdays £4 for adults; weekends £5.20.*
A former Victorian pumping station that is a shrine to the steam engine and also an enlightening foray into the history of London's water supply. Superb value and best at weekends and bank holiday steam days, when the mighty Cornish beam engines can be seen in action. The biggest steam engine in the world, the 'Ninety', runs for half an hour from 1500 on Sundays. Also a waterwheel and mini slate mine train for the kids.

Syon House

ⓘ *To20-8560 0881. Gardens open daily 1000-1730 or dusk; house open summer only 1100-1700 Wed, Thu, Sun and Bank Holidays. Gardens only £4, £3.50 concession; house and gardens £7, £6.25 concession. London Butterfly House: To20-8560 7272; information on To20-8560 0378, www.butterflies.org.uk, 1000-1500; summer 1000-dusk. Adults £4.95, £3.95 children. Nearest train station Syon Lane.*
Opposite Kew Gardens, on the west bank of the river, Syon House is the grand art-stuffed home of the Dukes of Northumberland, with fine Capability Brown gardens, an adventure playground and in the grounds, the London Butterfly House. This, the oldest exhibition of its kind in the world, is a tropical indoor garden filled with fluttering butterflies and also, safely behind glass, scorpions, spiders, giant land snails and millipedes.

Chiswick House

ⓘ *Burlington Lane, To20-8995 0508. Apr-Sep 1000-1800, Oct 1000-1700. Adults £4, concessions £3. Free audio guide.*
Back downstream nearer the centre of London and Hammersmith is Chiswick House, less of an austere family seat and more of an aristocratic toy. Designed by owner-architect Lord Burlington to mimic the style of the archetypal Roman villa, the house, though surprisingly small, is decorated with fine interiors, paintings and furniture, while the sumptuously lavish Blue Velvet Room is a magnificent example of Romantic aristocratic decadence. The 18th-century classical ornamental gardens are a perfect foil to Burlington's masterpiece and a very pleasant place to take a summer stroll.

Hogarth's House

ⓘ *T020-8994 6757. Tue-Fri 1300-1700, Sat and Sun 1300-1800; closed Jan. Free.*
A touch confusing to hunt down (beware contradictory signposts), the 18th-century residence of painter William Hogarth lies just 50 m from the frenetic Hogarth roundabout, on Hogarth Lane, and within a stone's throw of Chiswick House. The house and exhibition tell the story of the artist's life and work, with many of Hogarth's major works being on display, including the witty social criticism of *The Rake's Progress* and *The Harlot's Progress*. Not all of them are genuine, though copies are undoubtedly better than nothing at all.

Richmond

On exiting the tube/train station in Richmond, it is readily apparent that you are in the shopping centre of the borough. The road is lined on both sides of the street with high street branches (Gap, Laura Ashley, etc) which make up the staple of the average Richmond shopper. Richmond Hill itself is lined with expensive antique shops.

Richmond Park

ⓘ *T020-8948 3209. Mar-Sep, 0700-dusk, Oct-Feb 0730-dusk.* Europe's largest city park and a former Royal hunting ground dating from the 13th century, Richmond Park is popular largely because of its freely roaming deer and the historic attraction of the panorama over Surrey and London (especially from **King Henry VIII's Mound**, the highest point in the park). There is more than just this however: **Pembroke Lodge**, once the childhood home of Bertrand Russell and now an ornate tea-house, the bird sanctuary that is **Sidmouth Wood**, the beautifully landscaped **Isabella Plantation**, and the **White Lodge**, built on the command of George II though inhabited by Queen Caroline, his wife.

Museum of Richmond

ⓘ *Old Town Hall, Whittaker Av, T020-8332 1141. May-Sep, Tue-Sat 1100-1700; Sun 1300-1600; Oct-Apr, Tue-Sat 1100-1700. Free.*

As a former Royal resort, it would be easy for the Museum of Richmond to focus on this aspect alone. To its credit, however, it charts the history of the area from prehistoric times to the present day with numerous exhibits to back it up, temporary exhibitions, and friendly and informed staff to boot.

Marble Hill House

ⓘ *English Heritage, Richmond Rd, Twickenham, T020-8892 5115. Apr-Oct daily 1000-1700; Nov-Mar, Wed-Sun 1000-1600. Adults £4, concessions £3, under-16s £2. Reached most easily from St Margaret's train station.*

North of the river, a rare survivor of the string of grand villas which once lined the Thames, Marble Hill House was built in the 1720s for Henrietta Howard, mistress of George II. Regally decorated and perfectly proportioned, this handsome Palladian mansion, refreshing in its authenticity, also possesses examples of early Georgian painting and furniture.

Next door, the **Orleans House Gallery** ⓘ *T020-8831 6000, www.richmond.gov.uk/orleanshouse, Nov-Mar Tue-Sat 1300-1630, Sun 1400-1630, Apr-Oct Tue-Sat 1300-1730, Sun 1400-1730, free*, is worth visiting for its intriguing early 18th-century Octagon Room and its regular interesting temporary exhibitions.

★ Five of the best views of the river

- **Waterloo Bridge**, South Bank, page 250.
- **Island Gardens**, Docklands, page 273.
- **The Embankment**, Putney, page 339.
- **Kew Gardens**, across to Syon Park, page 341.
- **King Henry VIII's Mound**, Richmond Park, page 346.

Ham House

① *T020-8940 1950, Mar-Oct Mon-Wed, Sat, Sun 1300-1700. Adults £7.50, £3.75 under-16s.*

Maybe because of its slightly disjointed position away from the rest of Richmond's box of delights, but easily reached by the foot ferry from the end of Orleans Road, **Ham House** is often overlooked by visitors to the area. It's a shame really as it's also one of the most appealing of the local estates with original 17th-century artwork (including van Dyck) and furniture, the ornate extravagance of the Great Staircase, and an enchanting garden with statutory tea-room.

● Sleeping

Richmond and Kew *p340, map p342*

A Richmond Gate Hotel, Richmond Hill, Richmond, TW10, T020-8940 0061, www.corushotels.com/richmondgate. With 68 bedrooms, an award-winning restaurant, well-equipped Cedars leisure club with sizeable indoor swimming pool and, to cap it all, a beautiful position at the top of Richmond Hill, the Richmond Gate is a 4-star treat, expensive but better value than many in the centre of town, price (as so often) depends on date and availability, 60 rooms.

A Richmond Hill Hotel, Richmond Hill, Richmond, TW10, T020-8940 2247, www.corushotels.co.uk/richmondhill. The Richmond Hill dates from 1726 and retains much of its original grandeur. With an astonishing view over the Thames Valley and convenient proximity to Richmond Park it offers impressive facilities. Owned by the same company though usually slightly cheaper than the Richmond Gate.

A Richmond Inn Hotel, 50-56 Sheen Rd, Richmond, TW9, T020-8940 0171, www.richmondinnhotel.com. Friendly, family-run independent and well located within a couple of mins walk from the tube, modern facilities do nothing to detract from its charm.

B Hobart Hall Hotel, 43-47 Petersham Rd, Richmond, TW10, T020-8940 0435, www.smoothhound.co.uk/hotels/hobarthall. In its time Hobart Hall has seen Royalty staying within its 4 walls. Well served by public transport, the hotel is within easy walking distance of the tube and train station, and Richmond Park, it also boasts cut-price student rooms.

B-C Doughty Cottage, 142a Richmond Hill, Richmond, TW10, T020-8332 9434, www.doughtycottage.com. Consisting of 3 sumptuous rooms, Doughty Cottage is a luxurious home with every comfort. The Florentine and Venetian rooms have a private patio garden, whilst the Sienna comes with a remarkable vista over the river Thames and Surrey. Free car parking. 5 mins from the tube.

C Chelwood House, 1 Chelwood Gdns, Kew, TW9, T020-8876 8733, www.ukbed.co.uk/chelwood. Tucked away down a sleepy cul-de-sac, Chelwood House is a small, accessible and welcoming b&b, can recommend others in the area, 2 double rooms and 2 singles, 7 mins walk to Kew Gardens station.

C Mr and Mrs Leach, 15 Pensford Av, Kew, TW9, T020-8876 3354, www.prokewbandb.demon.co.uk. Quiet B&B with 4 rooms, 8 mins walk from the tube, non-smoking.

For an explanation of sleeping and eating price codes used in this guide, see inside the front cover. Other relevant information is found in Essentials, see pages 44-46.

🍴 Eating

Richmond and Kew p340, map p342

🍴🍴 **The Canyon**, Riverside, near Richmond Bridge, Richmond, T020-8948 2944. A white airy building with a picturesque riverside setting. It is a good, though fairly pricey, establishment with an unmistakably American (rib-eye steak and apple pie) theme. The prices could prove a touch restrictive, though that does tend to go with the area, and by and large you get what you pay for.

🍴🍴 **Four Regions**, 102-103 Kew Rd, Richmond, T020-8940 9044. Classy decor and oodles of atmosphere give this superior Chinese restaurant an edge over its rivals. The quality of the service and the food is very high, though unfortunately so is the price. Hugely popular nonetheless.

🍴🍴 **The Glasshouse**, 14 Station Parade, Kew, T020-8940 6777. Sat neatly outside Kew Gardens tube station, has rapidly built itself a reputation for friendly service in a warm, intimate location with, perhaps above all, very good food and an extensive and varied European menu. The set meals offer very good value (dinner is £32.50 for 3 courses) though the wine is more expensive.

🍴 **Chez Lindsay**, 11 Hill Rise, Richmond, T020-8948 7473. An enclave of Northern France in leafy Richmond, is true to its origins in both authentic haute cuisine and even more authentically aloof staff, although with a sizeable 3-course meal on offer for under £16 it would be difficult for even the staunchest Eurosceptic to reject its Gallic offerings.

🍴 **Prego**, 106-108 Kew Rd, Richmond, T020-8948 8508. Well staffed and very stylish with an airy main section and a more intimate back area. The Italian food is pleasant and the atmosphere is appealing, despite fairly high prices. Open all day.

Cafés and sandwich bars

Chiswick House Café, Chiswick House, Burlington Lane, W4, located bang next door to the house itself. One of the better stately home cafés with a decent snack menu and a wide selection of refreshments. Anything with Chiswick Gardens as a backdrop can't be all that bad.

The Kew Greenhouse, 1 Station Pde, Kew, T020-8940 0183, on the main approach from Kew Gardens tube. A good place to study the native aspiring middle-class in their prime habitat. As floral as the name suggests, the conservatory and outdoor seating make it a prime summer spot (open all day).

Ma Cuisine, 9 Station Approach, Kew, T020- 8332 1923. One of the better places to languish near the gardens, laid back and breezy with plenty of gallic charm, a decent menu and rapid service, especially popular at lunchtimes.

Original Maids of Honour, 288 Kew Rd, Kew, opposite Kew Gardens on the road leading off the Common. A teashop as English as its environs. It was here that Maid of Honour tarts were baked for Henry VIII and his household, and the present incumbents resolutely continue the tradition along with the other fineries of olde Englishe tea culture.

Pembroke Lodge, Richmond Park, Richmond. A pretty tea-room with outdoor seating on the crest of Richmond Hill, a good place to relax and enjoy the view.

🍺 Pubs and bars

Kew p340, map p342

Bull's Head, 15 Strand on the Green, T020-8994 1204, and **City Barge**, 27 Strand on the Green, T020-8994 2148, are both on the north bank of the river over Kew Bridge and both have sunny, south-facing tables overlooking the river.

The Railway, Station Parade, Kew, T020- 8332 1162. Despite the odd chain-pub feature this is an honest-to-goodness and laid-back pub conveniently situated for a post/pre-wander pint having explored the expansive acres of Kew Gardens. Well partitioned with a conservatory backing onto the station platform.

Richmond p346, map p342

The Britannia, 5 Brewers Lane, Richmond, T020-8940 1071. Tucked away snug and cosy between busy George St and Richmond Green. Its tiny size gives it much of its charm along with an open fire, ensuring a warm and friendly atmosphere. A good little hideaway.

Cricketers, Maids of Honour Row, The Green, Richmond, T020-8940 4372. Named in honour of the bordering cricket pitch on the green, offering a decent selection of real ales and a (comparatively) reasonably priced menu of unspectacular pub fare lunch and supper. Conjures images of summer pints on the lawn.

The Marlborough, 46 Friars Stile Rd, Richmond, T020-8940 0572. A pretty pub perched on Richmond Hill, surprisingly intimate and secluded inside with good wine list, expansive garden and enchanting view over the Thames making it a very popular spot in summer.

Orange Tree, 45 Kew Rd, Richmond, T020 8940 0944. A pleasant if slightly sanitized pub across the way from the theatre with which it shares its name. Punters hoping for big screen football will be disappointed – this is a rugby only zone and the daytime clientele reflect this. A popular haunt for the pre-theatre crowd in the evening.

The White Swan, 26 Old Palace Lane, Richmond, T020-8892 2166. Hidden among cottages, this is a classic country boozer. Slightly off the beaten track and thus mostly populated by locals, it's worth the venture to avoid the crowds and have a peaceful pint or a bite of regular pub grub lunch or supper.

Isleworth

London Apprentice, 62 Church St, T020-8560 1915, a short walk along the river from Marble Hill House. A riverside pub popular with the rugby crowd but with a pleasant beer garden out front.

White Swan, Twickenham, T020-8892 2166, further upstream. Has more character and overlooks the river at Eel Pie Island, which was a haven for hippy chicks and rockers in the 1960s.

⊕ Entertainment

Richmond and Kew *p340, map p342*
Cinema
Odeon Hill Street, 72 Hill St, Richmond, Surrey, T0870-505 0007.

Odeon Studio, 6 Red Lion St, Richmond, Surrey, T0870-505 0007.

Richmond Filmhouse, 3 Water Lane, Richmond, Surrey, T020-8332 0030. Popular arthouse cinema for modern and classic films.

Theatre

The Orange Tree, 1 Clarence St, Richmond, Surrey, T020-8940 3633. Popular theatre in the round which regularly wins widespread critical acclaim for its treatment of old, new and neglected.

Richmond Theatre, The Green, Richmond, Surrey, T020-8940 0088. Well-respected theatre showing a varied range of productions, from Shakespeare to musicals to comedy, now often hosting touring productions. Laurence Olivier, Helen Mirren and Derek Jacobi have all graced the boards here in their time.

Waterman's Arts Centre, High St Brentford, Middlesex, TW8 DS, T020-8847 5651. A picturesque modern location for dance, theatre and the visual arts.

▲ Activities

Richmond and Kew *p340, map p342*
All England Lawn Tennis Club, Church Road, Wimbledon SW19, T020-8944 1066. Site of the annual tennis championships and also of a new interactive museum on the game and its stars. **London Welsh RFC**, Old Deer Park, Kew Road, Richmond, Surrey (Information T0336-421744; Tickets: T020 8940 2368). **Harlequins RFC**, The Stoop Memorial Ground, Craneford Way, Twickenham (information T020-8410 6000; tickets T0870-8870230).

❶ Directory

Richmond and Kew *p340, map p342*
Richmond tourist information office, Old Town Hall, Whittaker Av, Richmond, TW9, T020-8940 9125, www.visitrichmond.co.uk. Open Mon-Sat 100-1700, May-Sep Sun 1030-1330.

Hampton Court

Hampton Court is the most beautiful and engaging of the Royal palaces in London. It set the standard for grand houses along the river and is best seen at sunset, when its mellow old red brick glows with warmth and the riverside gardens take on an other-worldly quality. Best reached by boat, which explains its situation, the Palace is also easily reached by train from central London. What particularly marks it out as a visitor attraction is the variety of history on display, from the late-medieval architecture of Henry VIII's court to the Georgian splendour of the Cumberland Suite. Sir Christopher Wren was asked to demolish the Tudor palace, but thankfully ended up simply extending it. The contrast between his classical wings with their formal gardens and the crumbly old buildings erected by Cardinal Wolsey illustrates 300 years of Royal history over a period when England was in the process of turning itself into a world power. Most of the interiors have been successfully restored to their original state. Nearby the seemingly endless expanse of Bushy park stretches north, while Thames Ditton is a sweet riverside village, one stop down the line. ▶▶ *For Eating and other listings see page 354.*

History

Until the 16th century, Hampton was little more than a small settlement in the bend of the river, although there is also evidence of a Bronze Age settlement in Bushy Park in among the roe deer, boars and beavers that flourished in the woods around. In 1514, however, Henry VIII's adviser Cardinal Wolsey bought land between the hamlets of Hampton and Hampton Wick from the Order of St John of Jerusalem and set about building himself a palace of truly regal proportions. Some 500 staff served him in his 280 rooms until he fell out of favour for failing to secure a divorce for Henry VIII; in an attempt to win back his position he gave Hampton Court to Henry.

It soon became another of the monarchy's preferred residences, and over the next 200 years the Court flourished. Henry VIII enlarged and enriched it, adding the hammer-beam Great Hall, the Chapel Royal kitchens and both indoor and outdoor tennis courts. The boy-king Edward VI spent much of his time here before dying aged 16 at Greenwich Palace, while Elizabeth held banquets, masques, balls and plays, often to entertain one of her many suitors freshly arrived from the Continent. The enclosed parks either side of the Hampton Court Road offered plentiful sport, whether hunting stags or tilting or coursing. Even Protector Cromwell took up residence here during the Commonwealth, and although Charles II had to conduct considerable repair work, William and Mary extended the Palace further by commissioning Wren to build the State Apartments.

It was also a place of refuge – for Charles I fled here just before the start of the Civil War, for fashionable Londoners escaping the Great Plague, and for George I, unpopular and homesick, who would hide away down here. Meanwhile, courtiers built fine houses nearby. The Old Court House and Prestbury House sat on the green, what are now known as Garrick's Villa and House along Hampton Court Road, and Orme, Barham, Old Grange and Grove houses in Hampton itself.

After the death of George II in 1760, the palace ceased to be used by reigning monarchs, but it wasn't until Victoria's reign that the Palace's treasures were opened to the public. Londoners would come to play in the grounds, get lost in the maze, or picnic under the chestnut blossom in Bushy Park. Hampton itself expanded towards New Hampton, but until the middle of the 20th century the area was still covered by up to 50 flourishing market gardens and nurseries.

During the First World War Bushy Park was home to Canadian troops, and in the Second, much of the park was taken over by American forces. Wire camouflage

★ Five of the best riverside pubs

- **The Dove**, Hammersmith, page 339.
- **City Barge**, Strand on the Green, Kew, page 348.
- **London Apprentice**, Isleworth, Richmond, page 349.
- **White Swan**, Riverside, Twickenham, page 349.
- **Fox on the River**, Thames Ditton, Hampton Court, page 354.

netting covered a military post of 400 huts, five office blocks and several of the ponds. Chestnut Avenue was used as an airstrip, and it was here that Eisenhower and his staff met for the initial planning stages of the D-Day landings.

Sights

Hampton Court Palace

ⓘ *T020-8781 9500, recorded information T0870-7527777, www.hrp.org.uk. Nov-Easter Mon 1015-1630, Tue-Sun 0930-1630 (last admission 1545), Easter-Oct Mon 1015-1800, Tue-Sun 0930-1800 (last admission 1715). Adult £12, under-16s £7.80, under 5s free, concessions £9, Privy Garden only £4, under-16s £2.50, maze only £3.50, under-16s £2.50. Self-service cafeteria in the grounds and coffee shop in the Palace. Hampton Court can be reached by boat from Westminster Pier or Richmond during the summer, the journey from Westminster can take up to 4 hours, depending on the tides, Westminster Passenger Services T020-7930 2062 or Turks Launches T020-8546 2434; by train (35 mins) from Waterloo (the palace is a 2-minute walk across the bridge from the station); or by train (connecting with the Waterloo service) from Wimbledon tube station on District Line.*

Like the Tower of London, Hampton Court Palace is run by Historic Royal Palaces and bears some of that company's hallmarks: lively costumed tours, clarity in the signposting, and division into different themed areas of interest. Unlike the Tower however, the history of the Palace and its presentation to the public focuses mainly on two particular reigns: Henry VIII (1509-1547) and his many wives, and William and Mary (1689-1702) who until Mary's death in 1694 were unique in sharing the monarchy.

Six different routes around the interior take in Henry VIII's State Apartments, the Tudor Kitchens, the Wolsey Rooms and Renaissance Picture Gallery, the King's Apartments (William's), the Queen's State Apartments (Mary's) and the Georgian Rooms (decorated by George II – 1727-1760 – the last monarch to use the Palace).

The main entrance is at its west front via William III's **Trophy Gate** through the gatehouse built by Cardinal Wolsey. Originally two storeys higher, the gatehouse was found to be unstable in the late 17th century. Beyond, the **Base Court** is still much as Wolsey intended it, although Anne Boleyn's Gateway straight ahead was heavily restored in the 19th century.

The next courtyard is the **Clock Court**, the best place to orientate yourself and appreciate the conflicting range of styles and eras the palace presents. Above the gate on the western Tudor side is the **Astronomical Clock**, designed for Henry VIII in 1540 and showing the phases of the moon and the sun revolving around the earth. To the north is Henry's Great Hall and his State Apartments. To the south is Wren's colonnade leading to William and Mary's State Apartments. And to the east are the Cumberland Suite and Georgian rooms behind a façade displaying William Kent's attempt to imitate the Tudor style. Through the George II Gate on this side is Wren's Fountain Court.

Highlights of the Tudor Palace are **Henry VIII's State Apartments**, especially the **Great Hall**, with its massive hammerbeam roof, and the **Chapel Royal**, with an equally extraordinary ceiling. This is all that remains of the original chapel, although the 18th- and 19th-century interior is splendid too, some of it designed by Wren for Queen Anne.

Nearby are the **Tudor Kitchens**, set up as if in preparation for a late-medieval banquet. Only the cauldrons in the Great Kitchen are original, with its three enormous open fireplaces, although the other kitchenware is convincing repro. Round about are the Boiling House, the Spicery and Pastry House, Larders and Sculleries, the Fish Court and the Cellars. The best feature of the Wolsey Rooms is their superb linen-fold panelling, while the Renaissance Picture Gallery contains works by **Correggio**, **Cranach**, **Titian** and **Brueghel** from the Royal Collection.

The **King's Apartments**, built by Wren, are reached via a grand staircase painted by Antonio Verrio. After being severely damaged by fire in 1986, the apartments have been immaculately restored to how they would have looked in 1700. Passing through the Guard Chamber, Presence Chamber and Eating Room, the worst damage was sustained by the Privy Chamber, now hung with magnificent tapestries telling the story of the life of Abraham. The Little Bedchamber contains some priceless Chinese porcelain, while the closet next door was William's study, featuring his writing desk and a 17th-century lavatory made for Charles II.

On the ground floor are more of the king's private apartments, including the beautifully panelled East Closet carved by **Grinling Gibbons**. Beyond the Orangery, paved with distinctive purple and grey Swedish limestone, the King's Private Dining Room has been laid as if for the third course of a small supper, overlooked by the Hampton Court Beauties, a painting by **Godfrey Kneller** of some of the ladies that attended on Queen Mary. The **Queen's State Apartments** seem considerably more 'modern' in appearance, their staircase designed by William Kent, while the playwright and architect Sir John Vanbrugh had a hand in the look of the Guard Chamber and Presence Chamber. The Queen's Drawing Room in the middle of the east front was designed by Wren to line up with the Long Canal in the gardens outside.

Highlights of the much more comfortable **Georgian Rooms**, several designed by William Kent, are **Wolsey's Closet**, for a taste of how the 19th century went about recreating Tudor interiors; the **Communication Gallery** hung with the Windsor Beauties by **Sir Peter Lely**, and portraying some of the women at the court of Charles II (although not his mistresses); and the **Cartoon Gallery**, with its copies of the Raphael cartoons in the V&A. The most exceptional original paintings in the Palace though are **Andrea Mantegna's** series of nine on the triumphs of Julius Caesar, completed in about 1492 and acquired by Charles I in 1629. These can be found in the Lower Orangery in the South Gardens, in a setting designed to evoke their original home in the Palace of San Sebastiano in 1506.

If weather permits, time should definitely be allowed for enjoyment of the Palace's beautiful gardens. The **Privy Garden**, in front of the King's State Apartments, has been restored to the way it may have looked in William's day, down to the original species known to have been planted then. The Great Vine was grown by Capability Brown in 1768 and claims to be the oldest in the world, still producing grapes,

● Ten historic houses near London

1. **Arundel Castle** Seat of the Dukes of Norfolk for over 500 years Arundel was rebuilt several times, most comprehensively in the 19th century, with fairy-tale towers and turrets. Inside are some of Mary Queen of Scots' possessions, 16th-century tapestries and portraits by Van Dyck and Gainsborough. ① *T01903-883136. Closed Sat. Adults £11, under 16s £7.50. Train from Victoria to Arundel.*

2. **Audley End** A Jacobean palace in landscaped grounds. The interior includes a magnificent carved oak screen, early 18th-century Gothick chapel and the painted beauty of the Robert Adam apartments. ① *T01799-522399. Closed Mon, Tue. Adults £8.95, under-16s £4.50. Train from Liverpool St to Audley End.*

3. **Chartwell** Sir Winston Churchill's home, and preserved by the National Trust as if the great man had just stomped out. The grounds include his painting studio and the garden wall he built. ① *T01732 868381, information T01732-866368. Adults £8, under 16s £4. Closed Mon. Victoria to Bromley South, then bus.*

4. **Chiddingstone Castle** Chiddingstone was rescued from dereliction by avid art collector the late Denys Bower. He filled his castellated Georgian home with an exotic collection including ancient Egyptian finds, Japanese lacquerwork and Jacobite memorablia. ① *T01892-870347. Open Thu 1400-1700, Sun 1130-1700. Adults £5, under 16s £2.50. Train from Victoria to Edenbridge, then bus or taxi ride.*

5. **Cliveden** A luxury hotel, although in the care of the National Trust, this Italianate villa was designed by Sir Charles Barry for the Duke of Sutherland, who sold up in 1893 to William Waldorf Astor. It was notorious as the base for Nancy Astor's political set and later the protagonists of the Profumo affair. ① *T01628-605069. House open Thu, Sun. Adults £7, 5-18 £3.50, under 5s free. Train from Paddington to Burnham, then 4-mile taxi ride.*

6. **Downe House** Charles Darwin's comfortable Victorian home features a reconstruction of his study and exhibitions on his life's work. You can also see the sand walk round the garden where he paced and ruminated on the origin of the species. ① *T01689-859119. Closed Mon, Tue. Adults £6.60, under 19s £3.30. Train from Charing Cross to Orpington, then bus R2 (except Sun).*

7. **Hatfield House** Another grand Jacobean palace, now home to the Marquess of Salisbury. Outside are the remains of Elizabeth I's childhood home and 4000 acres of parkland. ① *T01707-287010. Daily (except Thu and Fri). Easter Sat - 30th Sep. Adults £8, under 16s £4. Train from King's Cross or Finsbury Park to Hatfield.*

8. **Knole** The Elizabethan pile where writer and gardener Vita Sackville-West grew up. Once the largest private house in the country, it has an impressive art collection. ① *T01732 462100, T01732-450608. Closed Mon, Tue. Adults £6.40, under 16s £3.20. Train from Charing Cross to Sevenoaks, then a mile's walk.*

9. **Leeds Castle** The lovely lake-girt Leeds castle sits on a pair of small islands surrounded by wooded hills and parkland. The interior has rooms from a variety of periods. There's also a maze, underground grotto, aviary and series of gardens. ① *T01622-765400. Adults £13, under 14s £9, under 4s free.*

10. **Penshurst Place** A more modest version of Knole and the seat of the Sidney family since 1522. The Barons Hall at its heart was built in 1341 and is still kept much as it might have looked then. Outside, the 11-acre walled garden and Elizabethan formal walks are a delight. *T01892-870307. Adults £7, under 16s £5. Charing Cross to Tonbridge then bus or taxi ride.*

West Hampton Court

although it was outgrown by a cutting planted in the Royal Gardens at Windsor in 1775. In the gardens outside the East Front comical trembling topiary bushes line the Broad Walk down to the riverbank. To the north of the palace, the famous **Maze** is fun for all the family: stick to the right hand hedge on the way in and the left hand hedge on the way out if you don't want to be wandering around it all afternoon. Otherwise a visit to the Palace requires at least three hours.

Bushy Park

① *T020-8979 1586*. Beyond the Palace grounds to the north lies the expanse of Bushy Park, a royal demesne of over 1000 acres, home to over 300 deer, and putting on some spectacular floral displays: with its avenues of lime trees, in spring with carpets of daffodils; in May the flowering candles of the apparently endless Chestnut Avenue punctuated by Charles I's Diana Fountain, heading dead straight from the Palace up to Teddington.

● Eating

Hampton Court *p350*

¶¶ **Chu Chin Chow**, Bridge Rd, T020-8979 5993. Within walking distance of the Palace, Bridge Rd is the best bet, with this pricey but highly recommended Chinese restaurant.

¶¶ **Monsieur Max**, 133 High St, Hampton Hill, Middlesex, T020-8979 5546. For a special occasion, the superior and fairly formal French cuisine here needs booking well in advance but rarely disappoints.

¶¶ **Vecchia Roma**, Bridge Rd, T020-8941 5337. A traditional Italian.

¶ **Blubeckers**, 3 Palace Gate, T020-8941 5959, right opposite the gate. Open for American-English lunches and supper, £4 starter, £10 mains, with an excellent-value early-evening happy hour.

● Pubs and bars

Hampton Court *p350*

In Hampton Court itself there are sadly no pubs on the river.

The Albion, 34 Bridge Rd, East Molesey, Surrey, T020-8941 9421. A friendly local with a comfortable atmosphere.

The Prince of Wales, 23 Bridge Rd, East Molesey, Surrey, T020-8979 5561. Does food all day and can get very busy Sun.

Another option is to take the train back to **Thames Ditton** and stroll down Church Walk to the river.

The Crown, Summer St. The liveliest pub in the area, popular with a younger crowd, with a pool table and regular special events.

Fox on the River, Queen's Rd, Thames Ditton, T020-8339 1110. Does all-day food everyday right on the waterside opposite the Palace's east gardens.

● Entertainment

Hampton Court *p350*
Cinema
Kingston Odeon, T0871-2244007. Mainstream multiscreen.

Theatre
Rose and Crown, 61 High St, Hampton Wick (near Kingston Bridge), T020-8296 9100. Small fringe theatre above an excellent pub.

● Festivals and events

Hampton Court *p350*
Hampton Court Flower Show, **3-8 Jul**, T020-7834 4333. Royal Horticultural Society's annual flowerfest in the grounds. **Hampton Court Music Festival**, **7-16 Jun**, T020-8233 5000, booking T020-7420 1030, general information, T020-8233 6400, www.hamptoncourtfestival.com, in the Base Court of the Palace, kicked off in 2001 by José Carreras, also music from the West End musicals, Vivaldi fireworks, opera, Jools Holland, R&B and Royal Philarmonic classic fireworks finale. £32-75.

● *For an explanation of sleeping and eating price codes used in this guide, see inside the* ● *front cover. Other relevant information is found in Essentials, see pages 44-46.*

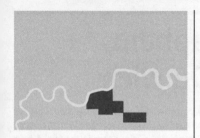

South London

Battersea, Clapham, Brixton and Dulwich

Most visitors to London rarely make it much further into south London than Waterloo or Bankside. Broader, more expansive and generally more suburban than the north, the south usually comes off worst in the traditional rivalry between the two. A brief glance at the tube map explains why, and apart from the area's inconvenience, many places of interest to the visitor in south London are usually much less given to hype. But Brixton is almost as popular as Notting Hill or Camden with European students, while parts of Clapham and Battersea have been optimistically dubbed 'south Chelsea'. In fact the vibrant shops, pubs, bars and clubs of SW2, 4, 8, 9 and 11 can make for just as rewarding browsing and carousing as some of their northern counterparts. The Dulwich Picture Gallery and the Horniman Museum are two of the city's most individual visitor attractions. But the best reason for taking a trip to Battersea, Brixton or Clapham is to enjoy some slices of 'real' London life: the clubs, venues, market and bars of multicultural Brixton; the restaurants, riverside park and cutting-edge live arts centre at Battersea; and the wide common, cafés and pubs of Clapham. ▸▸ For Sleeping, Eating and other listings see pages 363-366.

History

Apart from developments closer to the City, such as Southwark, and along the river's bank such as Putney, little of South London had developed by 1800. The Falcon Brook ran between Clapham and Wandsworth Commons to spill into the Thames at Battersea, a virtual island in the marshland. The River Effra rose at Norwood, passed through Dulwich and Brixton to the Thames at Lambeth. Saxon settlements – Badric's Isle (Battersea), Osgod Clapha (Clapham), 'Dile-wisc' ('the meadow where dill grew', Dulwich), and Brixistane (Brixton) – grew up around the rivers, but they grew slowly over the ensuing centuries. Each settlement had a common for water, fuel, grazing livestock (there were still sheep on Clapham Common in 1903) and fairs and meetings, and further afield, undulating farmland spread to a caravan of gypsies living on the hill to the south.

In 1619 the College of God's Gift at Dulwich (Dulwich College) was founded by the new lord of the manor, Edward Alleyn, a Shakespearian actor and bear-baiter. Although the village remained a relative backwater for the rest of the century, the fashionable spa at Dulwich Wells, the school and the rural setting saw the village grow.

For much of the 17th century, Clapham remained a wild and marshy tract, whose common was patrolled by highwaymen such as Robert Forrestor (dressed in drag), and prostitutes (presumably not in drag). Following the exodus here to escape the Great Plague and Fire in the 1660s, however, the village grew so much that by 1690 there was a stagecoach service to Gracechurch Street in the City. Captain Cook is reputed to have lived in the imposing Georgian mansions on the north side, dubbing his balcony the 'quarterdeck', but the area is better known as the home to the Clapham Sect. The evangelical group, or 'The Saints', which included the MP William Wilberforce, were instrumental in the fight for the abolition of slavery. Their place of prayer was Holy Trinity Church, and their 'African Academy' gave a home to 25 black children brought from Jamaica.

★ **Don't miss South London…**

1. **Battersea Park** Hire a bike to pedal around beside the river or over the bridge into Chelsea, page 357.
2. **Dulwich Picture Gallery** Ride the rails down to Dulwich for a look at some old masters in an antique setting, page 361.
3. **Brixton's music** Big yourself up in Brixton for some full-on sessions in the south's best clubs, bars and live music venues, page 365.

Sparked by the railways, Brixton and Battersea grew in the 19th century. Clapham Junction opened in 1863, and candle, glucose and glove factories and gas works were established in Battersea (the Power Station wasn't built until 1937). Workers moved into cottages on the Shaftesbury Park estate and went drinking in the Red House tavern, singing in the music halls near Clapham Junction or pigeon-flying in Battersea Park where, after 1896, the new craze of bicycling took off.

Electric Avenue in Brixton became one of the first electrically lit streets in Britain in the 1880s, as the market spread under the railway arches, and its houses converted to lodgings. After the Second World War, West Indian immigrants settled in Brixton, particularly in Somerleyton and Railton Roads. A generation later, economic decline and simmering racial tensions boiled up into riots against the police in 1981, 1985 and 1995.

Sights

South Battersea, Clapham, Brixton & Dulwich

Battersea ⊖ *Overland train: Battersea Park from Victoria. Buses: see p460.*

Just south of Chelsea Bridge, **Battersea Power Station** is one of London's best-known modern landmarks, its four towers unmistakeable when approaching Battersea from the north. Closed in 1983, the shell remains as a testament to industrial modernization and increasing environmental awareness, though only as a result of long-standing indecision over what should happen to the site.

‡ See map of Battersea park and around on the next page.

The latest plans once again include a multi-use development involving shops, cinemas, and affordable homes and a riverside park.

Across the Queenstown Road, along the south bank of the river between the Chelsea and Albert bridges, lies ★ **Battersea Park** ① *T020-8871 7530, 0800-dusk*, complete with adventure playgrounds, sports facilities and a children's zoo (see below), a beautiful boating lake, and a modern art gallery in the **Pump House** ① *T020-7350 0523*. Queen Victoria's gift remains a focal point of the borough. The riverside **Peace Pagoda**, donated by Japanese monks in 1985, and the **Festival Gardens**, designed for the Festival of Britain, are of special interest. A major £11 million restoration project in the park has recently refurbished these along with the Victorian lakeside areas, sub-tropical gardens, rosery garden and the riverside promenade. Sports facilities include an **all-weather pitch** ① *T020-8871 7535*, **tennis courts** ① *T020-8871 7542* and **running track** ① *T020-8871 7537* and the **Chestnut Centre** ① *T020-7924 5826*, a small zoo of native species, near the river. Bicycles can be hired from near the running track.

A 20-minute walk west from the park is the riverside **St Mary's Church** ① *Battersea Church Rd, SW11, T020-7228 9648, Jun-Sep Tue, Wed 1100-1500; all other times by appointment*. Dating from 1775, this old church is where William Blake was married, and Turner sat to sketch the river from the vestry window. Turner's favourite chair is exhibited in the chancel.

36 Battersea Park & around

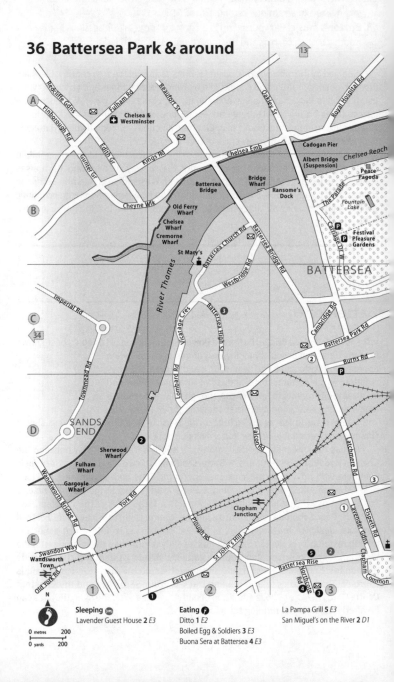

Sleeping 🛏
Lavender Guest House **2** *E3*

Eating 🍴
Ditto **1** *E2*
Boiled Egg & Soldiers **3** *E3*
Buona Sera at Battersea **4** *E3*

La Pampa Grill **5** *E3*
San Miguel's on the River **2** *D1*

Clapham

⊖ *Clapham North, Clapham Common.* ⊜ *Overland train: Clapham Junction from Victoria. Buses: see p460.*

Clapham Common is a picturesque stretch of commonly owned land which makes a pleasant walking ground at weekends when families and footballers are usually out in force. The long terrace of Georgian townhouses on the north side dates from

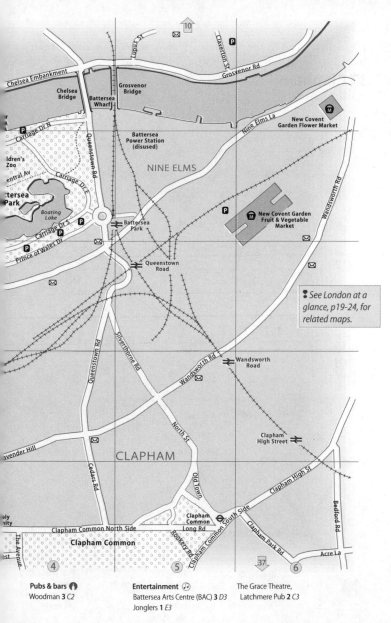

See London at a glance, p19-24, for related maps.

South Battersea, Clapham, Brixton & Dulwich

Pubs & bars 🍺	Entertainment 🎵	The Grace Theatre,
Woodman **3** *C2*	Battersea Arts Centre (BAC) **3** *D3*	Latchmere Pub **2** *C3*
	Jonglers **1** *E3*	

around 1720 and includes the former residences of Captain Cook and Charles Barry (architect of the Houses of Parliament).

Holy Trinity Church ① *Clapham Common North Side, SW4, T020-7627 0941*, was originally built in 1776 and partially rebuilt after The Second World War. Holy Trinity is the former headquarters of the zealously Anglican 'Clapham Sect' led by notable anti-slavery campaigner William Wilberforce. The fountain on the common donated by the local temperance society is an appropriately dry testament to their local influence.

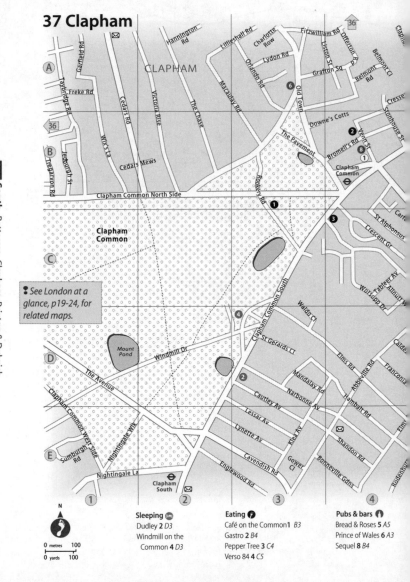

37 Clapham

❗ See London at a glance, p19-24, for related maps.

N

0 metres 100
0 yards 100

Sleeping 😴
Dudley **2** *D3*
Windmill on the Common **4** *D3*

Eating 🍴
Café on the Common **1** *B3*
Gastro **2** *B4*
Pepper Tree **3** *C4*
Verso 84 **4** *C5*

Pubs & bars 🍸
Bread & Roses **5** *A5*
Prince of Wales **6** *A3*
Sequel **8** *B4*

Brixton ⊖ *Brixton.*

Electric Avenue was one of the first streets in London to be supplied with electricity, and is nowadays the pulsating centre of ethnic Brixton. Dingy and verging on the dilapidated, the energy which emanates from **Brixton Market** (see below) represents the heart of this lively multicultural town at its effervescent best.

⁑ See map of Brixton on page 362.

Nearby is the **Black Cultural Archives** ① *378 Coldharbour Lane, SW9, T020-7738 4591, www.aambh.org.uk, Mon-Fri 1300-1600 or by appointment, free*. With frequent temporary exhibitions, the Black Cultural Archives is a good information point on black issues and a mouthpiece for Brixton's strong Afro-Caribbean cultural awareness.

Photofusion ① *17a Electric Lane, SW9, T020-7738 5774, www.photofusion.org, Tue, Thu-Sat 1000-1800, Wed 1000-2000, free*, have an extensive library of photos documenting contemporary British life with an emphasis on environmental and social issues. The facilities are for members only, but the galleries of regularly changing exhibitions are open to the public.

A short walk up Brixton Hill is the **Brixton Windmill**, Blenheim Gardens, a 19th-century windmill that's perhaps the last thing you'd expect to see in the down-trodden urban environs of South London. Ramshackle and forlorn, it diverts attention from the surrounding social decay and the dreadful prison next door; it's worth a visit for the juxtaposition alone.

East of here, on Dulwich Road, is **Brockwell Park**, with its lido swimming pool, hilltop café and walled lakeside garden giving wide views over London.

Dulwich

Although Dulwich – pronounced 'dullitch' – may not sound the most enticing of London's longer-haul destinations, its quaint village atmosphere and the wonderful old ★**Dulwich Picture Gallery** ① *Gallery Rd, Dulwich, T020-8693 5254, www.dulwichpicturegallery.org.uk, Tue-Fri 1000-1700, Sat, Sun 1100-1700, adult £4, concessons £3, trains (2 an hour) from Victoria to West Dulwich then 10-min walk; from Waterloo or London Bridge (4 an hour) to North Dulwich then 10-min walk*, both merit the trip. The Gallery claims to be the first purpose-built public art gallery in the world, specially designed by Sir John Soane

Entertainment 🎭
Clapham Picture House **1** *B4*
Upstairs at the Landor **2** *A6*

South Battersea, Clapham, Brixton & Dulwich

and opened to the public in 1817. A neo-classical temple to Old Masters, it has received a designer facelift and stands in peaceful gardens next to the house of Edward Alleyn, Christopher Marlowe's flamboyant manager, on the site of the original Dulwich College (relocated in the 19th century to much grander premises nearby). Inside, beneath elegant arches and restored roof lanterns, and above some rare antique furniture, hangs a small treasury of English, Italian, Spanish, French and Dutch paintings from the 17th and 18th centuries – by the likes of Gainsborough, Rembrandt, Van Dyck, Canaletto and Watteau.

Elsewhere around South London

The **Horniman Museum** ① *100 London Rd, SE23, T020-8699 1872, www.horniman.ac.uk, daily 1030 -1730, free, Forest Hill train station from London Bridge*, is one of the more eccentric museums in London and a lot of fun for kids. A permanent exhibition on Africa, along with a refurbished aquarium and natural history gallery now complements the museum's extensive and wonderful collection of strange musical instruments. The gardens give panoramic views over London and contain a small zoo of wallabies, turkeys, goats and guinea pigs.

The **Cuming Museum** ① *155 Walworth Rd, SE17, T020-7525 2163, Tue-Sat 1000-1700, free, www.southwark.gov.uk,* is a interesting curiosity worth a look if

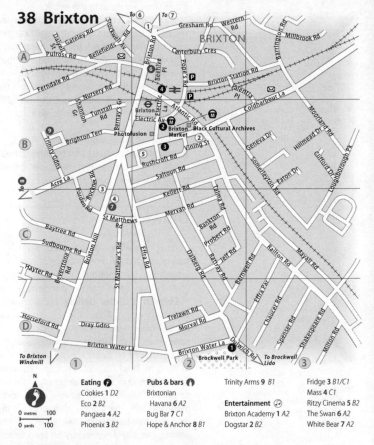

38 Brixton

N

0 metres 100
0 yards 100

Eating 🍴
Cookies 1 *D2*
Eco 2 *B2*
Pangaea 4 *A2*
Phoenix 3 *B2*

Pubs & bars 🍺
Brixtonian
Havana 6 *A2*
Bug Bar 7 *C1*
Hope & Anchor 8 *B1*

Trinity Arms 9 *B1*

Entertainment 🎵
Brixton Academy 1 *A2*
Dogstar 2 *B2*

Fridge 3 *B1/C1*
Mass 4 *C1*
Ritzy Cinema 5 *B2*
The Swan 6 *A2*
White Bear 7 *A2*

★ Five of the best pubs in south London

- **The Woodman**, Battersea High St, Battersea, page 364.
- **Bread and Roses**, Clapham Manor St, Clapham, page 364.
- **Prince of Wales**, Clapham Old Town, Clapham, page 364.
- **Dogstar**, Coldharbour Lane, Brixton, page 365.
- **Hope and Anchor**, Acre Lane, Brixton, page 365.

you happen to be on the No 12 bus route to Dulwich. Near the Elephant and Castle on the Walworth Rd, 'The Health of the People is the Highest Law' reads the inscription on a building that houses a bizarre collection of objects from round the world gathered together by archeaologist Henry Cuming about a hundred years ago. His study has been reconstructed, including ranks of drawers that can be opened to reveal peculiar things from the anthropological Lovett collection of superstitious charms and totems.

⊜ Sleeping

Clapham *p357, maps p358 & p360*

B Windmill on the Common, Clapham Common Southside, SW4, T020-8673 4578, windmillhotel@youngs.co.uk. A view over the Common, well-furnished rooms and a fancy restaurant make the Windmill a great base from which to see London, it is not cheap, however (reduced rates weekends).

C Dudley Hotel, 80-81 Clapham Common Southside, SW4, T020-8673 3534. Right next to the Common and very close to Clapham South tube station, the rooms all have en suite bathrooms and include a continental breakfast. £55 a double per night.

C Lavender Guest House, 18 Lavender Sweep, SW11, T020-7585 2767. Picturesque Victorian building with a pretty garden for guests' use. A standard double costs £60 a night with breakfast, though the lavish Executive Room, which might cost around £300 in the centre, is a snip at £85.

❶ Eating

Battersea *p357, map p358*

❦ Ditto, East Hill, SW18, T020-8877 0110, further afield, towards Wandsworth. A lively modern European gallery-bar restaurant with a comfortable sofa area.

❦ La Pampa Grill, 60 Battersea Rise, SW11, T020-7924 4774. Situated in the trendy restaurant strip leading off Clapham Common is this living shrine to all things

steak. Vibrant and atmospheric, it boasts a good list of Argentinean wines and 101 uses for sizzling red meat.

❦ Buona Sera at Battersea, 226 Northcote Rd, T020-7228 9925. Pizza, pasta and a full Italian country menu served up in an unfussy way at marble tables.

❦ San Miguel's on the River, Molasses House, Plantation Wharf, Battersea Reach, SW11, T020-7801 9696. Though the menu is relatively ordinary, the tapas on offers are well presented and low in price. Panoramic views of the river add value and there's also a much more expensive restaurant menu for those who want to splash out.

Clapham *p357, maps p358 & p360*

❦ Gastro, 67 Venn St, SW4, T020-7627 0222. Indeed a rare breed – unabashedly Gallic yet wonderfully uncontrived. The prices verge on the expensive, though the French provincial food is generally of a very high standard and the lively atmosphere itself merits the extra cost.

❦ Pepper Tree, 19 Clapham Common Southside, SW4, T020-7622 1758. Has long communal benches and tables ensuring an intimate experience in this busy Thai den. Bargain prices for some excellent Thai cooking.

❦ Verso 84, 84 Clapham Park Rd, SW4, T020-7720 1515. A tremendous Neapolitan pizzeria with a delightfully laid-back atmosphere.

Boiled Egg & Soldiers, 63 Northcote Rd, SW11, T020-7223 4894. A small family establishment offering spruced up traditional café fare. Kids abound unimpeded, so perhaps not the best place for a quiet snack, but otherwise a warm, clean and friendly local. And yes, boiled egg and soldiers are a speciality. Directly opposite is a more down-to-earth, good old greasy spoon where you can pile on the cholesterol while scanning the Sunday papers. Open Mon-Sat 0900-1800; Sun 1000-1700.

Café on the Common, 2 Rookery Rd, SW4, T020-7498 0770. A seemingly ramshackle café in the middle of Clapham Common serving amazingly good food, from standard café fare to almost gastronomic heights. There's precious little seating inside, so either wrap up warm or come on a summer's day and enjoy the scenery. Open daily 1000-1800.

Brixton *p361, map p362*

Eco, 4 Market Row, Brixton Market, Electric Lane, SW9, T020-7738 3021 (and also at Clapham, 182 Clapham High St, SW4, T020- 7978 1108). There are more pre-night-out kind of places than secluded dinner venues in this area, but this small chain provides decent pizza and pasta at a reasonable rate.

Pangaea, 15 Atlantic Rd, SW9, T020-7737 6777. About as authentic an Italian dinner destination as you can find. Colourful and friendly with a good range of pizzas, it's definitely worth a visit.

Phoenix Restaurant, 441 Coldharbour Lane, SW9, T020-7733 4430. An exceptionally cheap and cheerful caff, very typical of the area, doing filling platefuls of comfort food and all-day breakfasts in a warm fug.

Cafés and sandwich bars

Cookies, Brixton Water Lane, SW2, T020-7642 0380. Open daily 0900-1800, a welcome addition to Brixton café culture, with a good selection of coffees and snacks, as well as exhibitions.

ⓞ Pubs and bars

Battersea *p357, map p358*

The Woodman, 60 Battersea High St, SW11, T020-7228 2968. A fine, creaking, old-fashioned boozer with a cracking selection of ales, real and otherwise. Thankfully the food is not the usual bar-room stodge, the kitchen carrying off an interesting menu well. A place to sit back and watch the footy.

Clapham *p357, maps p358 & p360*

Bread and Roses, 68 Clapham Manor St, SW4, T020-7498 1779. Pick of the bunch, must be one of the finest pubs in the south, if not the whole of London. A Workers' Beer Company co-operative in the middle of bourgeois Clapham, it plays host to poetry and comedy (Wed).

Prince of Wales, 38 Clapham Old Town, SW4. Seek this place out for an eccentric pint, a small, low-lit, snug place full of bizarre bric-a-brac.

Sequel, 75 Venn St, SW4, T020-7622 4222, next door to the Clapham Picture House. Although a restaurant as well there's often room to sneak in for a shifty cocktail or 2 in this classy bar. Great for both a peaceful pre-movie concoction and pensive post-picture ruminations. Open Mon-Fri 1700-2300, Sat 1100-1600, 1730-2300, Sun 1200-1730, 1800-2230.

Brixton *p361, map p362*

Brixtonian Havana, Beehive Pl, SW9, T020-7924 9262, tucked away near the market. Serves cracking cocktails (including the infamous 'Brixton Riot') and the largest range of rum this side of the Antilles. Its stylish mock-colonial interior can get a little too busy for its own good at weekends, but it's well worth investigating. Open Tue, Wed 1200-0100, Thu-Sat 1200-0200.

Bug Bar, The Crypt, St Matthew's Church, SW2, beneath the massive church opposite the Town Hall and the Fridge Club, T020-7738 3184. The cavernous depths of St Matthew's crypt make for a loud and lively night beneath the town. The prevailing atmosphere is appropriately dance-driven

⬤ For an explanation of sleeping and eating price codes used in this guide, see inside the front cover. Other relevant information is found in Essentials, see pages 44-46.

and dangerous with seating provided by a few sofas and old oak pews, the only major downside being the admission charge after 2100 at weekends. Open Mon-Wed 1900-0100, Thu 1900-0200, Fri, Sat 1900-0300, Sun 2000-0100.

Hope and Anchor, 123 Acre Lane, SW2, T020-7274 1787. A standard and friendly pub with large and elaborately ornamented garden and an non-age specific clientele. Good beer, warm atmosphere and the best roast dinner in Brixton. Open Mon-Sat 1100-2300, Sun 1200-2230.

The Trinity Arms, T020-7274 4544, tucked away in Trinity Gardens. A cosy little local, pulling fine pints of Young's. Quiet and calm with a garden.

◉ Entertainment

Battersea, Clapham, Brixton and Dulwich *p356*

Cinema

Clapham Picture House, Venn St, Clapham, SW4, information T020-7498 2242, booking: T020-7498 3323. Pleasant independent cinema just off Clapham High St showing the old, the new and the cult.

Ritzy, Brixton Oval, Coldharbour Lane, SW2, information T020-7737 2121, booking: T020-7733 2229. Classy 5-screen cinema offering the best of both arthouse and mainstream and something of a Brixton institution.

Music

Rock, folk and jazz   Brixton Academy, 211 Stockwell Rd, SW9, Box Office T020-7771 2000. The mighty Brixton Academy is an old Victorian hall that has just enough capacity to attract the biggest of artists while not appearing over-large, and in any case it is invariably full. Much comment is made of the Academy's steeply sloping floor which, while ensuring a good view for all, has the disadvantage of making drunken dancing mildly perilous. For this reason, some of the big dance acts who occasionally play all-nighters prefer to level the floor artificially.

The Swan, 215 Clapham Rd, SW9, T020-7978 9778. Gigs from 2130 daily, £1.50-6 (usually free Mon-Wed and before 2100 Thu and Sun). The most Irish place you'll find south of, well, Kilburn. Though it

allows the odd rock act through its doors at weekends, you can guarantee semi-traditional Celtic stuff during the week along with a loud and lively atmosphere.

★ Nightclubs

Dogstar, 389 Coldharbour Lane, SW9, T020-7733 7515. Technically a bar/club crossover in the Bug Bar mould, the Dogstar is one of Brixton's most popular after hours venues, with decent DJs throughout the week and dodgy disco classics at the weekend. Furthermore, the beer is excellent.

Fridge, Town Hall Pde, Brixton Hill, SW2, T020-77326 5100. Banging trance and techno is the staple of Brixton's largest club, though it also hosts several popular gay nights. Admission is generally between £8 and £12.

Jongleurs, 49 Lavender Gdns, SW11, T020-7564 2500. The original branch of this expanding comedy chain, Jongleurs Battersea plays host to some of the biggest names on the UK comedy circuit. With 2 adjoining bars, *Bar Risa* and *Bar Risa Late*, a varied and riotous night is assured and booking essential.

Mass, St Matthews Church, Brixton Hill, SW2, T020-7738 5255. Situated above the Bug Bar, this dark and dingy converted church is renowned for its weekend hard house nights. Despite the mammoth exterior it can appear deceptively small and fills up quickly after midnight.

Theatre

Battersea Arts Centre, Lavender Hill, SW11, T020-7223 2223. An arts centre that enjoys a formidable reputation for fostering new and experimental theatre. Performances by touring companies include everything from stand-up comedy to opera and the centre's off-beat seasons of visual theatre.

The Grace Theatre, Latchmere Pub, 503 Battersea Park Rd, SW11, T020-7794 0022. A small middle-of-the-road theatre often staging fairly impressive productions, many of which later migrate to the more fashionable North. The *Latchmere* pub below is a luxurious and comfortable place for a pre-play pint.

Upstairs at the Landor, 70 Landor Rd, SW9 9PH, T020-7737 7276. A popular stopping off point for young writers showcasing their products. A good stage for new and innovative productions and a busy local with a strange nautical theme below.

The White Bear, 138 Kennington Park Rd, SE11, T020-7793 9193 (Kennington tube). A tiny theatre with an adventurous record behind a punk Irish pub.

O Shopping

Battersea *p357, map p358*

Hive Honey Shop, 93 Northcote Rd, SW11, T020-7924 6233, The name of this place says it all – honey shampoo, soap, health products, herbal treatments, pots and tableware – as well as a living and working beehive. An intriguing homage to apiculture. Open Mon-Fri 1000-1700, Sat 1000-1800.

Clapham *p357, maps p358 & p360*

Old Post Office Bakery, 74 Landor Rd, SW9. A venerable organic bakery. Get there fast at lunchtime because its popularity is entirely justified.

Brixton *p361, map p362*

Bookmongers, 439 Coldharbour Lane, SW9, T020-7738 4225. A well-arranged and comprehensive second-hand bookshop, also selling remainders and slightly damaged new copies. Open Mon-Sat 1030-1830.

Brixton Market, Electric Av, Pope's Rd, Brixton Station Rd, SW9. A melting pot of Afro-Caribbean food, fresh fish, clothes, wigs, bric-a-brac, reggae and religion. A surprising and wide-eyed shopping trip is guaranteed, with the streets around good for second-hand clothing bargains. Open Mon, Tue, Thu-Sat 0800-1800; Wed 0800-1500.

Collectable Furniture, 407 Coldharbour Lane, SW9, T020-7738 4141. An intriguing retro furniture shop, open Mon-Thu, Sun 1000-2300; Fri-Sat 1000-0200.

▲ Activities

Battersea, Clapham, Brixton and Dulwich *p356*

Latchmere Leisure Centre, Burns Rd, Battersea, SW11, T020-7207 8004. Swimming pool: Mon-Thu, Sun 0700-2130; Fri 0700-1800; Sat 0700-1930; £3.53 peak for adult non-members. Gym: Mon-Thu

0700-2230; Fri, Sun 0700-1000; Sat 0700-2000; £7.53 per session for non-members. Sports Hall also available for hire. Trial offers are worth looking into for cheaper deals, ask at reception.

Brixton Recreation Centre, 27 Station Rd, SW9, T020-7926 9779. Saunas, swimming pool, indoor tennis and basketball, badminton and even an indoor bowling green.

Battersea Park, Albert Bridge Rd, SW11, T020-8871 7542. Tennis: weekdays 0800-2200; weekends 0800-2000; £6.75 per hour peak; £4.65 per hour off-peak (before 1800 on weekdays). Athletics: weekdays 0730-2200; weekends 0730-1930; £2.30 for adults.

Foster's Oval, Surrey County Cricket Club's home ground, T020-7582 7764. Tickets £10 for county matches, £23-75 for one-day internationals, and £40-66 for test matches.

Brockwell Lido, Brockwell Park, Dulwich, SE24, T020-274 3088. Open-air swimming summer only: 0645-1000, 1200-1900, early morning £1.50, all day £4. Yoga and meditation all year. Poolside café. Theatre and art events.

Streatham Mega Bowl, 142 Streatham Hill, SW2, T020-8671 5021. Open 1000-2300, Sun, Mon, Tue-Sat 1000-0130. 36 bowling lanes, biggest in Europe, £4.75 adults, £3.75 under-16s per game including shoe hire. Burger King and two bars. Booking advisable for weekends.

Streatham Ice Rink, 386 Streatham High Rd, SW16, T020-8769 7771. Open daily 1030-1600 and at other times some evenings, ring to check. £7.30 including skates, last ticket sold one hour before closing. Large old local rink with a basic café.

Catford Stadium, Ardenmore Rd, SE, T020-8690 8000. Greyhound racing every Thu at 1920 until after 1000.

Crystal Palace National Sports Centre, Leddrington Rd, Upper Norwood, SE19, T020-8778 0131, www.crystalpalace.co.uk. One of the largest sports centres in the UK with 50-m swimming pool (£1.70 off-peak, £2.60 peak), gym (£2 off-peak, £3 peak), tennis (£6.80), squash (£3.60 off-peak, £7.50 peak), badminton (£3.65 off-peak, £8.20 peak), boxing events, running tracks. Crystal Palace train station.

Day trips

• Footprint features

Windsor and Eton

Everyone who loves anything royal loves Windsor. English Kings and Queens have lived in the impressive castle that glowers over the town since the 15th century and it remains the monarch's preferred residence. During the First World War it gave a good name to the current royal family (the Saxe-Coburg-Gothas), after a precedent established by Edward III in the 14th century. Easily accessed from London, tourists descend on the place in thousands during the summer and are generally not disappointed. Apart from the castle itself, the town centre is an attractive place to explore and the crowds can easily be escaped in the Great Park or along the river. Over the old bridge, visitors clog up Eton's quirky little High Street on their way to see the world-famous school, one of the oldest in the country. ▸▸ *For Sleeping, Eating and other listings, see pages 370-370.*

Ins and outs

Getting there
Rail South West Trains operate a twice-hourly service from London Waterloo to Windsor and Eton Riverside, taking about 50 mins. From London Paddington, **Thames Trains,** run regular connecting services from Slough (on the mainline from London to Reading) taking 6 mins. **National Rail Enquiries** T08457-484950.
Road Windsor is just south of the M4, 26 miles from London at Junction 6, a journey from central London that can take 30 mins to an hour, depending on the traffic. **Green Line,** T0870-6087261, operate bus services to Windsor from London.

Getting around
The Long Walk stretches dead straight for several miles from the castle gates into the Great Park, but Windsor town centre and the castle are easily small enough to walk around. Eton College is a 15-min walk from the castle over the river.

Information
Royal Windsor TIC, 24 High St, T01753-743900 (accommodation booking T01753-743907), www.windsor.gov.uk. Mon-Fri, Sun 1000-1600, Sat 1000-1700. Also small free exhibition upstairs on 'Town and Crown'.

Sights

Windsor Castle
① *T020-7321 2233, www.the-royal-collection.org.uk (24-hr information T01753-831118). Mar-Oct daily 0945-1715 (last admission 1600); Nov-Feb daily 0945-1615 (last admission 1500); Semi-State Rooms also open Oct-Mar only; State Rooms usually closed for 1 week mid- to late-Jun and occasionally at other times. Adult £12.50 (£6 when State Rooms closed), concessions £10.50 (£5), under-17s £6.50 (£3.50), under-5s free. There are guided tours of the restored areas not on the main public route including the medieval Undercroft and Great Kitchen each morning and afternoon on Tue and Wed, Oct-Mar only.*

Windsor Castle is hard to miss. Walk uphill anywhere in the town and you'll find yourself beneath its walls. It was built as part of a circle of Norman control around London. Unlike the other castles – Rochester, Tonbridge, Reigate, Berkhampstead, Ongar, Hertford and Guildford, all roughly equidistant from the Tower of London – it has survived intact and been much extended over the centuries. Today, the Royal control extends to banning dogs, radios, mobile phones, bicycles or alcohol from the castle precincts. Founded on a strategic sight affording far-reaching views by William the Conqueror within a day's march of the Tower of London, it ensured the dominance of the invading monarch over the western approaches to the city. The Queen still lives here most of the year. The public are admitted throughout the year (except on state occasions, phone first), to the **State Apartments**, including Charles II's apartments and the Waterloo Chamber, decorated with paintings from the Royal Collection by Van Dyck, Holbein, Rubens and Rembrandt and some very fine furniture; the castles' precincts and Henry VIII's gorgeous Gothic **St George's Chapel**, where 10 sovereigns are buried (and where Edward and Sophie tied the knot). The highlight of the State Apartments is **St George's Hall**, fully restored after the fire in 1992, where the Queen holds banquets and receptions.

From April to June, the **Changing of the Guard** happens here at 1100 Monday to Saturday. From July to March, the ceremony takes place on alternate days. The best vantage points are the Lower Ward of the Castle or outside on Windsor High Street. During summer, the Semi-State rooms are also open, featuring some of the Castle's most splendid interiors. One very popular curiosity is Queen Mary's Dolls' House, the most famous of its kind in the world, a complete palace built to a scale of 1 in 12 by at least 1,000 master craftsmen in the 1920s. All the little palace's fixtures and fittings are in full working order, including the bathrooms, lifts and electricity supply.

Windsor

Day trips Windsor & Eton

N

0 metres 100
0 yards 100

Sleeping
Christopher 2
Netherton 4
Park Farm B&B 6

Sir Christopher
Wren's House 7
YHA Windsor 8

Eating
Antico 1
Drury House 4

Other sights

South of the Castle stretches the wide expanse of the **Great Park**, most easily reached from town via the fine Georgian street Park Street. The Long Walk runs dead straight south for 3 miles towards a distant statue of George III on horseback. There are very fine views of the castle and Thames Valley from this giant statue.

Over the bridge, Eton High Street begins, running north for a few hundred yards before fetching up outside **Eton College** ① *includes the Museum of Eton Life, T01753-671177, Mar-Oct daily termtime 1400-1630, school holidays 1030-1630, adult £4.50, ordinary £3.50, guided tours 1415, 1515*. The guided tours illuminate the history of this the most exclusive boys school in the country, its high fees once described by 'old boy' George Orwell as "a tax the middle classes must pay to join the system".

● Sleeping

Windsor & Eton *p368, map p369*
L Sir Christopher Wren's House Hotel, Thames St, Windsor, T01753-861354. Individually designed rooms in Sir Christopher's old house which he designed himself down by the river bridge, as well as a top-notch restaurant.
A Christopher Hotel, 110 High St, Eton T01753-852359, www.christopher-hotel.co.uk. Best Western hotel in an old coaching inn with *Renata's* restaurant.
B Netherton Hotel, 98-98 St Leonard's Rd, Windsor, T01753-855508. Family-run hotel within walking distance of the Castle.
C Park Farm B&B, St Leonard's Rd, Windsor, T01753-866823. Smart and fairly central guest house.
F YHA Windsor, Edgeworth House, Mill Lane, Windsor, T01753-861710. In a big old house situated on the outskirts of the town itself.

● Eating

Windsor & Eton *p368, map p369*
♀♀ **Antico**, 42 High St, Eton, T01753-863977. Established Italian very popular with the locals.
♀ **Drury House**, 4 Church St, right opposite King Henry VIII gate. Tearooms abound in Windsor town and this is 'Windsor's oldest teashop', an archetypal example of the genre.

▲ Activities and tours

Windsor & Eton *p368, map p369*
French Brothers Ltd, Clewer Boathouse, Clewer Court Rd, Windsor, T01753-851900. Easter-Oct 1100-1700, boat trips.
Orchard Poyle Carriage Hire, T01784-435983, T07836-766027 (mob). 30 min £19, 1 hr £38. Victorian Hackney carriage pulled by 2 bay horses.
Walking along the Thames Path, contact National Trails Office, T01865-810224.

Oxford

Oxford's name means many things to most people: branding for shoes, trousers and cars, a bastion of snobbery and class distinction, a marriage market for the young idle rich. Above all though, it's still a university city of international standing. First-time visitors can hardly fail to be impressed by the sheer number of beautiful old colleges that make up this pinnacle of British academe. Christ Church is the grandest, Merton the oldest, New College the most authentic in its groundplan and Magdalen the most lovely, but all the colleges in the centre of the city are worth looking around. There's much else in the city to enjoy. Along with two of the most extraordinary museums in the country, the Ashmolean and the Pitt Rivers, there's punting on the river, almost a mandatory activity in summer for students and visitors alike. One of Europe's most remarkable cities, of course Oxford is mobbed in the high season. That said, it's never too difficult to escape the crowds, while even the passing visitor is likely to appreciate the highly charged meeting of cerebral old institutions with bright young things. ⟫ *For Sleeping, Eating and other listings, see pages 374-375.*

Ins and outs

Getting there

Rail **Thames Trains** run twice-hourly express services from London Paddington via Reading to Oxford, taking just under 1 hr. Stopping services (via Didcot Parkway and stations along the Thames valley) take 1 hr 30 mins. **National Rail Enquiries** T08457-484950. The main railway station is in the west of the city, where the Botley Road meets Hythe Bridge street, a 15-min walk into the centre.

Road Oxford is very well served by coach companies. The intercity and local bus terminus is at Gloucester Green, very close to the city centre. **National Express,** T08705-808080, for **London Victoria** and long distance. Also **City Link Oxford Express,** T01865-785400, **Oxford Tube,** T01865-772250 (24 hr London-Oxford Express, every 12 mins. Most local buses are run by **Stagecoach Oxford,** T01865-772250. **Jetlink** for airport buses T08705-757747, **Guide Friday,** T01865-790522, for open-top tours.

Getting around

Walking or cycling around central Oxford is one of life's real pleasures. For some of the slightly further-flung parts of the city, taxis are relatively cheap and the bus network from Gloucester Green along the High Street and around Carfax is regular and reliable.

Information

Oxford TIC, 15-16 Broad St, T01865-726871, www.visitoxford.org Mon-Sat 0930-1700, Sun 1000-1530. Accommodation booking service (including fee), **Oxford Guild of Guides,** walking tours, T01865-250551.

Day trips Oxford

Sights

The block of old streets and colleges formed by the Cornmarket, the Broad, Catte Street and the High Street is pretty much the heart of the university, embracing the University Church of St Mary the Virgin, the Radcliffe Camera, the Bodleian Library and Sheldonian Theatre, as well as Jesus, Exeter, and Brasenose colleges.

On the Broad, the **Sheldonian Theatre** ① *Broad St, T01865-277299, www.sheldon.ox.ac.uk, Apr-Oct daily 1000-1230, 1400-1630, Nov-Mar 1000-1230, 1400-1530 (subject to variations), adult £1.50, under-16s £1,* is the university's hall of ceremonies, also designed by Wren, who studied astronomy nearby at All Souls, its ceiling painted with the triumph of Truth, allied with Arts and Sciences, over Ignorance. An octagonal rooftop cupola above provides sheltered wraparound views of that famous skyline come wind or rain.

Its neighbour, the **Clarendon Building**, was constructed by Wren's pupil Hawksmoor, to the plans of Vanbrugh, architect of Blenheim Palace, as a printing house. Now it makes a grand front door for the **Bodleian Library** ① *Broad St, T01865-277000, www.bodley.ox.ac.uk, tours lasting 45 mins Apr-Oct Mon-Sat 1030, 1130, 1400, 1500, Nov-Mar Mon-Fri 1400, 1500, Sat 1030, 1130, 1400, 1500, £3.50 (no under-14s allowed), Divinity School and shop, usually an exhibition, donations requested, Apr-Dec Mon-Fri 1000-1600, Sat 1000-1230,* the university's chief academic resource and one of the greatest, certainly the oldest public libraries in the world. Its extraordinary Gothic Jacobean central courtyard has to be seen to be believed. Through the glass doors on the right, the 15th-century Divinity School is the oldest part of the building, with a magnificent vaulted stone ceiling. The library itself, one of the wonders of the western world, including its most ancient room, the mysterious and magical Duke Humphrey's, can be seen on guided tours that need to be booked in the summer.

The library makes up the north side of Radcliffe Square, effectively the centre of the university with 18th-century Scottish architect James Gibbs's majestic domed **Radcliffe Camera** plonked unceremoniously in the middle. On the south side of the square, the **University Church of St Mary** ① *University Church of St Mary's tower, 0900-1700 (Jul, Aug 0900-1900, last admission 50 mins before closing), adult £1.60, under-16s £0.80,* seals the university off from the High Street behind. The church itself did the job that the Sheldonian Theatre took over, and has a long history of ecclesiastical wrangling, but most visitors come for the climb up the tower to overlook the Radcliffe Camera, probably the best viewpoint (and the highest) in the centre of the city.

Day trips Oxford

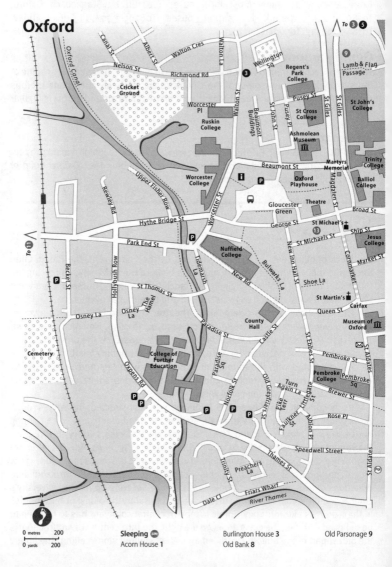

Oxford

| 0 metres | 200 |
| 0 yards | 200 |

Sleeping 🛏
Acorn House **1**

Burlington House **3**
Old Bank **8**

Old Parsonage **9**

The Ashmolean Museum

ⓘ Beaumont St, To1865-278000, www.ashmol.ox.ac.uk. Tue-Sat 1000-1700 (also Jun, Aug on Thu until 1900), Sun 1400-1700. Free. Cast Gallery, Pusey Lane, off St John St, Tue-Fri 1000-1600, Sat 1000-1300.

The oldest museum open to the public in the country. It was opened early in the 17th century by Elias Ashmole, one of Charles I's tax-men. Today it ranks as one of the most extraordinary collections under one roof outside London. The Ashmolean Museum's grand classical façade hides more than 50 rooms, some very beautiful, others not, all with stories to tell and on a very manageable scale. A wide staircase to the right of the front entrance leads up to the Founder's Collection, a right turn at the top of the stairs, displaying a few of gardener John Tradescant's 'curiosities', later purchased by Elias Ashmole. These include Powhatan's Mantle, 'perhaps the

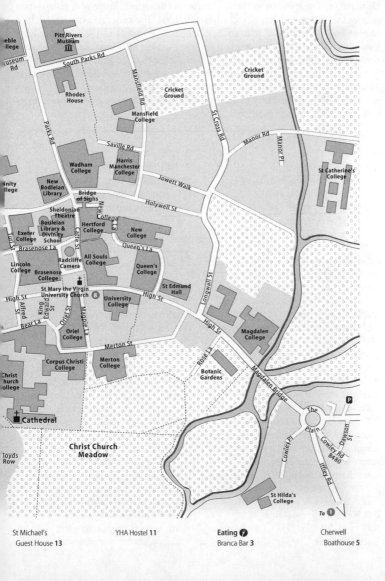

Day trips Oxford

St Michael's
Guest House **13**

YHA Hostel **11**

Eating ⑦
Branca Bar **3**

Cherwell
Boathouse **5**

most important North American Indian relic to survive anywhere' – four deerskins stitched together and decorated with shells. Sadly it's now thought unlikely that it was in fact worn by Pocahontas' dad.

Christy Church

ⓘ *College: T01865-286573, www.chch.ox.ac.uk. Mon-Sat 0930-1730, Sun 1200-1530. £4. Christ Church Cathedral: Mon-Sat 0900-1645, Sun 1300-1630. Hall: Mon-Fri 0930-1145, daily 1400-1730. Picture Gallery: Apr-Sep Mon-Sat 1030-1300, 1400-1730, Sun 1400-1730; Oct-Mar Mon-Sat 1030-1300, 1400-1630, Sun 1400-1630 (£2 additional fee).*

Christ Church, largest, most spectacular and most commercialized of the colleges, was founded by Cardinal Wolsey, (hence 'Cardinal College' in Hardy's *Jude the Obscure*), and re-founded by Henry VIII after his break with Rome who saved some money by making its chapel the city's cathedral. The college is the university's largest and in Tom Quad you know it. Used by Royalists in the Civil War as a cattlepen, during the 18th century it became famous for the antics of its equally bovine aristocratic undergraduates or 'junior members' as they're known at 'the house'. Tom Quad, the cathedral and the picture gallery are well worth a look round. The cathedral is the country's smallest. The picture gallery, housed in a purpose-built modernist block sunk next to the library, is particularly famous for its collection of Old Master drawings.

● Sleeping

Oxford *p370, map p372*
You should book well in advance, particularly for the budget accommodation options all year round and all others especially in the summer. The TIC runs the usual booking service.
L Old Parsonage Hotel, 1 Banbury Rd, T01865-310210. Oscar Wilde's undergraduate digs, since 1989 the Old Parsonage has been known as the poshest hotel in town.
A Old Bank Hotel, 92-94 High St, T01865-799599. One of the most stylish and central places to stay in the city, 42-individual room hotel (£155 a standard double, likely to have good views of the famous skyline).
B Burlington House, 374 Banbury Rd, T01865-513513, www.burlington-house.co.uk. Non-smoking little boutique hotel some distance up the Banbury Rd, 11 rooms, with a very good breakfast.
C Acorn House, 260 Iffley Rd, T01865-247998. 4 comfortable non-smoking double rooms, a 20-min walk into town.
D St Michael's Guest House, 26 St Michael St, T01865-242101. Central, £50 for a double.

F YHA Hostel, 2a Botley Rd, T01865-727275. Just behind the railway station, fairly smart and new with 180 beds in dorms and rooms, can be reached from the westbound platform through a little alleyway.

● Eating

Oxford *p370, map p372*
There are several restaurants well worth making tracks for just north of the centre. Some within walking distance are grouped around Little Clarendon St and Walton St.
Branca Bar Kitchen, 111 Walton St, T01865-556111. A newish Italian peasant favourite, with contemporary art on the walls, the kitchen upstairs on the balcony, above the snazzy low-lit dining room.
The Cherwell Boathouse, Bardwell Rd, T01865-552746. This is a more expensive gourmet option worth seeking out for a special occasion. The place to have a fine 'modern European' feast (about £30 a head for lunch) in a clapperboard hut, then hire a punt perhaps, or a more expensive and leisurely supper on the waterside.

▲ Activities and tours

Oxford *p370, map p372*
Boating
There are several places to hire boats and punts around Oxford.
Cherwell Boathouse, T01865-515978. This is the most rural place.
College Cruisers, Combe Rd Wharf, Combe Rd, T01865-554343,

www.collegecruisers.com. Hire out cruising boats on the river by the week.
Head of the River, Folly Bridge, T01865-721600. The one on the Thames.
Magdalen Bridge Punt Hire, T01865-761586. Punts can be hired here, which is the busiest place.
Salter Brothers, Folly Bridge, T01865-243421 www.salterbros.co.uk. Run boat trips on the Thames.

Salisbury and Stonehenge

Salisbury wins out in the league of beautiful cities of the south mainly because it has been lucky enough to keep out the way of big new road-building programmes. Which comes as some surprise given that nine major old roads meet here near the confluence of four rivers on the banks of the River Avon. The Market Square is the centre of things, alive and busy every Tuesday and Saturday, while the Close and its Cathedral remain very peaceful and serene behind their old walls a few hundred yards away. The Cathedral, with its magnificent spire, is still the main event, although Salisbury is large enough to boast some thriving nightlife and characterful pubs. Stonehenge, almost halfway to Exeter from London on the A303, and 7 miles north of Salisbury, is Britain's most famous and most visited prehistoric monument.
▶▶ *For Sleeping, Eating and other listings, see pages 377-377.*

Ins and outs

Getting there
Rail **Southwest Trains** run hourly services to Salisbury from London Waterloo, taking 1 hr 30 mins. **National Rail Enquirie**s, T08457-484950.
Road Relatively speaking off the beaten track, Salisbury is about 7 miles south off the main A303 between London and Exeter, and about 14 miles north of the main A31 between London and Bournemouth. Stonehenge is practically on the A 303. **National Express**, T08705-808080, run 3 direct services from London Victoria daily (around 3 hrs).

Getting around
Salisbury City Centre is small and charming enough to make walking around it a pleasure. Destinations further out of town can be reached on **Wilts and Dorset Buses**, T01722-336855. Buses for Stonehenge leave at regular intervals from the local railway station.

Information
Salisbury TIC, Fish Row, Salisbury, T01722-334956. May-Sep Mon-Sat 0930-1700 (Jun- Aug until 1800), Sun 1030-1630 (Jul and Aug until 1700); Oct-Apr Mon-Sat 0930-1700. Free accommodation booking service.

Sights

Salisbury

Although most visitors are inevitably drawn towards the Cathedral's towering spire, the city centre is also worth exploring. Unlike the twisting Saxon layout of Canterbury, the regular grid of old medieval streets around Market Square can reasonably claim to be one of the earliest examples of new town planning in Europe.

The **West Walk** ① *The King's House, 65 The Close, To1722-332151. Mon-Sat 1000-1700 (also Jul and Aug Sun 1400-1700), adult £3, concessions £2, under 16s £0.75*, backing onto the watermeadows of Queen Elizabeth Gardens, is home to the Salisbury Museum, an excellent example of its type, complete with Stonehenge and Early Man Gallery, the Pitt Rivers Gallery full of intriguing anthropological finds, the Brixie Jarvis Wedgwood Collection of almost 600 pieces of fine china and an award-winning costume gallery called 'Stitches in Time'.

Opposite these three stands the perfection of the west front of the **Cathedral** ① *Visitor Services, 33 The Close, To1722-555120, Cathedral services information To1722-555113, www.salisburycathedral.org.uk, daily 0730-1815 (Jun-Aug Mon-Sat until 2015), suggested donation £3.80, concessions £2.50, under-17s £2,*

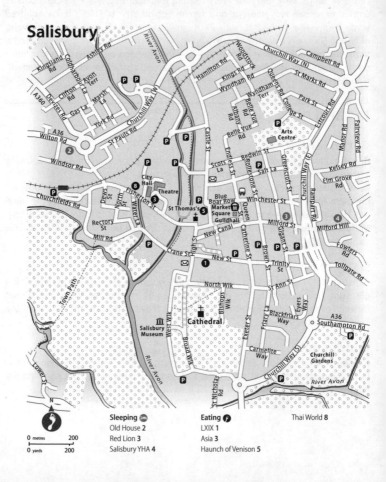

Salisbury

Sleeping 🛏	Eating 🍴	Thai World **8**
Old House **2**	LXIX **1**	
Red Lion **3**	Asia **3**	
Salisbury YHA **4**	Haunch of Venison **5**	

0 metres 200
0 yards 200

family £8. Along with St Paul's Cathedral in London, Salisbury is remarkable in representing the church-building achievement of a single generation. Sitting in probably the most beautiful and certainly the largest cathedral close in the country, it was built at miraculous speed between 1220 and 1258, in the style now known as Early English Gothic and almost too much of a piece for some tastes. Half a century or so later this great medieval palace of worship was blessed with a soaring 400-ft spire that has beautified distant views of Salisbury ever since. Famously portrayed by the painter John Constable as the centrepiece of a quintessentially English landscape, the story of its construction also inspired novelist William Golding's dark tale simply entitled *The Spire*.

Stonehenge

ⓘ T01980-624715, www.stonehengemasterplan.org, Jun-Aug daily 0900-1900, Mar 16-May and Sep-Oct 15 daily 0930-1800, Oct 16-Oct 23 daily 0930-1700, Oct 24-Mar 15 daily 0930-1600 (closed 25, 26 Dec, Jan 1), adult £4.20 including free audio tour, £3.20 concessions, £2.20 children, personalized out-of-hours tours, T01980-626267.

First impressions may be disappointing: big roads rush very close by; the whole place is often mobbed with visitors; walking among the stones is forbidden; and if you've only seen photographs, the standing stone doorways may seem unimpressively small. That said, the informative and entertaining audio guide quickly provokes a sense of wonder at humankind's achievement here during the Bronze Age. The main features of the monument are a circular ditch and bank (a henge), the ancient Heel Stone just outside it (the only naturally shaped stone on site), and in the middle the ruins of a circle of sarsens capped with lintels, a circle of bluestones, a horseshoe of trilithons and the fallen Altar Stone. Speculation continues as to the true purpose of the thing, broadly agreed to have been erected over the period 3000 to 1500 BC. It's sobering to think that it was probably in use for at least 3,000 years, the hub of one of the earliest cultures on the planet. Whether a temple to the sun, an astronomical clock, or gruesome site of ritual sacrifice, its importance can be judged from the fact that many of its stones were somehow transported all the way from the mountains of Wales.

● Sleeping

Salisbury & Stonehenge *p375, map p376*
A Red Lion, 4 Milford St, T01722-323334, www.the-redlion.co.uk. Founded in the 13th century, courtyard hotel in the middle of the city with a reliable restaurant.
C Old House, 161 Wilton Rd, T01722-333433. Beamed rooms and friendly family home with charming garden, within walking distance of the city centre.
F Salisbury YHA, Milford Hill, Salisbury, T01722-327572. Has 70 beds in one single, one double, 7 4-bedded and dormitory rooms, within walking distance of the Cathedral.

● Eating

Salisbury & Stonehenge *p375, map p376*
▼▼▼ LXIX, 67-69 New St, T01722-34000. The most stylish restaurant in the city, if not the whole of Wiltshire (and it knows it), booking essential for £30 a head modern British cuisine in sleek designer surroundings.
▼▼▼ Haunch of Venison, 1/5 Minster St, T01722-322024. A famous old pub with a very decent menu of pub grub in the restaurant upstairs (about £20 a head).
▼▼ Asia, 90 Fisherton St, T01722-327628. A reliable but quite pricey Indian restaurant.
▼▼ Thai World, off Fisherton St, T01722-333870. A good Thai alternative.

Bath

Quite a serious contender for top prize in the beautiful cities of Britain pageant, Bath attracts crowds in their thousands during the summer. If arriving by rail, first impressions may be a little disappointing, although it only takes a five-minute walk north to begin to appreciate what all the fuss is about. Eighteenth-century fashionable society's mania for the place is what makes it a sight to behold, the highlights of their architectural legacy being the neoclassical Palladian splendours of the Royal Crescent and Pulteney Bridge with its famous weir. Most visitors, though, still come to see the thing that's got everyone going for at least the last 2,000 years – the hot springs in the Roman Baths. They remain one of the country's most popular and intriguing archaeological sites. The city also does a fine line in other museums and just about manages to avoid being a museum itself. ▸▸ *For Sleeping, Eating and other listings, see pages 379-381.*

Ins and outs

Getting there

Rail **First Great Western** serve Bath Spa from London Paddington every 30 mins, direct services taking about 1 hr 30 mins. **National Rail Enquiries**, T08457-484950.
Road Estimated time from London by car is about 2 hrs. Total distance: 116 miles. From London take the M4 west (about 100 miles) exit at junction 18, head south on A46, and follow signs to town centre. From London, Victoria coach station, to Bath Spa, bus station, Manvers Street, the coach takes between 2 hrs 30 mins to 3 hrs 50 mins. **National Express**, T08705-808080.

Getting around

In the absence of Bath chairs, Bath is best walked around at a leisurely pace, although its hills can prove surprisingly wearing on the legs. Local buses are infrequent and unnecessary to take in the town centre. It's worth taking one of the double-decker tour buses for insight into the city's history and convenience. Taxi ranks are found outside the train station and the Abbey.

Information

Bath TIC, Abbey Chambers, T01225-477101, www.visitbath.co.uk. May-Sep Mon-Sat 0930-1800, Sun 1000-1600; Oct-Apr Mon-Sat 0930-1700, Sun 1000-1600. Accommodation booking, T0906-7112000, 10% deposit on first night's accommodation and booking fee.

Sights

Roman Baths

① T01225-477785, www.romanbaths.co.uk. Daily except 25 and 26 Dec, Nov-Feb 0930-1730; Mar-Jun, Sep-Oct 0900-1800; Jul-Aug 0900-2200, last entry 1 hr before closing, after 1800 daily torchlit evenings in Aug with last admission 2100, until 2200). Adult £9.50, concessions £8.50, unemployed/under-16s £5.30, family £25, (combined ticket with Museum of Costume for £11). Free guided tours on the hour every hour, free audio handset tours.

To this day the centre of Bath remains its hot springs and Roman Baths, now one of the most popular fee-paying visitor attractions in the country. Expect to have to queue (although it's generally quieter before 1000, and after 1800 in August) although they're well worth the wait. All in all, they provide one of the best insights in northwestern Europe into the Romans' achievement and their remarkably comfortable and sophisticated way of life. The Roman remains only began to be excavated in the late 19th century and first impressions today are still of the fine 18th-century neoclassical buildings erected on the site at the height of the hot springs fashionable heyday. After looking down into the open-air Great Bath from the Victorian gallery terrace, visitors descend to the water level. If you want to take the free guided tour, it's worth arriving half an hour early to have a look around the museum and Temple Precinct first. The variety of objects on display mean that a visit could easily last up to three hours, although two would be enough to do it justice.

The Royal Crescent

A stiff climb up Gay St through the Circus and down unassuming Brock Street, past the chi-chi shopping strip of Margaret's Buildings, the ground suddenly opens up in front of the most spectacular of Bath's 18th-century developments. The **Royal Crescent** ① *Number 1, T01225-428126, Feb-Nov Tue-Sun 1030-1700 (last admission 1630) and first two weekends of Dec, adult £4, concessions £3.50, family £10,* sweeps round to the right, facing south over Royal Victoria Park and the river valley with views right over to Beechen Cliff beyond. Completed by John Wood the Younger once the Circus was finished, over a period of seven years, its positioning, its rhythm, scale and scope, still give just as lively an impression of fashionable 18th-century life as any Jane Austen adaptation. And if it's period detail you're after, at No 1 the interior of the very grand end house was painstakingly returned to its Georgian condition in the late 1960s.

Pulteney Bridge

Walcot Street continues south into the High Street, back into the boundaries of the medieval city. To the left, down Bridge Street, is the last unmissable piece of 18th-century architecture in the city. Pulteney Bridge was designed by Robert Adam in the early 1770s and is unique in the country for still being lined with its original booths for shopkeepers. Along with the famous horseshoe weir on the Avon, it provides one of the most popular images of Bath. The bridge is best seen from North Parade, but a walk across it is mandatory in order to appreciate the splendour of Great Pulteney Street. The widest in Europe when it was built, wide enough for a horse and carriage to turn without having to back up, it provided the inspiration for the dimensions of the Champs Elysées. Up to the right are the dignified old pleasure gardens of Henrietta Park, a good spot for a picnic.

⊜ Sleeping

Bath *p378*
Central options are either budget or top-end, and should be booked in advance in summer.
L Royal Crescent Hotel, 16 Royal Cres, T01225-823333. The smartest hotel in the city, at the smartest address bang in the middle of its grandest architectural feature, with quiet back gardens and Roman-style spa facilities, oozing discreet Georgian elegance.
A Queensberry Hotel, Russell St, T01225-447928, www.bathqueensberry.com.

Stunning series of townhouses that are only marginally less grand than the Royal Crescent, very well-respected Olive Tree restaurant, and courtyard garden.
C Weston Lawn, Lucklands Rd, Weston, T01225-421362, www.westonlawn.co.uk. Friendly, traditional 3-room B&B in elegant family home 20 mins' walk from city centre. Fresh flowers in the very comfortable rooms and breakfast with home-baked bread in the conservatory overlooking a delightful garden.

E YMCA, International House, Broad St, T01225-460471, www.bath.org/ymca. Very central basic hostel with dorms (£12), singles and doubles (£32), including breakfast. Best budget option in town. Recommended.

F White Hart, Claverton St, Widcombe, T01225-313985, www.whitehartbath.co.uk. Recently refurbished pub south of the river, within 5 mins of station, providing some of the best value beds in town, from backpacker dorms at £12.50 per person to en-suite and family rooms. Self-catering kitchen, licensed café/bar, enclosed garden at the back.

🍴 Eating

Bath *p378*

🍴🍴🍴 **Fishworks**, 6 Green St, T01225-448707. Ardent piscivores can head confidently to this place. It's quite expensive but very wholesome and absolutely fresh, all served up in TV-cookery show-type surroundings.

🍴🍴🍴 **Moody Goose**, 7a Kingsmead Sq, T01225- 466688. Gourmets are catered for here. Top-notch modern British seafood and game with distinct French

Day trips Bath Listings

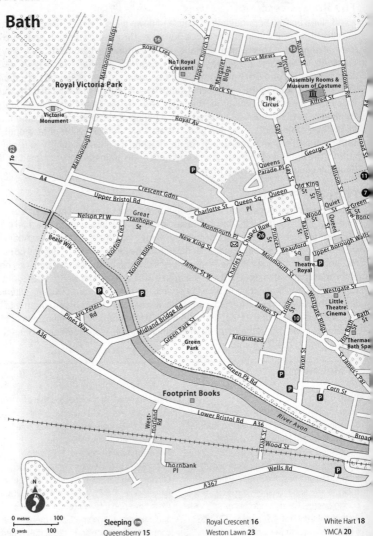

Bath

and Italian influences for about £35 a head in an inviting subterranean restaurant and cosy vaulted dining room. 2 Michelin stars for chef Stephen Shore.

Le Beaujolais, 5 Chapel Row, just of Queen Sq, T01225-423417. A French bistro-style restaurant, with plenty of ambience but rather small portions. Good value lunch menu.

Moon and Sixpence, 6a Broad St, T01225-460962. An intimate candlelit bistro, tucked away up a little passageway, in the middle of town. Eclectic dishes, including corn-fed chicken with spicy Thai risotto.

▲ Activities and tours

Bath *p378*
Walking tours
Bizarre Bath, T01225-335124. Comedy walk leaving the *Huntsman* every night, 2000 Apr-Sep.
Ghost Walks, from Garrick's Head T01225-463618. At 2000.
The Mayor's Corps of Honorary Guides, T01225-477411. Free 2-hr walking tours leave from outside the Pump Room throughout the year Mon-Fri, Sun at 1030 and 1400, Sat 1030 only, and also May-Sep Tue, Fri and Sat at 1900.

Day trips Bath Listings

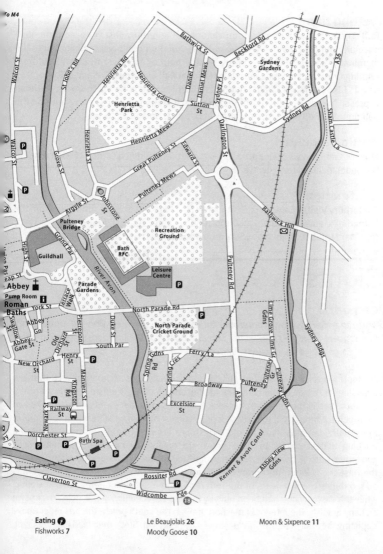

Eating 🍴
Fishworks **7**

Le Beaujolais **26**
Moody Goose **10**

Moon & Sixpence **11**

Canterbury

Canterbury is probably the single most popular tourist destination southeast of London. Not surprisingly it can become very congested, but the city also does an excellent job of combining its medieval roots with mass tourism on a charming and manageable scale. The pedestrianized heart of the city, within the medieval walls, is an enjoyable place to explore, despite the crowds, and thanks to its cathedral and university Canterbury has more style than anywhere else in east Kent. A trip here can easily be combined with Whitstable (see below). ▶▶ *For Sleeping, Eating and other listings, see pages 384-385.*

Ins and outs

Getting there
Rail There are trains from London Victoria to Canterbury East (1 hour 22 minutes) once an hour (twice with a change at Faversham) on the Dover mainline, or to the marginally more central Canterbury West (1 hour 25 minutes) twice an hour from Charing Cross on the Ramsgate line. **National Rail Enquiries,** T08457-484950.
Road Take the M2/A2 from London (about 1 hour 45 minutes) to Dover. **National Express,** T08705-808080, from Victoria coach station (2 hours) every hour on the half hour from 0830-2030, as well as at 0700, 2200 and 2330.

Getting around
Most of Canterbury's major attractions are within walking distance of each other in the pedestrianized town centre.

Information
Canterbury Visitor Centre, 34 St Margaret St, T01227-766567, a short walk from the Cathedral's main entrance at Christ Church gate. Apr-Oct Mon-Sat 0930-1730; Nov-Mar Mon-Sat 0630-1700, Sun 1000-1600 (closed Sun in Jan, Feb).

Sights

Cathedral
ⓘ *T01227-762862, www.canterbury-cathedral.org. Summer Mon-Sat 0900-1900, Sun 1230-1430, 1630-1730; winter Mon-Sat 0900-1700, Sun 1230-1430, 1630-1730. Adult £3.50, £2.50 concessions, under 5s free.*

The triple towers of the Cathedral still dominate the city. Most visitors quite rightly make a beeline for this medieval glory, the mother church of Anglicanism and most ancient Episcopal see in the kingdom, because it remains the main event and it's unlikely to disappoint. Although not the tallest, longest, oldest or even most beautiful cathedral in the country, the majesty of its old grey stones is awe-inspiring. Inside and out, the building almost seems to have grown up organically over the centuries, each generation adding, changing, removing or restoring parts, but never the whole. Most of the west end is late 14th-century. Bell Harry, as the great central tower is known, was added during the first years of the 16th century in magnificent Perpendicular Gothic, while the eastern choir had been built by the late 12th century, in the style now known as Early English. The interior is reached through the south porch, the bas-relief above depicting the Altar of Martyrdom destroyed by Henry VIII. Steps then lead into the Crypt, the earliest and most atmospheric part of the building. It's the finest Norman undercroft in the country, with remarkable stone-carving on pillars and capitals, especially on St Gabriel's chapel in the southeast corner which features a 13th-century painted ceiling. Back on ground level, the tourist route enters the long Quire, with Grinling Gibbons stalls at the west end, before heading to the famous Royal tombs (Henry IV and the Black Prince) in the Trinity Chapel behind the High Altar.

★ Whitstable

Six mile north of Canterbury, on the coast, Whitstable has long been associated with oysters. Those succulent molluscs have been happily breeding in the warm salty inshore waters here since Roman times. The town now depends on them for its popularity, if not for its livelihood, as it did a century ago when a dozen slithery mouthfuls were a staple meal for poor people across the land. The relatively high cost of oysters today, along with the mildly decadent frisson that eating them can

Canterbury

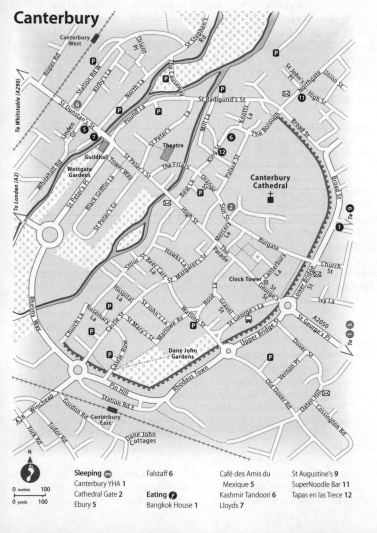

Sleeping 🛏	Falstaff **6**	Café des Amis du	St Augustine's **9**
Canterbury YHA **1**		Mexique **5**	SuperNoodle Bar **11**
Cathedral Gate **2**	**Eating** 🍴	Kashmir Tandoori **6**	Tapas en las Trece **12**
Ebury **5**	Bangkok House **1**	Lloyds **7**	

arouse, accounts for much of the town's current success with weekending Londoners. Also, unlike most of the towns on the coast to the east, Whitstable remains a working town, its hatchery in the harbour one of the largest in Europe.

Ins and outs

Getting there Whitstable is the first properly coastal, as opposed to estuarine, town on the North Kent coast, easily reached by **South East Trains** direct from London Victoria (1 hour 30 minutes) twice an hour. There's also a National Express coach service direct from Victoria (2 hours), **National Express**, T08705-808080.
Information TIC, 7 Oxford St, T01227-275482, www.whitstable.org

Sights

Never developed as a seaside resort, the High St casually turns its back on the sea, only a pebble's throw away. It's certainly not a quaint or even particularly attractive place, but the shingle beach (sandy at either end) affords beautiful sunsets looking across to the Isle of Sheppey and Southend beyond, the little harbour is still quite busy, and the rows of oyster huts (not all as yet converted into desirable holiday homes) were once sketched by Turner. The history of the place can be explored next door to the TIC at the **Whitstable Museum and Gallery** ① *5a Oxford St, T01227-276998, Mon-Sat 1000-1600 winter, summer also Sun 1300-1600, free*, through a diverting collection of local memorabilia, exhibitions on oysters and divers, as well as natural history (especially the local birdlife) and maritime history.

● Sleeping

Canterbury *p382, map p383*
Unfortunately Canterbury is not blessed with many outstanding hotels.
A-B Falstaff Hotel, 8-10 St Dunstan's St, T01227-462138, www.corushotels.com /thefalstaff. An antique hotel just outside the city walls (and one of the more expensive). Part of its building dates from the early 15th century, but the new building within and around blends in sympathetically enough.
C Ebury Hotel, 65-67 New Dover Rd, short walk from town, T01227-768433. 15 rooms, breakfast included. One 4-poster, 2 family rooms.
D-E Cathedral Gate Hotel, 36 Burgate, T01227-464381. Right next to Christ Church Gate and a creaking warren of rooms of all shapes and sizes, some quite basic. The views of the cathedral – beautifully floodlit at night – from the back rooms make it quite romantic and the best value place in the centre.
F Canterbury YHA, Ellerslie, 54 New Dover Rd, T01227-462911. Nearly a mile from Canterbury East station, fully equipped (85 beds).

Whitstable *p383*
Accommodation in Whitstable can be very difficult to find so book well ahead.
C Hotel Continental, 29 Beach Walk, T01227-280280, www.oysterfishery.co.uk.

The most stylish place to stay in Whitstable, with its fine Art Deco frontage and renovated rooms, some with balconies looking out to sea west of the harbour.
D-E Copeland House, 4 Island Wall, T01227-266207. A cosy B&B very close to the beach.

● Eating

Canterbury *p382, map p383*
♦♦♦ **Lloyds**, 89-90 St Dunstan's St, T01227-768222. One of the more recent openings and one of the more ambitious doing a sophisticated modern British and traditional French menu in a cunningly converted bank.
♦♦♦ **St Augustine's Restaurant**, 1 and 2 Longport, T01227-453063. Not quite as central as Lloyds, but similarly priced and with an enviable long-standing reputation, the place for some thoroughly civilized and well-prepared European dishes in a restrained atmosphere.
♦♦ **Bangkok House**, 13 Church St, T01227-471141. Genuinely Thai menu served up in a long narrow room decorated with some style.
♦♦ **Kashmir Tandoori**, Palace St. Specializes in tandooris from Kashmir, although the Tudorbethan dining room is unusual.

¶¶ **Tapas en las Trece**, 13 Palace St, T01227-762639. Does a reasonably priced Spanish menu in a laid-back atmosphere.
¶ **Café des Amis du Mexique**, 95 St Dunstan's St, T01227-464390. Mediterranean and Mexican cuisine in a bright, busy atmosphere, popular with students.
¶ **SuperNoodle Bar**, 87-88 Northgate St, T01227- 457888. For some very tasty, fast and inexpensive noodles, a good bet, bright and cheerful restaurant and takeaway.

Whitstable *p383*
Oysters can be had all year round, but the best homegrown varieties are only available in season (when there's an 'r' in the month).
Wheeler's Oyster Bar, 8 High St, T01227-273311. The best little place to enjoy oysters, open till 2100 Mon-Thu and Sun, 2130

Fri, 2200 Sat (closed Wed). Out front there's an old-fashioned and unpretentious counter serving a wide variety of fresh seafood and sometimes very good ginger ice cream. It's BYOB (available from *Thresher's* over the road) so a meal here is very good value, even if dining in the cosy parlour round the back.

▲▲ Activities and tours

Canterbury *p382, map p383*
Canterbury City Official Guide (tickets are available from the TIC). Walking tours lasting about 1 hr 30 mins and leaving from the centre at 1400 daily Apr-Nov, and also at 1100 daily from Jun-Aug.
Dr Thomson's Tours of Historic Canterbury, T01227-455922, 37 The Crescent. A private operator with considerable experience.

Brighton

From the good-time girls and gangsters of Graham Greene's Brighton Rock *via the mods and rockers of the cult film* Quadrophenia *to its current status as clubbing capital of the country, Brighton has always had that air of dangerous cool. This is Bohemia British style. Once the Prince Regent's coastal retreat, Brighton is now home to avant-garde artists and musicians, an exuberant gay and lesbian community, thousands of students and a few blue-rinse bungalow-dwellers who must be wondering where it all went wrong. The town has an atmosphere somewhere between hippy trail and Mediterranean sleaze-pit. In summer the streets around North Laine and the Prince's bizarre oriental Pavilion are a throng of trendy stalls and cafés, the pebbly beach awash with vocal youngsters and the clubs bursting at the seams seven nights a week. Brighton remains a highlight of any trip to the south coast. If you can't find fun here, you're unlikely to do so almost anywhere in the UK.* ▸▸ *For Sleeping, Eating and other listings, see pages 387-388.*

Ins and outs

Getting there
Rail   Brighton is excellently served by rail. There are 2 fast trains each hr from London Victoria (50 minutes), and 2 from London King's Cross, London Blackfriars and London Bridge (1 hour). **National Rail Enquiries,** T08457-484950.

Getting around
Brighton is a relatively small city, much of which can be reached by foot. If your feet are swollen, however, there's an extensive network of local buses which ply the city's streets (1 day pass, £2.80), many continue to nearby places of interest.

Information
The main TICs are at 10 Bartholomew Sq and Hove Town Hall, T09067-112255. Jun-Aug 0900-1700 Mon-Fri, 1000-1700 Sat, and 1000-1600 Sun; Sep-May 0900-1700 Mon-Sat.

Sights

Around The Lanes and the Seafront

Only Brighton could boast, as its most important piece of architecture, an Indo-Chinese royal palace inspired by an obsessive and mildly decadent half-German prince. Fresh from a thoroughly sensitive £10 million renovation programme, at the **Royal Pavilion** ① *Church St, T01273-290900, Jun-Sep 1000-1800 daily, Oct-May 1000-1700 daily, adult £5.80, child £3.40, concessions £4, family £15*, you can now enjoy John Nash's 1815-1823 masterpiece, with its dragon-shaped chandeliers and lotus-shaped lanterns, in its full glory. Nearby, is the splendid **Brighton Museum and Art Gallery** ① *Church St, T01273-290900, Tue 1000-1900, Wed-Sat 1000-1700, Sun 1400-1700, closed Mon, free*, which has just undergone renovation. There are also two local history galleries – one depicting life and work in Brighton – and one devoted to the seaside resort, double-entendre ridden postcards, et al.

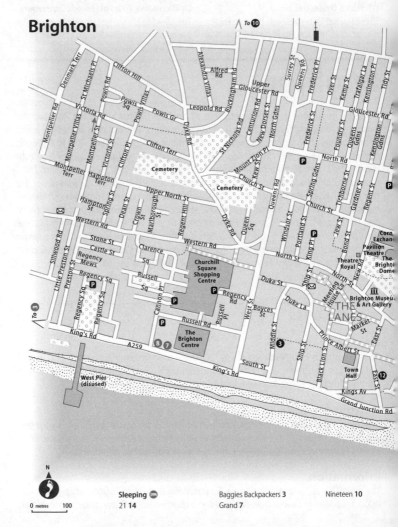

Brighton

N

0 metres 100

Sleeping 😴
21 **14**

Baggies Backpackers **3**
Grand **7**

Nineteen **10**

The area between West Street and the Steine was, until the 18th century, a small fishing village named Brighthelmstone. These days **The Lanes** are a maze of passageways containing antique and jewellery emporia of varying quality, and a host of cafés, restaurants and pubs. Few original features remain, but **English's Oyster Bar** occupies a former fisherman's cottage.

The Beach

Not exactly Copacabana, but a pebbly spot for a cheap ice cream, a pint in a plastic glass or, weather permitting, even a swim in the cold, green (and surprisingly clean) English water. In summer, come nightfall, the beach is awash with the local youth, drinking beer, lighting barbecues, patting bongos, smoking joints, fondling one another, falling in the sea, and generally making the place their own. There are also events like open-air cinema, fireworks, and live music. Perhaps the place's most captivating sight is the flocks of swallows that zig-zag around the ruined West Pier at dusk.

Much to the indignation of the locals, the 'Palace Pier' was renamed **Brighton Pier** ① *Madeira Dr, T01273-609361, dawn-dusk, daily*, to celebrate Brighton's recent entry in the great big A-Z in the sky under the section marked 'cities.' Corporate re-branding aside, it's still the unselfconsciously kitsch amalgam of fairground rides, money-swallowing machines and calorific cuisine that it always was. You can buy Brighton rock (the local sickly, minty sweet with the name running through it) by the yard here, and only the staunchest cultural snob wouldn't. Even Fatboy Slim has been known to frequent the Hog Roast here.

Around North Laine

This raggle taggle of trendy and secondhand shops, delis, cafés and pubs (between Trafalgar St & Church St) is the womb from which Brighton's current DJ-chic youth emerged. The denizens here are ridiculously fashion conscious, in a scruffy kind of way, and it's a great place to people-watch and pick up a few souvenirs. **St Bartholomew's Church** ① *Ann St, T01273-620491*, from the exterior looks like an outsize railway shed. For trivia fans, it is the highest church without a tower in the country, is grade I listed, and has some wonderful Art Nouveau furnishings.

● Sleeping

Brighton *p385, map p386*
There are myriad B&Bs (you ought to be able to get a bed for £20-£30 a night), in Kemp Town, and out towards Hove. They are all similar, so it's probably best to ask the TIC to make enquiries for you.

Eating ●
Bardsley's Fish & Chip Shop 1

Coach House 3
Seven Dials 10
Terre à Terre 12

Day trips Brighton Listings

L-A **The Grand**, King's Rd, T01273-321188. Saunas, jacuzzis, swimming pools, deferent room-service, good enough for conferencing PMs and IRA bombers. Don't argue about the price, just cough up, it's the best in town.

A **Nineteen**, 19 Broad St, T01273-67552. Hip Kemptown small hotel, very stylish
C **The Granville**, King's Rd, T01273-326302. The least grand of the expensive options.
D **21 Hotel**, 21 Charlotte St, T01273-686450. Clean and moderately trendy B&B.
E **Aquarium Hotel**, 13 Madeira Pl, T01273-605761. Clean, friendly, and close to the Pier.
F **Baggies Backpackers**, 33 Oriental Pl, T01273-733740. £11 dorms. Very well situated, Baggies is in quieter Hove and near the burgers, kebabs, and noodle bars of Preston St.

❼ Eating

Brighton *p385, map p386*
❢❢ **The Coach House**, Middle St, T01273-719000. Mediterranean cantina, with great value moules (£6/£8) and a small terrace.
❢❢ **Terre a Terre**, 7 East St, T01273-729051. The vegetarian and organic menu here is mind-bogglingly innovative. Mains start at around £10, and you'd be hard put to find a finer diner in its field.
❢❢ **Seven Dials**, 1-3 Buckingham Pl, T01273-885555. New kid on the block, this place has a fresh approach to British fusion cuisine without being too pretentious.
❢ **Bardsley's Fish and Chip Shop**, 106 Gloucester Rd, T01273- 681601. The best examples of the national dish are to befound in this little shop.

Cambridge

More than anything else, Cambridge is its university. For the last 700 years or so, academia has made its mark in this little place more impressively than just about anywhere else in the world. If it's specifically old colleges you want to see, with their medieval and Renaissance chapels, libraries, halls, gardens and courts, Cambridge is the place to come – and you won't be alone. Partly because of the tourist pressure, the whole town has a slightly unreal, self-conscious atmosphere, an impression compounded by the type of twee flannels-and-blazers pastoral idyll once promoted by the cult surrounding local poet Rupert Brooke. The city itself, only granted that status in the 1950s, now has a rapidly growing population of about 108,000, drawn in to work for the high-tech industries discreetly placed along the ring road. ▸▸ *For Sleeping, Eating and other listings, see pages 390-391.*

Ins and outs

Getting there

Rail Cambridge railway station is on Station Rd, a 20-min walk from the centre. The main operators are **WAGN** (West Anglia Great Northern Railway), T0870-8508822. Direct trains to Cambridge from London King's Cross (every 30 mins peak times, journey time 45 minutes to an hour); and London Liverpool St (1 hour 10 minutes).
Road From London take M11 north (which passes close to Stansted airport and Saffron Walden), at Junction 13 take the A1303 east and follow signs to city centre (1 hour 15 minutes, 63 miles from central London). Cambridge is well served by express coach services, all of which terminate at the Drummer St coach stands, adjacent to the bus station. The main operators are **Jetlink, Stagecoach** and **National Express**, T08705-808080. The travel office at the bus station has full details of all services and sells tickets for scheduled coach services and coach excursions to places of interest.

Cambridge town centre is only about a mile or so in diameter bordered to the north and west by the river Cam and the river Granta and its green banks including Midsummer Common and Jesus Green. The town centre is easily navigated by foot or by bicycle.

Information

Cambridge TIC, Wheeler St, To1223-322640, www.tourismcambridge.com. Mon-Fri 1000-1800 (until 1730 Nov-Mar), Sat 1000-1700, Easter-Sep Sun and bank holidays 1100-1600. Seems to charge for most things and has a rather indifferent/world-weary attitude. Walking tours (£7.35 per person) leave the office at 1030 (Jul-Sep, Mon-Sat), 1130 (Apr-Oct daily, Nov-Mar Sat only), 1330 (daily all year), 1430 (daily Jul-Aug), 1830. Costumed drama tours: £4.50 Tue in Jul and Aug.

Sights

Market Hill, a square where a general market of sorts still takes place Monday to Saturday, is the centre of Cambridge, with the Guildhall on its south side, and the TIC round the corner in the Old Library on Wheeler Street. Most of the colleges of particular interest to a visitor are lined up along Trinity Street a few steps to the west down St Mary's Street past the church of St Mary the Great.

South of Market Hill

Top of most visitors' places to visit is **King's College** ① *King's College Chapel, King's Parade, To1223-331250, www.kings.cam.ac.uk, during term-time: Mon-Sat 0930-1530, choral evensong 1730, Sun 1315-1415, choral evensong 1030, 1530, vacations: Mon-Sat 0930-1630, Sun 1000-1700 (no services), adult £3.50, concessions £2.50, under-12s free,* for the spectacular chapel on the north side of its Great Court. The simple elegance of the chapel's plan and exterior belie the wonders within: slender fan-vaulting soars overhead – surely one of the most impressive feats of ceiling-making in the western world – seeming to sprout organically from the walls, the whole space illuminated by a brilliant array of 16th-century windows, thankfully spared by the 17th-century iconoclasts. Construction on the chapel began in 1446 at the instigation of Henry VI, the centrepiece of his grand project for the University, and was completed by Henry VIII. The altarpiece at the east end of the simple rectangular plan is Rubens' *Adoration of the Magi*. The chapel's other pride and joy is its world-famous boys' choir, which can be heard at choral evensong most afternoons in term-time, as well as at the famous Christmas carol service.

Back on Trumpington Street, the continuation of King's Parade, on the left is **Pembroke College**, with a fine classical chapel designed by Wren. The college has a long list of famous alumni, including Pitt the Younger (Prime Minister at the age of 23) the poets Edmund Spenser and Ted Hughes, and comedian Peter Cook. Opposite Pembroke is **Peterhouse**, the smallest and oldest college in the University, founded by the Bishop of Ely in 1281. The college hall remains much as it was when built, while its well-kept garden and pretty octagonal courtyard are also worth a peek. The Fitzwilliam Museum is next door.

The Museums

Thanks to the University, for a market town Cambridge is blessed with an unusually large and well-endowed collection of museums, at least 10 in total. Next door to Peterhouse stands their flagship, the grand neoclassical façade of the **Fitzwilliam Museum** ① *Fitzwilliam Museum, Trumpington St, To1223-332900, www.fitzmuseum .cam.ac.uk, Tue-Sat 1000-1700, Sun 1415-1700, free,* without doubt one of the best reasons to visit the city in the first place. Founded in 1816, it houses a host of antiquities from Ancient Egypt, Greece and Rome, plus applied arts from sculpture and furniture to clocks and rugs, alongside precious manuscripts and an outstanding collection of Old Master paintings, drawings and prints. BLook up as you pass beneath its grand portico to enjoy its extraordinary gem-like Victorian coffered ceiling. Its main galleries recently refurbished, highlights of the collection on display in the magnificent Founder's Building include paintings by Titian, Vernonese, Rubens, Canaletto, Hogarth, Reynolds, Stubbs, Modigliani, Renoir, Cezanne and Picasso; Breughel's *Flowers in Stoneware Vase*, Monet's *Poplars*, and Vecchio's *Venus and Cupid*.

⌂ Sleeping

Cambridge *p388*
Accommodation is expensive.
L Garden House Moat House Hotel, Granta Pl, Mill Lane, T01223-259988, www.moat

househotel.com. The smartest hotel, with a lovely terrace bar and brasserie backing onto the punt-crammed Cam, as well as spacious, comfortable rooms with river views.

Cambridge

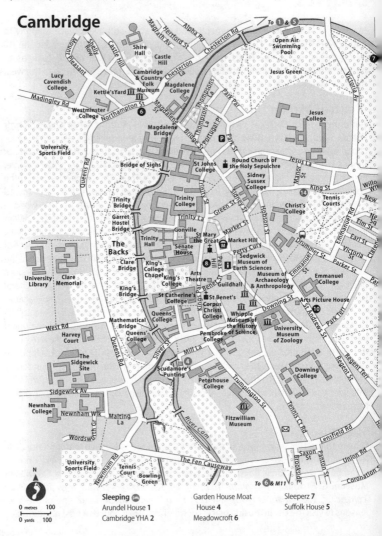

Sleeping ⌂		
Arundel House **1**	Garden House Moat House **4**	Sleeperz **7**
Cambridge YHA **2**	Meadowcroft **6**	Suffolk House **5**

0 metres 100
0 yards 100

A Meadowcroft Hotel, 16 Trumpington Rd, T01223-346120, www.meadowcroft .co.uk. A small, slightly chi-chi hotel with fine gardens.

B Arundel House Hotel, 53 Chesterton Rd, T01223-367701, www.arundelhousehotels .co.uk. Privately owned terraced Victorian hotel overlooking the river Cam at the top end of this bracket with reasonably priced menu in the restaurant.

C Suffolk House, 69 Milton Rd, T01223-352016. Family-run impeccably clean non-smoking guesthouse in a quiet area about 20 mins walk from the centre.

D Sleeperz Hotel, Station Rd, T01223-304050, www.sleeperz.com. Decent budget option in a converted granary by the station.

F Cambridge YHA, 97 Tenison Rd, T01223-354601. Close to the station, a Victorian townhouse about 15 mins' walk from the centre with 100 beds in 2-8 bedded rooms. Booking well in advance advisable.

🍴 Eating

Cambridge p388

🍴🍴🍴 **Michel's**, 21 Northampton St, T01223-353110. A modern Italian restaurant just over Magdalene Bridge, doing fairly good-value £9 3-course lunches.

🍴🍴🍴 **Midsummer House**, Midsummer Common, T01223-369299. Universally acknowledged to be Cambridge's best (and most expensive – about £50 a head for dinner, considerably less for lunch). It deserves all the praise. Innovative and delicious gourmet cuisine is served up with unfailing attention to detail in a delightful conservatory and garden, with a balcony area overlooking the Cam. Booking essential.

🍴🍴 **Curry Queen**, 106 Mill Rd, T01223-351027. One of the city's more reliable curry houses.

🍴🍴 **Rainbow Café**, 9a King's Parade, T01223-3211551. A vegetarian basement place tucked away right on the main tourist drag.

🍴🍴 **Varsity**, 35 St Andrew's St, T01223-356060. A 'continental' restaurant with a vaguely Greek theme, that has been around for years and remains popular.

🔺 Activities and tours

Cambridge p388
Punting

Scudamore's Punting Company, Granta Pl, Mill Lane, T01223-359750, www.scudamores .com. Mar-Oct 0900-dusk, Nov-Feb Sat, Sun only 1000-dusk. £12 an hr. In high season, expect to queue if you want a punt any time after 1300. Choose either an upriver boat, for Coe Fen and the 3-hr round-trip to Grantchester or a downriver boat for the Backs and the 2-hr, 2-mile round-trip to Jesus Green Lock. The upriver boats and the stretches of river they ply are generally less busy and more rural than the downriver ones.

Eating 🍴
Curry Queen **2**
Michel's **6**

Midsummer House **7**
Rainbow Café **8**
Varsity **10**

Day trips Cambridge Listings

⦂ Five more ideas for days outs from London

1. **Walk in the woods** Burnham Beeches is 540 acres of extraordinary old woodland maintained by the Corporation of London near Beaconsfield. The fantastic shapes of the trees are the result of more than 400 years of pollarding to provide a sustainable supply of wood for the City's carriage wheels – iron rims being banned from the Square Mile for cutting up the streets. There are plenty of unmarked trails, threading through grey poplar, Norway maple, juniper, Scots pine, holly, wild service and yew, as well as beech. ① *Open 0800-2100 Hawthorn Lane, Farnham Common, Near Slough, T01753-647358. Slough is 30 minutes by train from London Paddington. By car take the M40 to junction 2 and follow the A355 south to Farnham Common.*

2. **Stand on the white cliffs** Cuckmere Haven is one of the less crowded beaches on the south coast, partly thanks to the mile walk from Exceat bridge. From the shingle strand at the meandering river's mouth, the white cliffs of the Seven Sisters Country Park undulate east for 3 miles to Birling Gap and beyond. Rock pools and wonderful cliff walks. ① *Exceat is on the A259, 6 miles west of Eastbourne. By train, it's 1 hour 40 minutes from London Victoria, and then you'll need to take a bus. TIC T01323-411400.*

3. **Be beside the seaside** Southend is the most accessible resort for London, where acres of clean, supervised Blue Flag beach are backed up by some Regency architecture, loud pubs, amusement arcades and a formidable array of other attractions. Adventure Island on the Western Esplanade has rides for all ages that can be paid for one at a time, likely to please small children most, as will the train ride along the length (more than a mile) of the famous pier. ① *By car Southend is 40 miles east of London on the A13. Trains from London Fenchurch St usually reach Southend in under an hour. TIC 01702 215120.*

4. **Become a day-twitcher** In a quiet valley near lovely Arundel, the Arundel Wildfowl and Wetland Centre is home to a wide variety of wild birdlife. Set in 1100 acres of untampered downland, ideal for grassy strolls, the Centre itself provides 70 acres of wetland habitat including a spectacular reedbed in some former watercress fields, crossed by boardwalks, and the Icelandic Lake Myvatn enclosure. Kids enjoy feeding the Haiwain geese, the blue duck pen and the Discovery Trails, especially going Around the World in One Hour. ① *Take the train from Victoria to Arundel, then it's a 40-minute walk, up Mill Rd, or land train from town centre outside castle. T01903- 883355. Adults £5.50, under 16s £3.30.*

5. **Mess about on the river** River boating is a popular summer activity and not just for the carefree darlings of Oxford and Cambridge (see page 375 and 391). On the Thames, Salter Brothers are one of the oldest companies offering cruises, based in Oxford, Reading and Windsor, visiting many points between and beyond. Wallingford is particularly charming. They also do punts and dayboats. From Henley, Hobbs and Sons offer one-hour cruises down to Hambleden, as well as self-drive motorboats (£40 per hour), while J Hooper hire out smaller boats for trips down to Marsh Lock. French Brothers run cruises from Windsor and Maidenhead, as well as from Runnymede up to Hampton Court. ① *French Brothers T01753-851900; Hobbs and Sons T01491-572035; J Hooper T01491- 576867; Salter Brothers T01865-243421.*

Background

History

One hundred years ago, the novelist HG Wells wrote that "it is not too much to say that the London citizen of the year 2000 AD may have a choice of nearly all England and Wales south of Nottingham and east of Exeter as his suburb...And so the [city] centre will ...be essentially a bazaar, a great gallery of shops and places of concourse and rendezvous, a pedestrian place ... and altogether a very spacious, brilliant and entertaining agglomeration." His vision clearly overestimated the extent to which the urban sprawl of London would expand – the planning regulations of the Green Belt around the city have played their part – and it is neither spacious nor particularly friendly to the pedestrian, but much of what he says does ring true. The commuter belt now extends into the West Country. London has over 5000 pubs and bars and 30,000 shops, and 12,000 restaurants and cafés, and 28 million visitors arrive annually to sample the "brilliant and entertaining agglomeration". It is fitting that so many foreigners should visit the city, because ever since its founding 2000 years ago, London has been a prize and a haven for invading armies and fleeing refugees alike. It is, and has always been, "the mart of many nations".

The Romans are popularly believed to have established the first settlement where the City now lies, but prehistorians have uncovered evidence of habitation in this part of the Thames valley dating back half a million years. The Thames originally flowed through the Vale of St Albans, but was pushed south to its current position by the Ice Age. Flint handaxes have been found in Hillingdon, but perhaps its most fertile prehistoric era was during a warmer spell (about 130,000 BC-110,000 BC), when the landscape was brimming with exotic wildlife. Elephants and hippopotami grazed in what is now Trafalgar Square, lions in Charing Cross, buffaloes in St Martin-in-the-Fields, and wild bears in Woolwich. Remains of giant beavers and hyenas have also been found, and such was the broader nature of the Thames that shark remains have been found in Brentford.

Swamps, lagoons and marshes lined the river's course, fed by a series of rivers emerging from springs in the hills around, rivers that still flow beneath Londoners' feet. The Fleet rises in Hampstead, flowing from the ponds here and in Highgate down through King's Cross and Clerkenwell to spill into the Thames at Blackfriars. To the east, the Walbrook runs between Moorfields and Bishopsgate, and the more substantial river Lea down to Canning Town. To the west, the Tyburn runs through Regent's Park and under Buckingham Palace; the Westbourne through Hyde Park to Chelsea.

South of the Thames, the rivers Peck, Effra, Falcon and Wandle flowed through what was once marshland to the winding Thames. In total some 100 springs gave rise to over 100 miles of rivers beside which communities settled, to grow into villages and then suburbs, such that eventually most of the rivers were covered over by the ever-expanding city. The Thames itself seems to have been venerated by the people around – it has thrown up countless weapons and ceremonial artefacts (most notably the Battersea Shield and Waterloo Helmet), suggesting they were religious offerings made to the river.

By 3800 years ago there were farming settlements on Hampstead Heath, and remnants of Iron Age life have been found in places such as St Mary Axe, Gresham Street and Austin Friars, indicating that the Romans were not the first to settle here. Certainly, what with the abundance of fresh spring waters and fertile hillsides (Tower, Ludgate, Corn) surrounded by marshland, fens and the Thames, the site offered both natural protection and productive soil that was unlikely to have been overlooked by the generations that preceded the Roman invasion. Legend has it that a certain King Lud, buried by Ludgate, set out the original roads and walls of the city in the century

Roman London

Whatever the degree of prehistoric settlement here, it was the Romans who first established the town of Londinium as a major trading port, a role it played for almost two millennia. Despite distractions in further-flung regions of Britannia, such as the Scots spilling over the northern border or the Druids in Anglessey, and the city being razed to the ground by Boudicca, Queen of the Iceni, in AD 61, Roman London flourished in the second and third centuries.

A 20-ft wall and ditch surrounded the city, running from the Tower (a later addition) roughly to Blackfriars (the medieval City extended the walls to Temple), interspersed with gates (the medieval Ludgate, Newgate, Aldersgate, Cripplegate, where there was also a fort, Bishopsgate and Aldgate). The river Walbrook and its tributaries ran down the middle, leaping with salmon and trout. A huge marble-faced basilica, some 70 ft high, stood on the higher land at Cornhill, dominating the skyline; in its shadow business and trade would be conducted in the forum. Houses spread out from here, most made of a mixture of wood and thatch, but also some five-storey villas with courtyards and salmon-painted interiors.

To the north, an amphitheatre held gladiatorial contests and spectaculars, and shops, taverns and other commercial buildings ran down to the governor's palace on the banks of the river (at modern Cannon Street Station). Here the wharves and jetties were lined by ships laden with goods from the Continent, North Africa and the Middle East. Warehouses brimming with anything from olive oil to bronze tableware, ivory to dried fruit lined the banks. A wooden bridge, wide enough for traffic to pass both ways, spanned the river to Southwark, where commercial and industrial areas shared the land with homes and military bases.

Beyond the walls were farms and cemeteries, both growing in demand as the population reached 60,000 by the fourth century. Londinium was the fifth largest city in the Western Empire, and its reputation earned it the honorific title of 'Augusta'. Over the next 150 years, however, its prosperity declined with that of the Empire as a whole. When Saxons and Angles from northern Europe chose to establish settlements rather than simply make audacious raids, and pirate attacks on trading ships in the Channel became increasingly frequent, it signalled an end to Roman rule.

Saxon London

The new settlers, the Saxons, left Roman London abandoned for almost 200 years, and little record remains of the city until about the time of the first building of St Paul's in 604. They preferred to set up farms and villages in the land around such as Barking, Greenwich, Kingston or Hammersmith. By the mid-eighth century, however, the Venerable Bede could describe London as "the mart of many nations resorting to it by land and sea". He was referring to Lundenwic (London port), a town that grew up west of the River Fleet along the modern day Strand and Covent Garden (Aldwych maybe refers to the Saxon 'old-town'). Its flourishing trade invited unwanted attention as Viking raids in the mid-ninth century reduced the city to glowing embers.

Soon after, however, the Saxon King Alfred drove the Danes out, and began to rebuild London on the site of the Roman city. The Roman walls were repaired, jetties restored, streets laid out and markets established. Trade revived, mostly with the northern European and Scandinavian countries, as did industry, particularly metalwork (the abundance of water was a factor) and cloth-making. Further Danish raids in the 10th century resulted in Danish rule again, but not the destruction of the city (many settled in Hackney and Clapham). When Edward the Confessor moved his residence from the 'Wardrobe' in the City to Thorney Island in order to supervise his grand project, Westminster Abbey, politics and commerce were forever separated by the bend in the river. The merchants of the City could now concentrate on their own affairs secluded from court, an independence they have fiercely protected ever since. Tragically for Edward, when the Abbey was consecrated on Christmas Day 1065, he was too ill to attend, and just weeks later he was buried within it.

Norman London

It wasn't long before the Norman conqueror, William, having announced his arrival by burning Southwark, was being crowned at the Abbey. He granted privileges to the citizens of the City, being especially careful to keep the merchants sweet, but he was nonetheless wary enough of their independent streak to build three forts within the city walls – Montfichet's Tower, Baynard's Castle, and The White Tower. He introduced the Domesday Book, now the historian's guide to the state of Norman England, in 1086, documenting the size and livestock of each community. Although the City was granted exclusion from such investigations, it leaves us with a picture of a medieval city surrounded by hamlets and farms, fields and market gardens.

William, and many of his successors, held court at Westminster Palace, and the city within the walls was left largely as the residential and commercial heart of London. Ample mansions within spacious walled grounds housed the aristocrats, market gardens and orchards stretched either side of the city walls, and meadows, springs and babbling brooks spread beyond. Vibrant street markets sold imported wares and goods produced by craftsmen and artisans (both natives and Flemish, French, German and Dutch) working from home in the all parts of the city. Fairs and sports were regular events in the fields beyond the city walls, and miracle-plays, cock- and dog-fights, bear-baiting and the countless taverns provided the evening entertainment. But the aristocratic mansions propped up shacks, the babbling brooks were virtual sewers, and in the maze of streets the gutters and drains ran with offal. Although some tried to keep the stench at bay with perfumes and posies, it was often futile. Criminals were still left to slowly drown with the tide at Execution Dock in Wapping, refuse would at best be dumped outside the city walls in swamps such as Moorfields, and dead dogs were thrown aside in Houndsditch.

Medieval London

Wealth and poverty lived cheek by jowl, a feature of London throughout the centuries. Two markets, Eastcheap and Westcheap dominated the centre, the latter under the shadow of St Paul's. Eastcheap lay east of Poultry (another market), and was where the finer provisions were sold; Westcheap, now Cheapside, was a muddle of open stalls and kiosks lining the street, where frequent brawls would break out. On the river bank, Billingsgate, perhaps the oldest market, was where the 'wives' of Billingsgate drank and smoked and used foul language and earned the nickname the 'fish-fags'.

Smaller markets specialized in different provisions – Bread, Wood, or Milk Streets – while the fields at Smoothfield (Smithfield) became famed for the horse market. Laws were regularly passed to try to regulate the size, noise and criminal activity, but their regularity suggests they weren't very effective, as the bustling energy of the medieval city continued unabated. St Paul's, one of the largest covered spaces in the city, also played a part. Shops were set up in the portico (which became known as Paul's Walk), and attempts were made to prevent ball-playing. In 1560 it was described as a place for "all kinds of bargains, meetings, brawlings, murders and conspiracies".

The sound of eager tradesmen and industrious craftsmen resounded throughout the city. Cries of "Dumplins! Dumplins! Diddle, diddle, Dumplins Ho!"or "Buy! Buy! Buy! What d'ye lack? What'll you buy? What'll you buy?" would share the airwaves with the beating of the hammers and the pounding of the metal foundries, all riding over the steady hum of rushing water as the streams flowed through.

Craftsmen gathered in their own localities, eventually forming guilds to maintain the quality of their work and to support their own. They built halls and churches, making the spiritual health of their members one of their principal concerns. While their relations with God may have prospered, and their rights were firmly protected, the guilds were nevertheless constantly at odds with each other. Clubbings, stabbings, brawls and battles would regularly break out between rival apprentices, each often armed with the tool of his trade.

Some respite from the maelstrom could be found in the religious houses both within and without the city. Most of the monastic orders had established themselves in the 13th century – among them the White Friars, Black Friars and Grey Friars, named in accordance with the colour of their habits – and they were among the chief landowners in and around London. Church lands were everywhere – the farmlands of Soho, for instance, were owned by the abbey at Abingdon, and the pasture and market gardens north of the Strand by St Peter's Convent. Bishops' inns (in fact, large mansions and palaces) lined the road to Westminster, their gardens sweeping down to the river. Within the city, monastic orders settled among the poorer districts to do their good works, while the spires and towers of over 100 churches pricked the skyline.

Good works were much needed. Although the hospitals (St Bartholomew's and St Thomas's) provided some form of medical care, plagues were a regular threat, notably the Black Death, a bubonic plague brought by trading ships in 1348. It tormented the citizens in an agonizing and delirious death, swollen buboes growing in their armpits and groin, such that "after Easter in a newly made cemetery next to Smithfield more than 200 bodies were buried almost every day". Further outbreaks in the following decades ensured London, according to some estimates, lost two-thirds of its people. Those labourers that survived soon began to exploit their relative scarcity, and challenged the old feudal order.

The Peasants' Revolt of 1381, led by Wat Tyler from Kent and Jack Straw from Essex, involved up to 60,000 people laying waste to much of London in pursuit of airing their grievances to the king. Aided by the many city apprentices who joined the crowd, they dragged the Archbishop of Canterbury out of the Tower and beheaded him, burned down the Savoy Palace on the Strand, and ran amok in Clerkenwell where they opened the prisons and recruited the inmates. Wat Tyler finally perished on the dagger of the Mayor outside St Bartholomew's Hospital, and Jack Straw was beheaded at Smithfield.

The Peasants' Revolt presented, briefly, a genuine threat to government, but should be set against the backdrop of a London that often saw outbreaks of fights and small riots. Sometimes it might arise out of a scramble for the body dangling at Tower Hill or Tyburn Gallows, the relatives desperately fighting off those seeking to capitalize on the trade in bodies. Often it would be directed against foreigners, whether Dutch merchants in Westcheap or the Flemish in St Martin's, Vintry. In 1262 over 400 Jews were attacked and killed throughout the city (they were expelled in 1290 until the 17th century), and the Evil May Day Riots in 1517 were directed against the shops and houses of foreign merchants. Wrestling matches between the City and Westminster were known to break out into a full scale fights. Nevertheless, despite the explosions of violence, poor public health, and the virulent plagues, by the end of the 15th century when the Tudors came to power the population was almost 50,000 and growing.

Tudor London

The Tudors liked their palaces. Henry VIII, the most ostentatious, had about 50 residences spread throughout the country, most around the capital. Whitehall, Greenwich, Hampton Court and Richmond all found royal favour, each enhanced to display the magnificence of monarchy. Tilt-yards, bowling greens and tennis courts

Background History

were built, chapels erected, extensions built, and land such as modern Regent's Park and Soho given over to hunting. But his most lasting contribution to the development of the city, and indeed the country, came with his split with the Roman church, and his assumption as the Head of the Church in England.

Although this was prompted by his wish to father a healthy male heir, it also enabled him to claim the church lands as his own. Countless monasteries were 'dissolved', their treasures, buildings and lands either given or sold to courtiers and cronies. Religious houses were torn down and built on, empty sites taken over by tenements and chapels turned into taverns. Outside the city, the monastic lands were now in private hands so grand mansions emerged and land was sold off for building. Chelsea became known as the 'Village of Palaces' due to the grand houses built there. Within the city, migrants from the provinces and refugees from Catholic Europe swelled the numbers. Trestle tables in the markets increasingly turned to shacks and then to homes, thereby narrowing the streets such that the overhanging first floors almost touched over the street. There was some overspill outside the city, particularly to the east, around Whitechapel, Wapping and Spitalfields, and communities grew up around the various royal residences, and at the docks at Greenwich and Woolwich, so that by 1600 the population was 200,000, twice its number just 40 years earlier.

Nevertheless, life was no less colourful. Fields outside the city walls were alive with archers firing their arrows, wrestlers facing up, and any number of ball games – "hand-ball, foot-ball, bandy-ball, cambuck or cock-fighting". Moorfields, Lincoln's Inn and Gray's Inn Fields, Finsbury Park and Hyde Park all served as recreation grounds, protected by the crown from farmers' encroachment. In the winter, when the swamp of Moorfields froze, young men would tie animal bones to their feet and go skating; in the summer "the youths are exercised in leaping, dancing, shooting, wrestling, casting the stone and practising their shields". On the river, boats would charge towards each other in a jousting match, adversaries standing at the prow.

Fairs sprinkled the calendar, although they sometimes had to be closed down due to debauched behaviour. St Bartholomew's Fair, held on Smoothfields (Smithfield), was the longest established, Our Lady Fair in Southwark the most congested, and May Fair in Shepherd Market possibly the most unruly (it was eventually suppressed in 1708 for "drunkenness, fornication, gaming and lewdness"). Boxing, wild animals, plays and baiting competed for custom for up to six weeks a year.

Theatres opened up, notably the Globe and the Rose in Southwark, beyond the City's jurisdiction. Here was a sinner's paradise, where Winchester Geese (prostitutes) served the men spilling out from the raucous spews (taverns), theatres and bear or cock pits. Frost Fairs were held below London Bridge whose arches so slowed the Thames' flow that the river froze over (it was wider and shallower than it now is). Booths and tents, cook-shops and barbers' shops were erected beneath the bridge, while youths skated and chased across the ice. This "bacchanalian triumph, or carnival on the water" eventually died a natural death in the 19th century when a new London Bridge allowed a faster flow of water beneath its arches; and with the subsequent building of the Embankment, making the river deeper and faster, we are unlikely to see such sights again.

London Bridge itself was a fragile but magnificent sight. Rebuilt in stone in the 13th century, houses and shops clung to its edges, often arching over the road itself. A chapel dedicated to Thomas Becket was built in the middle, and criminals' heads were left to rot on spikes above the gatehouse at the Southwark end to serve as a constant reminder to those entering the city that retribution could be swift. Houses on the bridge were much coveted for the healthy air and spectacular views, although stalls, animals and traffic clogging up the thoroughfare and regular repair bills for the bridge meant living there was a mixed blessing.

Back on the shore, development tended to follow the movements of the monarch. As the 17th century passed, so building beyond the city walls increased, and the several-storey townhouse was born. Initially these were grand houses, along modern Piccadilly, in current Leicester Square, or along Great Russell Street, and a piazza, designed by Inigo Jones, in Covent Garden. His grand designs for Whitehall Palace were never fully executed, but the Banqueting House is a magnificent suggestion of what might have been.

During the Civil War, London sided with Parliament, forcing King Charles I to raise his army from Nottingham. Barricades were erected on all major roads in and out of the capital, and forts, batteries and ramparts built around the city. Troops turned out in numbers at Turnham Green to face off the king's army, and London was never threatened again. After Charles's defeat, the new regime under Oliver Cromwell confiscated royal treasures and property, and executed the king. One cold January morning in 1649, Charles walked out of Banqueting House to be beheaded. When the blow fell, there was "a dismal groan amongst the thousands of people who were in sight of it as I never heard before, and desire I may not hear again". The puritanical nature of Cromwell's rule, however, in which theatres were closed and Christmas celebrations banned, meant that following the restoration of the monarchy in 1660, his exhumed and rotting head remained on a spike on Westminster Hall for 25 long years without public protest.

Charles II entered the city to a carnival of welcome, "the ways strewed with flowers, the bells ringing, the streets hung with tapestry, fountains running with wine". But Restoration London soon faced a succession of disasters. Records of epidemics in London date back to the seventh century, whether the bubonic plague, or the 'ague' (malaria) which thrived in the open sewers and swamps caused by blocked gutters. The Black Death had swept away much of the city's population, and in the 16th century one outbreak of the plague "visited London with such violence that it carried off thousands in the space of five or six hours".

Towards the end of 1664 plague struck again. Beginning in the "deepe foul and dangerous" courtyards around Drury Lane, the 'sweating sickness' spread, reaching the City in July 1665. Shops closed and people retreated behind their doors, on which a red cross would be daubed if an inhabitant died. There was little traffic on the streets or on the river, only the sounds of the 'dead-carts', the "continuall ringing and tolling of bells", or people venturing out for supplies, sometimes collapsing in mid-transaction.

Fires burned at all major junctions to cleanse the air, and the Mayor ordered the killing of thousands of cats and dogs, thereby unwittingly ridding the flea-carrying rats of their principal predators. Those that could fled to outlying areas, particularly Hampstead and Clapham, but by September 1665, 8000 bodies a week were being thrown into the plague pits scattered outside the city, in some instances voluntarily joined by loved ones who had lost all hope of survival.

Superstitious remedies and quack potions were everywhere – amulets to ward off the evil spirits, potions, treacles and, immortalized in the children's nursery rhyme, pocketfuls of posies (they also stored posies in a large beak held over the nose). The citizens, according to Daniel Defoe, became "raving and distracted" making deathbed confessions while still healthy, and provided easy meat for the wealth of astrologers, fortune-tellers, "conjurors and witches" that capitalized on the people's fear. The plague finally subsided with the winter cold, so that Charles II felt safe to return in February 1666, but he returned to a city mourning almost half its population, some 100,000 dead.

Background History

Some notion of normal life was returning to the city when disaster struck again. As London suffered repeated visitations of the plague, so was it regularly alight. Fires often devastated huge areas of the city – in the 10th century what little that was left of Roman London was swept away in the flames, and in the 11th century the whole city from the River Fleet to the bridge was reduced to embers. Fires have destroyed huge palaces – Whitehall, Westminster and Crystal, as well as St Paul's countless times. Smaller conflagrations were more common still, often burning themselves out or being doused by the buckets of water kept outside every home.

So when a small fire began in the king's baker's in Pudding Lane, the Mayor's reaction – "Pish! A woman might pisse it out" – was not considered overly complacent. But aided by the dry summer and a fresh easterly wind, the fire spread out of control. Panicked residents brought their furniture and treasured items out onto the street, hampering the efforts of the chain of firefighters armed only with leather buckets and crude water hoses. A rush of refugees once more sought sanctuary outside the city in Islington and Highgate, or loaded their possessions onto boats and took to the river from where they could watch the blaze spread.

After four days and much prevarication by the authorities, streets were blown up to create a wasteland that the flames and sparks could not breach. The wind dropped, and the fire turned to smouldering embers. John Evelyn visited the site two days later, and found himself lost, bereft of accustomed landmarks while "clambering over heaps of smoking rubbish". The fire's impact was overwhelming. Not only were countless manuscripts and books destroyed when the roof of St Paul's collapsed, but also over 80 churches, 44 livery halls, and 13,000 houses. Although only six people were reported dead, thousands were made homeless, settling in tented villages in the fields and meadows north of the city.

Redevelopment of London

The fire, however, did provide the opportunity for the city to be rebuilt. Several plans were submitted, most proposing some form of grid street-plan, but merchants and residents alike could not afford to wait for these artistic visions to be approved. Greater thought was given to the style of house – the timber-frame overhanging Tudor houses were replaced by simpler stone and brick designs, and the streets were wider – but the familiar network of streets soon began to re-emerge. Sir Christopher Wren, the great architect of his time, devoted his energy to overseeing the construction of more than 50 churches, his signature piece being a further incarnation of St Paul's Cathedral, towering over the city with a splendour befitting the world's first Protestant cathedral. Beyond the city walls building also continued in earnest.

Charles II favoured St James's Palace, so the area around spawned squares, streets and grand mansions (Buckingham, Arlington and Clarendon houses) to accommodate the courtiers. Aristocrats moved west, so their previous residences were torn down and replaced by town houses as happened along the Strand, or taken over by merchants, as happened in Clerkenwell. Soho, swollen by the influx of Huguenots from France, developed around King's (now Soho) Square, and by the end of the century Bloomsbury (with Red Lion Square), and the area around the Seven Dials were established.

The West End continued to spread as the new century dawned. Squares, such as Hanover, Berkeley, and Grosvenor in Mayfair became fashionable, while Kensington drew greater interest following William III's decision to settle there. Proximity to the court did not preoccupy the East End so much. Huguenot refugees from France arrived in force following a clampdown by Catholic Europe, and Irish, Dutch and Jewish immigrants brought their varied crafts and trades to Spitalfields and Whitechapel, but were forced to settle among the small courtyards, dark alleys and low tenements notorious for crime and poverty.

66 99 When a small fire began in the king's baker's in Pudding Lane, the Mayor's reaction – "Pish! A woman might pisse it out" – was not considered overly complacent....

This was a time of true Bacchanalian indulgence. Prostitutes were plentiful, drink overflowing, and rioting frequent. Sex for sale was of course as old as the city, from the Roman 'fornixes' (shacks set up below arches) to medieval street names such as Maid, Cock and Love Lanes. Slang terms for prostitutes ran from the faintly sentimental 'Mother Midnights' to the plain infantile 'Trugmoldies'. In the 18th and 19th centuries business boomed. Whitechapel, Wapping and Spitalfields worked the lower end of the market, while The Strand, Covent Garden and Drury Lane weren't quite the match of the brothels in James and Curzon Streets in Mayfair.

Tourists could consult Harris's *New Atlantis* or Henry's *List of Covent Garden Ladies* for further details. Gays were served by 'Mollie' houses such as the Mother's Clap in Holborn, at alehouses such as the Fountain in the Strand, or by cruising the Royal Exchange. Those of better means kept mistresses in nearby hamlets like Brompton, and those seeking a mistress or a lover might hover under the portico of St Paul's church in Covent Garden. Haymarket and St James's Park were popular night haunts, where James Boswell met with "ugly and lean" and "monstrous big" prostitutes, or "a strong, jolly young damsel" and "a little girl". Child prostitution was common.

In the 19th century the number of 11- to 16-year-olds with syphillis in any one year exceeded 2,000, and Dostoevsky commented on mothers encouraging their daughters "to ply the same trade" in Haymarket. Some would be child mistresses – funded through school and put up in accommodation, in return for their sexual favours. Violence against prostitutes also proliferated, whether by Mohocks (gangs of youths) or in attacks on brothels, and gays had the added threats of blackmail or arrest. It was a century "dedicated to venereal pleasures", as one foreign observer put it, and by the mid-19th century there were estimated to be 80,000 prostitutes, the majority streetwalkers, and 3000 brothels.

If they weren't rutting, they were rioting. Scapegoating attacks on foreigners, price riots in theatres, brawls after football matches, food riots among workers and assaults on prisons. In 1780 the Gordon Riots ran a rampage of drunken thuggery through London over a number of days. Gathering in St George's Fields, it was intended as an anti-Popery march on Parliament to protest against the Catholic Relief Act. But the reality was much less contained. Gathering extras as they went (many of whom were simply along for the ride), they attacked Irish labourers and looted Catholic chapels in the East End, and attacked Downing Street, the Bank of England and prisons in Clerkenwell and Newgate. En route, they raided and set alight to a distillery. Many died in the smoke and flames when they ran into the cellars to grab gin, and others drank themselves to death in the rum running in the gutters. The government was worried, but the very substance that helped fuel the rioters was also a factor in their undoing. While approaching their next target, Kenwood House on Hampstead Heath, the mob were distracted by the offer of a free drink from the landlord of the Spaniard's Inn. The delay was sufficient to give time for the army to arrive.

Drink fuelled much of London life. Brown or pale ale, bitter beer or mellow porter, or the hangover remedy, 'saloop', were all served in a series of small rooms in private houses that acted as taverns and beer houses. In the early 18th century there were estimated to be over 6000 taverns, inns and beer houses, while in the cellars and workshops were gin-houses', serving the favourite spirit of the time. Many people would have a mug of ale for breakfast not least because it was probably 'cleaner' than the water and because drinking tea was considered "one of the worst habits". Beer was also not exclusively an adult pleasure. Children were often to be seen in taverns with a mug of ale, refilling their clay pipes with casual assurance.

A slightly more refined experience was to be had in the wealth of coffee-houses brewing up all over the city. A Swiss observer commented on them as where "you can partake of chocolate, tea or coffee, and all sorts of liquors served hot", but they also served as anything from auction rooms to postal addresses for the regulars. Charles II tried to have them banned, complaining that this was "where the disaffected meet and spread scandalous reports", but had to bow to public pressure to revoke the order.

Certainly they were important meeting places – the clergy in Child's (St Paul's Churchyard), Frenchmen in Giles (St Giles), artists in Old Slaughter (St Martin's Lane) or wits and authors at Will's in Covent Garden (Samuel Pepys, John Dryden, Aphra Benn and Jonathan Swift were among the regulars). Whigs met at St James's, the Tories at the Cocoa Tree. Batson's on Cornhill became a virtual doctors' consulting room, and Button's in Covent Garden became the editorial offices for the *Guardian* periodical. A French visitor described them as "the seats of English liberty" on account of the newspapers that lay on the tables, and the heated discussions that prevailed. Some houses, however, were less troubled by the state of the nation. Those that doubled as "temples of Venus" could be found where there hung the tell-tale sign of a woman's arm holding a coffee-pot, and others advertised auctions of slave boys.

Further developments

By the end of the 18th century, London had grown significantly, reaching a population of almost one million. Putney, Westminster and Blackfriars became the first bridges over the Thames since the Roman settlers built the stilted wooden affair across to Southwark. The New Road, now the Marylebone Road, was created as a ring road round the north of London for the traffic of cattle and sheep being driven to Smithfield Market. Bloomsbury, Fitzrovia, Mayfair and Marylebone all became fashionable, a multitude of Georgian terraces interspersed with grand squares.

Buckingham Palace became one of George III's favoured residences, although it was only later under Queen Victoria that it became established as the monarch's primary London residence. After the Tyburn Gallows had been removed from what is now Marble Arch in 1783, Oxford Street showed the early signs of its current role as a shopping street. With this expansion came slums. Intended developments such as Somers Town stopped abruptly when funds ran out, only to grow into dirty and dangerous slums with the arrival of French émigrés fleeing the Revolution. Nevertheless, the likes of Bow, Hackney, Islington and Chelsea remained as villages surrounded by fields and market gardens.

Regency London became grander still. In the West End architect John Nash linked St James's to Marylebone Park (later Regent's Park) with the broad and sweeping Regent's Street, and Thomas Cubitt built stuccoed squares, terraces and villas behind Buckingham Palace in Belgravia. In the East End, expansion continued apace with the development of the docks, and the digging of the Regent's Canal from the Thames at Limehouse to Paddington. The London, East India, Surrey, St Katharine's and West India Docks were all dug by 1830, many protected by 30-ft walls and marine police, such was the threat of criminal activity. Whitechapel was one of the most populous areas, close on the heels of fashionable Marylebone. A ribbon of industrial developments, warehouses and small factories sprang up along the Canal – in Camden, Islington, King's Cross and Paddington – and a new London Bridge was built across the Thames in 1831.

By the time Victoria came to the throne in 1837, London was at the centre of an Empire spanning one-fifth of the globe, its spoils contributing wealth and employment to the capital at its heart. Docks and warehouses blossomed with the growing trade and business boomed as goods were exported to all corners of the world. Large industry included the likes of ship building (Brunel's *Great Eastern*, the largest ship of its time, was built in Millwall docks), breweries and iron foundries, and Bryant & May's matchbox factory in Bow, employing some 5,600 people, but in 1851 over four-fifths of the capital's manufacturers employed 10 people or less. These businesses grew along the newly laid railway lines and the slightly older canals, or in the sweatshops of dark, damp and dingy basements and cellars, or in the one or two rooms that also served as the family home. At the other end of the scale, commercial enterprises such as banks, insurance and investment companies built fine offices in the City, slowly marking out their territory in what was to become the finance capital of the world.

By far the greatest transformation to the city's landscape was brought about by the transport revolution, particularly the arrival of the railways. In 1836 the first railway in London ran between the *Bricklayer's Arms* in Southwark and Deptford, although it was soon extended to London Bridge and Greenwich.

Over the next 20 years stations and large termini began cropping up across the city. Euston, Paddington, and King's Cross stations opened, and anything from shunting yards and engine huts to hotels sprang up nearby. Thousands were displaced as slums were cleared to lay tracks. Warehouses, small industries, and above all slum housing developed along the line of the tracks, and the population grew exponentially with the greater ease of movement. The railway opened up the suburbs, encouraging the growth of the likes of Norwood and Highgate.

In 1863 the Metropolitan Line, the world's first underground line, opened, ferrying a mixture of excited and sceptical Londoners across the city under the New Road from Paddington to Farringdon Road. Some feared that the tunnels would collapse, others considered the "mixture of sulphur, coal dust and foul fumes" unhealthy, although the Duke of Wellington's fear that an invading French army could now arrive unannounced at a station had less basis in reality.

Above ground, London's streets were awash with a multitude of vehicles. Horse-drawn trams and buses fought for right of way with hansom cabs, broughams, landaus and gigs, in a city still lit by gas and oil lamps. The advent of electricity, however, further transformed the city above and below ground. The first electric line, part of what became the Northern Line, opened in 1890; two years after, Electric Avenue in Brixton blazed electric light along its length. Horse-drawn trams soon turned electric, and continued to distribute commuters to their homes in the suburbs.

Omnibuses, horse-drawn when first introduced in 1829, grew in popularity – by 1900, there were 3000 of them carrying about 500 million passengers every year, even though the motorized bus only chugged on its way for the first time in 1904. By 1902, as Sir Halford Mackinder observed, London exhibited "the daily throb of a huge pulsating heart", whereby every morning and evening "half a million men are sent in quick streams, like corpuscles of blood through arteries, along the railways and the trunkroads".

Mile upon mile of Victorian terraces went up to accommodate the growing population of commuters. Victoria, Notting Hill, Holland Park, Camden, Islington and Finsbury in the north, and Brixton, Battersea, Lambeth and Kennington in the south all grew, the market gardens and fields slowly turning to brick fields and then streets and houses. The railway also brought shoppers to *Harrods*, *Liberty's*, and *Whiteleys*, and visitors to the Great Exhibition of 1851, a magnificent display of imperial power and confidence housed in a sparkling glass palace in Hyde Park. The Oval Stadium in Kennington hosted the first soccer cup final in 1871, soon followed by the first rugby international and cricket test match.

While the 19th century saw the most rapid expansion of London's suburbs to date, inner city slums continued to fester. The rapid expansion in the city's population meant huge overcrowding in the tenements – a census in Westminster uncovered an average of 40 people per house in the worst areas, while lodging-houses earned disapproval for the bed-sharing that was necessary to accommodate all the tenants.

Many slums were houses vacated by wealthier Londoners, still displaying their 'decayed glory' through the moulyd and crumbling 'stately edifices'. Others such as Agar Town, were virtual shanty towns, decried by Londoners as "a disgrace to the metropolis". The Seven Dials was particularly notorious for its criminal element, a crowd of alleys and courtyards and "dirty, straggling houses" (Dickens), hiding a network of escape routes carved through the buildings. One observer described London as "rattling, growling, smoking, stinking...pouring out poison at every pore".

Underneath most houses were cesspits to hold the pungent mixture of household and human waste. Streets were used as toilets, and the overflowing pits often seeped into the homes above. The sewage and water systems were part of the same cycle, with the former being tipped into the city's streams and rivers, only to be piped back through the street's water pumps.

Disease once again plagued the city. Cholera epidemics were severe and frequent, aided by the authorities' conviction that the carrier was a 'miasma' in the air that could best be solved by washing the streets' detritus into the very same waterways that were feeding the disease.

Public health campaigners such as Dr John Snow and Edwin Chadwick fought a sceptical and sluggish establishment to wake up to the links between poverty and disease, water and drainage. Countless studies and surveys put pressure on the authorities to take action, but it needed the 'Great Stink' of 1858 that infected the city with a stench previously unrivalled to force action.

The Metropolitan Board of Works constructed a drainage system that still forms the basis for London's drainage today. As one contemporary newspaper put it in Chadwick's obituary: "had he killed in battle as many as he saved by sanitation, he would have had equestrian statues by the dozen put up to his memory."

Nevertheless in 1883 Andrew Mearns still entered "courts reeking with poisonous and malodorous gases arising from accumulations of sewage and refuse scattered in all directions", and passed through "passages swarming with vermin" to "gain access to the dens in which these thousands of beings...herd together."

Housing programmes were enacted by parliament but it still required the diligence, money and concern of the likes of Lord Shaftesbury to really effect change. Slum clearances merely moved the problem to another part of the city, creating still more overcrowding there. Charities and philanthropists gave money, time and thought to easing the burden. George Peabody, an American millionaire and London resident, built model dwellings for the working classes; Angela Burdett-Coutts built blocks in Bethnal Green for "the very poorest", and Octavia Hill restored delapidated cottages for the poor inhabitants. Some, such as John Hollingshead, felt the charity was misplaced : "they have wasted their means on a class well able to help themselves...the industrious poor are still rotting up their filthy, ill-drained, ill-ventilated courts", in the likes of Somers Town and Agar Town. Ragged children still slept in alleys and under bridges, and most nights there were up to 400 people camped out in Trafalgar Square.

Alongside practical support, there was often spiritual and moral guidance to boot. The Society for Suppression of Vice, the Reformatory and Refuge Union, or the Christian Mission to the Heathen of our own Country (or the Salvation Army) all did good works in an attempt to steer their charges along the straight and narrow. Inspired by the horrors of St Jude's slum in Whitechapel, Canon Barnett founded the East London Dwelling's Company and the educational establishment at Toynbee Hall, while declaring that the "principle of our work is that we aim at decreasing not suffering, but sin!" Others opted prostitutes home in order to try to rectify their wayward ways.

Nevertheless, the housing shortage was rarely solved, merely moved. In 1901, a survey in Finsbury recorded that 45% of families still lived in one or two rooms, while in 1925 a Czech visitor described the East End as "miles and miles of grimy houses, hopeless streets...a superfluity of children, gin palaces and Christian shelters".

Immigration

This was what greeted many of the immigrants who reached London's streets in the 19th century. Chinese sailors settled in Limehouse in the 1850s, and in the following decades Russian and Polish Jews, escaping the pogroms in Eastern Europe, settled in Stepney. Italians congregated in Finsbury, the Irish in Docklands, and Germans in and around Camden. Elsewhere, Swedes, French, Spaniards, Americans and Turks sought to make a new home here.

London has had a history of ambivalence towards the immigrant population, not least because most of its residents were of immigrant stock themselves. Richard of Devizes' complaint that in London "all sorts of men crowd there from every country under the heavens. Each brings its own vices and its own customs to the city", is one that in its various forms has been echoed through time. Attacks on Jews were frequent until their expulsion in 1290, and were repeated over the centuries following their return under Cromwell; the Irish were also a particular source of suspicion, and subject to violent attacks for either being Catholic, or being prepared to work for less wages than an Englishman.

Bottom of the pile were blacks. By the late 18th century there were up to 20,000, most in domestic service, either as slaves or servants, having been brought over by plantation owners, sold in the coffee houses, or given as 'presents' to wealthy friends. But many were discarded by their owners or employers, and left scraping for a living in the likes of Wapping and St Giles. They were often the last to be given employment, and could be seen scavenging on the streets at dusk, keen to keep a low profile.

London also became a haven for radical thinkers and activists from abroad. Karl Marx lived in poverty in Soho (although aided by Friedrich Engels, a resident of Camden), plodding to the Reading Room at the British Museum to work on his potboiler, *Das Kapital*. Mahatma Gandhi and Mohammed Ali Jinnah both studied law here towards the end of the century; Jawarharlal Nehru (also a student at Harrow and Cambridge) completed the trinity when he studied at the bar at Inner Temple in 1910. Revolutionaries studied or worked here before returning to their homeland to act out their destiny. Sun Yat Sen (China), Marcus Garvey (West Indies), Michael Collins (Ireland) and Lenin (Russia) could all be found here in the early years of the century; Ho Chi Minh washed up dishes at the Carlton Hotel before doing much the same to American forces in his native Vietnam some 60 years later.

20th-century London

As the end of the century approached, much of London flourished. The growth of the railway network drew not only suburban commuters but also visitors from the country and abroad. Hotels sprung up in numbers – the *Westminster Palace*, the *Savoy*, the *Ritz* (often with shared bathrooms; at the Westminster Palace, 14 bathrooms served 300 rooms). Theatres boomed, and the likes of Henry Irving or Ellen Terry trod the boards at new theatres such as The Strand, Aldwych, or Lyric. In the music halls the bawdy song, dance and comedy routines of Max Miller or Marie Lloyd would also pack in the crowds.

The Olympics were held at White City in 1908. Piccadilly Circus glowed under neon lights in 1910, a more glamorous addition to a city now bathing in electric light. Cinemas began screening throughout the capital, and the Lyon's Corner House in Coventry Street offered more than palatable fare to over 4,500 people within many working men's budget. The *Café Royale* attracted the fashionable set, such as Oscar Wilde, Audrey Beardsley and Whistler, and London clubs in St James's basked in their exclusivity. The electric tram, the motorized bus and the motorcar began appearing on the streets, ferrying a population now grown to 6½ million.

First World War and after

The peace was broken by the outbreak of war in 1914. Young men turned up at recruitment offices across the capital, eager to fight for King and Country, unaware of the carnage that lay in wait. In 1915 London suffered its first air raid, when Zeppelins dropped incendiaries on Stoke Newington and Hackney. A few months later 39 people were killed near the Guildhall, and by the end of the war 650 had died in attacks from the air. Waterloo and Victoria stations became the setting of tearful and often final farewells for troops bound for the trenches, and Alexandra Palace took the German POWs. German and Austrian residents were rounded up as a precaution, and factories were given over to munitions production.

Due to the shortage of male labour, the women of the city took over half the factory jobs. In the build up to war, the Suffragette movement (a *Daily Mail* name) had moved to London from Manchester, setting up headquarters in Westminster, closer to government. From here, Emmeline Pankhurst and her two daughters Sylvia and Christabel orchestrated a campaign ranging from window-smashing in Parliament and Oxford Street, to chaining themselves to railings at Downing Street and Buckingham Palace, and slashing the *Rokeby Venus* in the National Gallery. With the outbreak of war, however, the campaigners were keen to demonstrate their patriotism, and they suspended the campaign and set to working for the war effort. There was some reward in legislation passed after the end of the war, but it was 1928 before they achieved parity with men.

Between the wars

Women continued to work in the factories such as Hoover and Firestone after the war, partly because the male labour force was depleted by casualties (some 125,000 Londoners are estimated to have died). Domestic service, however, was their main source of employment. Nannies, butlers, maids, sometimes all three, would live in the attic rooms of tall villas and terraces, Mary Poppins-like, or, if attached to any of the Mayfair mansions, from mews houses nearby.

American culture, promoted largely through the cinema, began to take grip. Cocktail and milk bars, jazz and the Charleston became a feature of the West End and in 1924 Woolworths opened a store on Oxford Street. Greyhound racing, another American import, was held at White City, no longer London's master stadium after Wembley opened in 1923.

Meanwhile, the London County Council set about improving the city's environment. Slums were cleared, houses built and parks extended. Nevertheless, Sir Arthur Conan Doyle was still moved to describe London as "a great cesspit into which all the loungers of the Empire are irresistably drained".

Elsewhere in the country, a slump in industries such as steel and textiles brought the government into conflict with the unions, and in 1926 the General Strike saw London almost grind to a halt. For several days volunteers and the army took over essential services – students tried to run the tube, volunteers to drive the buses, while the army escorted food convoys. But perhaps its most significant contribution was to establish the radio as a source of information and entertainment.

Home for many was now in the suburbs, in developments advertised in the enticingly titled *Metroland*. "Vast new wildernesses of glass and brick" sprang up in Cedars Estate in Rickmansworth, Becontree Estate at Dagenham (where there were just six pubs for 120,000 people), Ruislip, Edgware and Finchley, in the process swallowing up the market gardens and fields that hitherto surrounded London. One million new houses were built for a population fast approaching 8.7 million, a figure never matched before or since, so that in 1938 the notion of a 'Green Belt' of protected countryside around the growing city was widely welcomed. JB Priestley described an urban culture "of arterial and by-pass roads, of filling stations and factories..., of giant cinemas and dance halls and cafés, bungalows with tiny garages, cocktail bars, Woolworths, motor coaches, [and] wireless".

It was all that, but it was also a city facing war. Londoners were not unfamiliar with fascism. Sir Oswald Mosley, leader of the 'blackshirts', had held rallies at major venues such as the Albert Hall and Olympia, and then led his troops through the East End, creating a riot in Cable Street.

Second World War

The threat to the average Londoner was not from the ground, however, but from the air. In the year that followed, while the country armed itself for war, London prepared itself for imminent destruction. Schoolchildren and toddlers with mothers were evacuated north and west, some as far as Canada or Australia. Vacated buildings were taken over as reception centres for those bombed out, and the nation's treasures carefully stored. The army moved into the parks, setting up anti-aircraft guns to scan the skies.

"Britain's finest hour", as Churchill called it, began on Black Saturday, 7 September 1940. A raid of 400 bombers signalled the start of a bombardment that was to kill 20,000 Londoners, leave another 25,000 injured, and at its most intense, run for 57 consecutive days. The docks, law courts, The Tower, the House of Commons, Westminster Abbey, and even St Paul's, where "London was burning and the dome seemed to ride the sea of fire", all suffered some damage. After perhaps the severest night, December 29th 1940, a visitor commented that the "air felt singed. The air itself, as we walked smelt of burning", recalling images of John Evelyn in the rubble after the Great Fire.

Londoners' reaction was mixed – some were hysterical (there was an increased incidence of suicide), but many were defiant. They continued to go to work, stumbling across debris en route if necessary, and a Mass Observation survey held in the winter of the Blitz recorded more Londoners to be depressed by the weather than the bombing. During raids most people sought shelter in a basement or cellar, or under the stairs.

Many took refuge in the government-sponsored 'Anderson' shelters built out of soil and corrugated iron at the end of the garden. Railway arches became popular havens, and a network of trenches was built under Lincoln's Inn Fields, and in Bloomsbury and Russell Squares. Almost 150,000 people took to the underground itself. The platforms, corridors and stairs were swollen with people, but this "lice to lice" as some called it, gave people an attachment and loyalty to their shelter. Stations had their own libraries and canteens, there was underground theatre and at Swiss Cottage they produced a newsletter, the *Swiss Cottager*. One observer commented "the danger here is not bombs, or even burial or typhus, but of going native and not coming up again till after the war, when you will emerge with a large family and speaking another language".

East Enders took over massive subterranean warehouses, such as 'Mickey's Shelter' under Stepney. Mickey Davies, a dwarf hunchback, gave the shelter such a celebrity status that the American Presidential candidate paid a visit on his tour of London. Further shelters were excavated under a number of underground stations, most for the use of the public, although Stockwell was given over to American troops, and Goodge Street as General Eisenhower's headquarters.

The government moved underground too, Churchill's Cabinet War Rooms taking up just a fraction of the huge complex of rooms under Storey's Gate just off Parliament Square. But being underground did not guarantee safety. 600 people were drowned at Balham Station when a bomb burst a water main and flooded the tunnel, and at

Bank 117 people were killed by a bomb that bounced its way down the escalator and exploded on the platform.

Even when the 'Blitz' ended the following May, air raids were still a threat. In 1944, the VI, or 'doodle-bug', a pilotless plane of explosives that fell when its engines cut out, terrorized the capital. Witnesses recalled "holding one's breath, praying that they will travel on". Its successor, the V2, was still more destructive, killing scores of Saturday-afternoon shoppers in Woolworths on its first flight. The doodle-bugs damaged half the city's housing stock, some 1¼ million homes, but were cut short by the end of the war in May 1945.

Some 30,000 people had died in London in the course of the war, and another 50,000 had been injured. About a third of the City had been destroyed, including 20 churches and 18 livery halls on that December night alone. Large areas of the East End were devastated (Poplar and Stepney were largely flattened), to the extent that when Buckingham Palace was hit in September 1940, Queen Elizabeth, the late Queen Mother, is reputed to have said "now we can look the East End in the face". Communities had been disrupted, not only by the devastation from above, but by the mass exodus of residents to the suburbs, some of whom never returned. On top of this there were 1½ million Londoners who simply didn't have a home anymore.

Post-war London

The housing problem was given some temporary relief by the 'prefab' houses issued by the government, and by the unilateral actions of squatters who took over empty properties in the likes of Marylebone and Kensington. New towns such as Basildon, Stevenage and Harlow sprang up beyond the Green Belt as London raised itself from the ashes. The Olympics at Wembley in 1948, the Festival of Britain in 1951 and the Coronation of Queen Elizabeth II two years later all lent some sparkle to a time made lean by rationing. To add to the gloom, London suffered a particularly acute year of smog in 1952, causing up to 4000 deaths from associated illnesses. But theatres and cinemas were buoyant, football matches were well attended, and jazz could be heard in the pubs and clubs of Soho.

Heathrow and Gatwick both opened in the 1950s, and by 1956 the dockyards were dealing with up to 1000 ships a week. A skilled labour shortage prompted the likes of London Transport and the health service to seek employees from abroad. The 492 Jamaicans who disembarked from the *Empire Windrush* in 1948 had been broadly welcomed, but as economic pressures intensified and the West Indian population grew, local relations became strained. Riots in Notting Hill in 1958, where the homes of Trinidadians and Barbadians were attacked by "a crowd of a thousand white men and some women....tooled up with razors, knives, bricks and bottles", gave a different message to the thousands of immigrants who had been actively encouraged to come here.

In the 1960s many of Britain's colonies achieved independence, and were free to seek other markets. London's trade with the Commonwealth halved. Dockyards such as The East India and St Katharine's closed, often in the wake of union struggles that protected the workers' rights in the short term, but lost them their jobs in the long term. Pear's Soap closed its Isleworth factory in its centenary year of 1962, as unemployment in inner city areas such as Tower Hamlets grew. Between 1966 and 1976, London lost half a million manufacturing jobs, and over 7% of its population.

The laxness of planning authorities allowed over 400 tower blocks to be built across the city, a transformation of London's skyline comparable with that achieved by Wren. The result was hardly as picturesque, and the soulless blocks were regularly subject to vandalism, effectively imprisoning residents with the broken lifts and the fear of violence. The architectural, let alone social, failings of the towers were confirmed in 1968 when several storeys of a block collapsed in Ronan Point.

Meanwhile, in 1966, *Time* magazine confidently reported that London "swings, it is the scene". From the tentative appearance of the first coffee bar in Soho in 1953, and the bistros and the Mary Quant boutique in Chelsea, London was becoming the music and fashion capital of the world. Soho was invaded by media and music companies, and at its peak some quarter of a million Londoners were involved in photography, modelling, magazine publishing or advertising. Art-Deco was undergoing a renaissance at Barbara Hulanicki's boutique, *Biba* in Kensington, and Terence Conran's *Habitat* store in Fulham brought a sense of design to the home. The King's Road in Chelsea and Carnaby Street in the West End became the place to be seen.

The London music scene took off, fed by a vibrant student art scene in a London teeming with the young (some estimate that 40% of London's population were under 25). The Rolling Stones, The Who, the Small Faces and the Yardbirds all played in London venues, most notably on Eel Pie Island in the Thames by Twickenham. The club formed in the hotel that once stood here boasted 30,000 members (a number that would scarcely fit on the island itself), and became a magnet for that unholy trinity of the 1960s, sex, drugs and Rock 'n' Roll.

Meanwhile, demonstrations against the Vietnam War in 1968, and concerts in Hyde Park for some half a million people, represented a youth culture that challenged the establishment and dreamt of a life free of the threat of nuclear annihilation and at peace with itself. Cultural heroes, from 'Twiggy' in modelling, and East Enders David Bailey in photography or Vidal Sassoon in hair-styling, shared the spotlight with other photographers such as Lords Lichfield and Snowdon, as fashion became less trammelled by concerns over class and status.

Late 20th-century London

Thirty years later, in 1996, another American publication, *Newsweek*, announced that London was "the world's coolest city", a claim that for many was as ignorant as it was meaningless. Certainly many people had seen wealth and an improved lifestyle in the 1970s and 80s. The financial institutions in the City had adapted well to the decline of the Empire, and in the 1960s London became the world's largest source of borrowing. The Stock Exchange moved into a new building in 1972, and by the 1980s there were more foreign banks located within the square mile than anywhere else in the world. Prime Minister Margaret Thatcher favoured deregulation, and when in 1986 the Stock Exchange opened its doors to overseas members, businesses rushed to invest.

House prices reached a peak in 1988 as 'yuppies' (Young Urban Professionals), and 'dinkies' (Double Income, No Kids) helped fuel property prices. Georgian and Victorian properties were restored as fine family houses, or remodelled into smart bachelor pads, in areas as far afield as Clapham and Camberwell, Highbury and Paddington.

The story wasn't so sweet for everybody. Between 1973 and 1983 London lost half its manufacturing jobs. British Aerospace and the General Electric Company shed jobs in Hayes and Willesden. Companies sought out the cheaper labour and more efficient transport links offered by development along new motorway corridors such as the M4, around Reading, Swindon and Bristol. The last of the docks finally closed in 1981 – only Tilbury, further east, survives.

By 1990, 20% of the residents in Hackney and Haringay were unemployed, and 10% of all Londoners were on income support. Local councils became political footballs, having their central government subsidies cut or capped by successive governments from 1975. Conservative councils in Westminster and Wandsworth and Labour councils in Tower Hamlets and Hackney became flagbearers for their respective ideologies, though not without more than a whiff of corrupt practice.

In 1986 Margaret Thatcher abolished the Greater London Council, citing inefficiency and profligacy among its crimes, a decision no doubt made easier by the ideological gulf between the 'Iron Lady' and the council leader 'Red' Ken Livingstone. London was now the only major European capital without its own central authority (a situation only rectified by the incoming Labour government in 2000, when Londoners voted Livingstone back in as Mayor in a new Greater London Authority).

Reported crime rose, schools closed or awaited building repairs, and the underground and sewers, both in need of urgent investment, were left to age. Housing stock fell as government legislation forced councils to sell their homes to the tenants, but prevented them from building replacements with the proceeds.

By 1990, there were only 302 housing new starts, compared with over 9000 in 1979. Homelessness became apparent across the city, with up to 65,000 single homeless people seeking shelter in emergency accommodation. Cardboard cities grew up in Lincoln's Inns Fields, beneath Waterloo Bridge or off the Strand, and isolated figures in sleeping bags dotted the shop doorways. The *Big Issue*, written and sold by homeless people, attempted to give a leg up to those still awaiting the promised 'trickledown' effect of the 'economic miracle'.

Clashes between blacks and the police in Brixton and the Broadwater Farm Estate in Tottenham in the 1980s gave vent to simmering racial tensions. In 1986, a church report entitled *Faith in the City*, expressed concern over the degeneration of areas that "has now gone so far that they are in effect 'separate territories' outside the mainstream of our social and economic life". The Poll Tax riots of 1990 were partly sparked by a resentment at the widening gap between the 'haves' and 'have-nots', and Thatcher's resignation later in the year left John Major with an economy in recession and a party split over the touchy issue of Britain's role in Europe. Paradoxically, perhaps, a 1991 survey revealed that 48% of Londoners wanted to leave the city, at a time when tourism was booming (25 million tourists visited in 1990). The Conservative government squeezed through one further election, and then limped to sleaze-ridden defeat in 1997, as New Labour swept to victory on a wave of optimism. Six years later, the largest political demonstration in the history of the UK occurred when around a million people converged on Hyde Park to protest against the war in Iraq. In 2004, following the success of the traffic congestion charge imposed on central London the year before, Ken Livingstone was accepted back into the Labour Party and then re-elected Mayor.

21st-century London

So when future historians attempt to describe London around the turn of the 21st-century, as they most surely will, what will they say? They may marvel at the 200 museums and galleries, a staggering array of treasures bought, donated and appropriated from around the world, and envy the vast choice of food and drink available in the thousands of pubs and restaurants. They will paint colourful pictures of the theatre, the music, the lights and the sights, and show incredulity at the number and variety of shops.

They might gasp at the London Eye, puzzle over the Dome, snigger at the 'wobbly' Millennium Bridge or admire the Great Court at the British Museum. They may salute the City as the capital of commerce, which one-third of the world's dealings pass through, and will no doubt celebrate the 300 languages that can be heard on the streets or in the homes. There will be tales of clubbing, dancing, drinking and drugs, of fast cars, fast living and above all fast spending.

But they will also record the estates and tower blocks, the bedsits and the shelters, the doorways and the underpasses where many people still live. They will note the slowing beat of manufacturing, the stillness of the waters in the docks, and the creaking of the Underground. There will be tales of stabbings and muggings, of struggling schools and hospitals, of dirty air and the choking roads. But they will also recognize that such contrasts have been apparent throughout the ebb and flow of the city, perhaps all great cities. That slums have always rubbed shoulders with mansions, that business and manufacturing has constantly reinvented itself to adapt to changing circumstance, and that London will always regenerate.

One way or another, London will always be the object of much comment. It has been eulogized in poetry as "the fairest capital", and as "the flower of cities all". It has been labelled "the clearing-house of the world", and "the mansion-house of liberty". It is "immutable" and "eternal", "scattered" and "haphazard", "beautiful" and "uniquely seductive". One can speculate endlessly as to how and why London came to be as it is, but certainly the safest, and perhaps the wisest conclusion was given by the social historian Roy Porter in 1994 when he wrote: "London was always a muddle that worked".

Culture

Architecture

London is one of the world's most contradictory cities. It is at once ordered and chaotic, old fashioned and ultra-modern, opulent and squalid. It is also, for all its fine tailoring, gunmakers, hand-made shoes and posh accents, something of a mongrel: it has pretty much always been a home for successive waves of invaders and refugees, who over the centuries, have given the city its extraordinary global character. To see the world, and its architecture, in a single capital city, come to London.

Founded essentially by the Romans in the first century AD – certainly from an architectural perspective – London has always been like this. It had only just got into its first stride when Boudicca and her East Anglian warriors burned the place down. After that it rose to become one of the major cities of the western Empire, although, as far as we can tell, its architecture was often fairly crude and provincial compared with that of Rome or the great classical cities of what are now Turkey, Syria and Libya.

London declined after the Roman legions left in 410 AD, yet we know that Saxon architects travelled to Rome to study masonry and that the city was never as cut off from stylistic and technical developments during the Dark Ages as we were taught at school. In fact, what makes London such a delightful mongrel city is the way in which architectural currents lapped against the banks of the Thames on their way from other parts of the world – always a little late and always reinterpreted for the London market.

So, Gothic architecture (born in France) came late to London and was never as flamboyant as its continental precursors unless made for kings who were often French-speaking and who ruled much of France. Renaissance architecture was also slow off the mark, not really making much impact – with the exception of the works of Inigo Jones (the **Banqueting Hall, Whitehall**, from where Charles I walked out of a first storey window to the scaffold and his execution in 1649; **St Paul's Church, Covent Garden** – "the handsomest barn in England" the architect promised the Earl of Bradford; and the **Queen's House, Greenwich**), until after the Great Fire of 1666 when Christopher Wren began to rebuild the City with a necklace of imaginative parish churches gathered around the defining dome of his masterwork, **St Paul's Cathedral** (1675-1710). Even then, look how St Paul's is really an old fashioned Gothic cathedral in plan (which is what Wren's client, the Church Commission, wanted) clad in Renaissance garb and capped with that peerless dome. In other words St Paul's was a compromise – a brilliant one – and a grand example of London's mongrel spirit.

London came into its own, architecturally, from Wren. His unmissable buildings here are nearly all in the old City of London, with the exception of the exquisitely mannered **Royal Hospital, Chelsea** – home of the Chelsea Pensioners – and the magnificent Royal Naval complex downriver at Greenwich, now used by the **University of Greenwich**. This great gathering of Baroque towers, domes, courtyards, colonnades and painted halls overlooking the Thames is one of Europe's greatest architectural set pieces. Built over many decades, it includes work by Wren's famous assistants, Nicholas Hawksmoor and Sir John Vanbrugh, a former playwright and soldier whose exotic designs were inspired partly by extensive travels that took him as far as India.

Hawksmoor was quite simply one of the greatest architects of all time. A broody introspective man from a humble background but of great learning, he was very different from the urbane and gentlemanly Wren and the flamboyant and funny Vanbrugh. The character of his powerfully sculpted designs reflect his brilliant intensity. They include the nearly restored **Christ Church, Spitalfields**, its sky-piercing Portland stone tower soaring above gentrified streets of handsome Georgian terraced houses just a trader's shout from the brash new postmodern banks of the City of London and the organic foodstalls of the revitalized Spitalfields Market. His other great London designs are the churches of **St Mary Woolnooth** near the Mansion House and Royal Exchange, **St George's Bloomsbury** (which once featured a lion and unicorn chasing one another around its curious stepped tower based on the ancient Greek Temple of Helicarnassus; sadly there's only a statue of George I in a toga today) and a sequence of grand stone churches in London's Docklands.

London's Georgian streets lined with abstemiously decorated brick houses remain a quiet visual treat and some of the most sought after homes and offices in the capital. There are many to choose from, most designed by surveyors and builders working to designs reproduced from the prescriptive pages of 18-century pattern books. But no one would want to miss Bedford Square, Bedford Row, Doughty Street and Great James Street (Bloomsbury), Fournier Street (Spitalfields) or the dignified streets that constitute much of Marylebone and Mayfair, including Harley Street with its legions of private doctors.

Notable buildings of this long period of text-book Georgian good manners include **Somerset House**, a civic palace built around a grand courtyard overlooking the Thames on one side and facing the Strand with its ceaseless traffic on the other. Designed by Sir William Chambers, who acted as King George III's architectural tutor, Somerset House is, in fact, the first purpose-built office block in London. It was built for the Navy and other government offices and until recently was crammed with civil servants who parked their cars in the courtyard. Today the officials are on their way out; their cars have already gone. Their place has been taken by a mix of museums, including an outpost of the Hermitage (St Petersburg), the Courtauld Institute (a posh fine arts finishing school for impossibly grand young men and women), the Gilbert Collection and at least one very smart restaurant, The Admiralty.

The greatest talent of the late Georgian period was that of the manic depressive Sir John Soane (1757-1837). He designed the labyrinthine **Bank of England**, but, sadly, this was largely demolished, except for its superb defensive walls, in the 1920s. A part of Soane's magical interior has been rebuilt and is well worth a visit. Few architects before or since have handled the play of daylight inside buildings so well. Luckily, Soane's own truly fantastic house which was also his personal museum has survived inside three customized Georgian terraced houses in Lincoln Inn's Fields. The **Sir John Soane Museum** is an architectural sonnet. A time machine and shaper of dreams, it remains one of the best kept secrets in London. Because it's a house, visitors at quiet times have to ring the bell to gain admittance and sign the visitors' book; it's as if Soane is still in residence even though he lies buried in a curious Greek Revival tomb in old St Pancras churchyard, a haunt of drug-addicts and prostitutes alongside the Midland mainline railway today.

Yet, for all its Georgian inheritance, London, has largely been made by the Victorians. Grand Gothic Revival churches, the **Palace of Westminster** by Charles Barry and Augustus Welby Northmore Pugin and the **Grand Midland Hotel at St Pancras** by Sir George Gilbert Scott are the pinnacles of a wave of almost over-confident design that swept through London as the British Empire reached its peak. This wave kept on rolling up until the First World War. Modern architecture shuffled, soft-shoed, into London from the Continent in the 1930s. At first it was the work of emigré architects, from Russia, Hungary and other points east. The Modern Movement in London was a refugee movement to begin with, but after the Second World War was to distinguish the capital with its challenging concrete forms from giant housing estates to the National Theatre. Modern architecture was largely despised in London until the 1980s when not only did it become more glamorous – it had been a little on the wholemeal side before then – but it also became fashionable. By the beginning of the new century (the much vaunted new millennium), Londoners, and visitors to London, actually looked forward to seeing the latest addition to this complex and contradictory cityscape.

An architectural tour of modern London

The London Eye (2000) Not really architecture, but a very fine, if rather highly strung, big wheel was brought up to date for London's millennium celebrations by the architects David Marks and Julia Barfield. An immensely tall, yet remarkably unobtrusive Big Wheel from which London's streetscapes, its parks and architecture can be admired night and day (see page 250).

Waterloo International (1993) Prognathous Eurostar trains glide in and out under the great glazed roof of this super sleek modern-day railway terminus, linking London and Paris via the Channel Tunnel in just three tantalizing hours. The roof and platforms snake away from the airport-style concourse and ticket barriers following the line of the former Southern Railway main line towards Clapham Junction, still the world's busiest station. The only sad thing is that passengers are only allowed up to the platforms at the last moment so that the glory of Nicholas Grimshaw's fine roof is mostly experienced from outside the station.

Royal Festival Hall (1951) The handsome and popular music venue on the South Bank was designed by London County Council architects under Sir Leslie Martin; a showpiece of Festival of Britain design, its public spaces are awash with shimmering Thames light. A building with roots in Scandinavian and Revolutionary Russian ideas that brought modern architecture and design to a wide audience, it is currently being thoroughly renovated (see page 252).

Hayward Gallery (1967) Still controversial, this, the most brutal of Brutalist buildings was designed by the former London County Council's architects' department from the late 1950s. Like some kind of Mayan temple realized in mossy concrete, it is loved and loathed in equal measures. Its thick concrete walls were meant to baffle the noise of the London Heliport that was to have been built virtually alongside. It never happened. Despite its rough-hewn appearance, the Hayward Gallery is beautifully built; just look at all that bronze and brass inside. The gallery's entrance hall has been rebuilt to make room for a café and ease access to exhibitions, which are normally very good indeed (see page 252).

Royal National Theatre (1967-1977) The vast geological outcrop of concrete terraces and towers on the South Bank houses the Olivier, Lyttleton and Cottesloe theatres. The serious-minded and magnificent masterpiece of Denys Lasdun (1914-2000), it remains a great meeting place and is a fine institution with terraces which offer inspiring views of London's peerless riverscape.

Tate Modern (2000) This is mongrel London at its most heroic. Here the former Bankside Power Station, sited slap, bang opposite St Paul's, has been transformed into Britain's leading gallery of 20th century and contemporary art. The scale of the project demonstrates London's extraordinary commitment to modern art. The Brobdingnagian power station, finally completed in 1955, was given a handsome brick façade by Sir Giles Gilbert Scott, architect of Waterloo Bridge, Battersea Power Station (currently in ruins but possibly to be rebuilt as a culture and entertainment venue) and the Guinness Brewery in Park Royal, West London. This temple of power was converted into a cathedral of art by the Swiss architects Herzog and de Meuron (designers of the Laban Dance Centre, Deptford). The Tate has opened up the old and long-neglected borough of Southwark to Londoners and visitors alike; it is as much a place to crowd into on rainy Sundays as it is a huge vote of confidence in London's role as munificent patron of modern art (see page 238).

Millennium Bridge (2000) The famous – or is it infamous? – 'Wobbly Bridge'. Long awaited, London's first pedestrian Thames crossing wobbled dramatically as a vast crowd surged across when it first opened in May 2000. Modifications have been made and this exquisite suspension bridge, designed by Norman Foster, the sculptor Anthony Caro and the engineers Ove Arup & Partners, now carries hundreds of people safely across from St Paul's Cathedral to the Tate Modern and back every day.

Barbican (1958-1981) A vast concrete ocean liner of a housing estate and arts complex designed by architects Chamberlin Powell & Bon and come to berth in the City of London. Dominated by three 412-ft residential towers – Cromwell, Lauderdale and Shakespeare – the Barbican was originally built as affordable homes to rent; since its completion it has become a much-fêted middle-class bastion, offering well-built flats, many with inspiring views, minutes from the City's computer-driven counting houses. It also boasts an Arts Centre, famous for being more difficult to navigate than the Labyrinth (even Theseus might have missed the first act of a show here).

Broadgate (1984-2005) Ambitious US-style office scheme built to coincide with the deregulation of the City of London in Margaret Thatcher's heyday. This move led to a boom in City financial trading floors. The generously built and lavishly appointed Broadgate offices – acres of shiny marble, miles of polished brass – designed mainly by the US architects Skidmore Owings and Merrill were the answer. This massive development with its impressive public squares and notable artworks rode the roller-coaster of the Britain's economic ups and downs in the 1980s and 90s. It has since proved to be a big success. And, boy, is it BIG.

Lloyd's Building, City (1986) Richard Rogers' masterpiece is an astonishing space-age building infused with the spirit of *Blade Runner*, *Aliens* and, no less prosaically, North Sea oil rigs, rising above Leadenhall Market. Hard to believe that this titanic hi-tech finance house was commissioned by what was thought to be one of the most conservative bodies in Britain. Upper floors are reached by vertigo-inducing glass lifts that zoom up and down the outside of the building's stainless steel-clad towers. The whole edifice is gathered around a vast, Crystal Palace-style atrium and is full of delightful architectural surprises.

St Mary Axe (2004) An astonishing hi-tech moon rocket of a building (third tallest in town) on the site of the old Baltic Exchange, severely damaged by an IRA bomb in the 90s. Sir Norman Foster's latest contribution to the London skyline has been dubbed 'the Gherkin', which goes some way towards describing its snub-nosed, bullet-like shape but mocks the sophistication of its design. An extraordinary workplace for Swiss Re insurance brokers.

Canary Wharf (1980s-present) Movie-style Chicago architecture came to London's
former Docklands with this spectacularly banal new office city designed to drag the
bankers and brokers of the ancient City of London east along the Thames. Well built
and thoroughly landscaped, the postmodern office towers of Canary Wharf are suitably
vacuous symbols for the Thatcherite money culture they continue to celebrate. Canary
Wharf Tower, by the New York architect Cesar Pelli is, at 800 ft, the tallest building in
Britain. This stainless steel monolith is hard to avoid on the city's skyline; it does look
good, though, at sunrise and sunset when its smoking pyramid appears to burst into
flames, Towering Inferno-style. The Canary Wharf development also includes Norman
Foster's superb Jubilee Line station and is home to many water birds.

Jubilee Line Extension (2000) One of the most interesting journeys that any visitor
can make through east London, both north and south of the Thames, is by the new
Jubilee Line Extension from Westminster to Stratford. Without exception the new
stations have been designed to an exceptionally high standard under the aegis of the
project's Anglo-Italian architect Roland Paoletti (whose other previous achievements
include the super-efficient Hong Kong Metro). Each is a landmark, each the final fling of
publicly funded public architecture in a country crazy about privatization and where
trains and buses are increasingly run by cynical cowboys. It's hard to single out the best
stations, but Westminster (Michael Hopkins), Canary Wharf (Foster), Southwark
(MacCormac), North Greenwich (Alsop & Stormer) and the train depot west of Stratford
with its sweeping arched roof are all exceptionally good. See also tube map page .

Pumping Station, Millwall (1988) This is postmodernism at its best, as wilful
architectural folly. John Outram's pumping station enlivens a rather grim stretch of the
Thames as it winds eastwards to Greenwich from under Tower Bridge. It is a
grandiloquent play of ancient and classical themes. It also serves a very useful
purpose. Best seen from a boat.

The Dome (1999-2000) Nancy Banks-Smith, the *Guardian*'s TV critic, described
this heroic hi-tech tent as looking, by night, like a jellyfish glowing on the banks of the
Thames. Designed by the Richard Rogers Partnership to house the deeply
embarrassing Millennium Experience, a patronizing view of life in Britain in the year
leading up to the new millennium, the building itself is a romantic thing, a modern
cross-breeding of the two most celebrated structures at the 1951 Festival of Britain:
the Skylon, an ethereal space-age tower by Powell & Moya, and the Dome of
Discovery, a kind of *Boys' Own* flying saucer filled with the latest post-war British
technology. The Festival of Britain was much more popular than the Millennium
Experience; its legacy includes the cultural buildings on the South Bank. The future of
the Dome hangs in the balance. Most extravagant national exhibitions championed
by governments have tended to vanish in a puff of costly smoke.

Sainsbury Wing, National Gallery (1987) Limp-wristed attempt by US
postmodern architects Robert Venturi and Denise Scott-Brown to add a bit of classical
wit to the rather damp façade of William Wilkin's Neo-Greek National Gallery. As for
the paintings this otherwise well-planned gallery houses, what can anyone say that
would deflate a Bellini or give umbrage to an Uccello?

Charing Cross Station (1990) Big, brash, postmodern railway terminus remodelled
by Terry Farrell. Overscaled and finished in vile colours, the redevelopment of Charing
Cross was significant not so much for the way it intruded aggressively into the romantic
Thames riverscape, but because it showed how, if they could, developers would build
masses of office space above public buildings, stations especially, and leave those
who needed to use them, like commuters, in dismal dark spaces below. Great, eh?

416 **Portcullis House, Westminster (2000)** Hard to believe this ugly, bloated monster is by the same architects as the fine underground station beneath it. Designed as offices for members of parliament, previously squeezed indecorously into the Gothic Revival corridors of the Palace of Westminster opposite (Barry & Pugin, 1837-1860), Portcullis – even its name – is symbolic of Britain's politicians desire to hide themselves away from those dumb enough to elect them. Gathered around a glazed courtyard lined with fig trees, MPs while away their days in a kind of bombastic and lavish splendour. The chimneys on top of the building are simply ugly.

Centre Point (1967) Tall, slim beehive-style office tower at the eastern end of London's busiest shopping street. An icon of Pop architecture, designed by Colonel Richard Seifert, it seems odd now that it was much despised for many years, a symbol of aggressive high-rise property development. Fun to look at, it generates gale-force winds and so is hard to walk by. There is a bar low-down, but Londoners would flock to a stylish bar on the tower's coveted top (35th) floor.

London Telecom Tower (1966) Standing like some giant robot in the heart of Fitzrovia, the Telecom Tower was the showcase of Britain's white-hot technological 'revolution' championed by the Labour government of Harold Wilson in the 1960s. It beams zillions of telephone calls by microwave (keep your poodle well away) to lesser towers installed across the country. At 580-ft, it was until 1981 the tallest building in London. Visitors used to zoom up to the viewing galleries and revolving restaurant at its top. Sadly, these were closed permanently after the IRA exploded a bomb high in the tower. It was designed by the architects' section of the Ministry of Works, the team led by Eric Bedford.

Great Court, British Museum (2000) The breathtaking covered courtyard – Europe's largest – is at the heart of London's busiest museum (built, originally, to the designs of Robert Smirke between 1823 and 1847). The courtyard was a secret from 1857 when the famous circular Reading Room (by Smirke's younger brother, Sydney) was built inside it; the space left over was devoted to bookstacks. Now the courtyard, together with the Reading Room, has been opened up to the public, protected by a billowing and beautiful glazed roof. Under it you might like to try and identify the infamous South Portico, a classical design by the hi-tech Foster team; the design hasn't been in question – it is coolly elegant – but it is made of a French rather than good old English Portland stone from Purbeck in Dorset. This led to much huffing and puffing among those who felt the overcrowded museum should have been left as it was. A storm in an antique drinking vessel whipped up by the media, the South Portico will soon blend intrusively into this ambitious and truly grand design.

British Library, Bloomsbury (1997) Britain's most expensive building, the British Library, designed by Colin St John Wilson and Partners, took many years to plan and build. A red-brick colossus, it is pretty indigestible as seen from the street, yet the noble interiors are beautifully made, generous and a pleasure to use.

TV-am Camden Town (1982) Postmodern architecture came to London with this brash, flash and rather endearing broadcasting studio and offices for TV-am, a short-lived breakfast channel. A former garage, it was converted by Terry Farrell & Co into an entertaining three-dimensional map of the world (well, the flamboyant lobby at least). It was all done on a shoestring at a time when the British economy was still struggling out of a rut. It became known as Eggcup House, because of decorative glass-fibre eggcups (breakfast imagery, don't you know) set along its cornice lines. And the overall style? 'Depression Deco'.

Alexandra Road, Camden (1969-1979) The surreal housing scheme, comprising
520 homes, lined along one giant carless street, is hidden away from the world of
elegant white stucco-clad early Victorian houses all around. This is the last of
London's major public housing schemes, designed by the Greater London Council
architectural team led by Neave Brown, and it's quite mind-bending.

1-3 Willow Rd, Hampstead (1940) Pre-war, but this was the home of the Brutalist
architect Erno Goldfinger who designed the now fashionable Trellick Tower housing
brooding over Portobello Road (see below) and the former Sanderson Wallpapers
office, Fitzrovia, now the intensely fashionable Sanderson Hotel. Goldfinger (his
friend Ian Fleming borrowed the Hungarian architect's name and accent for his
famous Bond baddie) designed the house, one of a terrace of three, for himself and
his wife Ursula and lived here until his death in 1987. In 1994, the house was bought
by the National Trust. It is open to the public and is much as its designer left it.

Lord's Cricket Ground (1984-2000) Another old London institution – the home of
half-cut old gents asleep on summer days sporting panamas and
salmon-and-custard ties pretending to watch Test Matches – which invested, all of a
sudden, from the mid-1980s in adventurous new design. The white, tented Mound
Stand by Michael Hopkins set the tone for a pavilion with unobstructed views and real
elegance. The Press Pavilion by Future Systems is almost sensational: Britain's first
large-scale monocoque building (its structure is all of a piece), it seems quite happy
here in Marylebone even though it would be equally at home on Mars. It has been
cruelly nicknamed 'Cherie Blair's mouth'.

Trellick Tower, North Kensington (1973) The now fashionable Brutalist high-rise
concrete housing block designed by Erno Goldfinger overshadows Portobello Road
and its famous market. Highly expressive and not a little frightening, the flats are
gained by lifts running up a detached tower. The views from the flats are breathtaking.

Peckham Library (2000) The colourful new public library appears to stand on stilts
set at crazy angles and to be made of copper and stained glass. Designed by
architects Alsop & Stormer it is quite simply one of the most enjoyable new buildings
in London, set in one of its poorest quarters. The interior is a treat with its Sci-Fi
reading rooms housed in 'pods'. The views across north London from the London Eye
to the Greenwich Dome are dazzling.

Designed restaurants It's hard to single out London's best architect-designed
restaurants, but Tess and Julyan Wickham's **Kensington Place** (1987) is among those
that take pride of place. A sweeping, bright and sociable space, it was a deservedly
popular symbol of the moment when London began to fall in love with good modern
food and good modern architecture. It is still a fine, if noisy, place to eat.
   The Avenue (1998) Rick Mather's design rivals the Wickhams as one of the
essential architect-designed London restaurants. Big, classy and refined, it is also
sociable and an easy place to dine. Set in the heart of gloriously old-fashioned St
James's – Lock's the hatter and Lobb's the shoemakers are next-door neighbours.
The Avenue shows how class can take many forms.
   Sanderson Hotel (1999) An Erno Goldfinger office building transformed by the
New York hotelier Ian Schrager and Parisian designer Philippe Starck into one of the
most stylish new hotels in London. Wonderfully over-the-top furniture, a dazzling
white bar matched by a dark, sensual counterpoint elsewhere off the lobby and a fine
garden bar and café, it is a fine and fashionable place to meet as long as you pass the
doormen's intelligently astute gaze. Look like a star (or just a wannabe star) and
you're in.

Contemporary art

In 1976 the American artist RB Kitaj, then resident in London, coined the term 'School of London' to describe the "artistic personalities in this small island more unique and strong and I think numerous than anywhere in the world outside America's jolting artistic vigour". At a time when radical conceptual and minimal art by the likes of Richard Long (going on walks) or Gilbert & George (living sculpture) ruled the roost, Kitaj's polemic instead embraced primarily figurative artists of earlier generations such as Francis Bacon or David Hockney. For years art had barely figured in the wider cultural life of this island; it was thought to be something the French or Americans did better (a state of affairs that Kitaj was trying to redress).

In the 1990s things really seemed to change: the media fêted artists like Tracey Emin or Damien Hirst as if they were popstars and in the words of too many glossy magazine headlines 'London Swings Again'. Collected, anthologized, celebrated and promoted with an ad man's zeal, the best places to see art of the 90s is in the unlikely Edwardian office space of Charles Saatchi's Saatchi Gallery in County Hall on the South Bank. However, it was with the opening in May 2000 of Tate Modern in the giant landmark building of Gilbert Scott's Bankside Power Station that the British public's interest in art – particularly contemporary art – was confirmed by the millions of visitors attracted to the new museum. The original Tate Gallery, now renamed Tate Britain and situated on the north side of the river at Millbank, at first suffered from the attention given to the opening of Tate Modern, but its collection is still unrivalled and well worth a look (it's quieter there too).

The art map of London has always been determined by fashion and money, and in this it is no different from any other city. A century ago and until the 1930s, artists congregated in Chelsea in the triangle formed by Cheyne Walk and the Chelsea Embankment to the south, Sloane Street to the east and Fulham Road to the west and north. Although the purpose-built studio houses in the area are studded with blue plaques with the names of many distinguished artists of days gone by, very few artists today live and work in the area. The Chelsea Arts Club – for members only – is not the local it once was. Chelsea, however, was never really the place for the poor and starving artist.

In the first decades of the 20th century artists also lived and worked in what were then decidedly grubby and disreputable areas such as Fitzrovia (home to Wyndham Lewis and the Vorticists) or Bloomsbury (home to Virginia Woolf and the Bloomsbury Group). Other artists, especially in the 30s, opted for the rather more genteel atmosphere of Hampstead, home to many artist exiles from the continent, such as Piet Mondrian, who settled easily into what was described as a "gentle nest of artists" feathered by the likes of Henry Moore, Barbara Hepworth and Ben Nicholson. Now the area is home to the Camden Arts Centre (Arkwright Road), justly renowned for its exhibitions of contemporary and 20th-century art.

The 40s and 50s saw the rise of the louche dives and pubs of Soho and Fitzrovia as the backdrop for artists and poets at play from Francis Bacon to Dylan Thomas. In the 50s and 60s most young artists colonized the rundown territory of Notting Hill and Ladbroke Grove before moving east in the 70s and 80s to the still-deserted loft spaces of Docklands. In the 90s the location of choice was the run-down spaces of Shoreditch – now the grooviest place in London to live and one of the most expensive, it is now almost completely devoid of artists who have all been forced out further east by soaring rents.

For generations the centre of the commercial art world in London has been Cork Street and Bond Street on the edge of Mayfair and close to the Royal Academy. Save for a few survivors, most contemporary art galleries have moved away, or closed, long (always worth a look). Few contemporary art galleries can afford the rents or deal with the historical baggage of staying in the area. Those worth seeing are Stephen Friedman (Old Burlington Street), Asprey Jacques (Clifford Street), Waddingtons and Mayor Gallery (Cork Street), Anthony d'Offay Gallery (Dering St) and Anthony Reynolds (Great Marlborough St). For a slower pace one should move through the stately velvet-draped spaces of Agnew's Gallery (between Old Bond Street and Albermarle Street) – don't miss the upstairs gallery.

In 2000, Victoria Miro, dealer to Peter Doig and Chris Ofili, closed her small boutique space in Cork Street and moved to a huge warehouse building in Wharf Road on the edge of Shoreditch. Similarly, Jay Jopling, who has supported and promoted the careers of some of the most talked-about artists of the 90s, realized that the size of his Duke St gallery was disproportionate to the profile of his artists, and relocated into the epicentre of Shoreditch: Hoxton Square. East London has, indeed, been going through one of its periodic booms. One of the first dealers to open up shop in Hackney was the American Maureen Paley. Recently both Anthony Wilkinson and the Approach Gallery have also moved in to this area, which has always been rich in publicly funded and artist-run galleries such as the excellent Whitechapel Gallery, Matt's Gallery, the Showroom and the Chisenhale Gallery.

The location of the Institute of Contemporary Arts on the Mall, just down the road from Buckingham Palace, is even odder. Described as "an adult play centre" by one if its founders in the 1940s (when it had premises in Dover Street), things can still get quite anarchic there, with much to choose from between the bar, café, cinema, theatre and gallery.

Similarly incongruous is the Serpentine Gallery in a much-converted pavilion in the middle of Kensington Gardens. Its programme of young contemporary artists, 20th-century classics and timely group shows is outstanding and celebrated around the world. However, one of the most sympathetic public galleries, despite its uncompromising brutalist architecture, is the Hayward Gallery on the South Bank, a short walk westwards along the river from Tate Modern. Since it opened in 1968, the Hayward has produced some of the most exciting, significant and thought-provoking exhibitions to be mounted in London.

London in the movies

The city of London has never quite matched the celluloid magic of New York's skyscrapers or Hollywood's neon thrills. We try. James Bond launched a speed boat from the MI6 building by Vauxhall Bridge, and pursued yet another underdressed female kick-boxer all the way to that doomed symbol of modernity, the Greenwich Dome, in 1999. Michael Apted's opening sequence for *The World Is Not Enough* is the most frantic river trip through London any of us had ever seen, yet it wasn't quite enough after all. The film promptly ditched London and set off in search of other more interesting bits of the globe.

American cities seem to have it easier. Perhaps it's all that shimmering glass and helicopter-eye views of serial killers, stars and romance. The making and breaking of the American Dream is stitched into the very fabric of the buildings. The effortless glamour of it all is still Hollywood's hottest ticket, despite the complacency with which it is now served up. In the wrong hands, London can still look like a patchwork quilt of colloquial views and foggy heritage. And London is frequently in the wrong hands. Even now there are some whose celluloid view of the city is a caper comedy with randy cab drivers and saucy spinsters. For others, it's a starchy arrogant city full of stuffy drawing rooms, cobbled streets, and stiff upper lips. For an older generation of cinema-goers, the city was Boris Karloff in *Corridors of Blood* (1958), and Ingrid Bergman losing her marbles in *Gaslight* (1944). Fifty years later John Schlesinger wasn't doing much to change the tune with his 1997 version of *Sweeney Todd* complete with Ben Kingsley as the demon barber and Joanna Lumley with black teeth and grimy knickerbockers.

The 1960s provide rich pickings. Michelangelo Antonioni's *Blow-Up* (1966) is the vintage Swinging Sixties movie revolving around David Hemmings's strange adventures in Maryon Park off the Woolwich Road, and what he may or may not have seen there. The film ends with mime artists playing tennis without a ball. The park itself has barely changed since Hemmings went mad there. Michael Winner swung through London like Tarzan, perhaps most memorably with Oliver Reed and Michael Crawford in *The Jokers* (1967), a movie that moved seamlessly from Winner's South Kensington flat to the Tower of London via Tramp's nightclub and the old Stock Exchange. In a coup that belies the quality of this rough gem, Winner managed to get permission to hide the stolen jewels in the Scales of Justice on top of the Old Bailey. They don't make 'em like that anymore.

The sledge of ultra-violent gangster capers that stretch from Guy Ritchie's *Lock, Stock and Two Smoking Barrels* (1998) to his film *Snatch* (2000) (with Brad Pitt as a gypsy bare-knuckle boxer), has created yet more cock-eyed views of the city. Maybe we should blame the late great Stanley Kubrick for making London gangsters both hip and ridiculous when he banned his own film, *A Clockwork Orange* (1971), from being screened in Britain. Parts of it were shot in the basement of the Barbican Centre (as it was being built); other parts in the mean streets of the East End.

Ah, the East End. In Peter Medak's *The Krays* (1990), about London's two most infamous mobsters, the Krays's home turf turned out to be Caradoc Street in leafy Greenwich on the other side of the Thames. Fans of Meryl Streep and Charles Dance will doubtless remember the dilapidated lovebirds tottering down the same street in David Hare's *Plenty* five years earlier. Where would the East End be without Cheney Road, NW1 (note the post code). An amazing number of films (by British standards) were shot on this cobbled street, now almost obliterated by the channel tunnel rail-link into St Pancras. The street starred in *Alfie* (1966) with Michael Caine, *Shirley Valentine* (1989) with Pauline Collins, and most memorably in *Chaplin* (1992) with that clean cut young American actor, Robert Downey Jr. Here is where Alec Guinness pulled off a violent heist in *The Ladykillers* (1955).

That London is able to reveal so many conflicting faces is perhaps the greatest compliment one can pay the city. But the best way of discovering the myths behind the movies is to explore the locations yourself. The possibilities are endless. Films like Merchant Ivory's *Howard's End* (1992) are so stuffed with beautifully appointed location shots that they deserve an entire chapter to themselves: Roast beef at Simpson's-in-the-Strand; shopping at Fortnum and Mason's; a conversation by Admiralty Arch; a train to St Pancras; St James Court Hotel in Buckingham Gate doubling as a flat; and a hero's down-at-heel digs in Park Street in Southwark (home to Borough Market, the best food market in London), all these locations feature in this Oscar-winning Merchant Ivory film which starred Helena Bonham Carter, Anthony Hopkins, Vanessa Redgrave, Sam West, and Oscar-winner Emma Thompson. Further from the centre of town, Stephen Daldry's *The Hours* (2003) made use of the view from the Richmond Hill over the Thames and parts of Richmond High Street.

Young female romantics will probably find the journey to the Travel Bookshop (13 Blenheim Crescent, W11) a greater thrill. It's here that the shy Portobello bookshop owner, Hugh Grant, accidentally spills fruit juice over browsing superstar, Julia Roberts, in Roger Michell's *Notting Hill* (1999). The area has never quite recovered its bohemian cool, made famous by Hanif Kureshi's drug-dealing hero Clint (Justin

Chadwick) in the 1991 film, *London Kills Me*. More recently *Bridget Jones's Diary* (2001) featured various locations in the area, including the Notting Hill restaurant *192*. Richard Curtis, the writer of *Four Weddings* and *Notting Hill* did the same for tourist London as a whole with his directorial debut, the snapshot rom-com *Love Actually* (2004). Showing the city gearing up for Christmas, he managed to include the lights of Piccadilly Circus and Regent Street, the ice-rink at Somerset House, as well as Selfridges (with Rowan Atkinson as in-store assistant) the South Bank and Docklands and much more.

An actor responsible for a lot more juicy slaughter is David Naughton in *An American Werewolf in London* (1981). The extensive filming in some of London's busiest parts put a sharp comic chill on John Landis's cult classic. One of the most memorable meals was witnessed on the escalator at Aldwych tube station courtesy of an unwary passenger and a ravenous toothy Naughton. Naughton wakes up in a cage in London Zoo, Regent's Park the following morning, then brings Piccadilly to a standstill by running amok taking bites out of anything in sight. Eros has never before or since played host to a 20-car pile-up.

The most unusual angle on London arguably was pinched by Julian 'The Filth and the Fury' Temple who manages the remarkable feat of bringing Coleridge (Linus Roache) and Kubla Khan to life inside a Millennium Wheel pod in *Pandemonium* (2000). The chronicler of the Sex Pistols claimed to be the first director to shoot scenes inside the London Eye with its spectacular views over the city. But I doubt he or any other director will be able to top Kubrick's *Full Metal Jacket* (1987). Perhaps only Kubrick had the nerve to recreate the Vietnam War in the derelict Beckton Gas Works just beyond Docklands on the north bank of the Thames. Matthew Modine and his lads blew up so much of the property, and left so many of the old derelict office buildings unsafe, that the area had to be sealed off from the public. Much like Vietnam itself. Enjoy.

Music

It's true to say that in the field of popular music if you can't find what you're looking for in London then you probably won't find it anywhere. As the population centre of Britain it is the obvious and essential stopping-off point for the world's largest musical acts, whilst its unrivalled position as the hub of the British music industry means that numerous aspiring artists gravitate towards its plethora of pubs and clubs to showcase their potential. Along with your everyday pub, club and stadium acts, London also boasts the Notting Hill Carnival comprising two days of loud (invariably reggae and steel band) music, parades and dancing, and even a touch of sun if you're lucky. The Carnival takes place annually on the Sunday and bank holiday Monday of the last weekend in August. Of course, such is the scale of the scene that there are a number of places where one can sample some of the untapped talent trying to impose itself on an often fickle listening public. Everyone has to start somewhere after all, and the briefest venture into the music history books reveals how many of the world's greatest and most revered music acts could first be seen peddling future hits to a half-hearted London pub audience.

Aside from clubs and dancing there is still a lot of live music to be enjoyed in the capital. If there is a centre for **rock music** in London then it's definitely **Camden Town** in North London. Famous primarily for its weekend market, Camden also has a number of pubs which feature live music in their back rooms and present new groups on the first step of the ladder. Such well known groups as Blur, Travis, Suede and The Stereophonics, all got started by playing early gigs at Camden pubs and clubs like *The*

London in literature

Almost every English writer, as well as many writers in English, have been touched by London at some time in their lives. For centuries the city has been the place they have looked for both inspiration and a livelihood. In the late 14th century, the 'father of English literature', court poet Geoffrey Chaucer (1342-1400), started his pilgrims on the road from Southwark for his jaunty *Canterbury Tales*. Two centuries or so later, next door on Bankside, one William Shakespeare (1564-1616) was writing plays for the Globe theatre. A delightful replica of the theatre can now be seen in all its reconstructed glory close to the original site thanks to Hollywood film director Sam Wanamaker. Across the river, in the 17th century, the old cathedral of St Paul's had one of England's most intelligent poets, John Donne (1572-1631), for its Dean, while London found a vivacious, self-regarding observer and commentator in the diarist Samuel Pepys (1633-1703). He watched the cathedral and city go up in smoke in the Great Fire of 1666 from the steeple of All Hallows church next to the Tower of London. At the turn of the 18th century, Daniel 'Robinson Crusoe' Defoe (1660-1731) was making a name

for himself as a journalist and spy. In his *Journal of the Plague Year* he describes the panic and the body count with a creative flair that few modern correspondents would dare emulate. In 1726 he completed *A Tour through the Whole Island of Great Britain*, a guidebook in three volumes that gives an invaluable insight into the state of the nation at the time, describing the city as 'out of all shape, uncompact and unequal'. No change there then. The really big name in London during the 18th century though was Dr Samuel Johnson (1709-84) whose house just off Fleet St has been preserved. England's first true 'man of letters', his ground-breaking Dictionary and lengthy poems and miscellanies are now less popular than the image we have of the man and his Cheshire Cheese companions – the poet Oliver Goldsmith, Edmund Burke and Edward Gibbon among others – largely thanks to the efforts of his indefatigable young biographer James Boswell (1740-95). Infinitely quotable (way ahead of his time with his soundbites), he recorded Johnson

Dublin Castle (Parkway, NW1), *The Monarch* (Chalk Farm Road, NW1), and *The Underworld* (Camden High Street, NW1). All of these venues can be found within a short walk of Camden Town tube station and feature live bands most nights of the week. Entrance will be no more than around £6 and drinks are at pub prices.

In the **West End** of London there's a mixture of different-size venues featuring rock music. *The Astoria* (Charing Cross Road, WC1) plays host to big name groups from the UK and abroad, whilst smaller venues like *The Borderline* (Orange Tree Yard St, WC1) feature up and coming groups. The centre of London and particularly **Soho** is definitely the place to head if you want to hear jazz in London. The main venue is the world famous *Ronnie Scotts* (Frith Street) which has been open for over 30 years and plays host to many of the biggest and the best of the jazz world. There's also *The Pizza Express Jazz Club* (Greek Street) in Soho where you can eat pizza and listen to very good jazz. Outside Soho the main jazz venue is the excellent *Jazz Café* in Camden (Parkway, NW1). This beautifully designed venue usually has more funky jazz, Latin music and soul with very good food served upstairs. On the weekends DJs also perform at the *Jazz Café*.

remarking that 'When a man is tired of London, he is tired of life, for there is in London all that life can afford'. Boswell's own *London Journal* bears out the truth of the observation with energetic descriptions of his social climbing and sexual exploits in St James Park. Meanwhile, William Blake (1757-1827), England's greatest visionary poet and artist, was greeting visitors to his house in Lambeth sitting in the nude with his wife, also naked. Naturism may not have caught on just then, but Nature itself became all the rage. William Wordsworth (1770-1850), loved the Lakes of course, but also wrote of the city from Westminster Bridge that 'Earth has nothing to show more fair…'. As the 19th century gathered steam, London seemed far from fair to the likes of Shelley (1792-1822) who wrote that 'Hell is a city much like London'; Dickens (1812-70), who captured the law's interminable delay in *Bleak House* and whose home off the Grays Inn Road is now a museum; and Marx (1818-83), who lodged with his family in Dean St, Soho, while penning *Das Kapital* in the British Museum. Keats (1795-1821) did his best work in Hampstead, where his house can be visited; Byron (1788-1824) lived in Albany, Piccadilly, before his marriage; George Eliot (1819-80) wrote *Middlemarch* in St John's Wood; and Henry James (1843-1916) *A Portrait of a Lady* in Bolton St, Piccadilly. *The Golden Bowl* contains much vivid description of the London of his day. The Anglo-Irish flooded into the capital at the fin de siecle: after his marriage the celebrated wit Oscar Wilde (1856-1900) lived at 34 Tite St, Chelsea; before becoming a bearded sage, George Bernard Shaw (1856-1950) lodged in Fitzrovia as a young man; a dandified WB Yeats (1865-1939) strolled near his home on Primrose Hill. In the early years of the 20th century, TS Eliot (1888-1965) worked in a bank in the City. Bloomsbury gave its name to the group that included Virginia Woolf (1882-1941). George Orwell slept in Trafalgar Square during his research for *Down and Out in Paris and London* and also lived on the Portobello Road for a time. Contemporary London writers include Peter Ackroyd, Ian Sinclair, Martin Amis, Jeanette Winterson, Ian McEwan, Maureen Duffy, Michael Moorcock and Hanif Kureishi. And a younger generation like Nick Hornby, Will Self, Tim Lott, and Graham Swift.

Background Culture

For those wanting **folk and blues** there's a number of long-standing small venues which cater exclusively to these types of music. The *12 Bar Club* has been running for decades and is situated in a back alley off Denmark Street in the West End hidden amongst the street's renowned selection of guitar and musical equipment shops. Here you can find would-be folk pickers and blues players most nights of the week in a very sympathetic and charmingly low-key environment.

Classical and opera

One of the best places in Europe to hear excellent classical music, London boasts four world class orchestras and numerous notable ensembles. However, for many years, the city's esteemed classical music scene has been deeply troubled by financial difficulties. Still, as we enter the new century it is beginning to appear that the annual funding problems which have plagued classical music in London are beginning to ease. As new avenues of funding have opened up in the last few years many are beginning to feel a little optimism concerning the preservation of what is an otherwise healthy, vibrant and varied scene.

424 The **London Symphony Orchestra**, based at the notoriously difficult-to-find Barbican Centre (beware street signs pointing in opposite directions), is arguably the pick of the bunch, though it is closely followed by the **Philharmonia** and the **London Philharmonic Orchestra** (both resident at the Royal Festival Hall), as well as the itinerant and slightly weaker **Royal Philharmonic Orchestra**. In addition, there are a number of venues, large and small, which hold regular concerts by internationally renowned musicians, local artists and students. The **Barbican Centre** (see page), as well as housing the LSO, plays host to guest orchestras and is the domain for international acclaimed soloists and conductors, though the music is often safe and traditional.

The **South Bank Centre** (see page) is really three venues in one. The positively huge **Royal Festival Hall** holds large-scale symphonic orchestral and choral concerts, whilst the smaller **Queen Elizabeth Hall** and smaller still **Purcell Room** stick to chamber music, though the QEH can also stage opera.

The **Royal Albert Hall** (see page) is home to the world-famous Sir Henry Wood Promenade Concerts (Proms for short), the annual classical feast running from July to September with music ranging from the well-loved to the new and cutting-edge. Seats can be booked in advance, but to truly sample the essence of the season try slumming it with one of the dirt-cheap Arena standing tickets.

Wigmore Hall (see page) is ornate, intimate, affordable, acoustically perfect and its concerts and recitals are of a high standard. On the cheaper side of things, the **Royal College of Music** (see page) holds afternoon chamber concerts on term-time weekdays, most of which are free and open to the public. The standard is very high despite the musicians' amateur status, and well worth investigating. Look out also for some of the many festivals which take place throughout the year. The best and most interesting of these are the BOC Covent Garden Festival, the City of London Festival and the Spitalfields Festival.

Opera is best served in London by the **Royal Opera House** and the English National Opera at the **Coliseum** (see page 79). Despite the Royal Opera House's rather stuffy and conservative reputation, the old place appears to have loosened up a touch since its long-awaited refurbishment. Prices remain exorbitant (up to £115), though there are seats available in the gods for under £20. There is also a restaurant and bar in which to while away the day, and tours are available for the curious. The Coliseum, on the other hand, prides itself on being the antithesis to the ROH. Housing the English National Opera, its programme tends to be more ambitious, tickets are cheaper and the music is sung in English. In truth, both are of a high standard and the ROH has done much to regain its prestige after the public relations disasters of the last 10 years.

Background Culture

Books

Contemporary fiction

Ackroyd, Peter *Hawksmoor* (Penguin, 1993). Mystery chiller about rebuilding London after the Great Fire.

Al-Shaykh, Hanan *Only in London* (Bloomsbury, 2002). Elegant and witty account of the Arab diaspora in contemporary London.

Arnott, Jake *The Long Firm* (Hodder and Stoughton, 1999). Cockney gangster novel set in the 1960s, and *He Kills Coppers*. (Sceptre 2001), another London gangster story set in 60s Soho.

Baron, Alexander *The Lowlife* (Harvill Press, 2001). Guilt-racked life of an East End Jewish gambler.

Boyd, William *Armadillo* (Penguin, 1998). Accomplished comic thriller about a Pimlico loss-adjuster.

Duffy, Maureen *Capital* (Harvill Press, 2001). An amateur archaeologist looks to the city's future while searching for clues to its destruction in the Dark Ages.

Duncan, Glen *I, Lucifer* (Scribner, 2003). The devil incarnate takes a trip around the city.

Dunn, Nell *Steaming* (Amber Lane 1981). Very funny play about five women in an East London Turkish bath.

Emecheta, Buchi *Head Above Water* (Heinemann, 1994). Autobiographical account of a Nigerian woman settling in north London.

Frayn, Michael *A Landing in the Sun* (Picador, 2003). Quiet and erudite Whitehall civil servant crime caper.

Frewin, Antony *London Blues* (No Exit Press, 2000). Black and white blue movies and the Profumo scandal.

Green, Henry *Caught* (Panther 2001). A story of male friendship on active service with the Auxiliary Fire Service during the Blitz.

Hill, Tobias *Underground* (Faber and Faber, 1999). Punchy thriller located in the tube system.

Hoban, Russell *The Bat Tattoo* (Bloomsbury, 2002). Romance blossoms between an antique dealer and crash-test dummy designer on the steps of the V&A.

Hornby, Nick *Fever Pitch*. (Penguin, 2000), modern love among the Arsenal terraces and *High Fidelity*. (Penguin, 2000), modern love among the Holloway Road record stacks.

Kersh, Gerald *Fowlers End*. (Panther, 2001). Picture house politics in a run-down London community.

Kureishi, Hanif *Buddha of Suburbia* (Faber and Faber, 1991). South London mixed race life.

Kureishi, Hanif *London Kills Me* (Faber and Faber 1991). Drug dealer tries to improve himself in Notting Hill.

Lanchester, John *Mr Philipps* (Faber and Faber, 2001). A newly unemployed accountant goes walkabout round modern London.

Lott, Tim *White City Blue* (Viking, 1999). Comic west London buddy buddy novel.

Moorcock, Michael *King of the City* (Scribner 2000). A washed-up 60s waster recollects his London high life; and *Mother London* (Scribner, 2000), four 'mental patients' eavesdrop on the margins of the city.

Palliser, Charles *The Quincunx* (Penguin, 1995). Contemporary 19th-century murder mystery novel set in London.

Petit, Chris *Robinson* (Granta, 1993). Idiosyncratic Soho low life and high life.

Raban, Jonathan *Soft City* (Harvill Press, 1998). Early work on metropolitan life focusing on London and New York.

Richards, Ben *A Sweetheart Deal* (Review, 2000). Baroque love story set in the underbelly of the city.

Royle, Nicholas *The Director's Cut* (Abacus, 2000). Strange murder mystery in a cinematic West End.

Self, Will *Grey Area* (Penguin, 1996). Very articulate and funny divertimenti on Soho and London life.

Sinclair, Ian *Downriver* (Vintage, 1995). The legacy of Thatcherism with a Thames perspective.

Spark, Muriel *The Ballad of Peckham Rye* (Penguin, 1970). The devil arrives to shake up Peckham in the 1950s.

Swift, Graham *Last Orders* (Picador, 1997). Smithfield and East London grit and grime.

Thorne, Matt *Dreaming of Strangers* (Weidenfeld and Nicolson, 2000). A movie reviewer and movie buff meet in comedy of London manners.

Williams, Nigel *Fortysomething* (Viking, 1999). A sacked soapstar faces being 50 in Wimbledon.

Non-fiction

Ackroyd, Peter *London, The Biography* (Chatto and Windus, 2000). The story of the capital told with endless imagination, thought and humour. The best.

Archer, Caroline *Tart Cards* (Mark Batty, 2003). Arresting volume that transforms hundreds of prostitutes' calling cards left in phone boxes into design classics.

Barker, Felix and Jackson, Peter *A History of London in Maps* (Barrie and Jenkins, 1990). Fascinating insights into urban growth, illustrated by contemporary maps from the 16th century onwards.

Glinert, Ed *A Literary Guide to London* (Penguin, 2000). The movements of writers of all kinds systematically traced through the streets.

Hibbert, Christopher *London: The Biography of a City* (Longmans, Green and Co, 1977). An entertaining and fluent account of the city's history, finely illustrated.

Hibbert, Christopher and Weinreb, Ben (Ed) *The London Encyclopaedia* (Macmillan, 1983). The history of any building, park, street, statue that ever was part of London, or still is. A tome.

Jones, Edward and Woodward, Christopher *A Guide to the Architecture of London* (Weidenfeld and Nicolson, 1992). The A-Z (with photographs) of London's architecture, building by building, area by area.

Piper, David *The Companion Guide to London* (Spectrum, 1964). A personal and engaging walking tour of the historic areas of the capital.

Porter, Roy *London A Social History* (Hamish Hamilton, 1994). A lively, detailed and refreshing history of the Londoner.

Rasmussen, Steen Eiler *London The Unique City* (MIT Press, 1982). A study of the city and its people that has become a minor classic.

Rennison, Nick *The London Blue Plaque Guide* (Sutton, 1999). An alphabetical guide to those distinguished residents of London, and where they live.

Russan, Lilian and Ashmore *Historic Streets of London* (Marshall, Hamilton 1923). The historic and etymological origin of the capital's street-names.

Seatrobe, JB *Political London* (Politico's, 2000). A clear, simple guide to some of the locations of scandal, intrigue and historic events.

Trench, Richard and Hillman, Ellis *London under London* (John Murray, 1993). A wonderful study of the people, pipes, tunnels, and lost rivers of a fascinating subterranean world.

Wilson, AN (Ed) *The Faber Book of London* (Faber and Faber, 1993). An anthology of writing about London.

Wittich, John *Discovering London Street Names* (Shire, 1996). The historic and etymological origin of the capital's street names.

Restaurant guide

A quick reference guide to help you locate a restaurant to suit your taste and budget near to you.

🍴 under £20 🍴🍴 £20-40 🍴🍴🍴 over £40 (Two-course evening meal, without service charge or drink.)

Afghan

| Camden | The Afghan Kitchen | 🍴 |
| | T020-7359 8019 | ▸▸ 308 |

African

Covent Gdn	Calabash	🍴🍴
	T020-7836 1976	▸▸ 97
Mayfair	Momo	🍴🍴
	T020-434 4040	▸▸ 110

American

Chelsea	The Big Easy	🍴🍴
	T020-7352 4071	▸▸ 174
	Ed's Easy Diner	🍴
	T020-7352 1952	▸▸ 87
Covent Gdn	Christopher's	🍴🍴🍴
	T020-7240 4222	▸▸ 97
	Joe Allen	🍴🍴
	T020-7836 0651	▸▸ 97
East End	Arkansas Café	🍴
	T020-7377 6999	▸▸ 268
Fitzrovia	Eagle Bar Diner	🍴🍴
	T020-7637 1418	▸▸ 203
	Mash	🍴🍴
	T020-7637 5555	▸▸ 203
	RK Stanley	🍴🍴
	T020-7462 0099	▸▸ 203
Piccadilly	Planet Hollywood	🍴🍴
	T020-7287 1000	▸▸ 125
	Rainforest Café	🍴🍴
	T020-7434 3111	▸▸ 125
Richmond	The Canyon	🍴🍴
	T020-8948 2944	▸▸ 348
Soho	Ed's Easy Diner	🍴
	T020-7434 4439	▸▸ 87
	Hamburger Union	🍴
	T020-7437 6004	▸▸ 87
The Strand	Smollensky's	🍴🍴
	T020-7497 2101	▸▸ 71

Argentine

Battersea	La Pampa Grill	🍴🍴
	T020-7924 4774	▸▸ 363
Mayfair	Gaucho Grill	🍴🍴
	T020-7734 4040	▸▸ 110

Armenian

| Sth Kensington | Jacob's | 🍴 |
| | T020-7581 9292 | ▸▸ 166 |

Brazilian

Camden	Made in Brasil	🍴
	T020-7482 0777	▸▸ 302
Highgate	Sabor do Brasil	🍴
	T020-7263 9066	▸▸ 295

British *(See also Modern British)*

Bermonsey	M. Manze	🍴
	T020-7407 2985	▸▸ 247
Brixton	Phoenix Restaurant	🍴
	T020-7733 4430	▸▸ 364
Chelsea	Chelsea Bun	🍴
	T020-7352 3635	▸▸ 175
	The Chelsea Kitchen	🍴
	T020-7589 1330	▸▸ 175
Clerkenwell	Smiths of Smithfield	🍴🍴
	T020-7236 6666	▸▸ 216
	St John	🍴🍴
	T020-7251 0848	▸▸ 216
Covent Gdn	Plummers	🍴
	T020-7240 2534	▸▸ 98
	Rules	🍴🍴🍴
	T020-7836 5314	▸▸ 97
East End	Bluu	🍴🍴
	T020-7613 2793	▸▸ 268
Knightsbridge	Stockpot	🍴
	T020-7589 8627	▸▸ 166
Leicester Sq	Stockpot	🍴
	T020-7839 5142	▸▸ 77
	West End Kitchen	🍴
	T020-7839 4241	▸▸ 77

British cont.

Cantonese

Caribbean

Chinese

European *See also Modern European*

Fish and seafood

Fish and seafood cont.

Camden	Monkey Chews	♛♛	
	T020-7267 6406		▶▶ 302
The City	Livebait St Paul's	♛♛	
	T020-7213 0540		▶▶ 228
	Sweeting's	♛♛	
	T020-7248 3062		▶▶ 228
Covent Gdn	Livebait	♛♛	
	T020-7836 7161		▶▶ 97
	The Rock and Sole Plaice	♛	
	T020-7836 3785		▶▶ 98
Fitzrovia	Back To Basics	♛♛	
	T020-7436 2181		▶▶ 203
Holborn	The Fryer's Delight	♛	
	T020-7405 4114		▶▶ 215
Kensington	Lou Pescadou	♛♛	
	T020-7370 1057		▶▶ 325
Leicester Sq	J Sheekey	♛♛♛	
	T020-7240 2565		▶▶ 77
Marylebone	The Golden Hind	♛	
	T020-7486 3644		▶▶ 184
Mayfair	Bentley's	♛♛	
	T020-7734 4756		▶▶ 110
Notting Hill	Geales	♛	
	T020-7727 7528		▶▶ 317
Pimlico	Seafresh Fish Restaurant	♛	
	T020-7828 0747		▶▶ 153
Soho	Randall & Aubin	♛♛	
	T020-7287 4447		▶▶ 87
Sth Kensington	Bibendum	♛♛♛	
	T020-7581 5817		▶▶ 166
Southwark	Balls Brothers	♛♛	
	T020-7407 4301		▶▶ 246
	fish!	♛♛	
	T020-7407 3803		▶▶ 247
Tower	The Aquarium	♛♛♛	
	T020-7480 6116		▶▶ 235
	Yabo Sayo	♛♛	
	T020-7488 1777		▶▶ 236
Waterloo	Masters Super Fish	♛	
	T020-7928 6924		▶▶ 256
Westminster	The Laughing Halibut	♛	
	T020-7799 2844		▶▶ 146

French

Bermondsey	The Leather Exchange	♛♛	
	T020-7407 0295		▶▶ 247
Bloomsbury	Savoir Faire	♛	
	T020-7436 0707		▶▶ 204
Clapham	Gastro	♛♛	
	T020-7627 0222		▶▶ 363

French cont.

Camden	Camden Brasserie	♛♛	
	T020-7482 2114		▶▶ 301
Chelsea	Thierry's	♛♛	
	T020-7352 3365		▶▶ 175
The City	Chez Gerard Bishopsgate	♛♛	
	T020-7588 1200		▶▶ 228
Clerkenwell	Club Gascon	♛♛♛	
	T020-7796 0600		▶▶ 216
Covent Gdn	Incognito	♛♛♛	
	T020-7836 8866		▶▶ 97
	Mon Plaisir	♛♛♛	
	T020-7836 7243		▶▶ 97
Fitzrovia	Elena's L'Etoile	♛♛	
	T020-7636 1496		▶▶ 203
	Pied-à-Terre	♛♛♛	
	T020-7636 1178		▶▶ 203
Hampstead	Le Cage Imaginaire	♛♛	
	T020-7794 6674		▶▶ 294
Hampton Ct	Monsieur Max	♛♛	
	T020-8979 5546		▶▶ 354
Islington	Le Mercury	♛	
	T020-7354 4088		▶▶ 308
Sth Kensington	Maggie Jones	♛♛♛	
	T020-7937 6462		▶▶ 325
Marylebone	Villandry	♛♛♛	
	T020-7631 3131		▶▶ 184
Mayfair	The Mirabelle	♛♛♛	
	T020-7499 4636		▶▶ 109
	The Square	♛♛♛	
	T020-7839 8787		▶▶ 110
Notting Hill	Notting Hill Brasserie	♛♛♛	
	T020-7229 4481		▶▶ 317
Piccadilly	The Criterion	♛♛♛	
	T020-7930 0488		▶▶ 124
Putney	Putney Bridge	♛♛♛	
	T020-8780 1811		▶▶ 339
Richmond	Chez Lindsay	♛	
	T020-8948 7473		▶▶ 348
St James's	Le Caprice	♛♛♛	
	T020-7629 2239		▶▶ 124
	L'Oranger	♛♛♛	
	T020-7839 3774		▶▶ 126
South Bank	The People's Palace	♛♛♛	
	T020-7928 9999		▶▶ 256
	RSJ	♛♛♛	
	T020-7928 4554		▶▶ 256
Sth Kensington	La Brasserie	♛♛	
	T020-7581 3089		▶▶ 166
	Le Suquet	♛♛	
	T020-7581 1785		▶▶ 166

Fusion

Battersea	**La Pampa Grill**	¶¶
	T020-7924 4774	▶▶363
Bermondsey	**Delfina Studio Café**	¶¶
	T020-7357 0244	▶▶247
Camden	**Café Delancey**	¶¶
	T020-7387 1985	▶▶301
	The Engineer	¶¶
	T020-7722 0950	▶▶302
The City	**Prism**	¶¶
	T020-7256 3888	▶▶228
Greewich	**Inside**	¶¶
	T020-8265 5060	▶▶284
	The King William	¶¶
	T020-8858 4143	▶▶284
Hampstead	**Giraffe**	¶
	T020-7435 0348	▶▶294
	Toast	¶¶
	T020-7431 2244	▶▶294
Hampton Ct	**Blubeckers**	¶
	T020-8941 5959	▶▶354
Holborn	**Bleeding Heart**	¶¶¶
	T020-7242 2056	▶▶215
Islington	**Lola's**	¶¶
	T020-7359 1932	▶▶308
	Mesclun	¶¶
	T020-7249 5029	▶▶309
Kensington	**Arcadia**	¶¶¶
	T020-7937 4294	▶▶325
Leicester Sq	**Asia de Cuba**	¶¶¶
	T020-7300 5588	▶▶77
	Nobu	¶¶¶
	T020-7447 4747	▶▶109
Marylebone	**Providores**	¶¶¶
	T020-7935 6175	▶▶184
Notting Hill	**Ulli**	¶
	T020-7727 7511	▶▶318
Richmond	**Prego**	¶
	T020-8948 8508	▶▶348
St James's	**Shumi**	¶¶¶
	T020-7747 9380	▶▶125
Soho	**The Sugar Club**	¶¶¶
	T020-7437 7776	▶▶86
South Bank	**The Baltic**	¶¶¶
	T020-7928 1111	▶▶256
Tower	**Wine Library**	¶
	T020-7481 0415	▶▶235

Greek

Camden	**Andy's Taverna**	¶¶
	T020-7485 9718	▶▶301

Greek cont.

	Lemonia	¶
	T020-7586 7454	▶▶302
East End	**The Real Greek**	¶¶
	T020-7739 8212	▶▶268
Notting Hill	**Costas Grill**	
	T020-7229 3794	▶▶317
Soho	**Jimmy's**	
	T020-7437 9521	▶▶87

Hungarian

Soho	**Gay Hussar**	¶¶¶
	T020-7437 0973	▶▶86

Indian

Bayswater	**Khans**	
	T020-7727 5420	▶▶332
Chelsea	**Chutney Mary**	¶¶
	T020-7351 3113	▶▶174
	Vama	¶¶
	T020-7351 4118	▶▶175
	Zaika	¶¶
	T020-7351 7823	▶▶175
The City	**Bengal Tiger**	
	T020-7248 6361	▶▶228
Covent Gdn	**Punjab**	¶¶
	T020-7836 9787	▶▶97
East End	**Café Naz**	¶¶
	T020-7247 0234	▶▶268
	Le Taj	¶¶
	T020-7247 4210	▶▶268
	Saffron	¶¶
	T020-7247 2633	▶▶268
Euston	**Diwana Bhel Poori House**	
	T020-7387 5556	▶▶191
	Ravi Shankar	¶
	T020-7388 6458	▶▶191
Fitzrovia	**Rasa Samudra**	¶¶
	T020-7637 0222	▶▶203
Marylebone	**Kerela**	
	T020-7580 2125	▶▶184
Mayfair	**Tamarind**	¶¶
	T020-7629 3561	▶▶110
Notting Hill	**Malabar**	¶¶
	T020-7727 8800	▶▶317
Oxford Street	**Rasa W1**	¶¶
	T020-7629 1346	▶▶131
Regent Street	**Veeraswamy**	¶¶
	T020-7734 1401	▶▶110
Soho	**Masala Zone**	¶
	T020-7287 9966	▶▶87

	Villa Bianca	♟♟	
	T020-7435 3131	▸▸ 294	
Hampton Ct	**Vecchia Roma**	♟	
	T020-8941 5337	▸▸ 354	
Holland Park	**Cibo**	♟♟	
	T020-7371 6271	▸▸ 318	
Islington	**Casale Franco**	♟♟	
	T020-7226 8994	▸▸ 308	
	La Porchetta	♟	
	T020-7288 2488	▸▸ 308	
	Ristorante Portofino	♟♟	
	T020-7226 0884	▸▸ 308	
	Strada	♟	
	T020-7226 9742	▸▸ 309	
	Trattoria Aquilino	♟	
	T020-7226 5454	▸▸ 309	
Kensington	**Il Portico**	♟	
	T020-7602 6262	▸▸ 325	
	La Pappardella	♟	
	T020-7373 7777	▸▸ 326	
	Scoffs	♟	
	T020-7602 6777	▸▸ 325	
Knightsbridge	**The Pizza on the Park**	♟	
	T020-7235 5273	▸▸ 166	
	Zafferano	♟♟♟	
	T020-7235 5800	▸▸ 166	
Leicecter Sq	**Manzi's**	♟♟	
	T020-7734 0224	▸▸ 77	
	Pizzico	♟	
	T020-7839 3641	▸▸ 77	
Marylebone	**Locanda Locatelli**	♟♟♟♟	
	T020-7935 9088	▸▸ 184	
Mayfair	**Rocket**	♟	
	T020-7629 2889	▸▸ 110	
	Sartoria	♟♟♟♟	
	T020-7534 7000	▸▸ 109	
Notting Hill	**Assaggi**	♟♟♟♟	
	T020-7792 5501	▸▸ 317	
	Il Carratto Restorante	♟	
	T020-7229 9988	▸▸ 317	
	Mediterraneo	♟♟	
	T020-7792 3131	▸▸ 317	
	Osteria Basilico	♟	
	T020-7727 9372	▸▸ 317	
Pimlico	**L'Incontro**	♟♟♟	
	T020-7730 6327	▸▸ 153	
St James's	**Al Duca**	♟♟♟	
	T020-7839 3090	▸▸ 125	
	Il Viccolo	♟♟♟	
	T020-7839 3960	▸▸ 125	
	Mokaris	♟	
	T020-7495 5909	▸▸ 125	

Soho	**Centrale**		
	T020-7437 5513	▸▸ 8.	
	Kettners		
	T020-7734 6112	▸▸ 8.	
	L'Arena	♟	
	T020-7734 2334	▸▸ 8.	
	Pizzeria Malleti		
	T020-7439 4096	▸▸ 8.	
	Pollo		
	T020-7734 5917	▸▸ 8.	
	Spiga	♟	
	T020-7734 3444	▸▸ 8.	
	Tartuffo	♟	
	T020-7734 4545	▸▸ 8.	
South Bank	**Gourmet Pizza Company**		
	T020-7928 3188	▸▸ 256	
Sth Kensington	**Il Falconiere**		
	T020-7589 2401	▸▸ 166	
	Monza	♟	
	T020-7591 0210	▸▸ 166	
Tower	**Cantina del Ponte**	♟♟♟	
	T020-7403 5403	▸▸ 246	
	Il Bordello		
	T020-7481 9950	▸▸ 235	
Westminster	**Sorriso**	♟♟	
	T020-7222 3338	▸▸ 146	

Japanese

Bloomsbury	**Abeno**		
	T020-7405 3211	▸▸ 203	
	Hare and Tortoise	♟	
	T020-7278 4945	▸▸ 204	
	Roka	♟♟♟	
	T020-7580 6464	▸▸ 203	
	Wagamama		
	T020-7323 9223	▸▸ 204	
Camden	**Asakusa**	♟♟	
	T020-7388 8533	▸▸ 301	
	Bento Café	♟♟	
	T020-7482 3990	▸▸ 301	
	Wagamama Camden	♟	
	T020-7428 0800	▸▸ 302	
The City	**Japanese Canteen**	♟	
	T020-7329 3555	▸▸ 228	
Clerkenwell	**Japanese Canteen**	♟	
	T020-7833 3521	▸▸ 216	
Fitzrovia	**Ikkyu**	♟	
	T020-7636 9280	▸▸ 204	
Hampstead	**Jin Kichi**	♟♟	
	T020-7794 6158	▸▸ 294	

Japanese cont.

Korean

Lebanese

Mediterranean

Modern British

Modern British cont.

Modern European

Modern European cont.

Notting Hill	**Kensington Place**	♙♙♙	
	T020-7727 3184	▸▸ 317	
	Ladbroke Arms	♙♙	
	T020-7727 6648	▸▸ 317	
St James's	**The Wolseley**	♙♙♙	
	T020-7499 6996	▸▸ 125	
Soho	**Andrew Edmonds**	♙♙♙	
	T020-7437 5708	▸▸ 86	
South Bank	**Anchor and Hope**	♙♙♙	
	T020-7928 9898	▸▸ 256	
	Oxo Tower Restaurant	♙♙♙	
	T020-7803 3888	▸▸ 256	

Moroccan

Mayfair	**Mô**	♙	
	T020-7434 4040	▸▸ 110	

Nepalese

Euston	**Great Nepalese**	♙	
	T020-7388 6737	▸▸ 191	

Peruvian

Southwark	**Fina Estampa**	♙♙	
	T020-7403 1342	▸▸ 246	

Polish

Hammersmith	**Lowiczanka**	♙	
	T020-8741 3225	▸▸ 339	
Hampstead	**Zamoyski**	♙♙	
	T020-7794 4792	▸▸ 294	
Sth Kensington	**Daquise**	♙♙	
	T020-7589 6117	▸▸ 166	

Portuguese

Knightsbridge	**O Fado**	♙♙	
	T020-7589 3002	▸▸ 166	

Sardinian

Fitzrovia	**Sardo**	♙♙	
	T020-7387 2521	▸▸ 203	

Scottish

Belgravia	**Boisdale**	♙♙♙	
	T020-7730 6922	▸▸ 153	

Southeast Asian

Bloomsbury	**Bam-Bou**	♙♙	
	T020-7323 9130	▸▸ 203	
The City	**Singapura**	♙♙	
	T020-7329 1133	▸▸ 228	

Spanish

Battersea	**San Miguel's on the River**	♙♙	
	T020-7801 9696	▸▸ 363	
Camden	**Jamon Jamon**	♙	
	T020-7284 0606	▸▸ 302	
Clerkenwell	**Moro**	♙♙♙	
	T020-7833 8336	▸▸ 216	
Mayfair	**Destino**	♙♙	
	T020-7437 9895	▸▸ 110	
Notting Hill	**Galicia**	♙	
	T020-8969 3539	▸▸ 318	
Pimlico	**Goya**	♙♙	
	T020-7976 5309	▸▸ 153	
Putney	**La Mancha**	♙	
	T020-8780 1022	▸▸ 339	
Soho	**Mar I Terra**	♙♙	
	T020-7734 1992	▸▸ 87	
Southwark	**Mar I Terra**	♙	
	T020-7928 7628	▸▸ 247	
	Tapas Brindisa	♙	
	T020-7357 8880	▸▸ 247	
Waterloo	**Maisón Don Felipe**	♙♙	
	T020-7928 3237	▸▸ 256	

Sudanese

Bayswater	**Mandola**	♙	
	T020-7229 4734	▸▸ 332	

Tex-Mex

Camden	**Camden Cantina**	♙♙	
	T020-7267 2780	▸▸ 301	
Piccadilly	**The Hard Rock Café**	♙♙	
	T020-7629 0382	▸▸ 125	
Sth Kensington	**Cactus Blue**	♙♙	
	T020-7823 7858	▸▸ 166	

Thai

Bloomsbury	**Thai Garden Café**	♙	
	T020-7323 1494	▸▸ 204	
The City	**Silks and Spice**	♙♙	
	T020-7248 7878	▸▸ 228	
Clapham	**Pepper Tree**	♙♙	
	T020-7622 1758	▸▸ 363	

Thai cont.

Fulham	**206 Café**	Y	
			▶▶ 339
Greenwich	**Thai Chung**	Y	
	T020-8858 8588		▶▶ 284
Notting Hill	**Churchill Arms**	Y	
	T020-7792 1246		▶▶ 317
Soho	**Chiang Mai**	YY	
	T020-7437 7444		▶▶ 87
The Strand	**Thai Pot Express**	Y	
	T020-7497 0904		▶▶ 71

Turkish

Covent Gdn	**Papageno**	Y	
	T020-7836 4444		▶▶ 98
	Sarastro	Y	
	T020-7836 0101		▶▶ 98
Islington	**Gallipoli**	Y	
	T020-7359 0630		▶▶ 308
	Gallipoli Again	Y	
	T020-7359 1578		▶▶ 308
	Pasha	YY	
	T020-7226 1454		▶▶ 308

Mayfair	**Sofra Bistro**	YY	
	T020-7493 3320		▶▶ 110
Waterloo	**Tas**	Y	
	T020-7928 1444		▶▶ 257

Vegetarian and vegan

The City	**The Place Below**	Y	
	T020-7329 0789		▶▶ 228
Covent Gdn	**Food for Thought**	Y	
	T020-7836 0239		▶▶ 97
Hammersmith	**The Gate**	YY	
	T020-8748 6932		▶▶ 339
Soho	**Busaba Eathai**	Y	
	T020-7255 8686		▶▶ 87
	Country Life	Y	
	T020-7434 2922		▶▶ 87
	Mildred's Wholefood Café	Y	
	T020-7494 1634		▶▶ 87

Vietnamese

Camden	**Viet Anh**	Y	
	T020-7284 4082		▶▶ 302
East End	**Viet Hoa Café**	YY	
	T020-7729 8293		▶▶ 268

Check out...

WWW...

100 travel guides, 100s of destinations,
5 continents and 1 Footprint...
www.footprintbooks.com

Footnotes

Index

Number entries in bold denote maps. Text entries in bold denote chapter headings.

Maps

Credits

Footprint credits

Text editor: Sarah Thorowgood
Map editor: Sarah Sorensen
Picture editor: Robert Lunn
Editorial assistants: Emma Bryers and Laura Dixon
Proofreader: Stephanie Egerton

Publisher: Patrick Dawson
Editorial: Alan Murphy, Sophie Blacksell, Claire Boobbyer, Felicity Laughton, Nicola Jones, Angus Dawson
Cartography: Robert Lunn, Claire Benison, Kevin Feeney, Esther Monzón García, Thom Wickes
Series development: Rachel Fielding
Design: Mytton Williams and Rosemary Dawson (brand)
Marketing: Andy Riddle
Advertising: Debbie Wylde
Finance and administration: Sharon Hughes, Elizabeth Taylor and Lindsay Ditham

Photography credits

Front cover: Alamy, Big Ben
Back cover: Alamy, Piccadilly Circus
Inside colour section: Alamy

Print

Manufactured in Italy by LegoPrint
Pulp from sustainable forests

Footprint feedback

We try as hard as we can to make each Footprint guide as up to date as possible but, of course, things always change. If you want to let us know about your experiences – good, bad or ugly – then don't delay, go to **www.footprintbooks.com** and send in your comments.

Publishing information

Footprint London
2nd edition
© Footprint Handbooks Ltd
June 2005

ISBN 1 904777 35 X
CIP DATA: A catalogue record for this book is available from the British Library

® Footprint Handbooks and the Footprint mark are a registered trademark of Footprint Handbooks Ltd

Published by Footprint

6 Riverside Court
Lower Bristol Road
Bath BA2 3DZ, UK
T +44 (0)1225 469141
F +44 (0)1225 469461
discover@footprintbooks.com
www.footprintbooks.com

Distributed in the USA by

Publishers Group West

Neither the black and white nor colour maps are intended to have any political significance. Bus and cycle route information was sourced from Transport for London. For updates, consult www.tfl.gov.uk

Every effort has been made to ensure that the facts in this guidebook are accurate. However, travellers should still obtain advice from consulates, airlines etc about travel and visa requirements before travelling. The authors and publishers cannot accept responsibility for any loss, injury or inconvenience however caused.

About the author

Charlie Godfrey-Faussett has lived in London north and south of the river for the best part of the last 18 years. The author of *Footprint England*, he has also reviewed theatre and written guides for *Time Out* and contributes to a variety of national newspapers and magazines.

Acknowledgements

Charlie would like to thank all those who have contributed to this book, especially Andrew White for history, Jonathan Glancey for architecture, Andrew Wilson for art and James Christopher for film. And also the five writer-researchers who helped out with various areas north, south, east and west: Lizzie Taylor, Chris Moore, Tim Rowbottom, Tim Clark and Natasha Plowright. And everyone else in my home city who made researching the book so much more entertaining than strictly necessary. Thanks too are due to the whole team at Footprint, especially Sarah Thorowgood. And more love than ever to Addie.

Complete title listing

Footprint publishes travel guides to over 150 destinations worldwide. Each guide is packed with practical, concise and colourful information for everybody from first-time travellers to travel aficionados. The list is growing fast and current titles are noted below.
Available from all good bookshops and online at www.footprintbooks.com

(P) denotes pocket guide

Latin America and Caribbean
Argentina
Barbados (P)
Belize, Guatemala &
  Southern Mexico
Bolivia
Brazil
Caribbean Islands
Central America & Mexico
Chile
Colombia
Costa Rica
Cuba
Cusco & the Inca Trail
Dominican Republic (P)
Ecuador & Galápagos
Guatemala
Havana (P)
Mexico
Nicaragua
Patagonia
Peru
Peru, Bolivia & Ecuador
Rio de Janeiro (P)
South American Handbook
St Lucia (P)
Venezuela

North America
New York (P)
Vancouver (P)
Western Canada

Africa
Cape Town (P)
East Africa
Egypt
Libya
Marrakech (P)
Morocco
Namibia
South Africa
Tunisia
Uganda

Middle East
Dubai (P)
Israel
Jordan
Syria & Lebanon

Australasia
Australia
East Coast Australia
New Zealand
Sydney (P)
West Coast Australia

Asia
Bali
Bangkok & the Beaches
Bhutan
Cambodia
Goa
Hong Kong (P)
India
Indian Himalaya
Indonesia
Laos
Malaysia
Nepal
Northern Pakistan
Pakistan
Rajasthan
Singapore
South India
Sri Lanka
Sumatra
Thailand
Tibet
Vietnam

Europe
Andalucía
Barcelona (P)
Berlin (P)
Bilbao (P)
Bologna (P)
Britain
Cardiff (P)
Copenhagen (P)
Costa de la Luz
Croatia
Dublin (P)
Edinburgh (P)

England
Glasgow (P)
Ireland
Lisbon (P)
London
London (P)
Madrid (P)
Naples (P)
Northern Spain
Paris (P)
Reykjavík (P)
Scotland
Scotland Highlands & Islands
Seville (P)
Siena (P)
Spain
Tallinn (P)
Turin (P)
Turkey
Valencia (P)
Verona (P)

Lifestyle guides
Surfing Britain
Surfing Europe

Also available:
Traveller's Handbook (WEXAS)
Traveller's Healthbook (WEXAS)
Traveller's Internet Guide (WEXAS)

Footnotes Complete title listing

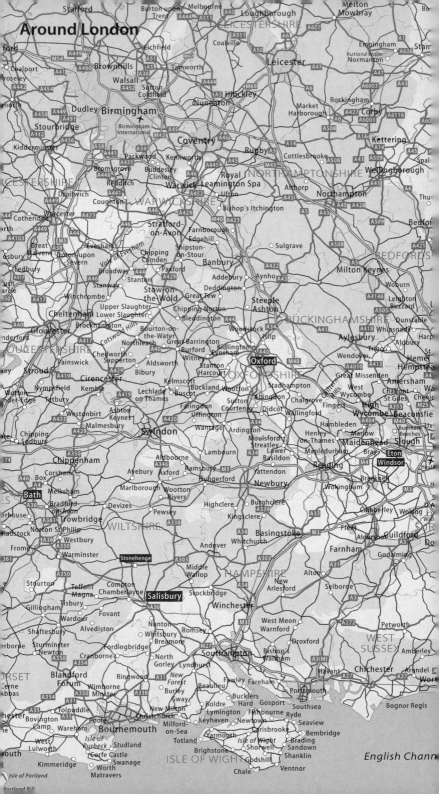

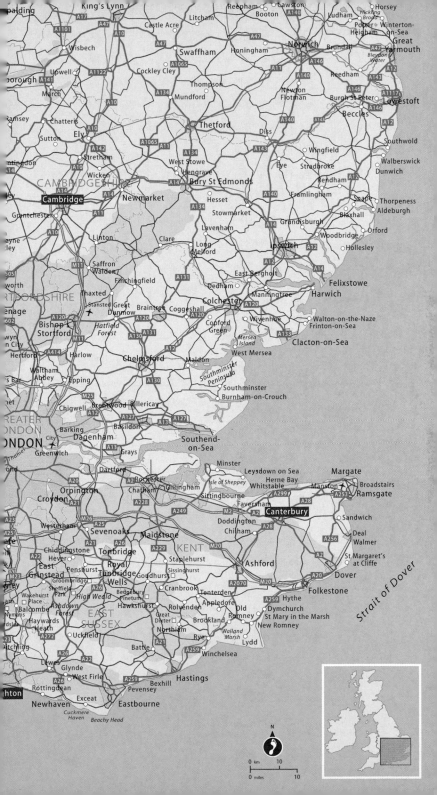

M25 & routes into London

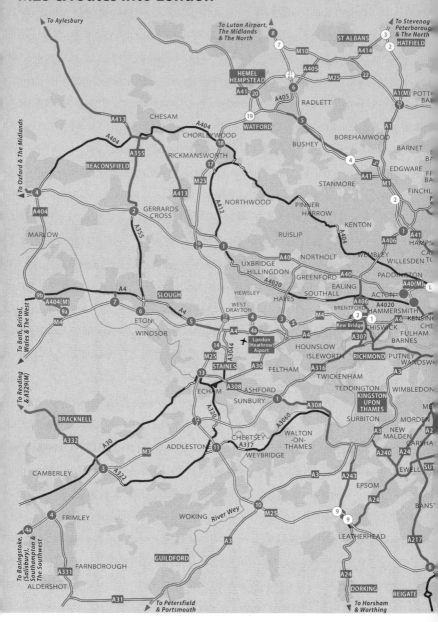

Congestion charge zone

N

| 0 km | 5 |
| 0 miles | 5 |

River Thames

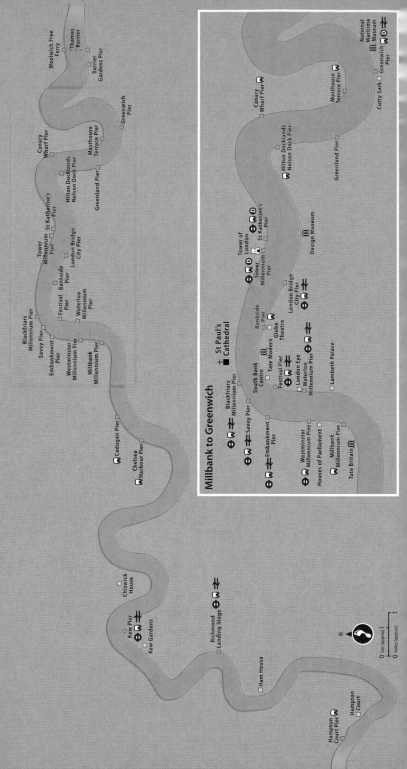

River services

Service	Timetable information	Cost
Savoy-Canary Wharf-Masthouse Terr-Greenwich	From Greenwich or Masthouse Terr and Savoy approx every 20 mins Mon–Fri. Restricted service at weekends and bank holidays	Adult single £2.50–£6.50, return £3.80–£10.50
Richmond-Kingston-Hampton Court	Four services westbound, three eastbound Tue–Sun	Adult single £4.50–£5.50, return £6–£7
Westminster-Kew-Richmond-Hampton Court	Four services westbound, five eastbound daily	Adult single £6–£13.50, return £9–£19.50
Westminster-St Katharine's	Circular service calling at Festival, Embankment, Bankside, London Bridge and St Katharine's about every 40 mins daily from 1100–1800	Adult single £3–£5.60, return £6.80
Westminster-Waterloo-Tower-Greenwich	Every 20 mins eastbound from 0940, westbound hourly services from Greenwich and about every 20 mins from Tower, daily	Adult single £5.60–£6.80, return £6.80–£8.60
Westminster-St Katharine's-Greenwich-Barrier Gardens	Every 30 mins from 1000-1700 eastbound daily, westbound hourly service from Barrier Gardens, half-hourly service from Greenwich	Adult single £5.60–£8.30, return £5.85–£10.50
Embankment-Waterloo-Bankside-Tower-Greenwich	Daily services every 40 mins eastbound from 1000-1700, westbound services from Greenwich every 40 mins or hourly	Adult single £3–£6.60, return £4–£8.20
Bankside-Waterloo-Millbank (Tate to Tate)	Daily services westbound every 40mins from 0955–1640, eastbound every 40 mins from 1020-1655	Adult single £3.40, return £5

Tickets and discounts

You should buy your ticket at the pier before starting your journey.

Travelcard holders receive a third off fares for most river services. Freedom Pass holders qualify for a 50% discount on the majority of services.

Some operators offer discounts to holders of London Student Union Cards.

For more information contact the relevant operator direct. Oyster cards are not valid on river services.

Further information

For up-to-date timetables and specific fare details, see the **Transport for London** website, www.tfl.gov.uk or call T020-7222 1234.

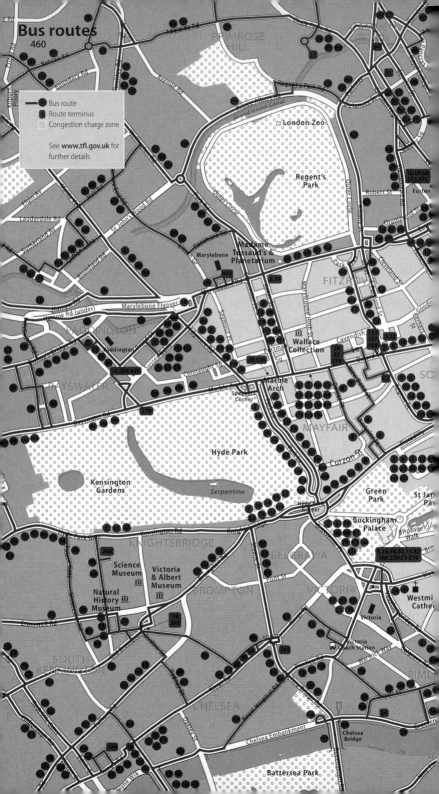

London Underground map

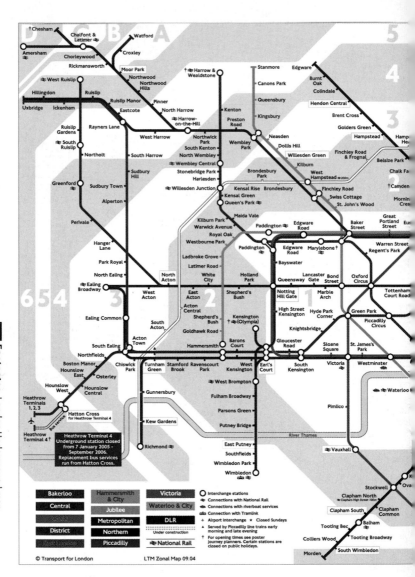

© Transport for London   LTM Zonal Map 09.04

Map symbols

Administration

- ◻ Capital city
- ○ Other city/town
- ⌇⌇. International border
- ⌇⌇. Regional border
- ⌇⌇. Disputed border

Roads and travel

- ═══ Motorway
- ─── Main road (National highway)
- ─── Minor road
- ---- Track
- ······· Footpath
- ⇌ Railway with station
- ✈ Airport
- 🚌 Bus station
- ⊖ Underground station
- 🄾 Docklands Light Railway
- ---- Cable car
- ++++ Funicular
- 🚢 Ferry

Water features

- ═══ River, canal
- ⬭ Lake, ocean
- ᵛᵛᵛ Seasonal marshland
- ⬚ Beach, sandbank
- 〽 Waterfall

Topographical features

- ⬭ Contours (approx)
- ⋀ Mountain
- ⛰ Volcano
- ⇌ Mountain pass
- ᴸᴸᴸᴸ Escarpment
- ⬚ Gorge
- ⬚ Glacier
- ▨ Salt flat
- ⬚ Rocks

Cities and towns

- ═══ Main through route
- ═══ Main street
- ═══ Minor street

Other symbols (right column continued)

- ⬚ Pedestrianized street
- Ↄ Ⅽ Tunnel
- ⟶ One way-street
- ⬚ Steps
- ⊨ Bridge
- ▰▰▰ Fortified wall
- ▱ Park, garden, stadium
- 🛌 Sleeping
- ❷ Eating
- ❶ Bars & clubs
- ⦿ Entertainment
- ▭ Building
- ▪ Sight
- ⸆⸆ Cathedral, church
- 🏯 Chinese temple
- 🛕 Hindu temple
- ⚲ Meru
- 🕌 Mosque
- △ Stupa
- ✡ Synagogue
- 🄸 Tourist office
- 🏛 Museum
- ✉ Post office
- ⓟ Police
- Ⓢ Bank
- @ Internet
- ♪ Telephone
- 🕿 Market
- ✚ Hospital
- 🄿 Parking
- ⛽ Petrol
- ⛳ Golf
- ◁1 Related map

Other symbols

- ⁘ Archaeological site
- ♦ National park, wildlife reserve
- ❁ Viewing point
- ⋀ Campsite
- ⌂ Refuge, lodge
- 🏰 Castle
- ⇲ Diving
- 🌲 Deciduous/coniferous/palm trees
- ⌂ Hide
- 🍇 Vineyard
- ⚗ Distillery
- ⤵ Shipwreck
- ✕ Historic battlefield